THE CAMBRIDGE HISTORY OF RELIGIONS IN THE ANCIENT WORLD

VOLUME II

From the Hellenistic Age to Late Antiquity

The Cambridge History of Religion in the Ancient World provides a comprehensive and in-depth analysis of the religions of the ancient Near East and Mediterranean world. The nineteen essays in this volume begin with the Hellenistic age and extend to the late Roman period. Its contributors, all acknowledged experts in their fields, analyze a wide spectrum of textual and material evidence. An essay by William Adler introduces the chapters of Volume II. The regional and historical orientations of the essays will enable readers to see how a religious tradition or movement assumed a distinctive local identity, and consider its development within a broader regional and Mediterranean context. Supplemented with maps, illustrations, and detailed indexes, the volume is an excellent reference tool for scholars of the ancient Near East and Mediterranean world.

Michele Renee Salzman is University of California Presidential Chair (2009–2012) and Professor of History at the University of California, Riverside. She is the author of three books and numerous articles, including *On Roman Time: The Codex-Calender of 354 and the Rhythms of Urban Life in late Antiquity* (1990); *The Making of a Christian Aristocracy* (2002); and *The Letters of Symmachus: Book 1*, translation (with Michael Roberts), Introduction, and Commentary (2011). She is on the Editorial Board of the *American Journal of Archaeology* and has served on the Executive Committee of the American Academy in Rome.

William Adler is Professor of Early Christianity and Judaism in the Department of Philosophy and Religious Studies at North Carolina State University. He has authored or coauthored six books dealing with early Christian literature and historiography and has served as a visiting professor at the Hebrew University of Jerusalem and as a visiting research scholar at the University of Adelaide, the Friedrich-Schiller-University of Jena, and the University of Basel.

THE CAMBRIDGE HISTORY OF RELIGIONS IN THE ANCIENT WORLD

VOLUME II

FROM THE HELLENISTIC AGE TO LATE ANTIQUITY

Michele Renee Salzman
General Editor
University of California, Riverside

Edited by

William Adler
North Carolina State University

CAMBRIDGE
UNIVERSITY PRESS

CAMBRIDGE
UNIVERSITY PRESS

University Printing House, Cambridge CB2 8BS, United Kingdom

One Liberty Plaza, 20th Floor, New York, NY 10006, USA

477 Williamstown Road, Port Melbourne, VIC 3207, Australia

314-321, 3rd Floor, Plot 3, Splendor Forum, Jasola District Centre, New Delhi - 110025, India

79 Anson Road, #06-04/06, Singapore 079906

Cambridge University Press is part of the University of Cambridge.

It furthers the University's mission by disseminating knowledge in the pursuit of education, learning and research at the highest international levels of excellence.

www.cambridge.org
Information on this title: www.cambridge.org/9781108703123

First published 2013
First paperback edition 2018

A catalogue record for this publication is available from the British Library

Library of Congress Cataloging in Publication data
The Cambridge history of religions in the ancient world : from the Bronze Age to the Hellenistic Age / [edited by] Marvin A. Sweeney, Michele Renee Salzman.
p. cm.
Includes bibliographical references and indexes.
ISBN 978-1-107-01999-7 (hardback set) – ISBN 978-0-521-85830-4 (volume 1) – ISBN 978-0-521-85831-1 (volume 2)
1. Religions. 2. Civilization, Ancient. I. Sweeney, Marvin A. (Marvin Alan), 1953– II. Salzman, Michele Renee.
BL96.C363 2012
200.93–dc23 2011049012

ISBN 978-0-521-85830-4 Volume I Hardback
ISBN 978-0-521-85831-1 Volume II Hardback
ISBN 978-1-107-01999-7 Two-volume Hardback Set
ISBN 978-1-108-70312-3 Paperback

CONTENTS

FIGURES AND MAPS

FIGURES

MAPS

CONTRIBUTORS

Albert de Jong is Professor of Comparative Religion at Leiden University, Leiden, the Netherlands.

Françoise Dunand is Professor Emerita, University of Strasbourg, Strasbourg, France.

Esther Eshel is Senior Lecturer in the Bible Department and in the Martin (Szusz) Department of Land of Israel Studies and Archaeology at Bar Ilan University.

Sidney H. Griffith is Professor in the Department of Semitic and Egyptian Languages and Literature and at the Institute of Christian Oriental Research at the Catholic University of America.

Robin M. Jensen is the Luce Chancellor's Professor of the History of Christian Art and Worship at Vanderbilt University, Nashville, Tennessee.

Ted Kaizer is Senior Lecturer in Roman Culture and History at Durham University, Durham, United Kingdom.

William Klingshirn is Ordinary Professor of Greek and Latin at the Catholic University of America.

Michael Kulikowski is Professor in the Department of History at Pennsylvania State University.

Giancarlo Lacerenza is Lecturer in Biblical and Medieval Hebrew at the University of Naples L'Orientale.

Hayim Lapin is Professor in the Department of History and in the Joseph and Rebecca Meyerhoff Program and Center for Jewish Studies at the University of Maryland.

Joseph Mélèze Modrzejewski is Professor Emeritus of Ancient History at the University of Paris, Paris, France.

Lynn E. Roller is Professor in the Department of Art and Art History at the University of California, Davis.

Brent Shaw is Professor of Classics and Andrew Fleming West Professor of Classics in the Department of Classics at Princeton University.

Michael E. Stone is Professor of Armenian Studies and Gail Levin de Nur Professor of Religious Studies at The Hebrew University of Jerusalem, Jerusalem, Israel.

Frank R. Trombley is Reader in the School of Religious and Theological Studies at Cardiff University, Cardiff, Wales.

Dennis Trout is Associate Professor and Department Chair in the Department of Classical Studies at the University of Missouri, Columbia.

William van Andringa is Professor of Roman History (History of Ancient Religions) at the University of Lille 3, Lille, France.

Pieter W. van der Horst is Professor Emeritus in the Faculty of Theology of Utrecht University, Utrecht, the Netherlands.

Jacques van der Vliet is Senior Lecturer of Coptic at Leiden University and Extra-ordinary Professor of Egyptian Religion at Radboud University Nijmegen, the Netherlands.

ABBREVIATIONS

AAAS	*Annales archéologiques arabes syriennes*
AB	Anchor Bible
ABD	*Anchor Bible Dictionary*, ed. David Noel Friedman. 6 vols. (New York, 1992)
AcOr	*Acta Orientalia*
ADPV	Abhandlungen des Deutschen Palästina-Vereins
AE	*L'Année epigraphique*
Aeg	*Aegyptus. Rivista italiana di egittologia e di papirologia*
AJA	*American Journal of Archaeology*
AJSR	*Association for Jewish Studies Review*
AMS	Asia Minor Studien
AnBoll	Analecta Bollandiana
Anc. Soc.	*Ancient Society*
ANRW	*Aufstieg und Niedergang der römischen Welt*
AnSt	*Anatolian Studies*
AntAfr	*Antiquités africaines*
AntTard	*Antiquité tardive*
ARG	*Archiv für Religionsgeschichte*
ASNSP	*Annali della Scuola Normale Superiore di Pisa, classe di lettere e filosofia*
ASPN	*Archivio Storico per le Provincie Napoletane*
BA	*Biblical Archaeologist*
BABesch	*Bulletin Antieke Beschaving*
BABeschSup	*Bulletin Antieke Beschaving*, Supplement
BAH	Bibliothèque Archéologique et Historique
BAIAS	*Bulletin of the Anglo-Israel Archaeological Society*
BAR Int. Ser.	*British Archaeological Reports, International Series*

BASOR	*Bulletin of the American Schools of Oriental Research*
BCTH	*Bulletin archéologique du Comité des travaux historiques et Scientifiques*
BGU	*Aegyptische Urkunden aus den königlichen (staatlichen) Museen zu Berlin, Griechische Urkunden, I–IV* (Berlin, 1895–1912)
BHG	*Bibliotheca hagiographica orientalis*, ed. François Halkin. Subsidia Hagiographica 47 (Brussels, 1969)
BIDR	*Bullettino dell' Istituto di Diritto Romano "Vittorio Scialoja"*
BJRL	*Bulletin of the John Rylands University Library of Manchester*
BKAT	Biblischer Kommentar. Altes Testament
BMC	*Catalogue of Greek Coins in the British Museum, Phoenicia*, ed. G. F. Hill (London, 1910)
BMGS	*Byzantine and Modern Greek Studies*
BO	*Bibliotheca Orientalis*
BSOAS	*Bulletin of the School of Oriental and African Studies*
C&M	*Classica et Mediaevalia*
CA	*Classical Antiquity*
CAG	*Carte archéologique de la Gaule* (Paris, 1988–)
CahRB	Cahiers de la Revue biblique
CBR	*Currents in Biblical Research*
CCL	Corpus Christianorum: Series latina (Turnhout, 1953–)
CdE	*Chronique d'Egypte*
CEFR	Collection de l'École Française de Rome
CH	*Church History*
CHJ	*The Cambridge History of Judaism*
CIJ	*Corpus inscriptionum judaicarum*, ed. J.-B. Frey (Vatican, 1936–52)
CIL	*Corpus inscriptionum latinarum* (Berlin, 1863–)
CILA	*Corpus de inscripciones latinas de Andalucía.* 6 vols. (Seville, 1989–96)
CIRG	*Corpus de inscricións romanas de Galicia*, ed. G. Pereira Menaut. 2 vols. (Santiago [Spain]: Consello da Cultura Gallega, 1991–94)
CIS	*Corpus Inscriptionum Semiticarum*
CP	*Classical Philology*
CPJud	*Corpus Papyrorum Judaicarum*, ed. Victor Tcherikover, Alexander Fuks, and Menahem Stern. 3 vols. (Jerusalem and Cambridge, Mass., 1957–64)
CPR	*Corpus Papyrorum Raineri*

CRAI	*Comptes rendus des séances*. Académie des Inscriptions et Belles-lettres
CRAIBL	Comptes rendus de l'Académie des Inscriptions et Belles-lettres
CRINT	Compendia rerum iudaicarum ad Novum Testamentum
CSCO	Corpus scriptorum christianorum orientalium
CSEL	Corpus scriptorum ecclesiasticorum latinorum
C.S.I.C.	Consejo Superior de Investigaciones Científicas
CSSH	*Comparative Studies in Society and History*
CTh	*Codex Theodosianus*
CTHS	Comité des travaux historiques et scientifiques
DHA	*Dialogues d'histoire ancienne*
DJD	Discoveries in the Judaean Desert
DOP	*Dumbarton Oaks Papers*
DSD	*Dead Sea Discoveries*
EA	*Epigraphica Anatolica*
EncJud	*Encyclopaedia Judaica*
EPRO	Études préliminaires aux religions orientales dans l'Empire romain
FCh	Fontes Christiani
FGrH	*Fragmente der griechischen Historiker*, ed. Felix Jacoby (Leiden, 1940–99)
FIRA	*Fontes Iuris Romani Anteiustiniani* (2nd ed.; Florence, 1940–43)
GCS	Die griechischen christlichen Schriftsteller der ersten [drei] Jahrhunderte
GLAJJ	*Greek and Latin Authors on Jews and Judaism*, ed. Menahem Stern. 3 vols. (Jerusalem, 1974–84)
GOTR	*Greek Orthodox Theological Review*
HAW	Handbuch der Altertumswissenschaft
Hen	*Henoch*
HEp.	*Hispania Epigraphica*
HO	Handbuch der Orientalistik
HR	*History of Religions*
HSCP	*Harvard Studies in Classical Philology*
HTR	*Harvard Theological Review*
HTS	Harvard Theological Studies
HUCA	*Hebrew Union College Annual*
HUCM	Monographs of the Hebrew Union College
ICI	*Inscriptiones Christianae Italiae*

ICUR	*Inscriptiones Christianae Urbis Romae*
IEJ	*Israel Exploration Journal*
IG	*Inscriptiones Graecae,* ed. Johannes Kirchner (2nd ed.; Berlin, 1916)
IGC-As. Min.	*Recueil des inscriptions Grecques Chretiennes d'Asie Mineure,* ed. Henri Gregoire (Paris, 1922)
IGLBibbia	*Iscrizioni greche e latine per lo studio della Bibbia,* ed. Laura Boffo (Brescia, 1994)
IGLS	*Inscriptions grecques et latines de la Syrie.* 13 vols. (Paris, 1929–)
IHC	*Inscriptiones Hispaniae Christianae,* ed. Emil Hübner (Berlin, 1871)
IJO	*Inscriptiones Judaicae Orientis,* eds. D. Noy et al. 3 vols. (Tübingen, 2004–)
ILAlg.	*Inscriptions latines de l'Algerie*
ILCV	*Inscriptiones Latinae Christianae Veteres*
ILER	*Inscripciones latinas de la España romana,* ed. José Vives. 2 vols. (Barcelona, 1975)
ILMM	*Inscripciones latinas del Museo de Málaga,* eds. Encarnación Serrano Ramos and Rafael Atencia Paez (Madrid, 1981)
ILPG	*Inscripciones latinas de la provincia de Granada,* eds. Mauricio Pastor Muñoz and Angela Mendoza Eguaras (Granada, 1987)
ILS	*Inscriptiones Latinae Selectae,* ed. H. Dessau. 5 vols. (Berlin, 1892–1916)
IRC	*Inscriptions romaines de Catalogne.* 5 vols. (Paris, 1984–2002)
IRCP	*Inscrições romanas do conventus Pacensis,* ed. José d'Encarnaçao (Coimbra, 1984)
IRG	*Inscripciones romanas de Galicia.* 4 vols. (Santiago de Compostela, 1954–68)
IRPL	*Inscripciones romanas de la provincia de León,* ed. Francisco Diego Santos (León, 1986)
IRPLugo	*Inscriptions romaines de la province de Lugo,* eds. Felipe Arias Vilas, Patrick Le Roux, and Alain Tranoy (Paris, 1979)
IstMitt	*Istanbuler Mitteilungen*
JA	*Journal Asiatique*
JbAC	*Jahrbuch für Antike und Christentum*
JBL	*Journal of Biblical Literature*
JDAI	*Jahrbuch des Deutschen Archäologischen Instituts*
JECS	*Journal of Early Christian Studies*
JEH	*Journal of Ecclesiastical History*

JHS	*Journal of Hellenic Studies*
JIGRE	*Jewish Inscriptions from Graeco-Roman Egypt*, eds. William Horbury and David Noy (Cambridge, 1992)
JIWE	*Jewish Inscriptions of Western Europe*, ed. David Noy. 2 vols. (Cambridge, 1993–95)
JJP	*Journal of Juristic Papyrology*
JJPSup	*Journal of Juristic Papyrology*, Supplements
JJS	*Journal of Jewish Studies*
JLA	*Journal of Late Antiquity*
JMedHist	*Journal of Medieval History*
JMS	*Journal of Mediterranean Studies*
JNES	*Journal of Near Eastern Studies*
JÖB	*Jahrbuch der Österreichischen Byzantinistik*
JQR	*Jewish Quarterly Review*
JRA	*Journal of Roman Archaeology*
JRAS	*Journal of the Royal Asiatic Society*
JRASup	*Journal of Roman Archaeology*, Supplementary Series
JRS	*Journal of Roman Studies*
JSAI	*Jerusalem Studies in Arabic and Islam*
JSav	*Journal des savants*
JSJ	*Journal for the Study of Judaism in the Persian, Hellenistic and Roman Periods*
JSJSup	*Journal for the Study of Judaism*, Supplement Series
JSNT	*Journal for the Study of the New Testament*
JSOTSup	*Journal for the Study of the Old Testament*, Supplement Series
JSP	*Journal for the Study of the Pseudepigrapha*
JSPSup	*Journal for the Study of the Pseudepigrapha*, Supplement Series
JSR	*Jewish Studies Review*
JSS	*Journal of Semitic Studies*
JTC	*Journal for Theology and the Church*
JTS	*Journal of Theological Studies*
KAI	*Kanaanäische und aramäische Inschriften*, eds. H. Donner and W. Röllig (Leipzig, 1919–23)
LCL	Loeb Classical Library
LIMC	*Lexicon Iconographicum Mythologiae Classicae*
MAMA	*Monumenta Asiae Minoris Antiqua*
Mansi	*Sacrorum conciliorum nova et amplissima collection*, ed. J. D. Mansi. 53 vols. (Paris, 1901–27)
MEFRA	*Mélanges de l'École française de Rome: Antiquité*

MGH AA	*Monumenta Germaniae Historica, Auctores Antiquissimi*
MH	*Museum Helveticum*
MHR	*Mediterranean Historical Review*
Mus	*Museon: Revue d'études orientales*
NAPSPMS	North American Patristics Society, Patristics Monograph Series
NovTSup	*Novum Testamentum*, Supplements
NTOA	*Novum Testamentum et Orbis Antiquus*
NTS	*New Testament Studies*
OCA	Orientalia Christiana Analecta
OGIS	*Orientis Graeci inscriptiones selectae*, ed. Wilhelm Dittenberger (Leipzig, 1903–5)
OLA	Orientalia Lovaniensia Analecta
OLD	*Oxford Latin Dictionary* (Oxford, 1996)
OrChr	*Oriens christianus*
OrChrAn	Orientalia christiana analecta
OrSyr	*L'orient syrien*
PAAJR	*Proceedings of the American Academy for Jewish Research*
Pan. Lat.	*XII Panegyrici Latini,* ed. R. A. B. Mynors (Oxford, 1964)
PCBE	*Prosopographie chrétienne du Bas-Empire*
PCPhS	*Proceedings of the Cambridge Philological Society*
PG	*Patrologia Graeca*, ed. J.-P. Migne (Paris, 1857–66)
PGL	G. W. H. Lampe, ed. *A Patristic Greek Lexicon* (Oxford, 1961)
PL	*Patrologia Latina*, ed. J.-P. Migne (Paris, 1862–65)
PLRE	*Prosopography of the Later Roman Empire*, eds. A. H. M. Jones et al. 3 vols. (Cambridge, 1971–92)
PMS	Patristic Monograph Series
P.Oxy.	*The Oxyrhynchus Papyri* (London, 1898–)
P.Polit.Iud.	James M. S. Cowey and Klaus Maresch, *Urkunden des Politeuma der Juden von Herakleopolis (144/3–133/2 v. Chr.). Papyri aus den Sammlungen von Heidelberg, Köln, München und Wien* (Wiesbaden, 2001)
PRSt	*Perspectives in Religious Studies*
PS	Patrologia Syriaca
PSI XVII	*Trenta testi greci da papiri letterari e documentari: editi in occasione del XVII Congresso Internazionale di Papirologia*, ed. M. Manfredi (Naples, 1983)
RA	*Revue archéologique*
RAC	*Reallexikon für Antike und Christentum*, ed. T. Kluser et al. (Stuttgart, 1950–)

RAE	*Revue Archéologique de l'Est*
RAESup	*Revue Archéologique de l'Est*, Supplement Series
RANarb	*Revue archéologique de Narbonnaise*
Reinach	*Textes d'auteurs grecs et romains relatifs au judaïsme*, ed. Théodore Reinach (Paris, 1895; repr. Hildesheim, 1963)
REJ	*Revue des études juives*
RevQ	*Revue de Qumran*
RGRW	Religions in the Graeco-Roman World
RHR	*Revue d'histoire des religions*
RICG	*Recueil des inscriptions chrétiennes de la Gaule antérieures à la Renaissance carolingienne*
RIT	*Die römischen Inschriften von Tarraco*, ed. Géza Alföldy. 2 vols. (Berlin, 1975)
RMI	*Rassegna Mensile di Israel*
RomBarb	*Romanobarbarica*
RRJ	*Review of Rabbinic Judaism*
RSR	*Revue des Sciences Religieuses*
RSSR	*Ricerche di Storia Sociale e Religiosa*
SBLSCS	Society of Biblical Literature Septuagint and Cognate Studies
SBLSP	*Society of Biblical Literature Seminar Papers*
SBLTT	Society of Biblical Literature Texts and Translations
SC	*Sources Chrétiennes*
SCI	*Scripta Classica Israelica*
ScrHier	Scripta hierosolymitana
SDHI	*Studia et documenta historiae et iuris*
SEG	*Supplementum Epigraphicum Graecum* (Leiden, 1923–)
SEL	*Studi epigrafici e linguistici*
SIG	*Sylloge Inscriptionum Graecarum*, ed. Wilhelm Dittenberger (3rd ed.; Leipzig, 1920; repr. Hildesheim, 1960)
SJLA	*Studies in Judaism in Late Antiquity*
SNG	*Sylloge Nummorum Graecorum*
SNG Cop	*Sylloge Nummorum Graecorum*, Copenhagen
SNTSMS	Society of New Testament Studies Monograph Series
SOC	*Studia Orientalia Christiana*
STAC	Studien und Texte zur Antike und Christentum
STDJ	*Studies on the Texts of the Desert of Judah*
StPat	*Studia Patristica*
SVTP	Studia in Veteris Testamenti pseudepigrapha
TALSup	*Travaux d'archéologie limousine*, Supplement

TAPA	*Transactions of the American Philological Association*
TED'A	*Taller Escola d'Arqueologia*
TGUOS	*Transactions of the Glasgow University Oriental Society*
TSAJ	Texte und Studien zum antiken Judentum
TUGAL	*Texte und Untersuchungen zur Geschichte der altchristlichen Literatur*
TZ	*Theologische Zeitschrift*
UPZ	*Urkunden der Ptolemäerzeit 1: Papyri aus Unterägypten* (Berlin and Leipzig, 1927)
VC	*Vigiliae Christianae*
VCSup	Supplements to *Vigiliae Christianae*
VDI	*Vestnik Drevnej Istorii*
VetChr	*Vetera Christianorum*
VT	*Vetus Testamentum*
WO	*Die Welt des Orients*
WUNT	Wissenschaftliche Untersuchungen zum Neuen Testament
YCS	Yale Classical Studies
ZA	*Zeitschrift für Assyriologie und Vorderasiatische Archäologie*
ZDMG	*Zeitschrift der Deutschen Morgenländischen Gesellschaft*
ZNW	*Zeitschrift für die neutestamentliche Wissenschaft*
ZPE	*Zeitschrift für Papyrologie und Epigraphik*

INTRODUCTION TO VOLUME II

WILLIAM ADLER

The nineteen chapters in this volume treat the religions of the ancient Mediterranean world from Iran and the Roman Near East to Gaul and the Iberian Peninsula. The bibliography accompanying each essay consists mainly of works cited. Under the heading "Suggestions for Further Reading," readers will find supplemental source material.

The temporal limits of each chapter vary according to region, available evidence, and subject matter. The profound transformation of the cultural and political landscape brought about by Alexander the Great and his Macedonian successors forms the natural backdrop for some of the chapters on the religions of Egypt, the Levant, Greece, and Asia Minor. For Iran and the western Mediterranean, other chronological limits are more suitable. The chapter on Iranian religion begins with the Parthian kingdom and extends to the fall of the Sasanian empire in 654. While archaeological evidence and the witness of Roman antiquarians and historians offer a glimpse, however faint, into an earlier age, the basic structures and practices of Roman and Italian religion become visible only in the last century of the Roman Republic. Similarly, the cult practices in pre-Punic and pre-Roman North Africa can only be known through inference from a scattering of later sources. The advent of Rome represents an obvious point of departure for the chapters dealing with the gods and cults of Gaul and Spain. Absent the epigraphic and material remains of Roman civilization in these regions, our knowledge of their religious traditions would be extremely limited.

Because the destruction of the Jerusalem temple and the end of the Jewish state marked a turning point in the history and character of Palestinian Judaism, two chapters cover this topic: one on Judaism in Palestine during the Hellenistic and Roman periods, the other on post-70 Judaism in Judea and the Near East. While relatively well documented for the Ptolemaic and early Roman period, Egyptian Judaism largely disappears from view after the brutal conflicts of the early second century, only to reappear in a different form in the fourth century. Jews living in Asia Minor and the West were less affected by the political and social upheaval of the late first and early second centuries. Although literary evidence for the Jews of Asia Minor is relatively sparse (and much of it from Christian sources), inscriptional evidence richly documents their presence in this region; drawing largely upon it, the chapter on the Jews of Asia Minor extends from their earliest attested settlements up until the rise of Islam. The chapter on Judaism in Rome and the West encompasses the period from its earliest attested appearance in Rome in the second century BCE up until the later fourth and early fifth centuries, depending on the evidence (again mostly epigraphic) from scattered Jewish communities throughout this area.

The chapters on Christianity begin with its first documented appearance in the region under consideration and extend either into Late Antiquity (Asia Minor), the early Middle Ages (Gaul and Italy), or the Islamic conquest (North Africa, Egypt, and Syria). Either because of the constraints of space or the paucity of evidence, some important religious movements of Late Antiquity have been folded into existing chapters. For example, the discussion of Manichaeism, a highly complex and international religious tradition, appears in the chapter on Iranian religion and in several chapters on Christianity.

One of the main editorial challenges in an undertaking of this scope is to ensure that the volume does not devolve into a series of disconnected studies, while at the same time taking full account of the inherent complexity of the subject and the extraordinarily mixed primary source material. Literary evidence varies in genre and represents, for the most part, the witness of the elite, educated classes. In many cases, they are either the product of a later age or skewed by polemical or apologetic interests. Inscriptions, coins, seals, and other archaeological remains are highly informative and unmediated witnesses to aspects of everyday religious practices and beliefs either slighted or undocumented in literary sources. But material evidence, often highly fragmentary, can be difficult to integrate with the literary record. We trust that the essays in this volume will serve as a guide to the critical evaluation and use of this sometimes intractable corpus of source material.

Thanks to the discovery of new sources and reevaluation of the older material, many of the neat organizing themes of previous studies of the religions of Late Antiquity are no longer defensible. No one today can seriously entertain the view that in the Hellenistic and Roman age, traditional religions had either declined into empty formalisms and artificial "syncretisms," or become mere extensions of political power (see Salzman, "Introduction to Volumes I and II"). If not carefully qualified, strict binary formulations (for example, "monotheism/polytheism" or "exclusivism/tolerance") run the risk of reading a set of static and even anachronistic categories into a highly fluid and dynamic religious landscape. Even for single religious traditions like Christianity and Judaism, it is a daunting task to construct a "master narrative" that does justice to their now well-documented varieties.

One variable that sometimes gets lost amid talk of the "religions of the ancient Mediterranean" is the formative influence of local and regional conditions (see further Salzman, "Introduction to Volumes I and II"). Recognition of the importance of this subject for understanding the religious world of the ancient Mediterranean underlies the ordering of chapters in this volume. Organizing the material in this way will, we hope, enable readers to see how a religious tradition or movement assumed a distinctive local identity, and compare its development both elsewhere and with other religions of the same region. To help orient readers to the chapters that follow, the following discussion identifies some of the major themes and trends that emerge from this approach.

ANCIENT MEDITERRANEAN RELIGIONS IN THEIR REGIONAL CONTEXTS

The eastern Mediterranean after the Macedonian and Roman conquests is a good example of the value of treating the religions of Antiquity in their regional settings. In Greece and Asia Minor, new political and social realities inevitably involved the religious realm as well. Well-known oracles ceased to exert the political influence they once had. With the decline of the *polis* and the deme came mounting dependence on royal patronage. Cult centers in western Asia Minor reaped the benefits of the diversion of resources in their direction. As the cult of Hellenistic rulers took up its place alongside more traditional cults, new festivals in honor of Macedonian kings found their way into the religious calendar (see Roller, Chapter 11). But despite these reforms, cult practices in Greece and western Asia Minor remained relatively stable. Panhellenic religious sanctuaries retained their standing as centers of ritual; sacrifices and festivals were performed as they always had been, and membership in local and regional cult activities continued to play a formative role in the creation of Greek civic and personal identity. With the support of philhellene emperors like Hadrian, traditional Greek cults and festivals remained undiminished by the advent of Rome. In some cases, such as the sacking and refounding of Corinth as a Roman colony, older sanctuaries were destroyed and civic cults valued by Roman settlers were introduced in their place. Even so, time-honored cult practices remained largely intact well into Late Antiquity. One measure of the dynamism of Greek religion and its "openness and adaptability to change" (Roller, Chapter 11) is the constructive and mutual relationships that Greek cities cultivated with Roman emperors. As Roller shows, the enthusiasm with which Greek cities embraced and pursued the conferring of cult honors on Roman rulers, and the seamless integration of the imperial cult into existing religious structures, suggest that it represented for them more than a hollow gesture of political expedience.

The notion of "Hellenistic religion" in Egypt and the Near East as an artificially imposed Greek veneer that can be neatly peeled away from an indigenous religious "core" misrepresents a process that was far more dynamic, adaptive, and regionally and locally specific. As Ted Kaizer points out in his study of religious identities in the Near East, the whole question of distilling, from its various local expressions, something that is identifiably and indigenously "Near Eastern" is itself fraught with difficulties. What Kaizer calls the "continuous renegotiation of religious elements taking place in the context of various open local cultures" is a more descriptive model than the still popular view of Hellenistic religion in the Near East as the accumulation of "stationary religious layers, of which the latest, the classical one, is believed to have no had real impact on indigenous religious elements" (Kaizer, Chapter 2).

In Hellenistic Egypt, as elsewhere, the introduction of new gods and the endowment of indigenous deities with Greek features and dress did change the face of traditional religion. But expressions of Ptolemaic beneficence in the form of publicly subsidized restoration of temples and the protection of priestly prerogatives ensured the continued vitality of traditional Egyptian religion. Egyptian subjects had little difficulty accommodating Ptolemaic dynasts to the ideology of the pharaoh as intermediary between the human and divine realms. Nor were the lines of influence unidirectional. Greeks in Alexandria, for example, gradually adopted the Egyptian practice of mummification. As Françoise Dunand points out in her chapter, adorning an Egyptian deity in foreign dress was not simply a matter of tailoring the god to the tastes of a non-native clientele. The goddess Akoris, dressed in Greek style and situated between two gods, might have reminded a Greek observer of Helen in the company of the Dioscuri. But an Egyptian onlooker, comfortable with representations of their deities in differing forms, would have had no difficulty in finding a traditional meaning for the same image (Dunand, Chapter 6).

While Rome had little incentive to reverse the religious and cultural policies of Hellenistic rulers in Egypt and the Near East, dislocations caused by a new political regime did sometimes intrude upon the religious order. Roman reliance on the educated Hellenized classes for advice and direction in administering Egypt accelerated official use of the Greek language, marginalizing the non-Greek-speaking Egyptian population in the process. Even in conservative priestly circles, Greek gradually overshadowed the native Demotic. The Roman government, wary of a powerful priesthood, instituted policies to keep holders of this office in check. Intrusive micromanagement – extending even to priestly vestments – along with confiscation of temple property, ruinous taxation, and the auctioning of high-ranking religious offices satisfied Rome's ever-growing appetite for revenue and sapped the Egyptian priesthood of the autonomy, wealth, and influence that it had previously enjoyed under the Ptolemies (Dunand, Chapter 6). Largely in response to the disruption of the social hierarchy brought about by Roman administration of Egypt, Alexandria, a city once known for its multiethnic cosmopolitanism, suffered an upsurge in religious and ethnic violence on a scale previously unknown there. For Egyptian Judaism, the consequences of escalating ethnic tensions created by Roman conquest were catastrophic (see Modrzejewski, Chapter 7).

From its earliest encounters with other peoples and cultures of the Mediterranean world, Rome was adept in embracing new cults and assimilating foreign deities to its pantheon. Prominent Romans sought and underwent initiation into the Greek mysteries. While enriching its culture with the myths and traditions associated with the whole panoply of Greek gods, Rome tended to favor deities that either embodied Roman virtues or were needed in times of crisis. Following a plague in the early third century BCE, for example, Rome built a temple to Aesculapius, the Greek god of healing. Cult practices that clashed with Roman values did not necessarily preclude their acceptance, albeit conditionally. A senatorial decree curbed what to Roman sensibilities were the excesses of the popular cult of Bacchus/Dionysus. When, at the end of the Punic Wars, the Romans learned from the Sibylline oracles that the goddess Magna Mater would protect them from foreign invasion, they imported her and her cult from Phrygia to Rome. But after her arrival, the Roman senate forbade Roman citizens from submitting to the rite of ritual castration that was a requirement for admission into her priesthood (see Salzman, Chapter 14).

In Rome's encounters with its neighbors in Italy and other provinces of the western empire, Rome found ways to forge an overarching religious framework flexible enough to accommodate regional and local particularities. As evidenced by her many epithets, a single deity like Venus could assume different identities and be worshipped according to prevailing local customs. A municipal charter from Spain of the Flavian age mandated the worship of certain deities and the performance of certain rites and dictated the formulation of oaths. But the same charter provided for the exercise of discretion in the choice of deities that local municipalities might choose to include in their pantheons. Rome's ready embrace and adaptation of foreign cults and deities might create the impression that this was purely a political calculation, meant either to satisfy strictly practical needs or to ensure social harmony. But as Michele Salzman's chapter demonstrates, that misconception has led to the false, albeit still prevalent, conclusion that only more private forms of religious practice (for example, the mystery cults) provided an outlet for the kinds of "real" (that is, personal) religious experiences lacking in Roman public religion in the imperial age. Rome's public cults were not purely the domain of the priests and magistrates who presided over them; nor were they simply an extension of state power. Although participation was not universally required, Rome's inhabitants were deeply invested in the city's festivals, sacrifices, and rites, from which they derived real material and spiritual benefit and a sense of collective and personal identity. As Salzman further points out, the fluidity of religious rituals and the multiple interpretations assigned to them are themselves testimony to the ongoing vitality of Roman religion (see Salzman, Chapter 14).

In his chapter on the religions and cities of Roman Gaul, William van Andringa disputes the common assumption that Rome pursued here a policy of religious "tolerance" and "coexistence" between indigenous and Roman gods – terms that in his view are more suitable to the modern nation-state than to imperial Rome. As he shows, the relocation of Gallic peoples into autonomous cities incorporated under imperial rule, and with it, the reorganization of cults and reshaping of sacred space within an urban context, created new community-defined pantheons and religious systems. Implementation of this policy depended on the conditions prevailing in what was by all accounts a patchwork of Gallic provinces with differing customs and relations with Rome. The Greek settlements of the Midi, for example, did not undergo the same social realignments as the territories farther to the west. In the Iberian Peninsula to the west, the Romans found a somewhat comparable situation. Before their arrival, the more geographically isolated areas of the Celtic and Iberian interior were less exposed to Mediterranean culture than the *polis*-style settlements of the coastal areas. The spread of Mediterranean gods and cults from the coastal areas to the interior, Augustus's urbanization of the entire peninsula, and the subsequent extension of the Latin right to every municipality under the Flavians thus introduced a degree of religious homogeneity previously unknown to the region (see Kulikowski, Chapter 19).

While the formal institution of the cults of the Roman state that commenced in the Augustan age, and with it the Romanization of local elites, helped to create at the official and administrative levels a "common" religion, these policies did not entirely efface differences in culture and religion. In the Iberian Peninsula, the geographic isolation of the interior was always a constraining factor. The physical terrain of North Africa also played a decisive role in the Romanization of religion and cult in North Africa. Because of its relative isolation, North Africa was less exposed to broader cultural movements in the rest of the Mediterranean basin. Once introduced, however, foreign deities and cults spread quickly, becoming deeply embedded in the cities and countryside of North Africa. During the period of the Roman republic, voluntary initiatives pursued by private parties and associations, not state policy, were the vehicle for the assimilation of Greek and Roman deities with local gods and spirits. As elsewhere in the western Mediterranean, the Augustan age first saw the deliberate introduction of Roman cults as part of official imperial policy. The embrace of these cults by civic elites, and their financing of the building of Capitolia and other Roman shrines and temples in town squares and forums, illustrate the contribution of the state religion to the process of "becoming Roman." But imperial initiatives, private benefactions, and the long-term impact of Roman-style urbanism on religious behavior are only one part of a much larger story. Collectively, the myriad local cults and hybrid gods, the remnants of older indigenous and Punic religious rituals and beliefs that survived after and sometimes in spite of Roman conquest, the religious entrepreneurs and specialists operating outside the confines of temples and priesthood, and the later arrival of Christianity produced a highly dynamic and identifiably "North African" brand of religious belief and practice. As Brent Shaw observes, it is hardly surprising that North Africa is difficult to incorporate into the standard narrative of Mediterranean religion in the ancient world. The "island of the West" was, in his words, "just different" (Chapter 9).

Incorporating Judaism into the narrative of ancient Mediterranean religions raises a very different set of problems. By the first century of the

Common Era, and largely as a consequence of the colonizing policies of Hellenistic kings, Jewish communities made up a sizeable segment of the populations of the Near East, Asia Minor, Egypt, North Africa, and Italy. The experience of these communities under Hellenistic and Roman rule and their interactions with the larger culture were hardly uniform. The assumption of an intrinsic and irreducible antagonism between Jewish monotheistic particularism and the universalizing ideals of Hellenism runs the danger of extrapolating the Maccabean uprising – the result of a unique confluence of events and conditions involving Jewish infighting over the Jerusalem temple and priesthood – to communities where the reception of Greek culture was less fraught and the boundaries separating Jews from non-Jews more fluid (see Eshel and Stone, Chapter 3).

The long and largely untroubled history of the Jews in Ptolemaic Egypt is probably the best-documented example of the latter case. Incorporation of the Torah in Greek translation into the Ptolemaic judicial system and official recognition of its standing as the "civic law" of the Jews allowed Jewish communities in Egypt to exercise autonomy in the administration of domestic affairs. For their part, the Jews found ways to adjust their beliefs and ancestral practices to the practical realities of life in Hellenistic Egypt. Jewish contracts drew upon Greek legal language and forms of documentation. Dedications of houses of worship in Egypt refer to the God of the Jews as "the highest god," a "great god," or "the god who hears," religious language more comprehensible to Greek speakers than the tetragrammaton or "Lord." The author of 3 Maccabees speaks with contempt of an Egyptian Jewish courtier named Dositheus, who deliberately "changed his religion and apostatized from the ancestral traditions" (1.3). But whether Dositheus's apparent participation in the cult of Alexander and the deified Ptolemies constituted self-conscious apostasy or merely a gesture of gratitude to a government that he had served with distinction is another question. In either case, his ability to do so reflects the wide range of religious and social options available to a people who, on the whole, "successfully negotiated the difficult feat of being simultaneously both Jewish and Greek" (Modrzejewski, Chapter 7).

While the history of the Jewish communities of Asia Minor is in some ways comparable to that of Egyptian Judaism, Roman colonization proved to be not nearly as disruptive. Beginning with the resettlement of Jews in Phrygia and Lydia by Seleucus III, Jewish communities were, by the first century CE, spread out over all of Asia Minor. For the most part, they managed to escape the turmoil engulfing Judea and the diaspora populations of Egypt and North Africa. In spite of local opposition, the Roman government protected their civic and legal standing. Jewish participation in the civic and cultural life of the cities of Asia Minor seems to have taken place at every level of urban society. At Sardis, Jews served on city councils, and the synagogue there is one of the most prominent features of the urban landscape. In the first century CE, Julia Severa, a priestess of the local emperor cult, contributed money to the restoration of a synagogue in Phrygia. Another member of her family is mentioned in an inscription as the "head of the synagogue." The relative inattention of Greek and Roman historians to the Jewish population of Anatolia should thus not be understood as a sign of their numerical or social insignificance. It means rather that their generally peaceful integration into Anatolian society was, in the words of van der Horst, too "uneventful" to earn their attention (van der Horst, Chapter 12).

One telling measure of this integration is the penetration of Jewish practice and traditions into non-Jewish settings. Coins from the third century found in Apamea include illustrations of biblical themes. An epitaph from Phrygia warns anyone contemplating abuse of burial privileges to remember the "law of the Jews." Evidence for the existence of God-fearers – that is, gentiles sympathetic to Judaism or observing some degree of Jewish practice – goes well beyond the famous Aphrodisias inscription (see van der Horst, Chapter 12). At Miletus, theater seats were reserved for "Jews who (are) also (called) God-fearers." A private altar at Aspendos dedicated to the god "not made with human hands" presumably refers to the god of the Jews. Because Jews were by law forbidden to make offerings to God outside of the Jerusalem temple, the existence of this inscription would suggest that cult veneration of the Jewish god had extended into non-Jewish circles. The most striking instance of this phenomenon is the cult of "Theos Hypsistos," a movement that, while originating in what van der Horst calls "pagan henotheistic circles," incorporated various features of Jewish beliefs and practices, including an imageless cult. The existence of a religious movement functioning quite viably in the interstices of Jewish monotheism and Greco-Roman polytheism demonstrates that the gap between the two was neither as wide nor as unbridgeable as sometimes imagined.

Epigraphic and literary sources from Asia Minor suggest that robust and ongoing exchanges between Judaism and the wider environment posed little threat to community cohesion and attachment to ancestral traditions (see van der Horst, Chapter 12). Anti-Jewish legislation by Christian emperors that began in the late fourth century did, however, impose hardships on Jewish life in Asia Minor, as it did elsewhere. For Jewish communities, that was only one of a series of reversals beginning with the ill-fated wars against Rome in the late first and early second centuries. Cumulatively, the outbreaks of ethnic tensions, the enormous toll in human life exacted by two wars in Judea, and the violent Roman suppression of Jewish uprisings in North Africa and the East destabilized relations between Jews and non-Jews. While these events, and the marginalizing effects of punitive imperial decrees, did not choke off all relations between the two groups, one result of the sharpening of the boundaries between Jews and non-Jews was an emerging and mutually shared consensus that "Jews were not entirely part of society" (Lapin, Chapter 4).

TRENDS TOWARD RELIGIOUS CENTRALIZATION

During the same period, Judaism itself was undergoing its own internal restructuring, most evident in the expansion of the influence of rabbinic Judaism, the increasing centrality of the synagogue, standardization of religious texts and the liturgical calendar, and the "rediscovery" of the Hebrew language. The process was gradual but insistent, ultimately extending even to Jewish communities in the western Mediterranean. In funerary and synagogue inscriptions from Rome and surrounding areas, for example, Hebrew, whose use for a long time was either decorative or confined to a few conventional phrases, had, by the fifth century, begun to rival Greek and Latin (see Lacerenza, Chapter 15). The destruction of the Jerusalem temple – a potent and unifying symbol of Jewish identity – and the disappearance of once flourishing forms of Judaism undoubtedly hastened this movement toward consolidation and normative self-definition. But as parallel developments in Christianity and Zoroastrianism illustrate, Judaism of Late Antiquity is only one instance of a broader cultural transformation.

Beginning in the middle of the third century, the new Sasanian regime that replaced the Parthian Arsacid dynasty radically changed the face of what would become the state religion of Zoroastrianism. Sasanian kings inherited from their predecessors a multiethnic state and a religious tradition of wide local variety. Parthian rulers, whose practice of Zoroastrianism took the form of a Hellenistic-style private dynastic cult, had neither the desire nor the means to enforce a unified understanding of the religion. In the far reaches of the Parthian empire, Zoroastrianism exerted either minimal influence or assumed forms that differed measurably from what would later be defined as "orthodox." While the religious autonomy that Arsacid kings extended to client kings and nobility may have ensured their loyalty, the Sasanian kings who succeeded them viewed their failure to promote religious uniformity as a symptom of weakness and faltering religious commitment. It was also at odds with the Sasanian vision of a unified Persian empire, strengthened by a single and overarching state religion. The campaign by Sasanian kings to bring this about was thoroughgoing, involving the eradication of heresy, reorganization of Zoroastrian rituals, destruction of sanctuaries to individual deities, and finally the codification of authoritative religious texts.

Repeated prohibitions against intermarriage and other forms of social interaction in the religious and legal texts of religious communities of Sasanian Iran create the initial impression of an empire evolving into self-segregating religious islands, living in virtual isolation from one another. But that is a deceptive impression, called into question by recent comparative studies of the legal and ritual systems of the various religious communities of the Sasanian empire. Religious centralization in Sasanian Iran did not spell cultural isolation. The Sasanian empire continued to act as an intermediary between India and the West. As Albert de Jong suggests in his chapter (Chapter 1), the idea of a state-sanctioned Zoroastrian orthodoxy was itself a reflection of and response to trends in Late Antiquity toward religious consolidation. In Sasanian Iran, other religions – most notably, Christianity and Manichaeism – also claimed possession of a single, textually codified, and revealed truth. The reorganization and centralization of Zoroastrianism enabled it to meet the challenges that they posed.

The brand of Zoroastrianism that came to embody orthodoxy in Sasanian Iran was only one of many expressions of the religion, alternative versions of which are much harder to recover. Were it not for Christian witnesses, for example, we would scarcely have known that the population of pre-Christian Armenia observed a kind of Zoroastrianism more closely aligned with the religious practices of Arsacid Parthia (de Jong, Chapter 1). The filtering effects of orthodoxy are also at work in Judaism and Christianity of Late Antiquity. From rabbinic sources alone, we would have little suspicion of the vast range of Jewish practices and beliefs of pre-70 Judaism, now so richly documented by recent archaeological and manuscript discoveries (see Eshel and Stone, Chapter 3; Lapin, Chapter 4).

Advocates of Christian orthodoxy engaged in their own brand of historical revisionism. To varying degrees, modern scholars are agreed that, almost from the very outset, diversity was organic to Christianity's early growth and development. But this was not the perspective of Eusebius's *Ecclesiastical History*, the single most important history of the early church. Eusebius was willing to acknowledge that proliferating heresies threatened to disrupt the teachings of Christ and the apostles faithfully preserved and transmitted by the champions of orthodoxy. But for him these were only later and transient distortions, meant to sow division and uncertainty. Eusebius's conviction that Christianity, no matter where it was established, shared from the very outset a common set of traditions and beliefs was hardly any more accommodating to the peculiar features of the various Christian communities scattered throughout the Mediterranean. To reconstruct the history and character of these communities, Eusebius's account must therefore be augmented with other sources, some of which have only recently come to light.

When, in the second century, the material and literary evidence becomes more plentiful, Christian communities stretching from Latin-speaking North Africa to Syria and Mesopotamia had already assumed distinctive regional identities. The first we hear about Christianity in North Africa is the story of the trial and beheadings of the twelve Scillitan martyrs (180), who refused even to consider an offer to renounce their beliefs. Age-old resentments of Roman colonial rule resurface in Tertullian's glorification of the martyr/gladiator and his mocking defiance of Roman power and religion. The hallmarks of North African Christianity of Tertullian's day – the cult of martyrdom and self-sacrifice, charismatic enthusiasm, and concern for individual and communal discipline and purity – are to be expected in a region known for its insularity, religious fervor, and rigorism (Jensen, Chapter 10). But Christianity in Roman North Africa was culturally far removed from Christian communities farther to the east, most notably in the cosmopolitan cities of Alexandria and, to the east of the Roman empire, Syrian Edessa. Lying on the borders between Rome and Parthia, Edessa, a semiautonomous Hellenistic city-state and cultural crossroads, proved to be a congenial environment for a rich variety of beliefs and practices. Bar Daysān, the cultured Edessene aristocrat, renaissance man, and friend of King Abgar, was worlds apart from Tertullian, the puritanical and alienated Latin-speaking polemicist of Roman Carthage (see Griffith, Chapter 5).

Over time, the transformative political events of the fourth century and institutional consolidation within the churches themselves brought those worlds closer together. Intensifying internal struggles about the sources of religious authority that had begun already in the second century were probably the single most important catalyst in this drive toward consolidation. Because the early history of Christian communities was often fragmentary or even inaccessible, attempts at self-legitimation by rival groups often required the creation of notional pedigrees, whether in the form of a chain of secret traditions or of episcopal succession lists extending back to the apostolic age. In Egypt, for example, the great Alexandrian gnostic teacher Basilides represented himself as the heir to the secret teachings of Jesus, handed down through the apostle Matthias. Orthodox Christian sources of the fourth and fifth centuries maintained their own succession lists, both of the teachers of the Alexandrian catechetical and of Alexandrian bishops extending back to Saint Mark, the follower of Peter and purported founder of the Alexandrian church (see van der Vliet, Chapter 8).

We are probably best informed about the stages in this process in the Christian community of Rome. The official record notwithstanding, institutional unity in Rome emerged slowly. Like other religious associations in Rome, Christianity began there as a confederation of loosely connected groups, meeting in houses and other buildings and subject to the changing demographics of its membership and the steady inflow of new doctrines and practices. While the earliest Christians were probably indistinguishable from Jews, at least in the eyes of the Romans, the apostle Paul's epistle to the Romans already suggests the existence of an unresolved dispute between Jewish and gentile members of the community over the meaning and significance of the Jewish law. In the second century, the growth of Marcionite churches contributed to an already pluralist religious environment, at the same time raising alarm among advocates of a more doctrinally unified church. A schism that had developed over the integration of those who had lapsed during the great persecution of the mid-third century further heightened the pressure for institutional unity, and with it concentration of power in the office of the episcopacy. By the end of the second century, claimed possession of a continuous list of Roman bishops extending back to the chief apostle Peter was a vital argument in the church's contest with heresy. Challenges to its authority from the emperor and the church of Constantinople in the post-Constantinian era intensified the campaign of the see of Rome to confirm its divinely sanctioned ecclesiastical primacy.

As Trout observes of Christianity in Rome, "internal diversity, tolerance and rivalry, undercurrents of distrust, and evolution toward institutional unity are primary themes of its social history" (Chapter 16). The same could be said of other Christian communities throughout the Mediterranean. But we need not assume that institutional formalization necessarily filtered down to everyday religious interactions. Differentiating "Montanist" from "non-Montanist" in epigraphic and archaeological sources in Asia Minor is far more difficult than might be expected from the rhetoric of schism that permeates official denunciations of Montanist liturgical structures and practices (Trombley, Chapter 13). Developments in post-70 Judaism and the increasingly gentile composition of Christian churches no doubt helped to widen the division between the two groups. But the boundaries between the two groups remained unstable, often to the dismay of heresiologists and church officials. In Phrygia, joint Jewish and Christian celebration of the Passover in 367 shows that official decrees issued at the time against participation in Jewish festivals were not merely anticipating, in the words of Pieter van der Horst, a "hypothetical possibility" (Chapter 12).

Increasing insistence on institutional unity and doctrinal conformity could itself sometimes produce the opposite effect. For centuries, the churches of Egypt remained divided over the polarizing Christological controversies of the fifth century. To judge from the inscriptions of Asia Minor from the fourth and fifth centuries, members of groups deemed "sectarian" or "heretical" actually became more assertive in expressing their distinctive identities (Trombley, Chapter 13). At least initially, coercive attempts by Christian emperors of the fourth century to abolish the Donatist church in North Africa only stiffened their resolve, at the same time reawakening anti-Roman resentments and the ideology of martyrdom. Contemporary witnesses describe Donatists actively pursuing death by hurling themselves over cliffs or by deliberate provocations against the local non-Christian population (Jensen, Chapter 10). In some cases, political boundaries stood in the way of institutional consolidation. Although the Syriac communities straddling the Roman and Persian frontiers were bound together by a set of shared traditions and customs, theological disagreements and the realities of living under different political regimes ultimately led to the division of these communities east and west (see Griffith, Chapter 5).

Over the longer term, however, the heterogeneity that marked Christian communities of the first three centuries gradually yielded to countervailing pressures. At the Council of Nicaea, there was no longer any disagreement on the date of the celebration of Easter, a subject that in the second century threatened a schism between Rome and the churches of Asia Minor. By the late fourth century, Syriac theologians, increasingly estranged from older representatives of their tradition, were now absorbed in the same divisive Christological controversies engulfing Christendom farther to the west. Thanks largely to Ephraem, himself an ardent advocate of Nicene orthodoxy, the once influential Bar Daysān was now a heretic in the class of Marcion and Mani. The Edessene church had also fashioned for itself a legitimating myth of origins. Records purportedly preserved in Edessa's archives established the ancient roots of Edessene orthodoxy and its early communion with the sees of Rome and Antioch (see Griffith, Chapter 5). The gradual transformation of Christian monasticism from private acts of ascetic withdrawal into strictly organized communities, subordinated to the authority of the bishop and the demands of orthodox doctrine, may be the most visible sign of the shift toward institutional consolidation and uniformity that is broadly characteristic of Christianity in Late Antiquity.

Repressive policies of Christian emperors exacted their own toll. While tolerating the divisive Christological disputes that roiled the churches of the fourth century, emperors, often acting on the advice of church officials, could be ruthless in rooting out threats to institutional unity. After raising the suspicions of local clergy, Priscillian, the leader of a rigorous Christian movement in Spain of the fourth century, was first banished by the emperor Gratian and then put to death on the charge of magic, a crime against the state. Montanist and Novatianist groups were still in existence in Asia Minor of the sixth century, but in the words of Trombley, "reduced to tiny remnants" (Chapter 13). Externally enforced uniformity did more than eliminate religious heterodoxy, however. In the case of North African Christianity, for example, once known for its defiance of "externally imposed conformity," the gradual erosion of its distinctive regional identity impaired its prospects for survival. In her chapter, Robin Jensen attributes the virtual disappearance of North African Christianity within a century of Arab conquest to "a history of successive conquests or domination by authorities who demanded religious conformity from the resident population.... Eventually, even the faith of the invading Arab Muslims may have seemed no more religiously foreign to indigenous African Christians than those of the previous ruling power – the Byzantine emperor and his delegates" (Chapter 10).

THE CHRISTIANIZATION OF THE MEDITERRANEAN WORLD OF LATE ANTIQUITY

In Eusebius's *Ecclesiastical History*, the single thread holding together the narrative is the story of the church triumphant: how it remained unified and true to the teachings of Jesus and the apostles, in the face of ceaseless threats to its existence from heresy and persecution. The ubiquitous shrines to martyrs and the stories of their heroism that crowd the historical memory of a later age add to the impression of early Christian communities living under constant siege. But the reality of Christian communities throughout the Mediterranean world was far more complex. For the first two centuries of their existence, sporadic persecutions against

Christian communities were left to the discretion of provincial governors, who implemented the policies according to their assessment of prevailing conditions. For the Roman government, well experienced in absorbing and domesticating new cults and beliefs, the socially destabilizing impact of the new religion was of greater concern than the specifics of Christian beliefs and practices.

While Christian monotheism was not an insuperable obstacle standing in the way of religious reconciliation, public refusals by Christian "atheists" to recognize traditional Roman deities did heighten suspicions about their loyalty to Rome. In his letter to Trajan seeking advice in dealing with Christians in Bithynia of Asia Minor, Pliny the Younger recalls that his own investigations revealed only a depraved, but essentially harmless, superstition. What he found more alarming was their obstinacy and the harm that the rapid growth of the religion was doing to the temple-based religion and economy. Even in the mid-third century, when Christians, especially influential figures in the Church, fell victim to a harsh general persecution, they were only the most conspicuous targets of a broader policy meant to ensure participation in the public cults (see Salzman, Chapter 14; Trout, Chapter 16).

In his letter, Pliny voiced his misgivings about a movement spreading from the cities into the countryside, and threatening to infiltrate all levels of society. His fears were warranted. Inscriptions from Asia Minor of the late third century show Christians serving as councilors, supervising public works, and even organizing public spectacles. Tertullian was exaggerating for effect when he gloats over Christians "filling your cities, fortresses, towns, assemblies, camp, palace, senate and forum" (*Apol.*, 37.4). Even so, contemporary sources from North Africa do confirm the existence of Christian landowners and members of distinguished families in North Africa of Tertullian's day. Inclusion of the educated classes in their ranks also enabled Christianity to compete more effectively in the arena of ideas. For the great teachers of the Alexandrian catechetical school, the allegorical method of interpretation popularized by Philo "succeeded in bringing the Bible up to the level of Homer and other classics of the dominant Hellenistic culture" (van der Vliet, Chapter 8). Through what Trombley describes as a "shared high culture of the Greek *paideia*" (Chapter 13), the language of divinity used in Christian literary and epigraphic sources was so conventional that it is often difficult to distinguish Christian from non-Christian inscriptions. During the thaw in Christian–Roman relations of the latter years of the Severan dynasty, Origen, the great Alexandrian theologian and scholar, even instructed the mother of the emperor Severus Alexander when she was traveling in Antioch (Eusebius, *Hist. eccl.* 6.21.3).

Increasing Christian participation in Greco-Roman culture did not always ease long-simmering resentments, however. In some cases, it merely offered a vehicle for Christian apologists to express their cultural and political disaffection more eloquently. In the late second century, the Syrian polemicist Tatian speaks of abandoning the Greek culture in which he was raised for the "barbarian philosophy" of Christianity (*Orat.* 42). With the tools and persuasiveness of the trained rhetor, Tertullian seethes against Rome and advises his coreligionists to avoid all interactions with pagan society. Occasional outbursts of apocalyptic enthusiasm, the appeal of the ascetic ideal, and the unexpected escalation of religious persecution that began in the mid-third century no doubt further fueled a sense of alienation from the broader environment. But once the political fortunes of Christianity and the Roman state had fused in the early fourth century, it was difficult to sustain the notion that Christianity, now the beneficiary of imperial largesse and privilege, was a movement at war with the world. In the aftermath of the conversion of Constantine, the influence, standing, and self-understanding of Christian communities throughout the Mediterranean entered into a completely new phase.

One highly revealing sign of this change is the growth in the sheer volume of Christian literature. For the first three centuries of its existence, Greek, and to a much lesser degree, Latin, were the primary languages of Christian writing. By the fourth century, however, Syriac and Coptic began to challenge Greek for supremacy in the Christian East. We should not assume that the flourishing of these languages either signified the repudiation of Greek language and culture, or followed unavoidably from the expansion of Christian communities into the non-Greek-speaking classes. Bar Daysān, one of the first Christian authors to write in Syriac, was deeply rooted in the highly Hellenized milieu of Edessa. Nor did the subsequent growth of Coptic and Syriac as literary languages leave Egypt and Syria isolated from Greek-speaking Christian communities to the west. Greek continued to be the official language of the Egyptian church. Starting in the late fourth century, Greek theological writings in translation were a staple of Egyptian and Syriac Christianity (see Griffith, Chapter 5; van der Vliet, Chapter 8). The engine driving this expansion of Christian literary culture was monasticism, a movement that by the early fourth century had in Egypt evolved into organized and thriving centers of authority, spiritual discipline, and learning. By recruiting their membership from the educated classes, monastic communities in

Egypt played an increasingly vital role in all aspects of scribal and literary culture (see van der Vliet, Chapter 8).

Endowments from wealthy patrons, the emulation of Egyptian-style communal monasticism in Syria and the West, and the growing appeal of monastic holiness made Christian monastic communities a highly visible presence in the landscape of Late Antiquity. In Egypt, some of them approached the size of small cities. But this is only one element in the dramatic transformation of public space. In keeping with the official recognition of Christianity, churches, once informal gathering places in homes and open spaces, were now publicly financed architectural monuments. As physical reminders of the heroic age of the church triumphant (a theme played out again and again in the literature), proliferating martyr shrines soon became popular destinations for religious tourists, the sites of healing miracles, the objects of cult, the focal point of intense competition between communities over possession of martyrs' relics, and even an incitement for fierce theological disputes about the proper way to honor them (see Trout, Chapter 16; van der Vliet, Chapter 8).

The active role that Christian bishops played in establishing and supervising these building projects, and in managing other aspects of the civic and religious life of Late Antiquity, is clear testimony to the professionalization of the office and the expansion of episcopal authority made possible by official enfranchisement. Bishops confirmed their leadership through alliances and networks of support, and the accumulation of moral, spiritual, and intellectual credentials. Some of the best-known bishops of the church of the fourth century were also exemplars of monastic piety and highly skilled rhetors. Like other aristocratic elites in Late Antiquity, bishops acted on behalf of cities by advocating for them before imperial officials and spending private wealth on civic projects. With the decentralization of political power caused by the decline of the Roman empire in the West, bishops even played roles once reserved for Roman officials. One project in which bishops took a direct interest was in rooting out the last vestiges of paganism, either by policing the behavior of the laity or by reconsecrating sacred groves and other sites of pagan cult with Christian churches and shrines (see Klingshirn, Chapter 18; Salzman, Chapter 14).

Imperial decrees, diversion of public funds to the churches, and occasional dramatic acts of mob violence against pagan monuments may have hastened the neglect and ultimate demise of the priesthood and public, temple-based religion. Even so, Christian laity continued to participate in traditional religious festivals, visit healing springs, and consult diviners for advice on everyday matters. Private expressions of traditional religious piety survived well into the fourth and fifth centuries, especially in geographically inaccessible places where Christianity had arrived late and had yet to become the majority religion (as for example in the north and west of the Iberian Peninsula; see Kulikowski, Chapter 19). In Rome itself, traditional religious practices were far from moribund. There, and in the absence of a resident emperor, civic elites played an increasingly important role in sponsoring and maintaining the traditional cults (see Salzman, Chapter 14). An empire now officially Christian, a landscape dotted with Christian churches and shrines, an increasingly influential clerical class, and religious calendars dense with the names of Christian saints collectively create the impression of a new religious order. But as the chapters on this subject amply illustrate, the institution of this new order was a far more incremental and locally variable process.

PART I

IRAN AND THE NEAR EAST

I

RELIGION IN IRAN: THE PARTHIAN AND SASANIAN PERIODS (247 BCE–654 CE)

ALBERT DE JONG

INTRODUCTION

Rich in natural resources and strategically located at the crossroads of the ancient world's civilizations, Iran has always been a sought-after prize for conquerors. Its history is thus one of both conquests and migrations, with many peoples and tribal federations entering the Iranian plateau in search of living space and pasture grounds. But human activity is only partly responsible for the great destruction that Iran has endured over its long history. Equally important are the earthquakes and other natural disasters that have engulfed the region periodically, often with devastating consequences, to which slow patterns of aridification and, locally, salination have further contributed.[1] Given its complicated socio-ethnic and natural history, it is hardly surprising that the cultural and religious history of pre-Islamic Iran is difficult to write.

To understand the religious history of the region, we must also take account of the attitude toward writing shown by the Iranian peoples who dominated the area. When the Achaemenid Persians gained control of much of the ancient world, the flourishing civilizations that they encountered employed writing for various purposes: administration, scholarship, religion, and literature. While they retained local administrative practices in those parts of the empire that had a functioning bureaucracy (for example, Babylonia and Elam, the heart of the empire), the lingua franca of the new imperial bureaucracy was Aramaic. For this administration, they relied initially on Aramaean scribes, who eventually taught their craft to local, Iranian-speaking boys, especially in the

[1] For overviews see Ambraseys and Melville, *Persian Earthquakes*; Christensen, *Decline of Iranshahr*; and Nützel, *Geo-Archäologie*.

23

outlying parts of the empire. This practice, already attested in the names of scribes found in a recently discovered fourth-century BCE archive from Bactria,[2] is especially visible a few centuries later, after the conquests of Alexander and the collapse of Seleucid rule over Iran and Central Asia. Independently, some of the former provinces of the Achaemenid empire continued to use Aramaic scribal conventions, but this time in Iranian languages: Parthian, Sogdian, and Khwarezmian.[3] We have to assume, therefore, that in the brief period of Macedonian and Seleucid rule over Iran, the traditional (Achaemenid) system of administration coexisted with a new administration in Greek.

While we can thus trace an unbroken administrative tradition for several Iranian peoples, none of them apparently ever extended the use of writing into two crucial areas of Iranian culture: literature, which in an Iranian context means poetry, and religion. Each had its own reasons for rejecting the use of writing. Poetry was the special domain of a highly trained class of professional minstrels, the *gosans*, who sang their lays for wealthy patrons, adapting them to local circumstances and interweaving old tales with items of local or historical interest.[4] In all likelihood, they did not master the craft of writing, the domain of yet another professional class, the scribes. But even apart from this, "freezing" their songs in writing must have seemed to them both unnecessary and undesirable.

In the religious domain, the situation was different. The two collections of Zoroastrian religious texts can be distinguished by the language(s) that they used. The first corpus, known nowadays as the Avesta,[5] differs from all other Zoroastrian texts by its use of an Old Eastern Iranian language known as Avestan. Although the texts preserved in Avestan are almost exclusively ritual texts, there is reason to assume that the corpus was originally larger, consisting of both legal and ritual texts and, perhaps, texts of a more narrative character. However, the majority of such texts, and in the case of the narrative texts, all of them, were eventually lost.[6]

---

[2] Shaked, *Satrape de Bactriane*, 22–7.

[3] For the evidence, see Henning, "Mitteliranisch"; see also Skjærvø, "Aramaic Scripts." While limited, Aramaic inscriptions from Armenia and Georgia suggest a similar development there as well.

[4] Boyce, "Parthian *gosan*."

[5] Although the frequent description of these texts as "the sacred books" of the Zoroastrians reflects the way they are regarded by modern Zoroastrians, it is deeply problematic for earlier periods of the religion.

[6] One "legal" text has been preserved, viz. the Vendidad (*Vidēvdād*), the structure of which is discussed by Skjærvø, "*Videvdad.*" Important fragments of texts discussing priestly and ritual matters in Avestan have further been preserved in the *Hērbedestān* and *Nērangestān*, on which see Kotwal and Kreyenbroek, *Hērbedestān and Nērangestān*.

The second corpus of Zoroastrian texts is known as *Zand* ("knowledge"). Unlike the Avesta, *Zand* texts are presumed to have been in the vernacular. The common presentation of the *Zand* as the "translation" of the Avesta into the vernacular is a wholly plausible interpretation from a modern point of view. But at least in Sasanian Zoroastrianism, the *Zand* was seen as the second part of the revelation, equally revealed to Zarathushtra by his god Ahura Mazdā. It was, furthermore, the basis for all Zoroastrian theology, the Avestan texts being gradually reduced in practical importance to specific ritual contexts.

These two collections, frequently referred to jointly as the *dēn*, "religion/revelation," were transmitted orally, but in distinct ways. For recitation in ritual contexts, the Avestan texts were memorized, syllable by syllable, line by line. Iranians believed that sacred words needed to be spoken in order to exert power. Mistakes in pronunciation and recitation of these sacred texts, in their own ritual language, would invalidate the ritual, with possibly disastrous consequences. The other corpus, the *Zand*, was evidently allowed to grow and change in transmission. The distribution of Zoroastrians over a number of Iranian languages and regions suggests that the priests of those linguistic communities all used their own *Zand*. But because the southwestern region of Iran emerged in Sasanian times as the dominant Iranian culture, the *Zand* of Pārs is the only preserved version. The fact that the *Zand* was preserved at all is the result of a process of scripturalization – the introduction of writing to preserve religious texts, a process that will be discussed more fully later in this chapter.

SOURCES AND PROBLEMS

Owing to the exclusively oral transmission of Zoroastrian texts almost up to the end of our period, there are no primary religious texts from which to reconstruct the history of ideas, beliefs, or rituals with any confidence. The sources we do have from the Iranian world itself are chiefly archaeological remains, documentary texts, royal and private inscriptions, coins, and seals. Like its twin sister, the religion of the Vedic Indians, Zoroastrianism is difficult to trace archaeologically. With roots reaching back to prehistory, in a nonsedentary setting, its basic requirements have always been simple. The characteristic rituals of lighting and tending a fire, animal sacrifice, rites of purification, and the exposure of corpses to be eaten by vultures and dogs do not require permanent (and thus traceable) installations. On the contrary, the evidence of the Avesta shows that the only requirement was a suitable ritual ground chosen and prepared for the occasion. It is true that modern Zoroastrians have numerous fire-temples, housing permanently tended sacred fires, and that a similar abundance of fire-temples is assumed to have existed in (late) Sasanian times. But we should not suppose that this was always the case. In fact, before the nineteenth century, the Parsis (the Zoroastrians of India) survived for eight centuries with a very small number of sacred fires.

Alongside this body of material evidence are the reports about the beliefs, rituals, and ideas of the Iranians in the writings of those who came into contact with them: Greeks, Romans, Jews, and Christians in western Iran, and Indians and Chinese in eastern Iran. If used judiciously, these sources are indispensable to the study of Iranian religions. Greek witnesses demonstrate, for example, that the basic Zoroastrian narrative about two primal spirits and their pact to test each other's strength in this world for a limited period was already fully developed in the fourth century BCE.[7] Because these Greek authors also show how Zoroastrian communities throughout the Iranian world differed in their performance of the rituals and observance of the laws of purity, they supplement the fairly homogeneous and normative picture provided by Zoroastrian priestly literature.[8] The same is true for the evidence in the literature of the Sasanian period in Armenian and various dialects of Aramaic (the Babylonian Talmud, Syriac Christian literature, and Mandaic).

The third, and possibly most controversial, source for our knowledge of the religious history of Parthian and Sasanian Iran is the later Zoroastrian tradition itself. Although it is generally accepted that most of the priestly texts are to be dated in the ninth century (that is, after the Arab conquests, at a time when Zoroastrians were gradually reduced to a minority), they contain vital information, especially for the Sasanian period.[9] This is also true for the living tradition, especially its rituals and some of its institutions. The Zoroastrian calendar has been the focus of particular attention. This calendar replaced an original one consisting of twelve months of thirty days (=360 days) with a 365-day year (with five intercalary days, still short of the natural year) in the Achaemenid period, on the model of the Egyptian calendar.[10] Because the original calendar regulated the ritual year, its reorganization, which is traceable in sources from all over the

---

[7] For a succinct statement, see De Jong, "Contribution of the Magi."

[8] This is treated in detail in De Jong, *Traditions of the Magi*.

[9] Zoroastrian Middle Persian ("Pahlavi") works are often referred to as the "ninth-century books" (thus Bailey, *Zoroastrian Problems*), since most of them are to be dated around that period. Some of them are earlier and some of them (much) later, however, and the continued use of this appellation especially distorts the history of Zoroastrianism in Islamic times.

[10] See De Blois, "Persian Calendar."

Zoroastrian world, was most likely enforced by a central government. The expected opposition to this reform is variously attested in sources from a wide geographic and chronological range.[11]

There are obvious dangers in using the living tradition (or evidence from the Islamic period) for the interpretation of much earlier material. All evidence dating from the Islamic period reflects a religious tradition that did not enjoy state support. In pre-Islamic times, however, the chief expressions of religiosity that we know of were closely tied to the state, the dynasts and their nobles, and the priestly organization they supported. It has been suggested, with good reasons, that the dynastic cult was little more than an appropriately grand version of the domestic cult, just as royal burials resembled those of commoners but on a different scale. But there are traces in the sources of profound changes taking place in late Sasanian times: a tightening grip by the central government on the organization of the priesthood, the collection and writing down of the sacred writings, and changes in the way the tradition was to be transmitted. This later process of unification produced a form of Zoroastrianism substantially different from that of the Parthian and Sasanian empires. To demonstrate this change, the following discussion will review developments of Zoroastrianism at three pivotal stages in its history: early imperial Arsacid times (the second century BCE), the shift from Arsacid to Sasanian rule (the third century CE), and the apogee of Sasanian power in the sixth century. Armenia deserves special attention, for it best exemplifies the substantial differences between Parthian and Sasanian Zoroastrianism.

THE HISTORICAL SETTING: THE RISE OF PARTHIA

For the obscure early history of the Parthian empire, only a few subjects have enjoyed general consensus.[12] One of them is the importance of the homeland of the Arsacids, the Iranian region known as Parthava in Old Persian sources, as Pahlav in Middle Persian texts, and as Parthia to the Romans. Its heartland is located in the northeastern part of Iran (Khorasan) and the southern part of the modern republic of Turkmenistan. Fronted by deserts on two sides (the Karakum to the north and the Kavir to the south), it

---

[11] For an overview, see Boyce, "Further on the Calendar."

[12] The following discussion of Parthian Zoroastrianism and Parthian history is based on Boyce and De Jong, *Parthian and Armenian Zoroastrianism* (in preparation). Indispensable for Parthian history are the many contributions in Wiesehöfer, ed., *Partherreich*. Wolski, *Empire des Arsacides*, is selective and controversial. See further Lerouge, *L'image des Parthes dans le monde gréco-romain;* Hackl, Jacobs, and Weber, eds., *Quellen zur Geschichte des Partherreiches.*

is defined chiefly by two parallel mountain chains – known mainly from their most impressive ranges, the Kopet Dagh and the Binalud – with a wide, flat, and fertile trough between them, richly watered by the rivers Atrak and Kashaf and countless other streams.[13] Despite its fame in later times as one of the most pleasant and fertile regions of Iran, some classical authors, and occasionally modern historians as well, present it as a rugged, barren, and inhospitable region (see Map 1).[14]

Originating in the north, the Arsacids were the only Iranian dynasty from the three pre-Islamic Iranian empires that did not come from Persia. With close cultural ties to the Hyrcanians and their western neighbors, the Medes, these northern Iranian regions were culturally dominant throughout the Arsacid period. Armenia and Georgia, ancient non-Iranian lands that adapted Parthian culture (and religion), provide additional evidence of this dominance. Parthian institutions also exerted a profound influence on the cultures of the buffer zone between the Parthian and Hellenistic-Roman worlds: Armenia, Mesopotamia, and Babylonia.[15]

There is also broad consensus about the importance of the year 247 BCE, the first year of the Arsacid era. Its importance is best explained on the assumption that this was the year in which Arsaces I, the founder of the dynasty, proclaimed himself king of an independent Parthia. He was not the first to do so, however. A few years earlier, the Greek satrap of Parthia, Andragoras, apparently broke away from his Seleucid suzerains and proclaimed himself ruler of Parthia. Although this act of independence is reflected only faintly in the sources, it appears to be confirmed by Andragoras's unexpected step of minting his own coins (including, significantly, gold coins), a few of which have survived.[16] These show him wearing the royal diadem, though otherwise bareheaded; the coin legend simply gives his name. At about the same time – that is, around the year 250 BCE – neighboring Bactria also claimed its independence under a Greek ruler, in this case Diodotus I.[17] The secession of Bactria was primarily a

[13] The best introduction is Fisher, "Physical geography," 62–72. Despite an outdated treatment of history and culture, Rawlinson's *Sixth Oriental Monarchy* and *Parthia* contain unsurpassed surveys of Parthian geography.
[14] Thus Sherwin-White and Kuhrt, *From Samarkhand to Sardis*, 84–8, to be read in conjunction with Bernard, "Asie Centrale."
[15] Both Armenians and Parthians are generally neglected, fatally it would seem, in Millar, *Roman Near East*.
[16] The best discussion is D'jakonov and Zejmal, "Pravitel' Parfii," with Alram, "Stand und Aufgaben," 369–71.
[17] Here too there is controversy over the date of the secession of Bactria. A late date for Bactria and Parthia is suggested by Lerner, *Impact of Seleucid Decline*; Holt, *Thundering Zeus*. For the likelihood of the earlier date see Bernard, "Asie Centrale."

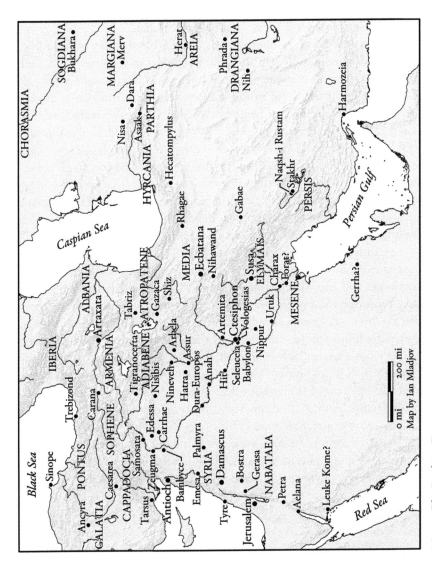

Map 1. The Parthian Empire

29

Greek affair, with Greek kings establishing a Greek realm in a country of mixed ethnic composition. Arsaces' conquest of Parthia, on the other hand, was an act of the local Iranian population striving for independence from "foreign" rule (in this case that of Andragoras).

Because of a dearth of sources, it is unclear to what extent feelings of ethnic and/or religious "identity" contributed to this uprising. An additional complication is the report of some Greco-Roman authors who say that Arsaces I, the founder of the dynasty, was not a Parthian at all, but rather the leader of a tribe of nomadic Aparnian Sakas who raided and then conquered Parthia.[18] Accepting their report would produce considerable problems for the religious history of the region. In particular, the Sakas are not known to have been Zoroastrians, while the Parthian kings are not known to have been anything other than Zoroastrians. There are many reasons to doubt the historicity of the Aparnian conquest, and preference must be given to the equally attested identification of Arsaces as a Parthian leading a Parthian uprising and establishing a Parthian kingdom.[19]

The early days of the Parthian kingdom, when Arsaces and his successors ruled their little province in northeastern Iran, saw the forging of traditions and institutions that lasted throughout the period of Arsacid rule, the longest of any pre-Islamic Iranian dynasty. One of these traditions was the practice, known already from the Achaemenid period, of lighting a dynastic fire, a special elaboration of the old custom of lighting a householder's fire. Arsaces' fire burned in the city of Asaak, the precise location of which is unknown.[20] Two further early Arsacid traditions remained virtually unchanged throughout the Parthian period: the use of only one throne name (Arsaces) and the design of Arsacid coins, the chief material for any reconstruction of Arsacid history.

At his accession, Arsaces' successor Tiridates also took the name of Arsaces, which he put on his coins.[21] His successor, whose name may have been Artabanus, followed suit, and from that moment onward, all Arsacid

---

[18] Following the many works of Jozef Wolski (and Rawlinson before him), most scholars have accepted the veracity of this tradition. For important objections, see especially Boyce, "Sedentary Arsacids," and Hauser, "Ewigen Nomaden."

[19] This is the version of early Arsacid history given in Arrian's *Parthica*.

[20] It is known only from a short mention in Isidore of Charax, *Parthian Stations* §11, ed. Shoff.

[21] Although now a minority opinion, it seems most likely to the present writer that Arsaces I did not live very long to enjoy his success – a mere two years – and that he was succeeded by his brother, Tiridates, who literally chose to rule in his name. This reconstruction, once accepted as true by all, has been attacked relentlessly by Jozef Wolski (and before him by Von Gutschmid, *Geschichte Irans*, 29–34) and has now been commonly abandoned. The "traditional" interpretation, suggested here, is better equipped to deal with the evidence of the Parthian ostracon 1760, as discussed by Lukonin, "Institutions," 686–9.

kings took the name Arsaces upon their accession.[22] They are distinguished by their personal, given names only in Greek and Latin sources. Documents surviving from the Parthian empire itself exclusively use the name Arsaces (unless there was uncertainty about which Arsaces was meant, in periods of coregency) – to the unending frustration of historians and numismatists trying to sort out the different reigns and attribute coins to different rulers. The coins themselves, at least the silver drachms and tetradrachms struck throughout the empire (but known especially from Seleucia-on-the-Tigris and Susa), are equally difficult to distinguish.[23] Their reverse design underwent virtually no changes, showing a figure known as the "royal archer" holding a bow and sitting on a backless throne. It is generally agreed that this image represents Arsaces, the founder of the dynasty. Because the example of Arsaces was faithfully followed, there was never any room on the coins for religious symbols. This practice contrasts with the coins of the neighboring Kushanas, which contain images of various divinities along with their Greek, Iranian, and Indian names.[24]

PARTHIAN ZOROASTRIANISM: THE NISA TEXTS

Apart from a few stray notices in classical writers of a much later period, there are no direct sources about the religion of the formative early period of Arsacid rule. These emerge only with the first written documents in their language, Parthian, and with the first tangible traces of their material culture. Both take us to Nisa, their first dynastic center, located in the vicinity of the modern city of Ashqabad in Turkmenistan. Excavations of the site, begun in the 1930s by Soviet archaeologists, continue to the present day.[25] Written evidence shows that the royal city, the layout of which was of staggering proportions, was known as Mithradatkird, "made by Mithradates"; this suggests that its royal buildings were commissioned by the first monarch of that name, Mithradates I (r. ca.171–32 BCE).

This written evidence comes from a large collection (more than 2,500) of ostraca found at various places during the excavations of Nisa.[26] The chief use of these ostraca for the historian of religion lies in their preservation of

---

[22] This is explicitly mentioned in Justin's *Epitome* of the *Philippic History* of Pompeius Trogus, 41.5.6.
[23] The standard work of reference is Sellwood, *Introduction*. Indispensable discussions can be found in Le Rider, *Suse*.
[24] See Staviskij, *Bactriane sous les Kushans*.
[25] For a *vue d'ensemble* of the results of the Soviet excavations, see Pilipko, *Staraja Nisa*. A joint Turkmen-Italian team of archaeologists directed by A. Invernizzi and C. Lippolis is currently conducting excavations, with regular reports being published in the journal *Parthica*.
[26] Published in Diakonoff, Livshits, and MacKenzie, *Parthian Economic Documents*.

a large number of names of local Parthians, of months and days, of some
places and temples, and of a few functions, including priestly ones.[27] The
Nisa ostraca have removed any possible doubt about Zoroastrianism as the
religion of the Parthians. Although they are more than a century later than
the early Arsacid kings – and thus stem from imperial Arsacid times – it
is unlikely that the abundant Zoroastrian elements in them represent an
innovation. The absence of even a single name of Saka origin from among
the hundreds of names recorded has dealt yet another blow to the image of
the Parthians as Saka invaders. The names, moreover, are generally recognizable as Zoroastrian, honoring a wide range of Zoroastrian divinities.
Not a single name has been found that "could not be borne by an orthodox
Zoroastrian."[28]

The Nisa ostraca provide the first post-Alexander evidence for the use of
the Zoroastrian calendar, recording a number of names of the Zoroastrian
months and days. Further evidence from Parthian documents of later
times[29] shows that the Parthian kings used the Zoroastrian calendar (in
combination with their own Arsacid era) only when dealing with other
Iranians in their empire. They did not impose the calendar on non-Iranian
subjects and client states, nor was it used by the Greek cities within their
realm. Its use is thus an emblematic one, a symbol of their allegiance to
Zoroastrianism as their native, ancestral religion.

Cumulatively, the Nisa texts firmly establish the Zoroastrianism of the
Parthians and their kings. They refer – sparingly, as is to be expected in this
type of document – to priests, both with the general western Iranian term
for a Zoroastrian priest, *magus*, and with the unique title "master of fire."
Finally, they mention a number of temples from the vineyards of whose
estates wine was brought to Nisa. Only one of these carries a further name,
indicating the deity worshipped there: it is Nanaia, originally a Sumerian
goddess, who was early incorporated into Zoroastrianism and whose cult is
well attested among the Parthians and generally in Central Asia.

The Nisa texts thus offer a unique insight into Parthian society and religion in a fairly early period of Arsacid rule. Because additional documents
are rare, recovering the further history of Zoroastrianism in the Parthian
period requires hypothetical reconstructions. Although the sources about
the Parthians themselves are much more extensive from this period

[27] For a good overview of their contents, see Bader, "Parthian Ostraca."
[28] Lukonin, "Institutions," 689, quoting their first publication (in Russian) by Diakonoff and Livshits.
   For the names, see Schmitt, "Parthische Sprach- und Namenüberlieferung."
[29] See, for example, the documents from Avroman. These are three parchment documents, two in Greek
   (Minns, "Parchments") and one in Parthian (Nyberg, "Pahlavi Documents"). Characteristically, the
   Zoroastrian calendar is used in the Parthian text, not in the Greek ones.

onward, they are one-sided, written almost exclusively by their enemies, the Seleucids and especially the Romans.

Mithradates I expanded the original kingdom of Parthia into the new Parthian empire by slowly but virtually unceasingly adding new territories to the Arsacids' possessions. While not all of Mithradates' conquests are known, the most important of them is recorded: the conquest of Babylonia, including the Greek city of Seleucia-on-the-Tigris, in 141 BCE. Although Babylonia was not held continually thereafter, whatever losses the Parthians suffered at the hands of the Seleucids and others were only temporary and reversible setbacks. Mithradates evidently did what he could to ease the pain of suddenly being cast from the Seleucid domain into the hand of the Parthians. As he did with a few other Greek cities, he accorded Seleucia a special status within the empire and put the epithet *philhellēnos*, "friend to Greeks," on his coins, a practice that was to be repeated by most, but not all, of his successors.

From this moment on, the Parthian empire became a truly multiethnic state, home to many different religions. Like their Achaemenid predecessors, and in the main – despite appearances – their successor (the Sasanians), the Arsacids did not impose their private religion on the inhabitants of the empire. Whatever information we possess strongly suggests that the religious life of the Arsacids themselves was mainly seen in terms of a family tradition, or a dynastic cult. This is shown by the many traces of veneration of the ancestors (in Zoroastrian terms the cult of the *fravashis*) at the royal court, as well as the practice of keeping dynastic fires. A further part of the religious life of the Arsacid dynasts must have been the celebration, with great pomp, of Zoroastrian festivals, for which nobles would assemble at the Parthian court. Because the celebration of these festivals is a fixed part of Persian literary works (from the early Islamic period) that have been shown to have originated in Parthian minstrel traditions, the written evidence for such celebrations comes only from much later times.[30] But the splendor of such public festivals is supported by the layout of some of the Parthian royal sites that have been preserved, with a marked example in far-away Georgia.[31]

---

[30] Especially the eleventh-century poem *Vīs u Rāmīn* of Gurgānī, the Parthian origins of which were established by Minorsky, "Vīs-u-Rāmīn."
[31] See Gagoshidze, "Dedoplis Mindori."

THE RELIGIONS OF THE ARSACID EMPIRE

Before we discuss the religions of the Parthian empire, it is perhaps useful to say something about its general structure. For various reasons, the Parthian empire is best conceived of as the private possession of the Arsacid dynasty. As it was crucial to the empire's enduring existence, its heartland – Parthia itself, Hyrcania, some Arsacid possessions on the Iranian plateau, and Babylonia – seems to have been governed centrally. Bordering these lands were various clusters of ancient kingdoms and satrapies, ruled by local dynasties or governed by some of the great Parthian noble families. An example of the latter case is eastern Iranian Zrangiana (modern Seistan), which was governed by the Parthian house of Suren. Several of the former satrapies within Iran were ruled by junior members of the Arsacid family, who were occasionally granted the honorary title of "king" (especially the kings of Media).

In the western territories of the Parthian empire, the Parthians, and any other Iranians, were a minority among the population. While the vitally important Babylonia was generally governed centrally, there were also semi-independent client states, ruled by local monarchs under Parthian suzerainty. Occasional battles and declarations of more formal independence have led to the assumption that this policy reflected the empire's weakness. But this estimation of the empire has now been generally rejected. Several of these kingdoms – the city of Hatra, Adiabene, Osrhoene – lay between the two superpowers of Parthia and Rome. Although they often bore the brunt of their military confrontations, in the main they showed unswerving allegiance to their Parthian overlords.[32] The history of these countries is in fact mainly known because of these battles between Parthia and Rome. None of them was decisive: the Euphrates remained by and large the border between the two empires.

Since Zoroastrianism obviously survived to emerge in the sources with the rise of the Sasanians, its existence during the reign of the Arsacids can hardly be denied. But Zoroastrianism during this period is difficult to trace archaeologically and did not transmit its traditions in writing. For these reasons, as well as Sasanian propaganda, the importance of that religion for the Arsacids and for the Iranian inhabitants of their empire has frequently been underrated. The impact of Greek culture on the Parthians,

---

[32] For two exemplary case studies of such vassal states, see Schuol, *Charakene*, which discusses the southern kingdom of Mesene, and Wiesehöfer, *Dunklen Jahrhunderte*, on the history of Pārs. The history of the more northerly regions in their Parthian context still needs to be written.

for example, has been cited as evidence of a weakened attachment to their religion or Iranian culture. There is, however, no reason to assume that the enjoyment of Greek art and literature in any way obviated the practice of Zoroastrianism. Interest in Greek culture did, however, shape the way in which the religion was practiced. As with most other Hellenistic dynasties, the kings had a private religious life, focusing on the dynasty and its ancestors, and offering them generous occasions for displaying their power, wealth, and status.[33]

They did this chiefly by organizing banquets and hunting parties. Here, as well as in other aspects of court life, they were followed by the dynasts of their client states in the West, who adopted or imitated Parthian costume and took over some institutional aspects of court life, such as accession rituals, and frequently Parthian names as well. This common culture is reflected in the easily recognizable Parthian costume[34] and what is often called "Parthian art" – that is, the sculptural traditions of the Near East and the subject of much confusion and controversy.[35] But this common culture did not extend to those aspects of Parthian culture that required language to be communicated and transmitted, including, of course, religion. Not a trace of Zoroastrianism has been found in the abundant epigraphic record from Hatra, nor at Dura-Europos, which, from the end of the third century BCE to 165 CE, was a Parthian possession. But the general assumption that Zoroastrianism either did not exist or did not amount to much in the western parts of the Parthian empire is wholly contradicted by the abundant evidence from Armenia. Because this evidence is crucial to our understanding of the later development of Zoroastrianism, it must be explored in somewhat greater detail.[36]

ARMENIA

The study of Armenian history depends largely on the historical record that the Armenians themselves produced shortly after the conversion of the (Arsacid) dynasty of that country to Christianity.[37] Within a few generations, the conversion of the Armenians to Christianity in the early

---

[33] On the interconnections between the Hellenistic/Near Eastern dynasties, see Sullivan, *Near Eastern Royalty.*
[34] See, for instance, Curtis, "Parthian Costume."
[35] The classic statement remains Rostovtzeff, "Problem of Parthian Art."
[36] The basic works of reference are Russell, *Zoroastrianism in Armenia,* and *Armenian and Iranian Studies.*
[37] For the three most important among them, see Thomson, *Agathangelos;* idem, *Moses Khorenats'i;* and Garsoïan, *Epic Histories.*

fourth century CE, and along with it the invention of a special Armenian alphabet, produced an abundant literature. The Armenians, who identified themselves with the heroic Maccabees, viewed their pre-Christian religion as a form of "paganism."[38] Although the use of this literature is therefore problematic, the enormous amount of information preserved in these early writings has established that the religion of the Armenians was Zoroastrianism – more specifically, a variety of Zoroastrianism with a strong Parthian flavor. Though it possessed its own distinctive culture, Armenia had old and very close ties with the Iranian world. The fact that the kings of Armenia were, from the beginning of the common era, Arsacids themselves made these ties even stronger.

The paucity of evidence for a temple cult of fire in Armenian Zoroastrianism can be easily explained; as we have seen, fire-temples were by no means necessary for the persistence of Zoroastrianism. The more interesting feature of Armenian Zoroastrianism is its abundance of temples for individual deities. It is becoming increasingly clear that these temples were a prominent part of pre-Sasanian Zoroastrianism and were the first to fall victim to the Sasanian wish for a unified version of the religion. For early Armenian historians, Zoroastrian temples – dedicated to Aramazd the creator, the highest god of the Zoroastrian pantheon; to Anahit the Lady, goddess of water and fertility; to Tir, the scribe of the gods; to Mihr (Mithra), god of contracts; and to Vahagn (Verethraghna), god of victory – offered a dramatic backdrop for their account of the country's Christianization.[39] By documenting the destruction of the temples and the erection of churches in their place, they have recorded innumerable details of the religious life of these places. Ironically, we know much more about Parthian Zoroastrianism from Armenia than we do from anywhere else.

After the Sasanians put an end to the Arsacid dynasty in Iran (but not in Armenia), they attempted both to conquer and pacify Armenia and to reconvert the Armenians to Zoroastrianism. But their version of Zoroastrianism was barely recognized by the Armenians as the same religion as that of their ancestors; even those Armenians who were still Zoroastrian did not welcome it. In order to explain the marked differences between Parthian and Sasanian Zoroastrianism, we must therefore examine the early Sasanian evidence.

---

[38] Thomson, "Maccabees."

[39] They function in this way especially in Agathangelos's *History of the Armenians* §§784–90 (Thomson, *Agathangelos,* 323–31).

THE RISE OF THE SASANIANS

The first Sasanian king, Ardashir I, began his life as the prince-in-waiting for the small principality of Stakhr in southwestern Iran.[40] There, his ancestors combined their rule of the city and its surrounding lands as vassals of the Parthian King of Kings with the hereditary guardianship of an important fire or an important temple. This was a land full of the ancient monuments of the Achaemenids. Even though now in ruins, they were still standing, evoking the former grandeur of important kings of the past. When Ardashir's father Pabag died, he was succeeded by Ardashir's older brother Shapur, who died unexpectedly, leaving the throne to his younger brother.

Ardashir apparently succeeded in uniting local noble colleagues to revolt against the Parthian king, Artabanus V. After defeating – and killing, according to the stories – the last Arsacid, he was crowned the new king of the Iranians in 224 CE. Immediately following this success, Ardashir evidently had to fight other battles to consolidate his reign. Although the stories of his success are deemed historically unreliable, they are highly useful for the study of the history of Zoroastrianism, as are the chosen coin design of the Sasanians and the rock reliefs commissioned by their first kings.

All of them stress the theme of unity. Ardashir chose for the reverse of his coins a representation of his own regnal fire, so indicated by its legend. The obverse bore his portrait, with a new and striking legend, presenting the new king as "the Zoroastrian Lord Ardashir, King of Kings of the Iranians."[41] Sasanian art and literary tradition help to explain why he chose to represent his own fire on the reverse. In the literary tradition, Ardashir fights heroic battles against evil creatures – including "the Worm" and a local queen – who reside in castles, there to be worshipped as living gods. He defeats them, takes away their treasure, destroys their sanctuaries, and replaces them with fire-temples. This is only reported of him and his son and successor Shapur, not of any later monarch.[42] It is to be read in connection with the *Letter of Tansar*, a Persian literary work that purports to reproduce a correspondence between Ardashir's high priest Tansar (Tosar) and the (Parthian vassal) king of Tabaristan (in northern Iran), recording his objections to Ardashir's seizure of the throne of Iran.[43] The most telling

[40] Although partly outdated, Christensen, *L'Iran*, remains indispensable. For the stories of the rise of the Sasanians, see Widengren, "Establishment."
[41] For early Sasanian coins, see Alram and Gyselen, *Sylloge I.*
[42] See De Jong, "One Nation under God?"
[43] Boyce, *Letter of Tansar.*

of his objections is that Ardashir extinguished many fires, a heinous sin in
Zoroastrianism. Tansar defends his king by stating that the "kings of the
peoples" had no right to have lit them in the first place. The "kings of the
peoples" is the technical term by which Sasanian propagandists referred to
the Parthians. To rob them of their legitimacy, they accused them of having divided Iran over a large number of "petty kings," thus denying to the
country the unity to which it was entitled.

The stories about Ardashir's destruction of the sanctuaries (fires or
temples in which living deities gathered treasure) and the choice of his
coin design clearly belong together: the message of the coin is not one of
Zoroastrian revival – as has often been claimed – but rather of the unity
of the realm, symbolized in his own dynastic fire, the only one to be left
burning. The most splendid visual illustration of the theme comes from
the impressive rock relief he commissioned at Naqsh-i Rustam, under
the tombs of the Achaemenid kings.[44] There the new king is represented
mounted on a horse, facing the god Ohrmazd (Ahura Mazdā) himself, also
mounted on a horse. Ohrmazd gives him the ring symbolizing sovereignty,
handing over to him the unique role of ruling the Iranians as the chosen
one of their god. Under the hooves of the horses are two figures. While
Ohrmazd's horse tramples the evil Ahriman, recognizable through a snake
coiling in his hair, Ardashir's horse tramples the defeated Parthian king.
The message is clear: just as there is only one king in heaven, Ohrmazd
himself, there can be only one king on earth.

The same theme recurs in the most extensive narrative we have of the
early Sasanian period, the "book of the deeds of Ardashir son of Pabag."[45]
Contrary to its (spurious) title, the book does not conclude with Ardashir,
or with his son Shapur, who did more than his father to consolidate the
empire. It ends rather with his grandson Hormizd I, the only of the three
early Sasanians to be credited with the crowning achievement of the narrative: the establishment of a single rule in all the lands of the Iranians.
Because his reign was both short (one year) and uneventful, it is most
likely that the book of Ardashir, despite later additions, was first produced
under him.

It was his father, Shapur, however, who did most for the expansion and
the consolidation of the empire. This is recorded in the extensive trilingual inscription he ordered to be engraved – in Parthian, Middle Persian,
and Greek – on the Ka'ba-i Zardusht at Naqsh-i Rustam, one of the other

---

[44] See Hinz, *Altiranische Funde*, 115–43.
[45] The best edition is Grenet, *Geste d'Ardashir*.

Achaemenid remains at that highly important place.[46] This inscription, sometimes known as *Res Gestae Divi Saporis*, describes the lands conquered by Shapur and his victories over the Romans – with the death of Gordian III and the humiliating defeat of Valerian. The inscription further mentions the organization of his court and ends with a long list of fires founded by him and religious observances for the care of the souls of his relatives paid for by generous donations.

The religious elements in his inscription, together with the evidence for Ardashir mentioned above, have created the not unreasonable impression that these early kings were devout Zoroastrians. Together with the anti-Parthian propaganda, it has also contributed to the notion that the Parthians were much less occupied with religion. While that was clearly the intention of some of these texts and traditions, their testimony can hardly be considered objective. The impression is strikingly enhanced, however, by what are arguably the most important written documents for religious history from the early Sasanian period: the inscriptions of the priest Kerdīr.[47]

THE INSCRIPTIONS OF KERDĪR

The inscriptions of Kerdīr, the only substantial epigraphic records of a commoner to have survived, were written on some of the most important sites of the early Sasanian state. Significantly, these include the same Ka'ba-i Zardusht where Shapur had commissioned his victory inscription to be engraved. Four versions are known, some of them accompanied by artistic representations of the priest himself. All this suggests a place of distinctive importance for Kerdīr at a certain stage of his career.

Kerdīr's inscriptions are divided into two sections, the first documenting his priestly career, the second his visionary journey to heaven, with proofs of the truth of the Zoroastrian religion.[48] What occasioned the unique honor of having these inscriptions engraved on such important places is still a matter of debate, but the texts themselves provide clues. In them, Kerdīr documents his rise to high office, from a comparatively humble court priest under Shapur to the clerical head of the whole realm under his successors. He boasts how, in attempting to establish a unified, organized, and "orthodox" version of the religion, he persecuted both Zoroastrian

---

[46] For the site, see Schmidt, *Persepolis III*; for the inscription, Huyse, *Dreisprachige Inschrift*.
[47] For a synoptic edition of these texts, see Gignoux, *Quatre inscriptions*.
[48] See Skjærvø, "Kirdīr's Vision."

"heretics" and their establishments and, famously, the religious minorities in the empire, some of whom he actually lists.

Whether or not Kerdīr actually did all this must remain uncertain; his persecutions of minorities are entirely undocumented in the traditions of those communities he mentions (Jews, Christians, Buddhists, and others). But the essence of his message ties in well with the requirements of the new Sasanian state: the creation of a unified nation for all Iranians, shielded by their ancestral religion. His description reveals important changes in particular features of the religion. For Kerdīr, a priest himself, the most important bearers of the tradition were the priests, the chief responsibility of whom was to care for the fires in their sanctuaries.

Although Kerdīr, unlike the Sasanian kings, frequently refers to the forces of evil – human and nonhuman – in his inscriptions, the first part of them is not a theological text. The second part, the famous vision of the hereafter, is different and unique, and thus difficult to contextualize. Kerdīr is granted the sole privilege of performing a ritual enabling him to gain knowledge of the hereafter, to have a visual experience of heaven and hell, and to be informed of his destined place in heaven. Kerdīr's vision seems to be part of a more widespread narrative tradition about chosen mortals to whom are revealed the most important tenet of the religion: that it and only it leads to a blessed afterlife. A few more examples of the same tradition have been preserved: the story of Vishtaspa, the patron king of Zarathushtra, and the book of the righteous Wiraz.[49] In all three cases, the urgent need to establish the truth about the religion constitutes the narrative background of their visit to the otherworld. Vishtaspa's vision is part of the narrative about the beginnings of the religion, for his conversion marks its first success. The book of the righteous Wiraz dates his visit to the otherworld to the mid- or late Sasanian period, a time of uncertainty caused by the activities of wicked priests and foreign faiths.

Viewed in the context of this literary *topos*, Kerdīr's vision served to justify some of the most important changes he advocated in the organization of the Zoroastrian religion and its rituals, imposing a single type of sanctuary – housing a consecrated fire – served by a hierarchy of priests, united by a common set of beliefs and doctrines, confirmed by his revelation.

MANICHAEISM

One of Kerdīr's most infamous acts was his campaign to bring about the death of the prophet Mani, the founder of Manichaeism. In interpreting

---

[49] For the latter see Gignoux, *Ardā Vīrāz*.

Kerdīr's inscription in this context, some scholars have seen the threat of this new religion as the occasion of his visionary journey to the other-world. There can be no doubt that Mani was tried and executed at the height of Kerdīr's power; Manichaean sources are in fact the only other texts to have preserved his name.[50] But such an interpretation of Kerdīr's inscriptions disregards the constant references to the correct performance of Zoroastrian rituals in these texts. These would be oddly out of place had the threat of Manichaeism been the main motive behind them.

Manichaeans are mentioned in the inscription only collectively, together with the other non-Zoroastrian religious communities that Kerdīr claims to have persecuted. But the rise of Manichaeism is an important part of the religious history of the early Sasanian empire, one that Kerdīr may have wished to conceal by ignoring it further in his inscriptions. Although the debate over Manichaean origins is far from settled, a clear majority among modern scholars have embraced the notion that it drew its main inspiration, initially, from Jewish Christianity.[51] Evidence for this comes mainly from the Cologne Mani Codex, a miniature parchment codex from fourth- or fifth-century Egypt containing a Manichaean Greek text on the early history of the prophet Mani and his community.[52] Much of that text is devoted to the initial split between Mani and the religious community he grew up in, referred to exclusively as a community of "baptists." In fictional discussions with its members, allusions in the text to passages from the Gospels and Paul have enabled scholars to establish that this community of baptists was a Christian one.[53] It has also drawn increasing attention to the Christian elements in Manichaeism, sometimes to the point of treating Manichaeism as a branch of Christianity.[54]

The chief flaw of this approach is that it perpetuates the notion that discussions of Manichaean origins must choose between Zoroastrianism on the one hand and Christianity on the other. Whereas Manichaeism was once conceived of as an exotic variety of Zoroastrianism,[55] it is currently presented as an equally exotic variety of Christianity. This robs Manichaeism of its striking originality and, as will be shown later in this chapter, perpetuates a decidedly obsolete vision of interrelations between

---

[50] See the Coptic "Recitation about the Crucifixion" from the Manichaean *Homilies* in Gardner and Lieu, *Manichaean Texts*, 79–84.
[51] See Gardner and Lieu, *Manichaean Texts*, 25–35. See further Griffith in Chapter 5 of this volume.
[52] The standard edition of the text is Koenen and Römer, *Kölner Mani-Kodex*.
[53] See especially *Cologne Mani Codex*, 91–3 (Gardner and Lieu, *Manichaean Texts*, 62–3).
[54] See, for example, Pedersen, *Demonstrative Proof*, 6–12.
[55] The classic statement is Widengren, *Mani and Manichaeism*.

various communities within the Sasanian empire – the undisputed place of origin of Manichaeism.[56]

RELIGIONS IN THE SASANIAN EMPIRE

The body of literature documenting the activities of the many religious communities active in the Sasanian empire is considerable. The most important communities are those of the Zoroastrians, Jews, Christians, Manichaeans, and Mandaeans. Zoroastrians and Jews, who had been in contact with each other for almost a millennium, shared important characteristics, such as an elaborate code of purity rules and the importance assigned to oral tradition. Although the origins of the Mandaeans are unclear, they too had much in common with the Zoroastrians, particularly in their rituals.[57] Christians and Manichaeans were newcomers to this scene and, unlike the other three groups, actively missionary. The literature of all these communities is frequently hostile to the others, abounding in ritual and legal prescriptions that would seem to preclude the possibility of friendly relations. Mixed marriages, for example, are forbidden in almost all sources, from whatever religious community, as is selling or consuming food prepared or procured by members of another religious community. With regard to marriage, it is difficult to be certain, but repeated warnings against mixed marriages imply that this practice was more common than the normative texts would suggest.[58]

Only recently have scholars begun to question the validity of the traditional view of the religions of the Sasanian empire as more or less fixed, impenetrable, and spiritual domains to be studied in comparative isolation from one another. This has happened in various fields. Apart from the artistic traditions referred to above, important studies of legal systems and of literary traditions have now shown how much the various communities interacted. The notion of a shared culture in the Sasanian empire's western regions is slowly but firmly gaining recognition.[59] The subject that has contributed most to this reassessment of relations is magic, as evidenced particularly in the unique Babylonian tradition of

---

[56] See De Jong, "Zoroastrian Religious Polemics."
[57] See Drower, *Mandaeans*; Rudolph, *Mandäer II: Der Kult.*
[58] Some examples are discussed in De Jong, "Zoroastrian Religious Polemics," 56–8. See further Lapin in Chapter 4 of this volume.
[59] For law, see Elman, "Marriage and Marital Property"; Macuch, "Servant of the Fire." For Iranian literary themes in Jewish texts, see Herman, "Ahasuerus" and "Iranian Epic Motifs." For Iranian themes in Christian literature, see Frenschkowski, "Parthica Apocalyptica"; Walker, *Mar Qardagh.*

making "incantation bowls," small earthenware bowls with protective texts written spirally inside. Hundreds of these bowls have already been published and hundreds more are known.[60] Although mostly written by Jews and Mandaeans, there are also many Christian and several Zoroastrian bowls, possibly even a few Manichaean ones. Much of the information in these texts is specific to the religious tradition that produced them: Talmudic sages and sayings characteristically appear on Jewish bowls, Mandaean spiritual beings on those in Mandaic. Even so, these bowls provide overwhelming evidence of religious interaction, with a notable Iranian element.[61]

The religious world of the Sasanian empire was thus a vibrant one, full of innovation and diversity. As if to underline this, there is growing evidence demonstrating the role of the Sasanians as a bridge between the Christian world in the West and India in the East. In this way, they enriched both cultures, mediating Indian science, stories, and ideas to the West, and Greek science and ideas to India, while adding their own distinctive Iranian traditions to both.[62]

It remains true, however, that the development of Zoroastrianism, the religion of the majority population, continues to be difficult to trace for most of the Sasanian period. One large body of evidence comes from the thousands of personal and official seals and sealings that have been preserved, while the documents to which the sealings were attached have almost entirely perished.[63] Detailed study of the seals, especially of the inscriptions on them, has enabled scholars to make enormous progress in our understanding of the organization – geographical and institutional – of the empire, and the prominent role played by priests in its administrative structure.[64] This, in turn, is fully confirmed by the relatively numerous Christian reports on the trials and executions of Zoroastrian apostates (or Christian converts). As far as the development of doctrine and ritual is concerned, however, the often conflicting information from Christian sources and from later Zoroastrian texts has made it difficult to arrive at a balanced picture.

---

[60] For recent publications of such bowls (with references to earlier collections), see Segal, *Catalogue*; Müller-Kessler, *Zauberschalentexte*. Hundreds more are currently being prepared for publication by Shaul Shaked.

[61] For an introduction, see Shaked, "Popular Religion."

[62] For literature, see, for example, De Blois, *Burzōy's Voyage*; for astrology, Pingree, *From Astral Omens to Astrology*.

[63] The most recent publication is Gyselen, *Sasanian Seals and Sealings*.

[64] See Gyselen, *Géographie administrative*; idem, "Sceaux des mages."

ZURVANISM

The case of Zurvanism illustrates the problem. Christian sources in Armenian, Syriac, and Greek show that in certain circles of the Sasanian court, there existed a version of Zoroastrian doctrine that placed a deity of time, Zurvan, above the two spirits Ohrmazd and Ahriman, and thus presented the two spirits – the basic notions in the Zoroastrian theology of the Pahlavi books – as twin brothers born of this single deity.[65] The Pahlavi books, which preserve barely a trace of such ideas, are thus thought to have been purged of this doctrine.[66] There is general agreement that "Zurvanism," the name given to this putative heresy, was largely indistinguishable from other varieties of Zoroastrianism in its rituals and its doctrines. The chief difference was its elevation, presumably effected also in ritual contexts, of the god Zurvan.[67]

Western scholars, for whom "Zurvanism" was the first known variant form of Zoroastrian theology, have made it the subject of intensive study. In the process, almost every variant idea or doctrine came to be attributed to it.[68] "Zurvanism" thus acquired a robust identity that has taken much effort to deconstruct. In all likelihood, it was one among many varieties of the crucial Zoroastrian narrative of the cosmogony. It has been suggested that it grew out of an alternative exegesis of a verse from the Gathas (Y. 30.3), which speaks of "the two spirits" as twins.[69] If this is correct, we must assume that this interpretation was accepted by priests working at the court, who handed their interpretation down to their students. It was evidently not the exegesis adopted by many other priests, whose traditions were preserved in the Pahlavi books. This both explains its prominence in reports on "court traditions" (in Syriac and Armenian) and its subsequent loss in the Zoroastrian tradition; because the court priests were the most affected by the Arab conquests, many such court traditions were lost.

A case in point is the supremely important theologian and politician Mihr-Narseh, active under the Sasanian king Bahram V (r.420–38). As the monarch's prime minister (*wuzurg-framādār*), he was actively engaged in the reconversion of Armenia, trying to impose Zurvanite ideas on the Armenians. One of his three sons, all of whom rose to high office, was

---

[65] See Boyce, "Reflections on Zurvanism"; eadem, "Further Reflections on Zurvanism"; Shaked, "The Myth of Zurvan."
[66] This is discussed critically in De Jong, "Jeh the Primal Whore?"
[67] See Boyce, *History of Zoroastrianism II*, 233–4.
[68] Especially in the one monograph devoted to the subject: Zaehner, *Zurvan*.
[69] Boyce, *History of Zoroastrianism II*, 232.

named Zurvāndād, "given by Zurvān."[70] Although this fact has been much highlighted, all other reports on Mihr-Narseh simply present him in the traditional activities of a Zoroastrian politician: accumulating offices for himself and his sons, founding temple-fires in his own name and the names of his sons, and endowing them with rich estates. Zurvandad became, it seems, the clerical head of the Zoroastrian scholar-priests, and he may have attempted to spread the doctrine of Zurvan throughout the empire. But other events quickly overtook such efforts.

THE MOVEMENT OF MAZDAK AND ITS CONSEQUENCES

This takes us to our final episode: the reign of Husraw I (r.531–39). The period before Husraw's reign was marked by intense religious turmoil, sparked by the movement of a certain Mazdak.[71] As the arch-villain of Zoroastrian history, he is the target of extremely hostile reports, fatally obscuring what really happened. While we must therefore be cautious with the evidence, it is certain that some of the most drastic reforms in Zoroastrian history followed on the trauma of this movement.

The Mazdakite movement appears in the sources chiefly as a movement of social reform, advocating the redistribution of wealth and property, including – famously – women. The sharing of women, which caught the attention of the opponents of the Mazdakite movement, has created a very lopsided image of the Mazdakites. The Sasanian law-book and later Zoroastrian legal texts make it clear that lineage was a crucial issue in Zoroastrian legal thought.[72] Every Zoroastrian man was obliged to produce a legitimate son and heir, who was indispensable not only for the management of his estate, but particularly for a set of ritual duties to commemorate his soul. If he did not have a son, he was expected to appoint one to perform these duties. The idea of obscuring the lineage by dissolving the institution of marriage was thus both a social and a religious problem. Even if one takes into account their particular focus, there are many indications in the sources that the Mazdakite movement was also a movement of religious reform. In fact, the Mazdakites presented their ideas in religious terms, claiming to offer an alternative, and better, interpretation of the *Zand*.

---

[70] The information comes from the Muslim historian Tabari; see Bosworth, *Sāsānids*, 103–6.
[71] See Klíma, *Mazdak*; Crone, "Kavad's Heresy"; idem, "Zoroastrian Communism"; Yarshater, "Mazdakism."
[72] For the Sasanian law-book, see Macuch, *Rechtskasuistik*.

The real threat to the status quo came when the Sasanian king Kawād was accused of supporting some Mazdakite ideas. The king was deposed, to return after an interregnum; in his second reign, he is said to have recanted his former support for the Mazdakites, and to have reigned long and successfully. It is his son, Husraw, who made decided efforts to end Mazdakism, by this time a full-fledged revolutionary movement.

For this, and for many other accomplishments, Husraw is remembered as the most successful and the most pious of the Sasanian kings.[73] In the domain of religion, the suppression of Mazdakism led to important reforms, with a lasting impact on the development of Zoroastrianism. One of them was the codification and writing down of the Avesta and its *Zand,* the two halves of the revelation. Because the recitation of the Avesta depended on a correct pronunciation of these texts in their own language, a special alphabet was developed for it, in which even the smallest of phonetic differences could be recorded.

The *Dēnkard,* a compendium of Zoroastrian theological works from the ninth century, has preserved a much-discussed passage on this process of codification, showing the attempts of many earlier kings – including, significantly, a Parthian king – to collect and codify the revelation, ending in the reign of "his present Majesty," Husraw I.[74] Apart from thus codifying the text and writing it down, it seems that even more drastic measures were taken by this king. Although Zoroastrians were enjoined to memorize the Avesta and to listen to the *Zand,* as it was expounded by scholar-priests (*hērbed*) in priestly schools (*hērbedestān*),[75] severe restrictions were imposed on this instruction. Every individual was to choose a priest who would be in a position of spiritual authority (*dastwar*) over him, and whose decisions in ritual and religious matters, based on his knowledge of the *Zand,* were binding.[76] According to several texts, the teaching of the *Zand,* in a further development, came to be forbidden to the laity.

This development is part of a process of scripturalization, and with it more intensive study of the now codified corpus of the revelation.[77] This is evident from the way in which passages from the Avesta and the *Zand* are quoted. Most often, quotations are vague. There are references only to "the revelation" (in the often occurring phrase "he/it says in the religion"),

---

[73] For a magisterial description, see Christenen, *L'Iran,* 363–440.
[74] The most reliable discussion of the text is Shaked, *Dualism in Transformation,* 99–103.
[75] See the introduction to Kotwal and Kreyenbroek, *Hērbedestān.*
[76] Kreyenbroek, "Spiritual Authority."
[77] Shaked, "Scripture and Exegesis."

followed by the quotation of small passages of Avestan text or – much more regularly – passages from the *Zand*. A new system made reference to one of the twenty-one sections of the Avesta-with-*Zand* that were devised in the sixth century ("it is stated in the Dāmdād Nask"), thus making it easier to check for accuracy among those who had memorized that particular section. A final system of reference specified chapters of text ("it is said in the fifth chapter of the Vendidad"), in which case we have arrived at an almost literate stage of the development. We can assume that scholar-priests now no longer relied exclusively on oral transmission, but also used written sources for reference.[78]

CONCLUDING REMARKS

The period of Zoroastrian and Iranian history we have been reviewing was a long and eventful one. At the beginning of the Arsacid empire, Zoroastrians lived in a religious world that had completely vanished by late Sasanian times. The Iranians in early Arsacid times shared their empire with Greeks and Babylonians, whose temples, festivals, and priests flourished as they had in the centuries before.[79] Their vassals – such as the kings of Elymais, Characene, and Hatra – reigned in kingly fashion, richly endowing sanctuaries devoted to their own ancestral gods.[80] Although their religion may have set an example, the Arsacids otherwise thought better of exerting their influence. The royal practice of religion, and its emulation by local nobles, must have been the professional domain of priests attached to the courts and estates, just as village communities were administered by community priests. Because of the lack of concrete evidence, the reconstruction of religion in the Arsacid empire is necessarily a static one. There is little hope of recovering stages of developments or of the ways in which the common people practiced and experienced their religion. One distinctive feature of it, however, was local variety: the cult of rivers, mountains, and other significant places. Another, better attested, aspect is the great importance of the cult of the ancestors.

What remains unseen is not only the religion of the ordinary Iranians in this period, but also the priestly tradition.[81] This is the first instance where

---

[78] The most recent discussion of the *Zand* in historical context is Cantera, *Pahlavi-Übersetzung*.

[79] For the great temples of Mesopotamia, see Van der Spek, "Cuneiform Documents"; the considerable evidence for Greek religion is collected in Canali de Rossi, *Estremo Oriente Greco*.

[80] For Elymais, see Hansman, "Great Gods"; for Hatra, Drijvers, "Hatra, Palmyra und Edessa."

[81] This is only slightly remedied by the evidence from Greek and Latin literature; for discussion, see De Jong, *Traditions of the Magi*.

we have to rely on the simple fact that the religion, with its Avestan texts, its high rituals, and its theological traditions, survived, to reemerge in written sources in the Sasanian period. The priests, as bearers of the tradition, are regularly found, moreover, in descriptions of the Persians in Greek and Latin literature. In addition, the evidence from Armenia suggests that the local and family-based characteristics of Parthian Zoroastrianism made that religion appealing to the Armenians. Although Zoroastrianism reached the Armenians long before the Arsacids, their version of the religion is strongly colored by Parthian traditions, evidently allowing the Armenians to combine their practice of Zoroastrianism with a strong and proud sense of their cultural distinctiveness.

In the third century, when the Sasanians removed the Arsacids as the rulers of Iran, the religious world had changed dramatically, with the rise of Christianity, the gradual erosion of traditional religion in Babylonia, and the impending rise of Manichaeism with its universal message. Official declarations by Ardashir and his successors about the restoration of former glories and especially of unity suggest that the capacity of the Parthian empire to forge loyalty to the Arsacid dynasty by allowing local and regional autonomy was now seen as a weakness. While the Zoroastrianism of the Parthians was not questioned in itself, this new vision of the empire was especially visible in the sphere of religion. One clear indication of this was the eradication of signs of regional diversity and the most important sources of local resistance: the dynastic shrines and the sanctuaries of individual deities.

While there is thus some truth in the image of the Sasanians as devout Zoroastrians, it is true only for a specific variety of that religion, the one that was to prove successful. Their version of the religion was arguably much better equipped to answer the threat of Christianity and Manichaeism. It was aniconic and hence less vulnerable to accusations of idolatry. It had its own version of universality, with a revealed message for all mankind. And it had a well-organized body of priests, a network of fire-temples, and institutions of learning. Zoroastrian priests dominated legal institutions and participated fully in the exchange of ideas that was characteristic of the Sasanian period.

Late Sasanian times present an image of Zoroastrianism similar to that of the other important religions of the empire, rabbinic Judaism and Christianity. The transformation of Zoroastrianism from a religion sharing important characteristics with the traditional religions of the ancient world to one resembling the religions of Late Antiquity shows the capacity of its priests and laymen to absorb new ideas and adapt to new circumstances. It also helps to answer the question: How did a religion apparently so closely connected to its kings survive the Arab conquests? Although it lost all of its territory and its adherents all came to live under Muslim rule, Zoroastrianism lived on as the only representative of an imperial religion dating back to the first millennium BCE.

BIBLIOGRAPHY

Primary

Alram, Michael, and Rika Gyselen. *Sylloge Nummorum Sasanidarum I. Ardashir I. Shapur I* (Vienna, 2003).

Canali de Rossi, Filippo. *Iscrizioni dello estremo oriente greco. Un repertorio* (Bonn, 2004).

Diakonoff, I. M., V. A. Livshits, and D. N. MacKenzie. *Parthian Economic Documents from Nisa*, 5 vols. (London, 1976–2002).

Gardner, Iain, and Samuel N. C. Lieu. *Manichaean Texts from the Roman Empire* (Cambridge, 2004).

Garsoïan, Nina G., trans. *The Epic Histories Attributed to P'awstos Buzand (Buzandaran Patmut'iwnk')* (Cambridge, Mass., 1989).

Gignoux, Philippe, ed. and trans. *Le livre d'Ardā Vīrāz* (Paris, 1984).

Les quatre inscriptions du mage Kirdīr. Textes et concordances (Paris, 1991).

Gyselen, Rika. *La géographie administrative de l'empire sassanide: les témoignages sigillographiques* (Bures-sur-Yvette, 1989).

Sasanian Seals and Sealings in the A. Saeedi Collection (Louvain, 2007).

Hackl, Ursula, Bruno Jacobs, and Dieter Weber, eds. *Quellen zur Geschichte des Partherreiches. Textsammlung mit Übersetzungen und Kommentaren.* 3 vols. NTOA (Göttingen, 2010): 83–5.

Huyse, Philip. *Die dreisprachige Inschrift Šābuhrs I. an der Ka'ba-i Zardušt (ŠKZ)* (London, 1999).

Minns, Ellis H. "Parchments of the Parthian Period from Avroman in Kurdistan." *JHS* 35 (1915): 22–65.

Müller-Kessler, Christa. *Die Zauberschalentexte in der Hilprecht-Sammlung, Jena, und weitere Nippur-Texte anderer Sammlungen* (Wiesbaden, 2005).

Schmidt, Erich F. *Persepolis III: The Royal Tombs and Other Monuments* (Chicago, 1970).

Segal, J. B. *Catalogue of the Aramaic and Mandaic Incantation Bowls in the British Museum* (London, 2000).

Shaked, Shaul. *Le satrape de Bactriane et son gouverneur. Documents araméens du IVe siècle avant notre ère provenant de Bactrie* (Paris, 2004).

Shoff, Wilfred H., ed. and trans. *Parthian Stations by Isidore of Charax* (Philadelphia, 1914).

Thomson, Robert, trans. *Agathangelos: History of the Armenians* (Albany, 1976).

trans. *Moses Khorenats'i: History of the Armenians* (Ann Arbor, 2006).

Wiesehöfer, Josef, ed. *Das Partherreich und seine Zeugnisse. The Arsacid Empire: Sources and Documentation* (Stuttgart, 1998).

Secondary

Alram, Michael. "Stand und Aufgaben der arsakidischen Numismatik." In *Das Partherreich und seine Zeugnisse*, ed. Josef Wiesehöfer (Stuttgart, 1998): 365–87.

Ambraseys, N. N., and C. P. Melville. *A History of Persian Earthquakes* (Cambridge, 1982).

Bader, A. "Parthian Ostraca from Nisa: Some Historical Data." In *La Persia e l'Asia Centrale, da Alessandro al X secolo* (Rome, 1996): 251–76.

Bailey, Herbert W. *Zoroastrian Problems in the Ninth-Century Books* (Oxford, 1971).

Bernard, Paul. "L'Asie Centrale et l'empire séleucide." *Topoi. Orient-Occident* 4/2 (1994): 473–511.

Bosworth, Clifford E. *The History of al-Ṭabarī V: The Sāsānids, the Byzantines, the Lakhmids, and Yemen* (Albany, 1999).

Boyce, Mary. "The Parthian *gōsān* and Iranian Minstrel Tradition." *JRAS* (1957): 10–45.

"Some Reflections on Zurvanism." *BSOAS* 19 (1957): 304–16.

The Letter of Tansar (Rome, 1968).

A History of Zoroastrianism II: Under the Achaemenians (Leiden, 1982).

"Some further Reflections on Zurvanism." In *Iranica Varia: Papers in Honor of Professor Ehsan Yarshater*, eds. D. Amin, M. Kasheff, and A. S. Shahbazi (Leiden, 1990): 20–9.

"The Sedentary Arsacids." *Iranica Antiqua* 29 (1994): 241–51.

"Further on the Calendar of Zoroastrian Feasts." *Iran* 43 (2005): 1–38.

Boyce, Mary, and Albert De Jong. *A History of Zoroastrianism IV: Parthian and Armenian Zoroastrianism* (in preparation).

Cantera, Alberto. *Studien zur Pahlavi-Übersetzung des Avesta* (Wiesbaden, 2004).

Christensen, Arthur. *L'Iran sous les Sassanides* (Copenhagen, 1944).

Christensen, Peter. *The Decline of Iranshahr: Irrigation and Environments in the History of the Middle East, 500 B.C. to A.D. 1500* (Copenhagen, 1993).

Crone, Patricia. "Kavad's Heresy and Mazdak's Revolt." *Iran* 29 (1991): 21–42.

"Zoroastrian Communism." *CSSH* 36 (1994): 447–62.

Curtis, Vesta S. "The Parthian Costume and Headdress." In *Das Partherreich und seine Zeugnisse*, ed. Josef Wiesehöfer (Stuttgart, 1998): 61–94.

De Blois, François. *Burzōy's Voyage to India and the Origin of the Book of Kalīlah wa Dimna.* (London, 1990).

"The Persian Calendar." *Iran* 34 (1996): 39–54.

De Jong, Albert. "Jeh the Primal Whore? Observations on Zoroastrian Misogyny." In *Female Stereotypes in Religious Traditions*, eds. Ria Kloppenborg and Wouter J. Hanegraaff (Leiden, 1995): 15–41.

Traditions of the Magi: Zoroastrianism in Greek and Latin Literature (Leiden, 1997).

"Zoroastrian Religious Polemics and their Contexts: Interconfessional Relations in the Sasanian Empire." In *Religious Polemics in Context*, eds. Theo L. Hettema and Arie van der Kooij (Assen, 2004): 48–63.

"The Contribution of the Magi." In *Birth of the Persian Empire*, eds. Vesta S. Curtis and Sarah Stewart (London, 2005): 85–99.

"One Nation under God? The Early Sasanians as Guardians and Destroyers of Holy Sites." In *Götterbilder, Gottesbilder, Weltbilder. Polytheismus und Monotheismus in der Welt der Antike. Band I: Ägypten, Mesopotamien, Persien, Kleinasien, Syrien, Palästina*, eds. Reinhard G. Kratz and Hermann Spieckermann (Tübingen, 2006): 223–38.

D'jakonov, I. M., and E. V. Zejmal. "Pravitel' Parfii Andragor i ego monety." *VDI*, no. 4 (1988): 4–19.

Drijvers, H. J. W. "Hatra, Palmyra und Edessa. Die Städte der syrisch-mesopotamischen Wüste in politischer, kulturgeschichtlicher und religionsgeschichtlicher Beleuchtung." *ANRW* II.8 (1977): 799–906.

Drower, E. S. *The Mandaeans of Iraq and Iran* (Leiden, 1962).

Elman, Yaakov. "Marriage and Marital Property in Rabbinic and Sasanian Law." In *Rabbinic Law in its Roman and Near Eastern Context*, ed. Catherine Heszer (Tübingen, 2003): 227–76.

Fisher, W. B. "Physical Geography." In *The Cambridge History of Iran 1: The Land of Iran*, ed. W. B. Fisher (Cambridge, 1968): 3–110.

Frenschkowski, Marco. "Parthica Apocalyptica. Mythologie und Militärwesen iranischer Völker in ihrer Rezeption durch die Offenbarung des Johannes." *JbAC* 47 (2004): 16–57.

Gagoshidze, J. M. "The Temples at Dedoplis Mindori." *East and West* 42 (1992): 27–48.

Grenet, Frantz. *La geste d'Ardashir fils de Pâbag. Kārnāmag ī Ardaxšēr ī Pābagān* (Die, 2003).

Gyselen, Rika. "Les sceaux des mages de l'Iran sassanide." In *Au Carrefour des religions. Mélanges offerts à Philippe Gignoux*, ed. R. Gyselen (Bures-sur-Yvette, 1995): 121–50.

Hansman, J. "The Great Gods of Elymais." In *Papers in Honour of Professor Mary Boyce. Acta Iranica 24* (Leiden, 1985): 229–46.

Hauser, Stefan R. "Die ewigen Nomaden? Bemerkungen zu Herkunft, Militär, Staatsaufbau und nomadischen Traditionen der Arsakiden." In *Krieg – Gesellschaft – Institutionen. Beiträge zu einer vergleichenden Kriegsgeschichte*, eds. Burkhard Meißner, Oliver Schmitt, and Michael Sommer (Berlin, 2005): 163–208.

Henning, W. B. "Mitteliranisch." In *Handbuch der Orientalistik 1.4. Iranistik 1. Linguistik* (Leiden, 1958): 20–130.

Herman, Geoffrey. "Ahasuerus, the Former Stable-Master of Belshazzar, and the Wicked Alexander of Macedon: Two Parallels between the Babylonian Talmud and Persian Sources." *AJS Review* 29 (2005): 283–97.

"Iranian Epic Motifs in Josephus' Antiquities (XVIII, 314–370)." *JJS* 57 (2006): 245–68.

Hinz, Walther. *Altiranische Funde und Forschungen* (Berlin, 1969).

Holt, Frank L. *Thundering Zeus: The Making of Hellenistic Bactria* (Berkeley, 1999).

Klíma, Otakar. *Mazdak. Geschichte einer sozialen Bewegung im sassanidischen Persien* (Prague, 1957).

Koenen, Ludwig, and Cornelia Römer, eds. *Der Kölner Mani-Kodex: über das Werden seines Leibes* (Opladen, 1988).

Kotwal, Firoze M., and Philip G. Kreyenbroek. *The Hērbedestān and Nērangestān*. 3 vols. (Paris, 1992–2003).

Kreyenbroek, Philip G. "On the Concept of Spiritual Authority in Zoroastrianism." *JSAI* 17 (1994): 1–15.

Le Rider, Georges. *Suse sous les Séleucides et Parthes. Les trouvailles monétaires et l'histoire de la ville* (Paris, 1965).

Lerner, Jeffrey D. *The Impact of Seleucid Decline on the Eastern Iranian Plateau: The Foundations of Arsacid Parthia and Graeco-Bactria* (Stuttgart, 1999).

Lerouge, Charlotte. "L'image des Parthes dans le monde gréco-romain: du début du Ier siècle av. J.-C. jusqu'à la fin du Haut-Empire romain." *Oriens et Occidens* 17 (Stuttgart, 2007).

Lukonin, V. G. "Political, Social and Administrative Institutions, Taxes and Trade." In *The Cambridge History of Iran 3: The Seleucid, Parthian and Sasanian Periods*, ed. Ehsan Yarshater (Cambridge, 1983): 681–746.

Macuch, Maria. *Rechtskasuistik und Gerichtspraxis zu Beginn des siebenten Jahrhunderts in Iran: Die Rechtssammlung des Farrohmard i Wahrāmān* (Wiesbaden, 1993).

"The Talmudic Expression 'Servant of the Fire' in the Light of Pahlavi Legal Sources." *JSAI* 26 (2002): 109–29.

Millar, Fergus. *The Roman Near East, 31 BC – AD 337* (Cambridge, Mass., 1993).

Minns, Ellis H. "Parchments of the Parthian Period from Avroman in Kurdistan." *JHS* 35 (1915): 22–65.

Minorsky, Vladimir. "Vīs-u-Rāmīn: A Parthian Romance." In *Iranica. Twenty Articles* (Tehran, 1964): 151–99.

Nützel, Werner. *Einführung in die Geo-Archäologie des Vorderen Orients* (Wiesbaden, 2004).

Nyberg, H. S. "The Pahlavi Documents from Avromān." *Le Monde Oriental* 17 (1923): 182–230.

Olbrycht, Marek J. *Parthia et ulteriores gentes. Die Beziehungen zwischen dem arsakidischen Iran und den Nomaden der eurasischen Steppen* (Munich, 1998).

Pedersen, Nils A. *Demonstrative Proof in Defence of God: A Study of Titus of Bostra's Contra Manichaeos* (Leiden, 2004).

Pilipko, Viktor N. *Staraja Nisa. Osnovnye itogi arkheologicheskogo izuchenija v sovetskoj period* (Moscow, 2001).

Pingree, David. *From Astral Omens to Astrology, from Babylon to Bīkāner* (Rome, 1997).

Rawlinson, George. *The Sixth Oriental Monarchy, or the Geography, History, and Antiquities of Parthia* (London, 1873).

Parthia (London, 1893).

Rostovtzeff, M. I. "Dura and the Problem of Parthian Art." *YCS* 5 (1935): 157–304.

Rudolph, Kurt. *Die Mandäer II. Der Kult* (Göttingen, 1961).

Russell, James R. *Zoroastrianism in Armenia*. Harvard Iranian Series 5 (Cambridge, Mass., 1987).

Armenian and Iranian Studies (Cambridge, Mass., 2004).

Schmitt, Rüdiger. "Parthische Sprach- und Namenüberlieferung aus arsakidischer Zeit." In *Das Partherreich und seine Zeugnisse*, ed. Josef Wiesehöfer (Stuttgart, 1998): 163–204.

Schuol, Monika. *Die Charakene. Ein mesopotamisches Königreich in hellenistisch-parthischer Zeit* (Stuttgart, 2000).

Sellwood, D. *An Introduction to the Coinage of Parthia* (London, 1980).

Shaked, Shaul. "The Myth of Zurvan: Cosmogony and Eschatology." In *Messiah and Christos: Studies in the Jewish Origins of Christianity presented to David Flusser*, eds. Ithamar Gruenwald, Shaul Shaked, and Gedaliahu G. Stroumsa (Tübingen, 1992): 219–40.

Dualism in Transformation. Varieties of Religion in Sasanian Iran (London, 1994).

"Popular Religion in Sasanian Babylonia." *JSAI* 21 (1997): 103–17.

"Scripture and Exegesis in Zoroastrianism." In *Homer, the Bible, and Beyond: Literary and Religious Canons in the Ancient World*, eds. Margalit Finkelberg and Gedaliahu G. Stroumsa. *JSRC* 2 (Leiden, 2003): 63–74.

Sherwin-White, Susan, and Amelie Kuhrt. *From Samarkhand to Sardis: A New Approach to the Seleucid Empire* (London, 1993).

Skjærvø, Prods O. "Kirdir's Vision: Translation and Analysis." *Archäologische Mitteilungen aus Iran* 16 (1983): 269–306.

"Aramaic Scripts for Iranian Languages." In *The World's Writing Systems*, eds. Peter T. Daniels and William Bright (Oxford, 1996): 515–35.

"The *Videvdad*: Its Ritual-Mythical Significance." In *The Age of the Parthians*, eds. V. S. Curtis and S. Stewart (London, 2007): 105–41.

Staviskij, B. Ja. *La Bactriane sous les Kushans: problèmes d'histoire et de culture* (Paris, 1986).

Sullivan, Richard D. *Near Eastern Royalty and Rome, 100–30 B.C.* (Toronto, 1990).

Thomson, Robert W. "The Maccabees in Early Armenian Historiography." *JTS* 26 (1975): 329–41.

Van der Spek, Robartus. "Cuneiform Documents on Parthian History: The Rahimesu Archive. Materials for the Study of the Standard of Living." In *Das Partherreich und seine Zeugnisse*, ed. J. Wiesehöfer (Stuttgart, 1998): 205–58.

Von Gutschmid, Alfred. *Geschichte Irans und seiner Nachbarländer von Alexander dem Grossen bis zum Untergang der Arsaciden* (Tübingen, 1888).

Walker, Joel T. *The Legend of Mar Qardagh. Narrative and Christian Heroism in Late Antique Iraq* (Berkeley, 2006).

Widengren, Geo. *Mani and Manichaeism* (London, 1965).

"The Establishment of the Sasanian Dynasty in the Light of New Evidence." In *Atti del convegno internazionale sul tema: La Persia nel medioevo* (Rome, 1971): 711–82.

Wiesehöfer, Josef. *Die 'dunklen Jahrhunderte' der Persis. Untersuchungen zur Geschichte und Kultur von Färs in frühhellenistischer Zeit (330–140 v.Chr.)* (Munich, 1994).

Wolski, Jozef. *L'empire des Arsacides* (Louvain, 1993).

Yarshater, Ehsan. "Mazdakism." In *The Cambridge History of Iran 3: The Seleucid, Parthian and Sasanian Periods*, ed. E. Yarshater (Cambridge, 1983): 991–1024.

Zaehner, R. C. *Zurvan, a Zoroastrian Dilemma* (New York, 1972).

2

CREATING LOCAL RELIGIOUS IDENTITIES
IN THE ROMAN NEAR EAST

TED KAIZER

The attentive visitor to the Fitzwilliam Museum in Cambridge may spot in room 24 a beautiful, large statue in basalt stone that, according to the accompanying label, represents a "syncretistic, Syrian military deity" (Fig. 1). The statue, from the Syrian Hauran region, circa 100km south to southeast of Damascus, was published in the acquisitions guide of the museum but has, to the best of my knowledge, not otherwise been discussed in scholarly literature.[1] In 1979 the Keeper of Antiquities, Dick Nicholls, described it in a slightly longer, unpublished report to the then director of the museum as follows:

This statue, possibly the finest of the Hauran sculptures now surviving, lacks its arms and legs but is otherwise splendidly preserved. The head is that of a goddess wearing drop ear-rings, a splendid late Roman link-in-link chain necklace with animal-head finials and a central medallion and, in her hair, the form of the Greek *stephanē* that had by Roman times evolved into a kind of crown worn by certain goddesses such as Venus and Diana.... Her hair is rendered in one of the developments from the much older Hellenistic "melon style" that became widespread in the eastern Roman provinces in the 3rd century AD, and more especially in the later part of that century. The figure wears a military cloak, fastened at the right shoulder by a brooch with ivy-leaf pendants hanging by chains, and a breastplate. The latter terminates below the androgynous breasts which mark the transition

I am very grateful to Bill Adler for asking me to contribute to this volume. Earlier versions were presented as seminar papers at Cambridge and Aarhus, and I should like to thank Rebecca Flemming and Rubina Raja for the respective invitations. I owe a special thank you to Lucilla Burn, Keeper of Antiquities at the Fitzwilliam Museum in Cambridge, for providing information about the statue with which this paper starts, and for allowing me to quote from her predecessor's unpublished report from 1979.

[1] Nicholls, *Fitzwilliam Museum Cambridge, Principal Acquisitions 1979–83*, 36, no. 224. Lucilla Burn informed me that there was an opportunity in 1979 or 1980 to analyze a sample of the stone, since the statue's head proved to have been detached and there were some problems mounting it, and that it was then confirmed to be "olivine basalt," common throughout Syria but especially characteristic for the Hauran.

Fig. 1. Statue of a "syncretistic, Syrian military deity" from the Hauran. Now in the Fitzwilliam Museum, Cambridge. Courtesy of the Syndics of the Fitzwilliam Museum.

from a female head to a male body and is worn without shoulder-guards. The preserved shoulders and struts from the body show that both arms were lowered to the sides. The right arm held a double-bladed battle axe, the blades and top of which are preserved against the right shoulder.... The left arm also held an attribute, of which the only part surviving is the head of a snake that extends over on to the breastplate. Almost certainly, what the statue held was the *kerykeion*, or herald's staff, of Hermes, twined with two snakes.

The report further recognized elements of different gods and goddesses in the figure: Zeus, Aphrodite, and Hermes, who were equated with the Syrian deities Hadad, Atargatis, and Simois, respectively, and connected with the planets Jupiter, Venus, and Mercury. Noting that sculptures from the Hauran – in the words of Nicholls, "possibly the most remarkable of all branches of provincial Roman art" – were not at all well presented in British museums, he was especially keen to buy the statue because it complemented the so-called shrine of Malikat already in the Fitzwilliam (Fig. 2).[2] This monolithic monument, with a preserved height of half a meter, and a hollow interior that originally housed a divine image or sacred object, owes its name to a Greek inscription referring to the lamp originally topping the shrine: Λύχνος Μαλειχάθου (Malikat being the very common indigenous name behind the Greek transcription). The monument is especially notable for its side reliefs: on the right, a bust of a sun-god with solar crown, wearing a *chiton*, and on the left, a bust of a moon-goddess with accompanying crescent. As is emphasized correctly in the museum catalog, this divine imagery does not necessarily hint at the deity or deities to whom the monument would have been dedicated. The view traditionally held among scholars – namely, that the supreme gods of most localities in the Near East had become solar deities by the Hellenistic period – was put straight by a classic article of Henri Seyrig. Seyrig pointed out that in virtually all cases the sun-god in the local religions of the classical Levant was never actually identified with the relevant supreme deity, but did instead become one of the latter's main manifestations.[3] Solar imagery – often, but certainly not always, in combination with a lunar representation – was in any case very present in many local Near Eastern religious contexts, where it could be used to portray, in some sort of abbreviated format, the cosmic settings of the divine world, as, for example, on the lintels of the Palmyrene temples of Bel and of Baal-Shamin.[4]

---

[2] Budde and Nicholls, *A Catalogue of the Greek and Roman Sculpture*, 78–9, no. 126 with pl. 42.
[3] Seyrig, "Le culte du soleil."
[4] Gawlikowski, "Aus dem syrischen Götterhimmel." For the lintels from the temples of Bel and of Baal-Shamin at Palmyra, see Drijvers, *Religion of Palmyra*, pl. II and pl. XXXII, respectively.

Fig. 2. Miniature "shrine," supporting lamp of Malikat, from the Hauran. Now in the Fitzwilliam Museum, Cambridge. Courtesy of the Syndics of the Fitzwilliam Museum.

The brief introductory remarks about these two relatively unknown sculptures in the Fitzwilliam have touched upon some of the issues that will be addressed in this chapter. There is something, whether it is in their material, style, or iconographic detail, that makes the sculptures instantly recognizable as inherently "Oriental" or, rather, "Near Eastern." Some elements, such as the busts of the sun and the moon deities on the sides of the miniature shrine, or the military breastplate of the statue, are similar to, or even identical with, evidence known from elsewhere in the Near East. Other aspects cannot be pinned down so easily, and it is especially the unprecedented combination of this particular set of iconographic features that turns the statue of the "syncretistic, Syrian military deity" into a unique, unparalleled divine figure. While we can withhold judgment on the report's precise identification of the statue, its characterization of the figure through iconographic features and requisites relating to different deities calls to mind the device applied in a well-known passage in the only contemporary account of pagan worship in the Roman Near East by someone claiming to be an insider: *On the Syrian Goddess*, attributed to the second-century satirist Lucian of Samosata. Here the author describes the statue of the main goddess at the large temple of Hierapolis (Mabog, in northern Syria) as follows:[5]

Certainly, the image of Zeus looks entirely like Zeus in features and clothes and seated posture; you could not identify it otherwise even if you wished. But when you examine Hera, her image appears to be of many forms. While the overall effect is certainly that of Hera, she also has something of Athena and Aphrodite and Selene and Rhea and Artemis and Nemesis and the Fates. In one hand she has a sceptre, in the other a spindle, and on her head she wears rays, a tower, and the *kestos* with which they adorn Ourania alone.

The description then continues, referring to precious stones sent to the goddess from far away and elaborating on the radiating *lychnis* she wears on her head. It may be known for certain from other sources, such as Strabo and Pliny the Elder, that she was Atargatis,[6] or rather Atar-ate, as

---

[5] Lucian, *Syr. d.* 32: Καὶ δῆτα τὸ μὲν τοῦ Διὸς ἄγαλμα ἐς Δία πάντα ὁρῇ καὶ κεφαλὴν καὶ εἵματα καὶ ἕδρην, καί μιν οὐδὲ ἐθέλων ἄλλως εἰκάσεις. ἡ δὲ Ἥρη σκοπέοντί τοι πολυειδέα μορφὴν ἐκφανέει· καὶ τὰ μὲν ξύμπαντα ἀτρεκέϊ λόγῳ Ἥρη ἐστίν, ἔχει δέ τι καὶ Ἀθηναίης καὶ Ἀφροδίτης καὶ Σεληναίης καὶ Ῥέης καὶ Ἀρτέμιδος καὶ Νεμέσιος καὶ Μοιρέων. χειρὶ δὲ τῇ μὲν ἑτέρῃ σκῆπτρον ἔχει, τῇ ἑτέρῃ δὲ ἄτρακτον, καὶ ἐπὶ τῇ κεφαλῇ ἀκτῖνάς τε φορέει καὶ πύργον καὶ κεστὸν τῷ μούνην τὴν Οὐρανίαν κοσμέουσιν. The translation follows Lightfoot, *Lucian, On the Syrian Goddess*, which is both an excellent edition and commentary on a complicated text and the most extensive study of Near Eastern religion in book form thus far.

[6] Strabo 16.1.27 (748): ἡ Βαμβύκη, ἣν καὶ Ἔδεσσαν καὶ Ἱερὰν πόλιν καλοῦσιν, ἐν ᾗ τιμῶσι τὴν Συρίαν θεὸν τὴν Ἀταργάτιν ("Bambyce, which is also called Edessa and Hierapolis, where the Syrian goddess Atargatis is worshipped" [LCL]); Pliny, *Nat.* 5.19.81: *Bambycen quae alio nomine*

coin legends from Hellenistic Hierapolis and Aramaic inscriptions from elsewhere in the Near East inform us.[7] But that is *not* how the treatise refers to her. Instead, it seems clear that this explicit syncretism (if the word may be used) – the invocation of other divine names in order to make a deity understandable – is a way to approach the uniquely local, indigenous deities of the Near East *not only* on the part of modern scholars but also in Antiquity. Of course, this is only Lucian, and if it was not Lucian, then it was at least an equally skilled literator who presents himself as someone able to give inside information while imitating the linguistic style of Herodotus with near perfection, as Jane Lightfoot has now established beyond reasonable doubt. Naturally, it could be argued that the fact that *On the Syrian Goddess* was first and foremost meant to be a linguistic play on its Herodotean model has a serious effect on its usefulness for historical purposes. But it should also be recognized that even if the piece was meant as tongue-in-cheek, the joke could only have worked if the author managed to portray a realistic representation of religious life in the wider Roman Syria. While the text may therefore not have given an accurate picture of what went on in this specific sanctuary at Hierapolis, it is emblematic of religious life in the Near Eastern lands as a whole.[8]

Moving away from the literary nuances, something similar can indeed be observed at the ostentatious *hierothesion* at Nemrud Dag, the tomb sanctuary of Antiochus I, king over Commagene from circa 70 to 36 BCE. The enormous statues on the west and east terraces of Mount Nemrud, among which the king himself is also seated, are explicitly identified in the inscriptions running on the back of the statues as Ζεὺς Ὠρομάσδης, Ἀπόλλων Μίθρης Ἥλιος Ἑρμῆς, and Ἀρτάγνης Ἡρακλῆς Ἄρης – the ultimate embodiment of the notion of syncretism, and the same gods with whom the king portrayed himself on the multiple *dexiōsis* reliefs that were set up throughout his kingdom (Fig. 3).[9] Naturally, these over-the-top remnants of the royal dynastic cult of Commagene do not seem to tell us much about the area's indigenous religious culture. However, even if they proceeded from the religious and political program of the slightly

---

Hierapolis vocatur, Syris vero Mabog – ibi prodigiosa Atargatis, Graecis autem Derceto dicta, colitur ("Bambyce which is also called by another name, Hierapolis, but by the *Syri* Mabog; there the monstrous goddess Atargatis is worshipped, but called Derketo by the Greeks" [LCL]).

[7] Lightfoot, *Lucian, On the Syrian Goddess*, 4–6 and 13–14 for references to coins and inscriptions, and 434–43 on the above-quoted description of the iconography of the temple's statue.

[8] I have made this point in Kaizer, "Introduction," 28–9.

[9] For the tomb sanctuary, see Sanders, *Nemrud Daği*; for the *dexiōsis* reliefs, see Petzl, "Antiochos I. von Kommagene," and for the epigraphic sources on Antiochus's ruler cult, see Crowther and Facella, "New evidence for the ruler cult of Antiochus." Cf. Facella, *La dinastia degli Orontidi*, 279–85.

Fig. 3. *Dexiōsis* relief of Antiochus I of Commagene with Artagnes Heracles Ares, *in situ* at Arsameia on the Nymphaios. Photo by Ted Kaizer.

megalomaniac Antiochus himself, they still needed to be sufficiently geared to his subjects in order to realize their potential as adherents to the cults.

The religious structures in Commagene are of course very distinct from those known from other areas within the Near East. But any bird's-eye view of the religious life of the wider region, even if far from comprehensive, will immediately reveal that the same can be said about most other places as well.[10] Patterns of worship in the many cities, villages, and subregions that constituted the Roman Near East (see Map 2) were above all very different from each other, despite some obvious similarities. It is true that the various local temple complexes were all embedded in subregions with quite specific geological characteristics, which obviously had a bearing on their relevant cultural developments. But the geographical divisions cannot explain all the variety, and neither should that variety be attributed to the undeniable imbalance in the spread of evidence. Literary sources are scant and – with the exception of the aforementioned *On the Syrian Goddess*, which has its own instruction manual, and Philo of Byblos's *Phoenician History*, which according to its title is geographically speaking of a more limited value – mostly useless. Still, they are interesting for their approach. The Church Father Tertullian's statement from the late second century that "each individual region and each locality had its own deity," linking Syria to the goddess Astartes and Arabia to the god Dusares, is a key example of the simplified treatment that the religious life of the Roman Near East suffered at the hands of Christian and other literary sources.[11] An enigmatic passage in the Syriac *Oration of Melito the Philosopher*, which claims to be a Christian speech addressed to a Roman emperor, gives a list of which deities received a cult where. The section, which possibly comes from a different source from that of the rest of the discourse, takes a euhemeristic form, describing how the respective gods and goddesses came to be worshipped as a result of their benefactions made while human. The often confusing passage states, for example, how "the Phoenicians worshipped Belti, queen of Cyprus" and "the Syrians worshipped Atti, a woman from Adiabene, who sent the daughter of *BLT*, a nurse, and she cured *SYMY*, the daughter of Hadad, the king of Syria," while "on Nebu then, who is in Mabog, why

---

[10] For an attempted bird's-eye view of local religious life in the Hellenistic and Roman Near East as a whole, see Kaizer, "Introduction," 2–10.

[11] Tertullian, *Apol.* 24.7: *unicuique etiam provinciae et civitati suus deus est, ut Syriae Astartes, ut Arabiae Dusares, ut Noricis Belenus, ut Africae Caelestis, ut Mauritaniae reguli sui* ("every individual province, every city, has its own god; Syria has Astartes; Arabia, Dusares; the Norici Belenus; Africa, her Heavenly Virgin, Mauretania its chieftains" [LCL]).

shall I write to you? For behold, all the priests who are in Mabog know that this is the image of Orpheus, the Thracian magian, and Hadaran, this is the image of Zaradusta, the Persian magian, because these two practised magianism to a well which was in the forest near Mabog."[12] Similarly, in the sixth century, Jacob of Serugh in his homily *On the Fall of the Idols* describes how Satan places Antioch under the protection of Apollo, Edessa under that of Nebu and Bel, Harran under that of the moon-god Sin and Baal-Shamin, and so forth.[13]

Such "fractionation"[14] of worship in the Near East, as the literary sources with their simplified treatment propagate it, was of course not reflected by the cultic realities. The cults of individual gods and goddesses were not restricted to particular places only, and many of them were worshipped throughout the wider region. It seems logical, then, that worshippers of a deity with the same name in different localities in the Near East (for example adherents to the cult of Bel at Palmyra, Apamea, and Edessa, among other places) must have shared a certain focus in their worship of that deity, even if they operated quite differently from each other within their respective local contexts. However, whether we should therefore assume that the multifarious idolization of individual deities was the result of one "central" cult of a particular deity being distributed over the Near East is a different matter. Such multiple occurrences of a god's idolization could also, and maybe better, be understood as being in the first place *local* cults, thanks to whose totality of pluralist identities the notion of a Near Eastern cult of that god would be shaped.[15]

If a Near Eastern religion in the Roman period may be hard to distinguish, several broad patterns of resemblance – such as the application of certain types of cult titles to deities, some specific rituals, and above all the presence of a number of nonclassical languages – have certainly assisted in the recognition (in any case on the part of modern scholars) of elements known from specific local contexts as generally Near Eastern. In his Burnett

---

[12] Cureton, *Spicilegium Syriacum*, 24, lines 15–25, line 23 (Syriac text). For a translation of the passage with further references, see Kaizer, "In search of Oriental cults," 30–5. For discussion, see now above all Lightfoot, "The *Apology* of Pseudo-Meliton"; eadem, "Pseudo-Meliton and the cults of the Roman Near East." While I would of course not want to suggest that it was Lucian himself who wrote the piece in his alleged mother tongue (*Bis. acc.* 27), it might be worth contemplating that the *Oration of Melito the Philosopher* (or at least its euhemeristic section) could also be read in a manner similar to *On the Syrian Goddess*, as a linguistic play on an unknown, perhaps only orally transmitted, Aramaic model of localizing religious history.

[13] Martin, "Discours de Jacques de Saroug," 110, line 42–112, line 91 (Syriac text).

[14] Kaizer, "Introduction," 1.

[15] As was argued in Kaizer, "In search of Oriental cults," 39–41.

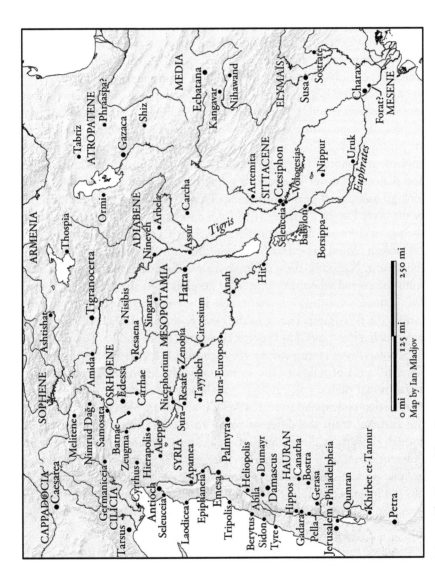

Map 2. The Roman Near East

lectures at Aberdeen University from 1888 to 1891, William Robertson Smith famously orated on the "religion of the Semites."[16] Scholars at least since then have searched for common characteristics of religious practice among the inhabitants of the Near East who spoke one of the Semitic languages. Mikhaïl Rostovtzeff formulated it as a "religious κοινή, familiar to all the Semites and to the semitized Greeks and Iranians throughout Babylonia, Mesopotamia, Syria, and Arabia."[17] As Fergus Millar has pointed out, this search is not only understandable, but also in principle legitimate: "Given the fundamental importance of language to the emergence of nationalism in the modern world, it is natural that we should pose the question, provided that we remain aware that it may embody completely inappropriate preconceptions."[18] However, one would need a large-scale study of the applied terminology for religious practices in the various Semitic languages and dialects in order to establish properly to what degree relevant phraseology was shared between different local and subregional communities in the Near East as a whole. The jury is still out over the degree to which the use of different Aramaic dialects, such as Palmyrenean, Hatrean, and Nabataean, could provide a "common link" for the pagan cult centers in the Levant. Naturally, these different dialects followed their own trajectory from the period when they started to develop from the dominant "imperial Aramaic" onward, but that is not to say necessarily that it was only Greek, the new lingua franca in the Near East since Alexander, that could meet such a need, as Glen Bowersock wanted to see it.[19]

Scholars have attempted to get around the apparent variety in Near Eastern forms of religious life in various ways. Maurice Sartre proposed a traditional division in multiple pantheons (Phoenician, Aramean, and Arab), "that correspond to each other without being identical."[20] However, the evidence from the different places in the Near East is seldom good enough to warrant the recognition of clearly structured relations between different divinities on the local level, let alone of a proper religious system on a larger scale, and talking of Phoenician, Aramean, and Arab pantheons is a huge oversimplification. Indeed, William Robertson Smith in his final lecture series on the subject already recognized that it is the physical

[16] Smith, *Lectures on the Religion of the Semites.*
[17] Rostovtzeff, *Dura-Europos and its Art,* 66. For useful criticism of his influential thesis, see Dirven, *Palmyrenes of Dura-Europos,* xix–xxii.
[18] Millar, *Roman Near East,* 11.
[19] Bowersock, *Hellenism in Late Antiquity,* 15–16. On the variety of Aramaic dialects in the Roman Near East, see most recently Gzella, "Das Aramäische in den römischen Ostprovinzen."
[20] Sartre, *L'Orient romain,* 490: "Le premier aspect qu'il faut souligner est la présence de panthéons différents, qui se recoupent sans être identiques. Il faut distinguer entre les panthéons phéniciens, araméens et arabes."

connection between a deity and its local sanctuary that is fundamental.[21] The idea that the divine worlds of the Roman Near East were "mixtures" of larger pantheons basically builds on the classic thesis of Otto Eissfeldt that nearly all Near Eastern sites were founded, or at least refounded, in the Hellenistic period; that they underwent influence not only from the Greco-Roman world (and in some cases from the Parthian and later also Persian spheres), but also from the surrounding "Arab" populations; but that ultimately, and most importantly, their local religious cultures remained at heart indigenous.[22] Consequently, it has often been argued that the assumed "indigenous nature of Near Eastern religion" was visible also in the Greco-Roman appearance of the Levantine temples. Above all, the separation of the innermost sanctuary, the adyton (θάλαμος in Lucian's terminology [*On the Syrian Goddess* 31]), from the cella, the temple building proper, is said to reflect the primitive chapel, which despite its "superficial" Greco-Roman veneer remains the home of the indigenous deity. The indigenous Near Eastern deities are believed to have remained untouched by the *interpretatio Graeca* from the Roman period, even if the classical cover layer at first glance suggests otherwise.

The religious history of the Roman Near East has, inevitably and invariably, been analyzed in terms of an intersection between "indigenous" and "foreign" (mostly classical) elements, between "local" aspects and those coming from, or at least ascribed to, different cultural spheres of influence. One way around this problem would be a radical appreciation that those elements of a local religion that were themselves not "local," or at least not local in origin, could over time become considered an intrinsic part of that same local religion, and would subsequently lose any foreign association to which they had been subject in an earlier phase. Thus, a relief from the temple of Bel at Palmyra showing a naked Heracles figure with club and lion skin, standing alongside three deities in traditional Palmyrene dress, ought really to be discussed as a relief of *four* gods, *all* of which are Palmyrene (Fig. 4). Although the iconography of the Heracles figure may be originally Greek, the style in which he is depicted on this relief is similar to that of the other deities, and hence very local. This is even clearer at Hatra, originally a Parthian stronghold in the northern Mesopotamian Jazirah steppe, where the Heracles figure could be depicted wearing typically Hatrene jewelry.[23] According to the available sources, both at Palmyra

[21] Smith, *Lectures on the Religion of the Semites. 2nd and 3rd Series*, 62–4.
[22] Eissfeldt, *Tempel und Kulte*, 9, 153–4.
[23] For example, Sommer, *Hatra*. Abb. 117.

Fig. 4. Relief of four Palmyrene deities, including a Heracles figure, from the temple of Bel at Palmyra. Courtesy of the General Director of Antiquities and Museums, Syria.

and at Hatra, the Heracles figure formed very much a part of the local religious setup.

In order to make sense of the often baffling evidence – and as an alternative to the still fashionable theory of an accumulation of rather "stationary" religious layers, of which the latest, the classical one, is believed to have had no real impact on the indigenous religious elements – it may be more helpful to postulate a process of continuous renegotiation of religious elements taking place in the context of the various open local cultures, a process that did not take place automatically in what moderns might view as a progressive or logical format.[24] That said, it remains a problem that the static nature of the documentary and visual evidence seems to show the opposite of the dynamism of the model of continuous renegotiation. But if the religious worlds of the Roman Near East may have been more dependent on tradition than this model seems to take into account, it is also a very risky assumption to conclude from the static nature of the evidence that pagan religious practice in the Near East was therefore unchanging and unchangeable in the Roman period.[25]

---

[24] For this model, see Kaizer, "The 'Heracles figure'," 225–6.
[25] Contra, for example, Teixidor, *Pagan God*, 6.

So far it has been argued that gods and their cults in the Near East ought to be interpreted first and foremost as conditioned by their direct local context, and that these local forms of religious life must have undergone continuing development, even if the nature of the evidence does not always help to reveal such development. But by what means were local religious identities created? In order to answer that question in full, attention ought to be paid to a variety of aspects, such as, for example, the language chosen by the worshipper to address his or her deity and to publicize his or her adherence to its cult; the actual terminology used in the inscriptions to describe the gods and to deal with the complicated divine worlds; the way the gods are depicted in sculptures and on coins; the sort of temple in which a particular deity was worshipped and that temple's location in relation to other sacred places within the locality; and the financial backing for a cult and its maintenance. These are only some of the issues related to the large and commonly ignored subject of the mechanics by which specifically *local* gods and goddesses could be created, by their worshippers and observers alike, in the Roman Near East. And only some of them can be dealt with in a little more detail in what follows.

It is fitting to look first at the widely spread worship throughout the region of so-called toponymic deities, gods and goddesses who were explicitly named after a specific locality. They provide important case studies, as it is clear that the local context is by definition of the utmost relevance for our understanding of the cult centered on a "universally known" god with an epithet that links him to his place of origin, whether a famous city in the case of Zeus *Damaskènos* or a village owned by a temple complex in the middle of the Jebel Ansariyeh in the case of Zeus *Baitokēkē*.[26] By means of such expressions, worshippers applied explicit labels of cultural identification to their deities. These can therefore illuminate the way in which the inhabitants of the Near East conceived of themselves – namely, above all belonging to a particular city or (even more common) a particular village. The Roman Near East has been described as "a world of villages."[27] Although the archaeological remains of these villages and small towns are scant and often lost, the multitude of inscribed dedications to their local gods show that they often formed the focal point in daily life.

---

[26] On Zeus *Damaskènos*: *IGLS* XIII.1 no. 9013 (an inscription actually found at Bostra), and see now Freyberger, "Im Zeichen des höchsten Gottes." On Zeus *Baitokēkē*: *IGLS* III no. 4028, with Steinsapir, *Rural Sanctuaries in Roman Syria*, 31–45. Further examples of toponymic deities are innumerable.

[27] Millar, *Roman Near East*, for example, 228, 250, 292, 390.

That is of course not to say that we can claim to know who these local deities really *were*, since we are handicapped by the nearly complete absence of sources that may have hinted at what the inhabitants of the Near East actually "believed." Inscriptions commonly form the basis of our investigations, providing the opportunity to attend first and foremost to the names and epithets actually given to the deities by their worshippers. In a way, therefore, as Fergus Millar phrased it, "the god is what the worshipper says he is."[28] This is certainly right in the sense that most of our knowledge of the divine world of the Roman Near East depends on the inscribed altars, stelae, and columns that individual dedicants and benefactors paid for in honor of specific inhabitants of that divine world. That said, an ancient worshipper would certainly not agree with this idea that he had "made up" his own god. Surely, he just addressed his deity in the manner that seemed to fit the appropriate situation best? In other words, and on a more theological level, the inhabitants of the local divine worlds within the Near East were there perpetually and invariably. Worshippers could simply adjust the divine names and approach deities in sometimes contradictory manners, depending both on the local context and on the worshippers' own perspectives.

In addition to the use of toponymic epithets, a strong *local* religious identity could also be expressed, and accordingly created, by using epithets that were not connected to the place name of the town or the village as such, but that were still restricted to one particular site. Two examples will show, in different ways, how unique and local forms of religion must be put in a wider context in order to gain full appreciation of the peculiarity that seems to characterize them in the first place. The first example is that of the well-known set of fascinating deities in the Limestone Massif, the hinterland of the cities of northwest Syria. They are characterized by unique epithets that simultaneously reveal some conceptual similarity lying underneath, namely a link with aniconic cult features.[29] At Burj Baqirha on the Jebel Barisha, the best-preserved temple of the Massif (Fig. 5) was dedicated by local benefactors, according to the lintel of the *temenos* gate, to Zeus Bōmos, Zeus "Altar." At Srir, also on the Jebel Barisha, a temple was built in classical style for Zeus Tourbarachos, the "ancestral deity," whose etymology is based on a junction of the Semitic roots *ṣwr* and *brk*, leading to something along the lines of "blessed rock." At Kalota on the Jebel Seman, to the northeast of Srir, a shrine belonged to Symbetylos,

---

[28] Millar, *Roman Near East*, 248–9, 270.
[29] For what follows, see Callot and Marcillet-Jaubert, "Hauts-lieux de Syrie du Nord"; Millar, *Roman Near East*, 250–6; and Gatier, "Villages et sanctuaires."

Fig. 5. The temple of Zeus Bōmos at Burj Baqirha. Photo by Ted Kaizer.

Zeus Seimos, and Leôn, thus to a deity whose name means "the one who shares the betyl (the aniconic stone)," a god whose name may be connected with the Semitic word for "name" (*shem*), and a divine figure called "lion."[30] A fourth pagan temple, on top of the dominant hilltop in the area, Jebel Sheikh Barakat, and hence from a topographical point of view the most important of the set, was dedicated to Zeus Madbachos (*mdbk*) and Selamanes. Whereas the latter may be connected with an old Assyrian divine name "Shulmanu," the epithet of Zeus, Madbachos, is in fact the Aramaic version of the Greek *bōmos*, "altar," since *mdbk* comes from the root *dbk*, "to sacrifice."

Whether all those involved in the worship of these deities fully realized the conceptual overlap between these cults is of course another matter. But despite the fact that the individual divine names appear only in the context of their own site, the idea of some sort of notional network between these sanctuaries and their gods is hard to escape. Nevertheless, even if the deities were named in similar fashion, the fact that their peculiar epithets seem to

---

[30] The latter, and especially his association with an aniconic cult object, calls to mind a passage in the early sixth-century *Life of Isidorus* (203) by the Neoplatonist Damascius, which is preserved in Photius's *Bibliotheca*, cod. 242 [348a-b]), in which an aniconic stone near Damascus replies to an oracular question that it belonged to a deity worshipped in Baalbek in the shape of a lion. The story may be suggestive, but of course it would be too far-fetched to look for any direct connection.

have been restricted to one particular place only implies that worshippers considered them individual deities. Simultaneously – and this is especially relevant considering the nonclassical elements of the divine nomenclature – it is worth emphasizing that the architectural expression given to these cults in the Roman period is not indigenous but Greco-Roman.[31] This observation may be used as a warning against too hastily drawn conclusions about the nature of these cults: despite the agreement in meaning between the divine names, it is not an automatic given that in the Roman period, the cults centered completely around aniconic imagery. Indeed, it has now been convincingly argued by Milette Gaifman that the long-held view that aniconic imagery was characteristic for the Near East as a whole is no longer tenable, and that the scholarly model that contrasts aniconic with anthropomorphic cult objects conflicts with the actual realities of worship.[32] As to the pagan temples in the Limestone Massif, it ought to be noted that some anthropomorphic figures are indeed present. At the start of the two roads leading up to the sanctuary at Srir, of the three roads leading to the top of Jebel Sheik Barakat, and also of a road leading up to Qal'at Kalota are inscribed reliefs of a reclining Heracles figure. The two reliefs at Srir differ from each other, and from the other ones, in one important aspect: while the relief at the northern approach is dated to 130 CE according to the era of Antioch (year 179), the one at the southern approach is dated to 131 CE according to the Seleucid era (year 445), showing how the sanctuary was situated right at the border between the civic territories of Antioch and of Chalcis, and hence raising questions about the logistics of the temple's administration and about the relevance that this local rural temple must have had for the civic communities of two major cities on either side.

The second example is that of Deir el-Qala, a place located on Mount Lebanon with a view over the nearby *colonia* Berytus that functioned as the center of worship of a god known as the "Lord of Dances."[33] His Latin and Greek names, *Jupiter Balmarcod* and *Theos Balmarkōs*, both attested only at Deir el-Qala, come from the Semitic phrase *b'l mrqd*, which has that precise meaning. And like his more famous toponymic counterparts from the Near East, the originally local gods of Doliche and Baalbek

---

[31] Thus Millar, *Roman Near East*, 255: "Continuity of cult over centuries is quite possible. Even if that must remain a mere hypothesis, our evidence from this rural area makes it certain that the Hellenistic cities did not wholly determine the nature of religious practices even at the heart of the most Hellenised part of the Near East. Yet the *expression* given to this cult in architectural form belongs, as always, to the Roman Empire."

[32] Gaifman, "Aniconic image." Cf. Stewart, "Baetyls as statues?"

[33] For what follows, see Rey-Coquais, "Deir el Qalaa."

(known throughout the empire as Jupiter Optimus Maximus Dolichenus
and Jupiter Optimus Maximus Heliopolitanus, respectively), the Lord of
Dances could receive dedications to Jupiter Optimus Maximus Balmarcod,
similarly turning a local cult into a nominal alternative to the deity who
presented Rome's most traditional and far-reaching parade of power. The
case of Deir el-Qala is of particular interest because it can provide a glimpse
into the role that mythology known from the classical world could play in
local religious contexts in the Roman Near East.[34] The Dionysiac epithet
κοίρανε κώμων, "leader of the processional band of revellers," which the
Lord of Dances received in at least one inscription, seems to confirm that
for at least some worshippers this indigenous divine figure was to be identified with Dionysus, the Greek god of merry-making, in whose cult processional and wild dancing played such a major part.

If that is correct, it may be possible to explain the surprising presence
of some of the other deities who are mentioned in the inscriptions from
Deir el-Qala, such as Mater Matuta (the Latin equivalent of Leucothea),
Juno, and Poseidon. As is well known, these deities play a role in the myth
of Ino-Leucothea. Ino was the daughter of Cadmus and second wife of
Athamas, who – by bringing up Dionysus (the son of Zeus by her sister
Semele) – provoked the anger of Hera. In her revenge, the goddess drove
them mad so that Athamas killed their son, Learchus, and Ino jumped
with their other son, Melicertes, to their death into the sea. There, of
course, they were received by Poseidon as sea-divinities, under the names
of Leucothea and Palaemon. Interestingly, coins from Berytus, the city
closest to Deir el-Qala that issued coinage, often show a dolphin, alongside
Poseidon or his trident,[35] and it could be that this imagery is connectable
to the version of the myth in which Melicertes-Palaemon is carried to the
Isthmus by a dolphin.[36] It is of course a valid question to ask how much
of this story would actually have been known in a Hellenized city on the
Phoenician coast that had become a Roman colony in the late first century
BCE, and especially why it is relevant to cultic practice in the immediate surroundings of Berytus. However, as Denis Feeney has emphasized, mythology functioned as a vital component of the continuous reproduction of
Greco-Roman religious culture.[37] And as regards the Roman Near East
in particular, the unfolding of local mythologies was further complicated

---

[34] For full details and references concerning the example that follows, see Kaizer, "Leucothea as Mater
Matuta," and now also Aliquot, *La vie religieuse au Liban*, 164–9.
[35] *BMC Phoenicia*, no. 11 (from the first century BCE); *SNG Cop.*, no. 102 (from the reign of Antoninus
Pius).
[36] Pausanias 1.44.7–8 and 2.1.3; Statius, *Theb.* 9.330.
[37] Feeney, *Literature and Religion*.

because there were no coherent "Oriental" mythological accounts that were spread all over the region, comparable to Homer and Hesiod, or to Ovid. The case of Deir el-Qala may therefore be used, with care, as a case study of how a mythological "package" from the classical world contributed to the creation of a local religious identity.

Further problems are encountered when considering visual representations of mythological stories: as long as there is no written evidence to tell us otherwise, it seems only natural for the modern scholar to assume that a Near Eastern depiction of a myth known from the classical world implies not only full knowledge of that classical myth on the part of the relevant worshippers, but also adherence to the prevalent version from the Greco-Roman world. In some cases, it must indeed have been a rather straightforward process of interpretation. A relief on a basalt lintel from the Hauran, now in the Louvre, represents – albeit in unclassically static fashion – the judgment of Paris.[38] For the observer unable to spot this dynamic story immediately from the inactive line-up of figures on the relief, the accompanying labels leave no space for doubt: from left to right the figures are named as Paris himself, Hermes, Aphrodite, Athena, Hera, and finally Zeus.

However, even if the divine figures are unambiguously identified by accompanying inscriptions, what we get is not always what we seem to see. In the late 1930s, excavations behind the temple of Bel at Palmyra laid bare a mosaic with the figure of Cassiopeia, identified by an inscription (Κασσιεπεια), revealing herself in all her naked beauty, with Poseidon standing in the center of the scene (Fig. 6).[39] When the mosaic was published, it was concluded that this was a depiction of the well-known story in which Cassiopeia, the wife of king Cepheus of Ethiopia, boasted that she was more beautiful than the Nereids, with the result that an angry Poseidon sent a sea-monster in revenge of Cassiopeia's slight of the sea-goddesses, with due consequences for Cassiopeia's daughter Andromeda.[40]

The interpretation seemed very logical indeed. However, many years later two mosaics were discovered at Apamea on the Orontes and at New Paphos on Cyprus, respectively, that clearly show Cassiopeia as the *victress* in her beauty contest with the Nereids, as she is crowned by a Nikē in the presence of a divine judge (Poseidon again, on the mosaic from Apamea).[41]

[38] Dunand, *Le musée de Soueïda*, 11–3, no. 1.
[39] Stern, *Les mosaïques*, 26–42.
[40] Apollodorus, *Bibl.*, 2.4.3.
[41] For the mosaic from Apamea, see Balty, *Mosaïques antiques de Syrie*, 82–7, nos. 36–8. For the mosaic from New Paphos, see Bowersock, *Hellenism in Late Antiquity*, pl. 3.

Fig. 6. Mosaic of Cassiopeia from Palmyra. Courtesy of the General Director of Antiquities and Museums, Syria.

No representation of the standard story, therefore, but an interesting twist on the classical myth, as was first noted by Jean-Charles Balty.[42] His theory was built on by Janine Balty, who put forward a Neoplatonic interpretation of the mosaic:[43] the victory of Cassiopeia, etymologically linked to the toponymic deity of Mount Kasios, probably the most famous hilltop in Syria, is believed to stand for the victory of the cosmic order over the chaos of the aquatic powers – of the unchanging, immaterial world, which is the real beauty, over the changing, material world, which is represented by the marine element. Indeed, the Suda identifies Cassiopeia as *hē kallonē*, Beauty personified.[44] Poseidon, standing in the center of the Palmyrene mosaic and seated on the one from Apamea, seems far removed from the raging sea-god acting out his revenge, as we know him from classical mythology. On these Near Eastern mosaics, he is instead acting as a wise judge and a more supreme deity. In fact, a bilingual inscription from 39 CE from Palmyra explicitly identifies Poseidon with Elqonera, "El the creator,"[45] and it does not come as a surprise, then, that his place on the mosaic from New Paphos has been taken by Aion (identified by an inscription, Ἀιων), the divine personification of the permanence of the

[42] Balty, "Une version orientale méconnue."
[43] Balty, "Composantes classiques"; eadem, "Zénobie et le néoplatonisme."
[44] Suda, *s.v.* Κασσιέπεια, ed. Adler.
[45] Hillers and Cussini, *Palmyrene Aramaic Texts*, no. 2779-IGLS XVII.I no. 318.

cosmos. It is argued by Balty that this unique mixture between Oriental cosmological conceptions and the Neoplatonic theory of the transmigration of souls could only have come into existence in the local circumstances of Palmyra, where the philosopher Longinus spent the last years of his life at the court of Zenobia, and that the idea was later copied at New Paphos and at Apamea. In any case, the clear diversion from the classical story on these three mosaics serves as a warning that our main sources for classical mythology are insufficient to provide a supraregional framework to which we can relate the indigenous deities of the Near East.

Nor can it be automatically assumed that ancient Mesopotamian mythology was transmitted to the Roman Near East without changes, as a discussion of the "battle relief" on one of the beams from the temple of Bel at Palmyra can clarify (Fig. 7). With a few early exceptions of scholars who wanted to see elements of the myth of Zeus and Typhon in the relief,[46] there has long been agreement that it depicts the fight against Tiamat, known from the Babylonian epic of creation *Enuma Elish* (in which the chief deity Marduk-Bel riding in his chariot had to overcome the monster Tiamat in order to create the world), and that therefore the famous Akitu festival from ancient Babylon was still celebrated in more or less identical format a thousand years later in the caravan city in the Syrian desert.[47] However, Lucinda Dirven has drawn attention to some important variations on the Babylonian myth.[48] The monster on the Palmyrene relief is represented with multiple legs in the shape of snakes. In addition, the figure in the chariot, on the far left of the relief (Fig. 8), is not the most important adversary of the chaos monster. Instead, the central position of the action scene seems to go to a horse rider, who is leading six other figures standing to the right of the relief.

If it is correct to view the figure in the chariot as Bel, this may be surprising, since Bel was by far the most important god of the city. Dirven's iconographic analysis concludes convincingly that nearly all the six figures who stand to the right of the horse rider can be identified with deities who received a cult in the temple "of Nebu" at Palmyra.[49] Nabu, as he was known in ancient Mesopotamia, was the son of Marduk-Bel, and his

---

[46] Note that Strabo (16.2.7) locates the mythical story of Typhon's stroke by lightning "somewhere" along the Orontes river, "formerly called Typhon."

[47] For example, Dalley, *Legacy of Mesopotamia,* 51; Tubach, "Das Akītu-Fest."

[48] For what follows, see Dirven, "The exaltation of Nabū"; eadem, *Palmyrenes of Dura-Europos,* 128–56.

[49] For the inscriptions and sculptures from this temple, see Bounni, Seigne, and Saliby, *Le sanctuaire de Nabū à Palmyre. Planches*; Bounni, *Le sanctuaire de Nabū à Palmyre. Texte.* Cf. Kaizer, *Religious Life of Palmyra,* 89–99.

Fig. 7. "Battle relief" from the temple of Bel at Palmyra. Photo by Ted Kaizer.

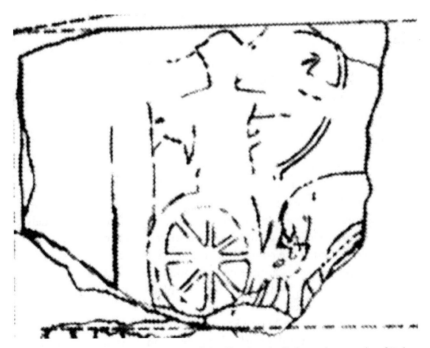

Fig. 8. Drawing of the missing part of the "battle relief" from the temple of Bel at Palmyra. *Source:* H. J. W. Drijvers, *The Religion of Palmyra* (Brill, 1976), pl. IV. 2.

leading role on the battle relief would not be incompatible with the fact that by the late Babylonian period he had reached a status virtually equal to that of his father – a rise to power reflected in an ancient Mesopotamian text known as *The Exaltation of Nabu*, and that scholars also believe to have been manifested in the proceedings of the Akitu festival. However, whether that says much about an Akitu festival at Palmyra is another matter. The temple "of Nebu" at Palmyra was, despite its central location, a relatively minor religious building, certainly compared to that of Bel. And the simple but often forgotten fact that Palmyra had no kingship (at least not before Odaenathus and Zenobia's episode) necessarily means that the rituals of the ancient Mesopotamian festival, which served to confirm the existing socio-political order centered around the king, cannot have had the same meaning at Palmyra. On the other hand, as will be seen later in this chapter, in 32 CE the temple of Bel at Palmyra was dedicated on the sixth day of Nisan (April), falling precisely in the period in which the Akitu festival was traditionally celebrated.

Thus far, we have seen how inscriptions, sculptures, and mosaics could contribute to the creation of local religious identities. It is only natural that different source materials provide different sorts of information on deities and their cults. Among the sources, the so-called Roman provincial coinage stands out as the medium par excellence by which cities in the eastern part of the Roman empire expressed their civic identity.[50] Because these coins were issued by the city *as a collectivity*, the religious imagery on such coinage was not the result of the piety of an individual or a small group like a family. They are therefore more significant than individual dedications for our understanding of local religious identity from a civic point of view. The religious imagery on these issues was supposedly recognized, and worshipped, by the entire population of the place where they were minted. However, as the following three examples illustrate, the numismatic evidence for gods, cults, myths, and rituals at a city does not provide a complete and impartial view of the patterns of worship of that city. The coinage of cities in the eastern provinces of the Roman empire presents a mere civic façade of religious life – indeed, a façade decided on by, and thus in the first place reflecting, the religious tastes of the local elites.

First, at Gerasa in the Syrian Decapolis, the earliest coins, struck from the reign of Nero onward, have both Artemis and Zeus on the reverse, but

---

[50] See Harl, *Civic Coins and Civic Politics,* and now Howgego, Heuchert, and Burnett, *Coinage and Identity.*

from Hadrian onward, only Artemis appears on coins, usually explicitly identified as the Tyche of the citizens of Gerasa.[51] It seems clear that this development signifies the increasingly important role of the goddess in the public presentation of the city outward, to such a degree that she even came to monopolize it. But it is not the whole story.[52] Both Zeus and Artemis occupied a large sanctuary at Gerasa. But whereas the temple of Zeus goes back to the late Hellenistic period, possibly even to a prehistoric grotto, the temple of Artemis was built only under Hadrian, resulting in a substantial reconstruction of the city's center. With the new temple built, the temple of Zeus became, in a geographical sense, a bit peripheral. But that is not to say that this temple ceased to perform an important function in day-to-day religious life, and inscriptions do indeed tell us that it continued to be well maintained throughout the second and third centuries CE.[53]

Second, at Scythopolis in the Decapolis, also known as Nysa – after the nymph who acted as nurse of the baby Dionysus and who was supposed to have been buried here – strong local traditions led to the complete domination of the city's coinage by Dionysus.[54] The god is depicted on issues from the early Roman period onward, but it is only in the late second century CE that a new visual program came to be introduced: Dionysus's mythological world now became directly connected with the local foundation legends, and a number of scenes appeared for the first time. Coins struck under the Severans and Gordian III show the second birth of Dionysus out of Zeus's thigh, after which he is handed over to the nymph Nysa, who is depicted on the coins with the *corona muralis* of the city protectress. Other coins from the early third century show how the baby Dionysus is cradled by Nysa, again depicted with a mural crown. And an issue from the reign of Gordian III shows the god riding in a *biga* drawn by two panthers, a reference to his triumphal return from India.[55] Taking all this into account, it seemed logical that at the beginning of the twentieth century, archaeologists chose to identify the large temple on top of the acropolis at Beth-Shean, the modern name of Scythopolis, as that of Dionysus. Who else? However, later epigraphic finds have revealed that this temple was actually dedicated to another god, to Zeus *Akraios*, according to his

---

51 Spijkerman, *Coins of the Decapolis*, 156–67; Lichtenberger, *Kulte und Kultur*, 195–200.
52 See now Lichtenberger, "Artemis and Zeus Olympios."
53 For a new discussion of the temple, see Raja, "Changing spaces and shifting attitudes."
54 See now Barkay, *Coinage of Nysa-Scythopolis*.
55 The respective coins are Spijkerman, *Coins of the Decapolis*, 194–5, no. 23; 198–9, no. 32, and 202–3, nos. 46–48; 208–9, nos. 60–1. Cf. Barkay, *Coinage of Nysa-Scythopolis*, 123–4, with clear drawings of the images.

epithet "dwelling on heights."[56] And according to recent excavations, the main cult of Dionysus at the city was located in a smaller sanctuary in the center.[57] Dionysus's domination of the civic coinage of Nysa-Scythopolis seems, then, not to have been the result of an actual or literal domination of the city's religious life. It could be suggested that it had rather more to do with the civic spirit that was of such importance in this period, the Second Sophistic, and that led cities throughout the eastern empire to highlight their Greek past, whether real or legendary, with a view toward self-promotion before other cities.[58]

Third, the coinage of Palmyra – generally poorly executed and badly preserved, and probably not minted before the second century CE – is very different from "regular" Roman provincial coinage. It has neither an imperial portrait on the obverse (with the exception of coins minted under Zenobia, but that is a different story), nor a legend to identify it as being "of the Palmyrenes."[59] Only a very few issues refer to the city at all, simply stating "Palmyra," without mention of *Palmyrēnōn*. The obverse, giving the Greek name of the city (ΠΑΛΜΥΡΑ), shows a Nikè holding scales and possibly a palm. The reverse shows three gods: the one in the middle wears a *kalathos*, while the two figures that flank the central figure wear a solar crown and a crescent, respectively.[60] The three gods on the reverse can be interpreted, on convincing iconographic grounds, as the "triad of Bel": Bel and his "acolytes" Yarhibol (the sun) and Aglibol (the moon). As is well known, these are the three gods to whom the north adyton of the great temple of Bel was dedicated in 32 CE, on the sixth day of Nisan, as an inscription from thirteen years later records.[61] The designation "temple of Bel," even if it does appear as such in a number of other inscriptions,[62] is a simplification of the actual cultic situation. Long before the dedication of the north adyton in 32 CE, a large number of other deities are recorded as receiving a cult in the sanctuary too.[63] And indeed, in addition to the inscriptions from the first century CE that refer to the temple as that "of

[56] Lifshitz, "Der Kult des Zeus Akraios"; Tsafrir, "Further evidence of the cult of Zeus Akraios"; Lichtenberger, *Kulte und Kultur*, 153–5.
[57] Foerster and Tsafrir, "Skythopolis," 80. Cf. Lichtenberger, *Kulte und Kultur*, 150: "Für Dionysos wäre allerdings zu erwarten, daß in Nysa-Scythopolis ein größeres Heiligtum errichtet war."
[58] Cf. Di Segni, "A dated inscription from Beth Shean"; Lichtenberger, "City foundation legends."
[59] See now Kaizer, "'Palmyre, cité grecque'?"
[60] Du Mesnil du Buisson, *Les tessères et les monnaies de Palmyre*, no. XCI. In Kaizer, "'Palmyre, cité grecque'?," 53. I have argued that there is just enough visible of an Aramaic *dalet* (-d-) to postulate that the reverse gave the indigenous name of the city, "Tadmor," which – if correct – matches the unique bilingualism of the city's public inscriptions and its countermarked coins.
[61] Hillers and Cussini, *Palmyrene Aramaic Texts*, no. 1347.
[62] Ibid., nos. 0270, 1352.
[63] Kaizer, *Religious Life of Palmyra*, 67–79.

Bel," others from the same time designate it – more correctly – as the "house of the gods of the Palmyrenes."[64] But while the latter name seems to have gone out of fashion, the conventional designation "temple of Bel" remained in use into the second century, as inscriptions show.[65] The fact that in 32 CE the temple was dedicated jointly to Bel and Yarhibol and Aglibol is generally interpreted as the direct result of a priestly intervention, the creation of a new "triad" on theological grounds. However, it is equally possible, if not more likely, that this joint dedication has to be explained simply as the initiative of the benefactor who paid for the north adyton.[66] Along the same lines, one could then argue that another benefactor, who was responsible a generation later for the addition of a second, south adyton, ought to be credited with the addition of the goddess Astarte to the most prestigious part of the temple. An inscription from 127 CE points to the group of Bel, Yarhibol, Aglibol, and Astarte having become a divine constellation in its own right by then.[67] If this hypothesis is correct, one could further suggest, with regard to the representation of Bel, Yarhibol, and Aglibol on the Palmyrene coin, that the so-called triad of Bel, originally put together at the whim of one benefactor, had grown into a true civic symbol for Palmyra by the second century, when the city started to mint its own coins.

The above examples of Gerasa and of Nysa-Scythopolis also show clearly to what degree the religious topography of a place – that is, the way in which temples are distributed over a city's territory and are related to each other – can give a very different impression of that site's religious life from the one gained through coins. At Gerasa, Zeus eventually lost out on the coinage, but the cult in his temple (the major religious building of the city alongside that of Artemis) remained of significance. At Nysa, the divine inhabitant of the largest temple on the city's acropolis (Zeus *Akraios*) did not make it at all to the coinage, which was instead dominated by Dionysus, who had to do with a more modest shrine. It may therefore be useful to focus briefly on Hatra, a city whose religious topography must form the basis of any study of its patterns of worship. Seemingly appearing out of the blue in the late first century CE and flourishing in the second and early third centuries, Hatra is characterized by a circular plan, dominated in its center by an enormous rectangular temple complex.[68] Central

[64] Hillers and Cussini, *Palmyrene Aramaic Texts*, nos. 0269, 1353.
[65] Ibid., nos. 0260, 2769.
[66] Kaizer, "Reflections on the dedication of the temple of Bel."
[67] Drijvers, "Inscriptions from Allât's sanctuary."
[68] Kennedy and Riley, *Rome's Desert Frontier*, 105, fig. 53.

to any understanding of Hatrene religion is the difference between, on the one hand, the temples within this central *temenos* and, on the other, the numerous minor shrines spread throughout the city. The deities who were worshipped in the central temple complex – above all, the unique family triad of Maren, Marten, and Bar-Maren, "Our Lord, Our Lady, and the Son of Our Lord and Our Lady" – appeared also in the smaller shrines. By contrast, the cults of deities such as Baal-Shamin and Atargatis were practiced only in one or more of the minor shrines, but never in the central complex.[69] In addition, the city's temples were differentiated by their respective building plans and architecture: the iwans in the *temenos*, enormous vaulted structures that were representatives of a new temple type in the Parthian period, contrasted with the "Breitraum" shrines elsewhere in the city, which were rooted in an older, Mesopotamian tradition. Both these aspects seem to point to a division between centralized cults that were important for the city as a whole and deities who were worshipped by a particular part of the population only.

The examples discussed in this chapter illuminate in various degrees the continuing process by which religious identities were created in the different localities that constituted the Roman Near East. The final case comes from Dura-Europos, a small town on the Euphrates that started life as a Seleucid fortress and fell under Parthian control for hundreds of years before it was occupied by Roman troops during the last age of its existence, finally being captured and destroyed by the Sasanians in the middle of the third century. The location of nearly all religious buildings at Dura was embedded within a gridiron city plan, which created conditions for the negotiation of religious space that were very different from those at Hatra. In one of those shrines, built against the wall and a tower in the southwest corner of the city, a relief was found showing a deity in cuirass (Fig. 9), the divine dress code generally taken to single out a god or goddess as protector of those traveling through the steppe and desert areas of the Near East,[70] and similar to the outfit worn by the statue from the Fitzwilliam that was discussed at the beginning of this chapter. Bearded like Baal-Shamin, the lord of the heavens, and wearing a *kalathos* like Bel, the god is standing on top of two griffons, resembling the near-canonical type of Jupiter Dolichenus, who in his characteristic representation is standing on the back of a bull.

---

[69] Kaizer, "Some remarks about the religious life of Hatra," 231.
[70] On the military outfit as a popular dress code among Near Eastern deities, see Seyrig, "Les dieux armés," and now also Downey, "Arms and armour as social coding," and Aliquot, *La vie religieuse au Liban*, 185–7.

Fig. 9. Relief of Aphlad from Dura-Europos. Courtesy of the General Director of Antiquities and Museums, Syria.

My choice to describe the figure by means of reference to other divinities is of course deliberate, and it would once again have been impossible to guess which god this was were it not for the accompanying inscription. This time, fortunately, it is recorded on the relief itself how "Hadadiabos son of Zabdibolos son of Sillos set up this ἀφείδρυσις from the sanctuary of Aphlad, named god of Anath, the village on the Euphrates, as a vow, for his own salvation and that of his children and of his whole house."[71] The divine name, otherwise unknown and transcribed differently in the available Greek inscriptions from the temple[72] (clearly reflecting a god whose name was originally spelled in a different language), has been explained as a combination of the Akkadian word *aplu*, "son," and Adda, meaning "son of Hadad," which matches the fact that an old Assyrian text had connected the "Son of Hadad" to this region along the Middle Euphrates.[73] The text establishes beyond doubt that the cult of Aphlad at Dura-Europos was considered as having its origins in the village of Anath. Indeed, the choice of the term ἀφείδρυσις implies that the image set up in the temple of Aphlad at Dura-Europos was a precise copy of the original cult statue.[74] However, what is most peculiar is the meticulous description of the god, which makes it very doubtful whether his cult at the Euphrates stronghold was adhered to only by villagers from Anath themselves. The inscription, referring explicitly to Aphlad, known as the god of Anath, a village on the Euphrates, must have been meant to communicate this specific information to a wider audience. It must be emphasized too that the relief is inscribed in Greek, despite the fact that not only the deity but also the dedicant and the village have nonclassical names.[75] This final example demonstrates once again clearly how a specific local religious identity could be created – from elements which seem typically Near Eastern – by labeling a deity whose very name ("Son of Hadad") locates him firmly in a supraregional divine world, as god *of* a particular village, and by doing so simultaneously expanding the local religious world of the small town Dura-Europos: "the religion of the locality interacts with principles, ideas and traditions which transcend space."[76]

---

[71] Rostovtzeff, *Excavations at Dura-Europos*, 112–13, no. 416: Τὴν ἀφείδρυσιν ταύτη[ν] ἱεροῦ Ἀφλαδ λεγομένου θεοῦ τῆς Ἀναθ κώμης Εὐφράτου ἀνέθηκεν Ἀδαδιαβος Ζαβδιβωλου τοῦ Σιλλοι εὐχὴν ὑπὲρ τῆς σωτηρί[ας] αὐτοῦ καὶ τέκνων καὶ τοῦ πά[ν]τος οἴκου.

[72] For example, ibid., 114, no. 418, a dedication Ἀπαλαδωι θεῶι, and 122–3, no. 426, a memento inscription, πρὸς τὸν Ἀφαλαδον θεὸν.

[73] Ibid., 118.

[74] Robert, *Hellenica*, 120, no. 4, and 124, no. 4.

[75] On the relation between cults and languages at Dura-Europos, see Kaizer, "Language and religion in Dura-Europos."

[76] Horden and Purcell, *Corrupting Sea*, 422.

BIBLIOGRAPHY

Primary Texts and Collections of Source Material

Budde, Ludwig, and Richard Nicholls. *A Catalogue of the Greek and Roman Sculpture in the Fitzwilliam Museum Cambridge* (Cambridge, 1964).

Cureton, William. *Spicilegium Syriacum* (London, 1855).

Dunand, Maurice. *Le musée de Soueïda: inscriptions et monuments figurés. Mission archéologique au Djebel Druze* (Paris, 1934).

Hillers, Delbert R., and Eleanora Cussini. *Palmyrene Aramaic Texts* (Baltimore, 1996).

Lightfoot, Jane L. *Lucian, On the Syrian Goddess. Edited with Introduction, Translation and Commentary* (Oxford, 2003).

Martin, M. l'Abbé. "Discours de Jacques de Saroug sur la chute des idoles." *ZDMG* 29 (1875): 107–47.

Spijkerman, Augustus. *The Coins of the Decapolis and Provincia Arabia*, ed. Michele Piccirillo (Jerusalem, 1978).

Stern, Henri. *Les mosaïques des maisons d'Achille et de Cassiopée à Palmyre* (Paris, 1977).

Secondary Sources

Aliquot, Julien. *La vie religieuse au Liban sous l'empire romain*. BAH 189 (Beirut, 2009).

Balty, Janine. *Mosaïques antiques de Syrie* (Brussels, 1977).

"Composantes classiques et orientales dans les mosaïques de Palmyre." *AAAS* 42 (1996): 407–16.

"Zénobie et le néoplatonisme." In *Zenobia and Palmyra. Proceedings of the International Conference (19–21 October 2002, Homs and Palmyra)*, eds. M. al-Hayek, M. Maqdissi, and M. Abdulkarim (Homs, 2005): 45–57.

Balty, Jean-Charles. "Une version orientale méconnue du mythe de Cassiopée." In *Mythologie gréco-romaine, mythologies périphériques: études d'iconographie*, eds. Lilly Kahil and Christian Augé (Paris, 1981): 95–106.

Barkay, Rachel. *The Coinage of Nysa-Scythopolis (Beth-Shean)* (Jerusalem, 2003).

Bounni, Adnan, Jacques Seigne, and Nassib Saliby. *Le sanctuaire de Nabû à Palmyre. Planches*. BAH 131. (Paris, 1992).

Bounni, Adnan. *Le sanctuaire de Nabû à Palmyre. Texte*. BAH 131. (Beirut, 2004).

Bowersock, Glen W. *Hellenism in Late Antiquity* (Ann Arbor, Mich., 1990).

Callot, Olivier, and Jean Marcillet-Jaubert. "Hauts-lieux de Syrie du Nord." In *Temples et sanctuaires*. Travaux de la Maison de l'Orient 7, ed. Georges Roux (Lyon/Paris, 1984): 185–202.

Crowther, Charles, and Margherita Facella. "New evidence for the ruler cult of Antiochus of Commagene from Zeugma." In *Neue Forschungen zur Religionsgeschichte Kleinasiens*. AMS 49, eds. Gudrun Heedemann and Engelbert Winter (Bonn, 2003): 41–80.

Dalley, Stephanie. *The Legacy of Mesopotamia* (Oxford, 1998).

Di Segni, Leah. "A dated inscription from Beth Shean and the cult of Dionysos Ktistes in Roman Scythopolis." *SCI* 16 (1997): 139–61.

Dirven, Lucinda. "The exaltation of Nabû. A revision of the relief depicting the battle against Tiamat from the temple of Bel in Palmyra." *WO* 28 (1997): 96–116.

The Palmyrenes of Dura-Europos. A Study of Religious Interaction in Roman Syria. RGRW 138 (Leiden, 1999).

Downey, Susan B. "Arms and armour as social coding in Palmyra, the Palmyrène, and Dura-Europos." In *Arms and Armour as Indicators of Cultural Transfer. The Steppes and the Ancient World from Hellenistic Times to the Early Middle Ages.* Nomaden und Sesshafte 4, eds. Markus Mode and Jürgen Tubach in cooperation with G. Sophia Vashalomidze (Wiesbaden, 2006): 321–55.

Drijvers, Han J. W. *The Religion of Palmyra* (Leiden, 1976).

"Inscriptions from Allât's sanctuary." *Aram* 7 (1995): 109–19.

Du Mesnil du Buisson, Robert. *Les tessères et les monnaies de Palmyre. Planches* (Paris, 1944).

Eissfeldt, Otto. *Tempel und Kulte syrischer Städte in hellenistisch-römischer Zeit* (Leipzig, 1941).

Facella, Margherita. *La dinastia degli Orontidi nella Commagene ellenistico-romana.* Studi Ellenistici 17 (Pisa, 2006).

Feeney, Denis. *Literature and Religion at Rome. Culture, Contexts, and Beliefs* (Cambridge, 1998).

Foerster, Gideon, and Yoram Tsafrir. "Skythopolis – Vorposten der Dekapolis." In *Gadara – Gerasa und die Dekapolis*, Sonderband der Antiken Welt, eds. Adolf Hoffmann and Susanne Kerner (Mainz, 2002): 72–87.

Freyberger, Klaus S. "Im Zeichen des höchsten Gottes: Kulte und religiöses Leben in Damaskus in hellenistischer und römischer Zeit." *Polis. Studi interdisciplinari sul mondo antico* 2 (2006): 157–70.

Gaifman, Milette. "The aniconic image of the Roman Near East." In *The Variety of Local Religious Life in the Near East in the Hellenistic and Roman Periods.* RGRW 164, ed. Ted Kaizer (Leiden, 2008): 37–72.

Gatier, Pierre Louis. "Villages et sanctuaires en Antiochène autour de Qalaat Kalota." *Topoi* 7.2 (1997): 751–75.

Gawlikowski, Michal. "Aus dem syrischen Götterhimmel. Zur Ikonographie der palmyrenischen Götter." *Trierer Winckelmanns-programme* 1–2 (1979/80): 17–26. Mainz, 1981.

Gzella, Holger. "Das Aramäische in den römischen Ostprovinzen: Sprachsituationen in Arabien, Syrien und Mesopotamien zur Kaiserzeit." *BO* 63 (2006): 15–39.

Harl, Kenneth W. *Civic Coins and Civic Politics in the Roman East, AD 180–275* (Berkeley, 1987).

Horden, Peregrine, and Nicholas Purcell. *The Corrupting Sea: A Study of Mediterranean History* (Oxford, 2000).

Howgego, Christopher, Volker Heuchert, and Andrew Burnett, eds. *Coinage and Identity in the Roman Provinces* (Oxford, 2005).

Kaizer, Ted. "The 'Heracles figure' at Hatra and Palmyra: problems of interpretation." *Iraq* 62 (2000): 219–32.

"Some remarks on the religious life of Hatra." *Topoi* 10 (2000): 229–52.

The Religious Life of Palmyra. Oriens et Occidens 4 (Stuttgart, 2002).

"Leucothea as Mater Matuta at *colonia* Berytus. A note on local mythology in the Levant and the Hellenisation of a Phoenician city." *Syria* 82 (2005): 199–206.

"In search of Oriental cults: methodological problems concerning 'the particular' and 'the general' in Near Eastern religion in the Hellenistic and Roman periods." *Historia* 55 (2006) 26–47.

"Reflections on the dedication of the temple of Bel at Palmyra in AD 32." In *The Impact of Imperial Rome on Religions, Ritual and Religious Life in the Roman Empire*. Proceedings of the Fifth Workshop of the International Network Impact of Empire, eds. Lukas de Blois, Peter Funke, and Johannes Hahn (Leiden, 2006): 95–105.

"'Palmyre, cité grecque'? A question of coinage." *Klio* 89 (2007): 39–60.

"Introduction." In *The Variety of Local Religious Life in the Near East in the Hellenistic and Roman Periods*. RGRW 164, ed. Ted Kaizer (Leiden, 2008): 1–36.

"Religion and language in Dura-Europos." In *From Hellenism to Islam: Cultural and Linguistic Change in the Roman Near East*, eds. Hannah M. Cotton, Robert G. Hoyland, Jonathan J. Price, and David J. Wasserstein (Cambridge, 2009): 235–53.

Kennedy, David, and Derrick Riley. *Rome's Desert Frontier from the Air* (London, 1990).

Lichtenberger, Achim. *Kulte und Kultur der Dekapolis. Untersuchungen zu numismatischen, archäologischen und epigraphischen Zeugnissen*. ADPV 29 (Wiesbaden, 2003).

"City foundation legends in the Decapolis." *BAIAS* 22 (2004): 23–34.

"Artemis and Zeus Olympios in Roman Gerasa and Seleucid religious policy." In *The Variety of Local Religious Life in the Near East in the Hellenistic and Roman Periods*. RGRW 164, ed. Ted Kaizer (Leiden, 2008): 133–53.

Lifshitz, B. "Der Kult des Zeus Akraios und des Zeus Bakchos in Beisan (Skythopolis)." *ZDPV* 77 (1961): 186–9.

Lightfoot, J. L. "The *Apology* of Pseudo-Meliton." *SEL* 24 (2007): 59–110.

"Pseudo-Meliton and the cults of the Roman Near East." In *Les religions orientales dans le monde grec et romain: cent ans après Cumont (1906–2006). Bilan historique et historiographique. Colloque de Rome, 16–18 Novembre 2006*, eds. Corinne Bonnet, Vinciane Pirenne-Delforge, and Danny Praet (Brussels, 2009): 387–99.

Millar, Fergus. *The Roman Near East, 31 BC – AD 337* (Cambridge, Mass., 1993).

Nicholls, Richard V. *Fitzwilliam Museum Cambridge, Principal Acquisitions 1979–83* (Cambridge, 1983).

Petzl, Georg. "Antiochos I. von Kommagene im Handschlag mit den Göttern. Der Beitrag der neuen Reliefstele von Zeugma zum Verständnis der Dexioseis." In *Neue Forschungen zur Religionsgeschichte Kleinasiens*, AMS 49, eds. Gudrun Heedemann and Engelbert Winter (Bonn, 2003): 81–4.

Raja, Rubina. "Changing spaces and shifting attitudes: revisiting the sanctuary of Zeus in Gerasa." In *Cities and Gods: Religious Space in Transition*. BABeschSup 22, eds. Ted Kaizer, Anna Leone, Edmund Thomas, and Robert Witcher (Leuven, 2012).

Rey-Coquais, Jean Paul. "Deir el Qalaa." *Topoi* 9 (1999): 607–28.

Robert, Louis. *Hellenica: recueil d'épigraphie de numismatique et d'antiquités grecques* XIII (Limoges, 1965).

Rostovtzeff, Mikhaïl, ed. *The Excavations at Dura-Europos, Conducted by Yale University and the French Academy of Inscriptions and Letters*. Preliminary Report of Fifth Season of Work, October 1931–March 1932 (New Haven, 1934).

Dura-Europos and its Art (Oxford, 1938).

Sanders, Donald H., ed. *Nemrud Daği. The Hierothesion of Antiochus I of Commagene* I-II (Winona Lake, Ind., 1996).

Sartre, Maurice. *L'Orient romain. Provinces et sociétés provinciales en Méditerranée orientale d'Auguste aux Sévères (31 avant J.-C. – 235 après J.-C.)* (Paris, 1991).

Seyrig, Henri. "Les dieux armés et les Arabes en Syrie." *Syria* 47 (1970): 77–112.

"Le culte du soleil en Syrie à l'époque romaine." *Syria* 48 (1971): 337–73.

Smith, William Robertson. *Lectures on the Religion of the Semites. 1st Series: The Fundamental Institutions* (Edinburgh, 1889).

Lectures on the Religion of the Semites. 2nd and 3rd Series. JSOTSup 183, ed. J. Day (Sheffield, 1995).

Sommer, Michael. *Hatra: Geschichte und Kultur einer Karawanenstadt im römisch-parthischen Mesopotamien.* Sonderband der Antiken Welt (Mainz, 2003).

Steinsapir, Ann I. *Rural Sanctuaries in Roman Syria: The Creation of a Sacred Landscape.* BAR Int. Ser. 1431 (Oxford, 2005).

Stewart, Peter. "Baetyls as statues? Cult images in the Roman Near East." In *The Sculptural Environment of the Roman Near East. Reflections on Culture, Ideology, and Power.* Interdisciplinary Studies in Ancient Culture and Religion 9, eds. Yaron Z. Eliav, Elise A. Friedland, and Sharon Herbert (Leuven, 2008): 297–314.

Teixidor, Javier. *The Pagan God: Popular Religion in the Greco-Roman Near East* (Princeton, 1977).

Tsafrir, Yoram. "Further evidence of the cult of Zeus Akraios at Beth Shean (Scythopolis)." *IEJ* 39 (1989): 76–8.

Tubach, Jürgen. "Das Akītu-Fest in Palmyra." *Aram* 7 (1995): 121–35.

3

JUDAISM IN PALESTINE IN THE HELLENISTIC-ROMAN PERIODS

ESTHER ESHEL AND MICHAEL E. STONE

THE "DARK AGES" OF THE FOURTH AND THIRD CENTURIES BCE

Although Alexander the Great's conquest of the Near East was a turning point in the region's history, Jewish historiography rarely marks this event as the beginning of a new era. The fourth (still mainly Achaemenid) and third (Ptolemaic) centuries are grouped together, bounded at their beginning by Ezra and Nehemiah and at their end by the Seleucid conquest of Judea (198 BCE). The reason for this neglect of Alexander's conquest is the darkness that shrouds Judaism in the fourth and third centuries.

Flavius Josephus provides little information about these two centuries apart from one document dealing with the Transjordanian Jewish principality ruled by the Tobiads in the third century (*Ant.* 12.4.157–236). From him, we learn that they intermarried with the aristocracies of Judea and Samaria, and that members of the Tobiad family, familiars at the Ptolemaic court, bid for and bought from the Ptolemies in Alexandria the right to farm the taxes of Judea. Information from the Zeno papyri intersects with Josephus. Zeno, the business manager of Apollonius, a financial minister of Ptolemy II Philadelphus, traveled in Syria and Palestine and traded with the Tobiads.[1] An inscription from the fifth century BCE and the last verses of Nehemiah also mention the Tobiads.

We know relatively little about the priestly aristocracy of Jerusalem and Samaria. Sanballat (Nehemiah 2, 4, 6, 13) was a member of a powerful governing family in Samaria,[2] while the Oniad priesthood of Jerusalem held an equivalent position in Jerusalem. There were thus two major districts inhabited by worshippers of the God of Israel, Samaria, and Judea.

---

[1] Tcherikover, "Palestine," 49–53; idem, *Hellenistic Civilization*, 39–89.
[2] Cross, "Samaritan and Jewish History," 201–5.

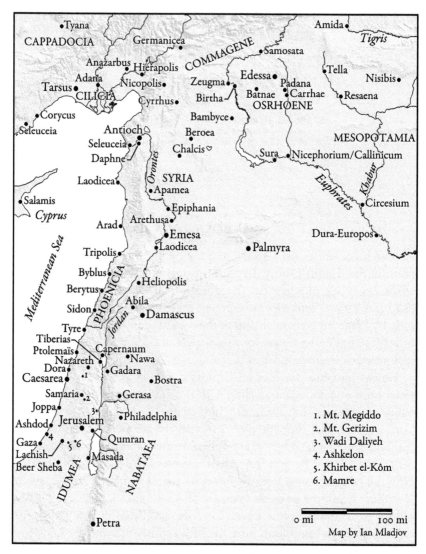

Map 3. Syria Palaestina

There was also a smaller, independent Jewish "barony" of the Tobiads in Transjordan (see Map 3). Samaria and Judea were each organized around a temple controlled by a priestly aristocracy, and the ruling classes were interrelated and often intermarried.[3]

[3] Grabbe, *History of the Jews*, 207–37.

The discovery since 1991 of around sixteen hundred ostraca from Khirbet el-Kôm (biblical Makkedah) has shown that under Alexander, the Macedonians continued to administer the province of Idumea (a region southeast of the Dead Sea) in the same way it was administered during the Persian period.[4] A bilingual ostracon found there attests to a shift from Aramaic to Greek.[5] The archaeological evidence of the late Persian and Ptolemaic periods paints a complex picture. *Favissae*, pits into which clay figurines and stone statues had been deposited, show that the pagan population of Idumea and the coastal area worshipped many gods.[6] The Idumean population used Aramaic, while Phoenician was spoken in the coastal area of Ashdod, Ashkelon, and Gaza.

Underlying the Jewish court tales of the Persian and early Hellenistic periods is a relatively benign attitude toward foreign rule. Daniel 2–6 and Esther record how a gentile king came to recognize the sovereignty of the God of Israel. Enterprising and wise Jewish courtiers like Zerubbabel (1 Esdras 3:1–5:6) and Daniel (Daniel 2–6 and Bel and the Dragon) functioned and rose to the highest positions in the pagan court.[7] One outcome of Achaemenid policy was that the Torah came to have the force of the law of the land, which led in turn to the creation of a hierocracy in Judea.[8] During this period, the Torah seems to have become authoritative in a written rather than oral form.[9] Once the transmundane norms of the religion of Israel were written down, or rather, once the written form of the tradition became authoritative, knowledge of the tradition was taken out of the priests' hands alone and became available for investigation by the learned. By the second century BCE, argument over the right of exegesis had thus become argument over power.

Before the discovery of the Dead Sea Scrolls, our sources for this early period were the latest of biblical writings, minimal material in Josephus,

---

[4] The name *mnqdh*, biblical Makkedah (Josh. 10:10, 16, 21; 12:16; 15:41), appears in numerous inscriptions included in these collections and is identified with Khirbet el-Kôm (Dorsey, "Location"). Eph'al and Naveh, *Aramaic Ostraca*, contains inscriptions dated to the Persian and Hellenistic periods that presumably also originated at Khirbet el-Kôm; see also Lemaire, *Nouvelles*; idem, *Nouvelles inscriptions* II.

[5] Geraty, "Khirbet el-Kom." For the history of the Idumeans and their incursion into the region of southern Judea, see Kasher, *Jews, Idumaeans, and Ancient Arabs*, 1–6.

[6] Stern, *Archaeology*, 490–505.

[7] Wills, *Jews in the Court*, 9–19, 22–3.

[8] Bickerman, "Historical Foundations," 70–114, esp. 73–4; Smith, "Jewish Religious Life," 219–78, esp. 260–9.

[9] Stone, "Three Transformations"; Carr, *Writing*; cf. Najman, *Seconding Sinai*. This is not to deny the importance of written documents in early periods; see Najman, "Symbolic Significance," 13–16, with references to earlier discussions.

some relatively minor books of the Apocrypha, certain fragments of Jewish writings in Greek, and some epigraphic and archaeological evidence. The early dating of a number of Qumran documents has shown that parts of the *Book of Enoch* (*1 Enoch*) originated in the third century BCE and *Aramaic Levi Document* (hereafter *ALD*) also originated in that period or slightly later. The *Temple Scroll* from Qumran, a work exhibiting an unusual attitude to authority and biblical law, and a book (or books) of Noah[10] may also have been composed at this time.

What we learn from these sources about Judaism of that time is not found in the "conventional" historical record. The Enochic *Book of the Luminaries* and *Book of the Watchers* presuppose a developed tradition about Enoch, a relatively obscure figure in the Hebrew Bible. The Enochic *Book of the Luminaries* promotes a 364-day solar calendar, different from the Babylonian lunar-solar calendar that the Jews took over after the Exile. Different calendars imply different sources of religious authority, and different branches or wings of Judaism. Whether the people sustaining this calendar formed a distinct group remains a mystery, but they were likely forerunners of trends and groups that emerge more distinctly on the stage of events in the second century BCE.[11] Documents from this early period, known only through the discovery of the Dead Sea Scrolls, also reveal the influence of the priesthood in the Persian and Ptolemaic periods. *ALD* transmits detailed priestly instructions that nicely relate to Noah's priestly role and that claim Noachic origin.[12] It gives regulations for sacrificial cult that agree neither with Pentateuchal nor with rabbinic sources. We are as yet unable to place these views in Jewish society or to relate them to the groups that appear in the following century, but their very existence means that Jewish expression in the third century BCE was multifaceted.

The *Book of Enoch* (*1 Enoch*) and the references to a *Book of Noah* show us other aspects of Jewish creativity in the period. *1 Enoch* is a vision book, an apocalypse. In addition to the revelation of the calendar in its *Book of the Luminaries*, its first part (*Book of the Watchers*)

---

[10] The existence of Book(s) of Noah is much debated. See Stone, Amihay, and Hillel, *Noah and His Book(s)*.

[11] What became the normative Jewish calendar originated in Babylon: see Talmon, "Calendar and Mishmarot," 112–16; Ben-Dov, "Babylonian Lunar Three"; "Tradition and Innovation." The calendar of *1 Enoch*, *Jubilees*, and *ALD* is a solar calendar of 12 x 30 days with one intercalated day every quarter. It resembles, but is not identical with, the Ptolemaic and old Persian calendars; see Samuel, *Chronology*, 145; Ginzel, *Chronologie*, 314.

[12] Levi was instructed by Isaac (*ALD* 5:8), who learned from Abraham (7:4), who, in turn, consulted the "Book of Noah" (10:10).

also preserves a very old instance of extrabiblical traditions (chs. 6–11).[13] Chapter 14 is the first ascent vision in postbiblical Jewish literature.[14] Enoch plays a role in the heavenly court. It describes the underworld (ch. 22), and discusses the distant parts of the earth (chs. 26–7, 33–6). Both *1 Enoch* and *ALD* suggest that the idea of two opposed spirits, one of truth and one of falsehood, had already emerged by the third century.[15] The work's developed angelology (ch. 20) and demonology contrast with First Temple writings. It has been stressed that this period saw the beginning of a process of "remythologization" of Judaism, in which time and metatime, space and metaspace, history and metahistory were emerging once more.[16]

JUDEA IN THE CONTEXT OF THE HELLENIZED EAST

While Greek penetration into the East preceded Alexander's conquest, Alexander's policies had far-reaching effects on the civilization of the eastern Mediterranean basin.[17] The Hellenization of the East brought about profound changes in the cultures of the Greeks and subject eastern peoples. In the third century BCE, ancient eastern civilizations, including the Jews, felt the need to present their traditions in Greek. Alexandrian Judaism of this period saw the translation of the Torah into Greek and the composition of the fragmentarily preserved work of Demetrius the Jewish "chronographer."

How pervasive was Hellenization in Palestine, where, in addition to a Jewish population, there were Greek cities and other pagan settlements? Although the exact extent of the Hellenization of Judea is unknown, it was no doubt considerable. The involvement of the Tobiads with the Ptolemaic court is well documented by Josephus and the Zeno papyri.[18] Zeno's reports on the Tobiads show the level of their participation in

---

[13] See Nickelsburg, *1 Enoch*, 29–30.

[14] It is not certain whether the idea of a separable soul is involved. Compare 14:8, which is not explicit.

[15] See Stone and Greenfield, "Prayer of Levi," 252.

[16] Stone, "Eschatology"; Cross, "New Directions"; cf. Cross, *Canaanite Myth*, 343–6; Boccaccini, *Origins of Enochic Judaism*.

[17] See Hengel, "Political and Social History," 35–6; Bickerman, *Jews in the Greek Age*, 13–19. Thirty-nine different seal impressions of the Wadi Daliyeh bullae, as well as one ring, were defined as stylistically Greek; see Leith, *Wadi Daliyeh*, 20–8, 35 (late fourth century BCE). The Aramaic of Daniel contains three Greek words (Dan. 3:5; all are names of musical instruments); see Coxon, "Greek Loan-Words." An Aramaic marriage contract found in Maresha, dated to 176 BCE, includes the Greek word *nomos* ("law" or "custom"); see Eshel and Kloner, "Marriage Contract"; Eshel, "Inscriptions in Hebrew, Aramaic, and Phoenician Script," 72–6.

[18] Tcherikover, *Hellenistic Civilization*, 60.

Hellenistic culture, an impression strengthened by Josephus's reports on the activities of Tobias's sons at the Ptolemaic court in Alexandria (*Ant.* 12.156–222, 228–36).[19] Out of 564 ossuaries with inscriptions discovered in the Jerusalem area, 187 (36%) were written in Greek, with the addition of 48 written in both Hebrew/Aramaic and Greek.[20] Even the list of early rabbinic authorities contains three individuals with Greek names.[21] According to one theory, the Maccabean revolt was not chiefly a reaction to the attempt of Antiochus IV Epiphanes (175–64 BCE) to impose Hellenism; it began rather as a response to a Hellenizing group in Jerusalem, aided by the monarch.[22] This theory assumes a substantial measure of Hellenistic penetration among the aristocracy, at least.[23]

Before the Maccabean period, court stories, for which the Joseph cycle in Genesis was the biblical prototype, became increasingly prominent. Although the conduct of these ideal heroes contrasts with the dissolute and avaricious *mores* of the Tobiad offspring, the context is not dissimilar. In these stories, the climax is the foreign potentate's recognition of the God of Israel as the true God.[24] Such stories disappeared after the Maccabean revolt, a reflection of the deteriorating relations with Hellenistic courts after that event. In a book like 3 Maccabees, God's intervention against the king's plans makes the point and not the wise Jewish courtier. The idea of a Jew in a high position in the pagan court has yielded to a more nationalist attitude pitting Jews against gentiles, as exemplified in the stories of Judith and Daniel 1.

DEVELOPMENTS IN THE SECOND CENTURY BCE

After the "dark ages" of the fourth and third centuries BCE, the sources for Second Temple Judaism become far more abundant. While these sources attest a great variety of groups, trends, and sects, they are largely known to us outside of received Jewish tradition. Rabbinic literature does refer to Pharisees and Sadducees, but its evidence is sparse and it foreshortens the Persian period, leaping from the generation of Ezra and Nehemiah to the

---

[19] On the Tobiads, see also 2 Maccabees 3:11; Josephus, *Ant.* 12.156–222, 228–236; see Gera, "On the Credibility."

[20] See Rahmani, *Jewish Ossuaries*, 13–15; Ilan, *Lexicon*, 11–13, 257–324; and lately, Cotton et al., *Corpus Inscriptionum Iudaeae/Palaestinae.*

[21] Tryphon (*m. Berakot* 1:3), Abtalion (*m. Abot* 1:10–11), and Antigonus of Socho (*m. Abot* 1:3); see Hengel, "Interpretation of Judaism," 217–18.

[22] See Bickerman, *God of the Maccabees*, 30, 38–42.

[23] For discussion of these issues see Victor, *Colonial Education*, 77–108.

[24] See, for example, Daniel 2:47, 3:28, 4:31–34, 6:27–28.

early second century BCE. The Dead Sea Scrolls, pseudepigrapha preserved in the Christian tradition, some apocryphal psalms, Josephus, Philo, and other Jewish-Hellenistic fragments provide information independently of the rabbinic tradition.[25] This plethora of sources contrasts strongly with the First Temple period, for which we have virtually no documents except the Hebrew Bible, a tendentious and quite carefully censored work, albeit a rich, variegated, and invaluable source.[26] It is difficult, therefore, to know whether religious phenomena appearing for the first time in Second Temple sources were new, or whether they came to light because of the different character of the transmitted sources. In all likelihood, both factors were at play.

In the second century BCE, Judaism underwent fundamental changes.[27] Early in this century (198 BCE), the Seleucid king Antiochus III defeated Ptolemy V at the Battle of Panium and gained control of Palestine. The ensuing conflict over Hellenism culminated in Antiochus IV Epiphanes' decrees against Judaism in 167 BCE, the outbreak of the Maccabean revolt in the same year, and the series of battles and subsequent political maneuvering that led to the independence of Judea under the Hasmonean high priest Jonathan in 152 BCE. The Hasmonean dynasty ruled until the Roman annexation of Judea in 63 BCE.

Throughout the Persian and Ptolemaic periods, a priestly aristocracy headed by the Oniad dynasty had led the Jewish polity until its replacement in 170 BCE. In that year, the high priest Onias IV fled to Egypt, where he established a temple in Leontopolis.[28] It continued to function down to the Jewish revolt when it was closed in 73 CE by the Romans as a precautionary measure (Josephus, *Ant.* 7.420–36). At the same time, the Tobiad family was ruling in Transjordan, while in Samaria to the north, leadership was in the hands of a family favoring the name Sanballat. The first known ruler of this name is mentioned in Nehemiah (2:10, 19; 4:1, 7; 6:1, 2, etc., and in Elephantine papyri). His family intermarried with the Jerusalem high-priestly families (Nehemiah 13:28), and he was associated with Tobiah (Nehemiah 6:4). In a *bulla* that sealed one of the Wadi

---

[25] Hippolytus also has a treatment of the Jewish sects. See Smith, "Essenes in Josephus"; Baumgarten, "Josephus and Hippolytus."

[26] On this issue, see Stone, *Scriptures,* 27–47.

[27] Gera, *Judaea and Mediterranean Politics,* 59–254.

[28] In *J. W.* 1.33, Josephus states that Onias III built the Leontopolis temple, but cf. *Antiquities* 12.387–8; 13.62–73, where he attributes the undertaking to Onias IV. For this reason, there is disagreement over which Onias established the Leontopolis temple; see Parente, "Onias III's Death," 70–80. On the Egyptian reaction to this temple, see Bohak, "CPJ III, 520."; see also Schwartz, *2 Maccabees,* 187.

Daliyeh papyri (no. 16), another ruler named Sanballat (fourth century BCE) is mentioned.[29]

After Judea became independent of both the Seleucids and Ptolemies in 142 BCE, Simon the Hasmonean ruled as both high priest and eventually ethnarch. The Hasmonean kingdom pursued a policy that, particularly under John Hyrcanus (135–104 BCE) and Alexander Jannaeus (103–76 BCE), led to a significant expansion of the boundaries of the country and the forced conversion of various surrounding tribes, including the Idumeans.

Despite Judaism's increased hostility to the pagan world, Hellenism had by the second century BCE made great inroads into Jewish society, not least in the Greek-speaking diaspora. Although it owed its position to a revolt against Antiochus's imposition of Hellenism, the Hasmonean court and its customs were deeply Hellenized. Like many other eastern peoples, the Jews entered into an intellectual dialogue with the Hellenistic world, developing an *interpretatio Graeca* of Judaism, a process that had already begun in the third century BCE. The same deeply ambivalent encounter with Hellenism was later exhibited in the philosophico-exegetical undertaking of Philo of Alexandria (late first century BCE to mid-first century CE) and in Josephus's *Jewish Antiquities,* a monumental work composed in Rome toward the end of the first century CE. These works, while clearly designed to demonstrate the superiority of Judaism, did so in literary forms and intellectual categories that were part of Hellenistic culture.

Over the course of the second century BCE, a number of religious movements (called "philosophies" by Josephus) appeared on the stage.[30] The Pharisees and Sadducees were involved in the court politics of Alexander Jannaeus and his wife Salome. It is unknown how much earlier they existed. Although the early history of the sect that lived at Qumran, on the northwestern corner of the Dead Sea, is disputed, these sectarians were established in their communal center by approximately the early part of the first century BCE. The stories surrounding the outbreak of the Maccabean revolt mention another group, the Hasideans (1 Macc. 2:29–42; 7:12–17; 2 Macc. 14:6). They disappear from our sources by the middle of the second century. Closely connected with the Temple, they were apparently a pietistic group who at the beginning of the revolt preferred death to fighting on the Sabbath.[31] An earlier conflict between the returnees from the

---

[29] Cross, "Samaria Papyri," 120–1.
[30] See Schürer, *History of the Jewish People,* 2.381–414, 550–9; Sievers, "Josephus."
[31] Kampen, *The Hasideans,* 45–62, 65–76, 128–35, argues for the identification of the Scribes and the Hasideans, 115–22. But cf. Schwartz, "Hasidim."

Babylonian exile and those remaining in the land is reflected in the books of Ezra and Nehemiah; the broad split between Judeans (that is, Jews) and Samaritans also goes back to that time or even earlier (if the highly biased account in 2 Kings 17 is to be believed, at least in general chronological terms).[32] So, by the end of the second century BCE, the existence of many religious groups and trends had become a defining feature of Judaism of the Greco-Roman period.[33]

One commonplace of biblical scholarship holds that from the time of the reforms of Josiah (622 BCE), the cult of the God of Israel was carried out exclusively in the Jerusalem temple. There is no doubt that the Temple played an absolutely dominant role in Judaism in the Greco-Roman period; its destruction by the Romans in 70 CE thus marked the end of an era in Jewish history. Disagreements over the Temple and over high-priestly legitimacy apparently played a major role in the formation of the Essene sect, as well as in the events subsequent to the victory of the Maccabees.[34] How, then, can we reconcile its apparent centrality with the establishment of a rival temple in Leontopolis by a refugee Oniad high priest?

Archaeological evidence and a rereading of Josephus suggest in fact that the centralization of worship in the Jerusalem temple, while an ideal of many, was not the practice of all. As early as the late sixth century BCE, a temple, built according to the architectural plan of the Jerusalem temple, existed in Arad on the southern border of Judea. An altar from the end of the First Temple period was found at Beer Sheba. A temple from the Persian period was discovered in Lachish. In the fifth century BCE, Jewish mercenaries in the Persian army in Elephantine, far up the Nile, had a temple dedicated to the God of Israel; when it was burnt, they had no inhibitions in writing to their brethren both in Samaria and in Jerusalem to ask for help in its rebuilding.[35] Based on the recently discovered ostraca from the Khirbet el-Kôm site, it seems probable that a temple for the God of Israel also existed there.[36] In addition to the temple in Leontopolis, there seems to have been a Jewish sacrificial cult in Sardis in Asia Minor (Josephus, *Ant.* 14.259–61). This situation seems to indicate that both diaspora Jews (see Philo's description of his pilgrimage, *Prov.* 2.64) and those in

[32] Nickelsburg and Stone, *Early Judaism*, 10–16; Coggins, *Samaritans and Jews*, 37–74; Karveit, *Origin of Samaritans*.

[33] Baumgarten, *Jewish Sects*, 57–8.

[34] Sanders, *Judaism*, 341–79; Baumgarten, *Jewish Sects*, 75–91, esp. 86–91.

[35] On the northern traditions in Second Temple Jewish writing, see Nickelsburg, "Enoch, Levi, and Peter"; Freyne, "Galileans," but cf. Eshel and Eshel, "Toponymic Midrash."

[36] Lemaire, *New Aramaic Ostraca*, 416–17; for the sanctity of Bethel at that period, see Schwartz, "Jubilees."

Judea did indeed recognize the uniqueness and centrality of the Jerusalem temple. Yet, at the same time it was possible to conduct sacrificial cult not only outside the Jerusalem temple, but also outside the land of Israel.[37]

THE DEAD SEA SCROLLS AND JEWISH SECTARIANISM

The Dead Sea Scrolls, discovered in eleven caves in Qumran between 1947 and 1956, constitute a library of about nine hundred documents and thousands of fragments (many unidentified). They include biblical writings, copies of known apocrypha, and pseudepigrapha together with other unknown but analogous works, as well as works of a distinctly sectarian character.[38] In this latter category of writings, we may discern the particular ideas and theological concepts of the Essene sect.[39]

It is not clear exactly where the Essenes originated. They must be related broadly to those third-century BCE circles that produced the Enochic *Book of the Luminaries* and the *Aramaic Levi Document*, circles that observed the 364-day solar calendar. Both groups also stressed the central role of the priesthood, but in different ways. Twelve manuscripts of *1 Enoch* and fifteen of *Jubilees* appear among the Qumran sect's manuscripts, though neither work bears the unique ideas or specific terminology typical of the sect. This indicates the overall continuity of this type of Judaism, but also that the Qumran sectarian form of it was quite distinctive. There is no evidence for the survival of the Essenes after the destruction of Qumran by the Romans in 68 CE.[40]

The Qumran sect and its lifestyle are chiefly known from three sets of sources. The first consists of documents from Qumran that prescribe the way of life of the group. The most important of these is the *Rule of the Community*, included in the *Manual of Discipline* (1QS). This book, found in numerous copies and versions at Qumran,[41] presents the way of life, laws, and customs of a communal sect living together, all subject to rigorous rules of conduct and discipline. Admission to the sect occurred in

---

[37] On Jewish cult outside Jerusalem, see Stone, "Judaism at the Time of Christ," 228; Smith, *Palestinian Parties*, 69–73; Campbell, "Jewish Shrines." On the Jewish temples at Elephantine and Leontopolis, see Mélèze Modrzejewski in Chapter 7 in this volume; on private altars in Asia Minor, see van der Horst in Chapter 12 of this volume.
[38] For the classification of the Qumran compositions, see Lange and Mittmann-Richert, "List of Texts."
[39] This seems the most reasonable identification, despite much debate. See VanderKam, *Dead Sea Scrolls Today,* 71–98; Beall, "Essenes," 262–3.
[40] For the *Songs of the Sabbath Sacrifice* found on Masada, see note 53.
[41] It was preserved in one copy from Cave 1 (1QS), and ten copies from Cave 4 (4Q255–264); see Qimron and Charlesworth, *Rule of the Community;* see also Metso, *Community Rule,* 69–155.

three stages: a preliminary year, a second year during which the candidate was a partial member, and then a final stage, when the candidate became a full, albeit junior member of the sect. Conduct, daily life, food, and dress were all regulated. This pattern of life may be compared with that of the Essenes described by Josephus in both of his descriptions of the Jewish sects, or "philosophies" as he calls them (Josephus, *J. W.* 2.119; *Ant.* 13.171; 18.11). Indeed, the writings of Josephus and Philo, Pliny the Elder, *Nat.* 5.15.73, and to a lesser extent of Hippolytus,[42] form the second source of information about the Essenes. The third source is made up of the archaeological finds at the site of Qumran. The nature of the installations uncovered there fits with the pattern of life that may be reconstructed from the *Manual of Discipline* and from the ancient sources.[43] Apparently, though, the sect living at Qumran was not the only type of Essene. Philo, in his treatises *Every Good Man Is Free* (75–91) and *Hypothetica* (11.1–18; preserved in Eusebius *Praep. evang.* 8.5.11–11.18), describes the way of life of Essenes living among others.[44]

This fits in overall terms with another intriguing ancient document. In 1910 a document was published from the Geniza in Cairo.[45] This document, later named the *Damascus Document*, was a puzzle to scholars until the discovery of the Dead Sea manuscripts, at which point it became immediately evident that it was cognate with them.[46] Afterward, copies of it were discovered at Qumran.[47] There are distinct differences between the way of life prescribed in the Qumran *Manual of Discipline* and that set forth in the *Damascus Document*. These probably reflect differing target audiences. While the *Manual of Discipline* was directed to a separatist, communal sectarian settlement, the *Damascus Document*, like Philo's description, addresses the way of life of Essene conclaves living in the towns and villages of Judea.

[42] Smith, "Essenes in Josephus."

[43] Milik, *Ten years*, 49–60; Magness, *Archaeology of Qumran*, 32–46.

[44] On the Essenes, see also Pliny the Elder, *Nat.* 5.15.73. See further Collins, "Sectarian Communities"; Taylor, "Classical Sources."

[45] The document was early discussed by Louis Ginzberg ("An Unknown Jewish Sect," 257–73) and included in Charles' *Apocrypha and Pseudepigrapha of the Old Testament* under the title "Zadokite Fragment." Ginzberg was of the opinion that it belonged to early zealot Pharisees; see Charles, *Apocrypha and Pseudepigrapha* 2. 785–834. See now Broshi, *Damascus Document Reconsidered*.

[46] A few months after he bought the first three scrolls, Eleazar L. Sukenik (after consulting with Chanoch Albeck) recognized the connection between the Dead Sea Scrolls and the Damascus Document.

[47] Eight copies were found in Cave 4 (4Q266–273), one from Cave 5 (5Q12), and one from Cave 6 (6Q15). See Baumgarten, *Damascus Document*, 1–22; Baumgarten, Charlesworth, Novakovitc and Rietz, *Damascus Document II*,; Hempel, *Damascus Texts*.

Before the discovery of these documents, the existence of separatist, indeed sectarian,[48] groups was not a familiar dimension of Judaism in Late Antiquity. The only prior reference to such groups, besides the Essenes in Josephus and Philo, was Philo's discussion of the Therapeutae, a Jewish sect living on the banks of Lake Mareotis in Egypt (*Contempl.* 1–90).[49] Scholars have debated the existence of this group and the accuracy of Philo's description. Was it influenced by Greek utopian ideas or by Greek ethnography that described groups of eastern sages such as the gymnosophists? No answer is known, although today, in light of Qumran, we may perhaps regard Philo's Therapeutae as reflecting a diaspora expression of the same impetus toward separation from daily life and toward pietism and communal living that characterized the Essenes in the land of Israel.

A typical expression of Essene religious ideas may be found in the cosmological dualism of the *Community Rule* (1QS 3:13–4:26). God, who is one, created two spirits, one of light and one of darkness. Humans and superhuman beings are divided into two camps under the leadership of these two spirits. It is unclear and debated whether the division between the sons of light and the sons of darkness was absolute or whether there was a mixture of the two spirits within humans. People are exhorted to piety, yet at the same time their lot in light or darkness has been fixed. This tension between determinism and piety was probably never resolved. In any case, such an approach to the world is quite different from what we find in rabbinic Judaism, for which human free will is the crucial factor in the religious life.[50] Qumran dualism has been compared with Zurvanism in Iran, both having a supreme deity below whom are two spirits, one good and the other evil. There are difficulties of chronology and of channels of contact, and Iranian influence on the Qumran sectaries cannot be asserted unambiguously.[51] Regardless, the dualism at Qumran does not resemble the "soul–body" dualism that characterized many Hellenistic religious viewpoints, pagan and Jewish.[52]

Although Josephus refers to Essenes in Jerusalem during the reign of John Hyrcanus and King Herod, it is difficult to trace their influence on

---

[48] On the term "sectarian," see Baumgarten, *Jewish Sects*, 5–15.

[49] See Hayward, "Therapeutae," 943–4; Taylor, *Jewish Women*, 74–104. For a survey of the literature, see Riaud, "Les Thérapeutes."

[50] *b. Ber.* 33b (= *b. Nid.*16b; *b. Meg.* 25a): "All is under the control of Heaven (i.e., God) except the fear of Heaven." See Urbach, *The Sages*, 255–85.

[51] Winston, "Iranian Component"; Frye, "Qumran and Iran"; Shaked, "Iranian Influence," 324–5. On problems in the study of Zurvanism, see also De Jong in Chapter 1 of this volume.

[52] See, for example, Wisdom 9:15: "for a perishable body weighs down the soul, and this earthy tent burdens the thoughtful mind."

the course of events in Judea in the last century BCE and the first century CE. A liturgical composition named *The Songs of Sabbath Sacrifice* was discovered in nine copies in Qumran caves, as well as in one copy at Masada. There is no scholarly consensus as to whether it is Essene or non-Essene in origin, and whether these prayers, which seem to have gained some popularity, were recited by the Qumran sect alone, or by other Jewish groups as well.[53]

The significance of the Qumran discoveries, then, reverberates in a number of different fields. The library contains the oldest surviving substantial manuscripts of books that became part of the Hebrew Bible, fragments of the lost Hebrew or Aramaic originals of known extrabiblical works, and many fragmentary works of similar character, as well as documents reflecting the ideas and practices of this sectarian community. It contains works in Hebrew, Aramaic, and Greek. From the evidence of this literature, we can see a group in which the priests played a major role that rejected the validity of the Jerusalem temple and its establishment, and that developed ideas of bloodless sacrifice and daily, weekly, and festival prayer cycles. In other words, this group cultivated a disciplined and ascetic way of life, designed, we may speculate, as a prolepsis of the eschatological state.[54] This, combined with the double determinism that dominated their cosmology, makes them remarkable in the history of Judaism.

During the same period as the floruit of the Qumran sect, sources also mention the Pharisees and Sadducees. Truth be told, our knowledge of these groups, especially of their early stages, is limited. According to Josephus, the Pharisees had a strong tradition of interpretation of the laws, which was crucial to their worldview. Although the process of committing oral tradition to writing took place earlier, during the Persian and Ptolemaic periods, its written form, particularly as embodied in the Torah, gradually became recognized as authoritative.[55] Once the oral tradition had been reduced to writing, it became available to larger circles in society, and was not limited to its oral tradents, who were most likely the priesthood. Much of the debate in Judaism throughout the Second Temple period, and particularly in its second part, was about the right to interpret the law.

---

[53] See Newsom, "Sectually Explicit," 179–85; Alexander, *The Mystical Texts*. For doubts about the sectarian character of *The Songs of Sabbath Sacrifice*, see Morray-Jones, "The Temple Within," 409–10.

[54] Cross, *Ancient Library of Qumran*, 37–79.

[55] Stone, *Three Transformations*. Earlier, particularly important documents were said to be "written"; cf. Najman, *Seconding Sinai*. On the question of canonical traditions and the extent of fluidity, see Trebolle Barrera, "A Canon within a Canon"; Carr, *Writing*, 217–18; Bowley and Reeves, "The Concept of 'Bible'"; McDonald and Sanders, *The Canon Debate*.

The Qumran sectaries thus made much of the inspired exegesis of the Teacher of Righteousness (see 1QpHab II:1–10; VII:3–5); they called their Pharisaic opponents the "Seekers-After-Smooth-Things" (e.g., 4ApNah Figs. 3–4, Col. 1:2).[56] The Pharisees were not only exegetes of the sacred writings with their own distinctive tradition and customs, but they also played a role in current events. In the first century BCE, we are told that the Hasmonean queen Salome gave them much power. Josephus's statement that most of the people later followed the Pharisees does not mean that in the first century CE most of the people were Pharisees themselves, but rather that they were considered the most influential group.[57] According to Josephus's characterization, the Pharisees also believed in the immortality of the soul. While the combination of Josephus with the New Testament Gospels and Acts provides a sort of checklist of Pharisaic beliefs, it is impossible to know how far this list reflects reality; it is wisest to regard it with a good deal of suspicion.

Even less is known of the Sadducees. Their name indicates their apparently priestly orientation. It derives from that of the Zadokite family, which had held the high-priestly position from the time of King David.[58] This group played a distinct role in politics and seems to have included wealthy aristocrats of priestly orientation.[59] The priestly aristocracy, as we have pointed out, held crucial political power through the Persian period and also down to the Ptolemaic. If the Sadducees were descended from that priestly aristocracy, their role in politics and the Temple is completely understandable. In 4QpNahum, there is some further support for the idea that they were the wealthy, upper-class group in society.[60] Like the Pharisees, however, they did not appear on the stage of history until the middle of the second century BCE. While both groups disappeared from the known historical record after the destruction of the Temple in 70 CE, it is the common view that the subsequent rabbinic tradition continued that of the Pharisees.[61]

Other groups existed in Palestinian Judaism at the turn of the era. Although not strictly "Jews" (that is, Judeans), the Samaritan worshippers

---

[56] See, e.g., CD I:18; 1QHa X:15,32; 1QpNah frags. 3–4, I:2.

[57] Josephus's motives for writing his histories, as well as for his presentation of the Pharisees, were very mixed, and it is difficult to tell how far he is serving his own aims in his description of their influence; see Baumgarten, *Jewish Sects*, 42, n. 2, 51–2, 62–3.

[58] Zadok is first mentioned in 2 Samuel 8:17 and in 2 Samuel and 1 Kings in connection with the Ark of the Covenant; see Ramsey, "Zadok."

[59] While this is the *communis opinio*, it may oversimplify things about which very little is known; see Regev, "Pharisees and Sadducees."

[60] Flusser, "Pharisäer."

[61] See Neusner and Chilton, *In Quest*.

of the God of Israel held different political and religious views. While the Sadducees rejected Pharisaic exegesis of the Torah, the Samaritans accepted only the Pentateuch as authoritative.[62] They identified with the northern kingdom of Israel and regarded Shechem, not Jerusalem, as the holy city and Mount Gerizim, not Mount Zion, as the holy site of the Temple. There were a number of Samaritan sects in the period under discussion and Samaritan communities also existed in the diaspora.[63]

ESCHATOLOGY AND APOCALYPTICISM

Scholars of the Hebrew Bible, for the most part, hold the view that during the period of the First Temple, the eschatology of the religion of Israel looked forward to events that would unfold in the ordinary course of history. At some point after the Restoration, this hope was transformed into the expectation of a momentous change in the historical order, an end of history, and finally the redemption of Israel and vindication of God. These events would take place beyond history. At some time, the arena of events changed from this created world alone and included the heavenly metaspatial world. We cannot trace the beginnings of this development in detail, but it was certainly well underway by the time the oldest parts of *1 Enoch* were written.[64] This hope for redemption beyond history and outside this world became a major force in the Judaism of the day, and of course in incipient Christianity.

George Nickelsburg has remarked that the persecutions of Antiochus IV in all likelihood played a significant role in the crystallization of eschatology. If theodicy, the flourishing of the wicked and the suffering of the righteous, was at the root of the eschatological solution, then the events of the Maccabean period brought this issue into sharper focus. The traditional explanation no longer held. With the death of the righteous for observance of the Torah under the decrees of Antiochus IV, people were dying *because* they observed God's commandments, not for disobeying them.[65] This made the issue of theodicy more acute, pushing the expectation of vindication and recompense beyond history and beyond the series of this-worldly events into the metahistorical. Without recompense of the righteous at the end of days, divine justice would be completely flaunted.[66]

---

[62] See Eshel and Eshel, "Dating the Samaritan Pentateuch's Compilation."
[63] Crown, "The Samaritan Diaspora"; Isser, *The Dositheans*; Coggins, *Samaritans and Jews*.
[64] See Hanson, *Dawn of Apocalyptic* and idem, "Rebellion in Heaven."
[65] Van Henten, *Maccabean Martyrs*; Nickelsburg, *Resurrection, Immortality*, 97–111.
[66] Nickelsburg, *Resurrection, Immortality*.

The hope of future redemption was often expressed in terms of the expectation of a redeemer figure(s) who would usher in the ideal future age. The Jews in the centuries before and after the turn of the era did not have a fixed and generally accepted belief about the details of such matters. The literature of the age expresses a yearning for a variety of redeemers and redemption. One pattern desired to see the restoration of the ideal polity of Israel as a sacred people living according to God's will and led by two figures, a king of the line of David and a Zadokite high priest. This hope is already expressed by the prophet Zechariah (6:11–12). Since both the king and the high priest were anointed with oil, they came to be called "Anointed Ones," or "Messiahs," a name symbolized by the two olive trees in Zechariah 4:16. The hope for two Messiahs was not widespread, but it is to be found in Essene documents from Qumran, which speak of the "Messiah" or "Messiahs of Aaron and Israel."[67] In the *Aramaic Levi Document*, we find the idea of a single, Levitical figure combining elements of the priestly and royal Messiahs.[68] The expectation of the restoration of the Davidic monarchy was bolstered by Nathan's prophecy to David (2 Samuel 7:13), as well as by prophetic expectations of the coming of a future ideal king (for example, Isaiah 11, and Balaam's oracle in Numbers 24:17–20). This hope is first expressed clearly in the apocryphal *Psalms of Solomon* 17:23–51. Although it later became the center of Jewish hope for a redeemer figure, during the Second Temple period it was only one among other expectations.

Another anticipated figure was the mysterious person of Melchizedek. He appears in Gen 14:18–20 as king of Salem (traditionally interpreted as Jerusalem) and priest of God Most High to whom Abraham brought tithes. Melchizedek is also mentioned suggestively in Psalm 110:4 where the king is told, "The LORD has sworn and will not change his mind, 'You are a priest forever according to the order of Melchizedek.'" In *2 Enoch*, Melchizedek is said to be Noah's nephew, to be assumed to heaven and to return to earth (71.33–37). In one version of the work, Melchizedek is called "my priest to all priests (71.79) … the head of the priests of another generation (71.37)." One Dead Sea Scroll also expresses the expectation of a Melchizedek figure who will come as a judge at the end of the present period (11QMelchizedek). The representation of Melchizedek in Heb 7:1–17 should also be understood in the context of the expectation of a non-Levitical priestly redeemer figure who returns to earth and whose

---

[67] See Evans, "Messiahs," 539–40; Collins, *The Scepter*.
[68] Greenfield, Stone, and Eshel, *Aramaic Levi*, 36–8.

final appearance will be eschatological. Unlike Hebrews, however, none of the other texts hint at a contrast or tension between Melchizedek and the eschatological expectation of an Aaronid Messiah. These traditions about Melchizedek, which cannot be reconciled or harmonized into a single system, must have coexisted within the spectrum of Second Temple Jewish thought.[69]

Another human type figure also expected at the end of days has been the subject of much discussion in the scholarly literature. This human figure bears one of the titles that the Gospels apply to Jesus, "Son of Man."[70] The title, in our texts, derives from the symbolic vision in Daniel 7, specifically from the description of the younger human figure who is to be associated in judgment with the Ancient of Days (Dan 7:9). The explanation offered by Daniel 7:22–28 is that this human figure represents the kingdom of the holy ones of the Most High, an ambiguous expression that can be taken to designate Israel or the saints, or else the angels.[71] These two figures, the Ancient of Days and the Son of Man, were taken up in the somewhat mysterious second part of *1 Enoch*, the *Similitudes (Parables) of Enoch*. There the Son of Man, also called the Elect One, is anointed and enthroned (46:1). He is hidden before creation and takes over part of God's function of judgment. This sort of depiction may lie in the background of the use of "Son of Man" in the Gospels.[72]

Other figures also served as redeemers or played a part in redemption. One is the eschatological prophet, a development of Malachi's reference to Elijah's future return as part of a new world order (Mal 3:23). Another actor in the eschatological drama is the leader of the forces of evil, expected to rally the armies in a final cataclysmic clash of the forces of good and evil. Following Ezekiel 38, this battle was called the war of Gog and Magog by later Jewish sources, while it is called Armageddon in Christian sources. That name possibly derives from Hebrew Har (Mount) Megiddo, where the battle was expected to take place (Rev 16:16).[73]

In the last century BCE and the first century CE, then, eschatological hopes assumed a special urgency. On the one hand, we hear of itinerant prophets such as John the Baptist, who according to the Gospels withdrew

---

[69] See Ellens, "Dead Sea Scrolls and the Son of Man"; and Roberts, "Melchizedek."

[70] See Nickelsburg, "Son of Man," with references to earlier discussions; also Yarbro-Collins, *Cosmology and Eschatology*, 139–58; Collins, *Daniel*, 79–89.

[71] Collins, *Daniel*, 278–94.

[72] In the *Testament of Abraham*, 13:2 (long recension) the eschatological judge is Abel, who is son of Adam = "man." See Allison, *Testament of Abraham*, 280–82; Boccaccini, *Enoch and the Messiah Son of Man*.

[73] See Meyers and Meyers, *Zechariah*, 343–4.

to the desert to preach the imminence of the eschaton and the requital of the righteous and wicked;[74] on the other, active anti-Roman agitation that seems to have been fueled, in part at least, by acute eschatological expectation broke out on a number of occasions.[75]

CHANGES IN JUDEAN SOCIETY AND RELIGION
UNDER ROMAN RULE

The civil war between the Hasmonean brothers Hyrcanus II and Aristobulus II resulted in the annexation of Judea by Pompey in 63 BCE. Succeeding it were the Idumeans Antipater, Herod, and his sons, the last of whom, Archelaeus, was deposed by the Romans in 6 CE.[76] Roman governors, under the authority of the governor of Syria, ruled the country thenceforth. A pattern of civil turmoil, stoked by Zealot activist tendencies, typified the first century CE, leading to full-scale revolt against Rome in 66 CE. Although Jerusalem was taken in 70 CE, the last of the fighters on the Herodian fortress of Masada were only overcome in 73 or 74 CE. Revolt erupted again half a century later under the leadership of Bar Kokhba (or son of Kosiba), lasting from 132 to 135 CE.

Judean history before the revolt saw major changes in Jewish society and religion. One factor that changed with Herod and Antipater was the removal of the high priesthood from the center of political power. The Temple played a central role in Jewish life in this period, and the high-priestly office carried great prestige. In seeking to concentrate all effective power in his own hands, Herod suppressed opposition fomented by scions of the Hasmonean family and took complete control of the office. The high priesthood thus became the object of manipulation under the Herodians and the procurators, and the holder of the office was frequently replaced.

Roman control of Judea brought about changes in Judean society and religion as far-reaching as those in political structures. The central role of the Temple in Jewish life continued, despite the divorce of the high priesthood from the monarchy.[77] Three major transformations, however, were to have considerable effects. In the early part of the first century CE,

[74] See Gray, *Prophetic Figures*, 122–3.

[75] On Judah the Galilean's "fourth philosophy," see Josephus, *J. W.* 2.117–119, 433; *Ant.* 18.4–10, 23–5. See also Hengel, *Zealots*, 76–145; cf. Horsley, *Bandits, Prophets, and Messiahs*, 118–27.

[76] Herodians continued to rule different parts of the land of Israel down to 100 CE. Members of this family, known for their loyalty to Rome, were even appointed as vassal monarchs elsewhere in the East; see Kokkinos, *Herodian Dynasty*, 225, 339–40.

[77] Sanders, *Judaism*, 47–72.

under the leadership of Judah the Zealot, the movement that Josephus calls the "fourth philosophy," or the Zealots, began to conduct activities with populist tendencies against the power elites and the Roman occupation.[78] The question remains open whether the nationalist enthusiasts whose actions played such a great role in the events leading up to the Great Revolt in 66–70 CE and in its aftermath were continuators of those early first-century agitators. The chief difficulty for the historian is that the only source with any detail is Josephus, whose jaundiced view of the Zealots makes him a suspect witness.

There seems no doubt, however, that in Judea and the Galilee in the first century CE, groups of individuals arose who, inspired by the expectation of divine intervention on behalf of the people of Israel and its Temple, cultivated activism against Roman rule. In the *Testament of Moses*, as Jacob Licht has pointed out, the symbolic figure Taxo with his sons sought, by direct action and martyrdom, to precipitate the divine redemption that they expected.[79] This layer of *Testament of Moses* certainly reflects events in the time of Archelaus.[80] The same sort of ideals permeated the rebels who formed the last pocket of resistance on Masada in 73 or 74 CE, choosing suicide rather than surrender.[81] Revolutionary activism seems to have been motivated by eschatological hopes interpreted in such a way as to become a program of military and political action.

LITERARY TYPES AND SOCIAL REALITIES

During the Greco-Roman period, the Jews produced a rich crop of literature, much of it in Greek. Attested already in the late fourth or early third centuries BCE, it included belletristic compositions such as the drama "Exodus" by Ezekiel the Tragedian, as well as philosophical, chronographic, oracular, sapiential, and other writings. In the diaspora, especially in Egypt, Greek was the language in which Jews usually chose to express themselves. There is good reason to think that Jews in the land of Israel also wrote original works in Greek. If the Eupolemus mentioned in 1 Macc 8:17 is the same as the fragmentary historian Eupolemus, then his work was perhaps composed in Jerusalem.[82] By the first century, many Jewish

---

[78] See note 75.

[79] Licht, *Taxo*, 95–100.

[80] Nickelsburg, "Antiochan Date," 36–7.

[81] Although Josephus's report of the speech of Eleazar, the head of the Masada fortress under Roman siege (*J. W.* 7.323–88), is fictitious, some aspects of it contain ideas that may have animated these activists.

[82] See Hummel, *Historiography*, 25–7; Wacholder, *Eupolemus*, 4–7; Cohen, "Masada."

sarcophagi from Jerusalem bore names written in Hebrew or Aramaic, Greek, or else Hebrew or Aramaic and Greek together.[83] Previously we alluded to Cave 7 at Qumran, which contained only Greek papyri, including translations of a few pseudepigrapha.[84] Thus, it is not implausible that some religious works (and nearly all Jewish literary writing of this period was religious) were composed in Palestine in Greek.[85]

Most of the hundreds of compositions that survive from the land of Israel were written in Hebrew and Aramaic. Most likely, the Aramaic ones antedate those in Hebrew. They include four of the five parts of *1 Enoch*,[86] Daniel 2–7,[87] *Aramaic Levi Document*, Tobit,[88] the *Genesis Apocryphon*, and others. The Hebrew works include an enormous range of writings from Qumran's sectarian documents, like the *Community Rule*, to pro-Hasmonean court propaganda, such as 1 Maccabees.[89] Books of psalms and prayers, such as the Thanksgiving Hymns from Qumran, the *Psalms of Solomon*, and the Apocryphal Psalms existed alongside sapiential writings such as the *Wisdom of ben Sira*. Many works, including some from Qumran, were pseudepigraphic – that is, they were attributed to authors who did not write them, most frequently biblical characters. Another substantial body of texts is anonymous, and there are almost no works from the land of Israel whose authors' names are known (*Wisdom of Jesus ben Sira* forming a notable exception).

The visionary texts, the apocalypses, which transmit teachings about cosmology, eschatology, and future redemption, have received great attention, at least in part because of their connection with the teachings of Jesus and his followers. These texts and the type of religious experience underlying

---

[83] See Cotton et al., *Corpus Inscriptionum Iudaeae/Palaestinae*.

[84] Compare also the late first-century BCE scroll of the Greek revision of the Septuagint version of the Minor Prophets found at Nahal Hever; see Tov, *Greek Minor Prophets*.

[85] For evidence of Greek influence in the early rabbinic period, see Lieberman, *Greeks in Jewish Palestine*, and idem, *Hellenism in Jewish Palestine*. See also the detailed statement by Hengel, *Judaism and Hellenism*, 1.83–106.

[86] The remaining part, the *Similitudes of Enoch*, might have been written in Aramaic as well, but this is unknown; see Nickelsburg and VanderKam, *1 Enoch 2*, 30–4, who prefer an Aramaic origin, although the Parables are attested only in an Ethiopic (Ge'ez) version. It is later than the other four parts and probably written around the turn of the era: see Knibb, "Parables of Enoch"; Collins, *Daniel*, 80–2.

[87] Though chapter 7 is problematic; see Collins, *Daniel*, 280–94, 323–4.

[88] For the assumption that Hebrew Tobit was translated from Aramaic, see Fitzmyer, "Significance," 419–23; idem, *Tobit*, 18–28. To date, no evidence is known for Hebrew translations of Aramaic compositions at that period, while there are examples of Aramaic translations of Hebrew texts (e.g., Targum Job from Qumran). Because people were fluent in Aramaic, it is possible that the Hebrew composition *Tobit* was translated into Aramaic.

[89] Of course, it is not always possible to determine the original language of works that survive only in Greek translation, or in daughter versions of the Greek.

them exhibit a form of Judaism that would not have been expected had they not survived.[90] In addition to apocalyptic and oracular literature, the psalmodic and prayer texts both in the Apocrypha and Pseudepigrapha and among the Dead Sea Scrolls exemplify the piety of the period. Personal religious sentiment, a sense of closeness to the deity and of divine providence, permeates these works. We can also discern simultaneous developments that stand close to the liturgical tradition of fixed prayer that became typical of Judaism toward the end of this period.[91] Speculative thinking, both about the nature of wisdom understood as a metaphysical element and about moral and ethical issues, is expressed in the sapiential books. Changes in the conception of time and history meant that the attempt to understand God's working by retelling the events of Israel's history was not undertaken again after Chronicles-Ezra-Nehemiah.[92] Instead, historiography found expression in apocalyptic reviews of history.[93] Of the major genres of biblical writing, the psalmodic and sapiential writings continue to be produced.

A major problem in writing the religious history of this period lies in the disjunction between this religious literature in all its genres and varieties and the numerous Jewish sects, trends, and movements attested in the historical sources. While the historical sources for the period give ample evidence of a great variety within Judaism, the ideas expressed in the literature of the period suggest that the various works originated from groups or individuals holding differing points of view. The only group to which we can attribute writings with any assuredness is the Qumran sect. That attribution is made on the basis of the archaeological find at Qumran and its relationship to the books found in the caves.[94] Even in this case, which of the documents actually reflect the ideas of the sect and which were just part of their library is debated.

Is it possible to speak of "normative Judaism" during the first century CE, a type of Judaism generally recognized and viewed as that from which other groups dissented? The only general ancient statement about this remains Josephus's assertion that most of the people followed the Pharisees. Yet, as observed previously, this statement may well be tendentious. Clearly, certain common institutions and practices characterized the Jews, such

---

[90] Stone, "Apocalyptic, Vision or Hallucination?"; idem, "A Reconsideration." *Ancient Judaism*, 90–121.
[91] Chazon, "Psalms," 710–11, 714.
[92] Flavius Josephus's major work, *Jewish Antiquities*, was modeled on Greco-Roman patterns.
[93] Stone, *Ancient Judaism*, 57–89.
[94] Magness, *Archaeology of Qumran*, 43–6.

as aniconic worship, the reverence for the Temple in Jerusalem, dietary laws, and Sabbath observance. Recent attempts to assess different groups in Jewish society taking advantage of sociological understandings of sectarianism have yielded some insights.[95] However, it remains impossible to declare one or another of the "sects," "parties," or "philosophies" to represent the norm from which the other groups differed. To pose the question in such a way is in all likelihood anachronistic. The impact of the destruction of the Temple in 70 CE, together with the loss of national autonomy, led to consolidation in many areas, including the biblical text and the rabbinic academies. It is difficult to reconstruct the situation before this process got underway.

Eschatological ideas lay at the root of much of the political unrest that characterized first-century Judea. It was exacerbated by a general eastern opposition to Rome [96] to which some must have subscribed, though the Jews, on the whole, were positive toward Rome.[97] In any case, this unrest issued in the Great Revolt, which broke out in 66 CE and continued down to 70 CE. Its end came with the destruction of the Temple in that year, though opposition continued in Masada down to 73 or 74 CE. The aftermath of the revolt brought further changes to Judaism and among the Jewish people.

BIBLIOGRAPHY

Alexander, Philip. *The Mystical Texts: Songs of the Sabbath Sacrifice and Related Manuscripts* (London, 2006).
Allison, Dale C. *Testament of Abraham* (Berlin, 2003).
Baumgarten, Albert I. "Josephus and Hippolytus on the Pharisees." *HUCA* 55 (1984): 1–25.
    The Flourishing of Jewish Sects in the Maccabean Era: An Interpretation (Leiden, 1997).
Baumgarten, Joseph M. *Qumran Cave 4. XIII: The Damascus Document (4Q266–273)*. DJD 18 (Oxford, 1996).
Baumgarten, Joseph M., James H., Charlesworth, Lidija Novakovitc, and Henry W. M. Rietz. "Damascus Document." In *The Dead Sea Scrolls: Hebrew, Aramaic, and Greek Texts with English Translations*. Vol. 3: *Damascus Document II, Some Works of the Torah, and Related Documents,* ed. J. H. Charlesworth (Tübingen, 2006): 1–185.
Beall, T. S. "Essenes." In *Encyclopedia of the Dead Sea Scrolls* 1, eds. L. H. Schiffman and J. C. VanderKam (Oxford, 2000): 262–9.

---

[95] For sociological approaches, see Baumgarten, *Jewish Sects,* 43–50; Regev, "Sectarian Practice." For recent works of a general character on Second Temple Judaism, see, for example, Sanders, *Judaism;* Cohen, *Beginnings of Jewishness;* Schwartz, *Imperialism.*
[96] On opposition ideology in the Roman East, see Fuchs, *Widerstand.*
[97] See Schürer, Vermes, and Millar, *History of the Jewish People,* 1.485–513, esp. 485–8.

Ben-Dov, Jonathan. "The Babylonian Lunar Three in Calendrical Scrolls from Qumran."
   ZA 95 (2005): 104–20.
"Tradition and Innovation in the Calendar of Jubilees." In *Enoch and the Mosaic Torah:
   The Evidence of Jubilees*, eds. Gabriele Boccaccini and Giovanni Ibba (Grand Rapids,
   Mich., 2009): 276–93.
Bickerman, Elias J. "The Historical Foundations of Postbiblical Judaism." In *The Jews: Their
   History, Culture, and Religion*, Vol. 1, ed. Louis Finkelstein (New York, 1949): 70–114.
From Ezra to the Last of the Maccabees (New York, 1962).
The God of the Maccabees: Studies on the Meaning and Origin of the Maccabean Revolt,
   trans. H. R. Moehring (Leiden, 1979).
Jews in the Greek Age (Cambridge, Mass., 1988).
Bilde, Per. *Flavius Josephus Between Jerusalem and Rome: His Life, His Works and Their
   Importance*. JSPSup 2 (Sheffield, 1988)
Boccaccini, Gabriele, ed. *The Origins of Enochic Judaism: Proceedings of the First Enoch
   Seminar. University of Michigan, Sesto Fiorentino, Italy, June 19–23, 2001* (Torino,
   2003).
Enoch and the Messiah Son of Man: Revisiting the Book of Parables (Grand Rapids,
   2007).
Bohak, Gideon. "CPJ III, 520: The Egyptian Reaction to Onias." *JSJ* 26 (1995): 32–41.
Bowley, James E., and John C. Reeves. "Rethinking the Concept of 'Bible': Some Theses
   and Proposals." *Hen* 25.1 (2003): 3–18.
Broshi, Magen, ed. *The Damascus Document Reconsidered* (Jerusalem, 1992).
Campbell, Edward F. "Jewish Shrines of the Hellenistic and Persian Periods." In *Symposia
   Celebrating the Seventy-Fifth Anniversary of the Founding of the American Schools of
   Oriental Research*, ed. Frank M. Cross (Cambridge, Mass., 1979): 159–67.
Carr, David M. *Writing on the Tablet of the Heart: Origins of Scripture and Literature*
   (Oxford, 2005).
Charles, Robert H. *The Apocrypha and Pseudepigrapha of the Old Testament*. 2 vols. (Oxford,
   1913).
Charlesworth, James H., and E. Qimron. "Rule of the Community." In *The Dead Sea
   Scrolls: Hebrew, Aramaic, and Greek Texts with English Translations*. Vol. 1: *Rule of the
   Community and Related Documents*, ed. J. H. Charlesworth (Tübingen, 1994): 1–103.
Chazon, Esther. "Psalms, Hymns, and Prayer." In *The Encyclopedia of the Dead Sea Scrolls* 2,
   eds. L. H. Schiffman and J. C. VanderKam (Oxford, 2000): 710–15.
Coggins, R. J. *Samaritans and Jews: The Origins of Samaritanism Reconsidered* (Atlanta,
   1975).
Cohen, Shaye J. D. "Masada: Literary Tradition, Archaeological Remains, and the
   Credibility of Josephus." *JJS* 33 (1982): 385–405.
The Beginnings of Jewishness: Boundaries, Varieties, Uncertainties (Berkeley, 1999).
Collins, John J. *Daniel: A Commentary on the Book of Daniel* (Minneapolis, 1993).
The Scepter and the Star: The Messiahs of the Dead Sea Scrolls and other Ancient Literature
   (New York, 1995).
The Apocalyptic Imagination: An Introduction to Jewish Apocalyptic Literature. 2nd ed.
   (Grand Rapids, Mich., 1998).
"Sectarian Communities in the Dead Sea Scrolls." In *The Oxford Handbook of the Dead
   Sea Scrolls*, eds. Timothy H. Lim and John J. Collins (Oxford, 2010): 151–72.

Cotton, Hannah M., Leah Di Segni, Werner Eck, Benjamin Isaac, Alla Kushnir-Stein, Haggai Misgav, Jonathan J. Price, Israel Roll, and Ada Yardeni, eds. *Corpus Inscriptionum Iudaeae/Palaestinae: A Multi-Lingual Corpus of the Inscriptions from Alexander to Muhammad, Volume 1: Jerusalem, Part 1: 1–704* (Berlin, 2010).

Coxon, Peter W. "Greek Loan-Words and Alleged Greek Loan Translations in the Book of Daniel." *TGUOS* 25 (1973–74): 24–40.

Cross, Frank M. "The Discovery of the Samaria Papyri." *BA* 26 (1963): 110–21.

"Aspects of Samaritan and Jewish History in the Late Persian and Hellenistic Times." *HTR* 59 (1966): 201–11.

Canaanite Myth and Hebrew Epic (Cambridge, Mass., 1973).

"A Reconstruction of the Judean Restoration." *JBL* 94 (1975): 4–18.

Crown, Alan D. "The Samaritan Diaspora." In *The Samaritans*, ed. Alan D. Crowe (Tübingen, 1989): 195–217.

Ellens, J. Harold. "The Dead Sea Scrolls and the Son of Man in Daniel, 1 *Enoch*, and the New Testament Gospels: An Assessment of 11Qmelch (11Q13)." In *The Dead Sea Scrolls in Context: Integrating the Dead Sea Scrolls in the Study of Ancient Texts, Languages, and Cultures*. Vol. 1, eds. Armin Lange, Emanuel Tov, and Matthias Weigold (Leiden, 2011): 341–63.

Eph'al, Israel, and Joseph Naveh. *Aramaic Ostraca of the Fourth Century BC from Idumaea* (Jerusalem, 1996).

Eshel, Esther. "Chapter 2: Inscriptions in Hebrew, Aramaic, and Phoenician Script." In A. Kloner, E. Eshel, H. Korzakova, and G. Finkielsztejn, *Maresha III: Epigraphic Finds from the 1989–2000 Seasons*. IAA Reports, No. 45 (Jerusalem, 2010): 35–88, 227–36.

Eshel, Esther, and Hanan Eshel. "Dating the Samaritan Pentateuch's Compilation in Light of the Qumran Biblical Scrolls." In *Emanuel: Studies in Hebrew Bible, Septuagint and Dead Sea Scrolls in Honor of Emanuel Tov*, eds. Shalom M. Paul, Robert A. Kraft, Lawrence H. Schiffman, and Weston W. Fields (Leiden, 2003): 215–40.

"Toponymic Midrash in 1 Enoch and in Other Second Temple Jewish Literature." *Hen* 24 (2002): 115–30.

Eshel, Esther, and Amos Kloner. "An Aramaic Ostracon of an Edomite Marriage Contract from Maresha, Dated 176 B.C.E." *IEJ* 46 (1996): 1–22.

Evans, C. A. "Messiahs." In *Encyclopedia of the Dead Sea Scrolls* 1, eds. L. H. Schiffman and J. C. VanderKam (Oxford, 2000): 537–42.

Fitzmyer, Joseph A. "The Significance of the Hebrew and Aramaic Texts of Tobit from Qumran for the Study of Tobit." In *The Dead Sea Scrolls: Fifty Years After Their Discovery*, eds. Lawrence H. Schiffman, Emanuel Tov, and James C. VanderKam (Jerusalem, 2000): 418–25.

Tobit. Commentaries on Early Jewish Literature (Berlin, 2003).

Flusser, David. "Pharisäer, Sadduzäer und Essener im Pescher Nahum." In *Qumran*, ed. Karl Erich Grözinger et al. (Darmstadt, 1981): 121–66.

Freyne, Sean. "Galileans, Phoenicians, and Itureans: A Study of Regional Contrasts in the Hellenistic Age." In *Hellenism in the Land of Israel*, eds. John J. Collins and Gregory E. Sterling (Notre Dame, Ind., 2001): 182–215.

Frye, Richard N. "Qumran and Iran: The State of Studies." In *Christianity, Judaism and Other Greco-Roman Cults: Studies for Morton Smith at Sixty, Part Three: Judaism Before 70*, ed. Jacob Neusner (Leiden, 1975): 167–73.

Fuchs, Harald. *Der geistige Widerstand gegen Rom in antiken Welt* (Berlin, 1964).

Gera, Dov. "On the Credibility of the History of the Tobiads." In *Greece and Rome in Eretz Israel: Collected Essays*, eds. Aryeh Kasher, Uriel Rappaport, and Gideon Fuks (Jerusalem, 1990): 21–38.

Judaea and Mediterranean Politics, 219 to 161 BCE (Leiden, 1998).

Geraty, Lawrence T. "The Khirbet el-Kom Bilingual Ostracon." *BASOR* 220 (1975): 55–61.

Ginzberg, Louis. *An Unknown Jewish Sect* (New York, 1976).

Ginzel, Friedrich K. *Handbuch der mathematischen und technischen Chronologie: das Zeitrechnungswesen der Völker*. Vol. 3 (Leipzig, 1914).

Grabbe, Lester L. *A History of the Jews and Judaism in the Second Temple Period. Vol. 1. Yehud: A History of the Persian Province of Judah* (London, 2004).

Gray, Rebecca. *Prophetic Figures in Late Second Temple Jewish Palestine: The Evidence from Josephus* (New York, 1993).

Greenfield, Jonas C., Michael E. Stone, and Esther Eshel. *The Aramaic Levi Document: Edition, Translation, Commentary.* STVP 19 (Leiden, 2004).

Hanson, Paul. D. *The Dawn of Apocalyptic*. Rev. ed. (Philadelphia, 1979).

"Rebellion in Heaven, Azazel, and Euhemeristic Heroes in 1 Enoch 6–11." *JBL* 96 (1977): 195–233.

Hayward, C. T. R. "Therapeutae." in *Encyclopedia of the Dead Sea Scrolls* 2, eds. L. H. Schiffman and J. C. VanderKam (Oxford, 2000): 943–6.

Hempel, Charlotte. *The Damascus Texts* (Sheffield, 2000).

Hengel, Martin. *Judaism and Hellenism: Studies in their Encounter in Palestine during the Early Hellenistic Period*, trans. J. Bowden (Philadelphia, 1974).

"The Political and Social History of Palestine from Alexander to Antiochus III (333–187 B.C.E.)." In *CHJ*. Vol. 2: *The Hellenistic Age*, eds. W. D. Davies and Louis Finkelstein (Cambridge, 1989): 35–78.

"The Interpretation of Judaism and Hellenism in the Pre-Maccabean Period." In *CHJ*. Vol. 2: *The Hellenistic Age*, eds. W. D. Davies and Louis Finkelstein (Cambridge, 1989): 167–228.

The Zealots: Investigations into the Jewish Freedom Movement in the Period from Herod I Until 70 A.D., trans. D. Smith (Edinburgh, 1989).

Henten, Jan W. van. *The Maccabean Martyrs as Saviours of the Jewish People: A Study of 2 and 4 Maccabees*. JSJSup 57 (Leiden, 1997).

Horsley, Richard, A. *Bandits, Prophets, and Messiahs* (Harrisburg, 1999).

Hummel, B. S. *An Analysis of the Historiography of 1 Maccabees: A Key to Understanding the Background of the Hasmonean Period*, diss. Southwestern Baptist Theological Seminary, 1996.

Ilan, Tal. *Lexicon of Jewish Names in Late Antiquity. Part I: Palestine 330 BCE–200 CE.* TSAJ 91 (Tübingen, 2002).

Isser, Stanley J. *The Dositheans: A Samaritan Sect in Late Antiquity* (Leiden, 1976).

Kampen, John. *The Hasideans and the Origin of Pharisaism: A Study of 1 and 2 Maccabees.* SBLSCS 24 (Atlanta, 1988).

Kartveit, Magnar. *The Origin of the Samaritans*. VTSup 128 (Leiden, 2009).

Kasher, Aryeh. *Jews, Idumaeans, and Ancient Arabs* (Tübingen, 1988).

Knibb, Michael. "The Date of the Parables of Enoch: A Critical Review." *NTS* 25 (1978–79): 345–59.

Kokkinos, Nikos. *The Herodian Dynasty: Origins, Role in Society and Eclipse.* JSPSup 30 (Sheffield, 1998).

Lange, Armin, and Ulrike Mittmann-Richert. "Annotated List of the Texts from the Judaean Desert Classified by Context and Genre." In *The Texts from the Judaean Desert: Indices and an Introduction to the Discoveries in the Judaean Desert Series*, ed. Emanuel Tov. DJD 39 (Oxford, 2002): 115–64.

Leith, Mary Joan W. *Wadi Daliyeh I: The Wadi Daliyeh Seal Impressions.* DJD 24 (Oxford, 1997).

Lemaire, André. *Nouvelles inscriptions araméennes d'Idumée au Musée d'Israël.* Transeuphratène Supp. 3 (Paris, 1996).

———. *Nouvelles inscriptions araméennes d'Idumée.* Transeuphratène Supp. 9 (Paris, 2002).

———. "New Aramaic Ostraca from Idumea and Their Historical Interpretation." In *Judah and the Judeans in the Persian Period*, eds. Oded Lipschitz and Manfred Oeming (Winona Lake, Ind., 2006): 413–56.

Licht, Jacob. "Taxo, or the Apocalyptic Doctrine of Vengeance." *JJS* 12 (1961): 95–103.

Lieberman, Saul. *Hellenism in Jewish Palestine* (New York, 1962).

———. *Greek in Jewish Palestine* (New York, 1965).

McDonald, Lee Martin, and James A. Sanders, eds. *The Canon Debate* (Peabody, Mass., 2002).

Magness, Jodi. *The Archaeology of Qumran and the Dead Sea Scrolls* (Grand Rapids, Mich., 2002).

Metso, Sarianna. *The Textual Development of the Qumran Community Rule.* STDJ 21 (Leiden, 1997).

Meyers, Carol L., and Eric M. Meyers. *Zechariah 9–14: A New Translation with Introduction and Commentary.* AB 25C (New York, 1993).

Milik, Josef T. *Ten Years of Discovery in the Wilderness of Judaea.* Trans. by John Strugnell (London, 1959).

Morray-Jones, Christopher R. A. "The Temple Within: The Embodied Divine Image and its Worship in the Dead Sea Scrolls and Other Early Jewish and Christian Sources." *SBLSP* 37 (1998): 400–31.

Najman, Hindy. *Seconding Sinai: The Development of Mosaic Discourse in Second Temple Judaism.* JSJSup 77 (Leiden, 2003).

———. "The Symbolic Significance of Writing in Ancient Judaism." In *The Idea of Biblical Interpretation: Essays in Honor of James L. Kugel*, eds. Hindy Najman and Judith H. Newman. JSJSup 83 (Boston, 2004): 139–73.

Newsom, Carol A. "'Sectually Explicit' Literature from Qumran." In *The Hebrew Bible and Its Interpreters.* Biblical and Judaic Studies 1, eds. William H. Propp, Baruch Halpern, and David Noel Freedman (Winona Lake, Ind., 1990): 167–87.

Nickelsburg, George W. E. "An Antiochan Date for the Testament of Moses." In idem, ed. *Studies on the Testament of Moses* (Cambridge, Mass., 1973): 33–7.

———. "Enoch, Levi, and Peter: Recipients of Revelation in the Upper Galilee." *JBL* 100 (1981): 575–99.

———. "Son of Man." In *Dictionary of Deities and Demons in the Bible (DDD)*, eds. Karel van der Toorn, Bob Becking, and Pieter Willem van der Horst (Leiden, 1999): 800–4.

———. *1 Enoch 1: A Commentary on the Book of 1 Enoch, Chapters 1–36, 81–108.* Hermeneia (Minneapolis, 2001).

———. *Resurrection, Immortality, and Eternal Life in Intertestamental Judaism.* HTS 26, expanded ed. (Cambridge, Mass., 2007).

Nickelsburg, George W. E., and Michael E. Stone. *Early Judaism: Texts and Documents on Faith and Piety* (Minneapolis, 2009).

Nickelsburg, George W. E., and James C. VanderKam. *1 Enoch: Vol. 2*. Hermeneia (Minneapolis, 2012): 2–332.

Parente, Fausto. "Onias III's Death and the Founding of the Temple of Leontopolis." In *Josephus and the History of the Greco-Roman Period: Essays in Memory of Morton Smith*, eds. Fausto Parente and Joseph Sievers (Leiden, 1994): 69–98.

Rahmani, L. Y. *A Catalogue of Jewish Ossuaries in the Collection of the State of Israel* (Jerusalem, 1994).

Ramsey, G. W. "Zadok." In *ABD* 6, 1034–6.

Regev, Eyal. "Comparing Sectarian Practice and Organization: The Qumran Sects in Light of the Regulations of the Shakers, Hutterites, Mennonites and Amish." *Numen* 51 (2004): 146–81.

"The Pharisees and Sadducees and the Sacred: Meaning and Ideology in the Halakhic Controversies between the Sadducees and Pharisees." *RRJ* 9 (2006): 126–40.

Riaud, Jean. "Les Thérapeutes d'Alexandrie et l'idéal Levitique." In *Mogilany 1989: Papers on the Dead Sea Scrolls offered in Memory of Jean Carmignac* 2, ed. Zdzisław J. Capera (Krakow, 1991): 221–40.

Roberts, J. J. M. "Melchizedek (11Q13 = 11Qmelch)." In *The Dead Sea Scrolls: Hebrew, Aramaic, and Greek Texts with English Translations. Vol. 6b: Pesharim, Other Commentaries, and Related Documents*, eds. James H. Charlesworth and Henry W. M. Rietz (Tübingen, 2002): 264–73.

Safrai, S., and M. Stern, eds. *The Jewish People in the First Century: Historical Geography, Political History, Social, Cultural and Religious Life and Institutions*. 2 vols. CRINT I.1–2 (Assen, 1974–76).

Saldarini, Anthony J. *Pharisees, Scribes and Sadducees in Palestinian Society: A Sociological Approach* (Grand Rapids, Mich., 1988).

Samuel, Alan E. *Greek and Roman Chronology*. HAW 1.17 (Munich, 1972).

Sanders, E. P. *Judaism: Practice and Belief, 63 BCE–66 CE* (London, 1992).

Schiffman, Lawrence H., and James C. VanderKam, eds. *Encyclopedia of the Dead Sea Scrolls*. 2 vols. (Oxford, 2000).

Schürer, Emil. *The History of the Jewish People in the Age of Jesus Christ (175 B.C.–A.D. 135)*, rev. ed. by Geza Vermes, Fergus Millar, and Martin Goodman. 3 vols. (Edinburgh, 1973).

Schwartz, Daniel, R. "Hasidim in 1 Maccabees 2:42." *SCI* 13 (1994): 7–18.

2 Maccabees. Commentaries on Early Jewish Literature (Berlin, 2008).

Schwartz, Joshua. "Jubilees, Bethel and the Temple of Jacob." *HUCA* 56 (1985): 63–85.

Schwartz, Seth. *Imperialism and Jewish Society: 200 B.C.E. to 640 C.E.* (Princeton, 2001).

Shaked, Shaul. "Iranian Influence on Judaism: First Century B.C.E. to Second Century C.E." In *CHJ. Vol. 1: Introduction: The Persian Period*, eds. W. D. Davies and Louis Finkelstein (Cambridge, 1984): 308–25.

Sievers, Joseph. "Josephus, First Maccabees, Sparta, the Three Haireseis — and Cicero." *JSJ* 32 (2001): 241–51.

Smith, Morton. "The Description of the Essenes in Josephus and the Philosophumena." *HUCA* 29 (1958): 273–313.

"Jewish Religious Life in the Persian Period." In *CHJ*. Vol. 1: *Introduction: The Persian Period*, eds. W. D. Davies and Louis Finkelstein (Cambridge, 1984): 219–78.

Palestinian Parties and Politics that Shaped the Old Testament, 2nd ed. (London, 1987).

Stern, Ephraim. *Archaeology of the Land of the Bible. Vol. 2: The Assyrian, Babylonian, and Persian Periods* (New York, 2001).

Stone, Michael E. "Judaism at the Time of Christ." *Scientific American* 228 (1973): 80–7.

"Apocalyptic, Vision or Hallucination?" *Milla-wa-Milla* 14 (1974): 47–56.

"Lists of Revealed Things in Apocalyptic Literature." In *Magnalia Dei: The Mighty Acts of God: Essays on the Bible and Archaeology in Memory of G. Ernst Wright*, eds. Frank M. Cross, Werner E. Lemke, and Patrick D. Miller (New York, 1976): 414–54.

Scriptures, Sects and Visions: A Profile of Judaism from Ezra to the Jewish Revolts (Philadelphia, 1980).

"Apocalyptic Literature." In *Jewish Writings of the Second Temple Period*. CRINT 2.2, ed. Michael E. Stone (Assen/Philadelphia, 1984): 383–441.

"Three Transformations in Judaism: Scriptures, History, and Redemption." *Numen* 32 (1985): 218–35.

"Eschatology, Remythologization, and Cosmic Aporia." In *The Origins and Diversity of Axial Age Civilizations*, ed. S. N. Eisenstadt (Albany, 1986): 241–51.

"A Reconsideration of Apocalyptic Visions." *HTR* 96.2 (2003): 167–80.

"The Book(s) Attributed to Noah." *DSD* 13 (2006): 4–23.

Ancient Judaism: New Visions and Views (Grand Rapids, Mich., 2011).

Stone Michael E., Aryeh Amihay, and Vered Hillel. *Noah and His Book(s)*. SBLEJL 28 (Leiden, 2010).

Stone, Michael E., and Jonas C. Greenfield. "Prayer of Levi." *JBL* 112 (1993): 247–66.

Talmon, Shemaryahu. "Calendars and Mishmarot." In *Encyclopedia of the Dead Sea Scrolls* 1, eds. L. H. Schiffman and J. C. VanderKam (Oxford, 2000): 108–17.

Taylor, Joan E. *Jewish Women Philosophers of First-Century Alexandria: Philo's 'Therapeutae' Reconsidered* (Oxford, 2003).

"The Classical Sources on the Essenes and the Scrolls Communities." In *The Oxford Handbook of the Dead Sea Scrolls*, eds. Timothy H. Lim and John J. Collins (Oxford, 2010): 173–99

Tcherikover, Victor. "Palestine under the Ptolemies (A Contribution to the Study of the Zenon Papyri)." *Mizraim* 4–5 (1937): 9–90.

Hellenistic Civilization and the Jews (Philadelphia, 1959).

Tov, Emanuel. *The Greek Minor Prophets Scroll from Nahal Hever (8 HevXIIqr; The Seiyâl Collection I)*. DJD 8 (Oxford, 1990).

Trebolle Barrera, Julio C. "A 'Canon within a Canon': Two Series of Old Testament Books Differently Transmitted, Interpreted and Authorized." *RevQ* 19 (2000): 383–99.

VanderKam, James C. *The Dead Sea Scrolls Today* (Grand Rapids, Mich., 2010).

"Daniel 7 in the Similitudes of Enoch (*1 Enoch* 37–71)." In *Biblical Traditions in Transmission: Essays in Honour of Michael A. Knibb*. JSJSup 11, eds. Charlotte Hempel and Judith Lieu (Leiden, 2006): 291–307.

Victor, Royce M. *Colonial Education and Class Formation in Early Judaism: A Postcolonial Reading* (London, 2010).

Wacholder, Ben Zion. *Eupolemus: A Study of Judaeo-Greek Literature*. HUCM 3 (Cincinnati, 1974).

Wills, Lawrence M. *The Jew in the Court of the Foreign King: Ancient Jewish Court Legends* (Minneapolis, 1990).

Winston, David. "The Iranian Component in the Bible, Apocrypha, and Qumran: A Review of the Evidence." *HR* 5 (1966): 183–216.

Yarbro Collins, Adela. *Cosmology and Eschatology in Jewish and Christian Apocalypticism.* JSJSup 50 (Leiden, 1996).

4

POST-70 JUDAISM IN JUDEA AND THE NEAR EAST

HAYIM LAPIN

The period between 70 CE and the Muslim conquests of the seventh century in the Near East saw the formulation of lasting features of Jewish ritual and practice. During this time, the authoritative legal texts, scriptural exegeses (*midrash*) and translations (*targum*), liturgical structures, and the basic liturgical calendar were all worked out in ways that would be adopted and perpetuated for centuries afterward. We know of these developments almost exclusively through the literary legacy of the rabbinic movement. For this reason, as well as for their traditional authority, rabbinic texts and traditions have been at the center of historiography on late antique Judaism.

To the surprise of nonspecialists (and some specialists), for much of the period under discussion, rabbis played rather marginal and geographically circumscribed roles. But the story of the rabbinic movement is part of larger developments in the complex and sometimes elusive history of late antique Judaism. Our goal in this chapter is to establish three main points about late antique Judaism: (1) In the first century, Jews already had a long history of porous boundaries within the non-Jewish settings they inhabited. If, by the end of our period, Jewish communities had higher and more articulated boundaries, the process requires explanation in terms of both the specific history of Jews in the Near East and the broad transformation of late antique religion. (2) We should resist the impulse to subordinate the fundamental diversity of Judaism in Late Antiquity to a "common Judaism." Common practices, institutions, or symbols that do emerge in our evidence thus require explanation in terms of the cultural work of Jews and others in creating commonality. Finally, (3) synagogues and emergent rabbinism, among the two best-documented developments in late antique Judaism in the Near East, underscore an increasing tendency toward high cultural boundaries between Jews and non-Jews from within Jewish communities. However, both can only be fully understood within the broader landscape of late antique society and religion.

The population of Jews in the Roman and Parthian empires at the end of the first century was almost certainly denser in the "fertile crescent" that linked Palestine, the Levant, Syria, and Mesopotamia than it was either in the plateau of Persia or in the western Mediterranean.[1] By the end of our period, there were also Jews in Arabia, particularly the Hijaz and Yemen.[2] At the start of the revolt of 66 CE in Palestine, Jews constituted a sizeable majority of the inland population of Palestine although not of the coastal cities, and were not necessarily a majority in the territories historically controlled by Judea on the eastern side of the Jordan (particularly in the cities).

The suppression of two revolts and the punitive measures that followed cost lives and prompted emigration. Some scholars have claimed a precipitous slide in the Jewish population in Palestine; a recent revisionist treatment has argued that the more significant transformation was the collapse of "Judaism."[3] By the fourth century, Jews were particularly concentrated (and predominated) in a small region south of Judea proper and in the eastern Galilee and the western "Upper" Golan. By the end of Antiquity, some Jews in Palestine, especially in most cities, lived as minorities within their immediate environs much as in the diaspora, while others, perhaps most, lived in ethnic enclaves.

Anecdotal literary evidence about the diaspora suggests that Jews in the Roman Near East lived as minority populations in cities and towns. In Mesopotamia before the first century CE, there existed a sizeable Jewish population that ancient and modern writers sometimes trace to the Judeans expelled in the sixth century BCE (2 Kings 25; Jeremiah 52). Antiochus III is said to have resettled Babylonian Jews in Asia Minor and Herod to have done the same in Batanaea.[4] In Late Antiquity, information is heavily weighted toward central and southern Iraq (from the Babylonian Talmud), but northern regions had significant, if less well-attested

---

[1] See the survey in E. Schürer, *History*, rev. ed. G. Vermes, et al. 3.1, 5–17. For northern Mesopotamia, see Segal, "Jews in Northern Mesopotamia"; Drijvers, "Jews and Christians."

[2] Newby, *Jews of Arabia*. Medinan Jews: Lecker, "Muḥammad"; Yemen: idem, "Conversion"; both reprinted in *Jews and Arabs*.

[3] Avi-Yonah, *Jews of Palestine*, 15–25; Schwartz, *Imperialism*, 103–10 and *passim*. See now Leibner, "Settlement."

[4] Josephus, *Ant.* 12.147–53; 17.23–31.

populations.[5] According to Josephus, in the Parthian period Jews lived in cities, much as in the Roman empire; the Babylonian Talmud may reflect a more dispersed Mesopotamian Jewish population in the Sasanian period. The apparent urbanism of Jews may represent the bias of our literary sources and the greater epigraphic profile of cities. In some parts of southern Syria (although generally in areas with limited urbanization in Late Antiquity), there is epigraphic evidence for synagogues in villages or other noncities.[6] In addition, Nawe was known both to rabbis and to Eusebius as a "city" east of the Golan with a predominantly Jewish population, suggesting the possibility of Jewish enclaves outside Palestine as well.[7]

Absolute numbers of Jews are unknown. Statistics provided by Philo (over a million Jews in Egypt [*Flacc.* 46]) or Josephus (innumerable myriads in Mesopotamia [*Ant.* 11.133]) are unreliable. The conventional estimates, ranging from four to eight million in the first century (7–13 percent of the population in the Roman empire) would most likely require demographic in-migration, or what scholars of Judaism tend to call, imprecisely, "prose-lytism." Even a far more conservative number of, say, one million (less than 2 percent of the population, although more concentrated and visible in the East) presupposes a rate of growth higher than one might expect from a premodern population over a substantial period of time.[8]

If the increase and spread in population were a result solely of repro-ductive growth, we would need to explain how Jews maintained a higher reproduction rate than expected – and higher than that of their diaspora neighbors – in both the diaspora and Palestine across very different settings in the Hellenistic and Roman periods. An alternative hypothesis is that Jewish communities grew through the slow but regular incorporation of non-Judeans into their numbers. Expansion of "Judaism" in Palestine in the Hasmonean period and later had its own complex dynamic, involving military conquest and political dominance, which was disrupted by the revolts against Rome.[9] As for the diaspora, there is anecdotal and epigraphic

[5] Gafni, *Babylonian Jewry*; idem, "Babylonian Jewry"; Neusner, *History*; Oppenheimer, *Rome and Babylon*; *Babylonia Judaica*; Segal, "Jews of Northern Mesopotamia"; Becker, "Anti-Judaism." On the size of the Jewish population in Sasanian Mesopotamia, see Beer, *Babylonian Amoraim*, 22–3, n. 14.

[6] *IJO* III Syr 34–41.

[7] Eusebius, *Onom.* 136.1, ed. Klostermann. See also *t. Shebi.* 4:8; *y. Dem.* 2:1, 22d; *IJO* III Syr 35–36 (54–56).

[8] Four to four and one-half million: Harnack, *Mission*, I, 8–12; eight million: Baron, *Social and Religious History*, I, 167–71, 370–2, n. 7. See also Juster, *Juifs*, 209–210; Simon, *Verus Israel*, 33–4; and criticism in McGing, "Population." Growth and proselytism: Feldman, *Jew and Gentile*, 293. My hypothetical one million merely doubles a conservative estimate of the Jewish population in Palestine in the first century CE.

[9] Smith, "Gentiles."

evidence for conversion to Judaism in the Near East both before and after 70 CE.[10] But growth through in-migration need not require or be mistaken for a "Jewish mission." It may simply mean that as religious associations, Jewish communities were able to absorb new members faster than they lost them through assimilation. Cultic devotion or philosophical interest, and a dose of exoticism, account for some new recruits in Hellenistic cities.[11] Recalling, however, that military colonists and war captives, enslaved or freed, dominate the accounts of diaspora origins,[12] we should also allow for more mundane incentives: marriage and family connections, community-provided services, and mutual aid (a feature of Hellenistic religious associations) traveling along established social networks.

This model of diaspora origins and maintenance has significance for understanding the late antique religious landscape that Jews in the Near East inhabited. It implies a role for Jews in the earliest spread of Christianity, as noted already by Harnack, and reasserted more recently by Stark and Hopkins, and not merely for the demographic reasons cited by them.[13] Without Jews and their social networks, one is left to wonder what kind of hearing this alien "new religious movement" would have received.[14]

The formation of more rigid ethnic and religious boundaries between Jews and others in Late Antiquity has partly to do with the specific history of Jews in this period. Long before Constantine, the outbreak and suppression of two revolts in Palestine in 66 and 132 CE, the interest of Roman emperors in regulating circumcision if not conversion, and the apparent state fiscal interest in determining who was eligible for the punitive *didrachmon* tax may all have contributed to the perception of Jews (also held by Jews themselves) as a distinct category of Roman subject.[15] Josephus points to unrest and hostility to Jews in the cities of Syria during and after the revolt of 66–74.[16] With the important exception of the (connected?) uprising of Jews in the territories of Parthian Mesopotamia newly conquered by

---

[10] Material for the later period is collected in Feldman, *Jew and Gentile*, 383–415. See also Goodman, *Mission*.

[11] See Isis (Plutarch, *Is. Os.*) or the Hermetic Corpus (Fowden, *Egyptian Hermes*).

[12] For example, Barclay, *Jews*, 20–2, 233, 261, 289–90.

[13] Harnack, *Mission*, ch. 1; Stark, *Rise*, 3–28; Hopkins, "Christian Number," 212–16.

[14] See the assimilation of Noah to the symbolic repertoire of Apamea in Phrygia (on which see also van der Horst in Chapter 12 of this volume).

[15] First Judean revolt (66 CE): Schürer (rev. Vermes), *History*, 1, 484–513; Bar Kokhba revolt (132): H. Eshel, "Bar Kokhba Revolt," 105–27; Roman restrictions on circumcision/conversion: *Dig.* 48.8.11 (Modestinus, citing a ruling of Antoninus Pius); Paulus, *Sententiae* 5.22.3–4, with Linder, *Jews*, nos. 1, 6; *didrachmon* tax and possible state interest in defining who was Jewish: Goodman, *Mission*, 121–6. Rabbinic tradition remembers the period of the Bar Kokhba revolt as one of persecution (*shemad*).

[16] Josephus, *J. W.* 2.461–80; 7.41–2, 54–62, 110–15.

Trajan, the Jews in the Near East seem to have avoided the massive outbreaks of violence that had devastating effects on the Jewish populations of
Egypt, Cyrene, and Cyprus in 115–17.[17] Punitive policies during or following
the Trajanic revolts cannot be excluded although these are ill attested.[18] If
there were episodes of persecution after 117 or after the Bar Kokhba revolt
of 132–35, analogy with persecution of Christianity suggests that these need
not in the long run have resulted in diminution of numbers (or even in
the slowing of recruitment from the outside). For both Jews and non-Jews,
however, they may well have accentuated Jewish "alterity."

Later developments further defined boundaries: Christianization of the
Roman empire; the increasing centrality of Zoroastrianism in official practices of the Sasanian state; the concomitant marking out of specific political
and religious places for Jews in the wider society; and, at least in the later
Roman context, increasing legal marginalization. Hardening of existing
internal divergences within Jewish communities may also have helped to
rewrite the boundaries between Jews and others in Late Antiquity. Debates
within Jewish communities over theology, eschatology, or membership
("conversion") may have contributed to sharpening divergence between
Judaism and Christianity.[19] This sharpening of boundaries should not be
overstated; at the end of the fourth century, it was much clearer to John
Chrysostom than to the Antiochene Christians against whom he railed.[20]
However, the phenomenon of mutually exclusive and highly bounded religious communities was also, paradoxically, a feature of late antique society
and consequently a measure of how Jews in Late Antiquity made up part
of the larger society.[21]

RELIGION OR ETHNIC PRAXIS: THE QUESTION
OF A COMMON JUDAISM

Thus far we have surveyed Jews. Analyzing the historical development of
"Judaism" – the overlapping clusters of descent, practice, belief, onomastics, language, and symbols that scholars use to identify an individual,

[17] Revolts and military action 115 (or 116) to 117: Pucci Ben Zeev, *Diaspora*.
[18] See the assignment of Lucius Quietus to Palestine, *SHA Hadrian* 5.8 (Stern, *GLAJJ* 2.618–19,
no. 510); the story of Pappos and Lulianos (Julianos) in Laodicea (if about Trajan), *Sipra*, Pereq 10:5,
99d; *y. Shebi.* 4:2, 35a-b and parallels; and the scholion of *Megillat Ta'anit* to 12 Adar (Lurya, ed.
189–90; No'am, ed. 117–18); see Pucci Ben Zeev, *Diaspora*, 99–119 (texts); 240–3 (discussion). For an
attempt to claim extensive persecution of Jews in the Roman Empire see Baer, "Israel."
[19] For example, Boyarin, *Radical Jew*; idem, *Border Lines*, but see my reservations on the latter in
"Boyarin, Critical Assessment."
[20] John Chrysostom, *Adv. Iud.* (*PG* 48); translation in Harkins, *Discourses*. In general, see Millar,
"Christian Emperors."
[21] R. Lim, "Christian Triumph"; Stroumsa, *La fin*, 147–86.

an artifact, or a community as "Jewish" – poses problems of its own. Although the term is inevitably anachronistic, it is still useful to ask: Was Judaism a "religion"?[22] In the period under review, the Mediterranean and Near Eastern world saw the emergence and spread of forms of individual identity and group association best described as "religions" in the modern sense. Christianity, Manichaeism, and later, Islam created primary identification through voluntary but exclusive adherence to a set of rituals, practices, and beliefs shared with other members and valued conformity to the group's values over broader societal, familial, or political norms.

Was Judaism a "religion" in the way that ancient Christianity was? The common answer is generally negative. Belonging in Judaism was ethnic; adherence flowed from membership (descent), not membership from voluntary adherence. Jews certainly were known and knew themselves to have peculiar beliefs and practices. But we would be hard put to define Judaism in every case *as* the belief in the one god, worshipped in a discrete set of ways (Sabbath rest, avoidance of pork, etc.), without also including a specific national or ethnic myth (exodus from Egypt, revelation, covenant, etc.) that locates Judaism and Jewishness in an ethnic identity.[23] This is because "Judaism" as a social formation both before 70 CE and after was complex. It was the distinctive beliefs and practices of the Judeans in their ancestral home, as practiced by a Jewish ethnos in a far-flung diaspora as well, but membership in the ethnos was not limited to those who shared common ancestry with their "brethren."[24]

Yet there are reasons to think that the ethnic definition of Judaism (what *Ioudaioi* do, believe, etc.) does not fully capture the experience or identification of ancient Jews. Conversion stories may give the best insight. In his account of Izates of Adiabene's conversion to Judaism (presumably in the 30s CE), Josephus has Izates assume that only circumcision would assure that he was Jewish (*Ant.* 20.38). However, what is principally at issue is not adoption into a community of ethnic Jews, but devotion to God after the Jews' ancestral manner (20.34, 41) or being brought over to their laws (*nomous*) (20.36) while practicing more or less alone. Moreover, for a time Izates followed the advice of one Ananias that God would forgive his failure to be circumcised for his own personal safety; a decision "to adhere to the ancestral practices of the Jews (*ta patria tōn Ioudaiōn*)" was "more

---

[22] Asad, *Genealogies*, 27–54, esp. 40–3; and for the period under discussion, Boyarin, *Border Lines*, 11; Satlow, "Defining Judaism," 837–60. See now Schwartz, "How Many Judaisms," 208–238.

[23] For the variety of types of identification, see Collins, *Between Athens*.

[24] Here, it is best to bracket the problem of "God-fearers" as a different kind of affiliation to the Jewish God. See Mitchell, "Theos Hypsistos," and van der Horst in Chapter 12 of this volume.

authoritative than circumcision" (20.41–42).[25] This, from a contemporary of the author of Acts about an older contemporary of Paul, suggests the possibility that the debates over proselytizing, circumcision, and belonging as they are described in Acts for first-century Christian groups may well have been "intra-Jewish" debates that also occurred in other Jewish communities.

Joseph and Aseneth, a text that may come from late antique Syria, describes the individual spiritual transformation of an Egyptian woman (the wife of the biblical Joseph) through direct divine intervention.[26] A paradigmatic description of "conversion" by a gentile, the text can also be read as a model of preelection, prayer, and revelatory illumination that applies to born Jews as well. An artificially sharp dichotomy between a Pauline, gentile Christianity of conversion and commitment and an ethnic Judaism of birth with a penumbra of converts and/or semiconvert "god-fearers" seems out of place at least in the first century, and may have continued to be so.

Intersecting the ethnos-or-religion dichotomy at several points is a second dichotomy of a single "Judaism" over against multiple "Judaisms." The plural "Judaisms" provides a necessary corrective against a tendency to harmonize fundamental differences in practices or beliefs among diverse Jewish groups. Unfortunately, there are no clear criteria as to what constitutes a "Judaism" as opposed to variation within a broader category. Although the impulse to identify identity groups with surviving or reconstructed texts has merit, it is rarely more than guesswork and risks treating in isolation indicators of a fluid cultural landscape.

The evidence for a diverse but fundamentally unitary "common Judaism" linking Jewish communities is impressive. However, the approach is marred by an inevitable circularity in how it selects and interprets data that are already distinctively "Jewish," such as synagogues, burial inscriptions with Jewish symbols or names, or literature that identifies its authors or audience as Jewish.[27]

---

[25] Accounts of fifth- and sixth-century conversions to Judaism by dynasts in southern Arabia, in which joining to the Jewish ethnos in the conventional communal sense does not fully apply and may be relevant in this context. See Newby, *Jews of Arabia*, 33–48; Tabari, 1, 901–6, 919–20, 924–6; trans. Bosworth, *History of al-tabarī* V, 165–72, 194–5, 202–4; Ibn Hisham, *Sīra*, 1, 12–24; trans. Guillaume, *Life*, 7–12, 17–18.

[26] Kraemer, *Aseneth*, 225–93, tentatively ascribing the text to the fourth century and Syria, leaning also toward identifying the text as Christian. Kraemer's is a revisionist reading in all three respects. The text is more conventionally seen as Jewish, considerably earlier, and from Egypt; for example, Collins, "Joseph and Aseneth."

[27] "Common Judaism" was coined by Sanders, *Judaism*, 46–9 and *passim*, followed subsequently by, for example, Rutgers, *Jews in Late Ancient Rome*, 206–9 and Fine, *Holy Place*; idem, *Art* (for the latter

VARIETIES OF JEWISH RELIGIOUS EXPERIENCE:
DIVERSITY AND COHERENCE

In many respects, Jews adhered to social norms current in the regions they inhabited. In Palestine and Iraq, rabbinic marriage norms and other social conventions may mirror broader Roman and Sasanian conventions, respectively.[28] The Jews of Arabia known to early Islamic tradition were embedded in the kin-based groupings ("tribes," "clans") of the other Arabs with whom they interacted.[29]

The experience of Jews where they formed substantial ethnic enclaves likely differed from those who inhabited cities and villages as resident minorities. Palestine contained the best-attested and (probably) largest of these enclaves, and these are not merely the survival of pre-70 settlement. Between 70 and 400 CE, the geographical distribution of Jews in Palestine underwent a dramatic transformation and, in the Golan at least, a specifically Jewish enclave may have formed and grown in Late Antiquity.[30] The Judaism of central and southern Mesopotamia richly attested in the Babylonian Talmud has features one might expect from an enclave population.[31]

Purpose-built synagogues are first attested archaeologically in Palestine centuries after synagogues developed in the diaspora, and in a deeply Christianized provincial context (see later discussion). The floors of some of those Palestinian synagogues were decorated with a depiction of the God of Israel, represented as the sun god Helios surrounded by the signs of the zodiac; one synagogue piously refrains from depicting the God of Israel himself, while another replaces depiction of the heavens with their textualization.[32] In Parthian or Sasanian Mesopotamia, synagogues also had images: the Babylonian Talmud discusses the presence of a statue, *'andrata*, that was seemingly a fixture of the Shap we-Yateb synagogue in Nehadea and that posed for rabbis the problem of seemingly idolatrous practice (*b. Rosh Hash.* 24b; *b. 'Abod. Zar.* 43b).

---

cf. Lapin, "Review"). "Judaisms" is the contribution of Neusner. See, for example, Neusner, *Judaic Law*, 9, characteristically insisting on texts as discrete "systems" (the volume specifically responds to Sanders: see especially 289–95). Collins, *Between Athens*, analogously treats writings of diaspora Jews from Antiquity as independent articulations of identity.

[28] Satlow, *Jewish Marriage*; Kalmin, *Sage*.

[29] Newby, *Jews of Arabia*, 50–5. Medinan Jews: Lecker, "Muḥammad."

[30] Lapin, *Economy, Geography*, 190; but the matter must be reevaluated in light of Ben David, *Settlement*; Leibner, "Settlement."

[31] Gafni, *Babylonian Jewry*.

[32] See Hachlili, "Zodiac." For textualization, see the synagogue inscription from En Gedi, Naveh, *Mosaic*, no. 70. My interpretation is influenced by Goodman, "Jewish Image," and Schwartz, *Imperialism*, 248–63.

In Palmyra, a doorway was inscribed with Deuteronomy 6:4–9 (the *Shema*) along with other verses (Deut 7:14, 15; 28:5), suggesting an apotropaic understanding of their purpose. The practice clearly parallels, but differs from, the rabbinic institution of *mezuzah* and has analogies in Samaritan practices and "magical" texts.[33] The same city has yielded an inscription of one Sadiq Kahana (or "the priest") b. Eleazar in the temple of Bel; a lamp with a fairly common late antique Jewish temple motif (menorahs flanking a conch) in the temple of Allat; and an inscribed altar whose dedicator may have been Jewish.[34] Participation by Jews in sacrificial practices,[35] and perhaps in non-Jewish temples, cannot be excluded. The Qur'an attributes to Jews the belief that ʿUzayr (Ezra) is the son of God just as the Messiah (Jesus) is for Christians and accuses them of treating their teachers (*aḥbārahum*) as "lords" in addition to God alone (9:30–31). Other early Islamic traditions attribute to Jews eschatological knowledge, magical expertise, and apparently some rabbinic traditions and practices.[36]

As with other late antique groups, some Jews gathered in conventicles of intense study and ritual practice. Rabbinic circles might well be described in this way for much of the period covered in this chapter, and even more certainly those responsible for the Hekhalot texts. It has long been conventional to distinguish between a nonascetic Judaism and the ascetic impulse guiding early Christianity (especially in Syria). Yet the Tosepta, a third-century rabbinic text, presents an unresolved exchange involving ben Azzai (early second century), who does not marry "for my soul yearns for Torah; let the world be maintained by others" (*t. Yeb.* 8:7); it also describes a debate in which a first-century rabbi convinces "abstainers" (*perushim*, sometimes to be read "Pharisees") that they must not abstain from meat and wine in perpetual mourning for the destroyed

---

[33] *IJO* III Syr 44–7; Naveh, Shaked, *Magic Spells*, 28–30.

[34] Temple of Bel: *IJO* III Syr48 (the assigned seventh-century date, after Christian re-use of the space as a church had ceased, is possible but circular); lamps in Temple of Allat: *IJO* III, 76; Krogulska, "Lampe," Ass'ad, Ruprechtsberger, *Palmyra*, 354–5, no. 110 (fourth century); inscribed altar: *CIS* ii.3.1.4029, cited *IJO* III, 78 (father of dedicator's is Yaʿaqob, Jacob).

[35] See the temple of Onias in Egypt (destroyed 73 or 74, Josephus, *J. W.* 2.433–6) or Josephus's description of the Jewish "place" at Sardis (*Ant.* 14.260); and the apparent practice of slaughtering of a paschal lamb in the manner of a sacrifice, the latter clearly post-70 (*t. Beṣah.* 2:15; and apparently presupposed by *m. Pes.* 10:4–5). See also Jerome, *Ep.* 112.15 (CSEL 55, 384), assuming Jerome is thinking of "real" Jewish practice. The emperor Julian argued that Jewish lay slaughtering was still "sacrificial" (*Gal.* 305D-306A; but cf. 351D; Stern, *GLAJJ* 2.513–48, no. 481a); might this reflect contemporary understandings? Jewish "pagan" sacrifice at Caesarea: *t. Ḥul.* 2:13.

[36] Eschatological knowlege: *Sīra* of Ibn Hisham, generally before the break between Muhammad and the Medinan Jews; magic by a Jewish *ḥabr*, 1, 352; trans. Guillaume, *Life*, 240. Rabbinization (?), *Sīra* 1, 383, 387; trans. Guillaume, 260, 263; see also 1, 659, trans. Guillaume, *Life*, 442.

Temple (*t. Soṭ.* 15:11–12).[37] In both cases, the texts seem to respond to tendencies within rabbinic circles or in groups with which rabbis were in conversation.[38]

Like late antique Christians and others, some Jews engaged in pilgrimage or religious tourism. One tradition in both the Palestinian and the Babylonian Talmud implies an itinerary and practices (for example, "the place where they take dust") associated with visiting the ruins of Babylon (*y. Ber.* 9:1, 12d; *b. Ber.* 57b). In Mamre in southern Palestine, Jews, Christians, and "Hellenes" (that is, pagans including local Arabs) were in the fifth century still visiting a religious festival and fair, where they had reportedly worshipped commingled – this in spite of the earlier intervention of the emperor Constantine, who at the behest of his mother-in-law provided a Christian basilica and separate enclosure and prohibited "pagan" sacrifice.[39] As late as the 380s, there was a Jewish shrine at Daphne that was the site of overnight ritual incubation (John Chrysostom, *Adv. Jud.* 1.6.2 [*PG* 48.852]).

Some Jews were influenced by eschatological expectations: a return by "Moses" to Crete reportedly led to suicidal enthusiasm (Sozomen, *Hist. eccl.* 7.38). There is also evidence for the continued survival, even flourishing, of apparent "hybrids."[40] Forms of "Jewish Christianity" – groups that understood themselves as Christian, but also as descendants of Jews and practitioners of some "Jewish law" – seem to have survived in Beroea in Coele-Syria and elsewhere in the region at least until the end of the fourth century, if we may believe Jerome and Epiphanius.[41] In addition, magic as practiced by Jews developed considerably in Late Antiquity in the form of magical amulets, bowls, and recipe books. Amulets from the vicinity of Palestine in Jewish Aramaic range from the invocation of biblical verses

---

[37] Compare the other views expressed in the whole pericope. See also *b. B. Qam.* 59b (symbolic mourning); *Pesiq. Rab.* 34.2, 3 ("mourners of Zion"; early medieval); *t. Ber.* 3:25; *m. Soṭ.* 15:11 (polemics against abstemiousness, *perishut*). Regarding sexual abstinence, see also the rabbinic discussions of Moses's prophetic celibacy in Koltun-Fromm, *Hermeneutics,* ch. 7 (in preparation; my thanks to Koltun-Fromm for making available portions of her manuscript); eadem, "Zipporah's Complaint"; Boyarin, *Carnal Israel,* 159–65.

[38] Note also Koltun-Fromm's argument that sexual renunciation in encratite Syrian Christianity was innovative in the third century, *Hermeneutics,* ch. 5. The alternative view that sees Tatian as instrumental still leaves these developments contemporary to rabbinic traditions.

[39] Sozomen, *Hist. eccl.* 2.4. See further Kofsky, "Mamre."

[40] See also Mitchell, "Theos Hypsistos" on late-antique evidence for hypsistarians and *theosebeis;* and van der Horst in Chapter 12 of this volume.

[41] Epiphanius, *Pan.* 29.7.7; Jerome. *Vir. ill.* 3 (claiming personal knowledge); texts in Klijn and Reinink, *Patristic Evidence* 172/173, 210/211; see also Kinzig, "Non-Separation," 27–35. For the Pseudo-Clementines, *Ascension of Isaiah,* and *Testaments of the Twelve Patriarchs,* see Baumgarten, "Literary Evidence"; Frankfurter, "Beyond 'Jewish Christianity'"; and Reed, "'Jewish Christianity.'"

alone to appeals to angelic and divine powers. Both amulets and bowls (from Mesopotamia) include the occasional appropriation of rabbinic personalities.[42] One literary collection of rituals, *Sepher ha-razim* (*Book of Secrets*), written in literate, biblically informed Hebrew, embeds such rituals in a distinctly "Jewish" cosmology, and includes an incantation for visionary experience that echoes at once the visionary incantations of late antique Jewish mystical texts (*Hekhalot* or *Merkabah* texts), Greek magical papyri, and philosophical and paraphilosophical interest in divinatory practices in Late Antiquity.[43]

Diversity, indeed differentiation, is what we should expect from a highly dispersed population in a period of substantial political, cultural, and religious change. Despite this, a significant body of evidence suggests coherence of Judaism around ethnic models of identity and around patterns of belief, practices, and symbolic representation with strong family resemblances among them (a "common Judaism"). It would be a mistake to view this coherence as simple, inevitable, or natural. It should be understood rather as the historical result of sustained cultural work.

In the pre-Christian and Christian Roman empire and in Sasanian Iraq, imperial, provincial, urban, and local actors performed some of that cultural work through formal and informal legal, religious, and social classification. But much of this work was carried out by Jews themselves. On the model of the propagation of Christianity, with its coalescence of a far-flung "proto-orthodoxy" in the second century and an episcopal network in the third, we should perhaps assume noncentralized intercommunication through emissaries and correspondence that might support and foster consolidation. Direct evidence for such intercommunication is very limited. There are, of course, traditions involving letter-writing in rabbinic literature.[44] Indirect evidence of communication appears in inscriptions where *archisynagogai* are honored or noted for their dedications in synagogues not their own.[45] Others include the emergence of the rabbinic movement in Babylonia and the tradition of *nahote*, rabbis who moved back and forth between Palestine and Babylonia; the appearance on an inscription from Bayt al Khadr in Yemen of a list of the twelve priestly

---

[42] For texts, see Naveh and Shaked, *Amulets*; idem, *Magic Spells*; Levene, *Corpus*, all with discussion of earlier publications. Verses alone: Naveh and Shaked, *Amulets*, Amulet. 13; cf. no. 15; *Magic Spells*, Amulet 22. Rabbinic personalities: Naveh and Shaked, *Amulets*, Bowl 5.5, 6; Levene, *Corpus*, no. 156.7. See also De Jong in Chapter 1 of this volume.

[43] Margulies (Margaliot), *Sefer Ha-Razim*; the invocation of Helios appears at 4.61–3.

[44] Hezser, *Jewish Literacy*, 267–75. See, for example, letters of recommendation discussed on p. 269 (*y. Ḥag.* 1:8, 76c [*y. Ned.* 10:8, 42b]; *y. Moʾed Qaṭ.* 3:1, 81c).

[45] E.g., *IJO* III Syr5, 54, although interpretation of both is disputed.

courses and their assignment to towns generally in the Galilee (the motif is otherwise epigraphically attested only in Palestine); and the utilization in the fourth-century *Apostolic Constitutions* of a liturgical formulary that echoes that of developing rabbinic statutory prayers.[46]

We can also identify attempts to centralize coherence. While the Jerusalem temple stood, it played this type of consolidating role for diaspora communities through the Temple priesthood, the custom of sending monetary tribute, the practice of pilgrimage, and the role of the high priests in acting as patrons of Jewish communities. In the wake of the Temple's destruction, there were no groups or institutions that could "naturally" step into such a role, although it is possible that rabbis and groups of priests or others tried. It is only in the fourth century or perhaps the third that the descendants of the Gamalielide patriarchs experienced some measure of success in extending their role as patrons and arbiters in diaspora communities, a role that is attested in inscriptions, Roman law, and literary texts.[47]

ASPECTS OF THE DEVELOPMENT OF JEWISH "RELIGION" IN THE NEAR EAST AFTER 70 CE

Let us turn, finally, to some features of Jewish practice that seem to be products of the post-70 era and help to mark out the higher boundaries that Jewish communities forged and maintained in Late Antiquity. We may begin with synagogues. This may seem surprising: Josephus, the Gospels, and Acts attest to synagogues before 70 in Jerusalem, Caesarea, Tiberias, Capernaum, Dora, perhaps Nazareth, and in the Near Eastern diaspora in Antioch, Damascus, and Salamis on Cyprus.[48] However, the archaeological attestation for synagogues is almost entirely later, from the latter half of the second century (Dura Europos) onward.[49]

[46] Oppenheimer, *Rome and Babylon*, 418–21; Bayt al Khadr: Degen, "Inscription"; *Apostolic Consitutions* 7.33–38.

[47] Inscriptions: *IJO* I Mac1; possibly Ach51 and *JIWE* I 145. Roman law: *CTh* 16.8.8 (392), 11 (396), 13 (397), 14 (399), 15 (404), 17 (404), 22 (415), 29; 2.1.10 (398), Linder, *Jews*, nos. 20, 24, 27, 30, 32, 34, 41, 53, 28. Literary texts: Julian, *Ad communitatem Iudaeorum* (Stern, *GLAJJ* 2.559–68, no. 486a); Libanius, *Epistulae* (texts in Stern, *GLAJJ* 2.589–603, nos. 496–504). See Schwartz, "Patriarchs"; cf. Levine, "Status," building on his own earlier contributions.

[48] Jerusalem: Acts 6:9 (assuming a building); Caesarea: Josephus, *J.W.* 2.285–92; Tiberias: Josephus, *Life*, 277, 280, 293; Capernaum: Mark 1:21 (Luke 4:33); Luke 7:4; John 6:49; by implication Mark 3:1 (Matt. 12:9; Luke 6:6); Nazareth: Luke 4:16 (cf. Mark 6:1; Matt. 13:54); Antioch: Josephus, *J.W.* 7.44; Damascus: Acts 9:1, 20: Salamis: Acts 13:5. Binder, *Temple Courts*, 156–61, 263–69; Levine, *Ancient Synagogue*, 42–69.

[49] Outside of Palestine: Roth-Gerson, *Jews of Syria*, 245–80. Dura-Europos dates from the mid-third century CE, with a previous phase in use as a synagogue from the late second century, White,

The widespread establishment of monumentalized synagogues paid for by donors whose names are commemorated in inscriptions coincides with broad reorganizations of religion and piety in the late antique eastern Roman empire, where the emergence of liturgies and architectures constructed Jewish, Christian, Manichaean, and ultimately Muslim congregations.[50] The spread of synagogues beyond larger towns reflects an emerging village culture in the Roman Near East.[51] In Palestine it dates largely to the fifth and sixth centuries, the period during which rural Palestinian churches, whose architectural features they echo, were also becoming numerous.

Within that broader framework, synagogues emerged as places where people articulated a communal ideology. Inscriptions wished that donors "be remembered for good." An inscription from Apamea honoring donors ends with the words "peace and mercy upon all your sanctified people."[52] Apamea in particular demonstrates the coexistence within communities of both a communitarian ethos that distributed blessings upon all members and also a dedicatory practice of contributing for the *sotēria*, "wellbeing," or perhaps in this late fourth-century context "salvation," of individuals, family members, and apparently whole households.[53]

While sharing much stylistically with the roughly contemporaneous Durene Mithraeum, baptistry, and other non-Jewish cultic sites, the synagogue at Dura manifests on its decorated walls two important features of communal formation that will be important in later Middle Eastern Jewish religious culture as well: the thematization of the Jerusalem temple, and with it a visual rhetoric of communal religious distinctiveness, even superiority.[54] The assimilation of synagogues to the Temple is a significant theme

---

Social Origins, 2, 276–87. For Palestine see Levine, "First-Century Synagogue"; Levine, *Synagogue*, 42–69. Pre-70 synagogues in Palestine: the Theodotus inscription from Jerusalem (*CIJ* 2, 1440; Lifshitz, *Donateurs*, no. 79; dating and context remain contested); modified "synagogue" spaces in rebel-occupied Masada and Herodium (special cases, reflecting the ideology of their occupiers); public building at Gamla (none of the remains implies a ritual function); and a number of proposed synagogues in Judea (Jericho: Netzer, "Synagogue"; Kh. Umm el 'Umdan: Levine, "First-Century Synagogue, 86–87; Qiryat Seper: Levine, *Ancient Synagogue*, 65–66). For the late dating of Palestinian synagogues, see, for example, Jodi Magness, "Question"; and "Heaven on Earth." (I cannot accept her position on either priests or the identity of Helios.)

[50] Stroumsa, *La fin*, esp. 148–49.

[51] Grainger, "Village Government"; Tate, *Les Campagnes*.

[52] See Lapin, "Palestinian Inscriptions," esp. 257–66. "Remembered [for good]": for example, Naveh, *Mosaic, s.vv. dkr, zkr*; Roth-Gerson, *Greek Inscriptions*, 1, 4, 7, 17; Weiss, Netzer, *Promise*, 41–2 and photos throughout; *IJO* III Syr23, Syr35, Syr83?, Syr84, Syr90–2. Apamea: *IJO* III Syr54, cf. Syr53.

[53] *IJO* III Syr53–71, esp. Syr61–6, Syr71.

[54] Elsner, "Cultural Resistance," esp. 281–99. For distinctiveness or superiority, see, for example, the depiction of Yahweh's victory over Dagon (represented as two (!) local deities, ibid. plate 12, with Goodenough, *Jewish Symbols*, 10, 74–80).

in the decorations and epigraphy from synagogues in Late Antiquity. As with much else, the evidence is overwhelmingly from Palestine; however, all or part of the synagogue at Apamea is called a *naos* (temple), and one of the sites preserving a list of priestly courses is in Yemen. Emerging liturgical poetry (generally from the end of our period) in particular expresses temple and priestly themes, and its performance may reflect a kind of sacerdotalization of worship.[55] We can say little about the actual liturgy of synagogues outside the rabbinized circles that produced and preserved surviving liturgical poetry. Early rabbinic traditions about liturgy suggest that rabbis were working with and standardizing forms, rubrics, and motifs, including some that may have predated 70 CE and were not unique to rabbis. The appropriation of a manifestly Jewish liturgical tradition in *Apostolic Constitutions* 7.33–8 suggests either a certain degree of rabbinization in a Greek liturgical context in Syria before the fourth-century date of the *Constitutions*, or a shared, if geographically dispersed and bilingual, tradition about how to construct at least some elements of a liturgy.

An explicit rhetoric of cultural distinctiveness is easiest to trace in the most significant Jewish literary corpus of Late Antiquity, that of the emerging rabbinic movement. Rabbis constructed an identity for Jews that was in but not of the Roman or Sasanian kingdoms, whose governments could be called simply *ha-malkut*, "the kingdom" (with or without the adjective "evil"). Although the rabbinic movement had a prehistory connected to Second Temple Jewish "sectarianism" and especially to Pharisees, the movement as we know it took shape only after 70. The development of textual and ideological consolidation is attested only in the second century, with the editing of the Mishnah in about 200 CE.[56] The production in something like their present form of the other corpora of classical rabbinic texts took shape after 200, with continued production of some significant texts after the Arab conquests of Palestine and Mesopotamia in the seventh century.[57] As historical artifacts, rabbinic texts are difficult to pin down. Palestinian texts do not cite rabbis or events any later than about 360 CE; the Babylonian Talmud extends the range of sages cited to about 500 CE. However, all draw on preexisting sources, and the durations of the collection and editing processes are unknown.

A mildly revisionist reconstruction understands the rabbinic movement as emerging first as a group of pietists and ritual experts who, in the third

---

[55] Temple themes: Fine, *Holy Place*, 95–126 (Palestine), 127–58 (Diaspora). Liturgy and Temple: Swartz, "Sage"; Yahalom, *Poetry*, esp. 107–36.

[56] This section draws on Lapin, "Origins."

[57] Discussion and bibliography in Stemberger and Strack, *Introduction*.

and fourth centuries, congregated in a number of cities of Palestine.[58] Also by sometime in the third century, a parallel rabbinic movement had set down roots in Mesopotamia.[59] The Babylonian Talmud, the sole, but monumental, "classical" product of rabbinic circles in Mesopotamia, draws heavily on Palestinian sources. Use of invented Palestinian traditions for a variety of rhetorical reasons implies an extended period of intellectual dependence. However, already within classical texts and especially in the early medieval (and largely Babylonian-oriented) Geonic literature, the relative authority of the two traditions and the superiority of Babylonia were matters of polemic and debate. In both Mesopotamia and Palestine, the rabbinic "movement" consisted of informal circles of masters, disciples, and other adherents who seem to have drawn their membership from wealthy, literate strata of the Jewish population.[60] By late Talmudic times, Babylonian rabbis may have developed formal academies.[61] Nothing quite so formalized seems to have existed in Palestine (although "academies" of some sort did develop) before the late Umayyad or early Abassid period.

The classical rabbinic texts reflect a situation in which rabbis and their legal norms or traditions did not dominate "Judaism" and in any case presuppose that rabbis were localized in certain areas of Sasanian Mesopotamia and Roman Palestine. Broadly speaking, the general piety that rabbis espoused and promoted made use of elements that preceded the origins of the movement, and were not unique to rabbis: male infant circumcision, a calendar whose major festivals were biblical, reading of scripture and particularly the Torah, synagogues, some liturgical formulae and structures, sabbath observance, and food avoidances. At the hands of rabbis, however, these features were given elaborate, specific treatments that do not necessarily reflect general Jewish practices. In certain cases, notably sabbath law, rabbinic innovations may mark this group's piety as peculiar, if not in fact "sectarian."[62] Rabbinic cases from Palestine largely reflect the concerns of adherents in the absence of means of enforcement, while Babylonian traditions about nonrabbis reflect a distinct corporate rabbinic identity verging on the separatist.[63] Yet by the early Middle Ages,

---

[58] Lapin, "Rabbis and Cities."

[59] Gafni, *Babylonian Jewry*; the essays on Babylonia collected in Oppenheimer, *Rome and Babylon*; and Gafni, "Babylonian Jewry"; Goodblatt, "Babylonian Academies"; Kalmin, "Babylonian Talmud," all in *CHJ* IV; and Elman, "Middle Persian Culture."

[60] Hezser, *Social Structure*; Lapin, "Rabbis and Cities"; Beer, *Babylonian Amoraim*.

[61] Rubenstein, *Culture*; cf. Becker, *Fear of God* on the Christian school of Nisibis.

[62] See Fonrobert, "Separatism" on rabbinic *'erub*.

[63] See, for example, Rubenstein, *Culture*, 123–42, Kalmin, *Sage*, 27–50, with differing emphases. The characterization as "separatist" or sectarian is my own, however.

rabbis seem to have imposed substantial hegemony on Jewish communities. In the Near East, full-fledged "rabbinization" may well be the product of the early Islamic period. However, there are several markers of an extension of rabbinic authority and influence beyond limited circles of adherents, particularly between the end of the fourth century and the early seventh. These markers include some limited knowledge on the part of Church Fathers of rabbinic tradition; Justinian's Novella 146 prohibiting some form of rabbinic teaching; inscriptions more or less unambiguously referring to rabbis; the Qu'ran's reference to rabbis and *ḥaberim* (*aḥbār*); the emergence of a corpus of liturgical poetry within the Palestinian Jewish community that is dependent upon rabbinic exegetical traditions; references to rabbinic personalities in magical bowls; and the development of a subrabbinic genre of Jewish mystical texts that appropriates the authority and power of early rabbinic figures.[64]

There are important political and social dimensions to even the limited rabbinization that we can trace at the end of our period of study. Roman law increasingly treated Jews as an administrative body with its own institutions, which it directly or indirectly authorized.[65] Legislation about the Palestinian Patriarchate, for instance, included laws giving them charge over *primates*, who in turn had charge over aspects of the religious or administrative life of Jewish communities.[66] Although these laws did not designate rabbis in such religious or juridical roles, rabbis in Palestine, with a long history of interaction with the Patriarchs, may have been among those with access to appointments or commissions where they could apply their influence. Nor did the discontinuation of the Patriarchate remove either the tendency to mark out Jews as legally and administratively distinct (some of these laws were carried over into the *Codex Iustinianus* of 529 and 534) or the opportunity for rabbis to fill communal roles.

From the point of view of Jewish "religion," rabbis and late antique synagogues of the Middle East contributed to the practices, beliefs, and identity of Jewish communities. Synagogues provided Jewish communal spaces

[64] Schwartz, "Rabbinization"; and Lapin, "Aspects" (forthcoming). Church Fathers: Jerome, *Ep.* 121.10 (CSEL 56, ed. Hilberg, 48–49); *Comm. Matth.* (22:23), (CCL 77, 204–5); *Comm. Isa.* 3, to 8:11–15 (CCL 73, 116–17, esp. 117); Epiphanius, *Pan.* 15.2.1; 33.9.3–4 (GCS, ed. Holl, 1, 209–10, 459). See also Augustine, *Contra adv. leg. et proph.* 2.1.2 (CCL 49, ed. K.-D. Daur, 87–88). Justinian, *Novella* 146: Linder, *Jews*, no. 66. Inscriptions: Naveh, *Mosaic*, 49 (Rehov); plausibly also 6 (Dabbura); *JIWE* I, 186 (Venosa, Italy). "Rabbi" existed as a general title in inscription, and cannot automatically be assumed to refer to the rabbinic movement (Cohen, "Epigraphical Rabbis") as in *IJO* III Syr36 (not in Cohen), Cyp1 (Cohen's no.7). Qu'ran: 5:44, 63; see also 3:79; 9:30–1, and above n. 39. Liturgical Poetry: Yahalom, *Poetry*. Magical bowls: see above. Mystical texts: Swartz, *Scholastic Magic*.
[65] Linder, "Roman Rule"; idem, *Jews*, 67–78, 87–9.
[66] See n. 50; see, esp., *CTh* 16.8.8 (392), 2.1.10 (398), 16.8.29 (Linder, *Jews*, nos. 20, 28, 53).

by drawing, not insignificantly, on the same technologies of architecture and ritual as Christian churches. Rabbinic tradition offered a totalizing alternative Jewish discursive world, the wherewithal to ritually enact and embody that world through festivals, liturgy, fasts, and dietary practices, a cognitive map of that world ranging from an anthropology and ethnography of Jews and gentiles to a mildly eschatological theodicy, and a disciplinary culture that fashioned rabbis through a lifetime of study and piety into lay experts who could navigate that discursive world. Yet rabbis, too, performed their cultural work in part by utilizing strategies (not least those of philosophical schools) appropriated from the wider world they inhabited.

In the end, one legacy of Late Antiquity for medieval Christian and Muslim societies was a consensus shared by Jews and non-Jews alike that Jews were not entirely part of society. A larger dynamic in the late antique formation of orthodoxies, and with it state engagement in religious enforcement, was the stigmatization as "foreign" of practices and groups of long standing within society and communal self-segregation. Late antique Jews contributed to their own alienation and demonstrated, paradoxically, that even in their cultural stigmatization Jews were firmly embedded within the late antique religious landscape they inhabited.

BIBLIOGRAPHY

Primary

Eusebius. *Das Onomastikon der biblischen Ortsnamen*, ed. E. Klostermann. GCS 11.1 (Leipzig, 1904).

Frey, J. B. *Corpus Inscriptionum Iudaicarum (= CIJ)* (Rome, 1936).

Harkins, Paul W. *John Chrysostom: Discourses against Judaizing Christians* (Washington, D.C., 1979).

Ibn Hishām, Abd al-Malik. *Kitāb sīrat Rasūl Allāh. Das Leben Muhammed's, nach Muhammed ibn Isḥāk*, ed. F. Wüstenfeld (Göttingen, 1858–60; repr. Frankfurt am Main, 1961).

The Life of Muhammad, trans. A. Guillaume (Oxford, 1955).

Lifshitz, Baruch. *Donateurs et fondateurs dans les synagogues juives, répertoire des dédicaces grecques relatives à la construction et à la réfection des synagogues*. CahRB 7 (Paris, 1967).

Linder, Amnon. *The Jews in Roman Imperial Legislation* (Detroit and Jerusalem, 1987).

Lurya, Ben Zion. *Megillath Ta'anith, with Introductions and Notes* (Jerusalem, 1964).

Margalioth, Mordecai. *Sepher Ha-Razim: A Newly Recovered Book of Magic from the Talmudic Period* (Jerusalem, 1966).

Naveh, Joseph. *On Mosaic and Stone* (Heb.) (Jerusalem, 1978).

Naveh, Joseph, and Shaul Shaked. *Amulets and Magic Bowls: Aramaic Incantations of Late Antiquity* (Jerusalem, 1985).

Magic Spells and Formulae: Aramaic Incantations of Late Antiquity (Jerusalem, 1993).

No'am, Vered. *Megillat Taḥanit: Versions, Interpretation, History* (Heb.) (Jerusalem, 2003).

Noy, David. *Jewish Inscriptions of Western Europe (= JIWE)* (Cambridge, 1993).

Noy, David, and Hanswulf Bloedhorn. *Inscriptiones Judaicae Orientis (= IJO)*. Vol. 3: *Syria and Cyprus. TSAJ* 102 (Tübingen, 2004).

Roth-Gerson, Lea. *Greek Inscriptions from the Synagogues in Eretz-Israel* (Heb.) (Jerusalem, 1987).

The Jews of Syria as Reflected in the Greek Inscriptions (Heb.) (Jerusalem, 2001).

Stern, Menahem. *Greek and Latin Authors on Jews and Judaism (= GLAJJ)* (Jerusalem, 1974–84).

Ṭabarī. *Annales quos scripsit Abu Djafar Mohammed ibn Djarir at-Tabari cum aliis edidit M. J. De Goeje* (Leiden, 1879–1901; repr. 1964).

The Sāsānids, the Byzantines, the Lakhmids, and Yemen, ed. and trans. C. E. Bosworth (Albany, 1999).

Secondary

Asad, Talal. *Genealogies of Religion: Discipline and Reasons of Power in Christianity and Islam* (Baltimore, 1993).

Assa'd, Khaled, and Erwin M. Ruprechtsberger. *Palmyra, Geschichte, Kunst und Kultur der syrischen Oasenstadt: einführende Beiträge und Katalog zur Ausstellung* (Linz, 1987).

Avi-Yonah, Michael. *The Jews of Palestine: A Political History from the Bar Kokhba War to the Arab Conquest* (Oxford, 1976).

Baron, Salo W. *A Social and Religious History of the Jews* (New York, 1952).

Baumgarten, Albert I. "Literary Evidence for Jewish Christianity in the Galilee." In *Galilee in Late Antiquity*, ed. L. I. Levine (New York/Jerusalem, 1992): 39–50.

Becker, Adam H. "Anti-Judaism and Care for the Poor in Aphrahat's Demonstration 20." *JECS* 10 (2002): 305–27.

The School of Nisibis and Christian Scholastic Culture in Late Antique Mesopotamia (Philadelphia, 2006).

Becker, Adam H., and Annette Y. Reed, eds. *The Ways That Never Parted: Jews and Christians in Late Antiquity and the Early Middle Ages* (Tübingen, 2003).

Beer, M. *The Babylonian Amoraim: Aspects of Economic Life* (Ramat Gan, 1974).

Ben David, H. "Settlement in the 'Lower Golan'," diss. Bar-Ilan University, 1999.

Binder, Donald D. *Into the Temple Courts: The Place of the Synagogues in the Second Temple Period* (Atlanta, 1999).

Bonz, Marianne P. "The Jewish Donor Inscriptions from Aphrodisias: Are They Both Third-Century, and Who Are the Theosebeis?" *HSCP* 96 (1994): 281–99.

Botermann, Helga. "Griechisch-jüdische Epigraphik: zur Datierung der Aphrodisias Inschriften." *ZPE* 98 (1993): 184–94.

Boyarin, Daniel. *Carnal Israel: Reading Sex in Talmudic Culture* (Berkeley, 1993).

A Radical Jew: Paul and the Politics of Identity (Berkeley, 1994).

Chaniotis, Angelos. "The Jews of Aphrodisias: New Evidence and Old Problems." *SCI* 21 (2002): 209–42.

Cohen, Shaye J. D. "Epigraphical Rabbis." *JQR* 72 (1981): 1–17.

Collins, John J. *Between Athens and Jerusalem: Jewish Identity in the Hellenistic Diaspora*, 2nd ed. (Grand Rapids, Mich., 1999).

"'Joseph and Aseneth:' Jewish or Christian?" *JSP* 14 (2005): 97–112.

Degen, R. "An Inscription of the Twenty-Four Priestly Courses from Yemen." *Tarbiz* 42 (1973): 302–4.

Drijvers, Hans J. W. "Jews and Christians at Edessa." *JJS* 36 (1985): 88–102.

Edwards, Douglas R., and Lee I. Levine. "The First Century Synagogue: Critical Reassessments and Assessments of the Critical." In *Religion and Society in Roman Palestine: Old Questions, New Approaches*, ed. D. R. Edwards (London, 2004): 70–112.

Elman, Yaakov. "Middle Persian Culture and Babylonian Sages: Accommodation and Resistance in the Shaping of Rabbinic Legal Tradition." In *The Cambridge Companion to the Talmud and Rabbinic Literature*, eds. Charlotte E. Fonrobert and Martin S. Jaffee (Cambridge, 2007): 165–97.

Elsner, Jaś. "Cultural Resistance and the Visual Image: The Case of Dura Europos." *CP* 96 (2001): 269–304.

Eshel, Hanan. "The Bar Kokhba Revolt, 132–135." In *CHJ*. Vol. 4: *The Late Roman-Rabbinic Period*, ed. S. T. Katz (Cambridge, 2006): 105–27.

Even Shemuel, Yehuda. *Midreshe ge'ulah* (Heb.) (Jerusalem, 1953).

Feldman, Louis H. *Jew and Gentile in the Ancient World: Attitudes and Interactions from Alexander to Justinian* (Princeton, 1993).

Fine, Steven. *This Holy Place: On the Sanctity of the Synagogue during the Greco-Roman Period* (Notre Dame, 1997).

  Art and Judaism in the Greco-Roman World: Toward a New Jewish Archaeology (Cambridge, 2005).

Fonrobert, Charlotte E. "From Separatism to Urbanism: The Dead Sea Scrolls and the Origins of the Rabbinic 'Eruv." *DSD* 11 (2004): 43–71.

Fowden, G. *The Egyptian Hermes: A Historical Approach to the Late Pagan Mind*, 2nd ed. (Princeton, 1993).

Frankfurter, David. "Beyond 'Jewish Christianity': Continuing Religious Sub-Cultures of the Second and Third Centuries and Their Documents." In *The Ways That Never Parted: Jews and Christians in Late Antiquity and the Early Middle Ages*, eds. A. H. Becker and A. Y. Reed (Tübingen, 2003): 131–44.

Gafni, Isaiah. *Babylonian Jewry and Its Institutions in the Period of the Talmud* (Heb.) (Jerusalem, 1986).

  "The Political, Social, and Economic History of Babylonian Jewry, 224–638." In *CHJ*. Vol. 4: *The Late Roman-Rabbinic Period*, ed. S. T. Katz (Cambridge, 2006): 792–820.

Gilbert, Gary. "Jews in Imperial Administration and Its Significance for Dating the Jewish Donor Inscription from Aphrodisias." *JSJ* 35.2 (2004): 169–84.

Goodblatt, David. "History of the Babylonian Academies." In *CHJ*. Vol. 4: *The Late Roman-Rabbinic Period*, ed. S. T. Katz (Cambridge, 2006): 821–39.

Goodenough, Erwin R. *Jewish Symbols in the Greco-Roman Period* (Princeton, 1953).

Goodman, Martin. *Mission and Conversion: Proselytizing in the Religious History of the Roman Empire* (Oxford, 1994).

Grainger, John D. "Village Government in Roman Syria and Arabia." *Levant* 27 (1995): 179–95.

Harnack, Adolf von. *The Mission and Expansion of Christianity in the First Three Centuries*, trans. James Moffatt, 2nd German edition, with additions from the 4th German edition, 1924, http://ccat.sas.upenn.edu/rs/rak/courses/535/Harnack/bko-TOC.htm. March 30, 2007.

Hezser, Catherine. *The Social Structure of the Rabbinic Movement in Roman Palestine.* TSAJ 66 (Tübingen, 1997).

Jewish Literacy in Roman Palestine. TSAJ 81 (Tübingen, 2001).

Hopkins, Keith. "Christian Number and Its Implication." *JECS* 6 (1998): 185–226.

Irshai, Oded. "Confronting a Christian Empire: Jewish Culture in the World of Byzantium." In *Cultures of the Jews: A New History*, ed. D. Biale (New York, 2002): 180–220.

Juster, Jean. *Les Juifs dans l'Empire romain: leur condition juridique, économique et sociale* (Paris, 1914).

Kaegi, Walter E. "Initial Byzantine Reactions to the Arab Conquest." *CH* 38 (1969): 139–49.

Kalmin, Richard. *The Sage in Jewish Society of Late Antiquity* (London, 1999).

"The Formation and Character of the Babylonian Talmud." In *CHJ.* Vol. 4: *The Late Roman-Rabbinic Period*, ed. S. T. Katz (Cambridge, 2006): 840–76.

Katz, Steven T., ed. *The Cambridge History of Judaism (=CHJ).* Vol. 4: *The Late Roman-Rabbinic Period* (Cambridge, 2006).

Kinzig, Wolfram. "'Non-Separation': Closeness and Co-Operation between Jews and Christians in the Fourth Century." *VC* 45 (1991): 27–53.

Klijn, A. F. J., and G. J. Reinink. *Patristic Evidence for Jewish-Christian Sects.* NovTSup 36 (Leiden, 1973).

Koltun-Fromm, Naomi. "Zipporah's Complaint: Moses Is Not Conscientious in the Deed! Exegetical Traditions of Moses' Celibacy." In *The Ways That Never Parted: Jews and Christians in Late Antiquity and the Early Middle Ages*, eds. A. H. Becker and A. Y. Reed, 283–306.

Hermeneutics of Holiness. In preparation.

Kraemer, Ross S. *When Aseneth Met Joseph: A Late Antique Tale of the Biblical Patriarch and His Egyptian Wife, Reconsidered* (New York, 1998).

Lapin, Hayim. "Palestinian Inscriptions and Jewish Ethnicity in Late Antiquity." In *Galilee through the Centuries*, ed. E. M. Meyers (Winona Lake, Ind., 1999): 239–68.

"Rabbis and Cities: Some Aspects of the Rabbinic Movement in Its Greco-Roman Environment." In *The Talmud Yerushalmi and Graeco-Roman Culture II*, eds. P. Schäfer and C. Hezser (Tübingen, 2000): 51–80.

"Daniel Boyarin, a Critical Assessment." *Hen* 28 (2006): 19–24.

"The Origins and Development of the Rabbinic Movement in the Land of Israel." In *CHJ.* Vol. 4: *The Late Roman-Rabbinic Period*, ed. S. T. Katz (Cambridge, 2006): 206–29.

"Review of Steven Fine, Art and Judaism in the Greco-Roman World: Toward a New Archaeology." http://www.bookreviews.org/pdf/5001_5267.pdf.

Lecker, Michael. "Muḥammad at Medina: A Geographical Approach." *JSAI* 6 (1985): 29–62.

"The Conversion of Ḥimyar to Judaism and the Jewish Banu Hadl of Medina." *WO* 26 (1995): 129–36.

Lehto, Adam. "Moral, Ascetic, and Ritual Dimension to Law-Observance in Aphrahat's Demonstrations." *JECS* 14 (2006): 157–81.

Leibner, Uzi. "Settlement and Demography in Late Roman and Byzantine Eastern Galilee." In *Settlements and Demography in the Near East in Late Antiquity*, eds. Ariel S. Lewin and Pietrina Pellegrini (Pisa, 2007): 105–30.

Levene, Dan. *A Corpus of Magic Bowls: Incantation Texts in Jewish Aramaic from Late Antiquity* (London, 2003).

Levine, Lee I. "The Status of the Patriarchate in the Third and Fourth Centuries: Sources and Methodology." *JJS* 47 (1996): 1–32.

The Ancient Synagogue: The First Thousand Years (New Haven, 2000).

Lim, Richard. "Christian Triumph and Controversy." In *Late Antiquity: A Guide to the Postclassical World*, eds. Glen W. Bowersock, Peter R. L. Brown, and Oleg Grabar (Cambridge, 1999): 196–212.

Linder, Amnon. "Roman Rule and the Jews during the Period of Constantine." *Tarbiz* 44 (1975): 95–143.

Magness, Jodi. "The Question of the Synagogue: The Problem of Typology." In *Judaism in Late Antiquity. Pt. 3: Where We Stand: Issues and Debates in Ancient Judaism. Vol. 4. The Special Problem of the Synagogue*, eds. A. J. Avery-Peck and J. Neusner (Leiden, 2001): 1–48.

"The Date of the Sardis Synagogue in Light of the Numismatic Evidence." *AJA* 109 (2005): 443–75.

"Heaven on Earth: Helios and the Zodiac Cycle in Ancient Palestinian Synagogues." *DOP* 59 (2006): 7–58.

McGing, Brian. "Population and Proselytism: How Many Jews Were There in the Ancient World?" In *Jews in the Hellenistic and Roman Cities*, ed. John R. Bartlett (London, 2002): 88–106.

Millar, Fergus. "Christian Emperors, Christian Church and the Jews of the Diaspora in the Greek East, CE 379–450." *JJS* 55 (2004): 1–24.

Mitchell, Stephen. "The Cult of Theos Hypsistos between Pagans, Jews, and Christians." In *Pagan Monotheism in Late Antiquity*, eds. Polymnia Athanassiadi and Michael Frede (Oxford, 1999): 81–148.

Netzer, Ehud. "A Synagogue from the Hasmonean Period Recently Exposed in the Western Plain of Jericho." *IEJ* 49 (1999): 203–21.

Neusner, Jacob. *A History of the Jews in Babylonia*. 5 vols. (Leiden, 1965–70).

Newby, Gordon D. *A History of the Jews of Arabia: From Ancient Times to Their Eclipse under Islam* (Columbia, S.C., 1988).

Oppenheimer, Aharon. *Between Rome and Babylon: Studies in Jewish Leadership and Society* (Tübingen, 2005).

Oppenheimer, Aharon, et al. *Babylonia Judaica in the Talmudic Period* (Wiesbaden, 1983).

Pucci Ben Zeev, Miriam. *Diaspora Judaism in Turmoil, 116/117 C.E.: Ancient Sources and Modern Insights* (Leuven, 2005).

Reed, Annette Y. "'Jewish Christianity'" after the 'Parting of the Ways': Approaches to Historiography and Self-Definition in the Pseudo-Clementines." In *The Ways That Never Parted: Jews and Christians in Late Antiquity and the Early Middle Ages*, eds. A. H. Becker and A. Y. Reed (Tübingen, 2003): 189–232.

Rubenstein, Jeffrey L. *The Culture of the Babylonian Talmud* (Baltimore, 2003).

Sanders, E. P. *Judaism: Practice and Belief, 63 BCE–66 CE* (London/Philadelphia, 1992).

Schürer, Emil, Géza Vermès, and Fergus Millar. *The History of the Jewish People in the Age of Jesus Christ (175 B.C.–A.D. 135)* (Edinburgh, 1973).

Schwartz, Seth. "Rabbinization in the Sixth Century." In *Talmud Yerushalmi and Graeco-Roman Culture*. Vol. 3, ed. Peter Schäfer (Tübingen, 2002): 55–69.

Imperialism and Jewish Society: 200 B.C.E. to 640 C.E. (Princeton, 2004).

"How Many Judaisms Were There? A Critique of Neusner and Smith on Definition and Mason and Boyarin on Categorization." *JAJ* 2 (2011): 208–38.

Segal, Judah B. "The Jews of Northern Mesopotamia before the Rise of Islam." In *Studies in the Bible Presented to M. H. Segal*, eds. Jehoshua M. Grintz and Jacob Liver (Jerusalem, 1964): 32–64 (English section).

Simon, Marcel. *Verus Israel: A Study of the Relations between Christians and Jews in the Roman Empire (135–425)*, trans. H. McKeating (Oxford, 1986).

Smith, Morton. "The Gentiles in Judaism 125 B.C.E.-C.E. 66." In *CHJ*. Vol. 3: *The Early Roman Period*, eds. William Horbury, W. D. Davies, and John Sturdy (Cambridge, 1999): 192–249.

Stark, Rodney. *The Rise of Christianity: A Sociologist Reconsiders History* (Princeton, 1996).

Stemberger, Günter, and Herman L. Strack. *Introduction to the Talmud and Midrash*, trans. Markus Bockmuehl. 2nd ed. (Minneapolis, 1996). [Contains guides to editions and translations.]

Stroumsa, Guy G. *La fin du sacrifice: les mutations religieuses de l'antiquité tardive* (Paris, 2005).

Sudilovsky, Judith. "Maccabean Hometown Uncovered? Modi'in Excavations Yield Synagogue, Tombs." *BAR* 29 (2003): 18.

Swartz, Michael D. *Scholastic Magic: Ritual and Revelation in Early Jewish Mysticism* (Princeton, 1996).

"Sage, Priest, and Poet: Typologies of Religious Leadership in the Ancient Synagogue." In *Jews, Christians, and Polytheists in the Ancient Synagogue*, ed. Steven Fine (London, 1999): 101–17.

Tate, Georges. *Les Campagnes de la Syrie du Nord du IIe au VIIe Siècle: un exemple d'expansion démographique et économique dans les campagnes à la fin de l'antiquité* (Paris, 1992).

Urman, Dan, and Paul V. M. Flesher. *Ancient Synagogues: Historical Analysis and Archaeological Discovery* (Leiden, 1995).

Weiss, Ze'ev, and Ehud Netzer. *Promise and Redemption: A Synagogue Mosaic from Sepphoris.* (Jerusalem, 1996).

White, L. Michael. *The Social Origins of Christian Architecture* (Philadelphia, 1996).

Yahalom, Joseph. *Poetry and Society in Jewish Galilee of Late Antiquity* (Heb.) (Tel-Aviv, 1999).

5

CHRISTIANITY IN SYRIA

SIDNEY H. GRIFFITH

The history of Christianity in Syria is a story of how this burgeoning religious movement of Late Antiquity came to take on a distinctively regional dress. Effectively a large frontier zone between the Roman and the Parthian (and later the Persian) empires, Syria was exposed to ever-changing cultural and political influences. While Aramaic, with many regional variations, was the dominant language in this milieu, from the late fourth century BCE onward Greek language and culture also gained a powerful presence. From the last third of the second century BCE, local circumstances allowed the development of the semi-independent kingdom of Edessa. Here the cultivation of the native Aramaic dialect eventuated in the appearance of Syriac, an Aramaic idiom that facilitated the growth of a unique Christian identity in cultural terms, defined largely in reaction to and/or in tandem with Greek thought and religious expression. While inscriptions and other archaeological evidence document the beginnings, for the most part the historical evidence is literary.

EDESSENE CHRISTIANITY

To the north and east of the Roman province of Syria, beyond the Euphrates and just within the borders of the province of Mesopotamia (Persian Osrhoene), lay the city of Edessa. Founded in 304 BCE by the Greek-speaking Seleucus I Nicator, the name Edessa recalled the city of the same name in Seleucus's native Macedonia. Syriac-speaking locals, however, have persistently called the city Ûrhāy.[1] In Parthian times, from around the year 132 BCE onward, the city and its associated territories

---

[1] Harrak, "The Ancient Name of Edessa."

became the kingdom of Edessa, a dignity it preserved until the year 214 CE, when it officially became a Roman colony.[2] In the environs of Edessa, sometime in the early first century CE, developments in the writing of Aramaic began to take the form that in due course would come to be called Syriac. From about the middle of the second century CE until well into Islamic times, Syriac, the standard Aramaic of a large corpus of mostly Christian texts, was, together with Greek, one of the principal vehicles of Christianity in Syria and eastward.[3] Indeed, by the fifth century Syriac and its associated ecclesiastical culture had extended its influence well to the west of the Euphrates.[4]

Culturally, theologically, and eventually jurisdictionally, the Greek-speaking city of Antioch, where "the disciples were for the first time called Christians" (Acts 11:26), exerted an enormous influence throughout Syria, beyond the Euphrates and even beyond the largely Syriac-speaking frontier areas between the Roman and Persian empires.[5] In all probability, Christianity first spread from the milieu of Antioch to the Syriac-speaking environs of Edessa, where Greek had also long been a language of intellectual and religious culture.[6] There too, again in all probability, Aramaic-speaking Christians also came from further to the east, from Persian territories such as the province of Adiabene and southern Mesopotamia, in Babylonia, where Jewish-Christian and other Christian communities had flourished at least from the third century.[7]

In the first decades of the fifth century CE, a now anonymous writer in Edessa, following in the footsteps of Eusebius of Caesarea in his *Ecclesiastical History*, composed the *Doctrina Addai* on the basis of records said to have been preserved in the city's archives. The narrative claims that at Jesus's own behest the disciple Addai was sent by the apostle Thomas immediately after Jesus's death to bring Christianity to Edessa. The text further specifies the city's communion with Rome, by way of its communion with the see of Antioch, and in set speeches espouses the themes of Edessene orthodoxy. While the legendary character of this narrative is

[2] Segal, *Edessa: The 'Blessed City'*; Ross, *Roman Edessa: Politics and Culture on the Eastern Fringes of the Roman Empire, 114–242 CE*.

[3] Van Rompay, "Some Preliminary Remarks on the Origins of Classical Syriac as a Standard Language: The Syriac Version of Eusebius of Caesarea's Ecclesiastical History"; Drijvers and Healey, *The Old Syriac Inscriptions of Edessa and Osrhoene: Texts, Translations and Commentary*, esp. 1–41.

[4] Millar, "Theodoret of Cyrrhus: A Syrian in Greek Dress?"

[5] Wallace-Hadrill, *Christian Antioch: A Study of Early Christian Thought in the East*.

[6] See the review of the pertinent literature in Murray, *Symbols of Church and Kingdom: A Study in Early Syriac Tradition*.

[7] Chaumont, *La Christianisation de l'empire iranien: des origines aux grandes persécutions du IVe siècle*.

clear, it nevertheless preserves the local memory of Edessa's ties with the Christians of Palestine.[8]

Historically reliable evidence for the beginnings of Christianity in Edessa and its environs is scarce. By the time of the Roman emperor Septimius Severus (r.193–211 CE), the Christian community in Edessa was large enough to support a church building of some sort. For the *Chronicle of Edessa* records the memory that in the year 201 CE, the church of the Christians was destroyed by a flood. The same sixth-century chronicle, presumably because of the popularity of his ideas in Edessa, dates the "apostasy" of Marcion to the year 138 CE. It also records the date of the birth of Bar Daysān, the local Christian philosopher, in Edessa in the year 154 CE.[9] Dated around the year 192 CE, the epitaph of Abercius Marcellus, bishop of Hierapolis in Phrygia, mentions the presence of Christians around Edessa. And Julius Africanus (ca.160–240), who in the year 195 CE may have come with Septimius Severus's expedition to Osrhoene, mentions in his *Cesti* or "Embroideries" that he had met Bar Daysān in Edessa.[10]

VARIETIES OF EARLY SYRIAC-SPEAKING CHRISTIANITY

An important Christian figure in the early history of the Syriac-speaking milieu is Tatian the Syrian (ca.160 CE); he says of himself that he was from Assyria,[11] by which he presumably meant northern Mesopotamia. In the works of early Christian heresiographers, Tatian is often accused of the "heresy" of the "Encratites,"[12] that is, ascetical rigorists – a charge that would long echo in accounts of Christianity in Syria. But the most important contribution of Tatian to church life in Syria and Mesopotamia was undoubtedly the *Diatessaron,* a work that he put together while in Rome. The original language of the composition is uncertain, either Greek or Syriac. But in the latter language, which many scholars think was in fact its original language, it had a wide circulation east of the Mediterranean.

---

[8] Griffith, "The *Doctrina Addai* as a Paradigm of Christian Thought in Edessa in the Fifth Century." The Addai legend is continued in stories of his missionary journeys from Edessa into Iraq and beyond, including the adventures of Mar Mari, his disciple. The accounts seem to have the purpose of making a claim for the early influence of Edessene Christianity well into the realms of the Parthians and the Persians. See Chaumont, *La Christianisation de l'empire iranien,* 8–29; see also the important introduction in Ramelli, ed. *Atti di Mar Mari,* esp. 19–144.

[9] Guidi, *Chronica Minora,* I, 2–3.

[10] Julius Africanus, *Cesti,* 1.20.39–53; Griffith, "Beyond the Euphrates in Severan Times: Mani, Bar Daysān, and the Struggle for Allegiance on the Syrian Frontier."

[11] Tatian, *Orat.* 42, ed. Whittaker.

[12] Grant, "The Heresy of Tatian"; Barnard, "The Heresy of Tatian – Once Again."

Although it was officially banned by Bishop Rabbula of Edessa (d.435), its influence was pervasive.[13]

Bishop Rabbula banned the *Diatessaron* in favor of another early literary accomplishment of Syriac-speaking Christians, the production of the so-called *Peshitta* translations of the scriptures into Syriac. The *Peshitta*, or the "simple" version of the Bible in Syriac as it was called from the ninth century onward, seems to have had its roots in the translation of the Torah and other Old Testament books made directly from Hebrew or Aramaic into Syriac and undertaken by Jews in Edessa already in the second half of the second century CE. By the fifth century, the process was complete, and the *Peshitta* itself becomes evidence of the early presence of a broad-based Christianity in the Edessene milieu.[14] In this connection, it is worth recalling the passages in Eusebius of Caesarea's *Ecclesiastical History* referring to the city's archives and to Edessa's participation in early, empire-wide doctrinal and liturgical controversies.[15]

Christian works in Syriac from the early period suggest a significant Christian presence by the Severan period, although there is some controversy over whether or not Syriac was actually their original language. There are, for example, the *Odes of Solomon*, the *Acts of Judas Thomas* (including the *Hymn of the Pearl*), and the *Gospel of Thomas*.[16] But the earliest Syriac writer among the Christians whose name and work we actually know is Bar Daysān (154–222).[17] We learn from Eusebius that Bar Daysān wrote polemical works against the teaching of Marcion of Sinope (d. ca.154), whose ideas had become popular among some people in Edessa, and that Bar Daysān was the author of a system of thought putting together elements from his own world beyond the Euphrates and the philosophy of the Greeks. Epiphanius of Salamis (ca.315–403) wrote in his *Panarion* that Bar Daysān was "a learned man in both Greek and Syriac,"[18] and Ephraem the Syrian called him "the Aramean philosopher."[19] Ephraem also presents Bar Daysān as a successful composer of *madrāshê*,[20] a genre of "teaching songs" in Syriac that became the effective vehicles of his teaching in the

[13] See Peterson, *Tatian's Diatessaron: Its Creation, Dissemination, Significance and History in Scholarship.*
[14] Weitzman, *The Syriac Version of the Old Testament: An Introduction*; Brock, *The Bible in the Syriac Translation.*
[15] See Ross, *Roman Edessa*, 127–8.
[16] For discussion and bibliography, see Murray, *Symbols of Church and Kingdom*, esp. 24–8; Patterson, "The View from Across the Euphrates," 411–31.
[17] Drijvers, *Bardaisan of Edessa*; Teixidor, *Bardesane d'Edesse: la première philosophie syriaque.*
[18] Epiphanius, *Pan.* 56, ed. Holl.
[19] Mitchell, *S. Ephraim's Prose Refutations of Mani, Marcion and Bardaisan*, 2.225.
[20] Ephrem, *Hymns Against Heresies*, 1.11,17; 53.6, ed. Beck.

Aramaic-speaking milieu. This genre was to become the preferred medium
for Ephraem's own teaching, and some modern scholars have suggested
that Bar Daysān had in fact been virtually its inventor in the form in
which Ephraem was to use it so effectively.[21] Bar Daysān is also thought to
have had a significant influence on the teaching of Mani (ca.216–76) and
Manichaeism, a suggestion made not only by modern scholars[22] but by
Ephraem himself. According to Ephraem, Mani, like Bar Daysān, composed *madrāshê*, presumably in Aramaic, in which "he published the fact
that he sold his freedom to his 'companion.'"[23]

Mani and Manichaeism had in fact a purchase in Edessa. Mani
was born near Seleucia-Ctesiphon, the capital of the Persian empire;
Ephraem said he was from Babylon.[24] Mani was religiously nurtured in
the Aramaic-speaking milieu of the Elkasaites, a Judeo-Christian group
in lower Mesopotamia.[25] The backbone of his mature teaching was based
in the epistles of St. Paul; it was gnostic in its inspiration and dualistic
in essence, featuring conflict between darkness and light. Manichaean
adepts, divided into two groups, the "perfect" and the "hearers," worked
to release the particles of light that according to their texts had been
captured by darkness in a primeval conflict. In this effort, they followed in the footsteps of the ancient prophets, the Buddha, Jesus, and
Mani himself.[26] In due course, after many vicissitudes, Manichaeism
spread from Mesopotamia west into the far Roman empire and eastward into Persia and beyond.[27] Mani is said to have addressed one of
his own epistles to a community of his followers in Edessa.[28] When
Ephraem the Syrian spoke of Mani's *madrāshê*, he presumably had in
mind the book of *Psalms and Prayers*, originally composed in Syriac, and
one of the seven works in the official canon of Manichaean scriptures.[29]
By the early fourth century CE, according to some authorities,

[21] McVey, "Were the Earliest Madrāshê Songs or Recitations?"; Griffith, "St. Ephraem, Bar Daysān
and the Clash of *Madrāshê* in Aram: Readings in St. Ephraem's *Hymni contra Haereses*."
[22] See, for example, Wessendonk, "Bardesanes und Mani"; Drijvers, "Mani und Bardaisan: Ein Beitrag
zur Vorgeschichte des Manichäismus"; Aland, "Mani und Bardesanes – zur Entstehung des manichäischen Systems."
[23] Ephraem, *Hymns against Heresies*, 1.16. The reference to Mani's "companion" here is presumably to
the *syzygos*, or "heavenly twin," from whom Mani was said to have received revelations.
[24] Ephraem, *Hymns against Heresies*, 14.8.
[25] Lieu, *Manichaeism in Mesopotamia and the Roman East*.
[26] BeDuhn, *The Manichaean Body: In Discipline and Ritual*.
[27] Lieu, *Manichaeism in the Later Roman Empire and Medieval China: A Historical Survey*. For
Manichaeism in the Sasanian empire, see De Jong in Chapter 1 of this volume.
[28] *The Cologne Mani Codex (P. Colon. Inv. Nr. 4780; 'Concerning the Origin of his Body'*, 50–1, ed.
Cameron and Dewey.
[29] Lieu, *Manichaeism in the Later Roman Empire*, 6.

Manichaeism had already gained a commanding presence in the environs of Edessa.[30]

By the dawn of the fourth century, the teachings of Marcion, Bar Daysān, and Mani, whom the Church of the Roman empire would in due course come to consider heretics, had thus already gained a hearing and a following in Edessa and the Syriac-speaking milieu at large. In a famous essay, Walter Bauer argued that these groups were actually the first Christians of Edessa; those who would come to be called "orthodox" were only organized later, in the days of bishop Qûnâ (r. ca.289–313), the last of the bishops named in the *Doctrina Addai*'s list of founders of the see of Edessa.[31] Significantly for Bauer, the names of both Bishop Qûnâ and Bishop Jacob of Nisibis (d.338) are on the list of attendees at the Council of Nicaea in 325 CE.[32] But Bauer's hypothesis seems unlikely on a number of grounds. Among other things, the teachings of all three groups presume the preexistence of a Christian community with whose views they were in dialogue; there are also references to earlier Christian activity in the larger Syrian milieu.

What is more, it is clear from the sources that in the first quarter of the fourth century, and extending to the beginnings of the fifth century, the controversies that engaged the attention of the Syriac-speaking Christians were for the most part the same religious and political issues that embroiled their coreligionists in the Greek-speaking Roman empire. In this connection, one must recall the fact that as Christianity was spreading in Persia in the third century, and experiencing tension with the Zoroastrian religious authorities, including some persecution, the Persian governmental policies at the same time, in the course of Persian conquests beyond the Euphrates, favored the deportation of a considerable number of Greek-speaking Christians from Roman Syria, even from the environs of Antioch, well into Persian territory and beyond the Tigris, a population shift that had important effects in the history of the church in Persia.[33]

APHRAHAT AND EPHRAEM THE SYRIAN

As it happens, after the time of Bar Daysān, the first important Syriac writers on religious themes whose names we know were from regions to

---

[30] Drijvers, "Addai und Mani, Christentum und Manichäismus im dritten Jahrhundert in Syrien."
[31] Walter Bauer, *Orthodoxy and Heresy in Earliest Christianity*, esp. 33.
[32] Gelzer, Hilgenfeld, and Cuntz, *Patrum Nicaenorum Nomina, Latine, Graece, Coptice, Syriace, Arabice, Armeniace, s.v.*
[33] Chaumont, *La christianisation de l'Empire iranien*; Fiey, *Jalons pour une histoire de l'Église en Iraq*; Brock, "Christians in the Sasanian Empire: A Case of Divided Loyalties."

the east of Edessa: Aphrahat, the "Persian Sage," who lived in northern Mesopotamia, and Ephraem the Syrian, the "Harp of the Holy Spirit," who served the church in Nisibis for most of his life. While little or nothing is known for certain about Aphrahat's biography, his *Demonstrations*,[34] the only writings we have from him, have survived along with the dates of their composition. The first ten of them carry the date of 336/337 CE, numbers 11 to 22 are dated to 344, and number 23 was written in 344/345 CE in the course of a major persecution of Christians in Persia. These dates allow us to suppose that Aphrahat's lifetime spanned approximately the years between 270 and shortly after 345. A number of significant themes emerge from the *Demonstrations* that shed light on the shape of Christianity in the Syriac-speaking milieu in the first half of the fourth century. Immediately evident to even the most casual reader is the biblical focus of the religious discourse; doctrinal themes are developed and their prose *Demonstrations* are composed in a process of scriptural reasoning that is expressed in a tissue of quotations from and allusions to passages in the Old and New Testaments, which are read through the lens of the Gospel. It is a multifaceted typological mode of scriptural reasoning, much akin to the modes of biblical theology to be found in contemporary Greek-speaking Christianity, but without any trace of the idiom of Hellenistic philosophy.[35] They address the major themes of Christian faith and practice, often vis-à-vis what is presented as their Jewish counterparts.[36] Church organization reflected in *Demonstrations* speaks of distinctively Syrian forms of the ascetical life, such as the institution of the "sons and daughters of the covenant" (VI); one *Demonstration* (XIV) is in the form of a letter from a church synod. There is no explicit trace of the theological controversies over Arianism, for example, that would engage Aphrahat's younger contemporary Ephraem, nor is there any hint of a line of thinking that could be traced to earlier figures such as Bar Daysān or Mani. What is distinctive in Aphrahat's expression of Christianity is its Syriac idiom rather than any departure from what in his time was quickly becoming conventional Christianity.

By way of contrast, Ephraem the Syrian (ca.306–73), whose works and thought would long remain authoritative for Syriac-speaking Christians, was embroiled in all the controversies, both religious and political, that

---

[34] Parisot, ed. *Aphraatis Sapientis Persae Demonstrationes;* Bruns, trans. *Aphrahat: Unterweisungen;* Pierre, trans. *Aphraate le Sage Persan: Les Exposés.*

[35] Bruns, *Das Christusbild Aphrahats des Persischen Weise.*

[36] Neusner, *Aphrahat and Judaism: The Christian-Jewish Argument in Fourth-Century Iran;* Koltun-Fromm, "A Jewish-Christian Conversation in Fourth-Century Persian Mesopotamia."

swirled throughout the fourth century in the Great Church.[37] For all but the last ten years of his life, Ephraem lived in Nisibis. There he served the local bishops, of whom Jacob of Nisibis (d.338) was the first. Perhaps a deacon, Ephraem was certainly a "teacher" (*mallpānâ*) and probably an ascetic, a "single man" (*îhîdāyâ*) in the service of the church.[38] He retained this same state in life during his service to the bishop of Edessa in his last decade. Ephraem was a prolific writer in Syriac, with a large number of probably inauthentic works in Greek also attributed to him; the number of pages it takes in the *Clavis Patrum Graecorum* to list the latter is second only to the number of pages it takes to list the works attributed to St. John Chrysostom! For all that, most of the Greek works attributed to Ephraem are more than likely by someone else.[39] His bibliography in his native Syriac is also long and includes all the major genres: prose, rhythmic and rhymed prose, verse homilies (*mêmrê*), "teaching songs" (*madrāshê*), and dialogue poems (*sûgyātâ*).[40] Due to their masterful literary quality and the acuity of the thought expressed in them, Ephraem's works, especially his *madrāshê*, remain classics in the Syriac language.[41] His literary and religious authority is unmatched in the whole Syriac tradition, and many of the works attributed to him were soon translated into the other languages of Late Antiquity: Greek, Armenian, Georgian, Arabic, Slavonic, and Latin.

Historically and politically, the major crisis in Ephraem's life was doubtless the death of the Roman emperor Julian deep in Persian territory in the year 363 CE. Ephraem loathed the emperor, who had renounced Christianity and had promoted the renewal of the old state religion, and composed a series of invective *madrāshê* in view of the slain emperor's catafalque placed before the gates of Nisibis on its return to the Romans.[42] The political consequence of the Roman defeat was the cession of the city of Nisibis to the Persians and the flight of many of its Christians, including Ephraem, to the city of Edessa in Roman territory. For the rest of his life, the frontier between Rome and Persia lay between Edessa and Nisibis, arguably the heartland of the Syriac-speaking peoples. And Ephraem became a vocal

---

[37] Murray, *Symbols of Church and Kingdom*, 3–34; Brock, *The Luminous Eye: The Spiritual World Vision of St Ephrem*; Den Biesen, *Bibliography of Ephrem the Syrian*.

[38] Griffith, "Images of Ephraem: The Syrian Holy Man and his Church."

[39] For overview, see Hemmerdinger-Iliadou, "Éphrem (Les versions). I. Éphrem grec; II. Éphrem latin," cols. 800–19; Den Biesen, *Bibliography*, 23–4.

[40] List of texts, editions, and translations in Den Biesen, *Bibliography*, 22–93.

[41] Survey and detailed study of the literary aspects of Ephraem's works in Den Biesen, *Simple and Bold: Ephrem's Art of Symbolic Thought*.

[42] Griffith, "Ephraem the Syrian's Hymns 'Against Julian': Meditations on History and Imperial Power."

champion in Syria and beyond of both Roman political alignment and Nicene orthodoxy.[43]

Marcion, Bar Daysān, and Mani remained major thinkers in the Syriac-speaking milieu. While Ephraem and Syriac writers after him continued to resist their ideas, they also responded to the challenges posed by the local indigenous religious communities, notably those whom they called *hanpê* in Syriac – that is, devotees of the local deities and their cults[44] – and the Jews, whose communities were widespread in the Syriac-speaking milieu.[45] Against this background, Ephraem, who became a champion of Nicene orthodoxy, arguably did more to advance its cause in Syriac than any other single writer of the fourth century. It is notable in this connection that the theological adversaries whose ideas Ephraem combated in Syriac came from the wider world of the Roman empire and wrote almost exclusively in Greek. This fact is of great significance for almost all the religious texts written in Syriac from the time of Ephraem onward. Indeed, Ephraem's own pedagogical and doctrinal accomplishments consisted largely in expressing artfully and accurately in Syriac ideas and doctrinal formulae that had become widespread first in Greek.

CHURCH-DIVIDING CONTROVERSIES FROM THE FOURTH TO SIXTH CENTURIES

For the most part, church councils convened by the Roman emperors set the agenda for Ephraem[46] and the Syriac writers who came after him, including even those living beyond the Roman frontier in Persia and eastward. Greek writers provoked the calling of these councils by espousing doctrines deemed officially unacceptable; others either inspired and defended the councils' decisions or attacked their decisions in writing.[47] This Greek-inspired agenda is especially visible in ongoing translations of the Greek theologians by Syriac writers and in the theological tracts they composed. Translation thus became an increasingly major factor in Syriac intellectual life from Ephraem's time onward, a phenomenon that would

---

[43] Griffith, "Ephraem, the Deacon of Edessa, and the Church of the Empire," 22–52; idem, "Setting Right the Church of Syria: Saint Ephraem's Hymns against Heresies," 97–114.

[44] Drijvers, *Cults and Beliefs at Edessa.*

[45] Drijvers, "Jews and Christians at Edessa," 350–64; Shepardson, *Anti-Judaism and Christian Orthodoxy: Ephrem's Hymns in Fourth-Century Syria.*

[46] Possekel, *Evidence of Greek Philosophical Concepts in the Writings of Ephrem the Syrian.*

[47] Brock, "From Antagonism to Assimilation: Syriac Attitudes to Greek Learning"; idem, "Greek and Syriac in Late Antique Syria."

play a major role in the church-dividing controversies that dominated the fifth century CE.

Ephraem and his Syriac-speaking contemporaries were very much *au courant* with mainline thinking in the Church of the empire.[48] In his Syriac *mēmrê* and *madrāshê* "On Faith," Ephraem's intention was to commend Nicene orthodoxy.[49] Although Ephraem wrote in a very different idiom from the Greek employed by Athanasius of Alexandria (ca.296–373) or the Cappadocian Fathers, such as Basil of Caesarea (ca.330–79) and Gregory of Nazianzus (329–89), his teaching echoed their doctrinal line. In the Syriac-speaking milieu, Ephraem, who was in the service of the bishops of Nisibis and Edessa, stands as a bellwether for ecclesiastical thinking in Syria in the fourth century CE. Other than his works, we have few sources of information about local Christian thought and practice in the fourth century.

Syria of the fifth century CE, with its multiple Christological controversies, conducted initially almost entirely in Greek, became the seedbed of the church divisions that would emerge in the Syriac-speaking milieu of the mid-sixth century, and which in due course would result in the development of new Christian church communities by early Islamic times. As was the case for the fourth century, so too the extant evidence for Christian life in Syria in the fifth century is almost entirely textual. Although archaeological and art-historical data are not totally absent, they are nevertheless in their present state meager resources for the historian's purposes.[50] Theological, and specifically Christological, issues consumed the attention of the Syriac writers of the period. But the stage was set for them by events transpiring outside the Syriac-speaking milieu. In the major sees of the Roman empire, theological controversies in Greek about the proper formulae to be used in affirming the divinity and humanity of Christ resulted in the calling of church councils. While decisions taken at these councils resolved the outstanding issues, they also incited further controversy.[51]

Developments began in earnest when in the year 429, Nestorius (d. ca.452/3), bishop of Constantinople (428–36), delivered a sermon in which he rejected the Greek term *Theotokos* (God-bearer, or Mother of God)

[48] Russell, *St. Ephraem the Syrian and St. Gregory the Theologian Confront the Arians.*

[49] Beck, *Die Theologie des hl. Ephräm in seinen Hymnen über den Glauben*; idem, *Ephräms Reden über den Glauben: Ihr theologischer Lehrgehalt und ihr geschichtlicher Rahmen*; Bou Mansour, *La pensée symbolique de saint Ephrem le Syrien.*

[50] For mostly later periods, see Leroy, *Les manuscrits syriaques à peintures conserves dans les bibliothèques d'Europe et d'Orient.*

[51] For discussion of parallel developments in Egyptian Christianity, see van der Vliet in Chapter 8 of this volume.

as a fitting or truthful epithet for the Virgin Mary. Nestorius's position elicited a strong, disapproving response from Bishop Cyril of Alexandria (d.444), who made his own position clear in a spirited correspondence he engaged in with Nestorius over the next several years.[52] A church council called by Emperor Theodosius II (401–50) and held in the city of Ephesus in the year 431 decided the matter in favor of Cyril. It approved the title *Theotokos* and deposed and excommunicated Nestorius, who was sent into exile in 436. But controversy continued. Another church council held in Ephesus in the year 449, under the domination of Cyril's successor in Alexandria, Bishop Dioscorus (d.453), failed to defuse the controversy, and the council was itself later repudiated. Then in the year 451 another council, called by Emperor Marcian (396–457) was held in Chalcedon in Asia Minor, where a decision was reached that would ultimately be recognized as expressing the orthodox position of the Church of the empire. The council proclaimed that Jesus of Nazareth, confessed to be the Son of God, was and is one divine person, one divine being or substance (*ousia*) in two natures (*physeis*), one divine and one human. After many vicissitudes, and a century after the Council of Chalcedon, its conciliar decision was systematically enforced in the Roman empire by Emperor Justinian I (ca.483–565). In 553, he called a council in Constantinople (Constantinople II), where actions were taken that would have a direct effect among the Syriac-speaking Christians.

These church councils and the Greek works of the scholars who participated in the councils or wrote about the issues decided in them were the prelude for developments among the Christians in Syria. Interest in the Greek works of an earlier Antiochene, biblical exegete, Theodore of Mopsuestia (ca.350–428), among some Syriac-speaking churchmen in Edessa and its environs inspired their translation into Syriac; they were thought by many to support the views of Bishop Nestorius of Constantinople, condemned at the Council of Ephesus. Meanwhile, among another group in the same Syriac-speaking milieu, the teaching of Cyril of Alexandria became popular, especially in the form in which it was presented in the anti-Chalcedonian, cathedral homilies of Bishop Severus of Antioch (ca.465–538, r.512–18). In due course, these texts were also translated into Syriac.[53]

---

[52] McGuckin, *St. Cyril of Alexandria, the Christological Controversy: Its History, Theology, and Texts*; Wessel, *Cyril of Alexandria and the Nestorian Controversy: The Making of a Saint and of a Heretic.*

[53] Lebon, *Le monophysisme Sévérien: étude historique, littéraire et théologique sur la résistance monophysite au Concile de Chalcédoine jusqu'à la constitution de l'Église jacobite;* idem, "La christologie du monophysisme syrien"; Menze, *Justinian and the Making of the Syrian Orthodox Church.*

From the beginning, bishops in the Syriac-speaking sphere had shown an interest in the controversies. Bishop Rabbula of Edessa (d.435), who had early on championed the views of Cyril of Alexandria, was even responsible for the translation of one of Cyril's works into Syriac; Rabbula also fought against the influence of the works of Theodore of Mopsuestia.[54] But Rabbula's successor in Edessa, Ibas (435–49; 451–57), associated himself with the policies of Theodoret of Cyrrhus (ca.393–460), who was friendly to the exegetical methods of Theodore; Ibas was deposed in the council of 449, but restored in 451. Theodoret's writings against Cyril of Alexandria and a letter of Ibas to another Syriac-speaking bishop, Mari, were together proscribed at the Council of Constantinople in 553. Meanwhile, Bishop Barsauma of Nisibis (d. ca.496) was an avid promoter of the works and thought of Theodore of Mopsuestia.[55] The struggle over the works of Theodore between rival scholarly circles reached such a pitch in Edessa that in the year 489, in the time of the Roman emperor Zeno (ca.450–91), the so-called School of the Persians in the city was closed. Those who supported the Antiochene exegete's views fled to Nisibis, in Persian territory, where they were welcomed by Bishop Barsauma. There they founded a new school, which would eventually become the famed "School of Nisibis."[56] Then, in the year 542 CE, Jacob Baradaeus (ca.500–78) became bishop of Edessa. He was the first bishop of the city to organize the church there in opposition to the Roman imperial policy of enforcing the decisions of the Council of Chalcedon. After being driven from his see, he continued in this enterprise; he and his followers became the nucleus of the community that would evolve into what is today called the Syrian Orthodox Church; in Late Antiquity they were often called "Jacobites," after Jacob Baradaeus. Their adversaries in the imperial church polemically and misleadingly called them, along with the Egyptian and Armenian followers of Cyril, "Monophysites" because of their espousal of Cyril of Alexandria's dictum that after the incarnation, Christ was "one incarnate nature (*mia physis sesarkomenē*)" and that divine, in one divine hypostasis or person.

The Syriac-speaking students of the doctrines and works of Theodore of Mopsuestia early on expressed their sympathy for Nestorius and included him as an honored father along with Diodore of Tarsus (d. ca.390) and Theodore. In the 540s, Mar Aba, who would become the Catholicos of Seleucia Ctesiphon (540–52), and thus hierarchical head of the church

---

[54] Blum, *Rabbula von Edessa, der Christ, der Bischof, der Theologe.*
[55] Gero, *Barsauma of Nisibis and Persian Christianity in the Fifth Century.*
[56] Becker, *Fear of God and the Beginning of Wisdom: The School of Nisibis and the Development of Scholastic Culture in Late Antique Mesopotamia.*

in Persia, brought works of Nestorius with him back into Persia after a sojourn in Alexandria and had them translated into Syriac. In due course, synods of the church in Persia held in the sixth and early seventh centuries adopted creedal statements that echoed both Chalcedonian teaching and the doctrinal positions of the Syriac-speaking scholars of the works of Theodore of Mopsuestia; their community had no participation in the councils of the imperial church in the Roman empire.[57] Their adversaries in the imperial church and among the "Jacobites" polemically called them "Nestorians";[58] they called themselves members of the "Church of the East" and, in modern times, the "Assyrian Church of the East."

Meanwhile, Syriac writers in the Edessene world, such as Philoxenus of Mabbug (ca.440–523)[59] and Jacob of Serugh (ca.451–521)[60] wrote homilies and treatises that favored the views of Cyril of Alexandria and Severus of Antioch; other Edessene writers, such as Narsai (ca.399–503),[61] wrote in support of the views of Theodore of Mopsuestia and of Nestorius. Further to the east, in Nisibis and Persia, Syriac writers associated with the School of Nisibis continued to write commentaries on the scriptures after the manner of Theodore of Mopsuestia, and theologians such as Babai the Great (d.628) articulated in Syriac the doctrinal views both of Theodore and of Nestorius.[62]

Church-dividing controversies about Christology were not the only developments in the life of the Syriac-speaking communities that straddled the frontier between the Roman and Persian empires in the fifth and early sixth centuries. At the beginning of the fifth century, in a synod at Seleucia Ctesiphon held in the year 410 CE under the influence of Bishop Maruta of Maipherqat/Martyropolis (d. after 410), the assembled bishops of the church in Persia formally accepted the teachings and canons of the Roman imperial council of Nicaea (325). In another synod in 424 CE, they are also said to have reaffirmed their juridical independence from the church in the West, that is, the sees associated with the patriarchates in the Roman empire.[63] Albeit independent, the church in Persia, as in the

[57] Brock, "The Christology of the Church of the East in the Synods of the Fifth to Early Seventh Centuries: Preliminary Considerations and Materials."
[58] Brock, "The 'Nestorian' Church: A Lamentable Misnomer"; Wilmshurst, *The Martyred Church*.
[59] De Halleux, *Philoxène de Mabbog: sa vie, ses écrits, sa théologie*.
[60] Bou Mansour, *La théologie de Jacques de Saroug*.
[61] McLeod, *The Image of God in the Antiochene Tradition*.
[62] Chediath, *The Christology of Mar Babai the Great*; Reinink, "Tradition and the Formation of the 'Nestorian' Identity."
[63] See, in connection with these developments, McDonough, "A Second Constantine? The Sasanian King Yazdgard in Christian History and Historiography."

West, was organized in bishoprics ranked under metropolitan sees. The bishop of the Persian capital city, Seleucia Ctesiphon, served as the chief hierarch, under the title *Catholicos*; this title was later supplemented with the addition of the term *Patriarch*, as it was used in the West from the mid-fifth century for the bishops of Rome, Constantinople, Alexandria, Antioch, and Jerusalem (after 451).[64] In the seventh century, beginning with Bishop Maruta of Tagrit (d.649), Christians in Persia who owed their creedal allegiance to the "Jacobite" community, and not to the "Church of the East," came under the jurisdiction of a bishopric first established in the Mesopotamian city of Tagrit just for them. Formally known by the somewhat enigmatic Syriac term *mapryānâ* ("fructifier"), or Maphrian, the bishop owed his allegiance to the "Jacobite" patriarch of Antioch in the Roman empire. Gradually other bishoprics for "Jacobites" in Persia and beyond came under the jurisdiction of the "Maphrianate."

Over the course of the fifth and sixth centuries, the West and East Syriac-speaking church communities gradually parted company with one another over theological and creedal issues, exacerbated by political division. They nevertheless shared a common religious heritage that had its roots in the earlier centuries, and particularly in the fourth century. They shared the *Peshitta*, the Syriac translation of the Christian scriptures; they shared a reverence for the Syriac patristic tradition, particularly for the name and the Syriac works of Ephraem the Syrian;[65] and they shared a common ascetical and monastic tradition.

FORMS OF ASCETIC AND MONASTIC PRACTICE

The ascetical and monastic traditions that developed in the Syriac-speaking milieu track an interesting trajectory. In their beginnings, they were very much the distinctive product of local ecclesiastical arrangements. In the fifth and sixth centuries, just as the Syriac-speaking hierarchs and theologians were setting their sails to catch the prevailing winds from the Greek-speaking churches in the Roman empire, so too the ascetical and monastic establishment in Syria became more and more attuned to the ever more popular ascetic and monastic literature emanating from Greek-speaking Palestine, and especially from Egypt.

[64] Baum and Winkler, *The Church of the East: A Concise History*, 14–41.
[65] It is interesting to note in passing that some writers, Philoxenus, for example, were somewhat diffident in their respect for Ephraem; see Van Rompay, "*Mallpânâ dilan Suryâyâ*: Ephrem in the Works of Philoxenus of Mabbog: Respect and Distance."

While a number of scholars have called attention to the rigorist and encratite character of Syrian asceticism,[66] the earliest texts actually speak of ascetical arrangements that developed within the everyday life of the local churches. The *Demonstrations* of Aphrahat and the *madrāshê* of Ephraem the Syrian refer to groups of men and women whom the texts call "sons" or "daughters" of the "covenant" (*bnay* or *bnāt qyāmâ*), in the customary translation. Living in loosely defined communities called *dayrê* or "sheep-folds" in Syriac, the inhabitants were designated as *dayrāyê*. Both terms are now usually anachronistically translated "monasteries" and "monks." Aphrahat, Ephraem, and Jacob of Serugh speak of these ascetics as "singles" (*îhîdāyê*), leading a single way of life (*îhîdāyûtâ*) as virgins or "holy ones" (*qadîshê*). "Holy ones" were persons who once may have been married, but who subsequently consecrated themselves to the single way of life. The term *îhîdāyâ* means simply "single one"; as the Syriac writers used it in the present context, it designates a person who in this life has taken on a special relationship with Jesus the Christ, the "Single One," the single son of God the Father.

In Syriac canonical texts, these "single ones," sons and daughters of the covenant, are seen to have had a special rank in the local church communities and at the liturgy, alongside the virgins and widows of whom the New Testament speaks.[67] It was presumably from among them that the earliest hermits and "monks" more properly so called came. Ephraem the Syrian wrote *madrāshê* to celebrate the memory of two of the earliest of them in the environs of Edessa: Julian Saba, whom Jacob of Serugh called the "father of the monks" of Syria, and Abraham Qîdûnāyâ, who came out of his solitude to help settle ecclesiastical affairs in far-away Antioch.[68] Later Syriac writers, such as the elusive Isaac of Antioch,[69] wrote long poems in praise of the monks and hermits of Syria. Referring to them with the colorful names of "mountain men," "mourners," or "loners," they lauded their wild and uncivilized behavior, including their unkempt, often unwashed appearance.[70] Some scholars have mistakenly assumed that the ascetic

---

[66] Vööbus proposed that monasticism developed independently in Syria, first in its anchoritic form, and that it had its origins in Manichaeism; see his *History of Asceticism*, 1. 143–6; 158–69. In developing these views, Vööbus was misled in part by mistaken dates assigned to a number of texts; see Mathews, "'On Solitaries': Ephraem or Isaac?" Even more recent scholars speak of the rigors of Syrian asceticism as a special characteristic; see Escolan, *Monachisme et église: Le monachisme syrien du IVe au VIIe siècle; un ministère charismatique*.
[67] Griffith, "Asceticism in the Church of Syria: The Hermeneutics of Early Syrian Monasticism."
[68] Griffith, "Julian Saba, 'Father of the Monks' of Syria"; idem, "Abraham Qîdûnāyâ, St. Ephraem the Syrian and Early Monasticism in the Syriac-Speaking World."
[69] Mathews, "The Works Attributed to Isaac of Antioch: A[nother] Preliminary Checklist."
[70] See the descriptions in Escolan, *Monachisme et église*.

rigors and bizarre excesses celebrated in these later texts are representative of an earlier Syrian asceticism.

A particular ascetic movement with its origins in the Syriac-speaking world of the fourth century eventually caused problems as far away as the Egyptian desert. Greek-speakers called it "Messalianism" or the heresy of the "Messalians"; the term has its origins in the Syriac word *mṣiallyānē*, basically meaning "people devoted to prayer." The so-called Pseudo-Macarian Homilies, surviving in Greek, seem in the judgment of modern scholarship to have had their origins in the Syriac-speaking ascetical milieu.[71] It is interesting to note in this connection that the Syriac writer Philoxenus of Mabbug claimed that a monk of Edessa named Adelphius, who had been a disciple of Julian Saba, was the inventor of the heresy of the Messalians.[72] However this may have been, the genuinely Syriac text most readily expressing ideas that Greek speakers might call "Messalian," namely that the "perfect" are free of the normal obligations of the faithful and of the ministrations of the hierarchy, is the now anonymous book of the late fourth century that in the West goes under the name *Liber Graduum*.[73]

By the early fifth century, under the burgeoning influence of monasticism in the Greek-speaking world, Greek writers began to incorporate the stories of the monks of Syria into the narrative that features Antony of Egypt (ca.251–356) and his countryman Pachomius (ca.290–346) as the fathers of monasticism. The Greek-speaking historian Sozomen (d. ca.445) was one of the earliest writers to mention Antony and Pachomius in connection with the history of monasticism in Syria. Sozomen, like his near-contemporary Palladius of Hellenopolis (d.431), and the younger Theodoret of Cyrrhus (d.460), in his *History of the Monks of Syria*, was full of enthusiasm for the Egyptian monastic experience.[74] Together with Palladius, Theodoret, and others, Sozomen sang the praises of the monastic movement in Greek in ways that quickly became standard in the Roman empire and wherever Greek culture exerted its influence, not least in Syria itself. As for the introduction of monasticism into Syria, Sozomen claims in his *Ecclesiastical History* that a monk named Eugene (Awgîn, Aones) played a role comparable there to that of Antony in Egypt. According to the story, Eugene was an Egyptian, a disciple of Pachomius, who with a

[71] Stewart, *"Working the Earth of the Heart": The Messalian Controversy in History, Texts, and Language to AD 431.*
[72] Ibid., 39.
[73] Kitchen and Parmentier, trans. *The Book of Steps: The Syriac Liber Graduum.*
[74] Canivet, *Le monachisme syrien selon Théodoret de Cyr.*

number of companions (variously numbered from seven to seventy) first brought monasticism to Syria when he settled at Padana, not far from Edessa and Charrān.[75] The trouble with this story is that while Sozomen may well have known of an Egyptian monk named Eugene who had settled with his companions in Syria, the claim that he introduced monasticism into the country can be found in Syriac only in later sources, the earliest of them dating from the ninth century.[76]

St. Jerome (ca.342–420) is another writer in the Roman world who connected the origins of monasticism in Syria with Egypt. Between 375 and 381 CE, Jerome spent four or five years as a hermit in Chalcis ad Belum, in the desert area of Syria Prima (Kennesrin). On the authority of his experience there, Jerome later remarked in his *Vita Hilarionis* that knowledge of the monastic way of life had come to Syria at the hands of St. Hilarion (ca.291–371). In 306 he had returned to his native Palestine from a sojourn in the Egyptian desert under the influence of Antony, and had settled as a hermit in the desert south of Majuma, near Gaza. According to Jerome, prior to Hilarion the Syrians knew nothing of monks and monasteries.[77]

By the early sixth century, even Syriac writers like Philoxenus of Mabbug were speaking of Antony, Evagrius of Pontus (346–99), and the other fathers of the Egyptian desert as the spiritual ancestors and teachers of record for the monks of Syria.[78] Philoxenus went so far as to suggest that Syria's own first eremitical monk whose name we know, Julian Saba, made something of an *ad limina* visit to Antony in Egypt when he, Julian, together with his disciple Adelphius, made a pilgrimage to Mount Sinai.[79]

Other Syriac writers of the same era and later also wrote about monasticism, asceticism, and growth in the spiritual life, now following the lead of Greek writers like Palladius, Sozomen, and Theodoret. They commended Syria's own early ascetics in the guise of the monastic figures of Egypt and the Holy Land, whose stories had achieved an almost canonical status in the Roman empire. To celebrate the person and writings of the Syriac community's own most notable father of the church, Ephraem of Nisibis and Edessa, they put him in the literary company of Basil of Caesarea and Antony of Egypt in the Syriac *Vita Ephraemi*, dressed him up in their icons in the monastic habit of the Greek-speaking fathers of desert asceticism,

[75] See Sozomen, *Hist. eccl.* 6.33.4.
[76] Fiey, "Aonès, Awun et Awgin (Eugène) aux origines du monarchisme mésopotamien"; idem, "Coptes et Syriaques; contacts et échanges," 310ff.
[77] Jerome, *Vit. Hil.* (*PL* 23.29–54, esp. col. 30).
[78] Graffin, "La lettre de Philoxène de Mabboug à un supérieur de monastère sur la vie monastique."
[79] See British Library add. MS 14,621, fol. 66 a-b, in Wright, *Catalogue of Syriac Manuscripts in the British Museum* 2.757.

and composed monastic texts in Greek, attributed to Ephraem.[80] This development seems to have gone hand in hand with the previously mentioned "Hellenization" of theology in Syriac in the fifth and sixth centuries. And in the same period, the lives of the holy men of Syria were used to promote the veracity of the theological positions espoused by their compilers, as in the instance of the works of John of Ephesus (ca.507–86), who supported the Syrian Orthodox cause.[81]

Several important Greek works in the ascetical and monastic tradition were translated into Syriac in the course of the sixth century, including such formative texts as the *Vita Antonii*, the first Letter of Antony,[82] and Palladius's *Lausiac History*.[83] But perhaps the most significant instance of Greek ascetical and mystical texts becoming religious classics in their Syriac translations involves the works of Evagrius of Pontus in Syriac. In fact, one of the most important of Evagrius's works, the *Kephalia Gnostica*, is preserved only in two Syriac recensions: the presumably original form of the text, and an expurgated form, seemingly produced in view of the condemnations of Origenism made at the Roman church council, Constantinople II, in 553 CE.[84] Interestingly, the two most important Syriac-speaking scholars who promoted the works of Evagrius were Philoxenus of Mabbug, a theological champion of the Syrian Orthodox Church,[85] and Babai the Great, the most prominent theologian of the "Church of the East." But the work with the most widespread influence in the later Syriac-speaking, monastic milieu was undoubtedly the *Paradise of the Fathers*, a compilation of originally Greek texts in Syriac translation, put together in the seventh century by the "Church of the East" monastic traveler, "Enânîshô" (fl. ca.630–70) of the monastery of Mount Izla. The compilation included such classics as the *Life of Antony*, Palladius's *Lausiac History*, the rule of Pachomius – that is, the *Asketikon* – Rufinus of Aquileia's *Historia Monachorum in Aegypto*, attributed to Jerome, and a collection of the *Apophthegmata Patrum*.[86]

[80] Griffith, "Images of Ephraem;" Amar, "Byzantine Ascetic Monachism and Greek Bias in the *Vita* Tradition of Ephraem the Syrian."
[81] Harvey, *Asceticism and Society in Crisis: John of Ephesus and the Lives of the Eastern Saints*; Brock and Harvey, *Holy Women of the Syrian Orient*.
[82] Rubenson, *The Letters of St. Antony: Monasticism and the Making of a Saint*; Draguet, *La vie primitive de s. Antoine conserve en syriaque*.
[83] Draguet, *Les formes syriaques de la matière de l'Histoire Lausiaque*.
[84] Guillaumont, *Les 'képhalaia gnostica' d'Évagre le Pontique et l'histoire de l'Origénisme chez les grecs et chez les syriens*.
[85] Watt, "Philoxenus and the Old Syriac Version of Evagrius' *Centuries*"; Young, "Evagrius in Edessa: Philoxenos of Mabbug's Use of Evagrius in the Letter to Patricius."
[86] Edition and English translation in Budge, *The Book of Paradise, being the Histories and Sayings of the Monks and Ascetics of the Egyptian Desert*.

Against this background of translated texts, a number of spiritual writers in Syriac emerged in the fifth and sixth centuries, whose works became classics in their own milieu. In this connection one might mention figures such as John of Apamea (fifth century), Abraham of Nathpar (ca.600), and from the seventh century, Sahdona and Isaac of Nineveh.[87] The latter writer, Isaac of Nineveh, or Isaac the Syrian, as he is sometimes called, wrote homilies on ascetic topics in Syriac, a selection of which were translated into Greek in the eighth or ninth century in the Judean Desert monastery of Mar Sabas. In the eighteenth century, extracts from the Greek translations were included by Sts. Macarius Notaras and Nicodemus of the Holy Mountain in the collection of ascetic homilies known as the *Philocalia*. In this way, Isaac, a monk and bishop of the "Church of the East," became a venerated spiritual writer of the western Orthodox Church.[88]

In the first half of the seventh century, the Syriac-speaking heartlands and their churches came into the world of Islam, where they continued their growth and development and for a time flourishing, spreading Christianity eastward along the so-called silk roads into China, and continuing their ties with daughter churches in south India, until finally, in modern times, in their historic homelands they have become demographically insignificant.[89]

BIBLIOGRAPHY

Primary

Aphrahat. *Demonstrations*, ed. J. Parisot. *Aphraatis Sapientis Persae Demonstrationes*. 2 vols. PS 1/2 (Paris, 1894/1907).

    Demonstrations, trans. M.- J. Pierre, *Aphraate le Sage Persan: Les Exposés*. SC 349/359 (Paris, 1988/1989).

    Demonstrations, trans. Peter Bruns. *Aphrahat: Unterweisungen*. 2 vols. FCh 5, 1–2 (Freiburg, 1991).

The Book of Paradise, being the Histories and Sayings of the Monks and Ascetics of the Egyptian Desert, trans. E. A. Wallace Budge. Lady Meux Manuscript 6. 2 vols. (London, 1904).

The Book of Steps: The Syriac Liber Graduum, trans. Robert A. Kitchen and Martien F. G. Parmentier (Kalamazoo, Mich., 2004).

---

[87] For an introduction, and some sample texts in translation, see Brock, intro. and trans. *The Syriac Fathers on Prayer and the Spiritual Life*.

[88] See Dana Miller, *The Ascetical Homilies of St. Isaac the Syrian*; Brock, ed. and trans. *Isaac of Nineveh (Isaac the Syrian): 'The Second Part', Chapters IV-XLI*; Alfeyev, *The Spiritual World of Isaac the Syrian*.

[89] Griffith, *The Church in the Shadow of the Mosque: Christians and Muslims in the World of Islam*.

The Cologne Mani Codex (P. Colon. Inv. Nr. 4780): 'Concerning the Origin of his Body,' ed. and trans. Ron Cameron and Arthur J. Dewey. Texts and Translations 15, Early Christian Literature Series 3 (Missoula, Mont., 1979).

Ephrem. *Hymns against Heresies*, ed. Edmund Beck. *Des heiligen Ephraem des Syrers Hymnen contra Haereses*. CSCO 169/170 Syri 76/77 (Louvain, 1957).

Epiphanius. *Panarion*, ed. Karl Holl. *Epiphanius: (Ancoratus und Panarion)*. GCS 31 (Leipzig, 1922).

Isaac of Nineveh (Isaac the Syrian). *'The Second Part'; Chapters IV-XLI*, ed. and trans. Sebastian Brock. CSCO 554/555 Syri 224/225 (Louvain, 1995).

Jerome. *Vita Hilarionis*. PL 23: 29–54.

Julius Africanus. *Cesti*, ed. J. R. Vieillefond, *Les "Cestes" de Julius Africanus* (Florence, 1970).

Sozomen. *Ecclesiastical History*, ed. J. Bidez. *Sozomenus. Kirchengeschichte*. GCS 50 (Berlin, 1960).

The Syriac Fathers on Prayer and the Spiritual Life, trans. S. Brock (Kalamazoo, Mich., 1987).

Tatian. *Oratio ad Graecos*, ed. and trans. Molly Whittaker (Oxford, 1982).

Secondary

Aland, Barbara. "Mani und Bardesanes – zur Entstehung des manichäischen Systems." In *Synkretismus im syrisch-persischen Kulturgebiet*, ed. Albert Dietrich (Göttingen, 1975): 123–43.

Alfeyev, Hilaron. *The Spiritual World of Isaac the Syrian* (Kalamazoo, Mich., 2000).

Amar, J. P. "Byzantine Ascetic Monachism and Greek Bias in the Vita Tradition of Ephraem the Syrian." *OCP* 58 (1992): 123–56.

Barnard, L. W. "The Heresy of Tatian – Once Again." *JEH* 19 (1968): 1–10.

Bauer, Walter. *Orthodoxy and Heresy in Earliest Christianity*, ed. and trans. R. A. Kraft et al., 2nd ed. (Philadelphia, 1971).

Baum, Wilhelm, and Dietmar W. Winkler. *The Church of the East: A Concise History* (London, 2003).

Beck, Edmund. *Die Theologie des hl. Ephräm in seinen Hymnen über den Glauben*. Studia Anselmiana 21 (Città del Vaticano, 1949).

Ephräms Reden über den Glauben: Ihr theologischer Lehrgehalt und ihr geschichtlicher Rahmen. Studia Anselmiana 33 (Rome, 1953).

Becker, Adam H. *Fear of God and the Beginning of Wisdom: The School of Nisibis and the Development of Scholastic Culture in Late Antique Mesopotamia* (Philadelphia, 2006).

BeDuhn, Jason David. *The Manichaean Body: In Discipline and Ritual* (Baltimore, 2000).

Biesen, Kees den. *Bibliography of Ephrem the Syrian* (Giove in Umbria, 2002).

Simple and Bold: Ephrem's Art of Symbolic Thought. Gorgias Dissertations 26; Early Christian Studies 6 (Piscataway, N.J., 2006).

Blum, Georg Gunther. *Rabbula von Edessa, der Christ, der Bischof, der Theologe*. CSCO 300 (Louvain, 1969).

Bou-Mansour, Tanios. *La pensée symbolique de saint Ephrem le Syrien*. Bibliothèque de l'Université Saint-Esprit 16 (Kaslik, Liban, 1988).

La théologie de Jacques de Saroug. 2 vols. Bibliothèque de l'Université Saint-Esprit 36 (Kaslik, Liban, 1993–2000).

Brock, Sebastian. "Christians in the Sasanian Empire: A Case of Divided Loyalties." In *Religion and National Identity*, Studies in Church History 18, ed. Stewart Mews (Oxford, 1982): 1–19.

"From Antagonism to Assimilation: Syriac Attitudes to Greek Learning." In *East of Byzantium: Syria and Armenia in the Formative Period*, eds. N. G. Garsoïan et al. (Washington, D.C., 1982): 17–34.

"The Christology of the Church of the East in the Synods of the Fifth to Early Seventh Centuries: Preliminary Considerations and Materials." In *Aksum-Thyateira: A Festschrift for Archbishop Methodios*, ed. G. Dragas (London, 1985): 125–42.

Brock, Sebastian, and Susan A. Harvey. *Holy Women of the Syrian Orient* (Berkeley, 1987).

The Luminous Eye: The Spiritual World Vision of Saint Ephrem. Cistercian Studies Series 124 (Kalamazoo, Mich., 1992).

"Greek and Syriac in Late Antique Syria." In *Literacy and Power in the Ancient World*, eds. Alan K. Bowman and Greg Woolf (Cambridge, 1994): 149–60, 234–5.

"The 'Nestorian' Church: A Lamentable Misnomer." *BJRL* 78 (1996): 53–66.

The Bible in the Syriac Translation. Gorgias Handbooks 7 (Piscataway, N.J., 2006).

Bruns, Peter. *Das Christusbild Aphrahats des Persischen Weise* (Bonn, 1990).

Canivet, Pierre. *Le monachisme syrien selon Théodoret de Cyr*. Théologie Historique 42 (Paris, 1977).

Chaumont, Marie Louise. *La Christianisation de l'empire iranien: des origines aux grandes persécutions du IVe siècle*. CSCO 499 (Leuven, 1988).

Chediath, Geevarghese, *The Christology of Mar Babai the Great* (Kottayam, Kerala, India, 1982).

Dietrich, Albert, ed. *Synkretismus im syrisch-persischen Kulturgebiet* (Göttingen, 1975).

Draguet, René. *Les formes syriaques de la matière de l'Histoire Lausiaque*. CSCO (Louvain, 1978): 389–90, 398–9.

La vie primitive de s. Antoine conserve en syriaque. CSCO 417/418 (Louvain, 1980).

Drijvers, Han J. W., *Bardaisan of Edessa*. Studia Semitica Neerlandica 6 (Assen, 1966).

"Mani und Bardaisan: Ein Beitrag zur Vorgeschichte des Manichäismus." In *Mélanges d'Histoire des Religions offerts à Henri-Charles Puech* (Paris, 1974): 459–69.

Cults and Beliefs at Edessa (Leiden, 1980).

"Addai und Mani, Christentum und Manichäismus im dritten Jahrhundert in Syrien." In *III Symposium Syriacum 1980*, OrChrAn 221, ed. R. Lavenant (Rome, 1983): 171–85.

Drijvers, Han J. W. and John F. Healey. *The Old Syriac Inscriptions of Edessa and Osrhoene: Texts, Translations and Commentary*. HO 42 (Leiden, 1999).

Escolan, Philippe. *Monachisme et église: Le monachisme syrien du IVe au VIIe siècle: un ministère charismatique* (Paris, 1999).

Ferguson, Everett, ed. *Early Christianity and Judaism* (New York, 1993).

Fiey, J.-M. "Aonès, Awun et Awgin (Eugène) aux origins du monarchism mésopotamien." AnBoll 80 (1962): 52–81.

Jalons pour une histoire de l'église en Iraq. CSCO 310 (Louvain, 1970).

"Coptes et Syriaques; contacts et échanges." *SOC Collectanea* 15 (1972–73): 297–356.

Gelzer, Heinrich, Heinrich Hilgenfeld, and Otto Cuntz. *Patrum Nicaenorum Nomina, Latine, Graece, Coptice, Syriace, Arabice, Armeniace* (Leipzig, 1898).

Gero, Stephen. *Barsauma of Nisibis and Persian Christianity in the Fifth Century*. CSCO 426 (Louvain, 1981).

Graffin, F. "La lettre de Philoxène de Mabboug à un supérieur de monastère sur la vie monastique," *OrSyr* 6 (1961): 317–52, 455–85; 7 (1962): 77–102.

Grant, Robert M. "The Heresy of Tatian." *JTS* 5 (1954): 62–8.

Griffith, Sidney H. "Ephraem, the Deacon of Edessa, and the Church of the Empire." In *Diakonia: Studies in Honor of Robert T. Meyer*, eds. Thomas P. Halton and Joseph Williman (Washington, D.C., 1986): 22–52.

"Ephraem the Syrian's Hymns 'Against Julian': Meditations on History and Imperial Power." *VC* 41 (1987): 238–66.

"Images of Ephraem: The Syrian Holy Man and his Church." *Traditio* 45 (1989–90): 7–33.

"Julian Saba, 'Father of the Monks' of Syria." *JECS* 2 (1994): 185–216.

"Asceticism in the Church of Syria: The Hermeneutics of Early Syrian." In *Asceticism*, eds. V. Wimbush and R. Valantasis (New York, 1995): 220–45.

"Setting Right the Church of Syria: Saint Ephraem's Hymns against Heresies." In *The Limits of Ancient Christianity: Essays on Late Antique Thought and Culture in Honor of R.A. Markus*, eds. W. E. Klingshirn and Mark Vessey (Ann Arbor, Mich., 1999): 97–114.

"The *Doctrina Addai* as a Paradigm of Christian Thought in Edessa in the Fifth Century." *Hugoye* 6.2 (2003), http:// Syrcom.cua.edu/Hugoye/Vol6No2/HV6N2Griffith.html.

"Beyond the Euphrates in Severan Times: Mani, Bar Daysān, and the Struggle for Allegiance on the Syrian Frontier." In *Philostratus's Heroikos: Religion and Cultural Identity in the Third Century C.E.*, Writings from the Greco-Roman World 6, eds. Ellen Bradshaw Aitken and Jennifer K. Berenson Maclean (Atlanta, 2004): 317–32.

"Abraham Qîdûnāyâ, St. Ephraem the Syrian and Early Monasticism in the Syriac-Speaking World." In *Il Monachesimo tra Eredità e Aperture: Atti del Simposio "Testi e Temi nella Tradizione del Monachesimo Cristiano" per il 50° Anniversario dell'Istituto Monastico di Sant' Anselmo, Roma, 28 maggio-1 giugno 2002*, Studia Anselmiana, 140, eds. Maciej Bielawski and Daniel Hombergen (Rome, 2004): 239–64.

"St. Ephraem, Bar Daysān and the Clash of *Madrāshê* in Aram: Readings in St. Ephraem's *Hymni contra Haereses*." *The Harp* 20 (2006): 1–25.

The Church in the Shadow of the Mosque: Christians and Muslims in the World of Islam (Princeton, 2008).

Guidi, I. *Chronica Minora.* CSCO 1/2 (Louvain, 1903).

Guillaumont, Antoine. *Les 'képhalaia gnostica' d'Évagre le Pontique et l'histoire de l'Origénisme chez les grecs et chez les syriens* (Paris, 1962).

Halleux, André de. *Philoxène de Mabbog: sa vie, ses écrits, sa théologie* (Louvain, 1963).

Harrak, Amir. "The Ancient Name of Edessa," *JNES* 51 (1992): 209–14.

Harvey, Susan Ashbrook. *Asceticism and Society in Crisis: John of Ephesus and the Lives of the Eastern Saints* (Berkeley, 1990).

Hemmerdinger-Iliadou, Democratie. "Éphrem (les versions). I. Éphrem grec; II. Éphrem latin." In *Dictionnaire de spiritualité ascétique et mystique, doctrine et histoire*, eds. Marcel Villier et al. 20 vols. (Paris, 1937–95).

Koltun-Fromm, Naomi. "A Jewish-Christian Conversation in Fourth-Century Persian Mesopotamia." *JJS* 47 (1996): 45–63.

Lebon, Joseph. *Le monophysisme Sévérien: étude historique, littéraire et théologique sur la résistance monophysite au Concile de Chalcédoine jusqu'a la constitution de l'Église jacobite* (Louvain, 1909).

"La christologie du monophysisme syrien." In *Das Konzil von Chalkedon: Geschichte und Gegenwart*, eds. Alois Grillmeier and Heinrich Bacht. 2 vols. (Würzburg, 1951–54): 425–580.

Leroy, Jules. *Les manuscripts syriaques à peintures conserves dans les bibliothèques d'Europe et d'Orient* (Paris, 1964).

Lieu, Samuel. *Manichaeism in the Later Roman Empire and Medieval China: A Historical Survey* (Manchester, UK, 1985).

Manichaeism in Mesopotamia and the Roman East. Religions in the Graeco-Roman World 118 (Leiden, 1994).

Mathews, Edward G. "'On Solitaries': Ephraem or Isaac?" *Mus* 103 (1990): 91–110.

"The Works Attributed to Isaac of Antioch: A[nother] Preliminary Checklist." *Hugoye* 6.1 (2003), http://syrcom.cua.edu/Hugoye/Vol6No1/HV6N1Mathews.html.

McDonough, Scott. "A Second Constantine? The Sasanian King Yazdgard in Christian History and Historiography." *JLA* 1.1 (2008): 127–40.

McGuckin, John A. *St. Cyril of Alexandria, the Christological Controversy: Its History, Theology, and Texts* (Leiden, 1994).

McLeod, Fredrick G. *The Image of God in the Antiochene Tradition* (Washington, D.C., 1999).

McVey, K. E. "Were the Earliest Madrāshê Songs or Recitations?" In *After Bardaisan: Studies on Continuity and Change in Syriac Christianity in Honor of Professor Han J. W. Drijvers.* OLA, eds. G. J. Reinink and A.C. Klugkist (Louvain, 1999): 185–99.

Menze, Volker-Lorenz. *Justinian and the Making of the Syrian Orthodox Church* (Oxford, 2008).

Millar, Fergus. "Theodoret of Cyrrhus: A Syrian in Greek Dress?" In *From Rome to Constantinople: Studies in Honour of Averil Cameron.* Late Antique History and Religion 1, eds. Hagit Amirav and Bas ter Haar Romeney (Leuven, 2007): 105–25.

Miller, Dana. *The Ascetical Homilies of St. Isaac the Syrian* (Boston, 1984).

Mitchell, C. W. *S. Ephraim's Prose Refutations of Mani, Marcion and Bardaisan.* 2 vols. (London, 1912/1921).

Murray, Robert. *Symbols of Church and Kingdom: A Study in Early Syriac Tradition*, rev. ed. (Piscataway, N.J., 2004).

Neusner, Jacob. *Aphrahat and Judaism: The Christian-Jewish Argument in Fourth-Century Iran*, new ed. (Atlanta, 1999).

Patterson, Michael J. "The View from Across the Euphrates." *HTR* 104 (2011): 411–31.

Peterson, William L. *Tatian's Diatessaron: Its Creation, Dissemination, Significance and History in Scholarship.* VCSup 25 (Leiden, 1994).

Possekel, Ute. *Evidence of Greek Philosohical Concepts in the Writings of Ephrem the Syrian.* CSCO 580 (Leuven, 1999).

Ramelli, Ilaria, ed. *Atti di Mar Mari* (Brescia, 2008).

Reinink, Gerrit J. "Tradition and the Formation of the 'Nestorian' Identity in Sixth- to Seventh-Century Iraq." *CHRC* 89 (2009): 217–50.

Rompay, Lucas Van. "Some Preliminary Remarks on the Origins of Classical Syriac as a Standard Language: The Syriac Version of Eusebius of Caesarea's Ecclesiastical

History." In *Semitic and Cushitic Studies*, eds. Gideon Goldberg and Shlomo Raz (Wiesbaden, 1994): 70–89.

"*Mallpânâ dilan Suryâyâ*: Ephrem in the Works of Philoxenus of Mabbog: Respect and Distance." *Hugoye* 7.1 (2004). http://syrcom.cua.edu/hugoye/Vol7No1/HV7N1VanRompay.html.

Ross, Steven K. *Roman Edessa: Politics and Culture on the Eastern Fringes of the Roman Empire, 114–242 CE* (London, 2001).

Rubenson, Samuel. *The Letters of St. Antony: Monasticism and the Making of a Saint* (Minneapolis, 1995).

Russell, Paul S. *St. Ephraem the Syrian and St. Gregory the Theologian Confront the Arians.* Mōrān 'Eth'ō Series 5 (Kerala, India, 1994).

Segal, J. B. *Edessa: The 'Blessed City'* (Oxford, 1970).

Shepardson, Christine. *Anti-Judaism and Christian Orthodoxy: Ephrem's Hymns in Fourth-Century Syria.* PMS 20 (Washington, D.C., 2008).

Stewart, Columba. *'Working the Earth of the Heart': The Messalian Controversy in History, Texts, and Language to AD 431* (Oxford, 1991).

Teixidor, Javier. *Bardesane d'Edesse: la première philosophie syriaque* (Paris, 1992).

Vööbus, Arthur. *History of Asceticism in the Syrian Orient.* CSCO (Louvain, 1958, 1960, 1988): 184, 197, 500.

Wallace-Hadrill, D. S. *Christian Antioch: A Study of Early Christian Thought in the East* (Cambridge, 1982).

Watt, J. W. "Philoxenus and the Old Syriac Version of Evagrius' Centuries." *OrChr* 64 (1980): 65–81.

Weitzman, M. P. *The Syriac Version of the Old Testament: An Introduction.* University of Cambridge Oriental Publications 56 (Cambridge, 1999).

Wessel, Susan. *Cyril of Alexandria and the Nestorian Controversy: The Making of a Saint and of a Heretic* (Oxford, 2004).

Wessendonk, O. G. von. "Bardesanes und Mani." *AcOr* 10 (1932): 336–63.

Wilmshurst, David. *The Martyred Church: A History of the Church of the East* (London, 2011).

Wright, William. *Catalogue of Syriac Manuscripts in the British Museum.* 3 vols. (London, 1870–72).

Young, Robin Darling. "The Influence of Evagrius of Pontus." In *"To Train His Soul in Books": Essays on Syrian Asceticism in Honor of Sidney H. Griffith*, eds. R. D. Young and M. J. Blanchard (Washington, D.C., 2011]: 157–75.

PART II

EGYPT AND NORTH AFRICA

6

TRADITIONAL RELIGION IN PTOLEMAIC AND ROMAN EGYPT

FRANÇOISE DUNAND

TRANSLATED BY WILLIAM ADLER

INTRODUCTION

Over the course of three centuries, two successive conquests profoundly altered Egyptian society. The introduction of a new ethnic group into the country resulting from the Macedonian conquest in 332 seems not to have brought about major changes. Greco-Macedonians and Egyptians coexisted without great conflict. And Egypt in the hands of the Ptolemies remained, at least up until the second century BCE, an independent and prosperous kingdom. But in integrating Egypt into a vast empire of which it was only one province among many, the Roman conquest of 30 BCE far more profoundly transformed its institutions, administrative and economic organization, and Egyptian society as a whole. (See Map 4.) Henceforth, the practice of the traditional religion of Egypt occurred within the framework of a nation subject to "foreign occupiers," but under very different circumstances.

RELIGION AND POLITICAL POWER

The religious policy of the rulers

The new regimes did not demonstrate any hostility to the native Egyptian religion. What interested the conquering powers was the domination and exploitation of the territory, not the diffusion of their own religious cults in the vanquished nation. Because they resided in Egypt, the Lagids found it necessary to heed the reactions of a people obviously committed to its traditional forms of worship. This was far less the case for the emperors; barring rare exceptions, they did not set foot in a country that for them was basically, in the words of Tiberius, "sheep for shearing" (see Cassius Dio 57.10).

Even before the accession of Ptolemy I to the throne in 305, the Lagids provided ample evidence of their benevolence to the traditional religion.

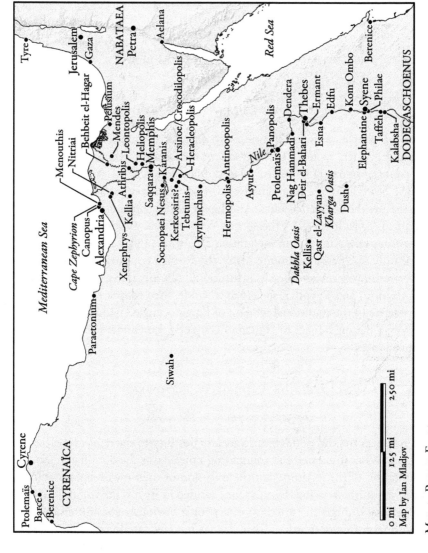

Map 4. Roman Egypt

166

These "benefits," enumerated in the decrees of assemblies of the third and second centuries BCE[1] and in royal edicts of the second century BCE,[2] extended from the restoration of temples and the support of sacred animals to the cancellation of debts and the exemption of the clergy from taxation. From the beginning of the third century, the extent of temple building and repair projects was also substantial. This period witnessed the building of the chief sanctuaries of Isis from Behbeit el-Hagar in the Delta to Philae on the Nubian frontier. The temples were arrayed all along the Valley: Dendara, Esna, Edfu, and Kom Ombo. Their own revenues, that is, the revenues from the lands under their control, constituted the main source of financing for both construction and renovation and for the upkeep of the buildings. But the government also must have made a contribution, and appeals could be made to the generosity of believers as well. This work continued up to the first and second centuries CE, extending from Esna to Philae as far as Nubia, as well as in the oases of the Western Desert, Dakhla, and Kharga. Although the temples bear the cartouches of Roman emperors from Augustus to Decius, we cannot know the extent to which the Roman administration contributed financially.

The Lagid administration, eager to appropriate as much of the resources of the country as possible, strove to take under its control the lands in the possession of the temple. According to Diodorus (1.21.7), this would have represented a third of the land of Egypt; but this estimate is surely inflated. Over time, the Ptolemies had to cede control and grant the priests the right to "administer the sacred *arourai*." Although Cleopatra VII expropriated temple property to replenish a treasury depleted by the ruinous policies of Ptolemy XII, the temples remained a source of considerable income. One of the first decisions of the Roman government was to confiscate this source of revenue, either by annexing it to the imperial estate or by distributing it to big Roman landowners. This measure allowed the new government to gain control over all the sectors of the economy.

It was also a means to keep watch over a suspect segment of the Egyptian population, namely the clergy. No longer able to administer the temple lands and their revenue, the priests found themselves obliged to resort to the closing of pieces of these territories, or even to receive, in exchange for their services, a subvention from the state, a *syntaxis*. This made them directly dependent upon and subject to the control of the Roman administration. Starting in 120 CE, a high-ranking civil functionary, "the high

---

[1] *OGIS*, 56, 90; Valbelle and Leclant, eds. *Décret de Memphis*, 41–65.
[2] Lenger, *Ordonnances des Ptolémées*, 53.

priest of Alexandria and all of Egypt," was responsible for the supervision
of the temples and their staff. The *Gnomon of the Idios Logos*, compiled
during the reign of Antoninus Pius, reveals the fastidiousness of the regulations imposed on members of the clergy and their activities.[3] Included
among its stipulations are conditions for admittance to priestly offices,
and regulations about authorized vestments and the participation of the
differing ranks of priests in cultural activities. Any infraction was subject to a fine. We might ask, of course, why the Roman administration
cared whether or not priests wore a linen garment or whether or not *pas-
tophoroi* were allowed to take part in processions. It is likely that this was
first and foremost a matter of making the existence of authority palpable
to members of the clergy. Because violations of such restrictive regulations would hardly be rare, it was also a means of extracting income from
their activities. Moreover, different taxes were deducted by the state on the
occasion of admission to the priesthood. Some offices, in particular the
most high-ranking in the priestly hierarchy, were put up for auction and
awarded to the highest bidder.

Compared to the general population, the Egyptian clergy in the
Ptolemaic era appears as a relatively privileged class. This continued to be
true even in the Roman period, their degraded status notwithstanding.
Priests and priestesses were entitled to a part of the food offerings, which
were distributed among them according to their function and rank in the
hierarchy. A text from Edfu reports that the priests are entitled to what
is found on the "table of god," while also making clear that this is "after
the god is served."[4] They possessed land, houses, and livestock, and even
lent money. In a society in which the majority of the people lived from
day to day, the position of the priest, and its attendant advantages, would
seem quite desirable. This is the reason why, just as had been the case in
previous centuries, those serving in these offices strove to keep them in
their family. Both in the lower echelons and in the uppermost ranks of
the hierarchy, there were always veritable priestly dynasties. As a matter
of course, inequalities in the priestly standard of living were substantial,
varying from one sanctuary to the next and depending on their relative
importance.

The Lagid government had to accommodate itself to a priestly class
that was both influential and powerful. As priestly offices could coexist

---

[3] *BGU*,V, 1210.
[4] Sauneron, *Les prêtres*, 83.

with civil and even military offices, there was no genuine conflict between the interests of the state and those of the clergy.[5] For its part, the Roman government very likely feared clerical influence over the populace and its potential to incite nationalist movements. Two centuries after the "pacification" of Egypt, an insurrection did take place in the Delta during the reign of Marcus Aurelius, under the leadership of a priest named Isidorus. Up until then, the Egyptian priests apparently had no inclination to oppose the Roman government.

Religious continuity

From the moment of his arrival in Egypt, Alexander was acknowledged by the clergy of Memphis as the legitimate successor to the pharaohs. This reaction was not at all surprising, as the kings of Persia had already been received in the same way. It is possible that he was enthroned according to Egyptian ritual. Although Ptolemy I did not receive this form of coronation, it was conceivably done for Ptolemy II, and in any case for Ptolemy IV and all his Lagid successors up to Cleopatra. Ptolemaic kings maintained a privileged relationship with the high priests of Memphis, who were responsible for their investiture.[6] Their images and cartouches regularly adorn the inner walls of several temples either built or refurbished during their reigns. The same is true of the emperors, who are depicted with the same features as their predecessors. If these images recur endlessly in the temples, it is because, irrespective of who was in power – a Ptolemy or an emperor – he was always regarded as the sole intermediary between human beings and the gods. Under the Lagids, the official titulature of a sovereign, inherited from pharaonic times, was always standard usage. The epithets that this titulature comprises might have been modified in the Roman period, as for example in the explicit formula "He whose power is unrivalled in the preeminent city that he loves: Rome."[7] But only those capable of reading hieroglyphs were able to appreciate the degree to which this formulation marked the difference between the pharaohs and the new masters. When the illiterate others – and they were the majority – saw the cartouches on the temple walls and knew that they contained the royal names, these cartouches affirmed the presence of a pharaoh, whom they of course had never seen.

---

[5] Hüss, *Makedonische König*, 73–93.
[6] Thompson, *Memphis*, 125–54.
[7] Grenier, "L'Empereur et le Pharaon," 3181–94.

What the temple texts proclaim in the Ptolemaic and Roman periods is the doctrine, in effect from the time of the Old Empire, of the sacred and hence inviolable character of pharaonic royalty. As son of and successor to the gods (who were thought to have been the first to reign over Egypt), the pharaoh was simultaneously both a god himself and servant of the gods. In the reciprocal arrangement existing between them, the gods gave to their son the authority to govern; he, on the other hand, was expected to bring to the land the rule of order that they desired, symbolized by the figure of Maat.[8] This power, of divine origin, could not be limited under any circumstance; nor could his decisions be subject to question. Potential opponents could only be treated as "impious," the "enemies of the gods." This is, for example, the way that the priests assembled at Memphis in 196 BCE described their countrymen from the Delta, whose rebellion was ultimately brutally crushed by Ptolemy V.[9]

The role assigned to the king of Egypt thus had a cosmic dimension. While universal order is the desire of the creator god, this world is constantly threatened by a return to primordial chaos. Every night, hostile forces, embodiments of the great serpent Apopis, engage in combat against the sun god Re, whose victory each morning recreates the world. In this endlessly recurring struggle, Re has his assistants, the chief one of whom is his son, the pharaoh. In this way, the king of Egypt was responsible not only for social order, but for the stability of the world as well.[10]

The ups and downs experienced by the Egyptian government, especially during crises in the transfer of power, are well known. It is clear that the Egyptians drew a distinction between the royal function, which was both divine and intangible, and the person of the king, who could be unimpressive and fallible. But the actual institution of the pharaoh was never challenged. The ideology on which it claimed to be based thus proved to be remarkably effective; it continued in operation up to the fourth century of the common era, at which time it was replaced by a new ideology, that of the Christian emperor, "vicar" of God on earth. From the moment when the clergy recognized in the Lagids, and then in the emperors, the heirs to the pharaohs, the traditional political-religious ideology did more than legitimize the power of the new rulers; it made it absolute.

[8] Assmann, *Maât*, 115–34.
[9] *OGIS*, 90.
[10] Bonhême and Forgeau, *Pharaon*, 110–20.

THE VITALITY OF THE TRADITIONAL RELIGION

The world of the temples

The great sanctuaries either built or restored during the Ptolemaic and Roman eras are in themselves a sign of the vitality of the traditional religion.[11] The temple of Horus at Edfu, constructed in the Ptolemaic period; the temple of Hathor at Dendara, built between the end of the second century BCE and the end of the first century CE; as well as the temple of Isis of Philae, the construction of which extended from Ptolemy II to Trajan, all adhere to a design of long standing. One passes in stages from the largest and most open space, the courtyard, to the enclosed space of the holy of holies, where one finds the cult statue, enclosed in its shrine. Some local sanctuaries conform to the same design, but on a smaller scale – for example, the temple of Osiris and Isis at Dush (the Kharga Oasis) and the temple of Amon at Deir el-Hagar (the Dakhla Oasis). Others are noticeably different, as, for example, the temples of Karanis (Fayyum) dedicated to various forms of the crocodile god and the temple of Amenebis (Amon of Hibis) at Qasr el-Zayyan (the Kharga Oasis). This latter temple, the restoration under Antoninus Pius of a building begun in the Ptolemaic era, consisted of a suite of two rooms, the second of which was meant to serve as the holy of holies. A simple niche, hollowed out of the room's interior wall and probably sealed off by a curtain or a wood shutter, was intended to shelter the cult statue. These small sanctuaries were widespread throughout all of Egypt. From the papyrological documents, we know that a village of middling importance like Kerkeosiris in the Fayyum numbered no fewer than fifteen temples in the second century BCE; we can thus imagine that quite a few of them were very modest buildings, little more than simple chapels.[12]

Depending on the importance of the temple, the number of officiants varied considerably. In a large temple like Dendara or Philae, we can suppose that, including auxiliary staff, they numbered in the hundreds. In the second century CE, the temple of the god Soknebtunis at Tebtunis, a building of modest significance, included several dozen officiants.[13] Strictly speaking, the priestly ranks were very hierarchical, each of its members assigned to clearly defined roles. Even so, it is likely that several smaller

---

[11] Arnold, *Temples of the Last Pharaohs*.
[12] Dunand and Zivie-Coche, *Hommes et dieux*, 300–4.
[13] Evans, "Social and Economic History," 145–83.

local sanctuaries consisted of a scaled-down staff. The existence of chapels having a single officiant, who might also be its owner, is attested in papyri from the Fayyum of the Ptolemaic period.[14]

The chief function of this priestly workforce remained "service to the god." Offerings made each morning, and accompanied by prayers and chants, were thought to assure the presence in the world of a god who, when "awakened" in this way, would take up residence in his cult statue. We know that this ritual, which was repeated over the course of the day, was performed in the heart of the sanctuary and excluded any "profane" presence. To the extent that they took place outside the temple proper, festival rites were, by contrast, open to all. The liturgical calendars that survive from Dendara, Edfu, and Esna record for each month a sizeable number of festivals, many of which would last for several days. Some of them were local festivals, like the "Creation of the Potter's Wheel" in honor of Khnum in Esna.[15] Others, like the festivals of the month of Choiak in honor of Osiris, would be observed throughout all of Egypt; as Herodotus notes (2.61), on the occasion of this festival, all the Egyptians "beat themselves" as a show of grief. The Dendara texts describe in great detail the complex rites, performed more or less in secret, of this combined agrarian and funerary festival commemorating Osiris's death and resurrection, marked most notably by the creation of the "gardens of Osiris." [16]

In the Ptolemaic and Roman eras, theological reflection on the part of the clergy of the great sanctuaries of Egypt led to the development of a subtle and complex synthesis of religious doctrines. The temple texts of Horus at Edfu, and Sobek and Haroeris at Kom Ombo, attest to this development. While each temple had its own "sacred discourse" to the gods, this did not prevent more extensive contemplation of the nature and powers of different gods and an attempt to synthesize varying traditions. Often inscribed on the walls of temples, these texts were also preserved in their libraries. As the inventory of the Edfu library shows, they contained all manner of treatises – on theology and liturgy, as well as astronomy, geography, and medicine.

Personal piety

In Egyptian religion, theological and liturgical activity was in principle reserved for the king, the mediator between the gods and human beings,

[14] Guéraud, *Enteuxeis*, 6, 80.
[15] Sauneron, *Fêtes religieuses d'Esna*, 71–244.
[16] Chassinat, *Mystère d'Osiris*.

but in practice performed by a clergy of specialists. Even so, starting with the New Kingdom, it would appear that men and women increasingly pursued direct and personal contact with their gods. This movement intensified once again in the first millennium, perhaps in response to the social and political upheavals of the age and the deep feelings of material and psychological insecurity that ensued.

In the Ptolemaic and Roman periods, displays of personal piety were ubiquitous. As copious graffiti attest, visits to temples were extremely common. Composed in both Demotic and Greek, they were inscribed on the walls of temples in places accessible to devotees, especially on doorposts. The pylon at Philae, covered with Greek inscriptions, is a striking example. To leave one's names, often accompanied by a small prayer or the simple formula *to proskynema*, "the act of adoration," meant leaving something of oneself with a god and under his care. Simply stroking or rubbing a wall was often considered enough, a way to collect a little of the sacred dust. This practice accounts for the deep fingerprints commonly visible in the courtyards and beside temple doors.

Visiting a temple might have as its sole objectives "contemplation of the god" and prayer. In other cases, however, the devotee had a petition to make or advice to solicit. This is what occurred in the oracular sanctuaries, widespread throughout all of Egypt.[17] Consultation of oracles increased considerably during the first millennium. In the Ptolemaic period, new "techniques" arose, especially the practice of incubation. Here one would spend the night in a temple in the hope that a god would appear in a dream. This technique was particularly popular in the temples of Serapis at Canopus and Memphis. Another widely employed technique involved writing a query on a slip that was then submitted to the god. The drawing of lots made it possible to "draw out" the divine response. Numerous notes of this type have been discovered in the temples of the crocodile gods of the Fayyum. The questions asked reflect an unshakable confidence in the gods who, it was believed, responded to concerns of the most basic and mundane type, among them family, marriage, and professional problems. As would be expected, the subject of health was a frequently recurring question. For the afflicted who might be able to visit a temple in search of a cure, the priests usually dispensed medical/magical knowledge. A building adjacent to the temple of Hathor at Dendara could be explained as a "sanatorium" set aside for the ill.[18]

---

[17] Valbelle and Husson, "Questions oraculaires d'Égypte," 1055–71.
[18] Dunand, "La guérison dans les temples," 4–24.

Particularly common were images of the gods in the form of stelae, amulets, and terra cotta (or more rarely bronze) figurines; these included Isis and Bes, guardians of women and childbirth, and especially the child god Harpocrates, son of Isis. His image, found in countless reproductions in homes and tombs, is a prime example of what we might call "popular piety." As patron of early childhood, he is a god who safeguards against everyday dangers, especially the bites and stings of snakes and scorpions. Devotees might deposit in the temples images of the gods as votive offerings. This is the case for the golden plates depicting Serapis or the Apis bull found in the hoard of Dush.[19] But they could also pray before images of the gods that they had in their homes. Dating from the second and third centuries CE, wall paintings have been found in homes at Karanis (Fayyum) with representations of Isis, Harpocrates, and the sphinx god Tutu (Tithoes).

The "cult of animals"

Although widely used, this expression is surely inappropriate. What is venerated in animal form is the special power that it embodies, above all its physical strength and fertility. Every deity in fact, or at least almost every one, could be represented simultaneously in human, animal, and hybrid form. What made this possible was that in the Egyptian worldview, god, human being, and animal all owe their origin to the work of the creator-god, without any difference existing between them either in nature or in the hierarchy of being. While the representation of the gods in animal or hybrid form is as common in the Roman period as it is in previous times, scholars have puzzled over the existence in this period of huge necropolises of mummified animals.

There is a twofold explanation for this practice. From the time of the New Kingdom, certain animals had been considered as the living image, the *ba*, of the gods with whom they were associated. This was especially true of the Apis bull, a "living image" of Ptah of Memphis; the Buchis bull of Armant, a "living image" of Montu; and the Mnevis bull, a "living image" of Re at Heliopolis. In the later period, the god Khnum was embodied by a live ram in Elephantine, and another ram (or goat?) embodied the god of Mendes, Banebdjedet. The crocodile-god Sobek could also be embodied by a live crocodile in the temples of the Fayyum. At Edfu, Horus was represented by a live falcon, enthroned for one year (while the

---

[19] Reddé, *Trésor de Douch.*

other divine animals were enthroned for life). These animals, selected by means of elaborately defined criteria, were supported over the course of their lives in the temple confines, lavished with care and honors, and of course ritually mummified and interred after their death.[20] Strabo offers a very vibrant account of a visit to a sacred crocodile of Arsinoë (Fayyum), which was fed all sorts of delicacies (Strabo 17.38).

As for the hundreds of thousands of animals of all species uncovered in tombs throughout all of Egypt, it is now known that they were deliberately put to death (usually while still young), after which they were mummified. Devotees could then purchase them and use them as votive offerings to the gods with whom they were linked. The great necropolises of Saqqara have, for example, revealed the existence of ibises offered to Thoth, falcons offered to Horus (mixed with shrews), and cats offered to Bastet. These mummies could obviously not be kept in the temples. It was necessary either to dig catacombs for their use or to stack them in unused human tombs. Because they would be put up for sale to people of varying wealth (or generosity), their presentation and quality were highly variable. There are also cases in which mummies that were carefully prepared with beautiful cloth contain only a single bone, if any at all. Their use as votive offerings evidently gave birth to a profit-making enterprise, and their preparation was made possible by the development in a later age of simplified and probably less costly methods of mummification.[21]

TRANSFORMATIONS IN THE RELIGIOUS UNIVERSE

A multicultural society

Although the Egypt conquered by Alexander preserved its identity, language, culture, and traditional religion, Greek was imposed as the dominant language and Greek education became progressively more pervasive. Different practices and customs were introduced. Indeed, a new society that could be described as multicultural was instituted in the Ptolemaic era.[22] It is likely that over time peoples living in Egypt, regardless of their ethnic origin, were increasingly influenced by the two dominant cultures. This was especially true for the upper echelons of the population. In the mid-second century, the vizier Dioscurides, the son of a Greek father and Egyptian mother, served as both a high officer in the Lagid court and

---

[20] Ikram, ed. *Divine Creatures.*
[21] Dunand and Lichtenberg, *Des animaux et des hommes*, 149–200.
[22] Johnson, ed. *Life in a Multicultural Society.*

high-ranking priest in the Egyptian temples.[23] In the second half of the
second century BCE, senior officers in the garrison at Edfu had themselves
buried with epitaphs on their tombs in both languages, in each case composed in the correct wording.[24]

Many things changed with the Roman conquest. The increasing
dominance of Greek, at the expense of the Egyptian language, extended
even into priestly circles, despite their conservatism. At the temple of the
crocodile-god Socnopaeus at Socnopaei Nesus (Fayyum), oracular questions, which were formerly composed in Demotic in the Ptolemaic era,
were drawn up in Greek in the Roman period. The policy of the Roman
administration, dependent on the Greek or Hellenized segment of the population, relegated the mass of the *Aegyptii* to subordinate status. Egyptian
culture was kept alive within the confines of the temples, which came to
represent the custodians of the traditions. Without doubt, it was also preserved in the *chōra* population, but under the most straitened conditions.

From the time of the Ptolemies, many foreign communities also arrived
from all over the Mediterranean, settling in the Delta and the Valley and
bringing with them their social organization, customs, and often their language as well. Egypt had never been closed to foreigners, especially since
the New Kingdom. From the sixth century BCE, it had been receptive to
Greek and Jewish communities. In the third century BCE, Jews in great
numbers settled in Egypt. In the second century, a sizeable community
arriving from Jerusalem settled in Tell el-Yahudiyeh, in the eastern Delta.[25]
The appearance of Jewish communities made for the emergence of a very
distinctive culture, Greek-speaking Hellenistic Judaism, one of whose most
conspicuous representatives was the philosopher Philo.

Alexandria, factory of the gods

The new capital founded by Alexander is the symbol of the diversity of
peoples and cultures characteristic of Egypt in the later period. Although
Alexandria, the largest city of the ancient world in the common era, was
a cosmopolitan city, coexistence did not continue free of discord. In the
first half of the first century CE, conflicts between Greeks and Jews were
unending. It would require a rather terse resolution of the problem by the

---

[23] Collombert, "L'exemple de Dioskouridès," 47–63.
[24] Yoyotte, "Bakhthis," 27–141.
[25] Mélèze Modrzejewski, *Juifs d'Égypte,* 107–26, 174–88; see also by the same author, Chapter 7 of this
volume.

emperor Claudius to restore a semblance of peace between them, which lasted until the Jewish war under Trajan (115–17 CE). The consequence of this war was the eradication of the Jewish communities of Egypt, lasting for almost two centuries. Even so, over the course of many centuries, the Jews were able to practice their religion freely, both in Alexandria and elsewhere in Egypt.

In Alexandria of the Ptolemaic era, the various religions coexisted peacefully.[26] Naturally, the Greeks brought their gods with them. At the top of the ranks was Dionysus, who had assumed a new importance throughout the entire Hellenistic world. This god was very popular with the Ptolemies. Following a practice that was widespread in great Greek families, they claimed Heracles and Dionysus as their divine ancestors. In the great festival of the Ptolemaea organized by Ptolemy II, the procession for the god held a separate place, marked by extraordinary pageantry and repeated evocations of the Dionysiac myth, in the form of statues or "live scenes." Ptolemy IV openly proclaimed himself an adept of Dionysus; during his reign there were numerous associations in Egypt devoted to him and performing initiations into his mysteries. Another deity widely worshipped in Egypt was Demeter. Just as in Attica, the festival of the Thesmophoria was celebrated in her honor, and perhaps as well her mysteries, modeled after the cult at Eleusis (whose name was given to a suburb of Alexandria). Beginning with Arsinoë II, Aphrodite, with whom several Ptolemaic queens were identified, had temples in the city and its surroundings. Among them was the temple at Cape Zephyrion, dedicated to Aphrodite Arsinoe Zephyritis and possibly the source of the beautiful statue recently discovered in the waters of Canopus. Other Greek gods, such as Zeus, Pan, and the Dioscuri, were also known, although no trace of their places of worship has been located.

But the god who most embodied this new city was Serapis.[27] Although his "creation" has been the subject of controversy, it is clear that we are dealing with a genuine Egyptian deity, the Apis bull, who after his death became an Osiris, under the name Osor-Hapi. As is shown by the "Oath of Artemisia," a Greek document dating to the fourth century BCE, the Greeks inhabiting Memphis before the founding of Alexandria knew him by the name "Oserapis."[28] But this Memphite deity received a Greek makeover. He is represented in the form of a Zeus or an Asclepius, with

---

[26] Fraser, *Ptolemaic Alexandria*, 189–301.
[27] Dunand and Zivie-Coche, *Hommes et dieux*, 285–94.
[28] *UPZ*, 1,1.

beard and long hair, dressed in *chitōn* and *himation,* and wearing as his
crown the *kalathos,* a basket-like grain measure. Cerberus, the dog of
the underworld, is often at his side. Without doubt, the legend of the
dream of Ptolemy came into existence as a way to explain this decidedly un-Egyptian appearance; the god of the Greek city of Sinope on
the Euxine city appeared to him and ordered him to bring his statue
to Alexandria (Plutarch, *Is. Os.* 361F–362E). This new god was probably
thought to take over the functions of the god of the dead, which belonged
to Osiris. Indeed, in the twosome made up of Isis and Osiris, Serapis
often took the place of Osiris. In funerary ideology and iconography,
however, Osiris continued to occupy the chief position. Serapis, on the
other hand, assumed Osiris's agrarian function. Quite soon, two of his
most prominent attributes involved healing and oracles; his temple at
Canopus was a healing center, the one at Oxyrhynchus the seat of a very
frequently consulted oracle.

While the Ptolemies supported the cult of this composite god, it was
certainly not with the intention of using it to promote a "mixing" of the
Egyptian and Greek populations. No suggestion of such a policy exists
elsewhere. On the other hand, in a new city, a Greek city in which the
Egyptian component also had its place, it was expedient to have a god
embodying both cultures. Although Serapis in Alexandria did not receive
the epithet *polieus,* "guardian of the city," until the imperial period, we can
assume that this was also the function he played at the very outset.

Even if the Serapis cult initially had somewhat the look of an implant
into the Greek environment of Alexandria, his popularity in the period of
the empire was well established throughout the entire country. His name
is prevalent in onomastic evidence, and the formula, "I pray to Serapis for
you," appears frequently in private letters. He was now well integrated into
the Egyptian pantheon.

New images

The depiction of Egyptian gods on temple reliefs of the Ptolemaic and
Roman eras adhered to age-old standards, which remained in effect for
as long as the decoration and restoration of buildings continued (third
century CE). But at the beginning of the Ptolemaic era, other images came
into use, translating a vision of the divine body into a form quite close to
that of the Greeks. In some cases, it was not merely a matter of modifying
existing iconographic rules; the new image of an Egyptian god expressed a
new way of conceptualizing his nature and powers.

The most significant of these transformations concerned the iconography and ideology of Isis.[29] From the third century BCE, and no doubt initially in an Alexandrian setting, there appeared statues representing the goddess in the Egyptian style: upright, with arms attached to her body. But her dress and hairstyle are of a new type, with a fringed sash and long ringlets. The same period witnessed the proliferation of bronze statuettes depicting the goddess in the same dress, and notably with an attribute of Greek origin, the cornucopia, the symbol of the prosperity and wealth that she distributes to humankind. She is also represented leaning on a rudder, bringing to mind the patronage she exercised over maritime affairs. Alexandria, a port city whose shipping traffic was vital to her existence, stood in need of a divine guardian. The choice of Isis for this function (no other deity had any special relationship with navigation) attests the importance that she held in this era. At the temple built in her honor near Pharos of Alexandria, she was invoked by the name Isis Pharia. But the rudder also symbolized the direction that she exercised over human affairs. She has become a Tyche, a benevolent embodiment of Fortune. Images of her, which proliferate, often present her with peculiar features. Assimilated to Renenutet-Thermuthis, the cobra-goddess and guardian of the harvest, she is a half-female, half-serpent figure. Identified with Aphrodite as Isis-Hathor, she is depicted nude, her flowing hair adorned with wreaths of flowers, above which is the Isianic crown. Often she even performs the action of Aphrodite Anadyomenē ("Aphrodite rising from the sea"), wringing out her hair as she emerges from the water. It is clear that these images reflect the norms of Greek iconography, which found nothing scandalous about depicting the body of a god unclothed.

If in the Ptolemaic era the figure of Isis was enriched by new features, she did not lose her Egyptian identity in the process. Traditional representations of her persisted in the great temples of Philae, Dendera, and Kalabsha, built during the Ptolemaic and Roman periods (Fig. 10). She remained essentially a "mother-goddess," giver of life, restorer of life to the dead, guardian of royal power, and guarantor of its continuity. At Philae, where she is depicted in the most conventional form, the hymns inscribed on the walls of the temple ascribe to her a power that she exercises both in the divine and human realms. She is even a power superior to Destiny, inasmuch as she "extends the years of the one devoted to her." But what is new in this age is the emphasis assigned to her universal character. The temple hymns of Narmuthis in the Fayyum, composed in Greek probably

---

[29] Dunand, *Isis, mère des dieux*, 41–62.

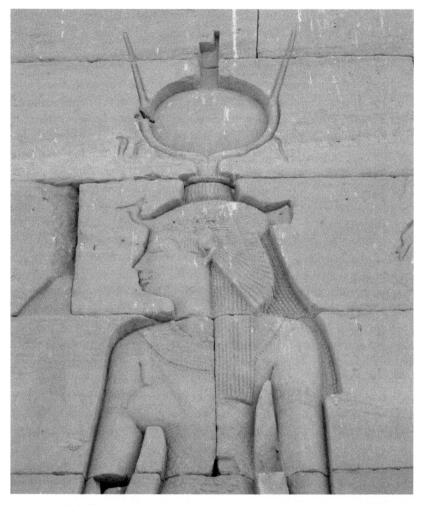

Fig. 10. Relief of the goddess Isis in the temple of Kalabsha at Aswan. Photo by
Françoise Dunand.

by a temple priest who declares his wish to "make known to the Greeks"
the Egyptian gods, proclaim that the goddess is worshipped by various
peoples under different names; but only the Egyptians know her by her
true name.[30]

Other Egyptian gods also underwent a transformation of their images.
This is the case for the Nile, depicted with the traits of a bearded old man,

---

[30] Bernand, *Inscriptions métriques*, 631–8.

along the lines of a Greco-Roman river-god. He carries the cornucopia, often surrounded by a swarm of little children, symbolizing the number of cubits equivalent to a "good" flood. But in the same era, Hapy, the demi-god of the Nile, continues to be represented as a fat young man (an expression of the prosperity that he personified), wearing a wig and false beard, as he appears on the monumental statue (also quite exceptionally) recently discovered in the waters of the port of Heracleum.[31]

Even more striking is the adoption, for various deities, of Roman military dress. Thus, Horus could appear as *imperator*, which is not all that surprising, seeing that he is a warrior-god, avenger of his father, and victor over the forces of evil. It is probably in virtue of the same role that Bes could be represented in military regalia, with sword and shield. Anubis, even though he is not a god of combat, is depicted as a Roman legionary on a wall of the main tomb of Kom esh-Shugafa in Alexandria.

One highly interesting innovation in the iconography of the Egyptian deities occurred in the Roman period. Various deities were at that time endowed with a crown of rays, Serapis in particular, whose solar character is highlighted in the Roman period. But it is also worn by Harpocrates, identified as the infant sun that emerges from a lotus flower at the origin of the world, and even by more unexpected divine personages, such as the crocodile Sobek or the sphinx Tutu. The crown of rays, a motif borrowed from Greco-Roman iconography, apparently carried in Egypt the double meaning of regeneration of power and regeneration of life.[32]

Many of these new images were disseminated through the medium of mold-cast terra cotta statuettes. These were manufactured in enormous quantities with a popular clientele in mind, and either kept in the home or deposited in tombs. Produced in the workshops of the *chōra* by artisans who also turned out everyday wares, they appear to have bypassed the rules governing the decoration of temples.[33] Even so, we cannot rule out the possibility that the Egyptian clergy had been gradually induced to integrate new features in both the figurative and textual representation of the traditional gods. The statuettes of Harpocrates on the lotus flower, ringing him with a crown of rays, reflect a doctrine elaborated in priestly circles, the so-called Hermopolitan cosmogony. The Nubian god Mandulis at Kalabsha is invoked under the name of Apollo and Aion in scholarly texts certainly composed by temple priests.

---

[31] Goddio, ed. *Trésors engloutis*, 94–5.
[32] Tallet, *Les dieux à couronne radiée* (forthcoming).
[33] Dunand, *Terres cuites gréco-romaines*, 5–17.

While the adoption of new images to represent traditional gods could be accounted for by the presence of foreign "customers," it would be much too simplistic to assume that the traditional images were intended for Egyptians and the new images for Greeks and other foreigners who had settled in Egypt. The latter are not at all hesitant about adopting the Egyptian vision of the gods. What is quite striking in this era is the coexistence of the divine images. A belief of long standing in Egypt allowed that a single deity could assume various forms, thereby accommodating the appearance of novel forms. As for these images, it was left for each person to interpret them in the context of his own culture. A relief discovered at Akoris depicts, dressed in the Greek style, a goddess between two gods. Although one might recognize here Helen in the company of the Dioscuri, another reading would make it possible to see in this triad Isis in the company of the two crocodile-gods (who, as we know, could be identified with the Dioscuri).[34] Graffiti from the temple of Deir el-Hagar (the Dakhla Oasis) portrays, side by side, Amon in the form of a bearded god, along the lines of Zeus or Asclepius, and in his Egyptian form as a ram. In Dush (Kysis) in the Kharga Oasis, at the end of the first century of the common era, the temple built in honor of Osiris depicts on its walls the traditional image of the god. But it is the classical image of Serapis (to whom the monumental inscription in Greek on the pylon is dedicated) that adorns the gold crown of the temple treasury. As for the votive offerings found in the treasury, they contain the image of Serapis, and that of the Apis bull in particular. The majority of the gods could be seen in various forms, which coexist with no trouble.[35]

AN UNCHANGING DOMAIN: FUNERARY BELIEFS AND PRACTICES

Universal mummification

From the Ptolemaic up to the late Roman period, the practice of mummification experienced considerable growth. The explanation for this trend is very likely the development over the course of the first millennium BCE of simplified techniques; these were much less costly than the "classical" technique, which had attained a high degree of sophistication toward the close of the New Kingdom. Herodotus reports that in his time (the middle of the fifth century CE), three "classes" of mummification existed, ranging from the most sophisticated, evidently the longest standing and most expensive,

---

[34] Drew-Bear, "Triade d'Akôris," 227–34.
[35] Dunand, "Syncrétisme ou coexistence," 105–15.

to the third class, used "for the poorer." There was also an intermediate category, simplified and thus accessible, but also of reasonably high quality (Herodotus 2.86–9). The study of mummies "in the field" attests to the accuracy of Herodotus's information. Necropolises of villages of the Kharga Oasis, dating from the Ptolemaic and Roman periods, confirm the existence of three classes of mummies. A few of them were prepared very well, according to the classical method, with evisceration, careful bandaging, and, in many cases, gilding of the body. Without doubt this was meant for prominent people. Many corpses have been mummified with the use of a simplified technique; although without evisceration, their preservation is often excellent. In other even more numerous cases, they are little more than skeletons; even so, they bear practically all the markings of mummification. It is necessary to add a fourth category to Herodotus's tableau: mummies of proper appearance that under X-ray show up as veritable "bags of bones."[36]

One should not, however, speak of a decline in mummification techniques in the Ptolemaic and Roman periods. Because the practice had become much more widespread during this period, the result was a lowering of the overall standard. Even so, embalmers often possessed the skill to prepare "good" mummies.

In addition, this practice spread into Greek circles in Egypt. In Alexandrian cemeteries, the oldest tombs were often for cremation, with funerary urns. But this practice gradually disappeared. From the beginning of the second century CE, the majority of tombs were for interment. The majority of the mummies discovered and described in excavation reports are in a poor state, due to the deplorable conditions of conservation in Alexandria.[37] With its close links to the affirmation of eternal life after death, mummification might well have seemed to the Greeks as expressing greater hope than their own practices did.

Visions of the afterlife

The traditional perception of the next life thus remained unchanged. Composed in the New Kingdom, the *Book of the Dead*, a "passport," as it were, for the journey to the next life, continued to be recopied and deposited in tombs in the Ptolemaic period. Although it was replaced by other funerary texts in the Roman period – the *Books of Respirations* and

---

[36] Dunand and Lichtenberg, *Mummies and Death*, 166–71.
[37] Charron, ed. *La mort n'est pas une fin*, 62–74.

the *Book of Passing through Eternity* – the objective remained unchanged. The countless images of the world of the dead illustrate these beliefs: the weighing of the heart performed by Anubis and Horus in the presence of Thoth, the presentation of the "justified" dead to Osiris, the voyage to the next world and the confrontation with the formidable demigods, the gate-keepers. These motifs are often reproduced on the sarcophagi and the "boxes" of painted stuccoed cloth into which corpses were very frequently deposited during this period.[38] The cartonnages could also depict the dead in "everyday" dress. An individualizing tendency appears also in the practice, dating to the beginning of the Roman period, which consisted of replacing the mask made of cartonnage or stucco with a portrait painted in tempera or in encaustic on a wooden backboard, sometimes directly on the shroud, following a tradition completely alien to Egyptian tradition.[39] This practice obviously was available only to an affluent and relatively privileged segment of the Egyptian population. This is also true of the practice that involved gilding the face and other parts of the corpse; this was a means of conferring divinity, inasmuch as gold, for the Egyptians, was the "flesh of the gods."

In this period, however, there are hints of a vision of the next world perhaps at odds with the traditional view. Before Alexander's conquest, texts insisted on the idea of retribution and the necessity of leading a just life in this world. But a literary text well known in the Roman period, the *Story of Satni,* provides a picture of the world of the dead relatively close to the Greek Underworld, including a series of "circles" in which various torments are inflicted on those who had lived bad lives.[40]

DECLINE AND DISAPPEARANCE OF THE TRADITIONAL RELIGION

One question remains open: the role that the diffusion of a new religion in Egypt – Christianity – played in the decline and disappearance of the traditional religion. The spread of Christianity appears to have been relatively late and rather slow. There are hardly any signs of it before the end of the second century, and the establishment of institutional structures was accomplished only gradually over the course of the third century. Even at the beginning of the fourth century, the position of Christians in Egyptian society was modest; judging from the onomastic evidence, they probably

---

[38] Walker and Bierbrier, ed. *Ancient Faces.*
[39] Parlasca, *Mumienporträts und verwandte Denkmäler;* Borg, *Mumienporträts.*
[40] Lichtheim, *Ancient Egyptian Literature,* III, 139–42.

numbered less than 20 percent of the population. This number slowly increased before undergoing a sudden acceleration toward the end of the century.[41] In other words, Christianity before the fourth century did not emerge as serious competition with the traditional religion. The Christian minority was evidently well integrated into a society within which there were no discernible conflicts. Persecutions officially carried out against the Christians under Decius, Valerian, and then Diocletian, the motives for which seem to have been of a political as much as a religious character, apparently did not have much of an impact in the *chōra*.

In Alexandria, on the other hand, troubles between the various communities erupted throughout the course of the fourth century. In 363, it was the mob-murder by the populace of the bishop George, who, being of Arian leaning, appears to have had enemies among both Christians and pagans (Amm. Marc. 22.11.3–10). But numerous conflicts erupted between different communities, often over the question of the possession or the recovery of a place of worship.

From the middle of the third century, the condition of the traditional cults is difficult to assess in its entirety. Up to this time, work continued to be done on the upkeep and restoration of the great sanctuaries; the cartouche of Decius is even present at Esna. But some temples have already collapsed, such as the one at Luxor. In the period of the tetrarchs, it was occupied by a Roman camp with a chapel of the emperor cult built in a room before the holy of holies. The only major temple providing indications of uninterrupted activity at a relatively late date was at Philae, where the last hieroglyphic inscription dates from the year 394 CE, and where the worship of Isis continued up until the beginning of the sixth century. But if the great temples of the Valley give little sign of activity starting in the middle of the third century, the reason probably has to do with the financial troubles observable at this time throughout the whole empire. After the Severan dynasty came a period of "military anarchy," from which the empire only recovered with the accession of Diocletian. All these years were marked by political and institutional crises, invasions, monetary disasters, and inflation. In Egypt, as elsewhere, the large temples must have been especially vulnerable. Their financial needs were substantial, because they involved maintaining buildings, organizing daily ritual and ceremonies, and providing for the livelihood of a sizeable staff. When public subsidies were lacking, the temples' own resources were certainly insufficient to ensure that they operated smoothly.

---

[41] Bagnall, *Late Antiquity*, 278–82. See further van der Vliet in Chapter 8 of this volume.

Small local temples, on the other hand, which essentially depended on the generosity of worshippers and were thus less exposed to political uncertainty, were not as vulnerable to major changes. The temples at Oxyrhynchus continued in operation in the fourth century, as well as the temple of the sphinx god Tutu at Kellis (the Dakhla Oasis).[42] In the same period, the little temple of Taffeh, to the south of Aswan, was rebuilt. Religious associations were active, like the one that came every year from Ermant to Deir el-Bahari to celebrate there a ritual banquet and sacrifice.

Religious life at that time experienced profound changes, and along with them the traditional role of the clergy. Possibly replacing the great official rites were practices more attentive to the expectations of worshippers; consultation of oracles and ritual magic assumed increasing importance. One can detect in Egyptian religion, over the course of the third and fourth centuries, a centrifugal tendency, placing more emphasis on local cults and expressions of personal piety.[43]

One central factor behind the disappearance of traditional religion was of course the religious policies of the emperors of the fourth century. Over the course of this century, measures intended to limit the practice of "pagan" cults followed one after the other. The edicts of Theodosius in 391/392 administered the coup de grâce. The Christians of Alexandria, under the direction of Bishop Theophilus, then seized the great temple of Serapis, looted it, and destroyed the statue of the god (Rufinus, *Hist. eccl.* 2.22–3). Even if Rufinus's report contains much rhetorical exaggeration, the event certainly had great repercussions. Beginning at this time, traces of the traditional religion were systematically effaced. Targeted for destruction were those countless little temples that in the words of Rufinus "fill all the country, the banks of the Nile, and even the desert" (*Hist. eccl.* 2.26). Even at Philae, an inscription proclaims, "The cross has triumphed, it triumphs forever."

Ancient practices endured nonetheless. At the end of the fifth century, monks invaded a private home in Menouthis near Canopus after a public accusation, and found there a stash of "idols," which they seized and destroyed. But even if private practices, more or less in secret, were still possible, the disappearance of the great temples, which for so long had been vibrant centers of theological reflection and ritual activity, brought about the end of traditional religious life.

---

[42] Kaper, *The Egyptian God Tutu*, 140–54.
[43] Frankfurter, *Religion in Roman Egypt*, 198–237.

BIBLIOGRAPHY

Arnold, Dieter. *Temples of the Last Pharaohs* (Oxford, 1999).

Assmann, Jan. *Maât, l'Égypte pharaonique et l'idée de justice sociale* (Paris, 1989).

Bagnall, Roger S. *Egypt in Late Antiquity* (Princeton, 1993).

Bernand, Etienne. *Inscriptions métriques de l'Égypte gréco-romaine; recherches sur la poésie épigrammatique des Grecs en Égypte* (Paris, 1969).

Bonhême, Marie Ange, and Annie Forgeau. *Pharaon: les secrets du pouvoir* (Paris, 1988).

Borg, Barbara. *Mumienporträts: Chronologie und kultureller Kontext* (Mainz, 1987).

Charron, Alain, ed. *La mort n'est pas une fin: pratiques funéraires en Égypte d'Alexandre à Cléopâtre* (Arles, 2002).

Chassinat, Emile. *Le mystère d'Osiris au mois de Khoiak* (Cairo, 1966–68).

Collombert, Philippe. "Religion égyptienne et culture grecque: l'exemple de Dioskouridès." *CdE* LXXV/149 (2000): 47–63.

Drew-Bear, Marie. "La triade du rocher d'Akôris." In *Mélanges Étienne Bernand*, eds. Nicole Fick and Jean-Claude Carrière (Paris, 1991): 227–34.

Dunand, Françoise. *Terres cuites gréco-romaines d'Égypte* (Paris, 1990).

"Syncrétisme ou coexistence: images du religieux en Égypte tardive." In *Les syncrétismes religieux dans le monde méditerranéen antique: actes du colloque international en l'honneur de Franz Cumont à l'occasion du cinquantième anniversaire de sa mort*, eds. Corinne Bonnet and André Motte (Rome, 1999): 97–116.

Isis, mère des dieux (Paris, 2000).

"La guérison dans les temples (Égypte, époque tardive)." *ARG* 8 (2006): 4–24.

Dunand, Françoise, and Roger Lichtenberg, with the collaboration of Alain Charron. *Des animaux et des hommes: une symbiose égyptienne* (Paris, 2005).

Mummies and Death in Egypt, trans. D. Lorton (Ithaca, N.Y., 2006).

Dunand, Françoise, and Christiane Zivie-Coche. *Hommes et dieux en Égypte* (Paris, 2006). Trans. David Lorton. *Gods and Men in Egypt: 3000 BCE to 395 CE* (Ithaca, N.Y., 2004).

Evans, J. A. S. "A Social and Economic History of an Egyptian Temple in the Greco-Roman Period." *YCS* 17 (1961): 145–283.

Frankfurter, David. *Religion in Roman Egypt: Assimilation and Resistance* (Princeton, 1998).

Fraser, P. M. *Ptolemaic Alexandria* (Oxford, 1972).

Goddio, Franck, ed. *Trésors engloutis d'Égypte* (Paris, 2006).

Grenier, Jean-Claude. "L'Empereur et le Pharaon." *ANRW* II.18.5 (1995): 3181–94.

Guéraud, Octave. *Enteuxeis: requêtes et plaintes adressées au roi d'Égypte au IIIe siècle avant J.-C.* (Cairo, 1931).

Hüss, Werner. *Der makedonische König und die ägyptischen Priester: Studien zur Geschichte des ptolemäischen Ägypten* (Stuttgart, 1994).

Ikram, Salima, ed. *Divine Creatures: Animal Mummies in Ancient Egypt* (Cairo, 2005).

Johnson, Janet H., ed. *Life in a Multicultural Society: Egypt from Cambyses to Constantine and Beyond* (Chicago, 1992).

Kaper, Olaf E. *The Egyptian God Tutu: A Study of the Sphinx-God and Master of Demons with a Corpus of Monuments* (Leuven, 2003).

Lenger, Marie-Thérèse. *Corpus des Ordonnances des Ptolémées* (Brussels, 1980).

Lichtheim, Miriam. *Ancient Egyptian Literature*. Vol III: *The Late Period* (Berkeley/Los Angeles/London, 1980).

Mélèze Modrzejewski, Joseph. *Les Juifs d'Égypte de Ramsès II à Hadrien* (Paris, 1997).

Parlasca, Klaus. *Mumienporträts und verwandte Denkmäler* (Wiesbaden, 1966).

Reddé, Michel. *Le trésor de Douch (oasis de Kharga)* (Cairo, 1992).

Sauneron, Serge. *Les fêtes religieuses d'Esna aux derniers siècles du paganisme* (Cairo, 1962).

 Les prêtres de l'ancienne Égypte (Paris, 1957). Trans. David Lorton. *The Priests of Ancient Egypt* (Ithaca, N.Y., 2000).

Thompson, Dorothy J. *Memphis under the Ptolemies* (Princeton, 1988).

Valbelle, Dominique, and Geneviève Husson. "Les questions oraculaires d'Égypte: histoire de la recherche, nouveautés et perspectives. " In *Egyptian Religion: The Last Thousand Years*, eds. Willy Clarysse, Antoon Schoors, and Harco Willems (Leuven, 1998): 1055–71.

Walker, Susan, and Morris Bierbrier, eds. *Ancient Faces: Mummy Portraits from Roman Egypt* (London, 1997).

Yoyotte, J. "Bakhthis: religion égyptienne et culture grecque à Edfou." In *Religions en Égypte hellénistique et romaine* (Paris, 1969): 127–41.

7

JUDAISM IN EGYPT

JOSEPH MÉLÈZE MODRZEJEWSKI
TRANSLATED BY WILLIAM ADLER

THE EGYPT OF THE BIBLE, THE PHARAOHS, AND THE PERSIANS

For the period of time from Abraham to Moses, we know the point at which ancient Israel took root in the Egyptian past. The Bible recounts a long sojourn of the Hebrews in Egypt, leading to the foundational events of Judaism: the Exodus, the giving of the Law, and the Mosaic covenant. For the historian, however, it is not an easy task to reconcile the biblical narrative with the historical and archaeological data now made available by Egyptology. The Bible and Egyptian hieroglyphs do not speak the same language. Points of intersection between the Egypt of the Bible and the Egypt of Egyptologists are both rare and a matter of dispute.[1]

The Egypt of the Bible is a reasonably accurate reflection of the various features of society in the Egyptian New Kingdom. History and archaeology allow us to verify its account with a certain degree of probability. Thus, the travails of the Hebrews described in the book of Exodus correlate with the projects undertaken in the Delta by the pharaohs of the eighteenth dynasty. The strict supervision of the workers, against which Moses revolts, today finds confirmation in Egyptian documents originating from a village laborer of Deir el-Medina.[2] This applies equally to quotas of bricks, the use of straw, and the allotment of vacation days. All of this was part of everyday life in Egypt of the thirteenth century BCE. In the ranks of the royal court, the figure of Aper-El, a Semite identified as vizier of Amenophis III, can be considered as a "prototype" of the biblical Joseph.[3] His success demonstrates that foreigners, who had either moved to Egypt or who had been born into an immigrant community in Egypt, could rise to high-ranking positions, including high office in the Egyptian court.

[1] Zivie, *La prison de Joseph.*
[2] Allam, *Arbeitersiedlung von Deir el-Medineh.*
[3] Zivie, *Le vizir oublié.*

189

Although Egyptology can furnish a historical and geographic framework into which the sojourn of the Hebrews in Egypt can be integrated, it cannot confirm the literary embellishments of a biblical text governed by doctrinal concerns extrinsic to this framework. The exodus of the Hebrews, for example, a critical moment in the sojourn in Egypt, could well be based on a historical event that would be tempting to date during the long reign of Ramses II (1279–12), around the year 1270 BCE. For the pharaoh's army, this was only a minor skirmish with a band of forced laborers who had managed to escape. The Jews, on the other hand, saw here a momentous event, a manifestation of the divine protection that had allowed them to escape their servitude and become an independent nation.

Properly speaking, the history of the Jews in Egypt begins with the Aramaic documents discovered in Elephantine, near Aswan. They constitute the "archives" of a Jewish military colony of the fifth century BCE, at a time when Egypt was a province (satrapy) of the Persian empire.[4] They inform us about the organization of a garrison of Syene/Elephantine, responsible for guarding the southern frontier of Egypt. In addition, they reveal details about the community life of this group, whose cultural and religious autonomy was ensured by the Persian government. Unique in the history of ancient Judaism, these documents raise fascinating questions about the enforcement of legal and social regulations within the community.[5] The issue of divorce will suffice as an example. As consecrated by biblical law, the only way to dissolve the marital bond – recognized in rabbinic law up to the present day – grants this privilege unilaterally to the husband. As a corollary to this right, the community of Elephantine extended this prerogative to the woman as well (Porten-Yardeni B 2.4).

The religious life of the colony revolved around the temple of their national God, "YHW," the tetragrammaton reduced to three letters. Its presence on the island did not continue without stirring up conflict with the neighboring Egyptians, worshippers of the ram-god Khnum, who also had his sanctuary there. The existence of a Jewish temple in Egypt in the fifth century BCE might appear to run afoul of the Deuteronomic principle of the unity of the sacrificial cult, reserved solely for the Jerusalem temple by the reforms of Josiah (622 BCE). Even so, the founding figures of postexilic Judaism, who adopted this principle, did not disown their fellow

---

[4] Porten, *Archives from Elephantine.*
[5] Yaron, *Introduction*; Muffs, *Studies.*

countrymen in Elephantine. Rather, they strove to absorb this peripheral Judaism into a movement of unification seeking to incorporate the various Jewish communities of Babylon and Jerusalem under the authority of the high priest. A document known by the name "Passover Papyrus" bears witness to this (Porten-Yardeni A 4.1). The purpose of the letter, written in 419/418 BCE and addressed to the leaders of the colony by a relative of Nehemiah, is to introduce Elephantine to the Passover calendar and the Feast of Unleavened Bread, which hereafter was to be celebrated at a fixed date – from the fifteenth to the twenty-first of the month of Nisan. Deuteronomic centralism, while fiercely opposed to "high places" in the land of Israel, spared the Elephantine sanctuary. Their reason for doing so could be that, during the entire period from the fall of Jerusalem in 586 BCE up to the reconstruction of the Temple after the return from captivity in Babylonia, Elephantine was the sole location where the temple cult was maintained.

To be sure, certain features of the religious practice of the Jews of Elephantine must have displeased the Jewish leaders in Jerusalem. Although the colonists respected the ancient commandments, such as the Sabbath rest, they continued the cultic practices that the reforms of Josiah attempted to abolish. The financial records of the temple reveal, for example, the existence of a female character, Anat-Yahu or Anat-Bethel, alongside the god venerated by the colonists (Porten-Yardeni C 3.15). This consort goddess is assuredly none other than the "Queen of Heaven," to whom the Jews of Egypt proclaim their devotion in response to the denunciations addressed against them by the prophet Jeremiah (Jer. 44:7). A "pre-Deuteronomic" Judaism lived on in Elephantine.

Despite these deviations, the dialogue between Elephantine and post-exilic Jerusalem resumed at the end of the fifth century. In the spring of 410 BCE, the sanctuary of YHW was sacked by Egyptian rebels with the support of a governor of Syene, who had split off from the central government. Although it would be rebuilt with the cooperation of the Persian regime, the sacrificial cult would from that point have to limit itself to vegetable offerings and incense; making burnt offerings of animals was discontinued (Porten-Yardenu A 4.9 and 4.10). This compromise would be of short duration. Everything came to an end at the beginning of the fourth century BCE, when the Jewish colony and its temple were eradicated by a surge in Egyptian nationalism. It would require the Macedonian conquest of Egypt in 332/331 BCE to see the revival of Jewish life on the banks of the Nile.

ALEXANDRIAN JUDAISM

The foundation of Alexandria by Alexander, king of the Macedonians, at the beginning of 331 BCE inaugurated a new era in the history of the Jews of Egypt and a new experience in Jewish history: Alexandrian Judaism, a nonrabbinic form of Judaism and the first Jewish diaspora in the West in the modern sense of the word.[6] In assimilating themselves to the conquering Greco-Macedonians – the "Hellenes" – the Jews of Hellenistic Egypt practiced their Judaism according to the terms of Greek language and culture, even while remaining faithful to the monotheistic tenets of their ancestral law.[7]

Inscriptions on the tombs of Alexandrian necropolises confirm Flavius Josephus's claims about the antiquity of the Jewish settlement in Alexandria (*J. W.* 2.487; *Ag. Ap.* 2.42f.). The oldest of them extend back to the times of Ptolemy I Soter (satrap in 323–282 BCE and then king, beginning in 305) and his son Ptolemy II Philadelphus (282–46 BCE). The names attested there are either Hebrew names in Greek form, or Greek names, some of which express devotion to the royal family (for example, "Ptolemaios" or "Arsinoë"). With two or three exceptions, the inscriptions are in Greek. They attest to the rapid integration of the Jews into the dominant group of Greek-speaking immigrants.

This integration did not entail the disappearance of Jewish identity, even though it aroused in pagan circles the hostility that comes to the fore in both literary sources and the papyri.[8] Adherence to Greek culture did not inevitably lead to apostasy, the abandonment of Judaism for the service of "other gods." One celebrated case of this occurring can be cited here, that of Dositheus, son of Drimylus. Dositheus, a Hellenized Jew, had a successful career in the service of Ptolemy III Euergetes, culminating in his commission in 223/222 BCE as eponymous priest of the cult of Alexander and the deified Ptolemies.[9] Despite the obviously political character of the priesthood of Alexander, Dositheus was, in the eyes of the author of 3 Maccabees, simply an apostate who "renounced his religion and apostatized from the ancestral traditions" (3 Macc. 1:3). His case is a rare one, however. On the whole, Hellenistic Judaism in Alexandria

---

[6] See Mélèze-Modrzejewski, *Juifs d'Égypte*; idem, "Espérances et illusions du judaïsme alexandrin." For a recent overview, see Schimanowski, *Juden und Nichtjuden in Alexandrien.*

[7] Mélèze-Modrzejewski, "Le statut des Hellènes." Jewish integration into Greek society is ratified by their fiscal status: *P. Count.* 2, 147–8.

[8] Mélèze-Modrzejewski, "Sur l'antisémitisme païen"; Schäfer, *Judaeophobia.*

[9] *CPJud.* I, 127a-d. See Fuks, "Dositheos Son of Drimylos."

and Egypt successfully negotiated the difficult feat of being simultaneously both Jewish and Greek.

According to latest estimates, the Jews at the beginning of the Roman era would have constituted one-third of the total inhabitants of the city, or between 150,000 and 180,000 people out of a total population of approximately 500,000 (the highest total population imaginable for an ancient megalopolis). Despite their numbers, they were not, barring extremely rare exceptions, citizens of Alexandria. In his *Letter to the Alexandrians* (*P.Lond.* VI 1912 = *CPJud.* II 153; November 41 CE), the emperor Claudius could thus remark that "they live in a city that is not their own," even though they had been settled there for more than three centuries. Although Alexandrians in the general sense – that is to say, inhabitants of Alexandria – they were not part of the Greek *polis* (city-state). They called themselves "Jews from Alexandria" (*Ioudaioi apo Alexandreias*: *CPJud.* II 151, 5/4 CE), a formula analogous to what one finds for local communities in the *chōra* – for example, the Jews of Xenephyris (Horbury-Noy, 24), Nitriai (Horbury-Noy, 25), Athribis (Horbury-Noy, 27), and Crocodilopolis (Horbury-Noy, 117).

We have little detailed information about the organization of their communities. Strabo, quoted by Josephus (*Ant.* 14.117), speaks of an ethnarch ("leader of the people") who administered Jewish affairs in Alexandria and settled legal disputes by means of arbitration. This function is not attested in the documentary material. Under the Roman empire, the sending of Jewish embassies to Rome presupposes the existence of a structured community with the means to select envoys invested with the authority to represent the Jews of Alexandria before the emperor. On the other hand, the existence of a *politeuma* of Alexandrian Jews, a quasi-civic community with aspirations to legal equality with the civic unit, the Greek *polis*, is far from proven. We shall return to this question later.

THE SEPTUAGINT

The religious and community life of the Jews in Greco-Roman Egypt was organized around the biblical law available in the Greek translation of the Torah known as the Septuagint. The historicity of this translation is confirmed by fragments from the Septuagint preserved in papyri dating to the pre-Christian era. On the other hand, historians are divided about its origins. According to one school of thought, the initiative for the translation came from the Lagid sovereigns. For the other school, it arose out of the rapid Hellenization of Jews in Ptolemaic Egypt. Because they no longer understood Hebrew, they required a version of the Scriptures that was comprehensible to them. The Greek version of the Torah was, therefore, initially only a Greek targum accompanying the reading of the Torah in the synagogue. What we now call the Septuagint would have only been a standardized and officially sanctioned later redaction.[10]

Examination of the documents preserved in the Greek papyri of Egypt enables us to break the impasse of this debate. At the same time, they disclose an important, but little-known, aspect of the Alexandrian Bible: its place in the judicial system of the Ptolemaic monarchy.[11] The need felt by the Jews to have a Greek version of the Torah available to them complements the goals of a royal policy anxious about guaranteeing respect for the national traditions of the kingdom's inhabitants. Translations of their "sacred books," undertaken during the reign of Ptolemy Philadelphus, were thus received favorably, if not materially supported, by the monarchy. A local counterpart of the Jewish Law, the Egyptian Priestly Case Book, a collection of rules and legal guidelines assembled by the native priests, was also translated into Greek under Ptolemy II. This translation has survived the Roman conquest, as a copy known to us from the Antonine era attests (*P.Oxy.* XLVI 3285).

Translations like these had significant practical value. For judges and royal functionaries, familiar only with Greek, they offered access to legal regulations relevant to the administration of justice but originally recorded in other languages. In a way comparable to the role that the Egyptian legal compendium played for the native population, the Septuagint version of the Torah could now be invoked by Jewish litigants before courts and officials. It thus received official sanction as the "civic law" (*politikos nomos*) of the Jews of Egypt.[12] For this reason, knowledge of the Bible in pagan circles pertained initially to legal matters and Ptolemaic administration. One must wait until the beginning of the Christian era to find an echo of the Septuagint in Greek literature (Ps. Longinus, *On the Sublime* 9, 9 = *GLAJJ* 1.364–65, no. 148: an allusion to Gen. 1:3).

In the eyes of some of the sages of the Talmud, the translation of the Torah into Greek was a quite legitimate, even inspired, undertaking, notwithstanding the alleged errors of the translators. R. Simeon b. Gamaliel, an admirer of Greek wisdom, goes so far as to privilege Greek as the only "other language" authorized for scripture (*b. Megilla* 8b-9b). To justify his opinion, the Gemara appeals to "the beauty of Japhet" (Gen. 9:27). The

[10] See Dorival, Harl, and Munnich, *La Bible grecque des Septante,* 39–82, 182–93.
[11] See Mélèze Modrzejewski, "Law and Justice in Ptolemaic Egypt"; idem, "Droit et justice dans l'Égypte des premiers Lagides."
[12] See Mélèze Modrzejewski, "The Septuagint as Nomos."

opposing opinion – which accepts only the Hebrew "square script" (*ktav ashuri*) and considers the day on which the Torah was translated into Greek for king Ptolemy "as disastrous as the day on which Israel fashioned the golden calf" (*Massekhet Soferim*, 7–10) – should be understood in its historical context. It represents the rejection of the Septuagint at a time when this translation, made by Jews for Jews, had, in the wake of the destruction of Alexandrian Judaism at the beginning of the second century CE, become the Bible of Greek-speaking Christians.

JEWISH BOOKS IN GREEK

The Septuagint version of the Torah is the first and most celebrated representative of Judeo-Alexandrian literature: a literature composed in the Greek language, while remaining Jewish both in content and in the goals that it sought to achieve.[13] With the exception of a few works, the most important of which were the Septuagint and the exegetical corpus of Philo, we know of them only in fragments that survive thanks to a chain of transmission extending from Alexander Polyhistor (first century BCE) to Eusebius of Caesarea (fourth century CE). A resource of inestimable value, they collectively reflect the various streams of thought, ideological choices, and political options available to Alexandrian Judaism.

Two works are directly connected with the Septuagint. Under the title *Letter of Aristeas to Philocrates,* the first work, possibly dating to the second part of the reign of Ptolemy VIII Euergetes II (ca.146–16 BCE), offers us an idealized account of the translation. Its author, a Hellenized Jew who represents himself as a Greek and approaches Judaism from a Greek perspective, asserts the adherence of the Greek version of the Torah to the norms of Alexandrian philology.[14] The position that he adopts supports the view that ascribes the initiative for the translation of the Torah to Ptolemy Philadelphus II.

The same view is also held by the Judeo-Alexandrian philosopher Aristobulus, the author of an exegetical work dedicated to king Ptolemy VI Philometer, around 176–70 BCE. Convinced that Greek philosophy has its origin in biblical wisdom, Aristobulus has no hesitations about claiming that Pythagoras and Plato were already inspired by the Jewish Bible. He thus posits the existence of a Greek translation, at least a partial one, prior to the Septuagint (in Eusebius, *Praep. Evang.* 13.12.1).[15] While the existence

---

[13] Nickelsburg, *Jewish Literature between the Bible and the Mishnah*, 191–230.
[14] Honigman, *The Septuagint*, 42–9.
[15] Walter, *Der Thoraausleger Aristobulos*, 27–9; 43–51.

of such a translation is highly doubtful, an Oxyrhynchus papyrus, known since 1972, now suggests that in fact some biblical themes, in this case Solomon's famous judgment scene (1 Kings 3:16–28), were already known in Greece before the death of Plato.[16]

The "chronographer Demetrius," who lived in Alexandria in the time of Ptolemy IV Philopator, is the first Greek-speaking Jewish historian known to us. Six fragments have survived from his work *On the Kings of Judea*.[17] Under the influence of Eratosthenes of Cyrene, Demetrius rationalizes Israelite history to an extreme degree, representing it as a series of chronological calculations, a method that he evidently regarded as the highest form of scientific discourse. He follows the biblical text of the Septuagint version, his sole source, for which he is the oldest historical witness.

In a work of the second century BCE, which is as much historical narrative as it is novel, another Jewish author, bearing the Persian name of Artapanus, portrays Joseph and Moses as the "first inventors," who taught the Egyptians the arts of astronomy, agriculture, philosophy, and religion (in Eusebius, *Praep. Evang.* 9.27.1–6).[18] In this way, Moses becomes, unexpectedly for us, the founder of the Egyptian worship of animals. The poet Ezekiel, inspired by Aeschylus and Euripides, describes the exodus from Egypt (*Exagōgē*) in the guise of Greek tragedy.[19] Another poet, Philo the Elder, recounts in archaizing hexameters the history of the holy city of Jerusalem.[20]

The novel *Joseph and Aseneth* (first century BCE), whose author remains unknown to us, addresses the problem of a mixed marriage between a Jew and a pagan and advocates conversion to Judaism as a solution.[21] An interpretation of this story in connection with the temple at Leontopolis has also been suggested.[22] A kind of historical-moral novel, also composed anonymously at the beginning of the first century BCE and preserved in some manuscripts of the Septuagint under the title *Third Book of the Maccabees,* recounts a conflict connected with the cult of Dionysus, pitting the Jews of Alexandria and Egypt against king Ptolemy IV Philopator.[23]

---

[16] See Mélèze Modrzejewski, "Philiscos de Milet et le jugement de Salomon."

[17] Text and translation in Holladay, *Fragments* 1: *The Historians,* 51–91. See Bickerman, "The Jewish Historian Demetrios."

[18] Artapanus's Jewish identity is contested by H. Jacobson, "Artapanus Judaeus."

[19] Collins, "Ezechiel."

[20] Gutman, "Philo the Epic Poet."

[21] Burchard, *Joseph und Aseneth.* cf. Chapter 4 above, p. 122.

[22] Bohak, *Joseph and Aseneth.*

[23] For a new English translation (replete with anachronisms), see Croy, *3 Maccabees.* For fuller exposition, see the edition of Mélèze Modrzejewski, in *La Bible d'Alexandrie.*

Criticized by modern philologists for its labored style, it conveys a message that places fidelity to the law over loyalty to the sovereign of the Jews' host country.

Judeo-Alexandrian literature culminates in the work of the philosopher Philo (ca.20 BCE–40 CE).[24] Only a portion of his purely philosophical treatises is extant, either in Greek (*Quod omnis probus liber sit, De aeternitate mundi*) or in an Armenian version (*Alexander, De providentia*). His political writings shed light on both the history of Alexandrian Judaism in the first century of the Roman empire (*In Flaccum, Legatio ad Caium*), and on the Jewish "sects," including the Essenes (*Apologia pro Iudaeis/Hypothetica*) and the Therapeutae (*De vita contemplativa*).

In the more than three-quarters of his writings devoted to the Torah, Philo, who is unfamiliar with Hebrew, uses the Greek version of the Septuagint for his commentary and interpretation. His exegesis is grounded in an allegorical reading that he pursues to its highest level. Proceeding from the principle that all language is symbolic, his method attempts to search out the deep meaning of the voice of God behind the terms of human discourse. In this way, Philo aspires to establish the perfect compatibility between the Torah and Greek reason.

At the heart of this exegesis stand the law and the law-giver: Moses, the unrivaled legislator, far superior to a Solon or a Lycurgus. Both the prophets of Israel and the Greek philosophers are his disciples. But while the former follow him faithfully, the latter preserve the revelation to Moses only in a partial and obscure form. Through the exegesis of scripture, Philo thinks it possible to restore the unity of the truth revealed to the world by Moses. The use of one universal language, namely Greek, the common language (*koinē*) of the civilized work (*oikoumenē*), would facilitate the undertaking. In this way, Philo hopes, the Mosaic law would end up triumphing on a universal scale.

Philo's influence on the Fathers of the Church and his role as intermediary between Greek philosophy and Christian theology are well known, even though the rabbinic sages pass over him in silence. Recent research, however, has attempted to delineate points of contact between his thought and rabbinic teaching of the same time.[25] This great sage was also an intrepid community leader. We see him at the head of a Jewish embassy

---

[24] For bibliographic inventory, see Goodhart and Goodenough, *General Bibliography of Philo Judaeus* (up to 1937); Radice, Runia, et al. *Philo of Alexandria* (1937–1986); Runia and Keitzer, *Philo of Alexandria* (1987–1996). For a good recent account intended for the general public, see Hadas-Lebel, *Philon d'Alexandrie*.

[25] Cohen, *Philo Judaeus*.

taking up the fight before the emperor Caligula in defense of the "civic rights" of his coreligionists.[26] What is at stake in this contest, one more religious than political, is a guarantee of the right of the Jews to live according to the precepts of the Torah.[27]

THE POLITEUMA

In discussion of Philo and his Alexandrian compatriots, several writers make use of the term *politeuma*, "a corporate civic body," as if it were an established fact. In fact, only the *Letter of Aristeas* (12.310) employs the term *politeuma* in connection with the Jews of Alexandria, in this case to distinguish the "people of the *politeuma*" (*hoi apo tou politeumatos*) from the "leaders of the people" (*hēgoumenoi tou plēthous*). One might as well say that the *politeuma* did not mingle with the "multitude" (*plēthos*) – that is, the Jewish population of the city. Flavius Josephus (*Ant.* 12.2.13), who paraphrases this text, does not even refer to it. Modern historians have inflated the significance of this isolated and temporally limited witness.

Papyrological discoveries now enable us to refine the terms of the debate. Until recently, we knew for sure of only one Jewish *politeuma* in a Hellenized province at the beginning of the Roman empire – that of Berenice in Cyrenaica (*IGLBibbia* 24; 24 BCE). Although evidence of the *politeuma* was at one time lacking for the Jews of the Egyptian *chōra,* this social structure, at once religious and military (consisting of soldiers who worshipped the same deity), was confirmed for other immigrant groups of shared origin: Idumeans, Cretans, Thracians, Boetians, Cilicians, Lycians, and Phrygians.

The 2001 edition of a score of documents scattered among the collections of Munich, Heidelberg, and Vienna (*P.Polit.Iud.*) now makes it possible to link these groups to a single Jewish *politeuma* established in the nome of Heracleopolis, at the entrance to the Fayyum, during the second part of the reign of Ptolemy VIII Euergetes II and after his restoration in 145 BCE (144/3 to 133/2 BCE).[28] It is described in these sources as the "*politeuma* of the Jews in Heracleopolis" (*to en Herakleou polei politeuma tōn Ioudaiōn*: *P.Polit.Iud.* 8.4–5, 133 BCE; cf. 20 v° 8–9, ca.143–32 BCE). Its members call themselves "those of the *politeuma*" (*ek tou politeumatos*) and

[26] Smallwood, *Philonis Alexandrini Legatio ad Gaium* (2nd ed.; Leiden, 1970); cf. Blouin, *Le conflit judéo-alexandrin de 38–41,* 38–137.
[27] See Mélèze Modrzejewski, "Les Juifs dans le monde gréco-romain," 10–12.
[28] The clarification of the term sought by Lüderitz, "What is Politeuma?," should now be answered in light of this archive. See Honigman, "Politeumata and Ethnicity."

proclaim themselves as "citizens" (*politai*) in contrast to the "foreigners" (*allophuloi*: *P.Polit.Iud.* 1.17–18, 135 BCE).

The politarch (*politarchēs*), the leader of the *politeuma*, and the archons ("magistrates"), who assist in the exercise of his duties, are petitioned by the members of the *politeuma* and other persons to settle disputes that arise in their domestic and community life. The business they engage in is thus of a judicial nature, in all likelihood by virtue of royal sanction. The petitions referred to them demonstrate that the Jews of Egypt appealed to biblical law as the system of justice regulating judicial practice. Formulae such as *kata ton nomon*, "according to the law" (*P.Polit.Iud.* 4.14–15, 30), to express conformity of an action to Jewish law, or *parabebēkotos ton patrion nomon*, "in violation of ancestral law" (*P.Polit.Iud.* 9.28–9), in connection with the violation of an oath, explicitly refer to the Mosaic law. The vocabulary is Septuagintal: *mneusteuomai* for a marriage proposal (*P.Polit.Iud.* 4.5–6; cf. Deut. 22:23–29 [LXX]), or *byblion tou apostasiou* for a writ of divorce (*P. Polit.Iud.* 4.23–4; cf. Deut. 24:1[LXX]). The documents from Heracleopolis thus establish that the Septuagint was not only the text that was read in the synagogues; it was also the law implemented in everyday life.

The archive of Heracleopolis also validates our doubts as to the continued existence of a Jewish *politeuma* in Alexandria. If one were to apply to Alexandria the official terminology used in Heracleopolis, we would expect to hear about a "*politeuma* of the Jews of Alexandria" (*to en Alexandreiai politeuma tōn Ioudaiōn*). But such terminology does not appear in any known source. All the evidence suggests that the Jewish community of Alexandria was not firmly organized as a *politeuma*. Nor is the *politeuma* the sole or even the dominant form of community organization of the Jews in Egypt. As a privilege extended to a group of soldiers, it is a social system reserved for military colonies like Heracleopolis and possibly Leontopolis (to be dealt with later).[29]

THE PRACTICAL AFFAIRS OF DIASPORA JUDAISM

The information provided by the archive of Heracleopolis offers us a realistic picture of the way in which Egyptian Jews practiced their Judaism in both their domestic and community life. A complaint addressed to the magistrates of the *politeuma* of Heracleopolis (*P.Polit.Iud.* 4) in 134 BCE is especially illustrative.[30]

---

[29] This is the conclusion of Cowey and Maresch, *P. Polit. Iud.*, 5–6.
[30] See Mélèze Modrzejewski, "La fiancée adultère."

After a member of the *politeuma* had proposed marriage to the daughter of another member of the community and the "betrothal" had been finalized, the father of the "fiancée" changed his mind and married his daughter to another man, without waiting to receive from his unfortunate son-in-law "the traditional writ of divorce" (*to eithismenon tou apostasiou byblion*). Believing that he had been wronged, the son-in-law demanded a judgment "in accordance with the law" (*kata ton nomon*). This document shows us that Jewish marriage in Ptolemaic Egypt was transacted, as it was elsewhere during the same time, in two successive stages: (1) *erusin* or *kiddushin* ("sanctification"), a term usually translated as "betrothed," but which actually designates a marriage that has already begun; (2) *nisuin* ("elevation"), the sealing of the conjugal bond through the introduction of the "fiancée" into the home of the husband. A period of several months could separate the two events, and a writ of divorce was necessary to dissolve the bond established by the *kiddushin*; if not, then the young woman would find herself in an unlawful state. In considering the question of her status, Philo of Alexandria (*Spec.* 3.72) wavers between adultery (*moicheia*) and seduction (*phthōra*), but opts for the first solution. The same problem also concerns his contemporary Hillel the Elder (*t. Ketub.* 4, 9, and parallels), who is more lenient than the Alexandrian philosopher on the subject of "betrothed adultery." In the time of Philo and Hillel, the pregnancy of Mary, the mother of Jesus, falls, from a judicial perspective, into the same category (Matt. 1:18–25). Thanks to the Heracleopolis papyrus, the texts of Philo, Hillel, and Matthew thus receive confirmation from a witness of unquestionable credibility.

The attachment of the Jews of Egypt to their ancestral law and the freedom they enjoyed in administering it in domestic affairs did not deter them from borrowing Greek terminology used by Hellenistic notaries for certifying contracts. In order to document in writing the rights and responsibilities of spouses, for example, they resorted to the *sungraphē sunoikisiou* ou *sunoikeseōs*, "a (written) agreement of cohabitation," corresponding in Alexandria to the *sunchōrēsis*, "judicial transaction," a type of document that is distinctively Alexandrian. References in the papyri dealing with Jewish couples in Egypt in the third and second centuries BCE[31] coincide with the story of the marriage of Tobias and Sarah in the book of Tobit (Tob. 7:13–14, in the version of codex Sinaiticus). Matrimonial practice in the diaspora thus sought to accommodate

---

[31] *CPR* XVIII 9, 180 (Samaria, Fayyum, 232 BCE); *P.Polit.Iud.* 3, 9 (Heracleopolis, ca.140 BCE); probably also *P.Ent.* 23 = *CPJud.* I 128.

the Jewish character of marriage to the practical necessities of life in a Greco-Roman setting.[32]

In business affairs, Jewish practice is illustrated by documents involving the biblical prohibition of loans with interest (Exod. 22:24; Lev. 25:35–37; Deut. 23:20–21). On this matter, the archive of Heracleopolis (*P.Polit.Iud.* 8, 133 BCE) confirms the assumption that a distinction was drawn between "a charitable loan" (a loan for consumption), for which interest was prohibited, and a "commercial loan" (an investment loan), in which case it was allowed. The prohibition against interest was thus in effect only when group solidarity came into play. Jewish practice in Egypt foreshadows rabbinic discussion of this same thorny question.[33]

Documents like those just cited allow us to uncover the state of *halakhah* in a Hellenized diaspora society more than three centuries before the redaction of the Mishnah. For the conduct of Jewish worship, we must now turn our attention to sources connected with the synagogue, the mainstay of the institutional framework of community life in the Jewish diaspora of Egypt.

SYNAGOGUE WORSHIP

Although archaeological remains are lacking, papyri and inscriptions attest the importance of synagogue worship in Greek and Roman Egypt.[34] In addition to this evidence, there is the description of the great synagogue of Alexandria attributed to R. Judah b. Ilai in the Talmud (*y. Sukkah* 5.1.55a). Built in the very heart of the Jewish quarter, it was, according to Philo (*Legat.* 134), "the largest and most famous of all." This "double colonnade" (*diplē stoa*), which evokes the account of the Talmud, is well deserving of the epithet "splendor of Israel" bestowed on it by R. Judah (*y. Sukkah* 5.1 cited previously).

Dedicatory inscriptions attest to the existence of "houses of prayer" (*proseuchai*) in the interior of the country from the middle of the third century BCE (Horbury-Noy, 22; 117). The fact that they were established by local communities implies a community effort and a certain sense of group solidarity. In placing the synagogue under the auspices of the king and his family, some dedications express the loyalty of the founders to the monarchy and the benevolence of royal authority, which both sanctions their

---

[32] Mélèze Modrzejewski, "Jewish Law and Hellenistic Legal Practice"; cf. Cowey, "Das ägyptische Judentum in hellenistischer Zeit," 37–9.

[33] For in-depth discussion, see Weingort, *Intérêt et crédit*.

[34] Levine, *The Ancient Synagogue*, 74–89.

initiative and on occasion even provides financial backing for it. Cases also occur in which a synagogue is founded by a single individual, possibly associated with a group, or in which a family makes a donation for furnishings (Horbury-Noy, 27 and 28).

The most ancient synagogue dedications do not specify the identity of the deity worshipped in the houses of prayer, on the pediment of which the inscriptions were engraved. The difficulty arose from the ineffable name of the God of the Jews. For the Greeks, the Hebrew tetragrammaton YHWH was indecipherable; *Kyrios*, "Lord," the Greek equivalent of the Hebrew *Adonai*, would have been highly enigmatic. Among the various divine names, one was finally found that could most favorably impress the religious sensibility of their Greek neighbors: *El Elyon*, "God most high" (Gen. 14:18–20), or *Theos Hypsistos* in Greek (Horbury-Noy, 9; 27; 105; 116). The word *hypsistos* evokes the supreme deity, comparable to Zeus, to whom Sophocles applies the same adjective.[35] But the God of the Jews is also a "great God" (*theos megas*: Horbury-Noy, 13; 116) and "one who hears" (*epēkoos*), an ability that was highly valued among the deities of the Hellenistic world (Horbury-Noy, 13).

In Egypt, as in Judea, the principal feature of synagogue worship was the reading of the Torah. When the passage from the Talmud cited above describes the reading of the Torah in the great synagogue, it in this respect surely expresses a historical reality. Fragments from scrolls of the Septuagint preserved on papyrus, the oldest of which date back to the end of the second century BCE, attest to the regularity of this practice in the synagogues of Egypt.[36] They complement the witnesses of the inscription of Theodotus (*IGLBibbia*, 31), Philo, Josephus, and the New Testament (Luke 4:16–22; Acts 13:13–16).

The administration of the synagogue required the presence of a specialized staff. Its direction was delegated to a *prostatēs*, the equivalent of the Hebrew "*rosh ha-knesseth*." This office could be a collective one, as the mention of two *prostatai* in Xenephyris suggests (Horbury-Noy, 24). A cantor (*hazzan*) was also employed in the great synagogue of Alexandria. The Greek equivalent of this term is *nakoros (neokoros)*; two attestations of the word are found in the papyri (*P.Ent.* 30 = *CPJud.* I 129, 218 BCE and *PSI XVII Congr.* 22, 114 or 78 BCE). The second document refers to a *nakorikon*, a word that in all probability denotes the contributions offered by

[35] Mitchell, "The Cult of Theos Hypsistos."
[36] Aly and Koenen, *Three Rolls of the Early Septuagint*.

the community for the cantor's salary. It is likely that this kind of financing of synagogue staff was widespread throughout all of Egypt.

In addition to the reading of the Torah, the synagogue could play a role in other community activities. In the first century BCE, an association (*synodos*) held its assembly (*synagogē*) in a house of prayer (*CPJud.* I 138); perhaps it was a kind of "funeral association" (*thiasos*), as was found among the Greeks in Egypt from the third century BCE. We also hear about a Jewish "club" (*CPJud.* I 139, first century BCE); its members, who include in their numbers a "sage" (*sophos*, the Greek equivalent of *hakham*), paid their share of the costs of holding the banquet.

Like pagan temples, the synagogues could also be beneficiaries of the privilege of asylum. That is, they could offer, with royal permission, a haven for people seeking refuge there. A bilingual inscription composed in Greek and Latin (Horbury-Noy, 125) records the granting of this privilege to an Egyptian synagogue by a Ptolemy Euergetes (Ptolemy VIII, rather than Ptolemy III), and its confirmation by a "queen and a king" (*regina et rex*). It is now thought that this was in reference to the last Cleopatra and one of her coregents, probably Cesarion, the son that she had from Julius Caesar.[37]

LEONTOPOLIS

Egypt was the only country outside the land of Israel in which a Jewish temple, at two different times, was in operation. The first was at Elephantine, at the time of the last pharaohs and Persian kings. The second was at Leontopolis, from the middle of the second century BCE up to 73 CE. It owes its origin to the high priest Onias IV, a refugee in the court of Alexandria during the Maccabean crisis. Leontopolis has now been identified with the site of Tell el-Yahudiya, "the mound of the Jews," near Shibin el-Qanatir, to the north of Heliopolis. The identification of the site, recognizable by its Arabic name, is confirmed by epigraphy; an epitaph informs us that we are indeed on the "land of Onias" (Horbury-Noy, 38), the equivalent of the "district of Onias" to which Josephus refers (*J. W.* 1.190; *Ant.* 12.287).

In describing the appearance of the sanctuary, Josephus evokes the image of a miniature copy of the Jerusalem temple (*Ant.* 13.73, 387–8). Elsewhere,

---

[37] Bingen, "L'asylie pour une synagogue." The use of the term *proseuchē* ("house of prayer") calls into question Rigsby's hypothesis ("A Jewish Asylum in Greco-Roman Egypt") that this inscription refers to the temple of Leontopolis.

however, he provides a different description, one more in keeping with an Egyptian setting: a tower (*purgos*), almost 30m (60 cubits) in height (*J.W.* 7.426–30) This tower could well have been a central component of a religious and military body (*politeuma?*) situated in Leontopolis.

The papyri assist in dating this construction, which is not reliable in Josephus's account. We find Onias serving in high office in the Alexandrian court in 164 BCE (*P.Paris* 63 = *CPJud.* I 132). He must have arrived in Alexandria well before this time, not as a child as Josephus states, but as a young man capable of moving swiftly through the ranks of the royal circle of Ptolemy VI. This dating enables us to assign the construction of the temple at Leontopolis to the years 167–64 BCE; its purpose would be, then, to ensure that the continuity of the Jewish sacrificial cult, which had been imperiled in Jerusalem, would be maintained in the "land of Onias."

This conclusion is corroborated by rabbinic sources. While aware of the existence of the Leontopolis sanctuary, the sages of the Talmud do not condemn it. They debate the legitimacy of Onias's undertaking (*b. Menaḥ.* 109b) and reach the judgment that a sacrifice or an oath could be made in Leontopolis, just as in Jerusalem. But they deny the service of the Jerusalem temple cult to the priests who exercised this function in Leontopolis (*b. ʾAbod. Zar.* 52b). The latter are likened to the officials of the "high places," which had formerly been targets of Josiah's reforms (2 Kings 23:9). In other words, for the sages, the Egyptian sanctuary, founded by Onias, was not at all "schismatic."[38] Far from being a rival to the Jerusalem temple, it was simply a temple for Jewish soldiers under Onias's command, just as, a few centuries before, the temple of Elephantine had been for the Jewish garrison stationed on the island.

The temple of Onias outlasted its counterpart in Jerusalem. Following the siege of Jerusalem, Josephus says (*J.W.* 7.420–36), those combatants who had escaped the disaster sought refuge in Egypt and began to incite a revolutionary movement there. When the prefect of Egypt, Tiberius Julius Lupus, informed the emperor Vespasian about this, he ordered the destruction of the temple of Leontopolis. As a dangerous symbol of Jewish nationalism, this vestige of the glorious past of the Oniads represented a direct challenge to Roman power. For Lupus and his successor, Valerius Paulinus, it was enough simply to put an end to the temple service and close the sanctuary. Its closing took place toward the end of 73.

[38] Against Momigliano, "Un documento."

DECLINE

For Alexandrian Judaism, the Roman conquest of Egypt in 30 BCE inaugurated a period marking both its cultural apogee, brilliantly exemplified by the work of Philo, and its political decline. Although the Romans did not interfere with the religious and cultural autonomy of the Jews, their conquest destroyed the social structure that allowed them to maintain both their national identity and their membership in a dominant group.[39]

The state of decline in which the Jews of Egypt found themselves under Roman domination revived old pagan-Jewish disputes. The first outburst occurred during the year 38 CE, under the government of A. Avilius Flaccus, a prefect of Egypt well known, thanks to Philo (*In Flaccum*), for his abuses.[40] At the time of the accession of Claudius in the beginning of 41 CE, a Jewish embassy from Alexandria confronted a Greek embassy in a court case unfolding before the emperor in Rome.[41] A certain kind of Greek universalism, espoused by the Alexandrian gymnasiarch Isidorus, son of Dionysius, denounces Jewish particularism, embodied in this case by Agrippa I, king of Judea. The lawsuit, known solely from papyrus sources, concluded with a capital sentence imposed against Isidorus and his associate, Lampo the registrar. Put to death for his homeland, Isidorus became the heroic archetype, whose example would be followed by other "pagan martyrs of Alexandria" (*Acta Alexandrinorum*).[42]

In 66 CE, under the reign of Nero, Tiberius Julius Alexander, nephew of Philo, who at that time was discharging the duties of the office of prefect, mercilessly crushed a Jewish uprising. Regarding this event, Josephus speaks of 50,000 Jewish victims in Alexandria (*J. W.* 2.490–97) – assuredly an exaggeration, although for the Jews of Alexandria, the year 66 was certainly an ordeal as severe as the pogrom of 38.

The outcome of these confrontations was one final test of strength at the beginning of the second century CE, culminating in the destruction of the Jewish communities of Alexandria and Egypt. Over the course of several months, from the end of the reign of Trajan to the beginning of the reign of Hadrian (the summer of 115 or the spring of 116 to August–September of 117), a bitter war incited the Jews of the diaspora (Cyrene, Egypt, and Cyprus), the East (Mesopotamia), and perhaps even Judea against Roman

[39] See further Dunand in Chapter 6 of this volume.
[40] Van der Horst, *Philo's Flaccus*.
[41] Mélèze Modrzejewski, "Le procès d'Isidôros."
[42] Musurillo, ed. *The Acts of the Pagan Martyrs*; idem, *Acta Alexandrinorum*; Rodriguez, "Les Acta Isidori."

power. The result of this uprising was calamitous for Alexandrian Judaism: it totally disappeared.[43]

A notice in Eusebius of Caesarea, citing pagan authors of the second and third centuries (*Hist. eccl.* 4.2.1–5 = Stern, *GLAJJ* 3, VII), sketches an escalating series of conflicts that is abundantly illustrated in the papyri. We see how a local disturbance (*tarachos*) rapidly evolved into full-scale war (*polemos*). The commander of the Roman expeditionary force, Marcus Turbo, massacres the Jewish rebels in the thousands. In Mesopotamia, a similar mission was entrusted to Lusius Quietus, whose name is known in rabbinic references to the "war of Quietus" (*polemos shel Qitos*). When a contemporary Greek observer, Appian of Alexandria, refers to "Trajan, who annihilated the Jewish nation in Egypt" (*Bell. civ.* 2.90), he echoes the Talmud's condemnation of the "massacre" that brought about the destruction of Alexandrian Judaism by the "vile Trajan" (*y. Sukkah* 5.1.55a, cited previously).

Accounting records preserved in Egyptian papyri and ostraca balance the books of this tragic revolt. They reveal the existence in Egypt of the mid-second century of two special accounts in the administration of the imperial domain: the "estate of Greeks who had died without heirs" (*pekoulion Hellēnōn aklēronomētōn*) and the "Jewish account" (*Ioudaïkos logos*). The Greeks in question are the combatants in the revolt who had died without leaving a will or legitimate heirs; the Jews are the rebels slapped with the confiscation of their property. We thus learn of a judgment from the emperor Hadrian passing sentence *post mortem* on the Jews complicit in sedition and ordering the seizure of their property.[44] After a reversal of such magnitude, it would not be a simple matter to reconstitute Jewish life in Egypt.

A NEW DIASPORA

In the wake of the failure of the revolt, Judaism in Egypt resembled a vast cemetery. Men have perished in conflict; their property, as we have seen, has been confiscated on the authority of a punitive sanction. On the Greek side, the destruction of Hellenistic Judaism in Egypt did not appear to have occasioned any sorrow. To the contrary, even at the very end of the second century CE, the Greek population of the town of Oxyrhynchus

---

[43] Sources and discussion in Ben Zeev Pucci, *Diaspora Judaism in Turmoil.*
[44] See further Mélèze Modrzejewski, "La fin de la communauté juive d'Égypte."

joyously commemorated the day on which the "impious Jews" had been reduced to nothing (*P.Oxy.* IV 705 = *CPJud.* II 450).

One must wait until the end of the third and the beginning of the fourth centuries to see the reappearance of Jewish settlements in Alexandria and on the shores of the Nile. Quite removed from the one that ceased to exist at the beginning of the second century, this new Jewish diaspora in Egypt foreshadows the way of life characteristic of Jewish communities in medieval and modern Egypt under Islamic rule. Hebrew and Aramaic are tending to replace Greek in prayer and funerary inscriptions as well as contracts and correspondence between community leaders. Even so, the preference for Semitic languages did not result in the elimination of Greek in the Jewish diaspora. Bilingualism took root, and along with it the inevitable interplay of influences and reciprocal borrowings.

Among the rare texts having to do with Jews in Egypt during this era,[45] a *ketubah* (marriage contract), the oldest one in existence (15 November 414 CE), beautifully illustrates this biculturalism. The contract was drawn up in Antinoopolis, a city founded by Hadrian in 130 as a memorial to his beloved Antinous, who had drowned in the Nile. It registers the marriage of a Jewish couple probably hailing from Alexandria.[46] Although the terminology used is indeed that of a Jewish *ketubah,* the Aramaic text is sprinkled with Greek words transcribed into square characters, rough breathing being rendered with a *chet.* Thus, the *mohar,* the "cost" of the bride paid by the groom to her father, is rendered by the word *hedna* ("nuptial gifts"). This archaic Greek word replaces the word *phernē* (dowry) that the Septuagint uses for *mohar,* reflecting common usage but to the detriment of judicial rigor. To reinstate the *mohar* into the marriage contract, the Jews of Byzantine Egypt revived a Homeric word that had been out of use for a long time. Here is how one could continue to be both a Jew and a Greek.

Hellenistic Judaism in Alexandria and Egypt did not therefore completely disappear at the end of Trajan's reign. It survived the turmoil of the years 115/116–17, not only as a social phenomenon, but as a major cultural force, of which the Septuagint and the exegetical work of the philosopher Philo are the most celebrated representatives. A noteworthy element of the cultural legacy of the Jewish people, it has left, via Christianity, a lasting imprint on the intellectual heritage of the ancient Mediterranean handed down to modern civilization.

---

[45] *CPJud.* III, supplemented by Fikhman, "Les Juifs d'Égypte à l'époque byzantine."
[46] Sirat, Cauderlier, Dukan, and Friedman, eds. *La ketouba de Cologne.*

BIBLIOGRAPHY

Allam, Schafik. *Das Verfahrensrecht in der altägyptischen Arbeitersiedlung von Deir el-Medineh* (Tübingen, 1973).

Aly, Zaki, and Ludwig Koenen. *Three Rolls of the Early Septuagint: Genesis and Deuteronomy. A Photographic Edition* (Bonn, 1980).

Bickerman, Elias. "The Jewish Historian Demetrios." In *Studies in Jewish and Christian History* 2 (Leiden, 1980): 347–58.

Bingen, Jean. "L'asylie pour une synagogue (CIL Suppl. 6583 = CIJ 1449)." In *Pages d'épigraphie grecque: Attique-Égypte (1952–82)* (Brussels, 1991): 45–50.

Blouin, Katherine. *Le conflit judéo-alexandrin de 38–41: l'identité juive à l'épreuve* (Paris, 2005).

Bohak, Gideon. *Joseph and Aseneth and the Jewish Temple in Heliopolis* (Atlanta, 1996).

Burchard, Christoph. *Joseph und Aseneth kritisch herausgegeben* (Leiden, 2003).

Cohen, Naomi G. *Philo Judaeus: His Universe of Discourse* (Frankfurt, 1995).

Collins, N. L. "Ezechiel, the Author of the 'Exagoge': His Calendar and Home." *JSJ* 22 (1991): 201–11.

Cowey, James M. S. "Das ägyptische Judentum in hellenistischer Zeit – neue Erkenntnisse aus jüngst veröffentlichten Papyri." In *Im Brennpunkt: Die Septuaginta: Studien zur Entstehung und Bedeutung der Griechischen Bibel* 2, eds. Sigfried Kreuzer and Jürgen P. Lesch (Stuttgart, 2004): 24–43.

Croy, N. Clayton. *3 Maccabees* (Leiden, 2006).

Le Dinahet, Marie-Thérèse, ed. *L'Orient méditerranéen de la mort d'Alexandre au Iᵉʳ siècle avant notre ère* (Nantes, 2003).

Dorival, Gilles, Marguerite Harl, and Olivier Munnich. *La Bible grecque des Septante: du judaïsme hellénistique au christianisme ancien* (Paris, 1988; 2nd ed. 1994).

Fikhman, Itzhak. "Les Juifs d'Égypte à l'époque byzantine d'après les papyrus publiés depuis la parution du 'Corpus Papyrorum Judaicarum' III." In *Wirtschaft und Gesellschaft im spätantiken Ägypten: kleine Schriften* (Stuttgart, 2006): 349–55.

Fuks, Alexander. "Dositheos Son of Drimylos. A Prosopographical Note." In *Social Conflict in Ancient Greece*, eds. Menachem Stern and Moshe Amit (Jerusalem, 1984): 307–11.

Goodhart, Howard L., and Erwin R. Goodenough. "A General Bibliography of Philo Judaeus." In *The Politics of Philo Judaeus: Practice and Theory*, ed. Erwin R. Goodenough (New Haven, 1938; repr. Hildesheim, 1967): 125–321.

Gruen, Erich S. "The Origins and Objectives of Onias' Temple." *SCI* 16 (1997): 47–70.

Gutman, Yoshua. "Philo the Epic Poet." *ScrHier* 1 (1954): 36–63.

Hadas-Lebel, Mireille. *Philon d'Alexandrie: un penseur en diaspora* (Paris, 2003).

Holladay, Carl R. *Fragments from Hellenistic Jewish Authors, 1: The Historians*, 51–91 (Chico, Calif., 1983).

Honigman, Sylvie. "Politeumata and Ethnicity in Ptolemaic and Roman Egypt." *Anc. Soc.* 33 (2003): 61–102.

The Septuagint and Homeric Scholarship in Alexandria: A Study in the Narrative of the Letter of Aristeas (London, 2003).

Horst, Pieter Willem van der. *Philo's Flaccus: The First Pogrom: Introduction, Translation, and Commentary* (Leiden, 2003).

Jacobson, Howard. "Artapanus Judaeus." *JJS* 57 (2006): 210–21.

Levine, Lee I. *The Ancient Synagogue: The First Thousand Years* (New Haven, 2000).

Lüderitz, G. "What is Politeuma?" In *Studies in Early Jewish Epigraphy*, eds. Jan Willem van Henten, and Pieter Willem van der Horst (Leiden, 1994): 183–225.

Mélèze Modrzejewski, Joseph. "Sur l'antisémitisme païen." In *Pour Léon Poliakov. Le racisme: mythes et sciences*, ed. Maurice Olender (Brussels, 1981): 411–39.

"Le procès d'Isidôros. Droit pénal et affrontements idéologiques entre Rome et Alexandrie sous l'empereur Claude." *Praktika tēs Akadēmias Athēnōn* 61 (Athens, 1986): 245–75.

"La fin de la communauté juive d'Égypte (115–117 de n.è.)." In *Symposion 1985* (Cologne, 1989): 337–61.

"Philiscos de Milet et le jugement de Salomon : la première référence grecque à la Bible." *BIDR* 91 [3rd ser., 30] 1988 (1992): 571–97.

"Les Juifs dans le monde gréco-romain: racines et antécédents d'une pensée juive du christianisme." In *Y a-t-il une pensée juive du christianisme? Les Nouveaux Cahiers* 113 (Paris, 1993): 5–13.

"Le statut des Hellènes dans l'Égypte lagide." In *Statut personnel et liens de famille* (Aldershot, Hampshire, 1993).

"Law and Justice in Ptolemaic Egypt." In *Legal Documents of the Hellenistic World: Papers from a Seminar*, eds. Markham J. Geller and Herwig Maehler, in collaboration with A. D. E. Lewis (London, 1995): 1–11.

The Jews of Egypt from Rameses II to Emperor Hadrian, trans. R. Cornman (Philadelphia and Jerusalem, 1995; online: Varda Books, 2001; 2nd ed. Princeton, 1997; French original: *Les Juifs d'Égypte, de Ramsès II à Hadrien*. Paris, 1991–92; 2nd ed. 1997).

"Jewish Law and Hellenistic Legal Practice in the Light of Greek Papyri from Egypt." In *An Introduction to the History and Sources of Jewish Law*, eds. Neil S. Hecht, et al. (Oxford, 1996): 75–99.

"Espérances et illusions du judaïsme alexandrin." In *Alexandrie, une mégapole cosmopolite* [*Cahiers de la Villa Kérylos* 9] (Paris, 1999): 129–44. = Anny Pikulska-Robaczkiewicz, ed. *Profesorowi Janowi Kodrębskiemu in memoriam [Mélanges à la mémoire de Jan Kodrębski]* (Lodz, 2000): 221–35.

"The Septuagint as Nomos: How the Torah became a 'Civic Law' for the Jews of Egypt." In *Critical Studies in Ancient Law, Comparative Law and Legal History: Essays in honour of Alan Watson*, eds. John W. Cairns and Olivia Robinson (Oxford, 2001): 183–99.

"Droit et justice dans l'Égypte des premiers Lagides." In *L'Orient méditerranéen*, ed. M.-Th. Le Dinahet (Nantes, 2003): 281–302.

"La diaspora juive d'Égypte" In *L'Orient méditerranéen*, M.-Th. Le Dinahet (Nantes, 2003): 330–53.

"La fiancée adultère: à propos de la pratique matrimoniale du judaïsme hellénisé à la lumière du dossier du politeuma juif d'Héracléopolis (144/3 – 133/2 av. n.è.)." In *Marriage: Ideal – Law – Practice: Proceedings of a Conference held in Memory of Henryk Kupiszewski*, eds. Zuzanna Służewska and Jakub Urbanik (Warsaw, 2005): 141–60. = Jean-Christophe Couvenhes, and Bernard Legras, eds. *Transferts culturels et politique dans le monde hellénistique* (Paris, 2006): 103–18.

Le Troisième Livre des Maccabées. Traduction du texte grec de la Septante, introduction et notes. La Bible d'Alexandrie 15.3 (Paris, 2008).

"Un peuple de philosophes". Aux origines de la condition juive (Paris, 2011).

Mitchell, Stephen. "The Cult of Theos Hypsistos between Pagans, Jews, and Christians." In *Pagan Monotheism in Late Antiquity*, eds. Polymnia Athanassiadi and Michael Frede (Oxford, 1999): 81–148.

Momigliano, Arnaldo. "Un documento della spiritualità dei Giudei Leontopolitani." *Aegyptus* 12 (1932): 171–2.

Muffs, Yochanan. *Studies in the Aramaic Legal Papyri from Elephantine* (Leiden, 1969; 2nd ed. New York, 1973).

Musurillo, Herbert A., ed. *The Acts of the Pagan Martyrs: Acta Alexandrinorum* (Oxford, 1954).

Acta Alexandrinorum (Leipzig, 1961).

Nickelsburg, George W. E. *Jewish Literature between the Bible and the Mishnah: A Historical and Literary Introduction*, 2nd ed. (Minneapolis, 2005).

Porten, Bezalel. *Archives from Elephantine: The Life of an Ancient Jewish Military Colony* (Berkeley, 1968).

Pucci Ben Zeev, Miriam. *Diaspora Judaism in Turmoil, 116/117 CE: Ancient Sources and Modern Insights* (Leuven, 2005).

Radice, Roberto, and David T. Runia, et al. *Philo of Alexandria: An Annotated Bibliography 1937–1986* (Leiden, 1988).

Rigsby, Kent J., "A Jewish Asylum in Greco-Roman Egypt." In *Das antike Asyl*, ed. M. Dreher (Cologne, 2003): 127–41.

Rodriguez, Chris. "Les Acta Isidori: un procès pénal devant l'Empereur Claude." *Revue Historique de Droit Français et Étranger*, 88–1, 2010, 1–41.

Runia, David T., and Helena Maria Keizer. *Philo of Alexandria: An Annotated Bibliography 1987–1996* (Leiden, 2000).

Schäfer, Peter. *Judaeophobia: Attitudes toward the Jews in the Ancient World* (Cambridge, Mass., 1997).

Schimanowski, Gottfried. *Juden und Nichtjuden in Alexandrien: Koexistenz und Konflikte bis zum Pogrom unter Trajan (117 n. Chr.)* (Münster, 2006).

Sirat, Colette, et al., eds. *La Ketouba de Cologne: un contrat de mariage juif à Antinoopolis* (Opladen, 1986).

Smallwood, E. Mary. *Philonis Alexandrini Legatio ad Gaium*, 2nd ed. (Leiden, 1970).

Walter, Nikolaus. *Der Thoraausleger Aristobulos: Untersuchungen zu seinen Fragmenten und zu pseudepigraphischen Resten der jüdisch-hellenistischen Literatur* (Berlin, 1964).

Weingort, Abraham. *Intérêt et crédit dans le droit talmudique* (Paris, 1979).

Yaron, Reuven. *Introduction to the Law of the Aramaic Papyri* (Oxford, 1961).

Zivie, Alain-Pierre. *Découverte à Saqqarah: le vizir oublié* (Paris, 1990).

La prison de Joseph: l'Égypte des pharaons et le monde de la Bible (Paris, 2004).

8

ANCIENT EGYPTIAN CHRISTIANITY

JACQUES VAN DER VLIET

More decisively than any other event in the country's history, the surrender of Alexandria to Arab troops in November 641 marked the end of Antiquity in Egypt. Egypt was irrevocably severed from the Hellenistic world to which it had belonged culturally ever since Alexander the Great, and from the Roman empire of which it had been part politically since the reign of Augustus.[1] Long before that crucial event, however, dramatic changes had already transformed the Egyptian landscape. In Alexandria itself around the middle of the fourth century, the Caesareum on the waterfront, completed in the time of Augustus as a temple in his honor, had been converted into the cathedral church of the city's Christian archbishops.[2] In the far south of the country, in Thebes, the age-old mortuary temple of Queen Hatshepsut in Deir el-Bahari experienced a different fate. In Ptolemaic and early Roman times, it had housed a thriving healing shrine patronized by the indigenous "saints" Amenhotep, son of Hapu, and Imhotep.[3] In the third and fourth centuries of the common era, part of the temple served as a cemetery; members of the corporation of iron-workers from nearby Hermonthis used another part of the building for social and ritual gatherings, which involved, among other things, the traditional sacrifice of a donkey.[4] At a much later stage, toward the end of the sixth century, it became the core of an impressive monastery. Dedicated to Saint Phoibammon, the monastery dominated the area until its remains were demolished by nineteenth-century archaeologists.[5] A process of

[1] Introductory: Bagnall, Rathbone, *Egypt*; for the later part of the period covered here, see now the essays in Bagnall, *Egypt in the Byzantine World*.
[2] Haas, *Alexandria*, 210–11.
[3] Laskowska-Kusztal, *Sanctuaire ptolémaïque*; Łajtar, *Deir el-Bahari*, 3–94.
[4] Łajtar, *Deir el-Bahari*, 94–104.
[5] Godlewski, *Monastère*.

irreversible Christianization had, at an unequal pace and with different outcomes, affected both the centers of official ceremony (like Alexandria's Caesareum) and the shrines that served the needs of local populations (as in Deir el-Bahari).

Egypt, as it was found by the Arab invaders, was a predominantly Christian land. On its southern borders, in Nubia, the Christian states that had developed there transmitted the culture of Byzantine Egypt to remoter parts of Africa.[6] Deeply divided over questions of Christological doctrine, Egypt's Christianity was not monolithic, however. As elsewhere in the East, church leaders and civil authorities perpetuated the conflicts over the divinity and the humanity of Jesus Christ that had arisen in the wake of the great church councils of the fifth century (Ephesus 430, 449; Chalcedon 451). Another notable characteristic of Egypt at the time was its bilingualism. Greek was the official language of church and administration alike, as well as the lingua franca of Egypt's intellectual elite. From the early fourth century onward, however, the indigenous language, Coptic in its various forms, had increasingly gained in status. The result was a profoundly bilingual society in which social and regional variables, not differences in ethnicity or nationality, determined linguistic preference. Other characteristics that might have struck the Arab conquerors concerned the specific forms of Christian Egyptian religiosity. Monasticism in its various forms occupied a central position within the religious and social life of Christian Egypt. Monasteries were more than places of continuous worship; they were also institutions of considerable symbolic and economic power, as were the numerous shrines devoted to the cults of the saints, in particular the holy martyrs.

On the eve of the Arab conquest, Egyptian Christianity had its own profile, shaped by a history extending over almost six centuries. The following discussion will present a brief outline of this history, not as a linear development, starting from obscure "roots" and ending in a predictable tree, but rather as the outcome of a series of transformations, determined by the interaction of religious ideas, cultural values, and social processes. Indeed, the whole concept of roots will be avoided here.

Our sources for the history of ancient Egyptian Christianity are both extremely rich and highly heterogeneous. The Greek works of the Alexandrian Church Fathers, from Clement (ca.150–215) down to Cyril (d.444) and his successors, have been transmitted carefully over the centuries. Among the chance manuscript finds preserved in Egypt's dry soil

---

[6] Welsby, *Medieval Kingdoms*.

is a corpus of gnostic and Manichaean scripture, mainly in Coptic; there are also countless Greek and Coptic papyri and ostraca, including magical and liturgical texts, that reflect the concerns of daily life. For the world of monasticism, descriptions of ancient visitors and hagiographical literature supplement archaeological witnesses and inscriptions on stone or wood. Although each of these sources may provide access to significant aspects of the life and thought of Egyptian Christians, they cannot be used indiscriminately. A cosmological treatise provides information different from that found in a business document.

An in-depth evaluation of these various sources and their respective contributions to the history of Egyptian Christianity is beyond the scope of this essay. Instead, the following pages will sketch some major processes of transformation from various perspectives. The first section concentrates on "transformations of the mind" – that is, on major trends in the development of Christian thought and ideology in Egypt. The second section is devoted to "transformations of authority," investigating the sources and structure of authority and the shifts that occurred in its attribution. Finally, a third section will deal with "transformations of the landscape," or the ways in which the Christian religion took shape on the level of local cult and piety.

TRANSFORMATIONS OF THE MIND

The first Christians who set foot on the Alexandrian wharf are unknown. Presumably, they were Jews, most likely from nearby Palestine. Several New Testament passages mention an early Christian missionary, Apollos, an Alexandrian Jew by birth (Acts 18.24–28; 1 Cor. 1:12; 3:6; 4:6; 16:12).[7] A later tradition connects the establishment of the Alexandrian church with the name of St. Mark the Evangelist.[8] Otherwise, the history of first-century Christianity in Egypt is a void. According to one widely held theory, the lack of surviving sources arose from the heretical, gnostic character of earliest Egyptian Christianity. Another explanation, more popular nowadays, maintains that Christian life, initially integrated into the Jewish community of Alexandria, became visible only after the great Jewish revolt of 115–17. Although both theories have strengths and weaknesses, they appear equally inadequate when confronted with the richness and diversity

---

[7] See Jakab, *Ecclesia alexandrina*, 41–2.
[8] Ibid., 45–9.

of Christian intellectual life in second-century Alexandria.[9] For the first
century, we simply lack information.

Descriptions of Alexandrian culture in Antiquity like to stress its cosmopolitan, multicultural, and multiethnic character, underlining the city's
status as a major international harbor. There can be no doubt, however,
that Hellenism was the predominant cultural paradigm. However cosmopolitan the city may have been, Hellenistic culture conveyed status and
prestige and thereby imposed its standards.[10]

Early Christian culture of Alexandria reflects both the variety of available models and the preeminence of the Hellenistic cultural paradigm.
As a missionary religion, Christianity had to find its place in this cultural
marketplace and choose its models accordingly. Papyrus finds from Upper
Egypt attest to both the early diffusion of what was soon to become the
canon of Christian scripture, the Greek Old and New Testaments, and
the popularity of the heterogeneous body of texts that came to be designated as extracanonical or apocryphal literature.[11] We can distinguish two
ways by which this material was processed into a Christian ideology in
Alexandria. One is the multifarious phenomenon of Gnosticism, represented in Alexandria by the names of Basilides (fl. ca.120–45) and Valentinus
(ca.100–65) among others. The other is the so-called Alexandrian catechetical school, with Clement of Alexandria and Origen (ca.185–253) as its
most brilliant representatives.

Gnosticism is a modern label that conventionally designates a wide range
of early Christian dualistic currents.[12] Our direct knowledge of Gnosticism
derives to a considerable degree from the fourth- and fifth-century Coptic
manuscripts of Upper Egypt. While some of them were found as early as the
eighteenth century, the so-called Nag Hammadi library is the best-known
representative of these manuscript finds. Stray discoveries include the
recently published papyrus codex, which, among other gnostic writings,
contains a Coptic translation of the so-called *Gospel of Judas*.[13] Several of
these texts may derive from second- or third-century originals composed
in Greek. A few of them have received considerable popular attention in
recent years. Most renowned are the *Gospel of Thomas*, a sapiential text
recycling sayings of Jesus,[14] and the *Gospel of Philip*, probably a set of notes

[9] Ibid., 38–41, 58–61; Pearson, *Gnosticism and Christianity*, 12–15.
[10] See Fraser, *Ptolemaic Alexandria*.
[11] Van Haelst, *Catalogue*; cf. Roberts, *Manuscript*.
[12] The term is contested: Williams, *Rethinking "Gnosticism"*; King, *What is Gnosticism?*; introductory:
Roukema, *Gnosis and Faith*; a good selection of original texts: Layton, *The Gnostic Scriptures*.
[13] Kasser et al., *Gospel of Judas*.
[14] Layton, *Nag Hammadi Codex II*, 37–128; introductory: Hurtado, *Lord Jesus Christ*, 452–79.

for a gnostic baptismal instruction.[15] Although these original writings are precious witnesses to the history of early Christianity, they are regrettably more often exploited for polemical and devotional purposes than taken seriously as historical sources.[16]

Two distinguishing features of Gnosticism are its negative view of the perceptible world and material man and its complicated relationship with Judeo-Christian scripture.[17] Accordingly, cosmology and anthropology occupy a central place within gnostic thinking. Many so-called Sethian writings (named after Seth, the third son of Adam and Eve) share a philosophical myth about the origin of the world and humanity that serves as a blueprint for the gnostic understanding of salvation.[18] It situates divinity and humanity in their various manifestations on a sliding scale between the extremes of the purely and ineffably spiritual and the gross ignorance of pure materiality. The Sethian myth, once discarded as a marginal aberration, is now seen as an important key to gnostic thought. Its very centrality explains its quasi-ritual repetition, its insertion into the most diverse contexts, and the insistence with which it is echoed in every aspect of Sethian gnostic teaching. In addition to its undeniable philosophical aspirations, which explain its ambivalent attitude toward the cosmogonical myth of the biblical book of Genesis, the Sethian myth showed an astonishing capacity to absorb diverse ritual and magical elements. The astrological, demonological, and angelological material derived from various scholarly traditions (Hellenistic, Jewish, and Egyptian) enhanced and expanded its ritual character. The famous *Apocryphon of John*, one of the most popular works of ancient Gnosticism, is a crowning witness to the magical and performative aspects of much of Sethian scripture.[19]

The figures of Basilides and Valentinus, the major representatives of Alexandrian Gnosticism in the second century, are not easy to grasp, as their works are largely lost. Both appear to have been speculative Christian theologians who borrowed their conceptual tools from contemporary philosophy.[20] Although Gnosticism has often been generally characterized as strongly Platonizing, in recent years due attention has been paid

---

[15] Layton, *Nag Hammadi Codex II*, 129–217; see Van Os, *Baptism*. See Roukema, "Historical context."

[16] This even applies to popular publications by scholars like Elaine Pagels and Gilles Quispel; cf. the ideologically tainted publicity around the recent rediscovery of the *Gospel of Judas*.

[17] For the latter: Luttikhuizen, *Gnostic Revisions*.

[18] Sethianism: Turner, *Sethian Gnosticism*.

[19] Waldstein and Wisse, *Apocryphon*; commentary: Tardieu, *Codex*; cf. Quack, "Dekane"; Van der Vliet, "The Coptic Gnostic Texts."

[20] Löhr, *Basilides*; on Valentinus: Thomassen, *Spiritual Seed*.

to the Aristotelian element in gnostic theology, particularly in Basilides.[21] Later Sethian gnostics tended to move away from Christianity toward neo-Platonism. That the major neo-Platonist philosopher Plotinus (205–70) expended the effort to attack them suggests that, in addition to sharing a common idiom, they also addressed similar audiences.[22]

A second major current in early Christian thought, which is no less indebted to Greek dualist philosophy, appears in the writings of the so-called Alexandrian catechetical school.[23] Although perhaps not a school in the strict sense, it represents a tradition stretching from Clement well into the fourth century with Athanasius (295–373) and Didymus the Blind (ca.313–98). This tradition took its lead from a current within Alexandrian Judaism best known from the work of Philo (ca.30 BCE–45 CE). "Gospel message" and "Hellenistic culture" (Daniélou 1955) are fused in a particular way of reading the Bible and of interpreting the figure of Jesus Christ. The so-called allegorical way of reading the scriptures attempted to reveal a symbolic meaning behind a text that need not have had this meaning originally. It was not just an arbitrary way of interpreting texts in terms of contemporary ideology, but rather a means of making them accessible to audiences who were not primarily interested in the details of Israelite history and cultic law or in the political and social conditions of early first-century Palestine. In terms of symbolic value, it succeeded in bringing the Bible up to the level of Homer and other classics of the dominant Hellenistic culture.

A similar cultural strategy can be observed in the even more central doctrine about Christ. Alexandrian Christian theology, again inspired by Philo, took up the Johannine notion of Christ as the Word of God, his Logos. In particular, Clement developed an all-embracing theological, cosmological, and historical concept of the Logos as the innate reason of God, who in the beginning had created the world and finally had become incarnate in Jesus Christ for the salvation of humanity. This tendency was even more marked in Origen's Christology, which sought to describe with greater precision the relation between the divine Logos and the incarnate Christ. In the fourth century, Athanasius's masterwork *On the Incarnation of the Word* would later set out from this broad concept of the Logos to sketch the history of human fall and redemption starting from the origins

---

[21] For example, Bos, "Prägung."
[22] See also Tardieu, "Recherches."
[23] Introductory: Jakab, *Ecclesia alexandrina*, 91–106; Pearson, *Gnosticism and Christianity*, 26–32; on Clement and Origen: Rankin, *From Clement*, 113–41. Still unsurpassed: Daniélou, *Gospel Message*; idem, *Origen*.

of the world.[24] The Alexandrian doctrine of the Logos again gave Christians access to Greek philosophical discourse on a high level.

From the half-magical, half-philosophical cosmology of Sethian Gnosticism to the refined theology of Origen and Athanasius, the whole spectrum of early Alexandrian Christian thinking reflects the appropriation at different levels of the various modes of discourse locally available. These could range from high-level Greek philosophy to liturgical and magical rites deriving their authority from (supposedly) Egyptian or Jewish models, passing through Stoic prescriptions for a "rational" lifestyle, as witnessed, for example, by the *Teachings of Silvanus*.[25] The various audiences of the Alexandrian Christian teachers were looking for such generally coveted symbolic goods as divine wisdom, personal salvation through spiritual or moral purification, or simply power over demons, rather than for creeds. Ancient Christian authors themselves recognized the intellectual and social differences underlying this variety. Thus, the modern word "gnostic" derives from a Greek term *gnōstikos*; defining Christian excellence in terms of access to superior intellectual and spiritual knowledge, the term was used by gnostics proper as well as by Clement of Alexandria and, later, Evagrius (345–99).[26] The domain in which these cultural distinctions and the corresponding doctrinal variety were expressed was probably that of liturgical and associated social practices. Although we know little of these practices, the remarkably fierce polemics of gnostic groups over baptism and the Eucharist confirm their importance at a quite early stage.[27]

The watershed of Late Antiquity, initiated by the reign of Diocletian, introduced entirely novel styles of Christian discourse, including in Egypt.[28] Following the Edict of Milan (313), Christianity developed, over a period of less than a century, from a persecuted minority to a rapidly spreading state-supported religion. But already before Constantine, social shifts and administrative reforms had changed the face of society. New religious movements – in particular, organized monasticism in its different forms – had moved ascetic lifestyles into a central position within the Christian culture of the period, making them a favorite option for those longing for purity and sanctity. What has been called "the politics of the body" would henceforth become a focus of much of Christian discourse.[29]

[24] Text: Thomson, *Athanasius*.
[25] Zandee, *Teachings*.
[26] On the term: Layton, "Prolegomena."
[27] Baptism: Sevrin, *Dossier*; Eucharist: *Gospel of Judas;* cf. Rouwhorst, "Gospel of Judas."
[28] General: Bagnall, *Egypt*.
[29] Brown, *Body*.

Traditional scholarship has often considered Egyptian monasticism as a kind of peasant movement, originating among the lower strata of indigenous society. The sources for fourth-century Egypt do not confirm this picture, however. From the standpoint of literary culture, fourth-century Egyptian monasticism was highly oriented toward learned Alexandrian theology. The letters attributed to St. Antony (ca.251–356), authentic or not, betray in their spiritual language a clear Origenist inspiration.[30] The Coptic gnostic manuscripts from Upper Egypt apparently circulated in monastic communities.[31] Monasticism is not an unreflective flight into primitivism, but a movement deeply rooted in Christian dualist thought. In fact, the most influential contribution to the construction of the spiritual profile of Egyptian monasticism, the *Life of Antony*, was probably written by Athanasius himself.[32] Ideologically, monasticism represented the influx of Alexandrian thinking in all its variety into the Egyptian countryside.

For all its spirituality, the discourse of late antique asceticism was paradoxically focused largely on human behavior, morally and socially, in its relation to the body, sexuality, kinship, and the world. Asceticism as an institutionalized way of life demanded a rethinking of man in his social and moral dimensions. A similar urge for new and more precise definitions characterized the development of the debate about the nature of Christ as the Godhead incarnate. From the perspective of a new, more practical anthropology, the traditional Alexandrian view of Christ as an abstract, extratemporal Logos was hardly apt to answer all questions that could be posed about Christ's humanity and divinity. While this had created tensions already before the fourth century, it now found a broader echo during the first great crisis over Christology, the Arian schism. Arius was a priest of the Alexandrian church (256–336), now best remembered as an exponent of what is called subordinationism. This is, roughly speaking, the tendency to make Christ inferior in position and in essence to the Father. What exactly Arius taught, however, is difficult to assess, and modern opinions on his theology are divergent.[33] The conflict ended in a triumph for another Alexandrian, Athanasius, bishop of that town from 328. His name remains connected with the term *homoousios*, "of the same substance," to define the relationship between the Father and the Son, over against Arian positions. During the Council of Nicaea (325), this term was

[30] Rubenson, *Letters*.
[31] Wipszycka, "Nag Hammadi Library."
[32] Text: Bartelink, *Vie*; cf. Brakke, *Athanasius*, 201–65.
[33] For a balanced view: Williams, *Arius*; cf. Grillmeier, *Jesus*, 1, 356–85. Arius as an Alexandrian: Haas, *Alexandria*, 268–77.

included in the Nicene Creed, which is still at the basis of most Christian denominations.[34] What have been called the learned and scholastic style of Arius, on the one hand, and the narrative and anthropomorphic style of Athanasius, on the other, were not merely matters of personal preference. Their opposing catechetic styles represent divergent modes of discourse attuned to different response groups.[35] The frictions that this divergence engendered on the level of theological definitions remained a source of conflict in the centuries to come.

As a way of solving doctrinal disputes, the ecumenical Council of Nicaea established a precedent. In the fifth century, the Christological debate flared up once again.[36] This time, the central theme was the relationship between the divine and the human in Christ incarnate. Facing Nestorius's provocative statements, which seemed to deny the essential unity of Christ, the Council of Ephesus was convened in 431. Once again, the council eventuated in a victory for an Alexandrian bishop and theologian, Cyril. But Cyril's almost scholastic use of the terms "nature," "hypostasis," and similar philosophical terms created confusions that persisted after his death during the Councils of Ephesus II (449) and Chalcedon (451), and continued thereafter. Whether one defined the union of divinity and humanity in Christ as "one single hypostasis in two natures" or as "the one nature of the Logos incarnate" had by the middle of the fifth century become shibboleths, opposing what are called, incorrectly, dyophysites and monophysites. Egypt was also embroiled in the controversy. In 451 the Council of Chalcedon condemned the Alexandrian bishop Dioscorus as an exponent of the latter option. The result was a violent conflict that split the Egyptian church for centuries to come. In the second half of the sixth century, what had formerly been a latent schism grew into an open one, with the development of parallel hierarchies and separate churches. Although the conflict over the nature of Christ arose out of a genuine interest in safeguarding the essential integrity of the Godhead incarnate, subtle but irreconcilable differences in discourse and the search for watertight definitions and purity of terminology came to dominate the debate. In spite of the efforts of, for example, the Alexandrian philosopher John Philoponus (ca.490–575), an important Aristotelian scholar,[37] the discussion was eventually decided by authority.

---

[34] Cf. Grillmeier, *Jesus*, 1, 386–413.
[35] Cf. Kannengieser, quoted in Williams, *Arius*, 112.
[36] For the theological issues involved: Grillmeier, *Jesus*, 1, 637–775, with vols. 2/1 and 2/4. Easier but partly antiquated: Frend, *Rise*. For Cyril's Christology, see now Van Loon, *Dyophysite Christology*.
[37] Grillmeier, *Jesus*, 2/4, 109–49; Lang, *John Philoponus*.

TRANSFORMATIONS OF AUTHORITY

Very little is known about the social organization of the earliest Christian communities of Alexandria. It can be inferred that they were organized according to a hierarchical model and that, at an early stage, inner-group dissension had led to the demarcation of subgroups.[38] The definition of such groups could involve their social setting, liturgical practices, and questions related to doctrinal correctness and access to wisdom and knowledge. Our earliest sources show how, in each of these domains, authority was defined and debated.

Real or spiritual genealogies were an important instrument in the process of establishing the authority of a group or an individual teacher. Thus, Basilides and his son Isidorus, both early Alexandrian gnostics, appear to have claimed access to secret teachings of Jesus himself, transmitted through the apostle Matthias. This is a rather simple, unequivocal way of mapping the transmission of authority. Other literary constructs are more complicated. As one moved away from the apostolic age chronologically, group dissension was projected onto the gospel narrative itself. By an identical procedure already found in the Synoptic Gospels (e.g., Matt. 16:13–20), the *Gospel of Thomas* (*logion* 13) and the *Gospel of Judas* (34:22–36: 9), for example, isolated privileged disciples (Thomas, Judas) and thereby created room for dissident views in a space where authority was defined traditionally. This does not mean that real-life Thomas or Judas communities existed. We are dealing rather with literary conventions meant to validate dissident views or positions. The same applies to the various representatives of the genre of the so-called gnostic dialogue, a literary setting in which Jesus answers the questions and remarks of some or all of his disciples, preferably in the forty-day period between his resurrection and ascension.[39] These dialogues were not particular to gnostic groups. It was a literary device that remained popular in Egypt and shaped much non-gnostic apocryphal literature. In a direct and straightforward way, this literary device lent authority to what has been called secondary teaching.

Genealogies were also important to the legitimation of the so-called catechetical school and the episcopal office, the main institutional sources of authority within the early Alexandrian church.[40] Fourth- and fifth-century sources give the succession of the school's supposed main teachers as well

---

[38] For general principles: Dorogovtsev and Mendes, *Evolution*.
[39] On the genre: Hartenstein, *Zweite Lehre*.
[40] Pearson, *Gnosticism and Christianity*, 19–21 and 27–8 (with further references).

as the pedigree of the Alexandrian bishops, beginning with St. Mark. The historicity of both traditions in the strict sense is hardly relevant. Their significance lies in the literary construction of a double genealogy of authority.

Whereas these two kinds of authority, of the teacher and of the bishop, were both tied up with an office, this was not the case with the authority of the martyr in the early church. Because it was linked to an individual's fate, the martyr's authority could not be translated into a genealogy. It is again Origen who at an early stage had designed the profile of the Christian martyr in his *Exhortation to Martyrdom*.[41] Like many other early Christians, Origen had desired from his youth to become a martyr – not in order to assert his authority, but out of a longing for Christian perfection that found its highest expression in the martyr's suffering and eventual death.[42]

The importance of martyrdom as a privileged way to obtain Christian perfection became apparent in a major crisis in the early fourth century, the Melitian schism.[43] This crisis pitted the Alexandrian bishop Peter, who died in 311 as one of the last victims of the persecutions under Maximinus Daia, against a local bishop, Melitius of Lycopolis (Assiout), in southern Egypt. According to the traditional view, the conflict involved the treatment of the so-called *lapsi*, Christians who, faced with persecution, had renounced their belief instead of accepting martyrdom. Peter took a lenient stand, allowing their readmission into the church under certain conditions, whereas Melitius's position was more rigorist. When a schism occurred, Melitius found wide support among bishops and clergy, who claimed for themselves the title "church of the martyrs." There can be no doubt that this conflict helped to thematize and popularize martyrdom during a time when it had properly become something of the past. After the persecutions had stopped, the debate no longer concentrated on the question of the *lapsi*, but rather on the proper forms and ways of honoring the martyrs. Access to martyrs' relics was apparently an issue, and their possession and authenticity were debated. In his *Life of Antony*, Athanasius, the major adversary of the Melitians, expressly situated the ascetic lifestyle in the spiritual lineage of the martyrs.

The traditional view of the Melitian schism should not go unchallenged, however. Essentially, the conflict may have been between the local bishop's authority and the traditional prerogatives of the Alexandrian bishop as the

---

[41] Text: O'Meara, *Origen*.
[42] Origen's ideal of perfection: Völker, *Vollkommenheitsideal*.
[43] Martin, *Athanase*, 215–98.

head of the Egyptian church. In any case, Athanasius reacted by forging the Egyptian church into a strongly structured unity kept in place by a great number of bishops with the bishop of Alexandria at their head.[44] Although the framework of episcopacies existed for the greater part before Athanasius, he unified election procedures and created new sees. Even centuries later, a marginal diocese like that of Philae traced its pedigree back to Athanasius.[45]

A perhaps more revolutionary move was Athanasius's close personal involvement in the rising ascetic movement of his time.[46] Although monasticism in its various fourth-century forms may have been ideologically prepared by Alexandrian theology, it gathered momentum only after becoming a broad communal movement. As such, it offered new forms of authority based on a distinct, ascetic lifestyle and on new forms of social organization. The typical monastic saint was not a theologian, but rather a mediator of spiritually based authority grounded in a particular lifestyle. If traditional research has perhaps been too focused on the spiritual ideals propagated by monastic pious reading, the scholarship of the last few decades, ever since Peter Brown, tends to isolate the heroic individual (the "holy man") as he is best known through hagiography, always a dangerous genre.[47] Thanks to the input of papyrological and archaeological research, there is a growing awareness that monasticism is mainly a communal effort with a strong institutional and economic basis.[48] Prescriptive literature demanded that the monk be an ascetic, turned away from the world, living in a symbolic desert, and feeding on the word of God. In reality, however, monks fulfilled a variety of economic and social roles. Otherwise, monasticism could never have become a viable lifestyle. In late antique Egypt, small and large monasteries fully integrated into the fabric of society covered both urban and rural regions. Society in its turn also favored this lifestyle: wealthy individuals became the founders and patrons of their own local monasteries.

Among the variety of authoritative models that characterized Egyptian monasticism as an institution, the two that became best known were the cenobitic and the eremitic lifestyles. The latter aimed at creating for

[44] Ibid., 637–763.
[45] Dijkstra, *Philae.*
[46] See particularly Brakke, *Athanasius.*
[47] Cf. Brown, "Rise."
[48] For example, Wipszycka, "Formes". Much current research aims at integrating the various strands of information (papyrological, archaeological, literary, etc.) for monastic centers like Bawit (Middle Egypt) and others; see in particular Wipszycka, *Moines.* For a reliable guide to the literary sources, see Harmless, *Desert Christians.*

the monk a real or supposed desert, where he lived in isolation, fighting demons.[49] It was perhaps most influentially propagated by the *Life of Antony*, but the same work shows the monk's isolation to be relative: Antony lived for a considerable part of his life surrounded by disciples and was visited by a sizeable clientele. His example, according to a well-known phrase from the *Life*, had turned "the desert into a city." The cenobitic lifestyle is traditionally connected with the name of Pachomius (ca.286– 346), whose ideal of a communal life, strictly controlled by a rule, a shared daily schedule of work and prayer, and the oversight of a superior, spread from Upper Egypt throughout the whole of the Empire.[50] In Egypt too, this model was developed, for example, by Shenoute (d. ca.465), from the region of Panopolis.[51] He stood at the head of a gigantic monastic confed- eration, comparable to a town in size and structure. His style of leadership, well documented by his own writings, was modeled after the prophets of the Old Testament. The main church of his monastery, which still stands, is by far the most impressive surviving building of late antique Egypt, the visible expression of the authority of monastic charisma in the fifth cen- tury.[52] But many other forms of monastic life are attested, sometimes by both archaeological finds and textual sources. In northern regions, mon- asteries tended to consist of modular units of modest size, rather than of great compounds, such as in the Kellia region.[53] Elsewhere, in particular in Middle Egypt, as it seems, cenobitic and eremitic lifestyles coexisted on the desert edge, as on the mountain of Naqlun in the Fayyum province.[54] A fourth-century house-size community of Manichaeans was discovered during excavations in the village of Kellis, in the Dakhla Oasis (Western Desert).[55]

Monastic authority was supported both by ascetic discipline and spir- itual charisma, and by high-profile literary and rhetorical activity. That is why the ascetic movement could provide the framework in which the indigenous language, Coptic, rose to the status of a fully fledged equiva- lent of Greek as a written language.[56] Coptic was not adopted because of the inability of some classes of society to write or read Greek, but because

[49] Desert: Goehring, *Ascetics*, 73–88; demons: Brakke, *Demons*.
[50] Best introduction: Rousseau, *Pachomius*.
[51] Emmel, *Shenoute's Literary Corpus*; Layton, "Rules."
[52] Grossmann, *Christliche Architektur*, 528–36.
[53] See the essays in Bridel, ed., *Site*.
[54] Wipszycka, "Rapports."
[55] Gardner et al., *Coptic Documentary Texts*.
[56] Various information about Coptic in Atiya, ed., *Coptic Encyclopedia*, vol. 8, 13–227; cf. Reintges, "Code-Mixing."

the native language had come to share the status and the authority of a successful new Christian lifestyle. Typically, monks were able to read and write, and to engage in scholarly activities like book production, medicine, and magic. Already the Manichaeans of Kellis maintained a lively correspondence in Coptic and Greek, which shows them active in copying sacred texts and magical spells.[57] The ascetic movement created literary genres of its own, like the spiritual letter of guidance or the monastic rule. Evagrius is still famous for his "handbooks," which provided psychological and spiritual guidance for the life of the monk.[58] The ability to preach was also a privilege of the educated. People flocked from all over the country to attend the sermons of the leaders of the Pachomian communities.[59] Likewise, the preaching of Shenoute, a prolific bilingual (Greek and Coptic) author, attracted the great names of his time, who in their turn sponsored the building of his great basilica.

Athanasius's *Life of Antony* has been described as a step toward the "domestication" of monasticism – that is, as a way of subordinating monasticism to the authority structures of the church at large and assuring its orthodoxy.[60] Although Athanasius does indeed stress Antony's orthodoxy, this is a somewhat reductionist view of the *Life*. Yet it cannot be denied that in the course of the fourth century, the struggle over authority within the Egyptian church and the debate over correct doctrine following the Arian crisis helped to shape the development of the rapidly growing monastic communities of the country. While the hoards of fourth- and fifth-century Manichaean and gnostic texts in Coptic discovered in Upper Egypt attest their wide diffusion, they also mark the end point of their manuscript transmission. In general, monastic discourse in the fourth and fifth centuries moved away from the tradition of Alexandrian dualism. It may be best, however, to see this development as a function of a far broader ideological change by which, on the one hand, spiritual authority had become anchored in a practical and physical lifestyle and, on the other hand, authority was increasingly coming to depend on doctrinal correctness.

The turning point in this trend was undoubtedly the so-called Origenist controversy of 399–400.[61] In this controversy, the Alexandrian bishop Theophilus (385–412) opposed an influential group of monastic intellectuals

[57] Gardner et al., *Coptic Documentary Texts*, 224–8.
[58] Guillaumont, *Philosophe*.
[59] Goehring, *Letter of Ammon*.
[60] Brakke, *Athanasius*, 201–65; the term is from M. A. Williams.
[61] Clark, *Origenist Controversy*, in particular 105–57.

in a dispute, as it appears, over the limits of anthropomorphism in the representation of God. The conflict signaled a development in which a more literal and moralizing interpretation of the Bible, stricter forms of organization, and greater attention to doctrinal orthodoxy came to characterize Egyptian monasticism. The Pachomian model, with its insistence on rules of communal behavior and biblical instruction, gained in authority, even if it had never become the sole model for the organization of monasticism in Egypt. Shenoute may be seen as a representative example of this tendency.

Another element that contributed to what might be called the ecclesiasticalization of Egyptian monasticism was the fusion of ascetic and pragmatic authority in the person of the bishop.[62] Athanasius not only favored the ascetic movement; he also appealed to it for the recruitment of clergy and bishops in particular. As several models of authority converged in the bishops of Late Antiquity, the bishop as monk became increasingly central to his makeup. From the biographies of Bishop Pisentius (569–632), it is hardly possible to discern what his proper episcopal role may have been institutionally or even practically. Judging from these hagiographical texts, he seems to have remained a monk who strayed from his cell more or less incidentally. Only his archives show the sharp edges, and even the limits, of his episcopal authority.[63]

The strong ties between the monastic movement, the local bishops, and the Alexandrian church as they had been forged since Athanasius are usually held responsible for the massive support that Egypt gave to the Alexandrian bishop Dioscorus during and after the Councils of Ephesus II (449) and Chalcedon (451). However, the still commonly held view of a predominantly monastic and Coptic Egypt that after 451 massively opted for monophysite positions and held to them against all odds is a myth that is at least partly born from hindsight.[64] Precisely within the monasteries, the Christological debates seem to have been particularly intense. In the course of the sixth century, the unity of Pachomian monasticism itself succumbed to the pressures of the conflict.[65] Several foundations of "double monasteries" are also reported: communities split up, and new monasteries were built at the threshold of old ones. The anti-Chalcedonian party itself was strongly divided, even if the moderate theology of Severus of Antioch (exiled in Egypt from 518–38) later succeeded in overcoming many

---

[62] Rapp, *Holy Bishops*; Sterk, *Renouncing*, pays less attention to Egypt.
[63] Hagiography: Gawdat Gabra, *Untersuchungen*; archives: Van der Vliet, "Pisenthios."
[64] Wipszycka, "Nationalisme."
[65] Goehring, *Ascetics*, 241–61.

of the divergent tendencies.[66] The sheer mass of the anti-Chalcedonian movement finally proved to be decisive. Nevertheless, what made up this mass was not nationalist or class sentiment (oppressed Copts against a ruling class of Greeks or even Byzantines), but rather the authority of local clergy and monks and the force of local practice. The case of John the Almsgiver, pro-Chalcedonian bishop of Alexandria (610–19) and not even an Egyptian, suggests that properly exercised local authority could cause shifts in loyalties.[67] The fate of schisms was decided by local alliances rather than by church councils.

TRANSFORMATIONS OF THE LANDSCAPE

The destruction of the Serapeum of Alexandria in 391 has been called an "iconic event."[68] The great temple of Serapis was indeed a visual and historical landmark. The very iconicity of the event also made it a symbol of Egypt's conversion to Christianity. Temples were demolished and replaced by churches and *martyria* (shrines for the relics of the saints). The Christianization of a country and its culture is not adequately described, however, in the dramatic events that epitomize it. It is rather the outcome of a process of gradual transformation. In this process, the primary role did not fall to theology or to church politics, but rather to the sum of local practices that is called landscape here.

The Christianization of the landscape involved more than the appropriation of its physical space; it also shaped and reshaped the symbolic associations that give the landscape its meaning. It could take the form of shifts in the localization of symbolic authority as it was distributed over the landscape by community rites and social habits; by liturgy and calendar; and by the establishment of chapels, churches, and monasteries. All religion, whatever its pretensions to universality, is lived locally, and Egyptian Christianity is no exception. Modern authors sometimes tend to emphasize the more sensational and, usually, violent incidents marking the Christianization of the country, in particular at the end of the fourth and the early fifth century. These, however, are the result rather than the engine of transformations that were already well underway. Christianity spread rapidly in the decades after Constantine's victory. Some authors claim that the demise of the traditional temples was already a fact before

---

[66] Allen and Hayward, *Severus.*
[67] Haas, *Alexandria,* 218–19, 258 (with n. 28).
[68] McKenzie et al., "Reconstructing," 107.

Constantine, which would explain the rapid success of Christianity.[69] While this may be true at the level of economic institutions, local religious practices, as distinct from the economic and political aspects of traditional pharaonic religion, were still very much alive.[70] The vitality of traditional religious knowledge and ritual expertise is well attested in Greek and late Demotic sources, mainly magical, from western Thebes.[71] Also in western Thebes, traditional ritual practices persisted until well into the fourth century, well anchored in the social life of the local community.[72] While imperial protection assuredly caused a steep rise in the cultural market value of Christianity after 313, the main explanation for the quick spread of Christianity over Egypt can be found at the level of local practices.

At this level, two aspects of Egyptian Christianity were particularly decisive: the cult of the saints and the rise of monasticism. From the beginning, the Christian saint par excellence was the martyr; even in late antique Egypt, most saints with an attested cult were martyrs.[73] Focused on the martyr's burial spot or the place where his relics were kept, such cults imparted a Christian character to the shape of the landscape. From the early fourth century onward, Alexandria became an important depository of martyrs' relics, including those of "Old Testament martyrs," such as the three youths of Daniel 3.[74] After 381, a *martyrium* for St. John the Baptist was built directly on the precincts of the Serapeum, as only one step in building the city's Christian identity.

In the wake of the spread of cults and relics over Egypt, the development of a rich martyrological literature assumed typically Egyptian forms.[75] Localizing holiness in the landscape was one of its primary functions. Coptic martyrdoms show the martyr traveling around the country from one tribunal to another, thus mapping his presence on the Egyptian landscape. The Alexandrian itinerary of St. Mark can be reconstructed from his Acts.[76] Whether or not the places indicated really did play a role in his life is less interesting than the role that reading these Acts played in shaping and perpetuating the Christian townscape of Alexandria.

Martyrs traveled even after their death. Their relics could be transferred more or less miraculously, and their journeys were the subject of a literary

[69] Bagnall, *Egypt*, 261–8.
[70] Frankfurter, *Religion*, esp. 97–144.
[71] Dieleman, *Priests*.
[72] Łajtar, *Deir el-Bahari*.
[73] Papaconstantinou, *Culte des saints*, 233–5.
[74] Ibid., 199; Frankfurter, "Urban shrine."
[75] Baumeister, *Martyr Invictus*; Zakrzewska, "Masterplots."
[76] Pearson, *Gnosticism and Christianity*, 100–11.

genre of its own, that of the *translatio*. The probably rather late *translatio* of St. James the Persian does more than simply explain the presence of his relics at a certain sanctuary in an insignificant village outside Oxyrhynchus. The complicated itinerary of his relics also attaches them to heroic episodes from the fifth-century resistance against the Council of Chalcedon. It thereby situated the cult of the saint not only spatially, but also historically and ecclesiastically by attaching it to the "correct" anti-Chalcedonian tradition.[77]

Miracles apart, relics did not travel on their own. In the fourth and fifth centuries, various witnesses attest to a widespread relics hunt.[78] The Melitians were sometime blamed for plundering cemeteries to obtain relics for their own churches. It is clear, however, that this was a much more pervasive phenomenon, unsuccessfully combated by moralists. But relics, once they had found their proper place, made people move in still another way. The mortal remains of several martyrs had become the center of famous cults, sometimes attracting pilgrims beyond the boundaries of the region itself. In some instances, the new pilgrimage centers assumed functions once performed by the traditional temples. The sanctuary of St. Menas to the west of Alexandria enjoyed an international reputation as a healing center. Pilgrims traveling to the site from all over the Mediterranean world took home with them the well-known oil flasks that can now be found in nearly every collection of antiquities. Excavations at the site revealed gigantic structures designed to receive and care for the pilgrims, confirming the prestige of this sanctuary.[79] Hundreds of oracle tickets have been found at the sanctuary of another healer-saint, St. Collouthos, near Antinoë in Upper Egypt. By soliciting advice about all kinds of daily life matters, these tickets were a direct continuation of pharaonic oracle practices.[80]

The cult of the saints played an important part both in the Christian appropriation of space and in shaping Christian time. The rhythm of pilgrimages was primarily determined by the liturgical calendar, much less by the private needs of the pilgrims. According to Shenoute, the authenticity of a martyr's cult must be hallmarked first of all by written acts and a date on the calendar.[81] The same author, and others as well, describes (and

---

[77] Van der Vliet, "Bringing home," 39–44.
[78] Lefort, "Chasse"; Horn, *Studien*, 1–9.
[79] Grossmann, "Pilgrimage Centre."
[80] Frankfurter, *Religion*, 145–97; on Egyptian oracle tickets, see also Dunand in Chapter 6 of this volume.
[81] Horn, *Studien*, 9. (Note that this passage is no longer attributed to Shenoute himself.)

criticizes) the festivals that took place on the occasions of the martyrs' commemoration. While primarily liturgical in form, they also included fairs and markets, as is still the habit in modern Egypt. Whether purely local or supraregional in scale, these were social events that bound communities around the liturgical commemoration of the saint. Complex activities focusing in particular on the martyrs' shrines had considerable social impact and made them an important factor in the Christianization of the Egyptian landscape.

The rise and development of the ascetic movement exerted a similar influence. The monk or the monastic community was clearly localized in a given landscape. As privileged habitation sites for monks, deserted temples or pharaonic tombs and quarries afforded them the opportunity to combat the demons inhabiting these places. This was not merely a literary topic, but a fact well confirmed by archaeological and epigraphical evidence – for example, from western Thebes. In the early phase, itinerant monks also contributed to the geographical spread of the movement. Monasticism did more than make the "the desert a city"; it turned the inhabited world into a metaphorical desert.[82]

Quite early, the monks – not only the isolated charismatic hero, but also those of the great monastic communities – became the object of monastic tourism, both from abroad and from elsewhere in Egypt. "Pilgrimage to living saints" inspired various literary works that propagated the monastic lifestyle.[83] On the local level as well, visitors sought out monasteries, either as sources of moral or material support, or as centers of economic and ritual activity; in this way, they assumed many of the roles of the traditional temples. As strongholds of literacy, they also played an active role in the transmission of intellectual and ritual expertise. By the fifth century, monks had become the experts in magic.[84] Ascetic and monastic circles modernized the traditional discourse of magic, thereby adapting it to a newly developing Christian culture. Although some traditional practices, such as those connected with the Isis-Horus mythology, retained their force remarkably long, by the fourth century a new magical literature had already arisen, steeped in biblical and liturgical language, and with a heavy emphasis on practical angelology.[85]

[82] Goehring, *Ascetics*, 89–109.
[83] For example, Goehring, *Letter of Ammon*; Frank, *Memory*.
[84] Frankfurter, *Religion*, 189–264.
[85] Christian Egyptian magic: Meyer and Smith, *Ancient Christian Magic*.

A rich literature, predictably often monastic and martyrological in character, supported the Christianization of the Egyptian landscape. One of the most characteristic and fascinating genres of Christian popular literature deserves to be mentioned separately: the so-called cycles. These are groups of literary works (martyrdoms, homilies, and revelations about the angelic world) that may in themselves be distinct units, with different protagonists and stemming from different authors. What connects them are common background narratives – for example, about the early history of the Diocletianic persecutions, the exiles of Athanasius, or the discovery of apostolic autographs on the dusty shelves of ancient libraries.[86] Like modern movies about World War II, they set different stories in a familiar frame, welding history and landscape into one single universe that toward the year 641 had become a world of its own: Christian Egypt.

BIBLIOGRAPHY

Allen, Pauline, and Robert Hayward. *Severus of Antioch* (London, 2004).
Atiya, Aziz S., ed. *The Coptic Encyclopedia* (New York, 1991).
Bagnall, Roger S. *Egypt in Late Antiquity* (Princeton, 1993).
    ed. *Egypt in the Byzantine World, 300–700* (Cambridge, 2007).
Bagnall, Roger S., and Dominic W. Rathbone, eds. *Egypt: From Alexander to the Copts* (London, 2004).
Bartelink, G. J. M., ed. *Athanase d'Alexandrie: Vie d'Antoine* (Paris, 1994).
Baumeister, Theofried. *Martyr Invictus: der Martyrer als Sinnbild der Erlösung in der Legende und im Kult der frühen koptischen Kirche* (Münster, 1972).
Bos, Abraham P. "Die Prägung des Gnostizismus durch den aristotelischen Dualismus." In *Philosophische Religion: Gnosis zwischen Philosophie und Theologie*, ed. Peter Koslowski (Munich, 2006): 37–55.
Brakke, David. *Athanasius and the Politics of Asceticism* (Oxford, 1995).
    Demons and the Making of the Monk: Spiritual Combat in Early Christianity (Cambridge, Mass., 2006).
Bridel, Philippe, ed. *Le site monastique copte des Kellia: sources historiques et explorations archéologiques* (Geneva, 1986).
Brown, Peter. "The Rise and Function of the Holy Man in Late Antiquity." In *Society and the Holy in Late Antiquity* (London, 1982): 103–52.
    The Body and Society (New York, 1988).
Clark, Elizabeth A. *The Origenist Controversy: The Cultural Construction of an Early Christian Debate* (Princeton, 1992).
Daniélou, Jean. *Origen* (London, 1955).
    Gospel Message and Hellenistic Culture (London, 1973).
Dieleman, Jacco. *Priests, Tongues, and Rites: The London-Leiden Magical Manuscripts and Translation in Egyptian Ritual (100–300 CE)* (Leiden, 2005).

---

[86] Preliminary: T. Orlandi, "Literature (Coptic)," in *Coptic Encyclopedia*, ed. Atiya, 1456–8.

Dijkstra, J. H. F. *Philae and the End of Ancient Egyptian Religion: A Regional Study of Religious Transformation (298–642 CE)* (Louvain, 2008).

Dorogovtsev, S. N., and J. F. F. Mendes. *Evolution of Networks: From Biological Nets to the Internet and WWW* (Oxford, 2003).

Emmel, Stephen. *Shenoute's Literary Corpus* (Louvain, 2004).

Frank, Georgia. *The Memory of the Eyes: Pilgrims to Living Saints in Christian Late Antiquity* (Berkeley, 2000).

Frankfurter, David. *Religion in Roman Egypt: Assimilation and Resistance* (Princeton, 1998).
   "Urban shrine and rural saint in fifth-century Alexandria." In *Pilgrimage in Graeco-Roman and Early Christian Antiquity*, eds. Jaś Elsner and Ian Rutherford (Oxford, 2005): 435–49.

Fraser, P. M. *Ptolemaic Alexandria* (Oxford, 1972).

Frend, W. H. C. *The Rise of the Monophysite Movement* (London, 1972).

Gabra, Gawdat. *Untersuchungen zu den Texten über Pesyntheus: Bischof von Koptos (569–632)* (Bonn, 1984).

Gardner, Iain, Anthony Alcock, and Wolf-Peter Funk, eds. *Coptic Documentary Texts from Kellis. Vol. 1, P. Kell V (P. Kell. Copt. 10–52; O. Kell. Copt. 1–2)* (Oxford, 1999).

Godlewski, Włodzimierz. *Le monastère de St Phoibammon* (Warsaw, 1986).

Goehring, James E. *The Letter of Ammon and Pachomian Monasticism* (Berlin, 1986).
   Ascetics, Society, and the Desert: Studies in Early Egyptian Monasticism (Harrisburg, Pa., 1999).

Grillmeier, Alois. *Jesus der Christus im Glauben der Kirche*. 5 vols. (Freiburg, 1979–90).

Grossmann, Peter. "The Pilgrimage Centre of Abû Mînâ." In *Pilgrimage and Holy Space in Late Antique Egypt*, ed. David Frankfurter (Leiden, 1998): 281–302.
   Christliche Architektur in Ägypten (Leiden, 2001).

Guillaumont, Antoine. *Un philosophe au désert: Evagre le Pontique* (Paris, 2004).

Haas, Christopher. *Alexandria in Late Antiquity: Topography and Social Conflict* (Baltimore, 1997).

Harmless, William. *Desert Christians: An Introduction to the Literature of Early Monasticism* (New York, 2004).

Hartenstein, Judith. *Die zweite Lehre: Erscheinungen des Auferstandenen als Rahmenerzählungen frühchristlicher Dialoge* (Berlin, 2000).

Horn, Jürgen. *Studien zu den Märtyrern des nördlichen Oberägypten*. Vol. 1, *Märtyrerverehrung und Märtyrerlegende im Werke des Schenute* (Wiesbaden, 1986).

Hurtado, Larry W. *Lord Jesus Christ: Devotion to Jesus in Earliest Christianity* (Grand Rapids, Mich., 2003).

Jakab, Attila. *Ecclesia alexandrina: évolution sociale et institutionnelle du christianisme alexandrin (IIe et IIIe siècles)*, 2nd ed. (Bern, 2004).

Kasser, Rodolphe, and Gregor Wurst. *The Gospel of Judas: Critical Edition* (Washington, D.C., 2007).

King, Karen L. *What is Gnosticism?* (Cambridge, Mass., 2003).

Lang, Uwe Michael. *John Philoponus and the Controversies over Chalcedon in the Sixth Century: A Study and Translation of the Arbiter* (Louvain, 2001).

Łajtar, Adam. *Deir el-Bahari in the Hellenistic and Roman Periods: A Study of an Egyptian Temple based on Greek Sources* (Warsaw, 2006).

Laskowska-Kusztal, Ewa. *Le sanctuaire ptolémaïque de Deir el-Bahari* (Warsaw, 1984).

Layton, Bentley. *The Gnostic Scriptures: A New Translation* (Garden City, N.Y., 1987).

ed. *Nag Hammadi Codex II, 2–7* (Leiden, 1989).

"Prolegomena to the Study of Ancient Gnosticism." In *The Social World of the First Christians: Essays in Honor of Wayne A. Meeks*, eds. L. Michael White and O. Larry Yarbrough (Minneapolis, 1995): 334–50.

"Rules, Patterns, and the Exercise of Power in Shenoute's Monastery: The Problem of World Replacement and Identity Maintenance." *JECS* 15 (2007): 45–73.

Lefort, L.-Th. "La chasse aux reliques des martyrs en Égypte au IVe siècle." *La Nouvelle Clio* 6 (1954): 225–30.

Löhr, Winrich Alfried. *Basilides und seine Schule: eine Studie zur Theologie- und Kirchengeschichte des zweiten Jahrhunderts* (Tübingen, 1996).

Luttikhuizen, Gerald P. *Gnostic Revisions of Genesis Stories and Early Jesus Traditions* (Leiden, 2006).

Martin, Annik. *Athanase d'Alexandrie et l'Église d'Égypte au IVe siècle (328–373)* (Rome, 1996).

McKenzie, Judith S., Sheila Gibson, and A. T. Reyes. "Reconstructing the Serapeum in Alexandria from the Archaeological Evidence." *JRS* 94 (2004): 73–121.

Meyer, Marvin W., and Richard Smith. *Ancient Christian Magic: Coptic Texts of Ritual Power*, 2nd ed. (Princeton, 1999).

O'Meara, John Joseph, ed. *Origen: Prayer, Exhortation to Martyrdom* (Westminster, Md., 1954).

Papaconstantinou, Arietta. *Le culte des saints en Égypte des Byzantins aux Abbasides: l'apport des inscriptions et des papyrus grecs et coptes* (Paris, 2001).

Pearson, Birger. *Gnosticism and Christianity in Roman and Coptic Egypt* (New York, 2004).

Quack, Joachim F. "Dekane und Gliedervergottung: altägyptische Traditionen im Apokryphon Johannis." *JbAC* 38 (1995): 97–122.

Rankin, David I. *From Clement to Origen: The Social and Historical Context of the Church Fathers* (Aldershot, Hampshire/Burlington, Vt., 2006).

Rapp, Claudia. *Holy Bishops in Late Antiquity: The Nature of Christian Leadership in an Age of Transition* (Berkeley, 2005).

Reintges, Chris. "Code-Mixing Strategies in Coptic Egyptian." *Lingua Aegyptia* 9 (2001): 193–237.

Roberts, Colin H. *Manuscript, Society, and Belief in Early Christian Egypt* (London, 1979).

Roukema, Riemer. *Gnosis and Faith in Early Christianity: An Introduction to Gnosticism* (London, 1999).

"The Historical Context of the Gospel of Judas and its Presentation to the Wider Audience." *JCS* 12 (2010): 1–18.

Rousseau, Philip. *Pachomius: The Making of a Community in Fourth-Century Egypt*, 2nd ed. (Berkeley, 1999; original, 1985).

Rouwhorst, Gerard. "The Gospel of Judas and Early Christian Eucharist." In *In Search of Truth: Augustine, Manichaeism and other Gnosticism*, eds. Jacob Albert van den Berg, Annemaré Kotzé, Tobias Nicklas, and Madeleine Scopello. NHMS 74 (Leiden, 2011): 611–25.

Rubenson, Samuel. *The Letters of St. Antony*, 2nd ed. (Minneapolis, 1995; original, 1990).

Schmid, Herbert. *Die Eucharistie ist Jesus: Anfänge einer Theorie des Sakraments im koptischen Philippusevangelium (NHC II 3)*. VCSup 88 (Leiden, 2007).

Sevrin, Jean-Marie. *Le dossier baptismal séthien: études sur la sacramentaire gnostique* (Quebec, 1986).

Sterk, Andrea. *Renouncing the World Yet Leading the Church: The Monk-Bishop in Late Antiquity* (Cambridge, Mass., 2004).

Tardieu, Michel. *Ecrits gnostiques: Codex de Berlin* (Paris, 1984).

"Recherches sur la formation de l'Apocalypse de Zostrien et les sources de Marius Victorinus." *RO* 9 (1996): 7–114.

Thomassen, Einar. *The Spiritual Seed: The Church of the "Valentinians"* (Leiden, 2006).

Thomson, Robert W. *Athanasius: Contra Gentes and De Incarnatione* (Oxford, 1971).

Turner, John D. *Sethian Gnosticism and the Platonic Tradition* (Quebec, 2001).

Van der Vliet, Jacques. "The Coptic Gnostic Texts as Christian Apocryphal Literature." In *Ägypten und Nubien in spätantiker und christlicher Zeit: Akten des 6. Internationalen Koptologenkongresses, Münster*, eds. Stephen Emmel, Martin Krause, Siegfried G. Richter, and Sofia Schaten (Wiesbaden, 1999): 553–62.

"Pisenthios de Coptos (569–632): moine, évêque et saint." In *Autour de Coptos: actes du colloque organisé au Musée des Beaux-Arts de Lyon (17–18 mars 2000)*, ed. Marie-Françoise Boussac (Lyon, 2002): 61–72.

"Bringing Home the Homeless: Landscape and History in Egyptian Hagiography." In *The Encroaching Desert: Egyptian Hagiography and the Medieval West*, eds. Jitse Dijkstra and Mathilde van Dijk (Leiden, 2006): 39–55.

Van Haelst, Joseph. *Catalogue des papyrus littéraires juifs et chrétiens* (Paris, 1976).

Van Loon, Hans. *The Dyophysite Christology of Cyril of Alexandria*. VCSup 96 (Leiden, 2009).

Van Os, Lubbertus Klaas. "Baptism in the Bridal Chamber: The Gospel of Philip as a Valentinian Baptismal Instruction," diss. Groningen, 2007.

Völker, Walther. *Das Vollkommenheitsideal des Origenes: eine Untersuchung zur Geschichte der Frömmigkeit und zu den Anfängen christlicher Mystik* (Tübingen, 1931).

Waldstein, Michael, and Frederik Wisse. *The Apocryphon of John: Synopsis of Nag Hammadi codices II,1; III,1; and IV,1 with BG 8502,2* (Leiden, 1995).

Welsby, Derek A. *The Medieval Kingdoms of Nubia: Pagans, Christians and Muslims along the Middle Nile* (London, 2002).

Williams, Michael A. *Rethinking "Gnosticism": An Argument for Dismantling a Dubious Category* (Princeton, 1996).

Williams, Rowan. *Arius: Heresy and Tradition*, 2nd ed. (London, 2001).

Wipszycka, Ewa. *Études sur le christianisme dans l'Egypte de l'antiquité tardive* (Rome, 1996).

"Le nationalisme a-t-il existé dans l'Égypte byzantine?" In *Études sur le christianisme dans l'Egypte de l'antiquité tardive* (Rome, 1996): 9–61.

"Les rapports entre les monastères et les laures à la lumière des fouilles de Naqlun (Fayoum)." In *Études sur le christianisme dans l'Egypte de l'antiquité tardive* (Rome, 1996): 373–93.

"The Nag Hammadi Library and the Monks: A Papyrologist's Point of View." *JJP* 30 (2000): 179–91.

"Les formes institutionelles et les formes d'activité économique du monachisme égyptien." In *Foundations of Power and Conflicts of Authority in Late-Antique Monasticism: Proceedings of the International Seminar Turin, December 2–4, 2004*, eds. Alberto Camplani and Giovanni Filoramo (Louvain, 2007): 109–54.

Moines et communautés monastiques en Égypte: IVe-VIIIe siècles. JJPsup 11 (Warsaw, 2009).

Zakrzewska, Ewa D. "Masterplots and Martyrs: Narrative Techniques in Bohairic Hagiography." In *Narratives of the Ancient Near East: Literary and Linguistic Approaches*, eds. F. Hagen, Hagen J. Johnston, W. Monkhouse, K. Piquette, J. Tait, and M. Worthington. *OLA* 189 (Louvain, 2011): 499–523.

Zandee, Jan. *The Teachings of Sylvanus (Nag Hammadi Codex VII, 4): Text, Translation, Commentary* (Leiden, 1991).

9

CULT AND BELIEF IN PUNIC AND ROMAN AFRICA

BRENT D. SHAW

The narrow belt of habitable lands that lines the southern shores of the Mediterranean – between Libya in the East and Morocco in the West – has always been an insular world. From their perspective, the Arab geographers logically named these lands the *Jazirat al-Maghrib*, the "Island of the West." The countries that make up North Africa today are thus collectively called "the Maghrib." The flow of sea currents and the predominant winds, the hard and rugged barrier formed by the coastal mountains, and a location between the world's largest desert and its largest inland sea, have produced a peculiar mix of connectivity and isolation that has affected both ideas and economies.[1] While moderating the exposure of its inhabitants to influences from elsewhere in the Mediterranean, these same forces have also promoted the rapid development of outside ideas and practices once they have entered North Africa.

One result of this double heritage of relative isolation and internalized intensity was the emergence of a bewildering variety, range, and localized identity of religious ritual and practice among Africans before the arrival of Christianity. In an area larger than that of the Iberian and Italian peninsulas combined, every environmental niche as small as a village or a valley came to have its own spirits, deities, rituals, and festivals. The practices and beliefs were so integrated into the life of each ethnic people, village, cultural or occupational group that they formed an almost out-of-mind part of daily routine. On the other hand, amid all this fragmentation and multiplicity, there was sufficient contact to encourage the formation of strands of unity that can be traced between Africa and the Mediterranean world of which it was part.[2] When a Christian empire during the later fourth

---

[1] Shaw, "Challenging Braudel," "A Peculiar Island," and *At the Edge of the Corrupting Sea*.
[2] Graf, "What Is Ancient Mediterranean Religion?," esp. 4–5, 11–12, gives eloquent expression to the nature of the problem.

century CE began to threaten the local festivals, pilgrimages, parades, and other performances, it was apprehension over the loss of this vital core of everyday life that provoked distress as much as any danger to deeply held beliefs.

Despite the complexity and range of deities and demons, ritual practices and sacred sites, the factor of isolation encouraged another, equally powerful tendency toward intensely local interpretations of various aspects of cult. The combination of these effects produced similarities in ritual and belief that were regionally specific to the Maghrib. Once they entered Africa, external cultural institutions tended to develop more rapidly and uniformly than they did elsewhere in the Mediterranean. In religion and ritual, this relative monism took the form of a pragmatic henotheism: a special emphasis on one deity around which other gods and goddesses oriented themselves as minor players. Within small regions in Africa, conflicts between local and Mediterranean-wide forces reproduced this larger pattern marked by strong polarities. Attempting to grasp the first of these processes, much less the second, as well as the complex interactions between the two, by deploying the traditional heavy armament devised for understanding big religions is bound to disappoint.

WHAT WAS AFRICAN CULT?

Although Africans came to share in a pan-Mediterranean *oikoumenē* of belief and practice, local forces working within regional ecologies strongly conditioned the manner in which elements of an external Mediterranean culture took root in an African environment. The striking absence of North Africa from recent surveys of Roman religion, however, reflects the perception of African cults as a peculiar thing within the context of the Roman empire.[3] Given the principal concerns of these surveys, the exclusion is understandable. These general accounts of ancient religions tend to mirror an eastern and northern Mediterranean arc of practice, and they take *that* constellation – for example, highlighting a classic mix of mystery religions and state cult, and the central roles of divinities like Isis and

---

[3] Among many general works, see, by way of example, Turcan, *Cults of the Roman Empire*; Scheid, *Religion et piété*; Beard, North, and Price, *Religions of Rome* despite some scattered references in the seventh chapter; and Ando, *Roman Religion*. Lane Fox, *Pagans and Christians*, who offers one of the finest evocations of the two worlds of religion, is still mainly devoted to this same arc of belief across the northern Mediterranean, with special emphasis on the Syria-Asia Minor nexus. MacMullen, *Paganism in the Roman Empire*, is a manifest exception. It would probably be an error, in any event, to postulate any one pattern as typically Mediterranean; see Woolf, "Sea of Faith."

Mithras – as the dominant norm. For the reasons just noted, however, Africa does not fit this paradigm. Its distinctive rituals and beliefs were fundamentally different from the styles and patterns found elsewhere in the empire. The student of African religion must therefore work with a looser and more dynamic paradigm that highlights the different constituent elements of pre-Christian "religion" in the Mediterranean world of the Roman empire.[4]

In the period of Roman military and political domination of Africa that extended from the mid-second century BCE to the sixth century CE, new developments were not inscribed on a blank slate. Additions, mutations, abatements, and intensifications of belief, structure, and practice grew out of and alongside an existing world of African and Punic religions that were dominant in the Maghrib down to the first century BCE and later. Given the nature of the evidence, it is difficult to estimate the state of belief and rituals in Africa before the Phoenician colonization of African lands that began in the mid-eighth century BCE. Because the conduct of cult before the advent of the Phoenicians took place wholly in a world of oral communication, the history of this early African phase of religion has been lost to us. The little material or archaeological evidence that survives or can be identified with confidence does not suggest much more than a generalized connection with animating forces resident in this tree or that water spring, in a rock outcrop, a mountain peak, a cave, or similar markers of a sacred landscape.[5] Local cults later glossed with specific Punic or Roman forms and names might suggest an element of continuity.[6] One example is the concentration of shrines and written dedications to Neptune from the Roman period found in small villages of no formal municipal rank, hamlets that were overseen by local African magistrates like the Eleven Men (*undecimprimi*) or the Elders (*seniores*).[7] Despite his name, in Africa Neptune was never a god of the sea or the ocean. He was, rather, a spirit of springs who embodied the living force of the waters that flowed from a local crevice or cliffside.

---

[4] Rives, *Religion in the Roman Empire*, provides a good model of an approach that is more useful for this investigation.

[5] For a general survey of what little can be known or estimated, see the overviews offered by Gsell, "Religion," ch. 2 in idem, *Histoire ancienne*, 6, 119–69; Charles-Picard, "La religion Libyque," in idem, *Religions de l'Afrique antique*, 1–25; and Bénabou, *La résistance africaine*, 267–308. Note that almost all the reliable evidence comes from the Roman period and that most of the rest consists of ethnographic parallels and guesswork.

[6] See Beschaouch, "Une fête populaire de Dougga," for a convincing demonstration of one case.

[7] A. Cadotte, *Neptune Africain*, and "Neptune, africain," ch. 8 in idem, *Romanisation des dieux*, 307–24; cf. Bénabou, "Neptune africain et le problème de l'eau," in idem, *La résistance africaine*, 356–8; Shaw, "The Elders," 27–9; and, on a closely related theme, Arnaldi, "Culto delle *Nymphae*."

Because detailed knowledge of local African practices is mostly lacking for pre-Roman or pre-Punic times, inferences, however risky, must be made from iconic representations and the physical design of sacred places. In the Roman period, written records sometimes accompanying material remains make more explicit the structure and meaning of cultic practice. In these few cases, it is possible to gain greater certainty. For example, hundreds, if not thousands, of cave sanctuaries once existed all over North Africa. Critical written documentation from the high Roman empire exists for exactly two of them. One is the cave on Jebel Taya (or Taïa), the mountain overlooking the Roman town of Thibilis in east-central Algeria. In the third century CE, the magistrates or *magistri* (ordinarily two of them) from the village of Thibilis made annual pilgrimages to the cave to offer sacrifices to the local deity Bacax who lived in it. On the rock surfaces of the corridor-like entrance to the cave, the magistrates of Thibilis recorded in Latin their annual votive promises, specifying the day and year of their visits. Because all of the attested pilgrimages date to the *kalends* (the first of the month) or the evening before the *kalends*, of March, April, or May, the annual journey to the mountain cave seems to have been a local spring ritual, albeit one now adapted to the timing of the Roman imperial calendar.[8]

A similar cave sanctuary was found on the Jebel Chettaba, to the southwest of the city of Cirta. Here inscriptions in Latin dating to the Roman period that recorded dedications to a local deity named Giddaba were crudely inscribed or painted over the walls of the rock shelter.[9] These, too, were made by the magistrates or *magistri* of the nearby town of Phua to the patron deity of the village and its surrounding rural lands. If the kinds of evidence that survive from the Roman period are extrapolated backward in time, they suggest a precontact field of religious and ritual behavior that was intensely fragmented and represented by cults primarily limited to specific locales. Other indicators suggest the same conclusion. The seven African deities named on a stele from the Roman period found near Baga (Roman Vaga) – Macurtam, Macurgam, Vihinam, Bonchor, Varsissima, Matilam, and Iunam – exemplify the general pattern. Individually and collectively, they are unattested anywhere else at

---

[8] Monceaux, "La grotte du dieu Bacax"; *ILAlg.* 2.2, 407–21, nos. 4502–85 (the inscriptions date from 210 CE [no. 4502] to 284 CE [nos. 4557–8]); J. and P. Alquier, *Le Chettaba*, 141–68, nos. 1–70; Toutain, *Cultes païens*, 48, 59–61. The god is often noted by the abbreviation G.D.A.S. (which is understood to mean *Giddabae Deo Augusto sacrum*).

[9] J. and P. Alquier, *Le Chettaba*, 129–68; Gsell, *Histoire ancienne*, vol. 6, 136; for the inscriptions, see *CIL* 8.6267–302; 19249–81; *AE* 1901: 54, and *BCTH* (1917), 227–38, nos. 60–3; all now conveniently gathered in *ILAlg.* 2.3 (Paris, 2003) 968–76, nos. 8907–70.

any other time.[10] Or there is the list of gods called the *Dii Magifae* found at a small locale west of Tébessa (Roman Theveste). The five African deities named – Masiden, Thililva, Suggan, Iesdan, and Masidicca – are unknown outside this small place.[11] This phenomenon of the fine localization of cult can be documented time and time again.

OPENING TO THE MEDITERRANEAN

When Phoenician colonists from Tyre, Sidon, and other places in the Levant began establishing colonial settlements along the African coast in the ninth and eighth centuries BCE, they brought to the western Mediterranean a fully developed panoply of deities. Along with the colonists, these were implanted along its shores from Tripolitania, through Sicily, Sardinia, and the Balearics, to the southern coasts of Iberia. The settlements in Africa were part of this larger process. New Phoenician cities, from Lepcis and Carthage in the East to Lixus and Volubilis in the West, belonged to the greater Phoenician colonial world in the West. Founded as colonies, these settlements had, by the sixth and fifth centuries BCE, acquired a distinctive "western" social, cultural, and political order that we call Punic. Although divinities, practices, and beliefs had been transplanted from their eastern homelands, in Africa they developed in specifically regional ways. The local western Mediterranean versions of Punic beliefs and rituals became core elements of western Phoenician self-definition. In a colonial society suffused with Greek and Hellenistic elements, Punic language and religion provided the people with their distinctive cultural identity.[12]

In its eastern Mediterranean homes, the Phoenician divine economy was already henotheistic, sharing a typical northwest Semitic emphasis on El, the one great god. This emphasis seems to have become only more pronounced in its overseas colonial developments in the western Mediterranean. The rapid spread and intense growth of western Phoenician cult in Africa produced a divine system that matched the greater sameness of the colonial culture of which it was a part, just as the latter developed a new and more uniform Punic identity in its western Mediterranean home. The result was a strongly henotheistic cosmic order, lorded over by a supreme earth-, sky-, and underworld-deity, Adôn or the Lord as he was called. The

[10] Merlin, "Divinités indigènes"; cf. Charles-Picard, *Religions de l'Afrique antique*, 22–3.

[11] *CIL* VIII: 16749 (Henchir Mektides); see Toutain, *Cultes païens*, 40 (and his list of such single occurrences of local deities on p. 41); and Charles-Picard, *Religions de l'Afrique antique*, 24, with another dozen examples of the local deities known nowhere except for the one place where they are attested.

[12] Lancel, *Carthage*, 193.

name of this great and powerful Lord was Ba'al Hammon or BL HMN in Punic.[13] His consort was a female deity who, like Ba'al, was at once Queen of the Skies, Queen of Nature, and Queen of the Underworld. In an important sense, she was not much more than his female alter ego, his "face" as she was often called: TNT PN BA'AL in Punic, Tinnit Pene Ba'al, meaning Tinnit the Face of Ba'al. Most often, however, she was named, simply, Tinnit.[14] The other spirits and deities that we hear of from time to time, like Shadrapha ("Shad" the Healer), Eshmûn, and Melqart ("God of the City"), were lesser bit players in this dominant single-god system. The latter two deities continued to have an important presence in the Roman period when they were identified with Aesculapius and Hercules.[15]

For the people who communicated with these deities, the ritual of sacrifice was at the very heart of practice.[16] The blood sacrifice of living beings at the core of the sacred ritual in the cult of Ba'al Hammon assumed an extreme form that required more than just an animal blood sacrifice.[17] Of living beings, the sacrifice of humans ranked as the most meaningful and powerful. It was the prince of sacrifices, so to speak. And among blood rituals, the rite of the sacrifice of living infants and children to the god Ba'al has drawn most modern attention. From descriptions of sacrificial sites found in the Hebrew Old Testament, modern students have labeled the sacred place of the sacrifice a *tophet*: a site specially set aside for the most important of all blood sacrifices, the *molk*.[18] In Africa, the main evidence comes from the sanctuary or *tophet* at Carthage, but the practice is also attested at other sacred sites found in Africa.[19] It is clear that these areas of sacrifice were specially delineated "sacred places."[20] Here vases containing the bones of infant humans and animals (mainly sheep and goats, but also birds)

[13] Although it is usually asserted that the "Hammon" means "of the perfumed ones," this is far from an established fact. For numerous conjectures about the significance of the name, see Lancel, *Carthage*, 195–8.
[14] There is uncertainty about the vowels in her name. She is most often called Tanit, but the Greek texts of the El-Hofra stelae vocalize her name as *T(h)innit(h)*.
[15] Cadotte, "Eshmoun/Esculape et Eshmoun/Apollon" and "Melqart, Milkashtart et Hercule," chs. 4 and 7 in idem, *Romanisation des dieux*, 165–200; 283–305.
[16] Recognized by Charles-Picard, *Religions de l'Afrique antique*, 130: as he noted, the vast majority of material records that we have are related to votives meant to memorialize a sacrifice.
[17] The eastern origin of the rite, however, seems to be more in the manner of a prompt. No clearcut evidence of a *tophet* has yet been found in Phoenicia. At Carthage, the role of Tinnit was later and peripheral. Mosca, *Child Sacrifice*, 99: "It was Baal Hammon who was and remained the great Punic god, the head of the Punic pantheon, and it was primarily to him that children were sacrificed."
[18] They were places set aside for this exceptional type of sacrifice: Mosca, *Child Sacrifice*, 102–3.
[19] Brown, *Late Carthaginian Child Sacrifice*; Hurst, "Child Sacrifice at Carthage"; Stager, "Rite of Child Sacrifice"; Charles-Picard, *Religions de l'Afrique antique*, 25–49.
[20] Bénichou-Safar, *Tophet de Salammbô*, 150–1: it was called a *shr hqdsh*, "a cut-off or defined holy place," in other words a *temenos*.

have been recovered in layers dating from the late eighth to the mid-second century BCE. In the period for which the most abundant evidence is available at Carthage, Ba'al Hammon and Tinnit received an estimated hundred child-sacrifices annually.[21] The *tophet* at Carthage was the largest of many such sacrificial sites known from various locales in the Phoenician western Mediterranean. Others have been found at Hadrumetum, Cirta, and Henchir el-Hami in Africa; at Motya and Lilybaeum in Sicily; and at Nora, Sulcis, Monte Sirai, and Tharros in Sardinia. The geographical distribution of these sites maps nicely onto the range of direct Carthaginian political, military, and cultural power. No *tophet* has yet been found either in southern Spain or in the far western parts of North Africa to the west of direct Carthaginian control.[22] At Carthage, a series of excavations strung out between the 1920s and the 1940s, and then resumed again in the late 1970s, uncovered about 3,000 burials in urns and an equal number of stelae connected with them.[23] The first analyses of the urns containing the remains of the sacrificed revealed a mixture of animal and human bones, the latter mainly those of infants and small children.

Detailed work done on the sacred precinct at Monte Sirai in Sardinia has confirmed the nature of these sacrifices. Some of the urns discovered there contained only the bones of infants or small children (some up to six months old). Others – about a third to a half of them – contained the bones of both animal sacrifices, mainly kids and lambs, and those of infants and children. It is now clear that this type of sacrifice was a central, permanent, and normal part of Punic cult.[24] Descriptions of the offerings written on the accompanying stelae designate them as a return payment for a promise or a vow that the devotee had made to the deity.[25] There is a vibrant debate over whether or not, in a demographic regime already marked by high infant mortality, the infants were already deceased at the time of their sacrifice.[26] The final verdict on this will

---

[21] Stager, "Rite of Child Sacrifice," 3.

[22] This distribution might well be the fortuitous result of archaeological finds. I think that Cic. *Pro Balb.* 43: inveteratam quandam barbariam ex Gaditanorum moribus disciplinaque [sc. Caesar] delerit, refers to the termination of this ritual at Gadir/Gades by the actions taken by Julius Caesar. It is just the case that we have not yet found the *tophet* there.

[23] For a survey of the historical background of the excavations, see Lancel, *Carthage*, 227–56.

[24] Mosca, *Child Sacrifice*, 97; see 24–5, 102, where he explains the propensity of some classical authors to identify these sacrifices with "great crises."

[25] Bénichou-Safar, *Tophet de Salammbô*, 151–3: the words *ndr* (he vowed) and *zbh* (a sacrifice) are used.

[26] Moscati, a supporter of the revisionist school – that is, that the majority of the infants were fetuses or stillborn births – arrays the evidence and arguments in support of this view in his *Gli adoratori di Moloch*, esp. 63–9; cf. Bénichou-Safar, *Tophet de Salammbô*, esp. 159–63, who also supports this view, developed by Fantar, Richibini, and others.

ultimately depend on much better analyses of the osteological data than is now available. In the view of this author, the weight of the evidence as it stands manifestly suggests the sacrifice of living infants and young children.

The rite of human sacrifice continued deep into the Roman period. In a famous if tendentious passage in his *Apology* (ch. 9.2 = CCL 1: 102), the Christian writer Tertullian claims:[27]

Throughout Africa, infants were openly sacrificed to the god Saturn up to the proconsulship of (the governor) Tiberius [n.b.: the name is certainly in error] who had the priests set out, crucified alive on crosses, on the same trees of the sacred area, in the shadows of which they had committed their crimes. I have my own father as a witness to this fact. He was among the soldiers who served the proconsul in this task. Even to the present day, this same sacred crime is still being perpetrated, although in secret.

Despite well-known problems with this passage, it is reasonably certain that for regions in proximity to the provincial metropolis of Carthage, human sacrifice continued in public until the lifetime of Tertullian's own father, that is, as late as the 170s and 180s CE, when a few known human sacrifices were made the object of official repression. In Tertullian's own day, that is in the 190s to 210s, human sacrifices were still being performed, even if as a secret ritual. Sacred burials from the town of Lambafundi, probably dating to this same time, as well as the new discoveries from the sacred area at Henchir el-Hami, confirm the long continuity of the practice.[28]

Sacrifices requiring the spilling of the blood of living beings were central to almost all Mediterranean religions of the time. Africa is no different in this respect. What is different about Africa is the peculiar intensity of the ritual. Here it involved human life – a human blood sacrifice that was central to the whole of the henotheistic system focused first on the worship of Ba'al and, later, on his Roman continuator, the omnipotent god Saturn. And it continued long after the rite of child sacrifice had been abandoned in Israel (Judea), Phoenicia, and elsewhere. In Africa, infant sacrifice represented an especially strong regional peculiarity of action and belief. Gradual changes in the practice over long periods of time, and its termination, varied from one region and site to another, depending on

---

[27] Charles-Picard, *Religions de l'Afrique antique*, 132–3; for a summary of problems with the text, including some new ones of his own, see Rives, "Child Sacrifice."

[28] Leglay, *Saturn africain. Monuments*, 2, 114–24, esp. 114–15: some of the vases buried in front of each stele contained the bones of infant children, while others contained the bones of sheep or of small birds. Leglay dated the stelae to the late second and early third century CE.

a mix of cultural influences, new interpretations of ritual meaning, and official repression.[29]

In response to both official Roman repression and cultural pressure, a substitute for human life was deemed both possible and preferable to the actual blood sacrifice of humans. In the Roman town of Nicivibus (modern-day N'gaous) in south-central Algeria, a series of five stelae set up to the god Saturn, dating to the end of the second and early third century CE – that is, from the period when the shift from human to stand-in was taking place – speak of the *molchomor* or the sacrifice of a sheep or a lamb as a substitute for a human life.[30] The texts on the stones, which variously call the sacrifice a *molchomor*, *morchomor*, or *mochomor*, explicitly mention the nature of the substitution: "spirit for spirit, blood for blood, life for life" (*anima pro anima, sanguine pro sanguine, vita pro vita*). The sacrifice is accompanied by a vow of the devotee, itself often provoked by a dream or a vision. The victim, however, is now a lamb, described as a substitute for a human, "the lamb serving in the place of another, the lamb as a substitute" (*agnum pro vikario*). This is the same type of sacrifice that is specified as a MLK' MR on the Punic stelae from the El-Hofra sanctuary at Cirta.

The long-term record of the *tophet* at Carthage, covering the entire period from the eighth century BCE to the second century CE, confutes easy ideas about the ameliorating effects of so-called civilizing forces on such rituals. In fact, the propensity to infant sacrifice only grew and intensified as time passed.[31] The worship of the supreme deities Ba'al and, later, Saturn, was this strongly attached to the idea of human blood sacrifice. The hypersacrality of the human victim and of the priest making the sacrifice remained at the core of local religious beliefs and values. A quasi-monotheism reinforced the peculiar intensity and meaning of the human sacrifice and the surrogates for this human blood. It is hardly accidental that in Christian times Africa became the land of the blood of the marytrs.

THE POST–AFRO-PUNIC WORLD

The dual propensity to the rapid adoption of outside Mediterranean ideas and their intense development in local forms remained just as

---

[29] See McCarty, "Representations of Ritual Change," on the particular case of the *tophet* at Hadrumetum.

[30] Charles-Picard, *Religions de l'Afrique antique*, 135–6; Carcopino, "Survivances par substitution"; Février, "Molchomor" and "Rite de substitution."

[31] Stager, "Rite of Child Sacrifice," 4–5, and Table 1; his results are questioned by Janif, "Sacrifices d'enfants," on the basis of the trends reported by Richard, *Étude médico-légale*, which I have not been able to consult.

true in the period following the conquest and incorporation of the former Carthaginian territory by Roman imperial power in 146 BCE. In this
new wave of Mediterranean colonization, Greek and Roman deities were
imported in abundance and began to populate African towns and their
rural territories. In the day-to-day reality of belief and practice in any one
of myriad places, gods and spirits associated, mixed, and merged with
others or aspects of others.[32] This mixing and migration of types was not
so much a conscious or even a subversive syncretism as it was a series of
associations and convergences suggested by local forces mostly beyond the
reach of our understanding. But we can see that the Roman state had an
impact on official ritual, at least at the three levels at which it was officially
represented: as an imperial state, as a provincial administration, and at
the local level of municipal government. But these influences were just as
insular in form as the terrain in which they worked.

There is very little evidence for the formal institution of Roman or Italic
cults in the Roman province of Africa from its inception in 146 BCE to
the end of the republic in the 40s BCE. Down to the reign of the first
Roman emperor, Augustus, such influences appear to have been mainly
private in nature, emanating from the practices of individual Romans and
Italians who came to Africa as settlers, businessmen, and soldiers, and from
the collective groups in which they associated. The large-scale deliberate
importing of official cult began in the Augustan Age. During the triumvi-
ral period at the end of the republic and the beginning of the Principate,
powerful generalissimos struggled to assert their control over Africa and
its strategic resources. In Africa, this global Roman conflict was marked
by the refoundation of Carthage as the great Roman colony that was to
become the imperial metropolis of all Africa. Everywhere else, the evidence indicates the continued practice of Punic cult, which only gradually
abated over the course of the first century CE. At Hadrumetum, the *tophet*
continued to receive typical inhumed burnt offerings – albeit of animals
only – that were marked by stelae until the 80s CE.[33] Further to the east,
the same practice also continued to the end of the first century at Sabratha
in Tripolitania.[34] And at Henchir el-Hami in the interior, human sacrifices
continued to the end of the second century CE. The widespread formal

---

[32] They are measured in epigraphical terms by Cadotte, *Les syncrétismes religieux en Afrique romaine*; in part 3.1, "Les associations divines," 416–76, the author notes dyads, triads, and even more complex juxtapositions and assimilations, groupings of imperial and local divinities, as just some of the ways in which these mixings happened.
[33] Charles-Picard, *Religions de l'Afrique antique*, 103–4, reporting the excavations of Cintas.
[34] Taborelli, *L'area sacra di Ras Almunfakh presso Sabratha*, 69–78: sacrifices only of animals such as goats.

introduction of Roman deities and cult that began in earnest only in the reign of Augustus corresponds to a generalized Roman imperial development observable around the whole circuit of the Mediterranean.[35]

After its refounding as a Roman colony in the 30s BCE, a massive demonstration of brute imperial power on African soil signaled the formal establishment of the cults of the deities of the Roman state at Carthage. The entire top of the great high hill at the center of Carthage, the so-called Byrsa, was systematically leveled to provide a large flat surface analogous in appearance, say, to the acropolis at Athens. Extensions of the platform formed at the top of the leveled Byrsa were supported by massive stone revetments and buttresses. The platform itself was a great stage of more than 30,000m^2 in area – one and a half times the combined size of the forums of Caesar and Augustus at Rome. It was a state project of staggering scale. On this stage were built the major structures of the Roman state: the forum, the basilica and law court buildings, and the temples.[36] The shrines that celebrated the imperial family and the cult of Concord (*Concordia*) looked out both over the harbors that were located to the southeast and over the city and its vast agricultural hinterland to the southwest – all from the focal point of the *groma*, or the Roman surveyor's central sight-point, from which all of the colony's territory had been systematically measured. Facing the provincial judicial basilica at the eastern end of the platform was the temple of the Capitoline triad on the western side.[37]

Everything on this high platform of state echoed not only the religious architecture of the imperial capital of Rome, but also that of the rebuilt Roman colony at Corinth. Corinth had been destroyed by the Romans in the same year that they had obliterated Punic Carthage, so it too was rebuilt in tandem. All of the cult innovations, like the systematic destruction of both cities in 146 BCE, were the result of both artifice and deliberation.[38] At both places, constructed as new imperial centers of the western and eastern Mediterranean, religion and the state intersected. To the very last years of Roman Africa, the imperial tribute for the province was displayed in front of the Capitolium on the height of the Byrsa at Carthage.[39] And it was before the Capitolium that the Christians, in the first state-driven persecutions, were compelled to demonstrate their loyalty by making public

---

[35] Woolf, "Unity and Diversity."
[36] Deneauve, "Le centre monumental de Carthage."
[37] Accepting the arguments of Ladjimi Sebaï, *La colline de Byrsa*, 260–6. They are, however, far from certain, as she herself admits; see Rives, *Religion and Authority*, 42–5, favoring a temple of Concordia.
[38] Purcell, "The Sacking of Carthage and Corinth."
[39] *CTh* 11.1.34, dating to 429 CE, the year of the Vandal invasion.

sacrifice.[40] Even from a great distance out in the countryside, anyone could look up to the monumental high place that defined the new metropolis of Africa. Lit up at night, it presented a brilliant spectacle: the African subjects of empire would have witnessed a symbol of imperial political unity and concord. "You overlords of the Roman empire, in public and on high, on the very summit of the city [sc. Carthage], there you preside to issue your judgments, openly to investigate matters and to examine us in public," remarked the Christian Tertullian, closely connecting the site with the religious and political ideology of empire.[41]

As the sign of a conscious identification with the Roman imperial state by local ruling orders, the building of Capitoline temples was one measure of "becoming Roman" in the province of Africa. Usually built in the main public square or forum of a town, they were a common project undertaken and funded by wealthy members of the local political elite. At Thugga, a mixed Roman-African city located about 100 miles inland of Carthage, a Capitoline temple was built by L. Marcius Simplex in the 160s CE.[42] The act and its timing are typical, so it is important to note the drag in the date of these developments. The delay in the introduction of the Capitoline deities by means of formal temples correlated with the solid wealth and power of local municipal elites in Africa in the Antonine age and later – and had little to do with official city status as such.[43] It was more a measure of the final acceptance of Roman identity by the urban elites of the African provinces than it was any preemptive strike by either side to incite a new sense of belonging.

DIVINE FORCES AND THEIR ECOLOGY

A census of the official gods of a Romano-Mediterranean pantheon celebrated in epigraphical texts reveals a normal top-down order, with Jupiter and other members of the Capitoline triad, Victory, and the Fortuna Augusta at the head of the list. Of the private or unofficial deities, a similar top-to-bottom order can be discerned: Saturn, Mercury, Magna Mater, Caelestis, Pluto, Frugifer, Hercules, Aesculapius, the Cereres,

---

[40] Cyprian, *Ep.* 59.13.3 (CCL 3C: 358); *Laps.* 8 (CCL 3: 225).

[41] Tertullian, *Apol.* 1.1 (CCL 1: 85).

[42] Barton, "Capitoline Temples," 278–9; Toutain, *Cultes païens*, 187–95; Rives, *Religion and Authority*, 118–22; Brouquier-Reddé, 285.

[43] Février, "Religion et domination," 801–3, believed that none were earlier than the Antonine age; Barton's list, "Capitoline Temples," 270–2, reveals some instances probably of Trajanic date. But they are few. Almost all are of Antonine date and later – as admitted by Ladjimi Sebaï, *La colline de Byrsa*, 264 n. 821, who makes the one at Carthage "a sort of peculiarity."

Mars, Neptune, Silvanus, Liber and Sol Invictus, approximately in that order.[44] Again, Africa differs from other areas of the Latin West of the empire.[45] Nor is Africa itself uniform. In the core "western" provinces of Proconsularis, Numidia, and the Mauretanias, for example, dedications to the chief Roman deity Jupiter came only from official functionaries and soldiers; the Saturn cult usurped all the "high ground." In Byzacena and Tripolitania, on the other hand, some local African adherents of Jupiter are found.[46] Although cult centers of Aesculapius, such as the one at Thuburbo Maius, might have been impressive, they were not numerous when compared with the god's Mediterranean profile. The same observation applies even more to the cult of Isis and Serapis. Other deities like Mercury and Silvanus seem to have been more heavily represented in Africa than elsewhere, although it is unclear why this was so.

The problem with simple lists of deities is that they falsely represent them as isolated individuals and occlude degrees of local intensity. The case of Isis, for example, is particularly problematic. The pilgrim's progress, from black magic to the true revelation of Isis, reported by the African philosopher Apuleius in his novel *The Metamorphoses,* is one of the best-known and most striking cases of conversion described for the high Roman empire.[47] But for Africa, the story is misleading. Apuleius is indeed a good representative of a new cosmopolitanism, a bearer of the pervasive cultural values and beliefs shared by the metropolitan classes of imperial Greco-Roman society during the age of the so-called Second Sophistic. As a cultural movement, it paralleled broad Mediterranean-wide fashions linking the social elites in the powerful arc between Asia Minor and Rome – styles like the worship of Isis. As a scion of the social elite, Apuleius was educated in Athens, and was widely traveled, having resided in both Alexandria and Rome. Although African born and raised, and long remembered in Africa for his involvements in philosophy and magic, Apuleius is only modestly representative of most Africans and their beliefs. Moreover, the cosmopolitan cultural movement that he exemplified was to die a hard death in the generation after his death. Trying to generalize about Africa from this exception is risky.[48] For it was not Isis, Mithras, Jupiter,

---

[44] Toutain, *Cultes païens,* 17; Smadja, "L'empereur et les dieux."

[45] MacMullen, *Paganism in the Roman Empire,* fig. p. 6.

[46] Leglay, *Saturne africain, histoire,* 233–4; cf. Foucher, "Paganisme en Afrique," 3.

[47] The classic case, even before Nock, "The Conversion of Lucius," ch. 9 in idem. *Conversion,* 138–55, made it central to modern conceptions.

[48] Isis does not figure anywhere, for example, in Cadotte's massive survey, *Romanisation des dieux;* for what can be said, see Leglay, "Paganisme en Numidie," 79–80.

or any of the other big gods and goddesses of the standard Greco-Roman pantheon, who dominated in Africa.

Divine power and identity, in fact, continued to concentrate in distinctively local African beliefs and practices. During the Roman period, the combination of African, Phoenician, and Punic beliefs that had earlier produced the dominant cult of Ba'al and his consort Tinnit manifested itself in the equally dominant cult of the Romano-African deity Saturn and his consort Caelestis.[49] Saturn and Caelestis were living continuators of Ba'al and Tinnit.[50] Connections with the Italic or Roman deity Saturn are very tenuous in any particular aspect and almost meaningless in general. Apart from his Latin name, this Saturn is an African creation who was the Roman-period manifestation of Ba'al Hammon, the single great deity of the previous Punic age. The cult of Saturn was the pervasive and dominant African practice of the Roman imperial age.

The ecological frontiers of Saturn worship can be mapped with reasonable accuracy. Evidence of the cult is concentrated in the main heartland of the Maghrib, between the plains of Sétif in the West and the borders of Byzacium in the East. This was the weight of its center and its peripheries. The cult of Saturn was not rooted elsewhere in Africa – not in Tripolitania to the east nor in Mauretania Tingitana to the west.[51] Their religious worlds reflect instead the fundamentally different circuits of Mediterranean communications in antiquity to which these two parts of North Africa belonged. Distinctions, however, were not just geographic; they were also social. New evidence has not fundamentally altered the analysis of social catchment of Saturn worshippers done a century ago. Members of the upper strata of Roman urban society under the empire – from emperors and governors and their imperial bureaucrats, to army officers and the local senatorial, equestrian, and municipal elites – are almost entirely absent from the recorded worshippers.[52]

---

[49] For what follows, see Leglay, *Saturne africain* and *Saturne africaine. Monuments*, vols. 1–2.

[50] On the nature of the translation from the one to the other, see Cadotte, "Baal Hammon/Saturne," ch. 1 in idem, *Romanisation des dieux*, 25–64; on Tinit or Tanit, see "Tanit/Caelestis," ch. 2 in ibid., 65–111.

[51] Toutain, *Cultes païens*, 89–90. For Tripolitania, see Brouquier-Reddé, *Temples et cultes*, who cites one possible, but questionable instance; cf. Charles-Picard, *Religions de l'Afrique antique*, 181. For Tingitana, see Shaw, *Edge of the Corrupting Sea*, 18–19.

[52] Toutain, *Cultes païens*, 98–102. For example, of the ten military men, all are footsoldiers whose names mark them as indigenous Africans (e.g., M. Porcius Easuctan, a centurion from Calama: *CIL* VIII: 2648). Toutain notes that at the Saturn sanctuary at Thurburnica there is not a single dedication from the imperial administrators of the mines at Simitthus, only ten kilometers away. Of the more than 1,400 dedicators to Saturn, at an absolute maximum there are only thirty who might have had any formal link with the Roman imperial order.

The numerous portraits, symbolic associations, and descriptions that survive of Saturn represent him as ruler over all the aspects of nature – skies, soils, and springs – responsible for Africa's great agricultural wealth. Insofar as any Roman influences might be discerned, Saturn could be said to be a divine projection of the harder Afro-Roman version of the patriarchal Roman *paterfamilias* or household head. His portrait was a local innovation, a pastiche of the elements of a common Hellenistic repertoire of expected physical characteristics in an anthropomorphic representation of a dominant male deity. He is portrayed as a heavily bearded mature man, often armed with a harvester's sickle that represented his role as a harvest-god, a divine reaper. One of his most frequent epithets indicated that he was, indeed, *the* Lord, just like Ba'al Hammon, whose cultural successor he was. Saturn was the *Dominus* – the Lord. This divine Lord was the owner of all lands, plants, and animals, and the patriarchal head of all humans. Saturn was called *Frugifer*, the bringer of bounty and plenty to the land and to each household. Finally, Saturn was the *Senex*, "the Old Man." And the African social system did in fact recognize and reward old age much more than any other circum-Mediterranean culture. Councils of elders or *seniores* governed the myriad hamlets and villages in which most Africans lived. In a later age, the highest-ranking Christian bishop in each African province would also be called the *Senex* or the "Old Man." Saturn was the exemplar of this power of seniority.[53]

In the Roman period, the other half of this divine power couple, the direct successor to Tinnit, was the universal sky-, earth-, and nature-deity, Caelestis. But, if anything, her presence and power had diminished considerably from Punic times. Her main temple at Carthage, however, was nothing to be despised. It was only finally decommissioned by imperial force in 420 CE, at which time the description of it by the Christian bishop of Carthage vividly evoked the image of a supreme deity around whom other quite lesser spirits oriented themselves: "There is at Carthage a vast temple to Caelestis, surrounded by lesser sanctuaries of the other gods of the country. The area is decorated with rich mosaics, beautiful stones, high columns, and a walled enclosure that is over two-thousand feet in length."[54] It was to be the end of almost a millennium of the goddess's dominant presence on African soil.

[53] Shaw, "The Elders."
[54] Quodvultdeus, *Lib. prom.* 3.38 (CCL 60: 185–6); cf. Charles-Picard, *Religions de l'Afrique antique*, 106–7.

URBAN POWER AND METROPOLITAN CULT

From the Augustan Principate onwards, but taking special hold with the concerns of the upstart Flavian emperors and their new dynastic rule of the empire, the worship of the emperors gradually added to the legitimation of their rule in the provinces. Despite its apparent significance for the central government, imperial ideology, and the identity of local elites, the general importance of the imperial cult or emperor worship is probably less than is perhaps suggested by the modern attention lavished upon it.[55] Most of the spectacular evidence, like the votive altars erected by imperial freedmen and their friends and associates, are Augustan in date and located in the large imperial urban centers anchored on the Mediterranean coast: Lepcis Magna, Carthage, and Caesarea.[56] So, too, evidence for the deliberate cultivation of an imperial cult in terms of representations of the *domus divina* in statuary or in special shrines in town forums, with some exceptions, are located in cities on the Mediterranean coast that functioned as important administrative centers, again like Lepcis Magna in Tripolitania. Apart from honorific dedications to the emperor, which were just as much if not more a part of a system of secular patronage, there is little to suggest the widespread impact of the cult as a pervasive form of religious belief and practice.

Granted, there are some striking examples of the iconography of the Augustan restoration. These include two altars whose reliefs feature members of the Augustan imperial family, and sacrificial scenes that reflect the program on the great Altar of Peace at Rome itself. Both were found in neighborhoods lying directly below the great imperial monumental complex atop the Byrsa at Carthage.[57] Although these do attest the direct impact of the new imperial religious ideology in the one great Augustan colony in Africa, they probably signify a lot less than is usually suggested. They were erected by freedmen, some of whom were the emperor's own servants, who were directly connected with the imperial family and whose economic interests made them direct beneficiaries of the new order. Naturally, they were energetic celebrants of its triumphalist ideology.

---

[55] Much that follows has been made clear by the studies of Fishwick, *The Imperial Cult in the Latin West*, esp. vol. 1.2, chs. 6 and 8; vol. 3.1, 128–32, 190–2; and vol. 3.2, ch. 6, on the foundational importance of the Augustan period, the importance of Flavian innovations, and yet the relative marginality of Africa in the whole apparatus of the cult when it is compared with the other western provinces of the empire; cf. Foucher, "Paganisme en Afrique," 24–8.

[56] Charles-Picard, *Religions de l'Afrique antique*, 170–4.

[57] Poinssot, *L'Autel de la gens Augusta*; Zanker, *The Power of Images*, 313–16 and fig. 247.

The role of the imperial cult in Africa was more comparable to the status that it had in Phoenicia, Syria, and Judea than that which it had in Asia Minor (for example). Notwithstanding examples of municipal adherence to the cult, there is very little evidence for the typical bearers of the imperial cult in the imperial age – the so-called *seviri Augustales*, under whatever name they were known. Unlike the other western provinces and Italy, these officials of the imperial cult are hardly attested at all in Africa. On the basis of the present evidence, it is safe to say that these core institutions of emperor worship are almost unknown in Africa.[58] A possible exception is the provincial council or *concilium provinciae*, which appears to have emerged from a general reform and regularization of the imperial cult by Vespasian and the Flavians – a more uniform reorganization that stressed the general western Mediterranean dimensions of the cult. Each city in the province that held the official status of a colony or a municipality chose a representative to this council, probably the same man who served as the local *flamen Augusti* or priest of the imperial cult. The council itself chose one man as the *sacerdos* of the whole group, a particularly high honor that they seem to have done their best to circulate among the various cities that were members of the council. The cult was important to the imperial court, and the ranks of its local administrators, but not much beyond.

Other official cults, however, had a wider reach and deeper impact. The worship of the Cereres, principally of the grain goddess Ceres, through the whole rural region of the new Roman colony at Carthage was established by Julius Caesar and confirmed by his adoptive son Octavian in 38 BCE. It was one of the official cults introduced in this axial age that was to have a long life.[59] Its priests and priestesses are found throughout the abnormally large *pertica* or rural surveyed lands that formed the territory of the imperial metropolis of Carthage. It encompassed dozens of towns and cities, like Thugga (mod. Dougga) and Thuburbo Maius (mod. Tébourba), that would only become independent municipalities in their own right at an artificially late date.[60]

Outside Carthage and its district, we find from Flavian times onward the steady elevations of towns to the formal status of colony (*colonia*), all of whose citizens become Roman citizens, or to the status

---

[58] Février, *Approches du Maghreb romain*, vol. 1, 195–6.
[59] Cadotte, "Les *Cereres*," ch. 10 in idem, *Romanisation des dieux*, 343–62 for a survey; see Gascou, "Les *Sacerdotes Cererum*," for a more specific study; cf. Leglay, "Paganisme en Numidie," 64–5.
[60] Pflaum, "La romanisation de l'ancien territoire de la Carthage," yet another regional and administrative peculiarity that helped determine the configuration of official cult in a large number of towns and villages in the whole hinterland of Carthage.

of municipality (*municipium*), where only the members of the ruling
elite became Roman citizens. In addition, there were many self-styled
"Romanizing" towns (*res publicae*) whose elites, seeking to mimic the
forms of Roman public life, developed their local forms of official cult.
In this new urban context, the temples, shrines, nymphaea, statues, and
public altars that constituted the public face of religion depended on
the generosity of powerful and wealthy local citizens. This was particularly true in Tripolitania, where almost all the big temples and their
iconic art were the result of such private subventions.[61] In the proconsu-
lar province of Africa, counts have shown that about three out of every
five large temple constructions were built by private benefactions.[62] The
general significance that local elites assigned to gods and deities must
be seen in this wider context of their patronal interests. Where did they
put most of their money? The overwhelming bulk of the evidence shows
that they were more interested in investing in the "living deities" of the
super-wealthy and the super-powerful among the living who could assist
them and their communities. By far, most laudatory dedications were set
up to imperial, senatorial, and other such elite patrons among the living
rather than to gods or goddesses.[63]

The one deity whom the urban elites of the burgeoning towns and cities
of Africa, especially in its ebullient Antonine age, associated with their celebration of wealth, power, success, and general improvement was Bacchus –
Dionysus in his world-conquering form, in his triumphal and festive
mood.[64] Dionysus is found everywhere and in every form of middle-rank
kitsch: in statues and paintings, in lavish and brilliant floor and wall mosaics, and in countless bric-a-bracs made of wood, marble, bronze, and glass.
There is some truth to the claim that Dionysus, as Liber Pater, simply continued the cult of Punic Shadrapha (or Shadrapa).[65] But this claim really
does not tell us more than the fact that this continuity was deemed to be

---

[61] Brouquier-Reddé, *Temples et cults de Tripolitaine*, 285–7.
[62] Rives, *Religion and Authority*, 178; and at 178 n. 6, where he notes that Duncan-Jones, "Who Paid for Public Buildings?" (30), found that the financing of all public building was divided roughly half and half between private benefaction and public expenditure.
[63] Rives, *Religion and Authority*, 179. In his "rough survey," Rives counts 18 dedications to deities as such, as against 162 to emperors and members of the imperial family, and 144 to civic patrons.
[64] Remarkably, there is still no in-depth study of this most important subject. Bénabou, "Bacchus africain," in idem, *La résistance africain*, 351–8 has some relevant remarks, as does Charles-Picard, *Religions de l'Afrique antique*, 115, 194–209, where he remarks on the profusion of mosaics alone. On the latter, see Dunbabin, "Dionysus," who remarks on the unusual importance of Dionysus in Africa and the exceptional profusion of artistic representations of the god and his story, a represen-tational art that has serious cultural significance.
[65] Charles-Picard, *Religions de l'Afrique antique*, 194–5.

useful.[66] What we are witnessing in this profusion of Dionysiac representations is a heady celebration of wealth and fecundity – one that drew on a cosmopolitan Hellenistic repertoire of images to rejoice in real African achievements. In his raucous celebration of the Happiness of the Times, the *Felicitas Temporum*, Dionysus rose above isolated individuals and individual communities to offer a general and unifying spirit of joy, one in which the civic elites of Africa in their Roman heyday could share.[67] If one is seeking the one divinity drawn from the classic Greco-Roman pantheon in which the well-off urbanites in Africa's heyday of empire invested their best and finest sentiments, that god was Dionysus.

In general, however, the process of identification, adaptation, continuity, innovation, synthesis, and mutation was a volatile and messy mix. The funerary monument built by the family of the Flavii at Cillium (modern Kasserine) is a good example of the problems.[68] The classic Afro-Punic mausoleum constructed in three stages was meant to house the body and the soul of the deceased, Titus Flavius Secundus, the 110-year-old *paterfamilias* of the family. After serving in the auxiliaries of the Roman army in the mid-first century CE, he had in consequence received citizenship from one of the Flavian emperors. A professional Latin poet was hired to compose a long eulogy in hexameters to the deceased – it is in fact the longest piece of verse epigraphy surviving in Latin. It was carved, although somewhat carelessly, on the face of the monument. The resulting cultural mélange of poem and monument can be seen either as a botched attempt at cultural identity or as a strange but powerful cultural amalgam. The Roman poet completely misunderstood the religious cult inherent in the monument. In consequence, he failed to mention the all-important rooster, perched on the peak of the pyramid-shaped top that crowned the whole monument.

When his patron drew this critical deficit to the poet's attention, he added another twenty lines of verse to compensate. Although ostensibly done to make up for his fault – and also to mention the all-important rooster – the poet did this somewhat disdainfully, in elegiac couplets. He finally did note the rooster in passing, otherwise using his new verses to suggest the superiority of elite Roman values of secular memory to their odd Punic superstitions. Perhaps not fully understanding the implied

[66] Cadotte, "Shadrapha/Liber," ch. 6 in idem, *Romanisation des dieux*, 253–82, for some of the complexities involved; cf. Foucher, "Paganisme en Afrique," 8–13, for a survey of the depth and range of Dionysian worship in Africa.
[67] Charles-Picard, *Religions de l'Afrique antique*, 195–205, with a host of examples.
[68] The studies in *Les Flavii de Cillium* are an insightful guide.

insult, the African Flavii dutifully had the additional verses carved on the face of their tomb. Even if the Latin verses simultaneously misunderstood and mocked their beliefs, as a form of imperial writing the formal and elevated language publicly proclaimed the middling success of the Flavii. The rooster, however, was not insignificant. Whereas the tomb itself housed the man's *nephesh*, his body, the bird represented the *rouah*, his eternal soul.[69] What Flavius Secundus held most significant in life and death was simply not transcribed by the Latin poem meant to celebrate his life and death.

MICRORELIGION AND INDIVIDUAL PRACTICE

With our attention drawn to the more visible and well-documented public levels of communal cult, it is easy to forget the far more pervasive micro-level of daily religious practice centered on the day-to-day concerns of most Africans: personal health and the well-being of friends and family; the fate of love and marriage; the birth of children; and success in gaming, gambling, and confronting personal enemies and threats to one's household, brutishly in the streets or more civilly in the courts.[70] A wide range of belief and practice therefore depended on the technical knowledge of experts outside the formal system of priests and temples. These private entrepreneurs could manipulate the power of protective amulets and apotropaic devices, or, more aggressively, summon the darker demonic forces of the Underworld to attack and coerce an intended victim.

The surviving evidence on these private practices points to a division between urban and rural.[71] In the rural world, where manipulative powers had been recognized and managed by holy men and holy women for a long time – in the second century BCE, the mother of the African king Massinissa was a renowned woman of magic – the same continued to be true in the Roman period. In the larger urban centers, on the other hand, professionals whose expertise could be acquired on the market for a price were now available. Ritual experts, it was known, commanded powers that could both harm and protect. Ennia Fructosa, a modest and much-loved wife of a tribune in the Third Augustan Legion at Lambaesis, was killed by curses; they first blocked her voice and then turned her into

---

[69] Fantar, *Eschatologie phénicienne-punique*, 32–8, whose ideas are significantly modified and extended by Bessi, "Il significato del gallo nel mondo semitico."

[70] See Sichet, *La magie en Afrique du Nord*, for a near-comprehensive collection of the texts and material evidence relevant to the problem.

[71] Most of the *tabellae defixionis*, for example, come from larger urban Mediterranean port centers in Africa, and of these almost all are from Carthage and Hadrumetum.

a mute.[72] In the more democratic world of the Roman empire, these powers could now be mobilized by anyone who could pay, not just by someone with patronal access to the mother of an African king.

The divine experts had access to a trans-Mediterranean body of technical knowledge and skills. A partial record of such curses-for-hire survives in the so-called *tabellae defixionum* or "binding tablets." These magical texts were inscribed, often on lead, before being sold to the patron.[73] A typical example, found at Carthage, was inscribed on a thin leaden sheet rolled up and buried in a grave. The client had purchased a curse whereby demonic spirits would impede the charioteer of the Blues racing team at Carthage.[74]

SEMESILAM DAMATAMENEUS IESNNALLELAM LAIKAM ERMOUBELE IAKOUB IA IOERBETH IOPAKERBETH EOMALTHABETH ALLASAN. A curse. I invoke you by the great names so that you will bind every limb and every sinew of Victoricus the charioteer of the Blues ... and of his horses.... Bind their legs, their onrush, their bounding, and their running. Blind their eyes so that they cannot see. Twist their soul and heart so that they cannot breathe. Just as this rooster has been bound by its feet, hands, and head, so tomorrow bind the legs and hands and head and heart of Victoricus the charioteer of the Blues.... Also, I invoke you by the god above heaven, who is seated upon the Cherubim who divided the earth and separated the sea. IAO ABRIAO ARBATHIAO ADONAI SABAO.... Now! Now! Quickly! Quickly!

Another leaden curse tablet, rolled up and provided with a hole through which it could be nailed into the ground, was found in the cemetery at Hadrumetum. Marked with a mixture of Greek and Latin found in the tablets from this city, the text also reveals a not atypical admixture of traditional magical spells along with elements from Greco-Jewish holy texts emanating from an Alexandrian milieu. Here, too, there is manifest evidence of the pervasive hybrids found in all other aspects of religious life. Copied out of a book of standard magical curses by the professional *magus*, it was provided for a female customer – on this occasion, to deal with a matter of the heart.[75]

I invoke you *daimonion* spirit who lies here, by the holy name AOTH ABAOTH, the god of Abraham, and IAO, the god of Jacob, IAO AOTH ABAOTH, god of Israma ... Go to Urbanus, to whom Urbana gave birth, and bring him to

---

[72] *CIL* VIII: 2756 (Lambaesis) = Gager, *Curse Tablets*, no. 136 (246); cf. Ogden, "Binding Spells," 27.
[73] Gager, *Curse Tablets*, 20f., and Ogden, "Binding Spells," 54–60 on "professionalism and specialisation."
[74] Gager, *Curse Tablets*, no. 12 (65–67) = *CIL* VIII: 12511 (Carthage)
[75] Gager, *Curse Tablets*, no. 36 (112–15) = Maspero, "Deux *tabellae devotionis*."

Domitiana to whom Candida gave birth so that loving, frantic, and sleepless with love and desire for her, he may beg her to return to his house and become his wife ... I invoke you ... to bring Urbanus, to whom Urbana gave birth, and unite him with Domitiana, to whom Candida gave birth, loving, tormented, and sleepless with desire and love for her, so that he may take her into his house as his wife.... Unite them in marriage and as spouses in love for all the time of their lives. Make him as her obedient slave, so that he will desire no other woman or girl apart from Domitiana alone, to whom Candida gave birth, and will keep her as his spouse for all the time of their lives. Now! Now! Quickly! Quickly!

These texts were urbane and answered to the citified concerns of courts and courting. But magical experts were also found out in the countryside. One of them was working in the area around the village of Aradi, deep in the hinterland of Carthage, and provided assistance to a landowner in the technical magical language of Greek.[76]

SSSEXI OREOBAZAGRA, OREOBAZAGRA, ABRSAX, MAKHAR, SEMESEILAM, STENAKHTA, LORSAKHTHE, KORIAUKHE, ADONAI, LORD GODS, prevent and turn away from this land and from the crops growing on it – the vineyards, olive groves, and the sown fields – hail, rust, the fury of Typhonian winds and the swarms of evil-doing locusts, so that none of these forces can gain a hold in this land or in any of its crops – all of them wherever they might be. Rather, keep them always unharmed and undamaged as long as these stones, engraved with your sacred names, are placed under the ground which lies around.

Magicians and astrologers, often not distinguished, represented themselves as skilled technicians who sold their expertise at a price. They were not priests. They had no temples. They practiced openly in the streets and alleyways of the towns, and in the fields and forests around them, where they sold their technical expertise to anyone seeking access to their knowledge and power.[77] But here, too, because of cost, expertise, and communications, there appears to have been a distinctive ecology of belief and practice. Almost all the known *tabellae defixionum*, for example, are found in Mediterranean port cities like Carthage and Hadrumetum, and so they reveal the presence of a more cosmopolitan and technically proficient aspect of magic. But other means of accessing this power were cheaper, and required less expertise. These material repositories of magical power, like symbols of phalluses; little statuettes; images of the god Mercury; and models of scorpions, eyes, lizards, sphinxes, and peacocks

---

[76] *AE* 1984: no. 933 (Aradi). Ferchiou, Gabillon, "Une inscription grecque magique de la région de Bou Arada"; cf. Rives, *Religion and Authority*, 193.

[77] Madden, *Pagan Divinities*, 18, citing Augustine, *Tract. Ev. Jo.* 8.11 (CCL 46: 89).

are much more widely distributed, especially in the rural centers of the African hinterland.[78]

WHAT WAS HAPPENING?

The fact of diversity was both a strength and a limit of cult. The enormous range of choice meant that each rural site, neighborhood, town, and social, ethnic or professional group could have its own deities and sacred things selected, as it were, from a smorgasbord of possibilities. If the modal commonalities in the whole repertoire of these choices were widespread, then the deity appears to have been a very popular one with a ubiquitous presence and cult. But this is a misleading impression. The effect is produced by the serial replication of similar circumstances. If they did not exist, the deity remained more narrowly confined. Serapis, for example, is indeed attested in Africa, but was limited to certain venues like the port areas of Carthage and to worshippers who were mostly expatriate Alexandrians. Both reveal how much Serapis remained a niche deity. The same is true of Mithras – no competitor at all for Christianity – whose cult was located sporadically and specifically in army camps and in urban milieus where the military servants and bureaucrats of the state found in its cult a heavenly and more perfect replication of their own hopes and values.[79] And that was that. Even more restricted were some Syrian deities, like the god Malagbel, that were found in small army encampments on the edge of the Sahara where Syrian detachments had been sent to serve the empire.[80] Other instances are provided by Mars as the city-deity of Roman colonies like Cuicul and Sitifis, settlements of veteran soldiers, or by Diana as the patron goddess of gladiators and professional wild-beast hunters in the

---

[78] Sichet, *La magie en Afrique du Nord*, vol. 1, 363–485; cf. Charles-Picard, *Religions de l'Afrique antique*, 247: mostly associated with "small people," like slaves, freedmen, and town and village commoners.

[79] See Leglay, "Paganisme en Numidie," 82–3; other than dedicatory inscriptions and a few altars – all by military men and administrative slaves – only three Mithraea are known, including one in the port city of Rusicade, a port where the *Familia Caesaris* was present, and another in the army base at Lambaesis: Clauss, "Africa," in idem, *Cultores Mithrae*, 246–52. Others probably existed in similar milieux, at Carthage and Hadrumetum, for example, but they were certainly specific in kind and never numerous. The locations conform with the known social catchment of Mithraic adherents: see Gordon, "Who Worshipped Mithras?"; Clauss, "Anhängerschichten," in idem, *Cultores Mithrae*, 261–79, and "Recruitment," ch. 6 in idem, *Roman Cult of Mithras*, 33–41, and distribution map, 26–7; see further Salzman in Chapter 14 of this volume.

[80] Charles-Picard, *Religions de l'Afrique antique*, 221–2, from his own excavations of Castellum Dimmidi: the unit of archers from Palmyra constructed a shrine with a painting of the god in Iranian costume; similarly, the god Theandrios was worshipped by Arabs at Manaf, and Illyrian immigrants in Numidia honored their Medaurus. For more of these Syrian "niche" deities linked to army units brought in from the East, see Leglay, "Paganisme en Numidie," 81–2.

arena.[81] So profuse and fragmented and mixed were the deities and their various presences, and so fragmentary is the evidence about them, that in most cases all we *can* see is this effect. We cannot understand what peculiar combination of local or personal interests produced the results that we witness in the surviving record. As with the unusual presence of the goddess Bellona in Cirta and its environs, the explanatory connections are simply missing.

The core problem, then, is that the defining characteristics of these practices, their great diversity and pliability, their morphing and matching, the fragmentation and disconnectedness of their parts frustrate analysis. We have to confront a huge and ever-changing kaleidoscope of possibilities. The modern label of "toleration" is a misleading description of these practices.[82] Over time, each individual and community could create their own worlds of practice and belief from a huge and varied repertoire. In center-periphery studies it has been argued that indigenous and other local cults represented a focus of resistance to the cultural impact of Romanization.[83] It is equally possible, however, to understand cult as an integrative force that was successfully manipulated to modulate and to mediate cultural difference.[84] Appeals to the "Gods of the Moors," the *Dii Mauri*, can be interpreted as solicitations of the benevolence of indigenous deities, as examples of the continuity of African cult that betokened a kind of resistance to foreign power, or as a way of manipulating the dedicators' picture of their African world – and all these interpretations can be simultaneously true.[85]

What, for example, is the significance of the cult of Neptune in Africa? Because the process of cultural change was complex and contradictory, rarely was any element – "this spring should be identified with Neptune" – consciously taken by any persons as a sign of their own subjugation or domination. Not at all. They surely thought of many of these elements as part of a shared cosmopolitan culture from which everyone had an equal right to filch ("to appropriate") with no necessary impairment of their own identity.[86] Was the worship of Neptune therefore a

---

[81] Leglay, "Paganisme en Numidie," 60 and 75.
[82] Garnsey, "Toleration" and O'Donnell, "Paganism" are model attempts. See further van Andringa in Chapter 17 of this volume.
[83] Bénabou, "La résistance religieuse."
[84] Février, "Religion et domination."
[85] Fentress, "*Dii Mauri*"; Camps, "Le problème des *Dii Mauri*" and "Qui sont les *Dii Mauri*?"; Bénabou, "Le problème des *Dii Mauri*: un culte ambigu," in *Résistance africaine*, 309–30; and Leglay, "Paganisme en Numidie," 76–7.
[86] Veyne, *Sexe et pouvoir*, 18f., is insightful on the process.

straightforward adaptation and sign of Romanization? A touchstone of African resistance? Did the cult serve an accommodating and enabling function? Or was it an instance of the "creolization" of cult? Or was it none of these, but rather a practice being manipulated by both sides in power negotiations over values and representations? All of these were possible in the same world, and all were present to some degree. One modern interpreter is as right on resistance as another is on integration – each catches part of how this dynamic and fragmented world could and did function in different contexts. As the monument and poem of the Flavii at Cillium dramatically demonstrates, they were both badges of Romanization and they were not. Our interpretations are both very sensible and problematic.

Every African, whether indigenous or settler, peasant or merchant, town councilor or imperial administrator, could select from a wide and varied repertoire. The sum of all choices could thus add up to anything from resistance to accommodation, from tradition to revolution. The kaleidoscope of belief and practice in Africa kept shifting over time and in fundamentally different patterns from one region to the next. The pattern of the more than one hundred different cults and as many temples and shrines attested for Tripolitania has almost nothing to do with the system of dozens of gods and numerous temples and shrines known for a well-defined rural region just to the north of Carthage.[87] Not only do the individual parts and building blocks of each matrix shift, but the whole that was produced for each region formed its own peculiar identity. Despite some specific connections and analogies – and therefore the ability of any participant readily to translate from the one to the other, it cannot be made the same as that of its neighbor. These regionally contained forces written on a larger scale for all of Africa reveal why the Maghrib cannot be easily assimilated into the religious narrative of the rest of the Mediterranean. The interrelated elements of worship and cult in Africa formed a world of shared characteristics having more in common with each other than with those of the other regions of the empire. The sum made this system separate from all the rest. Despite all of the prompts, similarities, and analogies, it was just different. And this distinctiveness was decisively to shape the contours of African Christianity.

---

[87] Brouquier-Reddé, *Temples et cultes,* 311–15 and "La place de la Tripolitaine," for Tripolitania, as compared to Peyras, *Le Tell nord-est,* 340–53, 425–7, for the region north of Carthage. The same could be said, for example, of the whole region of Mauretania Tingitana when compared to the rest of Africa: see Shaw, "A Peculiar Island," 106–16, and *At the Edge,* 16–19.

BIBLIOGRAPHY

Les Flavii de Cillium: étude architecturale, épigraphique historique et littéraire du Mausolée de Kasserine (CIL VIII, 211–216) (Rome, 1993).

Alquier, Jeanne, and Pascal Alquier. *Le Chettaba et les grottes à inscriptions latines du Chettaba et du Taya* (Constantine, 1929).

"Stèles votives à Saturne découvertes près de N'gaous (Algérie)." *CRAI* (1931): 21–6.

Ando, Clifford. *Imperial Ideology and Provincial Loyalty in the Roman Empire* (Berkeley, 2000).

ed. *Roman Religion* (Edinburgh, 2003).

Arnaldi, Adelina. "Osservazioni sul culto delle Nymphae nell'Africa romana." *Africa romana* 15 (2004): 1355–64.

Barton, Ian M. "Capitoline Temples in Italy and the Provinces (especially Africa)." *ANRW* 2.12.1 (1982): 259–342.

Beard, Mary, John North, and Simon Price. *Religions of Rome, 1: A History* (Cambridge, 1996).

Bénabou, Marcel. "La résistance religieuse." In *La résistance africaine à la romanisation* (Paris, 1976): 259–380.

Bénichou-Safar, Hélène. *Le tophet de Salammbô à Carthage: essai de reconstitution* (Rome, 2004).

Beschaouch, Azedine. "Epigraphie et ethnographie: d'une fête populaire de Dougga, en Tunisie, à la dédicace de l'aqueduc de Thugga, en Afrique romaine." *Comptes rendus de l'Académie des inscriptions et Belles-Lettres* (2000): 1173–81.

Bessi, Benedetta. "Un brano di al-Mas'udi e il significato del gallo nel mondo semitico: alcune osservazioni." [unpublished typescript].

Bonnet, Corinne. *Melqart: cultes et mythes de l'Héraclès tyrien en Méditerranée.* Studia Phoenicia 8 (Leuven [Namur], 1988).

Brouquier-Reddé, Veronique. *Temples et cultes de Tripolitaine* (Paris, 1992).

"La place de la Tripolitaine dans la géographie religieuse de l'Afrique du Nord." In *Actes du Ve Colloque international sur l'histoire et l'archéologie de l'Afrique du Nord* (Avignon, 1990) = *115e Congrès des sociétés savants* (Paris, 1992): 113–9.

Brown, Shelby. *Late Carthaginian Child Sacrifice and Sacrificial Monuments in their Mediterranean Context* (Sheffield, 1991).

Cadotte, Alain. *Les syncrétismes religieux en Afrique romaine d'Auguste à Dioclétien: étude épigraphique.* 2 vols. (Lille, 2001).

"Neptune Africain." *Phoenix* 56 (2002): 330–47.

La Romanisation des dieux: l'interpretatio romana en Afrique du Nord sous le Haut-Empire (Leiden, 2007).

Camps, Gabriel. "L'Inscription de Béja et le problème des *Dii Mauri*." *Revue africaine* 98 (1954): 233–60.

"Qui sont les *Dii Mauri*?" *BCTH* 20–1 (1984–85 [1989]): 157–8.

Carcopino, Jérôme. "Survivances par substitution des sacrifices d'enfants dans l'Afrique romaine." *RHR* 106 (1932): 592–9.

Charles-Picard, Gilbert. *Les religions de l'Afrique antique* (Paris, 1954).

Clauss, Manfred. *Cultores Mithrae: Die Anhängerschaft des Mithras-Kultes* (Stuttgart, 1992).

The Roman Cult of Mithras: The God and His Mysteries. Trans. R. Gordon (Edinburgh, 2000). Originally published as *Mithras: Kult und Mysterien* (Munich, 1990).

Deneauve, Jean. "Le centre monumental de Carthage: un ensemble cultuel sur la colline de Byrsa." In *Carthage et son territoire dans l'Antiquité*, eds. Serge Lancel, et al. (Paris, 1990): 143–55.

Dunbabin, Katherine M. D. "Dionysus." In *The Mosaics of Roman Africa: Studies in Iconography and Patronage* (Oxford, 1978): 173–87.

Duncan-Jones, Richard P. "Who Paid for Public Buildings in Roman Cities?" In *Roman Urban Topography in Britain and the Western Empire*, eds. Francis Grew, and Brian Hobley (London, 1985): 28–33.

Fantar, Muhammad. *Eschatologie phénicienne-punique* (Tunis, 1970).

"Ba'al Hammon." *Reppal* 5 (1990): 67–105.

Fentress, Elizabeth. *"Dii Mauri and Dii Patrii."* *Latomus* 37 (1978): 507–16.

Ferchiou, Naïdé and Aimé Gabillon. "Une inscription grecque magique de la région de Bou Arada (Tunisie), ou les quatre plaies de l'agriculture antique en Proconsulaire." *BCTH* n.s. 19B (1985): 109–25.

Ferjaoui, Ahmed. *Le sanctuaire de Henchir el-Hami: de Ba'al Hammon au Saturne africain, Ier s. av. J.-C.—IV s. apr. J.-C.* (Tunis, 2008).

Février, James Germain. "Molchomor." *RHR* 143(1953): 8–18.

"Le rite de substitution dans les textes de N'gaous." *JA* (1962): 54–63.

Février, Paul-Albert. *Approches du Maghreb romain.* 2 vols. (Aix-en-Provence, 1989–90).

"Religion et domination dans l'Afrique romaine." *DHA* 2 (1976): 305–36 = *La Méditerranée*, vol. 2 (Rome, 1996): 789–812.

Fishwick, Duncan. *The Imperial Cult in the Latin West: Studies in the Ruler Cult of the Western Provinces of the Roman Empire.* 3 vols. (Boston, 1987–2002).

Foucher, Louis. "Le culte de Bacchus sous l'empire Romain." *ANRW* 17.2 (1982): 684–702.

"Le paganisme en Afrique proconsulaire sous l'Empire romain. Bilan d'un demi siècle de recherche." [unpublished posthumous paper] (http://www.laportj.club.fr/maghreb/page10.html)

Gager, John, ed. *Curse Tablets and Binding Spells from the Ancient World* (Oxford, 1992).

Garnsey, Peter. "Religious Toleration in Classical Antiquity." In *Persecution and Toleration*, ed. W. J. Sheils (Oxford, 1984): 1–27.

Gascou, Jacques. "Les *Sacerdotes Cererum* de Carthage." *AntAfr* 23 (1987): 95–128.

Gordon, Richard. "Who Worshipped Mithras?" *JRA* 7 (1994): 459–74.

Graf, Fritz. "What is Ancient Mediterranean Religion?" In *Ancient Religions*, ed. Sarah Iles Johnston (Cambridge, Mass., 2007): 3–15.

Gsell, Stéphane. *Histoire ancienne de l'Afrique du Nord, 6: Les royaumes indigènes: vie matérielle, intellectuelle et morale* (Paris, 1927).

Hurst, Henry. "Child Sacrifice at Carthage." *JRA* 7 (1994): 325–8.

Janif, Moulay M'hamed. "Les sacrifices d'enfants à Carthage: l'hypothèse de L. W. Stage reconsiderée." *Reppal* 12 (2002): 73–8.

Ladjimi Sebaï, Leïla. *La colline de Byrsa à l'époque romaine: étude épigraphique et état de la question = Karthago*, vol. 26. (Paris, 2005).

Lane Fox, Robin. *Pagans and Christians* (New York, 1986).

Leglay, Marcel. *Saturne africaine. Monuments, 1: Afrique proconsulaire* (Paris, 1961).

Saturne africain. Histoire (Paris, 1966).

Saturne africaine. Monuments, 2: Numidie, Maurétanies (Paris, 1966).

"Le paganisme en Numidie et dans les Maurétanies sou l'empire romain: état des recherches entre 1954 et 1990." *Antiquités africaines* 42 (2006): 57–86.

MacMullen, Ramsay. *Paganism in the Roman Empire* (New Haven, 1981).

Madden, Mary Daniel. *The Pagan Divinities and their Worship as Depicted in the Works of Saint Augustine, exclusive of the City of God* (Washington, 1930).

Maspero, Gaston. "Sur deux *tabellae devotionis* de la nécropole romaine d'Hadrumète." *Bibliothèque égyptologique* 2 (1893): 303–11.

McCarty, Matthew. "Representations and the 'Meaning' of Ritual Change: The Case of Hadrumetum." In *Ritual Dynamics in the Ancient Mediterranean*, ed. A. Chaniotis (Heidelberg, 2011): 197–228.

Merlin, Alfred. "Divinités indigènes sur un bas-relief romain de la Tunisie." *CRAI* (1947): 355–71.

Monceaux, Paul. "La grotte du dieu Bacax au Djebel Taïa." *RA* 8 (1886): 64–76.

Mosca, Paul G. *Child Sacrifice in Canaanite and Israelite Religion: A Study in Mulk and [Molech]*, diss. Harvard University, 1975.

Moscati, Sabatino. *Gli adoratori di Moloch: indagine su un celebre rito cartaginese* (Milan, 1991).

Nock, Arthur Darby. *Conversion: The Old and the New in Religion from Alexander the Great to Augustine of Hippo* (Oxford, 1933).

O'Donnell, James J. "The Demise of Paganism." *Traditio* 35 (1979): 45–88.

Ogden, Daniel. "Binding Spells: Curse Tablets and Voodoo Dolls in the Greek and Roman Worlds." In *Witchcraft and Magic in Europe: Ancient Greece and Rome*, eds. Bengt Ankerloo and Stuart Clark (Philadelphia, 1999): 1–90.

Peyras, Jean. *Le Tell nord-est tunisien dans l'Antiquité: essai de monographie régionale* (Paris, 1991).

Pflaum, Hans-Georg. "La romanisation de l'ancien territoire de la Carthage punique à la lumière des découvertes épigraphiques récentes." *AntAfr* 4 (1970): 75–117 = *Afrique romaine: Scripta Varia 1* (Paris, 1978): 300–44.

Poinssot, Louis. *L'Autel de la gens Augusta à Carthage* (Tunis, 1929).

Purcell, Nicholas. "On the Sacking of Carthage and Corinth." In *Ethics and Rhetoric: Classical Essays for Donald Russell*, eds. Doreen Innes, Harry Hine, and Christopher Pelling (Oxford, 1994): 133–48.

Richard, Jean. *Étude médico-légale des urnes sacrificielles puniques et de leur contenu.* Institut Médico-Légal de Lille. Thèse pour le Doctorat en medicine (Lille, 1961).

Rives, James B. "Tertullian on Child Sacrifice." *MH* 51 (1994): 54–63.

Religion and Authority in Roman Carthage from Augustus to Constantine (Oxford, 1995).

Religion in the Roman Empire (Oxford, 2007).

Scheid, John. *Religion et piété à Rome*, 2nd ed. (Paris, 2001). Engl. trans. J. Lloyd as *An Introduction to Roman Religion* (Bloomington, Ind., 2003).

Shaw, Brent D. "The Structure of Local Society in the Early Maghrib: The Elders." *The Maghrib Review* 16 (1991): 18–54.

"Challenging Braudel: A New Vision of the Mediterranean." *JRA* 14 (2001): 19–53.

"A Peculiar Island: Maghrib and Mediterranean." *MHR* 18 (2003): 93–125.

At the Edge of the Corrupting Sea (Oxford, 2006).

Sichet, Sandra. *La magie en Afrique du Nord sous l'Empire romain.* 2 vols. (Villeneuve d'Ascq, 1992).

Smadja, Elisabeth. "L'Empereur et les dieux en Afrique romaine." *DHA* 11 (1985): 541–69.

Stager, Lawrence. "The Rite of Child Sacrifice at Carthage." In *New Light on Ancient Carthage*, ed. John Griffiths Pedley (Ann Arbor, Mich, 1980): 1–11.

Taborelli, Luigi. *L'area sacra di Ras Almunfakh presso Sabratha: Le stele = Rivista di Studi Fenici, vol. 20, supplemento* (Rome, 1992).

Toutain, Jules. "Les cultes africaines." In *Les cultes païens dans l'Empire romain.* Vol. 1 (Paris, 1907): 15–119.

Turcan, Robert. *The Cults of the Roman Empire.* Trans. A. Nevill (Oxford, 1996).

Veyne, Paul. *Sexe et pouvoir à Rome,* préface de Lucien Jerphagnon (Paris, 2005).

Woolf, Greg. "Unity and Diversity of Romanization." *JRA* 5 (1992): 349–52.

    "A Sea of Faith?" In *Mediterranean Paradigms and Classical Antiquity,* ed. Irad Malkin (London, 2005): 126–43.

Zanker, Paul. *The Power of Images in the Age of Augustus.* Trans. Alan Shapiro (Ann Arbor, Mich., 1988).

IO

CHRISTIANITY IN ROMAN AFRICA

ROBIN M. JENSEN

INTRODUCTION

No one knows exactly how or when Christianity arrived in Africa, and its demise under the Arabs is equally difficult to comprehend. While Christianity in other regions (for example, Egypt, Ethiopia, and Syria) survived under Muslim rule, African Christianity virtually disappeared within a century of the Arab conquest. A history of successive conquests or domination by authorities who demanded religious conformity from the resident population may partly explain the region's failure to establish a surviving local cult (or "national church"). At first, those authorities were Roman traditionalists who prosecuted Christians as such. Later, however, they were Christians themselves whose theology, ecclesiology, or rituals differed from established local practice. Rather than tolerantly accepting local difference in practice or dogma and being content merely to govern, these rulers sought theological and disciplinary acquiescence among the Christian communities they governed (Donatists, Nicenes, Arians, and Western Chalcedonians in turn). They enforced their demands by legal restrictions, confiscation of buildings and capital, and even persecution of nonconformists.

In each instance, existing Christian communities resisted such impositions, and evolving African churches were repeatedly challenged and transformed in ways that may have undermined the survival of an enduring established community – especially one associated with a dominant ethnic group. Moreover, from its beginnings, resistance to an often hostile secular authority was a hallmark of African Christianity. Thus, consecutive cycles of oppression, in most instances a case of one group of Christians attempting to impose its authority over another, ultimately resulted in the loss of a unified religious identity, either theological or cultural. Eventually, even the faith of the invading Arab Muslims may have seemed no more religiously foreign to indigenous African Christians than those of the previous ruling power – the Byzantine emperor and his delegates.

From the outset (although to varying degrees depending on time and place), African Christians esteemed rigorous individual and communal purity; valued martyrdom and self-sacrifice; argued that only one "mother Church" possessed the saving sacraments; and accented the importance of prophecy, dreams, and visions (given through the Holy Spirit). They typically understood themselves as disciplined athletes or soldiers allied with Christ against evil principalities and powers, and they claimed that whatever communion they belonged to was the unique true church. Repeated resistance to externally imposed conformity arguably made the community initially strong, authentic, and even attractive to converts. Over the centuries, however, political domination by successive alien powers eroded or changed the meaning of such resistance and thus diluted any single, coherent, or characteristically African brand of Christianity rooted enough to significantly survive the arrival of Islam over the long term.

THE EMERGENCE OF NORTH AFRICAN CHRISTIANITY: ITS CHARACTER, VARIATIONS, AND RELATIONS WITH OTHER RELIGIOUS CULTS

Evidence for North African Christianity includes an extensive corpus of theological and disciplinary documents, including the earliest Christian Latin treatises of Tertullian of Carthage and Marcus Minucius Felix. Both men were active around the turn of the third century, Tertullian's far more prolific output numbering more than thirty surviving treatises. From that time until the end of the Christian era, Africa produced some of the western church's most significant thinkers, including Cyprian of Carthage in the mid-third century and Augustine of Hippo, who lived and wrote from the end of the fourth century to the beginning of the Vandal era in the first quarter of the fifth century. Augustine's many theological treatises are balanced by sermons and letters, all revealing dimensions of lived Christianity during his time. Added to the works of individual writers are the records (*acta*) of the African church councils, as well as imperial legislation that impinged upon the practice of Christianity in the area.

In addition to a vast textual tradition, however, are extensive archaeological, epigraphic, and art historical remains that testify to the character of African Christianity in the Roman, Vandal, and Byzantine eras. Excavations have brought hundreds of church and church complexes to light that date from the fourth century through the eighth. These include urban cathedrals as well as saints' shrines and ex-urban pilgrimage and cemetery churches, many of them with baptisteries and living quarters for clergy. Along with church architecture at these sites, moreover, are polychrome mosaic pavements, inscriptions, epitaphs, funerary mensae, and tomb mosaics that are especially characteristic of Roman Africa.[1]

The first documented evidence of Christianity in Africa survives in what purports to be the official record of a trial held in Carthage on 17 July 180. The proconsul Saturninus attempted to persuade twelve Christians to take advantage of the legally allowed delay to consider the consequences of their adherence to Christ and then ordered them beheaded when they refused to recant or even reconsider.[2] The hometown of these Scillitan martyrs has not been identified, but some inscriptional evidence suggests that it might be located near Simitthu (Chemtou – see Map 5).[3] If so, Christianity had spread as far as 160km southwest of Carthage, no later than the mid-second century.

At this time, the local population was a blend of native African (Libyan) and Phoenician (Punic) peoples who had intermarried with occupying Romans and other immigrant groups (including Greeks, Spaniards, and Celts). The native languages (Libyan and Punic) persisted in the rural areas, but Latin had become the language of the governing elite, commerce, and high culture – including Christian intellectuals.[4] Often called "the father of Latin Christianity," Tertullian of Carthage (ca.155–230) authored what are arguably the oldest surviving Latin Christian documents apart from the *Vetus Latina* (Old Latin Bible) to which he referred. These documents contributed key Latin words to the western theological vocabulary, including "vetus testamentum," "novum testamentum," "Trinitas" and "sacramentum."

Despite its legal prohibition, African Christianity was well established by the early third century. Although probably exaggerating, Tertullian claimed that Christians constituted a majority in every city (*Scap.* 2.10). According to Bishop Cyprian (ca.200–58), seventy bishops from towns in Africa Proconsularis, Numidia, and Byzacena, attended a council in Carthage in the 220s or 230s. At a 256 assembly, the participants numbered

---

[1] The bibliography for both textual and material evidence for African Christianity is vast, of course. However, among the most significant recent publications on the archaeological side are Duval, *Loca sanctorum africae*; Gui et al., *Basiliques chrétiennes*; and Ennabli, *Carthage*.

[2] Musurillo, *Acts*, 86–9.

[3] Lancel, ed., *Actes*, vol. 373, 1456.

[4] Mattingly and Hitchner, "Roman Africa," 172–3. See Brown, "Christianity and Local Culture," 279–84 (on the problem of native languages in North Africa in Augustine's era).

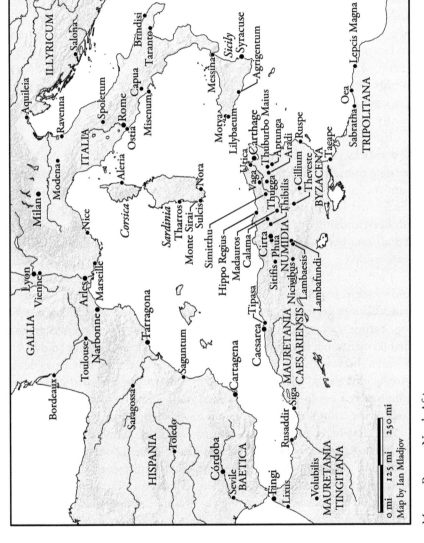

Map 5. Roman North Africa

o mi   125 mi   250 mi
Map by Ian Mladjov

eighty-seven.[5] These figures suggest that Christians were not only more or less tolerated, but secure enough to send representatives some distance to a meeting that must have been, to some degree, publicly known.

Moreover, the church attracted persons of status, family, education, and relative wealth. Tertullian's writings demonstrate his training in rhetoric and knowledge of Latin literature and philosophy. Perhaps himself the son of a Roman centurion,[6] he insisted that Christians populated every rank and station of life (*Apol.* 1.7).[7] Cyprian's execution by beheading and ownership of private estates indicate that he was an *honestior* (having both wealth and privileges). And the author of her *Passion* describes the martyr Perpetua (ca.202) as a member of a distinguished family, of good upbringing (or well educated), and a newly married matron (*Passio Perp.* 2.1).

These third-century African Christians established small congregations that met in private dwellings where they prayed together and shared an evening meal in addition to celebrating a eucharistic ritual.[8] They practiced baptism for adult converts and expected the initiated to follow a strictly disciplined life of fasting, prayer, and almsgiving, and avoiding idolatry, adultery, and other major sins. The church was the sacred "mother," whose womb was her baptismal font; outside of her protection, salvation was impossible.[9]

Their communities included consecrated virgins, dedicated widows, and councils of elders. Although the church to which Tertullian belonged had a bishop, presbyters, and deacons, other roles, such as reading, teaching, curing, and exorcizing were open to all males. Tertullian also argued that laymen could lawfully administer baptism in an emergency (*Bapt.* 17). Women, however, were restricted to seeking revelations, or living as dedicated widows and virgins. The bishop presided at the eucharistic banquet, administered baptism, and disciplined members who violated the moral code of the community. Clergy could be married, but only once.

As elsewhere, most third-century African Christians, including Tertullian, Minucius Felix, Perpetua, and Cyprian, were converts from traditional Roman religion.[10] The oath of commitment to Christ taken at baptism required almost complete separation from ordinary social and civic life, because renouncing the traditional gods meant shunning

---

[5] Cyprian, *Ep.* 71.1; *Sent.* 77 (CSEL 3.1.435–61); cf. Maier, *L'espiscopat*, 23–4.
[6] Jerome, *Vir. ill.*, 53.
[7] Groh, "Upper Class Christians," 41–7.
[8] Tertullian, *Apol.* 39.
[9] Jensen, "*Mater Ecclesia*," 140–4.
[10] See Tertullian, *Apol.* 18.

even casual contact with idols in the temples, marketplace, circus, and theater. In addition, Christians avoided passive (even accidental) presence at non-Christian rituals, because such occasions offered demons and evil spirits opportunities to pollute the unwary.[11] Undoubtedly, such behavior made them seem antisocial and secretive, especially because they excluded the uninitiated from their rituals.[12]

Christian-Jewish relations are less well understood. Although Tertullian denounced Jews for rejecting Christ, his writings refer only in passing to contemporary Carthaginian Jews.[13] Furthermore, Tertullian's attitudes toward Jews depended upon his audience. While taking a predictably supersessionist position in his *Answer to the Jews* (probably written for a Christian audience), his *Apology* (arguably directed at non-Christians) describes Jews as "dear to God" and their religion as allied to Christianity (*Adv. Jud.* 1.1; *Apol.* 16.11). He defended their scriptures as ancient and authoritative texts, but ones that would compel readers to Christian belief once fully understood (*Apol.* 18, 19, 21).

Potentially more problematic than idol-worshippers or Jews were heretical or deviant sects who, while considering themselves Christians and competing for adherents, held divergent views on the incarnation, the material world, and the biblical God of creation. Various such groups found their way to Carthage, among them the followers of Hermogenes, Valentinian gnostics, and Marcionites. Tertullian also encountered instances of deviant ritual practices, including a novel form of baptism administered by a woman whom he characterized as a pestilential viper. To his horror, she recruited a substantial following, including many of his fellow congregants (*Bapt.* 1).

The New Prophecy or Montanist movement also gained a substantial following in third-century Carthage. In this instance, Tertullian himself became an adherent, and perhaps also the martyr Perpetua and her comrades.[14] Followers claimed that the Holy Spirit commanded, through ecstatic human prophets, a tightening of Christian discipline. For example, Tertullian's rigorist later writings condemned second marriages, urged rigorous fasts, insisted on veils for unmarried women, and lauded the fortitude of the martyrs (*Mon.*, *Jejun.*, and *Virg*). On the basis of Montanist teaching, Tertullian also challenged the claims made by both bishops and

[11] Tertullian's treatises, *Idol.* and *Spect.*, treat this theme in general.
[12] See, for example, Minucius Felix, *Oct.* 9–10.
[13] Evidence for Jews in Carthage includes the Jewish necropolis at Gamarth. See Setzer, "Jews," 185–200; Stern, *Inscribing Devotion and Death.*
[14] See Tabbernee, "Perpetua." On Montanism, see Trombley, Chapter 13 of this volume.

martyrs to forgive significant sins committed by their members, insisting that the Spirit had forbidden tolerance of postbaptismal transgression.

The New Prophecy movement's emphasis on charismatic prophecy and visionary dreams was, however, compatible with more general North African Christian practice. For example, the *Passion of Saints Perpetua and Felicity* extols the validity and promise of continuing prophecy, the possibility of women as prophets, and the importance of dreams and visions (1, 4, 7, 8, 11–14). African Christians also assigned great value to martyrdom. Martyrs were the church's heroes, celebrated on their feast days (dates of death). Many (though not Tertullian) believed them to be endowed with the power of intercession for the forgiveness of sin because they went immediately to heaven (bypassing the interim time and final judgment that awaited ordinary believers after death). Although not all martyrs were dramatically killed in the arena or by the sword (some were imprisoned, exiled, or sent to the mines), their stories were exemplary lessons of courage and paralleled with those of exceptionally brave or steadfast Romans. Tertullian extolled the examples of Lucretia and Dido for women and Regulus for men, among others. Lucretia and Dido chose death over dishonor (at their own hands), and Regulus was a Roman general who endured torture at the hands of the Carthaginians rather than participate in a prisoner exchange (*Mart.* 4).

The Roman African love of blood sport may have also shaped the Christian perception of martyrs as athletes or gladiators.[15] That preoccupation is evident in many surviving mosaic pavements – some of which even depict victims going to their deaths in the arena (Fig. 11). On the night before they went to the beasts, Perpetua and her companions shared the "free banquet" that was traditionally served to combatants, but which they transformed into a Christian love feast (*Passio Perp.* 17).[16] The ancient Carthaginian practice of human sacrifice may also underlie the significance of the martyr cult in African Christianity. Both Minucius Felix and Augustine referred to that practice. Tertullian, in fact, claimed that no one should reproach the Christian God for requiring martyrdom, because the African Saturn was well known to have been appeased by human sacrifice (*Scorp.* 7).[17]

Early in 250, the emperor Decius required a general sacrifice to the Roman gods for the good fortune of the empire. Everyone was required

[15] Tertullian, *Scorp.* 6.
[16] Tertullian, *Apol.* 42.5, compares the two banquets.
[17] On the practice see Minucius Felix, *Oct.* 30.3; Tertullian, *Apol.* 9.2; Augustine, *Civ.* 7.26; and Rives, "Human Sacrifice," 65–85. See also Shaw, Chapter 9 of this volume.

Fig. 11. Detail from a third-century mosaic pavement, Thysdrus (El Djem), Sollertiana Domus. Now in the Museum of El Djem. Photograph by Robin M. Jensen.

to offer incense, pour a libation, or eat sacrificial meat to secure a certificate of compliance. Obstinacy resulted in exile, confiscation of goods, imprisonment, and torture. This first systematic challenge to Christian religious exclusivism had a devastating effect. Many Christians satisfied the edict to protect themselves or their families; others bribed officials by acquiring a certificate of compliance without actually performing the action. Widespread failure demonstrated that the church risked going out of existence unless it could find a means of accommodating severe sin (e.g., apostasy).

A series of councils led by Cyprian worked out a compromise between the hardliners, who would have excommunicated the lapsed, and the laxists, who would have readmitted them to communion through intercession of the martyrs. The compromise required fallen sinners publicly to repent while the church prayed that Christ would forgive them. After months or years, depending on the offense, the bishop allowed them to return in hope that they would be saved. Because they had rejected Christ, however, failed clergy had lost the power of the Spirit and so were demoted to lay status. Thus the ideal of purity was transferred from all members to representative clergy – especially to the bishop.

FOURTH-CENTURY CONSOLIDATION AND EFFORTS AT ENFORCING CONFORMITY

The great persecution at the beginning of the fourth century once again strained the competing ideals of purity and accommodation. As before, the Christian community faced the problem of Christians who failed the test of faith. In this instance, however, some of the lapsed were clergy and even bishops, who (it was claimed) cooperated with the persecutors by handing over holy books and other sacred objects.[18] Such defection undermined the theory that clergy representatively maintained the church's purity.

The election of Caecilian as bishop of Carthage (ca.311) provided a test case. Caecilian had made enemies during the persecution (allegedly) by refusing to allow congregants to bring food to Christians in prison, and (even worse) one of the bishops who consecrated him, Felix of Aptunga, supposedly turned over sacred scriptures to Roman soldiers.[19] Based on the compromise struck fifty years earlier, his consecrator's apostasy invalidated Caecilian's authority, and additionally infected any bishops (and laity) who accepted him into communion. Reacting to the urging (perhaps bribes) of certain interested local parties, the bishops of Numidia convened a council in Carthage, which tried, condemned, deposed, and replaced Caecilian in his absence.[20] Thus two competing communions were established – one led by Caecilian and the other by Donatus, whom the Numidians eventually chose as his replacement.

Because, after the peace, imperial funds financed the rebuilding of churches that had been destroyed in the persecution, the emperor Constantine needed to break the impasse between the two sides. He referred the case to episcopal courts in Rome and Arles, and by his own decision on the final appeal, Caecilian was affirmed as bishop while Donatus was condemned for schism. Meanwhile, the courts also required Caecilian's party to abandon the African practice of rejecting rituals (especially baptisms) performed in schismatic churches and to adopt the Roman church's policy of accepting them. This meant that Donatists who entered the

[18] See, for example, the accusations against Majorinus, *Brev. Coll.* 3.13.2.5; and the *Gesta apud Zenophilum* 2–5.
[19] See the proceedings against Felix of Abthungi, in Edwards, *Optatus*, 170–80.
[20] Mansi 2, 407–10; 4, 41; Maier, *L'épiscopat*, 25–6.

Catholic fold were not to be rebaptized, and their clergy could be installed in Catholic churches without being reordained.[21]

The party of Donatus refused to accept its condemnation. It claimed to be the true African church, unsullied by the apostasy of Felix and Caecilian, which, by virtue of its Roman recognition, also polluted the worldwide episcopacy. It also refused to accept baptisms performed by non-Donatist clergy. Both the emperors Constantine and Constans attempted to overcome the schism by suppressing the Donatists by force, but from a Donatist point of view, imperial persecution only confirmed the Caecilianists as collaborators and the Donatists as the authentic, pure Christian community.

Disputed claims over church buildings focused the struggle between the two rival communities. Throughout the fourth century, alternating periods of suppression and toleration of the Donatist churches meant that buildings often changed hands with losing parties forced to vacate and rebuild. In 330, for example, the Donatists seized the Catholic basilica in Constantine (built with funds from Constantine himself). Although appeals were made, the emperor simply supplied the Catholics with funds to build another.[22]

From Julian's restoration of their rights and property (361) until the end of the fourth century, Donatism grew to be the majority sect in Africa, especially in Numidia.[23] Bishops' lists from councils around that time show that nearly 60 percent of the towns in North Africa had both Donatist and Catholic bishops, and presumably at least two different church buildings served those separate congregations. Carthage, for example, had a Catholic cathedral (the Basilica Restituta)[24] as well as a Donatist one.[25] Timgad, the center of Numidian Donatism, also had both Donatist and Catholic cathedrals (the former built by Optatus himself).[26]

According to one thesis, Donatism's strength was an instance of native African identity asserting itself over against Roman culture, religion, and political domination. Allied with the rural population and the lower social classes (especially in Numidia), the Donatists opposed the more Romanized (i.e., less African) inhabitants of large urban centers (e.g., Carthage).[27] A different view, although acknowledging Donatism's Numidian dominance, claims that region's Donatists were no more rural and of no lower

[21] Mansi 4.48; Maier, *L'épiscopat*, 27–8.
[22] Optatus, *Don.* 10.
[23] Possidius, *Vita* 7, and Optatus *Don.* 7.1: Catholics were few in number.
[24] Augustine, *Serm.* 19, 29, 90, 112, 277.
[25] Augustine, *Ep.* 139.1; *Enarrat. Ps.* 80; and *Gest. Coll. Carth.* 411, 3.5.
[26] Gui, *Basiliques chrétiennes*, 263–86.
[27] Frend, *Donatist Church*; see review by Brown, "Religious Dissent," 237–59.

social status than their Catholic counterparts.[28] Whatever their situation, Donatist bishops occasionally allied themselves with rebellions against Roman imperial rule and used gangs of local (probably Punic-speaking) religious terrorists, the Circumcellions, to thwart the enforcement of laws restricting their activities.[29] The Donatist bishop of Timgad, Optatus, even formed an alliance with the rebel Mauretanian prince Gildo. Both were executed by Roman authorities (ca.398).[30]

In response to one particularly outrageous assault on a Catholic bishop, the emperor Honorius applied the Theodosian laws against Christian heretics to the Donatists in 405, and attempted to suppress the church by exiling its leading bishops and confiscating its property.[31] When this led to increased violence, he proposed a full judicial hearing of the cases of both sides in the spring of 411 in Carthage. The theological and legal arguments of the Donatist delegates were unsuccessful, and the imperial commissioner found for the Catholics. As a result, Donatist property was officially turned over to the Catholics, and civil penalties were reinstituted against individual Donatists. Enforcement was, of course, piecemeal, and the Donatist church continued to function, perhaps even to thrive.

Donatists were attached to their local martyrs, and especially to those who withstood what they perceived as unjust government coercion – in particular their model and patron, St. Cyprian. Not only did they revere those who had stood firm in the face of past persecution, but they viewed themselves as currently tested victims – sure proof that they were the authentic Christians while the others collaborated with God's enemies.[32] According to contemporary (Catholic) documents, some even sought out martyrdom by throwing themselves over cliffs, burning themselves alive, or by provoking local polytheists to kill them, presumably in fits of outrage, when they made a public spectacle of mocking their gods at traditional festivals.[33] The Donatists reflected on their plight and evaluated their place in history in the *Liber Genealogus*, a chronicle that was reedited multiple times in the first half of the fifth century. Although all extant versions begin with creation, they stop at successively later points, and include contemporary events (e.g., instances of Catholic persecution), and

---

[28] Mandouze,"Donatisme," 357–66; and Bénabou, *Résistance*.
[29] Shaw, "Circumcellions," 227–58. For a thorough study of the sectarian conflicts between Catholic and Donatist communities see Shaw, *Sacred Violence*.
[30] Augustine, *Parm.* 3.24; *Bapt.* 2.11.16; *C. litt. Petil.* 1.10, 11; 1.24.26; 2.83.184; *Ep.* 53.3.6.
[31] *CTh* 16.10.16–25.
[32] Augustine, *C. litt. Petil.* 2.92.202. See also *Gesta coll. Carth.* 411, 3.22.
[33] Augustine, *Parm.* 1.10.16; *Gaud.* 1.28.32; *Ep.* 185.3.12 and *Haer.* 69; Tilley, *Martyr Stories*, 77.

present themselves as heirs to such great biblical heroes as Abel, Daniel, and the Maccabees.[34]

Although the dominant struggle of the fourth and early fifth century was between Donatist and Catholic communions, other groups continued to exist and from time to time emerged to challenge religious authorities. Among these groups were Manichees and Tertullianists – or those who continued to follow the New Prophecy.[35] While the Tertullianists appear to have been still active only in Carthage, Manichees were a major focus of Augustine's attentions in the first years of his service at Hippo (ca.391–92).[36]

Unlike the Donatists, Manichees espoused a doctrine that ran counter to orthodox teaching. Even more significantly, their teaching contradicted some of the most deeply held African Christian values; they did not believe that martyrdom served any good, they denied the resurrection of the body, and they repudiated the use of material elements in the sacraments.[37] Different from their teachings elsewhere in the empire, moreover, African Manichees presented themselves using distinctively Christian language (invoking the Trinity and referring to the crucifixion) – which made them even more of a specifically regional threat.

Roman authorities associated Manichaeism with foreign (Persian) cults and magic and tried to suppress the cult. Diocletian's first rescript of persecution (31 March 297) actually was promulgated against Manichees and seems to have been triggered by complaints from Africa.[38] Like Christians, they survived persecution. Among their converts in fourth-century Carthage was young Augustine, who was initially attracted to their explanation of evil and probably also to their high-status adherents as potential patrons (*Conf.* 3.10). Much later, after his conversion to Christianity and arrival in Hippo, he twice persuaded the prominent Manichee Fortunatus to a debate over matters of doctrine. He also authored a series of anti-Manichaean treatises.[39]

In contrast to these variant forms of Christianity, devotees of the pre-Christian gods appear to have dwindled numerically by the mid-fifth century. At the beginning of the third century, traditional religion was robust

---

[34] Mommsen, *MGH* 9,154–96; Monceaux, *Histoire*, 247–58.

[35] Augustine, *Haer.* 86.

[36] Brown, "Diffusion," 92–103; Frend, "Gnostic-Manichaean Tradition," 13–26. See also Griffith (Chapter 5) and De Jong (Chapter 1), this volume.

[37] See Augustine, *C. du. ep. Pelag.* 4.4–5 and *Haer.* 46. On denial of the resurrection see Evodius, *Fide*, 40.

[38] Cited in Brown, "Diffusion," 95.

[39] Possidius, *Vita*, 6.

and, as elsewhere in the Roman empire, followed the practice of identifying local gods with their Roman counterparts. The Punic-African deities Ba'al and Tanit were thus secondarily named Saturn and Caelestis (also Juno, Cybele, or Magna Mater).⁴⁰ Even though the gradual establishment of Christianity as the state's official cult took its toll, the native Augustine described his attendance at festivals for Caelestis and Cybele (Berecynthia) in Madauros as a boy and in Carthage as a young man (*Civ.* 2.4, 2.26, 7.26). Quodvultdeus, bishop of Carthage (d. ca.453), bemoaned the continuing popularity of the gods in a sermon preached to catechumens in the 430s, and at least a decade later the Gallican historian Salvian claimed that supposedly Christian Carthaginians still paid homage to Juno Caelestis.⁴¹

Perhaps in response to this, by the end of the fourth century Christian emperors began to pass laws against the old Roman cults. Theodosius I (347–95) promulgated edicts abolishing sacrifices. Honorius moved to confiscate temples for public use, actions directed specifically at African traditionalists.⁴² Simultaneously, Christians began taking over those temples and transforming them into churches. While still a deacon, Quodvultdeus had witnessed Aurelius's seizing of Carthage's temple of Caelestis on Easter, probably sometime after 407.⁴³ Bishop Aurelius and his entourage entered the temple and placed the bishop's throne in the place of the goddess's statue. Augustine preached in one of these transformed temples, renamed the Basilica Honoriana, around 417 (*Serm.* 163). Its new name suggests that the emperor himself sanctioned and possibly even funded that particular conversion.⁴⁴

Similar transformations were probably less dramatic but no less permanent – an indication that the Christian faith had replaced the older Roman cult. For example, churches in Sufetula (Basilica III, called the Church of Servus and possibly also Basilica I, "of Bellator"), Thuburbo Maius, and Djebel Oust were all installed within former temple structures, the last within a former temple of Asclepius. In all three cases, the formerly open *peristyle* was transformed into the nave, its columns serving as the supports for a roof over nave and aisles. The *cella* of the temple became its baptistery, a small chamber now attached to the side of the building rather than being its inner sanctum.

⁴⁰ Tertullian, *Apol.* 24, Augustine, *Civ.* 7.26; *Conf.* 1.23.36. See Mohamed Kheir Orfali, "De Baal Hammon à Saturne africaine," 142–9.
⁴¹ Quodvultdeus, *Symbol.* 2.3.1; Salvian, *Gub. Dei.* 8.2, see discussion below.
⁴² *CTh* 16.10.16–25. See Augustine, *Civ.* 18.54.
⁴³ Quodvultdeus, *Lib. prom.* 3.38.44. Regarding the date (407), see *CTh* 16.10.2.1–2.
⁴⁴ Hanson, "Transformation," 257–67.

Meanwhile, the sack of Rome by the Goths brought an influx of Roman refugees to North Africa, among them the British monk Pelagius, with whom Augustine had one of his last theological disputes. Presumed to have been initiated by a line in his *Confessions* (10.2) in which Augustine asked God to "command what you will, and give what you command," this dispute has often been characterized as a debate about the transmission of original sin, although its substance was more focused on Augustine's contention that humans were incapable of consistently choosing and doing the good.[45] Although the bishops of Africa backed it fully, his view that divine love not only assisted human goodness but constituted it undercut the autonomy of human choice and was not accepted or understood by eastern Christians. In modified forms, however, it eventually passed into the tradition of Latin (western) Christianity.

FIFTH-CENTURY CONFLICTS — VANDAL ARIANS AND AFRICAN CATHOLICS

As Augustine lay dying in the summer of 430, Vandal armies surrounded Hippo. In a letter to a brother bishop in Thiabe, he referred to the enemy army as "subverters of Romanity," in contrast to the local population who, in his view, were the heirs of Roman civilization.[46] According to his biographer, Possidius, the invaders were a mixture of Germanic Vandals, Iranian Alans, Goths, and various other ethnic groups (*Vita*, 28). These peoples had united, crossed the Rhine in 406, and by 409 were in Spain – where the Romans (and their Visigothic allies) accorded them rights to residency but not to property. Caught in an imperial power struggle following Honorius's death, Augustine's friend, the African governor Boniface, revolted against Rome and, according to Procopius, invited the Vandals into Africa (he had married a Vandal woman, Pelagia, through whom he had connections to the Vandal king, Gunderic). Later, after regaining the favor of the empress Galla Placidia, he defended the province against the united Vandal tribes, led by Gunderic's brother Gaiseric.[47]

Although composed of different languages and ethnicities, the majority of the Vandal people adhered to an Arian form of Christianity, probably having been converted during the reign of the Arian emperor Valens. Unlike other Arian groups (e.g., the Visigoths and Ostrogoths), the Vandals were

[45] As reported by Augustine himself, *Praed.* 2.53.
[46] Possidius, *Vita*, 30.
[47] Procopius, *Vand.* 3.3.22, 25–34.

intolerant of Christians who confessed the Nicene faith.[48] In their defense, they claimed the Councils of Ariminum and Seleucia, presided over by an earlier Arian emperor Constantius.[49] If this is accurate, Vandal theology was probably more Homoean than truly Arian, and taught that the Son was like (rather than unlike) the Father, although not of the same essence.

Augustine's understanding of Arianism likely was based on his encounter with Gothic Arians in Milan, and he agreed to debate the Arian bishop Maximinus, who came to Africa with the Gothic Count Sigiswulf in 427 or 428.[50] According to Augustine, the Donatists tried to win the Arians over to their cause, purporting to hold similar beliefs (*Ep.* 185.1.1). However, he pointed out, the Donatists confessed that the Trinity has one substance, while the Arians held differently. For their part, the Vandals (like the Goth Maximinus) considered themselves true "Catholics." The dramatic differences, illuminated in a theological debate called by the Vandal king Huneric in 484, show that historians may justifiably argue that the Vandals were engaged in a religious war as much as in territorial conquest (*Hist.* 2.56–101).[51]

Under the leadership of their king Gaiseric, the Vandals swept east across Mauretania from Spain taking city after city until they reached Carthage. According to Possidius and Victor of Vita (both fifth-century eyewitnesses), they demolished and burned churches, dispersed their congregations, and captured – and even killed – some clergy. They also took over cathedral churches in major cities (Hippo, Cirta, and Carthage) and installed their own bishops.[52] The Donatist editors of the *Liber Genealogus* saw these events as signs of the end time, and characterized Geiseric as the Antichrist (*Lib. Gen.* 618F) – a term removed at the king's insistence from subsequent editions. Victor also reported that the Catholic bishop of Carthage, Quodvultdeus, with a number of other clerics was herded naked onto a rudderless ship and put out to sea.[53] Catholics and Donatists alike were forced to rely on their rural congregations, and to practice the passive resistance to state power that the Donatists had perfected.

Vandals occupied Carthage's Basilica Maiorum, Basilica Celerina, and the Scillitan Martyrs (perhaps two different basilicas), Mensa Cypriani,

[48] Heather, "Christianity and the Vandals."
[49] Victor of Vita, *Hist.* 3.5; Shanzer, "Intentions," 271–90.
[50] Augustine, *Arian.; Maxim.*
[51] Modéran, "Une guerre de religion," 21–44.
[52] Possidius, *Vita* 28, Victor of Vita, *Hist.* 1.15–16.
[53] Victor of Vita, *Hist.* 1.15; Quodvultdeus, *Temp. barb.* 11 and 12. Quodvultdeus arrived in Naples safely and died in exile.

Memoria Cypriani, and Basilica Restituta (the Catholic cathedral).[54] Although their churches had been confiscated and their bishops exiled, one can infer from Victor of Vita's account that Nicenes were yet permitted to hold services in basilicas outside the city walls (the Basilicas Fausti and Novarum [*Hist.* 1.25]). And although they initially refused to replace bishops who died in exile, after an intervention of Emperor Valentinian III, they allowed the Africans to consecrate Deogratias as primate of Carthage to replace Quodvultdeus. Nevertheless, when Deogratias died in 457, the post again went empty. According to Victor of Vita, the number of Catholic bishops in Africa Proconsularis dwindled to three from an original 164 (*Hist.* 1.24–9).[55]

Between 457 and 480, the Vandals reportedly clamped down further, prohibiting assemblies and forcing the Nicenes to celebrate in secret.[56] However, about 480 or 481, Gaiseric's successor, Huneric (477–84), adopted a more moderate stance and, acceding to the wishes of emperor Zeno (474–91) and Placidia (sister to Huneric's wife Eudocia), once again allowed the Nicenes a bishop. This was granted on condition that the Arians be allowed to practice their own religion elsewhere in the empire, and preach in whatever language their people could understand. The election of Eugenius (481–84) took place soon after, to general joy among Catholics.[57]

Jealousy soon shattered the momentary peace. Because Vandals were seen going into Nicene churches (raising questions about loyalty), Huneric required all court officials to follow the Arian faith and reinstituted persecutions.[58] He tortured consecrated virgins, and (according to Victor [*Hist.* 2.23–37]) sent nearly five thousand Nicene deacons, priests, and bishops into exile in the desert. Intending to show himself as theologically motivated, Huneric ordered the beleaguered bishops to a *Collatio* (484) to argue their case. The African Nicenes, led by Eugenius, presented the king a book containing their confession of faith. Ultimately they were denied an actual hearing, in part because the Arians immediately objected to the Nicenes calling themselves "catholics," because they also claimed that nomenclature for themselves.

---

[54] Victor of Vita, *Hist.*, 1.9, 15, 16; Procopius, *Vand.* 1.21.18–19.
[55] Heather, "Christianity and the Vandals." The number of bishops (fifty-four) at the 484 *collatio* suggests that not all were exiled and that some remained in their sees. E.g., see Merrills and Miles, *Vandals*, 177–203 (Chap. 7, "Religion and the Vandal Kingdom").
[56] Victor of Vita, *Hist.*, 2.1; 1.41; 2.39, 3.4.
[57] Victor of Vita, *Hist.*, 2.2–6; ibid., 2.18, 47–51 also mentions Eugenius as bishop from about 480–84, and exiled in 484, *Hist.*, 3.34.
[58] Victor of Vita, *Hist.*, 2.8–9.

The uproar at this perceived insult moved the king once again to grant all African churches and property to Arian bishops, and to threaten to exile any Nicene cleric who persisted in holding services.[59] Finally, by means of a subterfuge, Huneric rounded up the destitute clergy and demanded that they swear to uphold a document naming his son, Hilderic, as his successor. Whether they succumbed to this demand or not, all were sent into exile – on one hand, for disloyalty; on the other, for swearing an oath, contrary to the Gospel (Matt. 5:13).[60]

Huneric's plan failed in any case. He was succeeded not by his son, but by his (older) nephew Gunthamund (484–96). King Gunthamund returned to a policy of appeasement and granted the shrine of St. Agileus to Eugenius, the bishop of Carthage, when he returned from exile.[61] The expanded shrine served as the Catholic cathedral for most of the rest of the Vandal era in Africa.[62] Gunthamund also allowed some clergy to return from exile. When his younger brother, Thrasamund, came to power (496–523), however, the tide turned again, as he collaborated with the Ostrogothic King Theodoric and once again exiled the Catholic bishops, including Fulgentius of Ruspe, the Nicenes' leading theologian.[63] At the end of his life, Thrasamund allowed the establishment of parallel churches.[64]

Thrasamund was succeeded (finally) by Huneric's son Hilderic (523–30), whose mother was the Byzantine princess Eudocia (the daughter of Valentinian III). Probably because of this lineage, Hilderic broke with the Ostrogoths, allied himself with the Byzantines, allowed exiled clergy to return once again, and reopened the churches. Bonifatius was installed as bishop of Carthage and presided over a council in 525.[65] The returnees included Fulgentius of Ruspe, who had been recalled earlier (515) to mediate a dispute on the nature of the Trinity (but as he had then refused to cooperate, he was returned).[66] The homecoming of the exiled clerics was a triumphant moment for the African Nicenes. Recorded by Fulgentius's biographer Ferrandus, a Carthaginian deacon, these heroes were their generation's martyrs for the true faith.[67]

---

[59] Victor of Vita, *Hist.*, 3.7–14, the Decree of Huneric.

[60] Victor of Vita, *Hist.*, 3.17–21.

[61] Victor of Tunnuna, *Chron.*, 52; *Laterculus reg. Wand.* (annals of the Vandal Kings); Steinacher, "Laterculus Regum Vandalorum," 177.

[62] Perhaps to be identifed with Bir el Knissia; see Ennabli, "Carthage," 38–9, 114–20.

[63] Stevens, "Fulgentius," 327–41.

[64] Courtois, *Vandals*, 304.

[65] Victor Tunnuna, *Chron.*, 523.2, 535; *Laterculus reg. Wand.* A. 16; Ferrandus, *Vita Fulgentii*, 26–7.

[66] Victor of Tunnuna, *Chron.*, 78–9.

[67] Lapeyre, *Vie de Saint Fulgence*; Stevens "Fulgentius," 327–41.

In 530 Gelimer deposed Hilderic, claiming that he had become more Roman than Vandal, and even colluded with the emperor to hand over the kingdom. Gelimer's action outraged Emperor Justinian, who demanded that Gelimer return the throne to Hilderic. Gelimer's refusal to acknowledge the emperor's demand only compounded Justinian's outrage and led him to launch a final attempt to retake Africa for the empire. Four years later, the Byzantine navy arrived on African shores.[68]

The Gallican historian Salvian (ca.400–80) may have been one of the earliest witnesses to everyday life in Vandal Carthage, although it is not certain that he ever visited the city. His treatise *The Governance of God* (written ca.439–51) explained the incursions of barbarian tribes as God's punishment for Christian moral laxity and misbehavior (*Gub. Dei* 7.13).[69] In his view, while ancient Carthage had been home to apostles and martyrs, in latter times it had become a city filled with all kinds of iniquities, from effeminate men to unchaste women. Salvian reported that while Vandal besiegers encircled the walls, Christians in Carthage were oblivious, reveling in the theaters and going mad in the circuses (*Gub. Dei* 6.12). Furthermore, he claimed, supposed Christians had continued to worship the Roman goddess Caelestis (*Gub. Dei* 8.2). Although Salvian was probably no less biased than Victor of Vita, his view of the Vandal Arians offers a useful counterpoint. He described Vandals rehabilitating prostitutes by compelling them to marry and as enforcing chastity within marriage. In Salvian's view, Vandals merely took possession of a corrupt population's property, as it deserved (*Gub. Dei* 7.22).

Whatever they were, the Vandals do not seem to have been builders.[70] Few Vandal-built churches (or significant renovations) can be identified, which suggests that when the invaders appropriated available buildings for their religious services, little in the Vandal liturgy required architectural adaption. The main evidence of Vandal occupation of a formerly Catholic or Donatist church is inscriptional, especially Germanic names on funerary plaques. One such inscription, found in what was probably Augustine's basilica in Hippo, identifies a certain Gulia Runa as a *presbyterissa* – a title that has led some scholars to suggest that she attained some type of clerical standing.[71]

---

[68] Procopius, *Vand.*, 3.9.6–26.
[69] Cleland, "Salvian," 270–4.
[70] See A. Ben Abed and N. Duval, "Carthage, la capitale du royaume et les villes"; Merrills and Miles, *Vandals*, 228–55, Chap. 9, "Justinian and the End of the Vandal Kingdom."
[71] See Madigan and Osiek, *Ordained Women in the Early Church*, 197–8.

THE LAST CENTURIES: FROM BYZANTINE RULE
TO THE ARAB CONQUEST

Procopius, a native Palestinian, also witnessed life in Carthage under the Vandals, although at the end of the era and during another power shift. He accompanied Justinian's general Belisarius in the successful campaign to drive the Vandals out of Africa. In his chronicles – one on the Vandalic War and another describing Justinian's building programs – he recounted the retaking of Carthage and its rebuilding, which included new churches (one dedicated to the Theotokos) and a monastery (*BV* and *Aed.* 6.5.8–11). Other African cities benefited from this era of reconstruction and elaboration. Byzantine forts were planted, using large blocks of dressed stone in place of the older style of building known as *opus Africanum* (uprights and horizontal courses filled with mortared loose rubble), and new churches were built in nearly every important center.

In a later chronicle, Procopius described the harsher realities of the reconquest and imposition of Byzantine rule – the deaths of countless Vandals (as well as Romans and Moors), and the violent repression of Arianism (*Anec.* 18.5–10). The Byzantines, no more tolerant of Arian Christians than the Vandals had been of African Nicenes, reestablished the Nicene faith and restored the native Catholic hierarchy to their former churches. Despite their reinstatement, the African bishops soon learned that their Byzantine liberators were actually only a new set of colonial rulers. The army and civil administration were controlled by an elite group of Greeks who kept largely to themselves; in matters of religion, however, they expected the Africans to conform to orthodoxy as it was defined in Constantinople.[72]

Although the churches retained Latin, their liturgies were inevitably influenced by Byzantine customs. New buildings were often dedicated to Greek saints. Altars that had been traditionally close to the center of the main aisle were gradually shifted toward the apse and surmounted with ciboria. Domes were constructed over the nave and vaults set over aisles, instead of the former wooden roofs, covered by decorative terra cotta tiles. Nevertheless, some distinctively African traditions were maintained and some developed that were specific to the region, including the use of polychrome mosaic tomb covers – often covering burials in the floors of churches (Fig. 12) – and more elaborately designed and decorated baptismal fonts (Fig. 13). Counter apses were added to many African churches in

---

[72] Cameron, "Byzantine Africa," 45.

Fig. 12. Mosaic tomb cover from Furnos Minos, mid-fifth century. Now in the Bardo Museum, Tunis. Photograph by Robin M. Jensen.

Fig. 13. Baptismal font from Kélibia, Basilica of Felix, sixth century. Now in the Bardo Museum, Tunis. Photograph by Robin M. Jensen.

this period to accommodate the African practice of burying clergy within the church.

Nevertheless, while the cult of the Theotokos was evident in the Byzantine palace chapel at Carthage, neither the veneration of the Virgin nor that of icons in general seems to have taken hold beyond the capital. Thus, the architecture reflected the continuity of African tradition, and though it incorporated certain elements imported by the new rulers, it appears to have blended those with typically indigenous characteristics.

Based on the rarity of Greek names on bishops' lists for councils in the 540s and 550s, it appears that African clerics also managed local ecclesiastical politics. Furthermore, African Catholics continued to turn to Rome (rather than to Constantinople) as their closest ecclesiastical ally, just as they had during the Donatist controversy. Now, however, they were even more inclined to agree with Roman policies. For example, when in 535, under the leadership of Bishop Reparatus of Carthage, the bishops called a council to decide what to do with Arian converts to Nicene orthodoxy, they called upon the bishop of Rome, John II, for advice and validation of their decrees. The decision not to admit former Arians to orders and to reduce their converted clergy to lay status conformed to the Roman handling of reconciled schismatics at the beginning of the fifth century (contrary to their earlier African position).[73] The strengthening of these ties may have been the result of the years that many African bishops spent in exile in Sicily and Italy.

Meanwhile, a series of Mauri uprisings in the late 530s and 540s, combined with rebellions of Vandals who had been brought into the imperial army, caused the Byzantine general, Solomon, to flee to Syracuse. Simultaneously, a resurgence of ancient ethnic identity also threatened the fragile alliance as Romanized, Latin-speaking Africans found themselves caught between suddenly energized Mauri tribes and a government made up of Greek-speaking foreigners. In the 540s the Mauri, perhaps in another instance of native nationalistic feeling, instigated a revolt against their new rulers. Corripus, the chronicler of this era, although an African himself, had no sympathy with the rebels, whom he described as uncouth and violent worshippers of a bull-god called Gurzil. His writings supply precious but undoubtedly biased evidence on contemporary Berber tribes and customs.[74] His hero, John Troglita, a general in Justinian's service, successfully restored Byzantine control and military discipline.[75]

Having come through more than a century of political, economic, and military disruption and disorder, native clergy resented efforts from the imperial court to impose doctrinal conformity, especially when they judged compliance as drawing them into heresy. Thus, another religious crisis erupted in 546 when Justinian wrote to the African bishops, ordering them to accept the condemnation of the "Three Chapters" (writings of Theodore of Mopsuestia, Theodoret of Cyrrhus, and Ibas of Edessa). Although Justinian's edict was aimed at reconciling eastern Monophysites, in the eyes of African Catholics it profoundly undermined Chalcedonian orthodoxy. The Africans, not especially attuned to Justinian's desire for unity, refused his demand.[76]

A series of dogmatic treatises produced from the late 540s to the early 560s summarized the Africans' reasons for dissent. These works, produced by Ferrandus (author of the Life of Fulgentius), Bishop Facundus of Hermiane, and the archdeacon of Carthage, Liberatus, show that African clerics presumed the right to independently judge matters of dogma and

---

[73] Cameron, "Byzantine Africa," 46; *Collectio Avallana*, 85–7.
[74] Ibid. 39–40, 46–9. Corippus's writings give some precious but problematic evidence on Berber tribes and customs at this time.
[75] Kaegi, "Arianism," 23–53.
[76] Modéran, "L'Afrique reconquise," 39–82.

discipline. Further, they showed that the Africans were unconvinced that Theodore's views were in any way heretical, although their knowledge of his theology came largely from a textbook based on the teachings of Paul of Nisibis, a student of Theodore's.[77] Facundus's treatise, *The Defense of the Three Chapters*, came to the attention of Justinian himself in 551, who specifically denounced it in his second edict of 551.[78]

Although at first allied with the Africans, Rome's bishop Vigilius (537–55) succumbed to Justinian's pressure to conform, prompting the Council of Carthage (550) to excommunicate him.[79] This council's action provoked Justinian to summon the ring-leaders to Constantinople to justify themselves – apparently to no avail. At the fifth general council (II Constantinople, 553), all were deposed or exiled, including Bishop Reparatus of Carthage.[80] The main chronicler of these events, Bishop Victor of Tunnuna, was himself imprisoned for his resistance, first in the monastery that Justinian had earlier established in Carthage (the Mandracium), and subsequently in Egypt. African resistance to the imperial government continued until Justinian's death in 565.

Meanwhile, the African church may have experienced a Donatist revival. In the 590s, Gregory I wrote to Gennadius, the exarch of Africa, to request that he suppress the Donatists and take steps to bar former Donatists from the episcopate (*Ep.* 1.74–7). This effort seems to have failed, however, because several subsequent letters refer to bishops handing churches over to Donatist clerics or permitting the establishment of Donatist sees. Gregory insisted that the heresy of Donatism was spreading and that many Catholics had received rebaptism (*Ep.* 2.48). In a letter to Pantaleo, prefect of Africa, he claimed that Donatists were throwing Catholic priests out of their churches and rebaptizing their congregants (*Ep.* 4.34).[81] Finally, Gregory, apparently frustrated by lack of cooperation, went straight to the top and wrote to the emperor Mauricius, pleading with him to enforce the laws against the Donatists and punish the disobedient (*Ep.* 6.65). At least one scholar thinks that Gregory's letters reveal that he was more concerned about Donatists and Catholics forming a practical alliance than he was about Donatist resurgence, however.[82]

[77] Cameron, "Byzantine Africa," 46; the textbook was Junillus's *Instituta regularia divinae legis*. See Honoré, *Tribonian*, 237–42.
[78] Cameron, "Byzantine Africa," 47.
[79] Ibid., 47–49. Victor of Tunnuna, *Chron.*, 141 (550).
[80] Victor of Tunnuna, *Chron.*, 145 (552)–152 (555).
[81] See also Gregory, *Ep.*, 6.37 (to Columbus, Primate of Numidia).
[82] Markus, "Donatism," 118–26.

At the least, these letters suggest that Donatism never totally disappeared, despite centuries of church and state efforts at coercion. The tenacity of this ethnically African movement perhaps demonstrates a continued disaffection of the native population from a Catholic, Romanized hierarchy as well as from foreign secular authorities.[83] Editions of the Donatist chronicle, the *Liber Genealogus*, were published between 427 and 453, Leo I wrote a letter to the bishops of Gaul about possible Donatist refugees in the 450s (*Ep.* 168.18), and Victor of Vita may have mentioned Donatists as late as 480 (a passing mention and possible interpolation – *Hist.* 3.71). Archaeological evidence of Donatism in the Vandal and Byzantine era includes certain church inscriptions that mention characteristically Donatist themes (e.g., purity and sanctity), record so-called Donatist watchwords (e.g., "*Deo laus*"), or employ the term "unitas" (perhaps indicating anti-Donatist sympathies).[84] Apart from these slim indications, however, no literary or archaeological records of Donatists in Africa exist for the century before Gregory's writings.

The doctrinal debate over Monotheletism in the first half of the seventh century represents the last significant theological or ecclesiological output from Christian North Africa and (for the last time) demonstrates its continued sense of doctrinal independence. By this time, based on surviving documentary evidence, all of the discussion was carried on in Greek rather than in Latin. As with the earlier efforts of Justinian to reach a rapprochement with Monophysites, the emperors Heraclius (610–14) and Constans II (641–68) attempted to impose the dogma that the two natures of Christ (human and divine) shared a single activity or energy. As before, the African church resisted. This time, however, their opposition was supported by Gregory, the imperial exarch of Africa along with the orthodox theologian Maximus the Confessor, who had come to Africa from Palestine to escape the Persian advance and had been living in a Carthaginian monastery. This monastery was also home to another major orthodox figure from the seventh century, Sophronius, the patriarch of Jerusalem (634–39), who had also fled from the invading Muslims and who, like Maximus, viewed Monotheletism as a heresy. Thus, Byzantine governors and theologians rather than native Catholic clergy represented the African church in this last major controversy.

Gregory sponsored a debate between the Maximus and Pyrrhus, the Monothelite patriarch of Constantinople. Pyrrhus was no match for

[83] Frend, *Donatist Church*, 300–14.
[84] Ibid., 306–8; Duval, Cintas, "L'eglise du prêtre Felix," 139–49.

Maximus, and the confrontation ended in his recantation.[85] As always, the African bishops looked to Rome for support, and both Maximus and Pyrrhus sailed there to seek the assistance of Pope Martin I. Under political pressure, the now-deposed Pyrrhus changed his position again and returned to Constantinople, where he was reinstated as patriarch. In the meantime, the African bishops joined forces with Maximus and Martin at a Lateran synod (649) to anathematize Monotheletism. Meanwhile, because Emperor Constans had forbidden any further inquiry into Christ's "single activity," both Martin and Maximus were accused of rebellion and were arrested and extradited to Constantinople. Martin died *en route*, but Maximus was tried, exiled, and tortured. He died in exile (662). Gregory, meanwhile, had been killed in a first battle with invading Arabs, possibly at Sufetula in 648 – his death the beginning of the end of Christian Africa.[86]

Little is known about the African bishops who returned from the Lateran synod, or how they coped with the next fifty years of Arab conquests. From the middle of the seventh century, the written record of Christianity in Africa dies out entirely; the only sources are Arabic histories that concentrate on the conversion of the region to Islam and its transformation from a set of Roman provinces into the Maghreb. Carthage held out longer than many other places, finally falling to the Arabs in 698 after a siege of some months and help sent too late from Constantinople.

Although Christianity may have survived for another century or two, and possibly even longer in rural areas among native tribes who never fully converted to the new religion (Islam), the story of one of the most influential and robust of early Christian communities seems to end here.[87] The reasons for its ultimate extinction may not be so puzzling, however, in light of the previous centuries of successive foreign occupation and divisive doctrinal controversies that arose when those occupying ruling powers attempted to repress distinctively African Christian teachings and traditions. Had the African church been united from the outset, rather than torn apart by competing claims of purity and legitimacy, a coherent and sustainable community may have been established and survived, even in the face of continuous opposition and even oppression from the outside. Given this history of internal conflict and external threat, however, the Arab arrivals may have been viewed as no more "foreign" than any of the other invading groups, and perhaps in some respects sharing some of

---

[85] Maximus, *Disputatio cum Pyrrho* (*PG* 91.288–353).
[86] Theophanes, *Chronographia*, 343.24–9, ed. de Boor (A.M. 6139); Nicephorus, *Breviarium*, 39.
[87] On the survival of Christianity in Africa see Prevost, "Les dernières communautés."

the ancient indigenous values of African Christianity – their emphasis on rigorous individual and communal purity, the importance of heroic martyrs and saints, and the belief that the righteous community both guarded and guaranteed authentic religious faith.[88]

BIBLIOGRAPHY

Primary

Actes de la Conférence de Carthage en 411, ed. Serge Lancel. 4 vols. *SC* 194, 195, 224, 373 (Paris, 1972–91).
Optatus. *Against the Donatists*, ed. and trans. Mark Edwards (Liverpool, 1997).

Secondary

Ben Abed, Aïcha, and Noel Duval. "Carthage, la capitale du royaume et les villes de Tunisie à l'époque Vandale." In *Sedes regiae (ann. 400–800)*, eds. Gisela Ripoll and Josep M. Gurt (Barcelona, 2000): 163–218.
Bénabou, Marcel. *La résistance africaine à la romanisation* (Paris, 1976).
Brown, Peter. "Christianity and Local Culture in Late Roman Africa." In *Religion and Society in the Age of Augustine* (London, 1972): 279–300.
  "Religious Dissent in the Later Roman Empire: The Case of North Africa." In *Religion and Society in the Age of Augustine* (London, 1972): 237–59.
  "The Diffusion of Manichaeanism in the Roman Empire." *JRS* 59 (1969): 92–103.
Cameron, Averil. "Byzantine Africa –The Literary Evidence." In *Excavations at Carthage 1978* VII, ed. John H. Humphrey (Ann Arbor, Mich., 1982): 29–62.
Cleland, D. J. "Salvian and the Vandals." *StPat* 10.1 (1970): 270–4.
Clover, Frank. "Carthage in the Age of Augustine." In *Excavations at Carthage, 1976* IV, ed. John H. Humphrey (Ann Arbor, Mich, 1978): 1–14.
  "Carthage and the Vandals." In *Excavations at Carthage 1978* VII, ed. J. H. Humphrey (Ann Arbor, Mich., 1982): 1–22.
Courtois, Christian. *Les Vandales et l'Afrique* (Paris, 1955).
Decret, François. *Early Christianity in North Africa*. Trans. Edward L. Smither (Eugene, Oreg., 2009).
Duval, N., and J. Cintas. "L'eglise du prêtre Felix (région de Kélibia)." *Karthago* 9 (1958): 157–265.
Duval, Yvette. *Loca sanctorum africae: le culte des martyrs en Afrique du IVe au VIIe siècle*, 2 vols. (Rome, 1982).
Ennabli, Liliane. *Carthage: une métropole chrétienne du IVe à la fin du VIIe siècle* (Paris, 1997).
Frend, William H. C. *The Donatist Church* (Oxford, 1952).
  "The Gnostic-Manichaean Tradition in Roman North Africa." *JEH* 4.1 (1953): 13–26.
Fournier, Eric. *Victor of Vita and the Vandal 'Persecution': Interpreting Exile in Late Antiquity*, diss., University of California, Santa Barbara, 2008.

---

[88] For a helpful summary of various theories regarding the reasons for the disappearance of Christianity in Africa, see Handley, "Disputing the End of African Christianity."

Groh, Dennis E. "Upper-Class Christians in Tertullian's Africa: Some Observations." *StPat* 14 (1971): 41–7.

Gui, Isabelle, et al. *Basiliques chrétiennes d'Afriques du nord.* 2 vols. (Paris, 1992).

Handley, Mark A. "Disputing the End of African Christianity." In *Vandals, Romans, and Berbers*, ed. Andrew H. Merrills (Aldershot, Hampshire, 2004): 291–310.

Hanson, R. P. C. "The Transformation of Pagan Temples into Churches in the Early Christian Centuries." *JSS* 23 (1978): 257–67.

Heather, Peter. "Christianity and the Vandals in the Reign of Geiseric." In *Wolf Liebeschuetz Reflected: Essays Presented by Colleagues, Friends, and Pupils*, eds. John Drinkwater and Benet Salway (London, 2007): 137–46.

Honoré, Tony. *Tribonian* (Ithaca, N.Y., 1978).

Jensen, Robin. "Baptismal Rites and Architecture." In *A People's History of Christianity 2: Late Ancient Christianity*, ed. Virginia Burrus (Minneapolis, 2005): 117–44.

   "*Mater Ecclesia* and *Fons Aeterna*: The Church and Her Womb in Ancient Christian Tradition." In *Feminist Companion to Patristic Literature*, ed. Amy-Jill Levine (Sheffield, 2008): 137–56.

Kaegi, Walter E. "Arianism and the Byzantine Army in Africa, 533–46." *Traditio* 21 (1965): 23–53.

Lapeyre, Gabriel. *Saint Fulgence de Ruspe. un évêque africain sous la domination vandale* (Paris, 1929).

Leone, Anna. *Changing Townscapes in North Africa from Late Antiquity to the Arab Conquest* (Bari, 2007).

Madigan, Kevin, and Carolyn Osiek, *Ordained Women in the Early Church* (Baltimore, 2005).

Maier, Jean-Louis. *L'épiscopat de l'Afrique Romaine, Vandale, et Byzantine* (Rome, 1973).

Mandouze, André. "Le donatisme represente-t'il la résistance à Rome de l'Afrique tardive?" In *Assimilation et résistance à la culture Greco-Romane dans le monde ancient: travaux de Vie congrès internationale d'études Classiques 176*, ed. D. M. Pippidi (Madrid, 1974): 357–66.

Markus, Robert A. "Donatism: The Last Phase." *Studies in Church History* 1 (1964): 118–26.

Mattingly, D. J., and R. B. Hitchner. "Roman Africa: An Archaeological Review." *JRS* 85 (1995): 172–3.

Merrills, Andrew H., ed. *Vandals, Romans, and Berbers: New Perspectives on Late Antique North Africa* (Aldershot, Hampshire, 2004).

Merrills, Andrew H., and Richard Miles. *The Vandals* (Oxford, 2010).

Modéran, Yves. "Une guerre de religion: les deux églises d'Afrique à la époque Vandale." *An Tard* 11.2 (2003): 21–44.

   "L'Afrique reconquise et les Trois Chapitres." In *The Crisis of the Oikoumene*, eds. Celia Chazelle and Catherine Cubitt (Turnhout, 2007): 39–82.

Monceaux, Paul. *Histoire littéraire de l'Afrique chrétienne depuis l'origines jusqu'a l'invasion arabe* (Paris, 1901–23).

Musurillo, Herbert. *The Acts of the Christian Martyrs* (Oxford, 1972).

Orfali, Mohamed Kheir. "De Baal Hammon à Saturne africain: Les traces du culte en Algérie." In *Algerie Antique: catalogue de l'exposition 26 avril au 17 août 2003, Musée de l'Arles et de la Provence antiques*, eds. Claude Sintès and Ymouni Rebahi (Arles, 2003): 142–50.

Prevost, Virginie. "Les dernières communautés chrétiennes autochtones d'Afrique du Nord." *RHR* 224 (2007): 461–83.

Rives, James. "Human Sacrifice among Pagans and Christians." *JRS* 85 (1995): 65–85.

Religion and Authority in Roman Carthage from Augustus to Constantine (Oxford, 1995).

Setzer, Claudia. "Jews, Jewish Christians, and Judaizers in North Africa." In *Putting Body and Soul Together: Essays in Honor of Robin Scroggs*, eds. VirginiaWiles, et al. (Valley Forge, Pa. 1997): 185–200.

Shanzer, Danuta. "Intentions and Audiences: History, Hagiography, Martyrdom, and Confession in Victor of Vita's *Historia Persecutionis*." In *Vandals, Romans, and Berbers*, ed. A. H. Merrills (Aldershot, Hampshire, 2004): 271–90.

Shaw, Brent. *Rulers, Nomads, and Christians in Roman North Africa* (Aldershot, Hampshire. 1995).

"Who were the Circumcellions?" In *Vandals, Romans, and Berbers* (Aldershot, Hampshire, 2004): 227–58.

Sacred Violence: African Christians and Sectarian Hatred in the Age of Augustine (Cambridge, 2011).

Steinacher, Roland. "The So-called Laterculus Regum Vandalorum et Alanorum: A Sixth-century African Addition to Prosper Tiro's Chronicle?" In *Vandals, Romans, and Berbers* (Aldershot, Hampshire, 2004): 163–80.

Stern, Karen. *Inscribing Devotion and Death: Archaeological Evidence for Jewish Populations of North Africa* (Leiden, 2008).

Stevens, Susan. "The Circle of Bishop Fulgentius." *Traditio* 38 (1982): 327–41.

Sumruld, William A. *Augustine and the Arians* (Selinsgrove, Pa., 1994).

Tabbernee, William. "Perpetua, Montanism, and Christian Ministry in Carthage." *PRSt* 32 (2005): 421–41.

Tilley, Maureen. *Donatist Martyr Stories: The Church in Conflict in Roman North Africa* (Liverpool, 1996).

Van Slyke, Daniel. *Quodvultdeus of Carthage: The Apocalyptic Theology of a Roman African in Exile* (Strathfield, NSW, 2003).

PART III

GREECE AND ASIA MINOR

II

RELIGIONS OF GREECE AND ASIA MINOR

LYNN E. ROLLER

Greek cult practice comprised a broad spectrum of ritual activities that acknowledged and communicated with the multiplicity of deities in the Greek pantheon. Rather than presupposing a body of revealed truth, Greek cult reflected the cumulative expression of the Greeks' conceptions about the general order of existence and their need to interact with the divine beings that created and controlled that order.[1] Because the Greeks had no authoritative text(s) or central organization that served to codify and interpret their religious system, the best way to approach the topic of Greek religion is to examine the actual rituals and cult observances of the Greeks. Essential rituals included the time-honored practices of prayer and votive offerings to a deity, augmented by animal sacrifice and shared meal on a group level. Cult activities were woven into the lives of virtually all Greeks living in Greece and Asia Minor, and the shared activities of cult practice articulated social networks that strengthened bonds of affiliation with family, community, and state. Such activities could be more elaborate for a larger and wealthier unit, such as a civic festival, while an individual or small group with fewer resources celebrated simpler rites. In the absence of any sacred writings to explain Greek cult practices to us, our principal evidence lies in the physical remains of Greek religion – the sanctuaries, temples, cult images, and votive offerings – and the written texts that discuss these, both literary and epigraphical. Taken together, this material gives us a rich picture of a multifaceted religious experience that was an important component of individual lives.

---

[1] In this approach I am following the conceptual framework of the study of ancient Greek religion as defined by scholars such as Nock, "Cult of Heroes," and Burkert, *Greek Religion*, and more broadly the anthropological approach of Geertz, "Religion as Cultural System," esp. 4 and 42.

Religious practice was an essential part of the Greeks' consciousness of their own ethnic identity as something different from that of neighboring peoples.[2] It was one of the factors that contributed to the development of the *polis*, the independent Greek city-state, in the ninth and eighth centuries BCE and to religious institutions, such as panhellenic sanctuaries, that played a key role in mediating relationships between Greek city-states.[3] By the latter part of the fourth century BCE, Greek ritual practice was established along well-recognized lines. While ending the independent *polis*, the advent of Hellenistic monarchies and Roman hegemony did not dislodge the fundamental sense of a compact between human and deity. However, the changed circumstances of Greek cities in the eastern Mediterranean led to several significant developments in Greek religious practice. The new political landscape resulted in the creation of cults honoring rulers, including Alexander and his Hellenistic successors and the cult of Roma and Roman emperors. Throughout the Greek world, the construction and maintenance of cult centers relied increasingly on the patronage of monarchs and their representatives. The Greek cities of Asia Minor gained markedly in wealth and prominence during the Hellenistic and Roman periods, and their enhanced resources enabled them to build or restore significant cult installations. Yet despite altered political and economic conditions, the rhythm of religious practice in the Greek world continued with surprisingly little change. Greek cult practice continued to be centered on the cyclical patterns of sacrifices, festivals, and rituals administered by communities and individual groups. Sanctuaries such as Olympia, Eleusis, and Delphi, which had long been regarded as sacred places, continued to serve as important centers of cult ritual. The interwoven layers of membership in local and regional cult activities remained influential in shaping a Greek's sense of civic and personal identity (see Map 6).

In this chapter, the time span from the late fourth century BCE to the early fourth century CE is treated as a continuum. While this long period brought many changes in political alliances and in the status of individual cities and regions in the eastern Greek world, the major elements that constituted Greek cult practice retained their basic identity until Late Antiquity. For this reason, the elements of Greek cult practice during this time period are examined thematically, with comments on chronological

---

[2] On Greek cult as a marker of Hellenic identity, see Herodotus 8.144.

[3] For good introductions to Greek cult practice during the Archaic and Classical periods, see Burkert, *Greek Religion*, and Bremmer, *Greek Religion*. On the relationship of religious practice to the Greek polis, see Sourvinou-Inwood, "Polis Religion," and "Further Thoughts"; De Polignac, "Sanctuaries and Festivals."

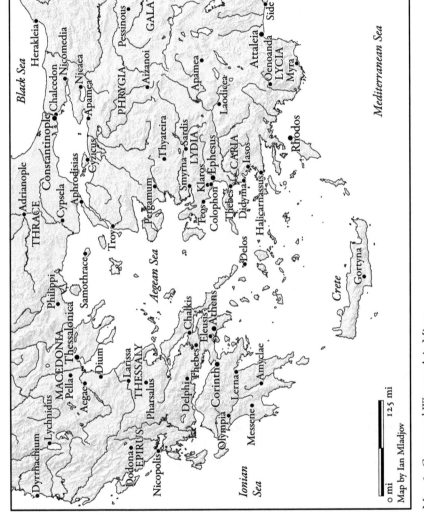

Map 6. Greece and Western Asia Minor

development within a thematic unit where appropriate. Because of the
abundance and complexity of the material, it is not feasible to offer a comprehensive treatment of every facet of Greek cult during the Hellenistic
and Roman periods. Detailed treatment of a few selected examples of representative features of Greek cult will make it possible both to explore the
evidence more fully and to convey a sense of the emotional content and
meaning that cult practice brought to Greek society. The main emphasis
is on cult practice from the third century BCE through the second century
CE, although some later Roman material is discussed.

CIVIC AND PANHELLENIC CULTS

Every Greek city acknowledged the presence of its own tutelary deities,
both the gods of Olympus and the deities and heroes with more local and
regional significance. The rhythm of civic life had long been punctuated
by regular offerings and festivals to honor these divine beings. These festivals, open to citizens, were organized and supported by the community
and conducted by priests who were regular citizens of the community.
Service as a priest was a civic duty that brought prestige to the participant;
some priesthoods were hereditary, while others were actively sought after
for the status they conferred.[4] Priesthoods could be held by both men and
women, with special priesthoods reserved for women, who normally held
them for a limited time and during a specific stage of their lives.[5]

Athens offers one well-documented example of cult practice in civic
life. During the Hellenistic and Roman eras, cult practice, as before, centered on the Acropolis and the Agora. The quadrennial celebration of the
Greater Panathenaia was still the most important civic festival, and provided an opportunity for Athenians to display their pride in their patron
goddess Athena. The new political realities, however, soon became apparent: the Panathenaia was occasionally omitted when warfare or other
forms of civic stress prevented it, and increasingly the expense of produc-
ing the Panathenaia was borne not by the city, but by individual donors
such as Hellenistic monarchs.[6] Royal patronage also contributed to the

---

[4] Clinton, "Eleusis and the Romans," 169–74, gives examples of hereditary priesthoods at Eleusis
that continued into the Roman period. An inscription of the third century BCE from Erythrae, in
Asia Minor, details the sale of priesthoods (in Engelmann and Merkelbach, *Inschriften von Erythrai*,
287–327, no. 201); most cost a considerable sum of money and formed a source of profit to the civic
government.

[5] Connelly, *Priestess*, 27–55.

[6] On changes in the Panathenaea, see Mikalson, *Religion in Hellenistic Athens*, 99–101, 108–10
(Panathenaea canceled in 286 and 282 BCE), 196–9.

construction of the grandiose temple of Zeus Olympios, supported by the Seleucid monarch Antiochus IV.[7] The new political realities of the Hellenistic era resulted in further changes in cult practice in rural Attica. The gods and heroes of Attica still exerted their presence in Attic life, but the role of the deme, the rural district or village, in the religious life of the average Athenian diminished sharply in the third century BCE and disappeared in the second.[8] With this ends the series of deme calendars with their richly detailed lists of sacrifices and group obligations. The average rural resident of Attica may well have retained his sense of affinity with regional shrines, but there was little organizational or financial structure in the Hellenistic and Roman eras to encourage the cult rituals that had been supported by membership in a deme or genos (ancestral clan group).

During the Roman imperial period, a major innovation in Athenian cult practice was the introduction of the Roman imperial cult (discussed in greater detail below), which became a conspicuous feature on the Acropolis and in the Agora. The status of the Agora as a cult center was also reinforced by the placement of older cult structures in its center, including the altar of Zeus Agoraios and the temple of Ares. While this development has been attributed to the impoverishment of the Attic countryside, it more likely reflects Augustus's decision to enhance the status of the Agora as a sacred museum of religious art and architecture, paralleling the Augustan use of Athenian models in Rome.[9] The new prominence of the temple of Ares may also suggest the higher prestige accorded by the Romans to the cult of the god Mars.[10]

Civic cult in Corinth, in contrast, reflected the discontinuity of its history during the Hellenistic and Roman periods.[11] Hellenistic Corinth was a venerable Greek city with a rich range of temples and shrines, including cults of well-established Olympian deities like Apollo, Athena, and Zeus, and cults with strong local connections, such as the shrines for the children of Medea and several Corinthian heroes. There were also prominent sanctuaries outside the city, including that of Demeter and Kore on the slope of Acrocorinth and of Aphrodite on its height. Many of these shrines were destroyed in the sack of Corinth by Mummius in 146 BCE. When the city was refounded in 44 BCE, a new series of cults was initiated, reflecting the concerns of the new Roman settlers. These

[7] Mikalson, *Religion in Hellenistic Athens*, 200.
[8] Parker, *Athenian Religion*, 264.
[9] On transplanted temples, see Thompson, *Athenian Agora* XIV, 160–8; on the Agora in the Augustan period, Walker, "Athens under Augustus," 69–72.
[10] Spawforth, "Early Reception," 193. See also Alcock, *Graecia Capta*, 195–6.
[11] Bookidis, "Religion in Corinth," 141–64.

include cults connected with official imperial patronage, such as Apollo (protector of Augustus), Venus, and the imperial cult, and cults of Greek deities that meant much to the Romans, including Asclepius, Demeter, and Kore. Some cults with a distinctively Corinthian identity, like that of Medea's children, seem to have been preserved primarily for their nostalgia value.[12]

Ephesus furnishes a good example of civic cult practice in Asia Minor. Ephesus had long been celebrated for its sanctuary of Artemis, for whom a magnificent new temple was built in the later fourth century BCE after the older one was burned down.[13] The Artemis sanctuary and its distinctive cult image continued to play a major role in the religious life of the newly refounded Hellenistic city, along with cults for many other divinities, including Zeus, Athena, Aphrodite, Apollo, Hephaestus, Dionysus, Demeter, Asclepius, and the Egyptian deities Isis and Serapis.[14] The Anatolian Mother-goddess retained an important shrine on the slope of the mountain east of the city.[15] These cults continued to flourish during the Roman-period city as well, although the evidence for them comes largely from epigraphical and sculptural evidence; few actual temples and sanctuaries have been found. The most prominent sanctuaries in the Roman city were connected with the imperial cult, particularly in the upper Agora.[16] They provide vivid evidence for Ephesus's status as the capital of the province of Asia, and for the dominant role played by imperial freedmen and Roman emissaries in the religious life of the city.

The civic cults of Pergamum offer a different model of cult practice in an Asiatic city. As the center of a new Hellenistic monarchy, the Pergamene kings placed their city under the protection of the gods, especially Athena Polias, who was given pride of place on the acropolis. Cults of major Olympian gods, including Zeus, Demeter, and Dionysus, were also established in the city.[17] The altar of Zeus on the Hellenistic acropolis may represent cult honors to both Zeus and the Pergamene hero Telephos, the mythical city founder.[18] The pre-Greek cult traditions of the region also left a mark on the city; the Anatolian Mother-goddess and her consort Attis received a prominent shrine near the entrance to the acropolis, and

---

[12] Pausanias 2.3.7.
[13] Knibbe, "Via Sacra Ephesiaca," 141–54.
[14] Knibbe, "Nicht nur die Stadt Artemis"; Walters, "Egyptian Religions," 281–311.
[15] Knibbe, "Via Sacra Ephesiaca," 142–3; Roller, *God the Mother*, 200–2.
[16] Scherrer, "Historical Topography of Ephesos," 69–71, 74–8.
[17] Ohlemutz, *Kulte in Pergamon*; Radt, "Urban Development," 48, 53.
[18] Stähler, "Pergamonaltar."

in mountain sanctuaries nearby.[19] There were also provisions for the ruler cult of the Attalid monarchs.

The cults of Roman Pergamon were even more varied. The older sanctuaries of Athena, Demeter, and Dionysus continued to be important in the city, while a new sanctuary came to dominate the acropolis, dedicated jointly to Zeus Philios and the Roman emperor Trajan.[20] Noteworthy sanctuaries were also erected in the lower city. One, the Roman-period Asklepieion, was a revival of an older cult; its magnificent complex, which included facilities for the god's healing cult and a theater, gained wide renown for Pergamon.[21] The impressive sanctuary of the Egyptian deities Isis and Sarapis, the so-called Red Hall, was a new foundation, representative of the popular appeal of Egyptian deities in Asia Minor and indeed throughout the eastern Mediterranean.[22] All of these structures, built during the second century CE, attest to the prosperity of the city and the desire of the citizens to use their wealth to advertise cult affiliations.

In addition to cults and sanctuaries supported by individual cities, the major panhellenic sanctuaries in Greece lost little of their luster during the Hellenistic and Roman periods. The celebration of the Olympic Games remained unbroken until the closure of the games in 396 CE. The fabled chryselephantine cult statue of Zeus continued to excite admiration: the orator Quintilian (*Inst.* 12.10.9) stated that the statue added something to the conventional religion, while the orator Dio Chrysostom (*Or.* 12.25) praised it as the work most dear to the gods. Changed political realities were evident; the Philippeion at Olympia, gift of Philip II, father of Alexander, attests to the impact of the Macedonian rule, while the Metroon, the temple of Rhea, mother of Zeus, was furnished with statues of Roman emperors. The sanctuary of Apollo at Delphi also continued as one of the most prominent oracular shrines in the Greek world, although its influence on political affairs was noticeably less prominent (see more on this later in this chapter).

VOLUNTARY CULT ASSOCIATIONS

In addition to cults administered by civic and panhellenic authorities, many individual groups were formed to celebrate cult rituals. Known primarily

---

[19] Roller, *God the Mother*, 206–12.
[20] Radt, "Urban Development of Pergamon," 49; Schowalter, "Zeus Philios and Trajan Temple," 233–49. See also n. 75 on the imperial cult.
[21] Hoffman, "Asklepieion," 41–59.
[22] Nohlen, "Red Hall," 81–3. On Egyptian deities in Asia Minor, see Koester, "Egyptian Deities," 111–33.

through inscriptions that describe the obligations of their members, these groups constituted an increasingly vital part of Greek religious life. Documentation from the Piraeus, the port city of Athens, describes several such cult groups, called *orgeōnes* and *thiasoi*.²³ Because they fell outside the structures for conducting Greek civic cults, cults for deities of non-Greek origin were often administered in this way. The cult of the Thracian deity Bendis furnishes a well-documented example. The worship of Bendis had been known in Athens since the fifth century BCE and became an increasingly prominent part of the city's religious life during the Hellenistic period. The Thracians resident in Attica received the right to own land and to establish a temple and conduct rites in honor of their goddess. These were special privileges not granted lightly to any group outside the Athenian citizen body, and their implementation needed the sanction of the oracle of Zeus at Dodona.²⁴ Plato's vivid description of the festival of Bendis conveys some of the emotional fervor of the goddess's rites (Plato, *Republic* 1), and also portrays the festive celebrations that involved both Thracians and Athenians. Another Attic cult administered by *orgeōnes* and *thiasoi* was the cult of Meter, the mother of the gods. While this deity, originally a Phrygian goddess, had long had a civic cult in the Athenian Agora, she also enjoyed a substantial following in the Piraeus during the Hellenistic period. The Piraeus group administered a separate cult whose members included Athenian citizens, noncitizens, and freedmen, all of whom seem to have been treated on equal footing in the context of the cult. Rites could include both the standard Greek practices of sacrifices and communal banquets, and rites that were specific to Meter and involved her consort Attis. Members also contributed to a common burial fund.²⁵ Membership in the cult offered a mix of religious observances and social activity.

There were also individual cult groups in Athens that honored Egyptian deities, primarily Isis, but also Serapis, Anubis, and Osiris.²⁶ The cult of Isis is first attested in the late fourth century BCE and continued through the early Roman period. This could have been initiated by an Egyptian emigrant community in Attica, but it may have resulted as well from Athenian commercial interests and from contact with emporia such as that on Delos, where Isis had a reputation as patroness of sailors.²⁷ Political motives also played a role: an inscription from the later first century BCE recording

²³ For a general discussion of individual cult groups in Athens, see Mikalson, *Religion in Hellenistic Athens*, 140–55.

²⁴ *IG* ii² 1283; Mikalson, *Religion in Hellenistic Athens*, 140–2.

²⁵ Roller, *God the Mother*, 218–24.

²⁶ Pollitt, "Egyptian Gods"; Mikalson, *Religion in Hellenistic Athens*, 275–7.

²⁷ On Isis in Athens and Delos, Mikalson, *Religion in Hellenistic Athens*, 276–7.

the cult of Isis in Athens may signify Athenian support for Antony and Cleopatra. Egyptian deities were worshipped during the Roman period also, as attested by a calendar of a local group recording sacrifices to Nephys and Osiris along with the Greek deities Demeter and Kore, Apollo and Artemis, Zeus, Poseidon, Dionysus, Cronus, and Heracles.[28] Clearly the traditional Olympic pantheon had broadened to include several deities not of Greek origin, whose presence reflected both political realities and personal needs.

Voluntary associations were also involved in the cults of established Hellenic divinities. A second-century-BCE text from the Piraeus describes a cult of Dionysus in which a father and son, both Attic citizens, were honored, the father as former priest and the son as the next holder of the priesthood; both gained these honors by contributing a substantial sum of money to the group.[29] This association did not supplant the civic cult of Dionysus in Athens, but rather served the group, whose members had monthly meetings to honor the god and undoubtedly to enjoy social conviviality. In some cult associations, the social life may have superseded the sacred activity. The cults administered by the Iobacchi in Athens are a well-documented example. Attested in an inscription of the second century CE, this seems to have been a men's club for an exclusive group of wealthy donors.[30] Deities honored by the Iobacchi included Dionysus, Kore, Palaemon, Aphrodite, and Proteurythmus (an otherwise unknown figure). The occasion of the inscription is the induction of Herodes Atticus, one of the wealthiest men in Greece, who was to take over the leadership of the group. The group was to meet monthly and hold regular festivities, including drinking wine; club members appointed as "horses" were to maintain order. Membership brought together social festivities, religious piety, and, for the priests, the potential for public prestige.

Individual cult could also be set up by the bequest of an individual donor to perpetuate the memory of the individual's family. A third-century-BCE inscription from the island of Thera is typical: it records that a generous sum of money was given by a woman named Epikteta to fund a cult honoring the Muses and the "heroes," a term used here to designate Epikteta's deceased husband and sons and presumably also Epikteta herself after her death.[31] The text describing the bequest makes it clear that the cult

---

[28] *IG* ii[2] 1367, Sokolowski, *Lois sacrées*, no. 52.

[29] *IG* ii[2] 1326; cf. *IG* ii[2] 1325.

[30] *IG* ii[2] 1368; Sokolowski, *Lois sacrées*, no. 51; translation and commentary by Tod, *Sidelights*, 85–93; discussion by Lane Fox, *Pagans and Christians*, 85–9.

[31] Laum, *Stiftungen*, II, 43; Sokolowski, *Lois sacrées*, 230–3, no. 135.

honoring this family was to be a lavish affair, one that lasted three days and included an elaborate feast.

MYSTERY CULTS

Another important form of religious experience was the mystery cult, so called because practitioners had undergone rites of initiation that required secrecy from them about the nature of those rites. Some mystery cults attracted a wide international following, while others were of local significance. Mystery cults were very widespread throughout the Greek-speaking Mediterranean world; even a rural district like Arcadia celebrated no fewer than thirteen mystery cults,[32] and comparable numbers probably existed in other regions of Greece. Older cults such as the Eleusinian mysteries continued to flourish during the Hellenistic and Roman eras, and there were also new foundations and revivals of older rituals. The deities most often associated with mystery cult were Demeter, goddess of agriculture, and her daughter Kore, but there were many others, including the unnamed Great Gods of Samothrace, and the Kabeiroi, worshipped on Lemnos and near Thebes.[33]

The mysteries of Demeter and Kore celebrated at Eleusis continued to be the most prominent and venerable of Greek mystery cults. Their presence brought prestige to Athens, which administered the rites.[34] Inevitably, the mysteries were affected by the politics of the age: powerful men such as Demetrius Poliorcetes were allowed to bypass the normal progression of rites of initiation and complete initiation into all grades of the mysteries within one day.[35] Many Romans of high rank were initiated into the mysteries also; among the noteworthy are Cicero and his friends Atticus and Appius Claudius Pulcher in the late Republic, and the emperors Augustus, Hadrian and his favorite Antinous, and Marcus Aurelius, along with the empresses Sabina and Faustina.[36] The Roman era witnessed extensive building activity in the sanctuary: an impressive Propylon was erected, along with extensive facilities such as hotels and baths for the large crowds of pilgrims. The Telesterion, the main hall of rituals, was rebuilt during the reign of the Roman emperor Marcus Aurelius after its

---

[32] Jost, "Mystery Cults in Arcadia," 143.
[33] Schachter, "Theban Kabiroi."
[34] Clinton, "Eleusinian Mysteries," 1500. Athens' benefits from the prestige of Eleusis, Isocrates, *Paneg.* 28–31; Xenophon, *Hell.* 6.3.4–6; *IG* ii² 1134.
[35] Plutarch, *Demetr.* 26.
[36] Clinton, "Eleusinian Mysteries," 1499–1539.

destruction in 170 CE, and the sanctuary remained in use until the sack of Alaric in 395 CE.[37]

The mysteries celebrated on the island of Samothrace offer a further example of a mystery cult with wide appeal. The Samothracian pantheon chiefly honored the *Megaloi Theoi*, the Great Gods, but also included a number of other deities, Greek and non-Greek.[38] The rites were held from at least the seventh century BCE, but an impressive set of cult structures from the Hellenistic period attests to the growing importance of the mysteries during this time and to their ability to attract adherents from many parts of the Greek world. Like the mysteries at Eleusis, the rites celebrated at Samothrace were held in strict secrecy; even the identity of the Great Gods is not entirely certain. Dancing seems to have been a key part of the rituals, and we hear of those who had reached a higher grade of initiation dancing ecstatically around the new initiates.[39] The mysteries seem to have had a special appeal to sailors and seafarers and attracted dedications for naval victories, such as the famed Nike of Samothrace, a Rhodian dedication. Samothrace too attracted powerful patrons: the Macedonian Philip II was initiated into the mysteries and important structures were donated by Ptolemy II and Arsinoë, wife of Lysimachus. There were also many prominent Roman initiates at Samothrace, although no emperors; Hadrian took a personal interest in the cult but was probably never initiated into it.[40] The mysteries of the Great Gods enjoyed a wide following beyond the island of Samothrace; followers of the Samothracian gods spread the rites throughout Greek cities in the eastern Mediterranean, and also to Thrace, the Black Sea region, and North Africa.[41]

In addition to mystery cults of long standing, new mystery cults became prominent. The mysteries celebrated at Andania in Messenia provide one example.[42] According to Pausanias, the Andanian mysteries traced their origin to the heroic age and the Messenian hero Kaukon, their founder. The tradition of the legendary past, however, may have been invoked to confer prestige and authority on a set of rites that were linked to the more recent history of Messenia and its liberation from Spartan rule in 371 BCE. Pausanias reports that the Messenian rites were derived from the Eleusinian

---

[37] Mylonas, *Eleusis*, 186.
[38] Burkert, *Greek Religion*, 283–5; Cole, *Theoi Megaloi*; Matsas, "Problems in Island Archaeology."
[39] Clinton, "Stages of Initiation," 61–70. Marconi, "*Choroi*, *Theōriai* and International Ambitions," 123–133.
[40] Plutarch, *Alex.* 2.2, initiation of Philip II; Cole, *Theoi Megaloi*, 22 (on Philip and Arsinoë), 87–103 (Romans at Samothrace). For a plan, see Clinton, "Stages of Initiation," 62, fig. 3.2.
[41] Cole, *Theoi Megaloi*, 57–86; also at Ilion, Lawall, "Sanctuary," 79.
[42] Pausanias 4.1.5–8; Guarducci, "I culti di Andania," 174–204; Graf, "Lesser Mysteries," 242–6.

mysteries and were dedicated to several deities, including Demeter and Kore, here called Hagne (the Pure One), Apollo Karneios, and Hermes; he also states that the mysteries, whose contents he would not divulge, were second in holiness only to the Eleusinian rites.[43] Pausanias's information is augmented by a lengthy inscription of 92/1 BCE, after Messenia came under Roman control.[44] According to this text, the mysteries were celebrated for the Megaloi Theoi (the Great Gods), Demeter, Hermes, Apollo Karneios, and Hagne. The text offers rich detail on issues such as cult administration, acquisition of animals for sacrifice, and musicians. A strict code of behavior and dress was prescribed for the participants, along with regulations limiting the types of lodging available during the ritual period; methods of accounting for the money were also spelled out. There is, however, no information about the actual rituals; these were clearly much too sacred to reveal in a public document.

These descriptions of processions and sacrifices and dispersal of funds convey the importance that the Greeks attached to mystery cults but do little to explain why people found them so moving. Yet the frequency, ubiquity, and richness of the documentation on mystery cults indicate that their rites became, if anything, even more important to people during the Hellenistic and Roman periods. In part, this may reflect the fact that mystery cults were open to all who were willing to undergo the rites of initiation. Several of them drew adherents from places far from their location, and many were open to non-Greeks; the Andanian mystery regulations contain comments about the role of slave initiates, although the greater severity of punishment for slaves who broke the rules clearly implies that even here a slave initiate retained his inferior status. But apart from the more fluid social groups that mystery cults encouraged, we sense that the mysteries offered some form of deep emotional experience that people found satisfying. The comments of Dio Chrysostom (*Or.* 12.33) on the spiritual insight gained from the mystery rites are revealing:

If one would bring a man, Greek or barbarian, for initiation into a mystic recess of overwhelming beauty and size, so that he would behold many mystic views and hear many sounds of the kind, with darkness and light appearing in sudden changes and other innumerable things happening, ... would it be possible that such a man should experience just nothing in his soul, that he should not come to surmise that there is some wiser insight and plan in all that is going on, even if he were one of the most remote and nameless barbarians?

[43] Pausanias 4.33.4–6.
[44] *SIG³* 736; Sokolowski, *Lois sacrées*, no. 65.

Indeed, the term *epopteia*, or seeing, was used to describe the more advanced stage of initiation rites. The statement in the early Homeric Hymn to Demeter, that the man who had seen the Eleusinian mysteries was blessed and would not fear death, implies a personal experience of a profound nature. This sentiment was reiterated in the first century BCE by Cicero (*De legibus* 2.14.26):

For by means of these mysteries ... we have learned the fundamentals of life, and have grasped the principle not only of living with joy but also of dying with better hope.

This promise of hope and inviolability remained a forceful and meaningful part of the Greek religious experience until the end of Antiquity.

ORACLES

The practice of divination, or consulting a deity for guidance about the unknown, had a long and respected tradition in the Greek world, and that tradition continued during the Hellenistic and Roman eras. Subtle changes can be noted, however; some oracular shrines that had earlier had a history of involvement in affairs of state became less influential, while others gained prominence. Reasons for these developments lie in political grounds: because the independent city-state was no longer the principal unit of political organization, there was little need for a divinely mandated institution that mediated between states. The geographical focus shifted also, as oracular sanctuaries in Asia Minor became more prominent, reflecting the greater political patronage and economic resources that they enjoyed during the Hellenistic and Roman eras.

Several oracular sanctuaries on mainland Greece, like the oracle of Zeus at Dodona and the Boiotian sanctuary of Apollo Ptoios, continued to exert influence, but the most prestigious oracle in the Greek world remained the oracle of Apollo at Delphi. Regular inquiries to the god continued unabated in the Hellenistic and Roman eras, as the inscriptional record, both in Delphi and in the inquirer's home community, indicates; however, the nature of these inquiries suggests that the oracle was consulted primarily about religious, not political, questions.[45] There are a few noteworthy exceptions: the Romans consulted Delphi in 216 BCE, on the occasion of their early defeats in the Second Punic War, and again in 204 BCE,

---

[45] Fontenrose, "Delphic Oracle," 244–354, lists historical and quasi-historical responses continuing until the fourth century CE. Parker, "Greek States and Greek Oracles," 101–5.

to clarify the command from the Sibylline Books to bring the Anatolian Mother-goddess, the Magna Mater, to Rome.[46] Numerous inscriptions also demonstrate the prestige of Apollo as a witness in the establishment of asylum and the manumission of slaves. The reality of Hellenistic power politics can be seen in dedications by the Pergamene kings Attalus I and Eumenes II, and by the Roman general Aemilius Paullus, to celebrate his victory over the Macedonians in 168 BCE. The majority of the questions to the oracle, however, are less concerned with political matters than with the establishment of cult rituals and shrines for deities and heroes in the inquirer's home community. Decisions about inter-state relations lay in the hands of Hellenistic monarchs, as a telling passage about Demetrius Poliorcetes makes clear: instead of Delphi, a petition was sent to Demetrius and the king's pronouncements were considered "oracles."[47] Even Plutarch, a priest of the oracle at Delphi, was conscious of the oracle's loss of political influence.[48]

In addition to Delphi, there were several oracular sanctuaries of Apollo in western Asia Minor, and these enjoyed a marked revival. The sanctuary at Didyma provides an excellent illustration. The sanctuary, about 20km south of Miletus and controlled by that city, had been an important cult center during the Archaic period. Its fortunes waned when western Asia Minor came under Persian control, then rose again with the liberation of the Greek cities by Alexander of Macedon. In the early third century, a magnificent new temple to Apollo, largest in the Greek world, was begun under the patronage of the Seleucid kings; after a lapse of several centuries, its construction was further advanced by Hadrian, but it was never fully completed. The building is an imposing testimony to the strength of the oracle. The main structure is an unroofed shell that surrounds a small shrine and sacred spring; its exterior is marked by a theatrical arrangement of steps, platforms, and towers that allowed the priests to address a crowd gathered on the steps of the building. The sanctuary of Apollo at Claros is a product of similar circumstances. This sanctuary, under the control of the Ionian Greek city of Kolophon, also had a local following in the early Archaic period, but its main period of prominence began in the third century BCE with the construction of a new temple dedicated to Apollo, Artemis, and Leto, and other facilities to support the sacred oracular spring and shrine. A propylon added visual magnificence. As at

[46] On the Punic Wars: Plutarch, *Fab.* 18.3; Appian, *Hann.* 5.27. On the Magna Mater: Livy 29.11.5–6.
[47] Plutarch, *Demetr.* 13. Parker, *Athenian Religion*, 103.
[48] Plutarch, *Obsolescence of Oracles. Moralia* 5.408–38.

Didyma, the sanctuary was provided with structures that contributed a theatrical element to the delivery of the god's oracles – in this case, vaulted underground structures.[49] As the vivid description of Iamblichus makes clear, the consultations took place at night, and the journey in the dark to the god's underground oracle added a heightened sense of drama to the proceedings.[50]

Petitioners came to both Didyma and Claros from great distances, attesting to the prestige of both oracles. The delegations to Claros were often accompanied by a choir of children, and the varied ages and character of the group must have taken on the air of a religious pilgrimage.[51] At Claros, petitioners were delegates of cities, while at Didyma most of the inscribed oracles are responses to individuals. No oracular texts from Claros survive,[52] but we have oracles from Apollo at Claros that were inscribed in the delegation's home city; the oracle at Oenoanda, discussed below, furnishes a vivid example. Responses from the oracle at Didyma were inscribed on stone, although the surviving total is roughly a tenth of those known from Delphi, suggesting that even with imperial patronage, Didyma did not surpass the prestige of Apollo's oldest and best-known oracle.[53] The responses from Didyma cover a wide spectrum of topics, including political issues and cult administration. One telling example that illustrates the influence of Didyma comes from the reign of the Roman emperor Diocletian, who consulted the god to learn if he should pursue Christians; the god answered affirmatively.[54]

RULER CULT

Cult honoring a monarch or emperor was a phenomenon that appeared in the Greek world with the power of Alexander of Macedon and lasted until the Christianization of the Roman empire. The concept of cult for a living or recently deceased person was not entirely new, for such honors had been given to several successful military commanders in the fifth century BCE.[55] Cult honors paid to a living ruler, though, were something different

---

[49] Parke, *Oracles of Apollo*, 137–9.
[50] Iamblichus, *On the Mysteries*, 3.11.
[51] Robert, *La Carie*, 214–16; Lane Fox, *Pagans and Christians*, 177–80.
[52] Parke, *Oracles of Asia Minor*, 205; Lane Fox, *Pagans and Christians*, 180.
[53] Fontenrose, *Didyma*, 86, 179–244, lists 61 recorded responses from Didyma, in contrast to 535 from Delphi.
[54] Lactantius, *Mort.* 11. 7; Fontenrose, *Didyma*, 206.
[55] Heroic honors for Miltiades in the Chersonesos (Hdt. 6.38), Brasidas in Amphipolis (Thuc. 5.11); divine honors for Lysander on Samos, Duris, *FGrHist* 76 F 71 and F 26; Habicht, *Gottmenschentum*, 3–6.

in both concept and scale. Such cults became a way for Greek cities to acknowledge the power of an outside ruler, frequently one who had been a special benefactor to the community.[56]

The cult of a ruler became a forceful presence in the Greek world with the prominence of Alexander and the exceptional nature of his accomplishments. Alexander's visit to the oracle of Zeus Ammon in Siwah had prepared the way for his acceptance as a son of Zeus,[57] and divine honors soon followed. Divine cult to Alexander was established in a number of Greek cities in Asia Minor in gratitude for their liberation from Persian rule.[58] On the Greek mainland, divine cult appears after Alexander's death, and did not always meet with approval, as the disparaging comment by the orator Hyperides illustrates: "We [Athenian citizens] are forced now to accept sacrifices for men, and statues and temples and altars are established for both gods and men."[59] Yet the reality of Macedonian politics not only encouraged such cult but made it desirable. Only twenty years after Alexander's death, the Macedonian commander Demetrius Poliorcetes was honored with divine cult by the Athenians. A hymn to Demetrius from the early third century BCE helps convey the sentiment behind this: "The other gods are far away or do not have ears or do not exist or do not pay attention to us, but you are present among us, not of wood or stone, but real."[60] The cult of the ruler was not created solely for political expediency, but was a genuine expression of support and gratitude.

This concept reappears regularly in the cults of Hellenistic rulers. Ruler cult was not a routine, birth-to-death ritual automatically given to every sovereign on the pharaonic Egyptian model, but was an honor given to individual monarchs from individual Greek cities in appreciation of special benefits. Thus, Antiochus III of Syria was awarded an altar in 197 BCE by the city of Iasos in Asia Minor, in thanks for liberating the city from Philip V of Macedon. Similar cult and sacrifices were paid to his wife Laodike III, who among other things endowed a fund to provide dowries for poor girls in the city.[61] In Teos, in Asia Minor, a cult for Antiochus III and his wife Laodike was established in the temple of Dionysus. Cult statues of the king and queen stood next to those of the god; an inscription explains this: "by sharing in the temple and other matters with Dionysus, they (the king

---

[56] See the discussion in Price, *Rituals and Power*, 25–40.

[57] Bosworth, "Alexander and Ammon."

[58] Habicht, *Gottmenschtum*, 17–25.

[59] Hyperides, *Epitaphios*, 8.21–2. Badian, "Deification," favors Athenian worship of the living Alexander; Cawkwell, "Deification," argues against it.

[60] Athenaeus, *Deipn.* 6.253.

[61] Price, *Rituals and Power*, 30.

and queen) should become the common saviors of our city and should give us benefits in common."[62] Such sentiments help us understand how a living flesh-and-blood human being could be viewed on par with the traditional gods of the Hellenic pantheon; just as the divinity of the gods was manifest through their power to help or hurt mankind, so the same status was accorded a powerful human figure. Ruler cult could also vanish with the disappearance of power. Cult to Philip V of Macedon was formally ended in Athens after the Athenians broke their alliance with him, and cult to Antiochus III ended with his defeat by the Romans and the Peace of Apamea in 188 BCE.[63]

The ruler cult for Hellenistic kings took on a more potent dimension when Greece and Asia Minor came under Roman control in the second century BCE. Cult for the goddess Roma was established, and several outstanding Romans were worshipped as deities; Mark Antony and his wife Octavia, for example, received divine cult at Eleusis.[64] The whole concept of ruler cult, however, changed markedly with the accession of the emperor Augustus. Greece and Asia Minor had supported Mark Antony in his struggle against Octavian, and so the supremacy of the successful ruler of the Mediterranean world had to be acknowledged.[65] While Augustus was given the title of *divus* in Rome only after his death in 14 CE, cult honors for Octavian/Augustus were initiated by the Greek cities in Asia in 29 BCE, shortly after the battle of Actium. The new emperor insisted that the cult be dedicated both to Roma and Sebastos (Augustus), probably to avoid the image of self-aggrandizement that had been associated with Mark Antony. Yet it is clear that Augustus himself was the cult's principal subject. In documents dated to 9 BCE, the Roman proconsul of Asia described Augustus as "most divine," and the cities of Asia followed suit, praising Augustus as a god and savior who ended war and established all good things for the people.[66]

It would be easy to dismiss the imperial cult as an empty gesture of flattery or a calculated statement of political expediency.[67] Recognizing the new master of the Roman world, however, was more than a matter of expediency. Both Greece and Asia Minor had undergone a tumultuous period of warfare and impoverishment in the first century CE. The

---

[62] Ibid., 30–1.
[63] Ibid., 30–40.
[64] Mellor, *Worship of Goddess Roma*; Clinton, "Eleusis and the Romans," 165.
[65] Friesen, *Twice Neokoros*, 7–15.
[66] Sherk, *Roman Documents*, 328–37, no. 65; Price, *Rituals and Power*, 54–5.
[67] As Mellor, *Worship of Goddess Roma*, 21–2, does.

advent of Augustus brought stability and prosperity that deserved the thanks owed to a divinity. Moreover, the enthusiastic response to the cult of the emperor continued beyond Augustus to many of his successors. In some cases, the emperor personally requested worship; the emperor Gaius (Caligula) demanded divine cult, an action not inconsistent with his unstable character, but Hadrian also established new shrines or rededicated older ones to himself during his travels in Greece and Asia Minor.[68] Usually, though, the initiative came from the Greek East, and the physical presence of the emperor was not necessary. Cities in Greece, and more especially in Asia Minor, openly competed for the honor of establishing a cult of the emperor, applying to the imperial house in Rome for permission to establish a cult shrine and/or an honorific statue.[69] It was considered a privilege when such requests were granted.

In addition to the encomium of the texts, the monuments created for the imperial cult convey its importance and intensity. In some cases, monuments celebrating the Roman emperors appropriated space within pre-existing cult structures. The fourth-century-BCE Metroon in Olympia housed statues of emperors and imperial family members from the Julio-Claudian and Flavian dynasties; Augustus as Zeus was given the position of honor.[70] In Athens too, the imperial cult appears among venerable monuments of the Classical era: a temple to Augustus and Roma was erected on the Acropolis, and the priest of the cult of Augustus was given a special seat of honor in the Theater of Dionysus. In the Agora, a statue of Tiberius was placed in front of the Stoa of Attalus, and the imperial cult was incorporated into the temple of Apollo Patroos and the stoa of Zeus.[71] A cult to Hadrian was added to the temple of Zeus Olympios in Athens, which the emperor was responsible for finishing.[72] In Corinth, the imperial cult was integrated into the buildings of the new Roman Forum, including a basilica and market as well as temples designated for this purpose.[73] In Asia Minor, the cult of Antoninus and Faustina was placed in the venerable temple of Artemis at Sardis, while a shrine to the imperial cult was added to the Asklepieion at Pergamum.

[68] Price, *Rituals and Power*, 68–9, 244–5.
[69] Tacitus, *Ann.* 4.55–6; Mellor, *Worship of Goddess Roma*, 14–15; Friesen, *Twice Neokoros*, 18–21, 49.
[70] Pausanias 5.20.9; Price, *Rituals and Power*, 160, fig. 9. Alcock, *Graecia Capta*, 189–91. These were honorific statues, not cult images, Price, *Rituals and Power*, 179.
[71] Hoff, "Athenian Imperial Cult"; Spawforth, "Early Reception," 183–6; Clinton, "Eleusis and the Romans," 168–9. On the imperial cult in Greece, see Alcock, *Graecia Capta*, 181–91.
[72] Wycherley, *Stones*, 162–5.
[73] Walbank, "Imperial cult in Corinth"; Bookidis, "Religion in Corinth," 156–7.

Even more striking were altars, shrines, and temples that were constructed specifically for the imperial cult. Asia Minor is particularly rich in this regard. The temple of Augustus and Rome was and still is a conspicuous feature of Roman Ancyra (Ankara). Ephesus had several such cult installations, including a temple to Domitian and the great Antonine altar with its elaborate sculpted frieze; the city proudly boasted that the cult of the Sebastoi (the imperial cult) was equal to that of Ephesian Artemis.[74] In Pergamum, the temple dedicated by Hadrian to Trajan occupied the most conspicuous point of the acropolis, and formed the focal point for the orientation of the rebuilt Roman city.[75] The extensive array of monuments devoted to the imperial cult in Asia Minor vividly illustrates its importance to the social and religious life of this region.

SURVIVALS OF PRE-GREEK ANATOLIAN CULTS AND SHRINES

Along with a wide range of Greek cults, Asia Minor was also home to a number of religious cults of the pre-Greek peoples who had dominated the region for many centuries before the advent of Greek influence. While these peoples, including the Carians, Mysians, Lydians, Lycians, and Phrygians, had long since lost their political independence and, in most cases, their native languages,[76] many sanctuaries and cults of traditional Anatolian deities were still in evidence as late as the fourth century CE.

In some cases, the Anatolian deity was identified with a Greek deity, with only an epithet or distinctive attribute to give evidence of a pre-Greek identity. The best example is the dominant male deity, who was identified with the Greek Zeus and addressed with a wide variety of regional epithets in Phrygia, Lycia, Lydia, Caria, and Galatia.[77] Others retained their Anatolian name. The Anatolian Mother-goddess Matar, or Meter in Greek, was widely worshipped throughout Asia Minor. Sanctuaries to her existed both at long-established cult centers such as Midas City in Phrygia and Pessinous in Galatia and at many smaller local shrines, where regional epithets stress her association with a specific place.[78] An interesting melding of

---

[74] Friesen, *Twice Neokoros*, 56–7.

[75] These are but a few of the best known examples. Price, *Rituals and Power*, 249–74, gives a complete list. On the temple of Trajan at Pergamum, see Radt, "Urban Development," 49–50.

[76] Epigraphical texts in the Phrygian language continued to be written until the second or early third centuries CE; see Haas, *Sprachdenkmäler*; Lubotsky, "Phrygian Inscription," 115–30; Brixhe, "Interactions," 246–66.

[77] Mitchell, *Anatolia*, II, 22–4. Note also the cult of Zeus Sabazios (see Roller, "Sabazios") and the cults of Zeus Alsenos, Zeus Petarenos, Zeus Ampeleites, and Zeus Thallos (see Drew-Bear, Thomas, and Yildizturan, *Phrygian Votive Steles*).

[78] Mitchell, *Anatolia*, II, 19–22; Roller, *God the Mother*, 334–43.

314 Lynn E. Roller

the cults of Zeus and Meter is found at Aizanoi in Phrygia; here a striking pseudodipteral Greek temple, constructed during the Flavian period, was dedicated to Zeus, while a shrine in a nearby cave was dedicated to Meter, recalling the goddess's traditional association with caves and hollows.[79] Another traditional Anatolian deity widely worshipped in Roman Asia Minor was Men. A prominent sanctuary dedicated to him near Pisidian Antioch includes two impressive temples and more than twenty small houses for worshippers' banquets. His cult had long been important in Lydia, and is also attested in the regions of Phrygia and Lycaonia.[80]

Anatolian cult practice also gave a prominent position to deities that represented ethical values. One example is the divine pair Hosios and Dikaios, the gods Holy and Just. Often shown holding a balance symbolizing the scales of justice, the pair is frequently depicted as two male figures, although a female counterpart, Hosia, is also known.[81] They could be worshipped jointly with deities such as Meter and Apollo, stressing the local connection of these Hellenized deities to traditional Anatolian cults and values. Other deities whose cult reflects a concept of divinity based on ethics and moral values include Theos Hypsistos, the Highest God, object of many dedications in the second and third centuries CE in central Anatolia; Helios, the Sun, the deity whose rays see all; and Aither, the air.[82] The gods were considered a powerful force for inflicting divine justice and retribution on those who did not live up to expected standards of integrity. This is vividly illustrated by a series of texts known as confession inscriptions, from the region near the Lydian-Phrygian border zone, where both anthropomorphic deities and personifications combined to uphold justice.[83]

As a final example, we may note an inscription from Oenoanda in northern Lycia. The text, a response to a question posed to the oracle of Apollo at Claros, defined the nature of god:

Self-born, untaught, motherless, unshakeable,
Giving place to no name, many-named, dwelling in fire,
Such is god: we are a portion of god, his angels.
This, then, to the questioners about god's nature

---

[79] Roller, *God the Mother*, 336–41; Rheidt, *Aizanoi und Anatolien*, 18–19; Jes, Posamentir, and Wörrle, "Das Tempel des Zeus in Aizanoi."

[80] Mitchell, *Anatolia*, I, 191; II, 24–5.

[81] Ricl, "Hosios kai Dikaios, Premiere partie." 1–69; idem, "Hosios kai Dikaios, Seconde partie," 71–103; Mitchell, *Anatolia*, II, 25–6.

[82] Mitchell, *Anatolia*, II, 43–6; Mitchell, "Theos Hypsistos."

[83] Petzl, *Die Beichtinschriften Westkleinasiens*; Chaniotis, "Watchful Eyes."

The god replied, calling him all-seeing Aither: to him, then, look
And pray at dawn, looking out to the east.[84]

The text illustrates the strength of traditional Greek practices such as prayer and sacrifice as applied to all deities, seen and unseen, named and unnamed.

CONCLUSION

The evidence for the religious life of Greece and Asia Minor during the Hellenistic and Roman periods is diverse and diffuse, but several patterns emerge. Taken together, they produce a picture of a dynamic and active tradition of cult practice that was fundamental to the ways in which people lived their lives and viewed themselves in the social, political, and cosmic hierarchy. One key part of the picture is continuity. Places that had been considered sacred well before the Hellenistic era remained sacred until Late Antiquity; this could include sites such as the oracle of Apollo at Delphi and the Eleusinian Mysteries, where the tradition of cult practice remained unbroken, and also sites such as the oracle of Apollo at Didyma, which underwent a significant revival during the Hellenistic and Roman eras. The sense of continuity was not static, for cults could and did respond to shifting political and social circumstances as needed. Athens provides an excellent example of this: the cults of the Athenian Agora, including the Panathenaic Procession that had been practiced since the first half of the first millennium BCE, continued even as a new temple to Ares and a center for the imperial cult, both reflecting an increased Roman presence, were established in the center of the Agora. The city of Pergamum continued to honor the cults of Athena and Demeter, established by the Attalid monarchs, but also incorporated a major new cult structure dedicated to Isis and Serapis into the city. Overall, a sense of sanctity associated with a deity's territory was an enduring feature of the religious experience.

Another key part of the polytheistic cult system was its openness and adaptability to change. As the Greek cities in Greece and Asia Minor came under the dominance of Hellenistic monarchies and later of the Roman empire, the cult of rulers became an increasingly important element of the religious experience, offering cities a means to honor a living or deceased

---

[84] On the Oenoanda text, see Robert, "Oracle." I follow the translation of Lane Fox, *Pagans and Christians*, 169. On its relationship to Claros and Didyma, see Lane Fox, *Pagans and Christians*, 168–77; Mitchell, *Anatolia*, II, 44.

ruler and to increase their status and visibility. These honors did not replace honors due to the gods, and were often combined with them, such as the cult of Zeus Philios and the emperor Trajan at Pergamum. Honors due to a ruler were not a one-way street, for several emperors were active patrons of traditional Greek cults and festivals. Hadrian was particularly conspicuous in this regard, donating funds to the sanctuary of Zeus Olympios in Athens and the sanctuary of Apollo in Didyma and completing the rites of initiation at Eleusis. On a more personal level, voluntary cult associations became an increasingly prominent part of the spectrum of religious activities. These could be formed to administer rituals for deities from outside the Greek world, such as Bendis, the Phrygian Mother, and Isis and Osiris, and also became a way for individuals to honor traditional Greek deities within a setting that encouraged social interactions between fellow members of the association.

The evidence also provides a vivid picture of different levels of engagement with cult activities. As members of a political community, citizens participated in rituals of their city's deities even as they joined individual cult groups. People took part in public festivals and public sacrifices that were open to all, while some chose to undergo rites of initiation in mystery cults that offered meaningful spiritual experiences on an individual level. The open system of polytheism permitted – even encouraged – such flexibility. Throughout this variegated picture, the one constant is the importance of cult practice for the individual and the community. The text from Oenoanda summarizes this sense of regular interaction with the gods: "Unnamed and many named, such is god, and we are a portion of god." It encapsulates a key feature of Greek religious practice – namely, the deeply rooted sense that deity, whether one specific deity or an abstract concept of divinity, was the center of human existence.

BIBLIOGRAPHY

Alcock, Susan E. *Graecia Capta: The Landscapes of Roman Greece* (Cambridge, 1993).
Badian, Ernst. "The Deification of Alexander the Great." In *Ancient Macedonian Studies in Honor of Charles F. Edson*, ed. Harry J. Dell (Thessaloniki, 1981): 27–71.
Bookidis, Nancy. "Religion in Corinth: 146 B.C.E. to 100 C.E." In *Urban Religion in Roman Corinth*, eds. Daniel N. Schowalter and Steven J. Friesen (Cambridge, Mass., 2005): 141–64.
Bosworth, A. B. "Alexander and Ammon." In *Greece and the Eastern Mediterranean in Ancient History and Prehistory: Studies presented to Fritz Schachermeyr on the Occasion of his Eightieth Birthday*, ed. Konrad H. Kinzl (Berlin, 1977): 51–75.
Bremmer, Jan N. *Greek Religion.* (Oxford, 1994).

Brixhe, Claude. "Interactions between Greek and Phrygian under the Roman Empire." In *Bilingualism in Ancient Society: Language Contact and the Written Text*, eds. J. N. Adams, Mark Janse, and Simon Swain (Oxford, 2002): 246–66.

Burkert, Walter. *Greek Religion: Archaic and Classical.* Trans. John Raffan (Cambridge, Mass., 1985).

Cawkwell, G. L. "The deification of Alexander the Great: a note." In *Ventures into Greek History*, ed. Ian Worthington (Oxford, 1994): 293–306.

Chaniotis, Angelos. "Under the watchful eyes of the gods: divine justice in Hellenistic and Roman Asia Minor." In *The Greco-Roman East: Politics, Culture, Society*, ed. Stephen Colvin (Cambridge, 2004): 1–43.

Clinton, Kevin. "The Eleusinian Mysteries: Roman Initiates and Benefactors, Second Century BC to AD 267." *ANRW* II.18.2 (Berlin, 1989): 1499–1539.

"Eleusis and the Romans: late Republic to Marcus Aurelius." In *The Romanization of Athens. Proceedings of an International Conference held at Lincoln, Nebraska (April, 1996)*, eds. Michael C. Hoff and Susan Rotroff (Exeter, 1997): 161–81.

"Stages of Initiation in the Eleusinian and Samothracian Mysteries." In *Greek Mysteries: The Archaeology and Ritual of Ancient Greek Secret Cults* (London, 2003): 50–78.

Cole, Susan Guettel. *Theoi Megaloi: The Cult of the Great Gods at Samothrace* (Leiden, 1984).

Connelly, Joan Breton. *Portrait of a Priestess: Women and Ritual in Ancient Greece* (Princeton, 2007).

Drew-Bear, Thomas, Christine Thomas, and Melek Yildizturan. *Phrygian Votive Steles* (Ankara, 1999).

Engelmann, Helmut, and Reinhold Merkelbach. *Die Inschriften von Erythrai und Klazomenai* (Bonn, 1973).

Fontenrose, Joseph. *The Delphic Oracle: Its Responses and Operations with a Catalogue of Responses* (Berkeley, 1978).

Didyma: Apollo's Oracle, Cult, and Companions (Berkeley, 1988).

Friesen, Steven J. *Twice Neokoros: Ephesos, Asia, and the Cult of the Flavian Imperial Family* (Leiden, 1993).

Geertz, Clifford. "Religion as a Cultural System." In *Anthropological Approaches to the Study of Religion*, ed. Michael Banton (New York, 1966): 1–46.

Graf, Fritz. "Lesser Mysteries – Not less mysterious." In *Greek Mysteries: The Archaeology and Ritual of Ancient Greek Secret Cults*, ed. Michael Cosmopoulos (London, 2003): 241–62.

Guarducci, Margherita. "I culti di Andania." *Studi e materiali di storia delle religioni* 10 (1934): 174–204.

Haas, Otto. *Die phrygischen Sprachdenkmäler* (Sofia, 1966).

Habicht, Christian. *Gottmenschentum und griechische Städte*, 2nd ed. (Munich, 1970).

Hoff, Michael C. "The politics and architecture of the Athenian imperial cult." In *Subject and Ruler: The Cult of the Ruling Power in Classical Antiquity*, ed. Alastair Small (Ann Arbor, Mich., 1996): 185–200.

Hoffman, Adolf. "The Roman Remodeling of the Asklepieion." In *Pergamon, Citadel of the Gods: Archaeological Record, Literary Description, and Religious Development*, ed. Helmut Koester (Harrisburg, Pa., 1998): 41–59.

Jes, Kai, Richard Posamentir, and Michael Wörrle. "Der Tempel des Zeus in Aizanoi und seine Datierung." In *Aizanoi und Anatolie*n, ed. Klaus Rheidt (Mainz, 2010): 58–87.

Jost, Madeleine. "Mystery Cults in Arcadia." In *Greek Mysteries: The Archaeology and Ritual of Ancient Greek Secret Cults*, ed. Michael Cosmopoulos (London, 2003): 143–68.

Knibbe, Dieter. "Ephesos – nicht nur die Stadt der Artemis." In *Studien zur Religion und Kultur Kleinasiens*, ed. Sencer Şahin, Elmar Schwertheim, and Jörg Wagner (Leiden, 1978): 489–503.

"Via Sacra Ephesiaca: New Aspects of the Cult of Artemis Ephesia." In *Ephesos: Metropolis of Asia*, ed. Helmut Koester (Cambridge, Mass., 1995): 141–54.

Koester, Helmut. "The Cult of the Egyptian Deities in Asia Minor." In *Pergamon, Citadel of the Gods: Archaeological Record, Literary Description, and Religious Development*, ed. Helmut Koester (Harrisburg, Pa., 1998): 111–33.

Lane Fox, Robin. *Pagans and Christians* (New York, 1987).

Laum, Bernhard. *Stiftungen in der griechischen und römischen Antike: Ein Beitrag zur antiken Kulturgeschichte* (Leipzig, 1914).

Lawall, Mark. "'In the Sanctuary of the Samothracian Gods': Myth, politics, and mystery cult at Ilion." In *Greek Mysteries: The Archaeology and Ritual of Ancient Greek Secret Cults*, ed. Michael Cosmopoulos (London, 2003): 79–111.

Lubotsky, A. "New Phrygian inscription No. 48: palaeographic and linguistic comments." *Frigi e Frigio. Atti del 1° Simposio Internazionale. Roma, 16–17 ottobre 1995* (Rome, 1997): 115–30.

Marconi, Clemente. "Choroi, Theōriai and International Ambitions: The Hall of Choral Dancers and its Frieze." In *Samothracian Connections: Essays in honor of James R. McCredie*, eds. Olga Palagia and Bonna D. Wescoat (Oxford and Oakville, 2010): 106–135.

Matsas, Dimitris. "Problems in Island Archaeology: Towards an Archaeology of Religion on Samothrace." In *Samothracian Connections: Essays in honor of James R. McCredie*, eds. Olga Palagia and Bonna D. Wescoat (Oxford and Oakville, 2010): 33–49.

Mellor, Ronald. ΘΕΑ ῬΩΜΗ: *The Worship of the Goddess Roma in the Greek World* (Göttingen, 1975).

Mikalson, Jon. *Religion in Hellenistic Athens* (Berkeley, 1998).

Mitchell, Stephen. *Anatolia: Land, Men, and Gods in Asia Minor*. Vol. 1: *The Celts and the Impact of Roman Rule*. Vol. 2: *The Rise of the Church* (Oxford, 1993).

"The Cult of Theos Hypsistos between Pagans, Jews, and Christians." In *Pagan Monotheism in Late Antiquity*, eds. Polymnia Athanassiadi and Michael Frede (Oxford, 1999): 81–148.

Mylonas, George. *Eleusis and the Eleusinian Mysteries* (Princeton, 1961).

Nock, A. D. "The Cult of Heroes." In *Essays on Religion and the Ancient World*, ed. Zeph Stewart (Oxford, 1972): 575–602.

Nohlen, Klaus. "The 'Red Hall' (Kızıl Avlu) in Pergamon." In *Pergamon, Citadel of the Gods: Archaeological Record, Literary Description, and Religious Development*, ed. Helmut Koester (Harrisburg, Pa., 1998): 77–110.

Ohlemutz, Erwin. *Die Kulte und Heiligtümer der Götter in Pergamon* (Würzburg, 1940; repr. 1968).

Parke, H. W. *The Oracles of Apollo in Asia Minor* (London, 1985).

Parker, Robert. *Athenian Religion: A History* (Oxford, 1996).

"Greek States and Greek Oracles." In *Oxford Readings in Greek Religion*, ed. Richard Buxton (Oxford, 2000): 76–108.

Petzl, Georg. *Die Beichtinschriften Westkleinasiens. EA* 22 (1994).

De Polignac, François. "Sanctuaries and Festivals." In *A Companion to Archaic Greece*, eds. Kurt A. Raaflaub and Hans van Wees (Malden, Mass. and Oxford, 2009): 427–43.

Pollitt, Jerome J. "The Egyptian Gods in Attica: Some Epigraphical Evidence." *Hesperia* 34 (1965): 124–30.

Price, S. R. F. *Rituals and Power: The Roman Imperial Cult in Asia Minor* (Cambridge, 1984).

Radt, Wolfgang. "The Urban Development of Pergamon." In *Urbanism in Western Asia Minor: New Studies on Aphrodisias, Ephesos, Hierapolis, Pergamon, Perge and Xanthos*, ed. David Parrish (Portsmouth, R.I., 2001): 43–56.

Rheidt, Klaus. *Aizanoi und Anatolien* (Mainz, 2010).

Ricl, Marijana. "Hosios kai Dikaios, Premiere partie: Catalogue des inscriptions." *EA* 18 (1991): 1–70.

"Hosios kai Dikaios, Seconde partie: Analyse." *EA* 19 (1992): 71–103.

"Hosios kai Dikaios, Noveaux monuments." *EA* 20 (1992): 95–100.

Robert, Louis. *La Carie II. Histoire et géographie historique* (Paris, 1954).

"Un oracle gravé a Oinoanda." *CRAI* (1971): 597–619.

Roller, Lynn. *In Search of God the Mother: The Cult of Anatolian Kybele* (Berkeley, 1999).

"The Anatolian Cult of Sabazios." *Ancient Journeys: A Festschrift in Honor of Eugene Numa Lane*. http://www.stoa.org/lane/ (2002).

Schachter, Albert. "Evolutions of a mystery cult: The Theban Kabiroi." In *Greek Mysteries: The Archaeology and Ritual of Ancient Greek Secret Cults*, ed. Michael Cosmopoulos (London, 2003): 112–42.

Scherrer, Peter. "The Historical Topography of Ephesos." In *Urbanism in Western Asia Minor: New Studies on Aphrodisias, Ephesos, Hierapolis, Pergamon, Perge and Xanthos*, ed. David Parrish (Portsmouth, R.I., 2001): 57–87.

Schowalter, Daniel N. "The Zeus Philios and Trajan Temple: A Context for Imperial Honors." In *Pergamon, Citadel of the Gods: Archaeological Record, Literary Description, and Religious Development*, ed. Helmut Koester (Harrisburg, Pa., 1998): 233–49.

Sherk, Robert K. *Roman Documents from the Greek East: Senatus Consulta and Epistulae to the Age of Augustus* (Baltimore, 1969).

Sokolowski, Franciszek. *Lois sacrées des cites grecques* (Paris, 1969).

Sourvinou-Inwood, Christiane. "What is *Polis* Religion?" In *Oxford Readings in Greek Religion*, ed. Richard Buxton (Oxford, 2000): 13–37.

"Further Aspects of *Polis* Religion." In *Oxford Readings in Greek Religion*, ed. Richard Buxton (Oxford, 2000): 38–55.

Spawforth, Antony J. S. "The Early Reception of the Imperial Cult in Athens: Problems and Ambiguities." In *The Romanization of Athens: Proceedings of an International Conference held at Lincoln, Nebraska (April 1996)*, eds. Michael C. Hoff and Susan I. Rotroff (Exeter, 1997): 183–201.

Stähler, K. "Überlegungen zur architektonischen Gestalt des Pergamonaltars." In *Studien zur Religion und Kultur Kleinasiens*, eds. Sencer Şahin, Elmar Schwertheim, and Jörg Wagner (Leiden, 1978): 838–67.

Thompson, Homer A. *The Athenian Agora XIV: The Agora of Athens. The History, Shape and Uses of an Ancient City* (Princeton, 1972).

Tod, Marcus N. *Ancient Inscriptions: Sidelights on Greek History* (Oxford, 1932).

Walbank, Mary E. Hoskins. "Evidence for the imperial cult in Julio-Claudian Corinth." In *Subject and Ruler: The Cult of the Ruling Power in Classical Antiquity*, ed. Alastair Small (Ann Arbor, Mich., 1996): 201–13.

Walker, Susan. "Athens under Augustus." In *The Romanization of Athens: Proceedings of an International Conference held at Lincoln, Nebraska (April 1996)*, eds. Michael C. Hoff and Susan I. Rotroff (Exeter, 1997): 67–80.

Walters, James C. "Egyptian Religions in Ephesos." In *Ephesos: Metropolis of Asia*, ed. Helmut Koester (Cambridge, Mass., 1995): 281–311.

Wycherley, R. E. *The Stones of Athens* (Princeton, 1978).

12

JUDAISM IN ASIA MINOR

PIETER W. VAN DER HORST

INTRODUCTION

Map B VI 18 of the *Tübinger Atlas des Vorderen Orients* (the map with the title *Die jüdische Diaspora bis zum 7. Jahrhundert n. Chr.*)[1] reveals a striking concentration of Jewish settlements in Asia Minor (modern Turkey). As is to be expected, there is a higher density of Jewish communities in the west of Asia Minor than in the east, especially in great coastal cities such as Ephesus, Miletus, and Smyrna. The interior of Anatolia, however, also has a very high number, especially in Lydia, Caria, and Phrygia (see Map 7).

The history of the Jewish diaspora in Asia Minor is a long one, probably starting as early as the fifth century BCE and continuing until the present day.[2] This chapter will focus on the roughly one thousand years between the beginnings of Jewish settlement there and the end of the Talmudic period (or the rise of Islam). Unfortunately, the literary sources at our disposal are relatively scarce: only a handful of references in pagan literary sources, several more in Josephus and the New Testament, and some also in the Church Fathers and in canons of church councils. On the other hand, we have no fewer than some 260 Jewish inscriptions, the overwhelming majority in Greek and only a handful in Hebrew.[3] Because there is no scholarly consensus as to whether or not we possess Jewish writings from Asia Minor (perhaps some of the *Oracula Sibyllina* and 4 Maccabees), we will have to leave this question out of account.[4] Archaeological remains are

---

[1] Wiesbaden, 1992. For a helpful but less complete map, see Trebilco, *Jewish Communities*, xvi. For a good and concise survey of the evidence, see F. Millar in Schürer, *History*, III 17–36, with the additions by H. Bloedhorn in Hengel, "Der alte und neue 'Schürer,'" 195–6.

[2] Hirschberg and Cohen, "Turkey," 1456–62.

[3] All relevant material has been conveniently collected in Ameling, *Inscriptiones Judaicae Orientis II* (hereafter *IJO*).

[4] See Trebilco, *Jewish Communities*, 95–9 on *Or. Sib.* I-II; Buitenwerf, *Book III of the Sibylline Oracles*, 130–3; Waßmuth, *Sibyllinische Orakel*, 475–86; Norden, *Kunstprosa*, 416–20 (on 4 Maccabees).

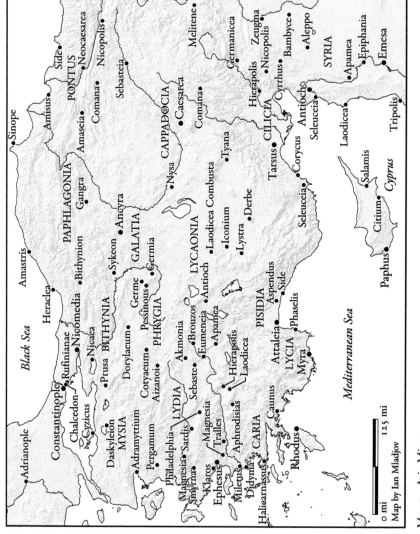

Map 7. Asia Minor

Black Sea

Sinope
Amisus
Side
PONTUS
Neocaesarea
Nicopolis
Comana
Amaseia
Sebasteia

Melitene
Germanicea
Zeugma
Nicopolis
Bambyce
Aleppo
SYRIA
Apamea
Epiphania
Emesa

Adrianople
Amastris
Heraclea
Rufinianae
Chalcedon
Constantinople
Cyzicus
Nicomedia
Bithynion
PAPHLAGONIA
Gangra
Sykeon
Ancyra
GALATIA
Germia
CAPPADOCIA
Caesarea
Comana
Nysa
Tyana
Hierapolis
Cyrrhus
CILICIA
Tarsus
Antioch
Seleuceia
Laodicea
Tripolis

Prusa
Nicaea
BITHYNIA
Dorylaeum
Germe
Pessinous
PHRYGIA
Coryaeum
Aizanoi
Akmonia
Brouzos
Antioch
Eumeneia
Apamea
Hierapolis
Laodicea
LYCAONIA
Laodicea Combusta
Iconium
Lystra
Derbe
Corycus
Seleuceia

Daskyleion
MYSIA
Adramyttium
Pergamum
Philadelphia
LYDIA
Sardis
Magnesia
Sebaste
PISIDIA
Antioch
Side
Aspendus
Attaleia
LYCIA
Phaselis
Myra

Klaros
Smyrna
Ephesus
Tralles
Magnesia
Mileros
Didyma
Aphrodisias
CARIA
Caunus
Rhodus
Haliearnassus

Cyprus
Salamis
Citium
Paphus

Mediterranean Sea

0 mi   125 mi

Map by Ian Mladjov

not very numerous (apart from the epigraphic material), but some of them are spectacular (see below on Sardis).

HISTORICAL ASPECTS

The beginnings of a Jewish presence in Asia Minor may go back to the fifth century BCE, although the evidence is controversial. The problem originates from the contested meaning of a word in Obadiah 20. There the prophet says that the exiles of Jerusalem who live in Sepharad will possess the towns of the Negev. Because Sepharad (the designation for Spain only in later Hebrew) is a name that occurs nowhere else in the Hebrew Bible, it is uncertain which place or region the prophet had in mind.[5] That uncertainty is also reflected in the ancient versions: the Septuagint renders it Ephratha (or Sephratha), the Vulgate has Bosporus, and the Peshitta and the Targum read Spain. According to some modern scholars, however, the city of Sardis is meant here.[6] They base this on an Aramaic inscription from the Persian period (KAI no. 260: fifth century BCE) found in 1916 in the ancient necropolis of Sardis. In this inscription, the name Sepharad (in the same spelling as in Obadiah 20: *sprd*) was used for the capital of the Persian satrapy Sparda (= Sardis). The publication fifty years later of another Aramaic inscription from the Persian period (ca.450 BCE) revealed that a Jewish family had settled in Daskyleion, not far from Sardis.[7] It is thus possible that the prophet did indeed have in mind Jewish exiles in the Lydian capital of Sardis. But because that cannot be strictly proved, some scholars remain understandably skeptical.[8]

According to the Jewish historian Flavius Josephus, some two centuries later, in the year 205 BCE, the Seleucid king Antiochus III issued a letter ordering that two thousand Jewish families be transferred from Mesopotamia to serve as military colonists in the most important cities of Lydia and Phrygia. The purpose of the decree, a characteristic example of the colonization policy of the Seleucids in Asia Minor, was to maintain the

---

Rabbinic references to Jewish communities in Asia Minor are extremely rare and have little or no historical value (e.g., *t. Meg.* 2:5; *b. Mo'ed Qat.* 26a).

[5] See the survey in Wineland, "Sepharad," 1089–90.

[6] See, for example, Lipinski, "Obadiah 20," 368–70; Wolff, *Dodekapropheton 3: Obadja und Jona*, 47–8. Wineland, "Sepharad," is also inclined to see a reference to Sardis here.

[7] For details, see the publications mentioned in the previous note.

[8] For example, Trebilco, *Jewish Communities*, 38; and F. Millar in Schürer, *History*, III 1, 20–1. The story that in the middle of the fourth century BCE, Aristotle met a learned Jew in Asia Minor (Clearchus *ap.* Josephus, *Ag. Ap.* 1.179–82) is to be regarded as nonhistorical; see Tcherikover, *Hellenistic Civilization*, 287; Stern, *GLAJJ* 1.47, no 7.

king's control over the region (*Ant.* 12.148–53).⁹ These Jews were allotted arable land for cultivation and a plot for building a house. We can thus be reasonably sure that at least by the end of the third century BCE, these two Anatolian provinces numbered Jewish families among their inhabitants. Most probably, these families laid the foundations for what was to become the rapidly expanding Jewish diaspora in Asia Minor. Some six decades later (ca.140 BCE), a letter from the authorities in Rome "to the kings and to the countries" (1 Macc. 15:15) urged them to refrain from harming the Jews or waging war upon them because they are "our friends and allies" (15:17). The reference to Caria, Pamphylia, Lycia, Halicarnassus, Phaselis, Side, Kos, Rhodos, etc. (15:23) among the "countries" enumerated implies that within two or three generations Jews had spread out over most of Asia Minor.¹⁰

Josephus also preserves a long series of decrees and resolutions, taken by either the Roman rulers or the Greek city councils, concerning the rights of the Jews in Asia Minor. Among the places named are Ephesus, Miletus, Smyrna, Tralles, Pergamon, Halicarnassus, Laodicea, Sardis, and the islands of Paros and Cos.¹¹ These documents, all dating from the period between 50 BCE and 50 CE, show that when friction did arise between the Jews and the local authorities in the early Roman period, the basic cause was usually "tension over questions concerning the civic status of the resident diaspora communities vis-à-vis the Greek citizen bodies of the host cities."¹² Apparently, at least some Jews were claiming admission to Greek citizenship, while the Greeks felt that "such admission should entail integration into pagan civic life and that the Jews could not expect to temper the privilege of citizenship with exemption from its uncongenial features."¹³ The secure position of the Jews in the cities did not come to them automatically. Roman authorities had granted the Jewish communities certain rights and privileges (for example, exemption from military service), and the Jews had to struggle to maintain them. But

---

⁹ See Schalit, "The Letter of Antiochus III." There are some scholars, though, who doubt the authenticity of the letter of Antiochus III; see Barclay, *Jews,* 261 with note 8; but see also Tcherikover, *Hellenistic Civilization,* 287–8; Hegermann, "The Diaspora," 146; Mitchell, *Anatolia,* II, 32 n. 181.

¹⁰ Perhaps also the Jewish woman Plousia, who is mentioned in *P. Polit.Iud.* 8 (from 132 BCE) as Gargarissa, should be taken as a testimony of Jewish presence in Gargara (in the Troad); see Cowey and Maresch, *Urkunden des Politeuma der Juden von Herakleopolis,* 97.

¹¹ Most of them are in *Ant.* 14.185–267; 16.160–78; 19.278–312. On the question of the historicity of these documents as preserved in Josephus see Pucci ben Zeev, *Jewish Rights.* On the reasons why the tensions apparent in these documents disappear after the first half of the first century CE, see Ameling, "Die jüdischen Gemeinden," 49–50.

¹² Smallwood, "The Diaspora," 177.

¹³ Ibid., 179.

they apparently had sufficient influence and good will to get things done as they wanted.

On the whole, the documents leave the impression that "in a number of cities in Asia Minor, Jews often met with local opposition to their rights and privileges and had to appeal to Roman authorities who always ruled in their favour."[14] The picture we get is that although Jewish communities, keen to retain their own identity in the midst of a pagan society, often met with resistance, that very same society enabled them over the long run to maintain their way of life without insurmountable problems. Occasionally, however, we do get glimpses of more serious conflicts. Josephus says, for example, that in the time of Augustus, the Jews of Asia Minor were mistreated by the Greeks and saw no limit to their inhuman behavior (*Ant.* 16.161; but see note 14 for Augustus's reaction).[15]

Cicero further corroborates the impression of a growing diaspora in Asia Minor. He informs us that in 62 BCE the Jews accused Flaccus, the Roman governor of Asia Minor, of having confiscated money (that is, the annual half-shekel payment for the temple in Jerusalem) from the Jewish inhabitants of Apamea, Laodicea, Adramyttium, and Pergamum (*Flac.* 28.68).[16] The New Testament adds further evidence, especially in the book of Acts, which mentions Jewish communities in Cappadocia, Phrygia, Pamphylia, Pontus, Ephesus, Smyrna, Philadelphia, Pisidian Antioch, Tarsus, Lystra, Derbe, and Iconium (2:9–10; 13:14; 14:1; 16:1–3; 19:17; see also Rev. 3:9).[17] Philo states that "in every village" of Asia and Syria there were innumerable Jews (*Legat.* 245; in 281 he mentions Jewish "colonies" in Cilicia, Pamphylia, and "most of Asia as far as Bithynia and the remote corners of Pontus").

The literary sources make it clear that by the first century CE, Jewish settlement had spread all over Asia Minor. This is confirmed by epigraphic evidence: we have inscriptions from at least some seventy-five Anatolian cities

[14] Levinskaya, *The Book of Acts*, 143. As a good example, at pp. 141–2, Levinskaya quotes the important edict issued by Emperor Augustus in 12 BCE stating that the Jews "may follow their own customs in accordance with the law of their fathers ... and that their sacred monies shall be inviolable and may be sent to Jerusalem and delivered to the treasurers in Jerusalem and they need not give bond (to appear in court) on the Sabbath or on the day of preparation for it after the ninth hour; and if anyone is caught stealing their sacred books or their sacred monies from a synagogue or an ark (of the Law), he shall be regarded as sacrilegious and his property shall be confiscated to the public treasury of the Romans" (*Ant.* 16.163–4).

[15] It should be kept in mind that, as Pucci Ben Zeev states, the rights given to the Jews "may not be regarded as proof of a special consideration for Jewish needs, but rather an application of common principles of Roman policy" (*Jewish Rights*, 482). On the legal status of the Jewish communities, which falls outside the scope of this article, see Ameling, "Die jüdischen Gemeinden," 34–7.

[16] Marshall, "Flaccus and the Jews of Asia."

[17] See Levinskaya, *The Book of Acts*, 137–52.

and villages, most of them from the early centuries CE. This literary evidence is insufficient, however, to write a history of the Jews in ancient Asia Minor. Jewish life in Anatolian cities was typically probably too uneventful to earn the attention of ancient historians. Even so, we do observe that, compared with the situation of cities such as Alexandria and Rome, friction and tension between Jews and non-Jews were relatively scarce. It would seem that Jews gradually attained a high degree of integration into Greek city life.

SOCIO-RELIGIOUS ASPECTS

Only some of the more striking instances of this high degree of integration can be mentioned here. A very intriguing inscription (*IJO* II 168) from Phrygian Acmonia informs us that some prominent members of the local Jewish community had seen to the restoration of the synagogue built by Julia Severa. This woman is well-known to us – she is also mentioned in other inscriptions and on coins from Acmonia – as the priestess of the local emperor cult in the fifties and sixties of the first century CE. Definitely not Jewish, she played a prominent role in an important pagan cult in the city. Even so, this inscription testifies to her warm interest in the Jewish community (which recalls the story of the Roman centurion in Capernaum, who, according to Luke 7:5, loved the Jewish people and for that reason had a synagogue built for them at his own cost). Julia Severa, an aristocratic woman whose son later became a senator in Rome, had close connections with the prestigious Roman emigrant family of the Turronii. One of them, Turronius Rapo, was also a priest of the emperor cult and together with Julia Severa is mentioned on the coins of the city. Another member of the same family, Turronius Cladus, is mentioned in our inscription as the "head of the synagogue (*archisynagōgos*)" that had undergone the renovations![18] We see here how a woman of high social standing, with a prominent role in the pagan community of Acmonia, extended a largesse to the Jewish community – a sure sign of the successful integration of the Jews of that city and of the sympathy they enjoyed among non-Jewish inhabitants.[19]

Some inscriptions referring to the book of Deuteronomy also originate in Phrygia, but now two centuries later. They threaten anyone who buries someone in a tomb other than the person for whom it was intended with

---

[18] See Mitchell, *Anatolia*, II, 9.
[19] For other instances, see Feldman, *Jew and Gentile*, 310, although I disagree with his statement that "we may conclude that she [Julia Severa] later converted to Judaism and then built the synagogue" (576 n.120).

"the curses that are written in Deuteronomy" (*IJO* II 173 and 174; a third instance is from Laodicea, *IJO* II 213). This is an interesting variant on the curse formulas that are so frequent on Phrygian graves.[20] The reference is undoubtedly to Deuteronomy 28, where we read, inter alia, "The Lord will affect you with consumption, fever, inflammation, with fiery heat and drought, and with blight and mildew" (22) and "The Lord will afflict you with madness, blindness, and confusion of mind; you shall grope about at noon as blind people grope in darkness, but you shall be unable to find your way" (28–29). And thus more curses follow, not only in the Hebrew text but also in the Septuagint, which the authors of the inscriptions used. The blindness motif mentioned in vv. 28–29 also occurs in another epitaph from Acmonia: "If someone opens this grave, he will be struck by the curses that are written against his eyes and all the rest of his body" (*IJO* II 172). While Deuteronomy is not mentioned explicitly, the allusion is unmistakable.[21] In this connection it is interesting to see that another Phrygian epitaph, *IJO* II 179 from Apamea, states that whenever anyone dares to bury here another person, "he knows the Law of the Jews!" This formulation ("the Law *of the Jews*") seems to indicate that the non-Jewish population of the region had some knowledge of the Torah, however partial and superficial.[22]

This suggestion is further confirmed by evidence of quite a different nature but from the same place, namely the curious Noah coins from Apameia. In this city, coins found from the first half of the third century CE depict Noah and his wife together with the ark (and the name *Nōe* added). In a number of ancient sources, the city of Apamea is also called Kibōtos (= ark).[23] (In the Septuagint, *kibōtos* is the word used for Noah's ark.) There circulated a legend that Noah's ark had landed on a hill in the neighborhood of the city. Is this a case of Jewish influence? The coins were struck by the pagan authorities of the city, showing that the legend was accepted outside Jewish circles. And the fact that as early as the first century BCE the Greek geographer Strabo says that Apamea was also called Kibōtos (*Geogr.* 12.8.13)[24] would seem to be proof that Christians did not introduce the legend into Phrygia. But doubts about the Jewish origin of the legend arise when one sees that some earlier coins of the city, from the

[20] For which see Strubbe, "Curses Against Violation of the Grave." See also Trombley, Chapter 13 of this volume.
[21] See van der Horst, *Ancient Jewish Epitaphs*, 56–7.
[22] See Trebilco, *Jewish Communities*, 100. Cf. an inscription from Catania on Sicily: *adiuro vos per legem quem Dominus dedit Iudaeis* (*JIWE* I, no. 145).
[23] See for references Schürer, *History*, III.1, 28–30; Trebilco, *Jewish Communities*, 86–95.
[24] In the 60s of the first century CE, Pliny the Elder says the same (*Nat.* 5.29.106).

time of Hadrian, use the plural *kibōtoi* and depict *five* chests. That seems
to indicate that this nickname of the city had a "non-Noachidic" origin
(otherwise unknown to us) and that only at a later stage did this nickname give the Jewish inhabitants the occasion to localize the landing of
Noah's ark there. However uncertain much of this remains, the depiction
of a biblical scene on the city's coins is a clear case of Jewish influence on
a non-Jewish population. But influence could also work the other way, as
is demonstrated by a Phrygian tombstone (*IJO* II 171) that stipulates that
each year at a fixed day the tomb should be adorned with roses; if the surviving relatives neglect this duty, they will have to account for that before
God's justice (*tēn dikaiosynēn tou theou*). This is an interesting threat in that
the said ritual (the *rosalia*) was an originally pagan usage that had arrived
in Asia Minor from Rome.[25]

Another striking example of peaceful coexistence of Jews and non-Jews
is the recently discovered inscription from Aphrodisias in Caria on a huge
marble block or pillar. Almost 3m high and some 45cm wide, it is inscribed
on two sides with a long Greek inscription of 86 lines (*IJO* II 14).[26] It most
probably – but not certainly – dates from the late fourth or fifth century CE.[27] The greatest part of the text consists of lists of some 125 names[28]
mentioned as donors or contributors to a local synagogue institution.
Although tentatively identified by the editors as the Jewish community's
soup kitchen, it may have been the collective burial place of that community.[29] The 125 or so names of the benefactors are subdivided into three
categories: 68 are Jews (although they are not explicitly so described, the
overwhelming preponderance of biblical and Hebrew Jewish names leaves
no room for another conclusion); 54 are called "God-fearers (*theosebeis*)";
three are proselytes.

This strikingly high percentage of God-fearers – that is, pagan sympathizers with Judaism – in a list of benefactors and contributors to a
Jewish institution, is the great surprise of this inscription. We know from
the book of Acts and from Josephus that in many cities of the ancient
world, synagogues had sympathizers in the form of a body of permanent or

[25] See Williams, *The Jews Among Greeks and Romans*, 128; Mitchell, *Anatolia*, II, 35. A sign of Greek
philosophical influence is perhaps the frequent use of *Pronoia* (Providence) as a designation of God
in the inscriptions from Sardis.
[26] Reynolds and Tannenbaum, *Jews and Godfearers at Aphrodisias*; van der Horst, "Jews and Christians
at Aphrodisias."
[27] On the problems of dating this inscription, see esp. Chaniotis, "The Jews of Aphrodisias."
[28] The uncertainty about the exact numbers of persons is due partly to the damaged state of the stone,
partly to the fact that it is not certain whether or not some names are patronymics; see Reynolds and
Tannenbaum, *Jews and Godfearers*, 93–6.
[29] See for the latter interpretation Ameling's commentary on *IJO* II 14.

semi-permanent catechumens.[30] The author of Acts leaves us in no doubt about the presence of a sizeable body of God-fearers in the major cities of Asia Minor. Josephus even reports, with characteristic exaggeration, that most of the pagan women of Damascus belonged to this category, and that in Syrian Antioch the number of sympathizers was also extremely great (*J. W.* 2.560; 7.43–5).[31] It was among these God-fearers that, according to Acts, Paul made most of his early converts.

If we leave out of account Josephus's exaggerated reports, it is not possible either from Acts or from inscriptional evidence to gauge the exact extent of this phenomenon of pagans sympathizing in various degrees with Judaism (although the literary and epigraphic attestation for God-fearers in Asia Minor is not negligible).[32] Now we have for the first time an indication of the degree of influence of the synagogue on local pagans in a middle-sized city of Asia Minor. And we have to bear in mind that this inscription records only the names of the contributors – that is, probably of only a part of the more well-to-do citizens among the God-fearers. Even so, 54 of them are listed.

The occupations of the God-fearers, of which some 22 are given in the inscription, cover a wide range, only very few of which indicate lower social status.[33] Most remarkable is the fact that nine of them are *bouleutai*, city councillors. In the later Roman empire, this office imposed heavy financial obligations and could only be exercised by the wealthy of a city. So what we are now able to see is that, in Aphrodisias at least, the Jews attracted large numbers of local gentiles – again, the people recorded undoubtedly form only a part of the total group of God-fearers – and persons of high standing and great influence at that. When pagan local magistrates heartily support and partly pay for the foundation of a Jewish institution, one cannot but conclude that the Jewish community of that city was influential to a degree hitherto hardly imaginable. Its members appear to have been self-confident, accepted in the city, and evidently able to attract the favorable attention of many gentile fellow Aphrodisians.

God-fearers, who were not full converts to Judaism, had relative freedom to follow or not follow the commandments of the Jewish Bible. One of the commandments required sacrifices to the God of Israel to be

---

[30] Wander, *Gottesfürchtige und Sympathisanten*, 143–54, 180–203; and Trombley, Chapter 13 of this volume.

[31] On these and other cases of "adherence" and "conversion" in Josephus see Cohen, "Respect for Judaism by Gentiles."

[32] Mitchell, "The Cult of Theos Hypsistos," 117–18.

[33] Reynolds and Tannenbaum, *Jews and Godfearers*, 116–23, esp. 119–22.

offered only in the temple of Jerusalem. A recent find may indicate that God-fearers felt free to sacrifice to this God in their own home town as well. *IJO* II 218 is an inscription on a small private altar found in Aspendos in Pamphylia and probably dating from the first or second century CE.[34] It reads, "For the truthful god who is not made with hands (in fulfillment of) a vow (*theōi apseudei kai acheiropoiētōi euchēn*)." The interpretation of this inscription is debated.[35] Although the terminology (especially the use of *acheiropoiētos*) suggests a Jewish origin, it is hard to imagine a Jewish altar outside the Jerusalem temple.[36] It seems much more credible to look for the origin of this altar inscription in the circles of God-fearers. If the God-fearer was in a position to decide which elements of the Jewish way of life to adopt, then the problem of a Jewish altar outside a Jewish temple disappears. The centralization of the sacrificial cult in Jerusalem (or the cessation of that cult after 70, if the inscription was engraved after the destruction of the Temple) was no constraint on a pagan Judaizer who wanted to confess belief in the one true God who is not made with hands. As a non-Jew, one was free to bring sacrifices to the God of the Jewish people wherever one wanted.

A private altar, erected by oneself before one's own house or in the backyard, was one of the possibilities. Indeed, in the soil of Pergamon, a small altar was discovered with an inscription that several scholars regard as having been engraved by a God-fearer.[37] At the top of the altar, we read *theos kyrios ho ōn eis aei*,[38] "God the Lord is the one who is forever" (or "God is the Lord who is forever"); the lower part of the altar reads, "Zopyrus (dedicated) to the Lord this altar and the lampstand with the lantern." In this case, too, the clearly Jewish terminology and the fact that it is an altar from the second century CE are together sufficient reason to regard the inscription as belonging to a pagan sympathizer or Judaizer, that is, a God-fearer. Throughout Antiquity, the bringing of sacrifices, as Elias Bickerman has rightly recognized, was part and parcel of the daily life of Greeks or Romans. "Rabbinic doctors of the Law," he writes, "approved of gentile altars to God.... The situation was paradoxical. While the sons of Abraham, after the destruction of the Temple, were no more able to make

---

[34] For what follows see van der Horst, "A New Altar of a Godfearer?"

[35] For a survey see Ameling, *IJO* II, 458–61.

[36] We do know of Jewish temples in places other than in Jerusalem, but not of private altars; see Eshel and Stone in Chapter 3 and Mélèze Modrzejewski in Chapter 7 of this volume.

[37] See Nilsson, "Zwei Altäre aus Pergamon"; Delling, "Die Altarinschrift eines Gottesfürchtigen in Pergamon"; Bickerman, "The Altars of Gentiles." This inscription has not been included by Ameling in *IJO* II.

[38] Note the allusion to Exod. 3:14, *egō eimi ho ōn*.

offerings to God, a sweet savor continued to go up to the God of Abraham, Isaac, and Jacob from sacrifices offered by God-fearing gentiles. Yet the rabbis abetted this impairment of the privileges of the chosen people."[39]

The best-known example of Jewish integration into Greco-Roman city life is Sardis.[40] In 1962, American archaeologists unearthed the greatest ancient synagogue ever in the city of Sardis, capital of ancient Lydia. The colossal basilica-shaped building measures almost 20 by 100m and could accommodate some 1,000 people. This richly decorated basilica is an integral part of a huge municipal bath-and-gymnasium complex with a shopping mall in the city center. As such, it is a monument to the integration of the Jewish community into this Greco-Roman city.[41] The building is one of the most prominent features of the city's urban landscape, as every modern visitor can now easily see. Even apart from the enormous size, it points to the fact that the Jewish community of Sardis was definitely not a "quantité négligeable." Minorities in a city do not usually get hold of a central and prestigious building if they do not have any clout and influence there.

That the Jews did indeed have this influence is amply confirmed by the more than eighty inscriptions found in the synagogue. No fewer than nine of the Jews mentioned are *bouleutai*, that is, members of the city council (*boulē*), the highest administrative body of the city.[42] Here we see Jews who have climbed up to the highest rung on the social ladder, for "the councils of Greek cities under the late empire were open only to the wealthier families, with membership, once purchased, being hereditary and held for life."[43] Distinguished and well-to-do Jewish families thus participated here in the government of the city.[44] No wonder that here, unlike elsewhere in the fifth and sixth centuries, Christians did not expropriate the synagogue for conversion into a church building. Although this basilica could have been a magnificent church, during the fifth and sixth centuries the Christians in Sardis had to make do with a building much smaller than the synagogue. The famous Aphrodisias inscription also mentions nine

---

[39] Bickerman, "The Altars of Gentiles," 344.
[40] From the abundant literature, I refer *exempli gratia* only to Seager and Kraabel in Hanfmann, *Sardis*; van der Horst "The Synagogue of Sardis"; and Levine, *Ancient Synagogue*, 242–9, where further references can be found.
[41] Seager and Kraabel, "The Synagogue and the Jewish Community."
[42] Note that here, again, six non-Jewish donors are explicitly called "God-fearers" (*theosebeis*, nos. 67, 68, 83, 123, 125, 132). See now the caveat by Martin Goodman in his "Jews and Judaism in the Mediterranean Diaspora."
[43] Kroll, "Greek Inscriptions," 10.
[44] Also elsewhere, we have evidence of the relative affluence of Jewish families, for example, in Phrygian Acmonia; see Mitchell, *Anatolia*, 35. *IJO* II 172 and 173 are striking cases.

bouleutai. But there the city councillors are all gentiles, whereas in Sardis they are Jews. "The Sardis dossier stands out for its sheer richness and scale, and for the striking vitality of late Roman Judaism that it conveys, a vitality that appears all the more remarkable because of the growing strength of Christianity at the same period in history."[45]

Finally, we have to discuss a very significant form of rapprochement between Jews and gentiles in Asia Minor – namely, the cult of *Theos Hypsistos*, God Most High.[46] Stephen Mitchell has collected almost 300 inscriptions of worshippers of this god from the second and third centuries CE,[47] mainly from the eastern Mediterranean, but especially from Asia Minor. Almost half of these inscriptions, some 140, are from Asia Minor.[48] In most cases, it is impossible to determine whether the inscription is pagan, Christian, or Jewish; arguments for assigning them to any of these three categories are rarely decisive. That is so because *Theos Hypsistos* is a designation that was current as an epithet for the highest god in paganism, Judaism, and Christianity.[49] It is highly probable that this rather elusive cult concerned a syncretistic religious movement that made a conscious effort to bridge the gap between polytheism and monotheism. Its origins lie not in Jewish but in pagan henotheistic circles, where the attraction of Judaism was strong enough to cause them to seek common ground.

Hypsistarians chose to address their god by a name befitting both pagan and Jewish patterns of belief. Quite often they combined their worship of *Theos Hypsistos* with that of angels, another trait with monotheistic, or at least henotheistic, overtones.[50] As Mitchell says, "We are evidently dealing with an area of belief, where Jews, Judaizers, and pagans occupied very similar territories.... The cult of *Theos Hypsistos* had room for pagans and

---

[45] Kroll, "Greek Inscriptions," 48. That the growing strength of Christianity could also have the effect of Jews stressing more and more their distinctive Jewishness (e.g., by more frequently adopting Hebrew names) is illustrated for Cilician Corycus by Williams, "The Jews of Corycus."

[46] For what follows, see esp. Mitchell, "The Cult of Theos Hypsistos."

[47] It is important to realize that whereas the epigraphic evidence is mainly from the second and third centuries, other evidence makes clear that this cult was not a development of these centuries, "but occurred at least sporadically during the late Hellenistic or early Roman periods, (...) for which there is little or no epigraphic attestation" (Mitchell, "The Cult of Theos Hypsistos," 209). Mitchell also points out that there is still evidence for the Hypsistarians in the fourth and fifth centuries CE.

[48] The greatest density of inscriptions outside Asia Minor is to be found in Athens (23), Cyprus (23), and the Bosporan Kingdom (22). For its relatively frequent occurrence in Phrygia (23 items so far), see Drew-Bear and Naour, "Divinités de Phrygie," 2032–43.

[49] See esp. Simon, "Theos Hypsistos."

[50] Sheppard, "Pagan Cults of Angels in Roman Asia Minor"; Mitchell, "The Cult of Theos Hypsistos," 102–5; van der Horst, "Hosios kai Dikaios." Sheppard's no. 8 even mentions an "association of the lovers of angels" (*philangelōn symbiōsis*). For a hymn "for God (...) and his first angel, Jesus Christ" see Mitchell, *Anatolia*, II, 100–2 with n. 406.

for Jews. More than that, it shows that the principal categories into which we divide the religious groupings of Late Antiquity are simply inappropriate or misleading when applied to the beliefs and practices of a significant proportion of the population of the eastern Roman empire" (114–15).[51] The lack of any representations of the god and the absence of animal sacrifice from the rituals "distinguish the worship of *Hypsistos* from most other pagan cults in Greece, Asia Minor, and the Near East."[52]

Mitchell also shows that what we know about pagan "God-fearers" (*theosebeis*), or sympathizers with Judaism, agrees so closely with the information we have about the worshippers of *Theos Hypsistos* that both groups could very well have been identical. Hypsistarians often used the term "God-fearers" (*theosebeis*) as a technical term to describe themselves. "Dedications to *Theos Hypsistos* occur at almost all the places [in Asia Minor] where God-fearers appear."[53] A very strong argument Mitchell adduces for identifying Hypsistarians with God-fearers is what he calls the "uncanny parallel" (120) between Josephus's description of God-fearers and the Cappadocian Father Gregory of Nazianzus's description of Hypsistarians. Josephus says about the God-fearers, "The [non-Jewish] masses have long since shown a keen desire to adopt our religious observances, and there is not one city, Greek or barbarian, not a single nation to which our custom of abstaining from work on the seventh day has not spread, and where the fasts and lighting of lamps and many of our prohibitions in the matter of food are not observed."[54] Compare this with what Gregory says about the Hypsistarians (to which his own father had belonged!): "This cult was a mixture of two elements, Hellenic error and adherence to the Jewish law. Shunning some parts of both, it was made up from others. Its followers reject the idols and sacrifices of the former and worship fire and lamplight; they revere the sabbath and are scrupulous not to touch certain foods, but have nothing to do with circumcision."[55] A pagan confirmation of these Jewish and Christian descriptions can also be found in Juvenal's famous *Satire* 14.96–106.[56]

Occasional references in the inscriptions to gods other than *Theos Hypsistos* (for example, Zeus, Helios, Men, Cybele, Larmene) do not plead against their association with Hypsistarians and God-fearers.[57] This

[51] For an elaborate presentation of the problems of categorization see Mitchell, *Anatolia*, II, 11–51.
[52] Mitchell, "The Cult of Theos Hypsistos," 108.
[53] Ibid., 119 [my addition].
[54] Josephus, *Ag. Ap.* 2.282.
[55] *Or.* 18.5 (*PG* 35.989–91).
[56] See *GLAJJ* 2.102–7, no. 301.
[57] Instances can be found easily in Mitchell, "The Cult of Theos Hypsistos," 129–47.

apparent polytheism does not militate against the essentially henotheistic nature of the cult. In Hypsistarian circles, gods other than the Most High were often regarded as his angels. A second- or third-century-CE inscription from Oenoanda, for example, contains a Clarian oracle in which Apollo says that he and other gods are no more than angels of the highest god (SEG 27 [1977] 933 = no. 233 in Mitchell's list).[58] In general, it can be said that in the century between 150 and 250 CE, the oracles of Apollo at Claros and Didyma forged a kind of new theology which can be seen as "a persistent effort to integrate the pantheon of paganism into a system governed by a single guiding principle or a supreme god."[59] An impressive testimony to that effort is another oracle of the Clarian Apollo, in which he says that Yahweh (Iaō) is the Highest God, who is called Hades in winter, Zeus in spring, Helios in summer, and Iakchos (=Dionysus) in autumn.[60]

If God-fearers and Hypsistarians were identical, that would be another confirmation of the important role that Jewish communities in Asia Minor played in religious and social interactions. It would explain, for instance, the identity of the persons for whom the theater seats in Miletus were reserved according to the much-debated inscription *IJO* II 37. If this text – *topos eioudeōn tōn kai theoeebion* [sic] (= *topos Ioudaiōn tôn kai Theosebiōn*) – is to be translated as "place of the Jews who (are) also (called) God-fearers," it may imply that the connections between Jews and Hypsistarians (*theosebeis*) were so close that Jews managed to obtain reserved seats in the city theater by parading as Hypsistarians, the latter possessing enough clout with the municipal authorities to provide these seat reservations for their "coreligionists."[61]

Before the Council of Nicaea in 325 CE, Christians in Asia Minor generally "mingled with their non-Christian fellows without friction and confrontation in a territory which was familiar to all of them."[62] We also know of Christian priests who worshipped *Theos Hypsistos*.[63] As is to be expected under these circumstances, interrelationships between Jews and non-Jews did not remain restricted to gentiles. This is apparent, among other things, from the canons of the synod of Laodicea (in Phrygia) from the middle

---

[58] See also Zuntz, *Griechische philosophische Hymnen*, 89–94; Lane Fox, *Pagans and Christians*, ch. 4.

[59] Mitchell, *Anatolia*, II, 43.

[60] Quoted by Cornelius Labeo, *De oraculo Apollinis Clarii*, fr. 18 Mastandrea (*ap.* Macrobius, *Sat.* 1.18.19–20). See Mastandrea, *Un neoplatonico latino*, 159–92 (160–1 on the text-critical problem of the last name); Zuntz, *Griechische philosophische Hymnen*, 76. For a general discussions of these oracles see van der Horst, "Porphyry on Judaism."

[61] See Baker, "Who Was Sitting at the Theatre at Miletos?"

[62] Mitchell, "The Cult of Theos Hypsistos," 122. But there is anti-Jewish Christian literature from Asia Minor; see Trebilco, *Jewish Communities*, 27–32.

[63] Mitchell, "The Cult of Theos Hypsistos," 122–3.

of the sixties of the fourth century CE. These decrees issue severe warnings to Christians against participation in all sorts of Jewish practices.[64] That this was more than a hypothetical possibility is made very clear by a passage about exactly this period (namely, the year 367) in Theophanes's *Chronographia* (62.17–19). It tells us that in that year Christians in Phrygia celebrated Passover *together with the Jews*. (Here one is reminded strongly of the situation a couple of decades later in Antioch-on-the-Orontes, where the many strongly Judaizing Christians were heavily castigated by John Chrysostom.[65]) It is also to be noted that both Jewish and Christian epitaphs from Phrygia use as a standard warning to grave robbers the so-called Eumeneian formula ("he/they will have to reckon with God"), which often makes it very hard to distinguish one group from the other.[66] "The later fruits of this close relationship between Anatolian Jews and the Christian communities living alongside them are clear in the Judaizing strain of Novatian Christianity, which is attested above all in Phrygia in the late fourth and fifth centuries."[67] Celebrating Easter at the time of the Jewish Passover was only one of these Novatian practices. The seventh-century *Life of Saint Theodore of Sykeon* tells us that the Jews of the village of Goeleon were present at this saint's greatest miracle of exorcism.[68]

On the other hand, it should be added that there was not always a peaceful coexistence between Jews and Christians. In the *Acta Pionii*, we read about the martyrdom of Pionius in Smyrna in 250 CE. In chapters 13–14, Pionius launches an attack on the Jews that is more vehement than his attack on his pagan persecutors. As it appears from his words, the Jews of Smyrna, who we know formed a prominent and influential community in the city,[69] tried to make proselytes among persecuted Christians. Conversion to Judaism was of course as efficacious in avoiding martyrdom as a sacrifice to idols. Even in the Diocletian persecution, the emperor explicitly exempted the Jews from the necessity of offering sacrifice, thus confirming an old privilege of Judaism. And, as Marcel Simon has observed, "it is very difficult to believe that Jewish attempts to convert persecuted Christians were made without the cognizance of the Roman

[64] For the texts, see Jonkers, *Acta et symbola*, 86–96, esp. canons 29 (keeping Sabbath), 35 (angelolatry), 37 (festivals with Jews), and 38 (celebration of the Jewish Passover); discussion in Trebilco, *Jewish Communities*, 101–3.
[65] See van der Horst, "Jews and Christians in Antioch." For a map showing the many sites with both Jewish and Christian presence in Phrygia see Mitchell, *Anatolia*, II, 42.
[66] Trebilco, "The Christian *and* Jewish Eumeneian Formula."
[67] Mitchell, *Anatolia*, II, 35; cf. ibid., 96–108.
[68] See Mitchell, *Anatolia*, II, 139–43, for extensive discussion.
[69] See Lane Fox, *Pagans and Christians*, 481–3, and Ameling, *IJO* II, 174–95, for the evidence. Note that almost a century earlier the Jews of Smyrna opposed Christianity according to *Mart. Pol.* 12:2.

authorities.... It looks as if the state, in its desire to eliminate Christianity by making apostates and not martyrs, accepted the two recognized religious categories, Jewish and pagan, and left to the defecting Christians themselves the choice."[70] If Simon is right, we see here one of the most threatening consequences for the church of the Jewish-pagan coalition. Robin Lane Fox has also proposed that the "Great Sabbath" (mentioned in *Acta Pionii* 2) marking the occasion of the persecution was the festival of Purim, which the Jews in Smyrna celebrated at the same time as the pagan celebration of the Dionysia (!). If he is correct, then we see that the church had to face a bizarre form of that coalition in an easy relationship between a Jewish and a gentile festival.[71]

In spite of the many proofs of peaceful coexistence and rapprochement between Jews and non-Jews (both pagan and Christian) in Asia Minor, we should not doubt that many of these Jews attached great importance to maintaining their Jewish identity and singularity. This is most visible in the epigraphic material, but not only there. One finds their central institution, the synagogue, mentioned many times (sometimes as "most holy synagogue");[72] the functions they had in their religious community (*archisynagōgos, archōn, presbyteros, gerousiarchēs, grammateus, diakonos, anagnōstēs, hiereus, psalmologos, phrontistēs*);[73] the repeated references to their Bible (see above on the curses from Deuteronomy[74]) and to reading and studying the Bible (*IJO* II 14,2–5 from Aphrodisias; 131 from Sardis); the mention of their religious festivals (Pesach and Festival of Weeks in no. 196,7 from Hierapolis); their commitment to the annual collecting of the temple tax before 70 (see Augustus's decree in Josephus, *Ant.* 16.163–4); the regulations for kosher food in Sardis and no doubt elsewhere (see the decree in Josephus, *Ant.* 14.259–61); their request for exemption from military service in order not to desecrate the Sabbath (Josephus, *Ant.* 16.163–4);[75] the references to God's punishment and judgment on tombstones (see above

---

[70] Simon, *Verus Israel*, 111.

[71] Lane Fox, *Pagans and Christians*, 486–7. Note that *CTh* 16 8,18 (from 408 CE) prohibits the Jews from mocking Christianity on Purim by burning Haman's effigy on a cross.

[72] See *IJO* II, p. 624 *s.v.* See also the term *sambatheion* (synagogue?) in no. 149.

[73] On the meanings of these designations (quite often obscure), see van der Horst, *Ancient Jewish Epitaphs*, 85–101; Levine, *Ancient Synagogue*, 387–428. Note that there is no mention of rabbis, who apparently had no influence at all in Asia Minor until the early Middle Ages (*IJO* no. 184 is only an apparent exception; see Ameling, *ad locum*). It is telling that in at least some, but probably more, places women even had leading positions in the communities (*IJO* II 14, 25, 36, 43); see Brooten, *Women Leaders*, and Trebilco, *Jewish Communities*, 104–26.

[74] In *IJO* II 175 and 176, one also finds references to Zech. 5:1–4.

[75] See the discussion in Trebilco, *Jewish Communities*, 16–18.

on the curses in epitaphs); the numerous representations of the menorah; and last but not least, the frequent self-identification as *Ioudaios* (especially in Hierapolis). It is clear that for most of the imperial period the Jews of Asia Minor formed self-conscious communities that were in intense interaction with their surroundings, both pagan and Christian. It is only from the end of the fourth century CE onward that the anti-Jewish legislation of Christian emperors began to make Jewish life increasingly difficult.[76]

APPENDIX: SAMARITANS IN ASIA MINOR?

Alongside a Jewish diaspora, in Antiquity there was also a Samaritan diaspora that was much more extensive than is often assumed.[77] From Rome to Mesopotamia there were Samaritan communities, so it stands to reason that there were also Samaritans in Asia Minor. But what is the evidence? Apart from a late (fifth-century) literary reference to the effect that the city of Tarsus had two synagogues, a Jewish and a Samaritan one,[78] we have a very limited number of inscriptions. *IJO* II 11 (second century CE, from Rhodos) mentions a Rhodocles *Samaritas*, but here the problem is that ancient sources use one and the same term for "Samaritan" (a member of the religious community of the Samaritans) and for "Samarian" (an inhabitant of Samaria, who could be a Jew, a gentile, or a Samaritan). Without further indicators we cannot know whether Rhodocles was a Samaritan. The same applies to no. 243 (fourth to sixth century, from Corycus in Cilicia), where a woman is called *Samarissa*. This woman, however, is also called *diakonissa* and there is a cross on the stone, so she was most probably a Christian from Samaria. Finally, there is no. 24 (first century BCE–CE, from Caunos in Caria), where five persons are called *Sikimitai*, people from Sichem. Here we most probably have to do with a self-designation of Samaritans, who sometimes named themselves after the biblical site at the foot of their holy mountain, Mount Gerizim. Even if this interpretation is rejected, it still remains highly probable that Samaritans were part of the religious landscape of Asia Minor. Most of the evidence may not be traceable for the simple reason that in many cases it is impossible to distinguish Jewish from Samaritan inscriptions.

---

[76] Quite telling is a recently discovered inscription from the fifth or sixth century, found in a church on the island of Icaria, which says, "It is impossible that you will ever hear the truth from Jews at Icaria!" (*IJO* II 5a).

[77] See van der Horst, "Samaritan Diaspora."

[78] See Palladius, *Dial. de vita Joh. Chrys.* 20 (*PG* 47.73). The implication of the passage may be that there were Samaritan synagogues in other cities of Asia Minor as well.

BIBLIOGRAPHY

Ameling, Walter. "Die jüdischen Gemeinden im antiken Kleinasien." In *Jüdische Gemeinden und Organisationsformen von der Antike bis zur Gegenwart*, eds. Robert Jütte and Abraham P. Kustermann (Vienna, 1996): 29–55.

Inscriptiones Judaicae Orientis II: Kleinasien. TSAJ 99 (Tübingen, 2004).

Baker, Murray. "Who Was Sitting at the Theatre at Miletos? An Epigraphical Application of a Novel Theory." *JSJ* 36 (2005): 397–416.

Barclay, John M. G. *Jews in the Mediterranean Diaspora* (Edinburgh, 1996).

Bickerman, Elias. "The Altars of Gentiles: A Note on the Jewish 'ius sacrum'." In *Studies in Jewish and Christian History* II (Leiden, 1980): 324–46 (596–617 in vol. II of the new edition, Leiden, 2009).

Blanchetière, Francois. "Le juif et l'autre: la diaspora asiate." In *Études sur le judaïsme hellénistique*, eds. Raymond Kuntzmann and Jacques Schlosser (Paris, 1984): 41–59.

Brooten, Bernadette J. *Women Leaders in the Ancient Synagogue: Inscriptional Evidence and Background Issues* (Chico, Calif., 1982).

Buitenwerf, Rieuwerd. *Book III of the Sibylline Oracles and its Social Setting* (Leiden, 2003).

Chaniotis, Angelos. "The Jews of Aphrodisias: New Evidence and Old Problems." *SCI* 21 (2002): 209–42.

Cohen, Shaye J. D. "Respect for Judaism by Gentiles according to Josephus." *HTR* 80 (1987): 409–30.

De Boor, Carl, ed. *Theophanis Chronographia*. 2 vols. (Leipzig, 1883–85).

Delling, Gerhard. "Die Altarinschrift eines Gottesfürchtigen in Pergamon." In *Studien zum Neuen Testament und zum hellenistischen Judentum* (Göttingen, 1970): 32–38.

Drew-Bear, Thomas, and Christian Naour. "Divinités de Phrygie." *ANRW* II 18, 3 (Berlin, 1990): 1908–2044.

Feldman, Louis H. *Jew and Gentile in the Ancient World* (Princeton, 1993).

Goodman, Martin. "Jews and Judaism in the Mediterranean Diaspora in the Late-Roman Period: The Limitations of Evidence." In *Ancient Judaism in its Hellenistic Context*, ed. C. Bakhos (Leiden, 2005): 177–203.

Gutsfeld, Andreas, and Dietrich-Alex Koch, eds. *Vereine, Synagogen und Gemeinden im kaiserzeitlichen Kleinasien*. STAC 25 (Tübingen, 2006).

Hegermann, Harald. "The Diaspora in the Hellenistic Age." In *CHJ*. Vol. 2: *The Hellenistic Age*, eds. W. D. Davies and Louis Finkelstein (Cambridge, 1989): 115–66.

Hengel, Martin. "Der alte und der neue 'Schürer'." In *Judaica, Hellenistica et Christiana. Kleine Schriften II* (Tübingen, 1999): 157–99.

Hirschberg, H. Z., and H. J. Cohen. "Turkey." *EncJud* 15 (1971): 1456–62.

Jonkers, E. J. *Acta et symbola conciliorum quae saeculo quarto habita sunt* (Leiden, 1954).

Kroll, John H. "The Greek Inscriptions of the Sardis Synagogue." *HTR* 94 (2001): 5–127.

Lane Fox, Robin. *Pagans and Christians* (Harmondsworth, 1986).

Levine, Lee I. "The Hellenistic-Roman Diaspora CE 70 – CE 235: The Archaeological Evidence." In *CHJ*. Vol. 3: *The Early Roman Period*, eds. William Horbury, W. D. Davies, and John Sturdy (Cambridge, 1999): 991–1024.

The Ancient Synagogue: The First Thousand Years (New Haven, 2000).

Levinskaya, Irina. *The Book of Acts in its First Century Setting, 5: Diaspora Setting* (Grand Rapids, Mich., 1996).

Lipinski, Edward. "Obadiah 20." *VT* 23 (1973): 368–70.

Marshall, Anthony J. "Flaccus and the Jews of Asia." *Phoenix* 29 (1975): 139–54.

Mastandrea, Paolo. *Un neoplatonico latino: Cornelio Labeone (testimonianze e frammenti)* (Leiden, 1979).

Mitchell, Stephen. *Anatolia: Land, Men, and Gods in Asia Minor*. 2 vols. (Oxford, 1993).
"The Cult of Theos Hypsistos between Pagans, Jews, and Christians." In *Pagan Monotheism in Late Antiquity*, eds. Polymnia Athanassiadi and Michael Frede (Oxford, 1999): 81–148.

Nilsson, Martin P. "Zwei Altäre aus Pergamon." *Eranos* 54 (1956): 167–73.

Norden, Eduard. *Die antike Kunstprosa*. 2 vols (Darmstadt, 1980 = Leipzig, 1909).

Noy, David. *Jewish Inscriptions of Western Europe*. Vol. 1 (Cambridge, 1993) (=*JIWE*).

Pucci ben Zeev, Miriam. *Jewish Rights in the Roman World* (Tübingen, 1998).

Reynolds, Joyce M., and Robert Tannenbaum. *Jews and Godfearers at Aphrodisias* (Cambridge, 1987).

Schalit, Abraham. "The Letter of Antiochus III to Zeuxis Regarding the Establishment of Jewish Military Colonies in Phrygia and Lydia." *JQR* n.s. 50 (1960): 289–318.

Schürer, Emil. *The History of the Jewish People in the Age of Jesus Christ*. Rev. ed. by Geza Vermes, Fergus Millar, and Martin Goodman. 3 vols. (Edinburgh, 1973–87).

Seager, Andrew R., and A. Thomas Kraabel. "The Synagogue and the Jewish Community." In *Sardis from Prehistoric to Roman Times*, ed. George M. A. Hanfmann (Cambridge, Mass., 1983): 168–90.

Sheppard, A. R. R. "Pagan Cults of Angels in Roman Asia Minor." *Talanta* 12–13 (1980/81): 77–101.

Simon, Marcel. "Theos Hypsistos." In *Le christianisme antique et son contexte religieux*. WUNT 23. Vol. 2 (Tübingen, 1981): 495–508.

Verus Israel: A Study of the Relations between Christians and Jews in the Roman Empire (AD 135–425) (Oxford, 1986).

Smallwood, E. Mary. "The Diaspora in the Roman Period Before CE 70." In *CHJ*. Vol. 3: *The Early Roman Period*, eds. William Horbury, W. D. Davies, and John Sturdy (Cambridge, 1999): 168–91.

Stern, Menahem. *Greek and Latin Authors on Jews and Judaism* (= *GLAJJ*). 3 vols. (Jerusalem, 1974–84).

Strubbe, Johan H. M. "Curses Against Violations of the Grave in Jewish Epitaphs from Asia Minor." In *Studies in Early Jewish Epigraphy*, eds. Jan Willem van Henten, and Pieter Willem van der Horst (Leiden, 1994): 70–128.

Tcherikover, Victor A. *Hellenistic Civilization and the Jews* (1959; repr. New York, 1975).

Trebilco, Paul R. *Jewish Communities in Asia Minor*. SNTSMS 69 (Cambridge, 1991).
"Asia." In *The Book of Acts in Its First Century Setting, 2: Graeco-Roman Setting*, eds. David W. J. Gill and Conrad H. Gempf (Grand Rapids, Mich., 1994): 291–362.

"The Christian *and* Jewish Eumeneian Formula." In *Negotiating Diaspora: Jewish Strategies in the Roman Empire*, ed. John M.G. Barclay (London, 2004): 66–88.

Van der Horst, Pieter W. "Jews and Christians in Aphrodisias in the Light of Their Relations in Other Cities of Asia Minor." In *Essays on the Jewish World of Early Christianity*. NTOA 14 (Fribourg/Göttingen, 1990): 166–81.

"The Samaritan Diaspora in Antiquity." In *Essays on the Jewish World* (Freiburg, 1990): 136–47.

Ancient Jewish Epitaphs: An Introductory Survey of a Millennium of Jewish Funerary Epigraphy (300 BCE – 700 CE) (Kampen, 1991).

"A New Altar of a Godfearer?" In *Hellenism – Judaism – Christianity: Essays on Their Interaction*, 2nd ed. (Leuven, 1998): 65–72.

"Hosios kai Dikaios." In *Dictionary of Deities and Demons in the Bible (DDD)*, 2nd ed., eds. Karel van der Toorn, Bob Becking, and Pieter W. van der Horst (Leiden, 1999): 427–8.

"Jews and Christians in Antioch at the End of the Fourth Century." In *Christian-Jewish Relations through the Centuries*, eds. Stanley E. Porter and Brook W. R. Pearson (Sheffield, 2000): 228–38.

"Inscriptiones Judaicae Orientis: A Review Article." *JSJ* 36 (2005): 65–83.

"The Synagogue of Sardis and Its Inscriptions." In *Jews and Christians in Their Graeco-Roman Context* (Tübingen, 2006): 43–52.

"Porphyry on Judaism: Some Observations." In *"Follow the Wise." Studies in Jewish History and Culture in Honor of Lee I. Levine*, eds. Zeev Weiss, Oded Irshai, Jodi Magness, and Seth Schwartz (Winona Lake, 2010): 71–83.

Wander, Bernd. *Gottesfürchtige und Sympathisanten: Studien zum heidnischen Umfeld von Diasporasynagogen* (Tübingen, 1998).

Waßmuth, Olaf. *Sibyllinische Orakel 1–2: Studien und Kommentar*. AJEC 76 (Leiden, 2011).

Williams, Margaret H. "The Jews of Corycus – A Neglected Diasporan Community from Roman Times." *JSJ* 25 (1994): 274–86.

The Jews Among the Greeks and Romans: A Diasporan Sourcebook (Baltimore, 1998).

Wineland, J. D. "Sepharad." *ABD* 5 (1992): 1089–90.

Wolff, Hans W. *Dodekapropheton 3: Obadja und Jona*. BKAT XIV/3 (Neukirchen, 1977).

Zuntz, Günther. *Griechische philosophische Hymnen*, eds. Hubert Cancik and Lutz Käppel (Tübingen, 2005).

13

CHRISTIANITY IN ASIA MINOR

OBSERVATIONS ON THE EPIGRAPHY

FRANK R. TROMBLEY

Asia Minor is one of the few areas of the Mediterranean where the continuous development of Christianity can be traced from the first century CE.[1] Apart from Rome, other regions are by comparison devoid of specific literary references to the physical layout of Christian communities, the trades they practiced, their position in local social strata, and their interactions with non-Christians, excluding of course those with imperial and provincial authorities in times of sporadic persecution.

For a long time, the ecclesiastical histories of Eusebius and his successors provided the basic evidence for Asia Minor. Starting with the last decades of the nineteenth century, however, there began systematic exploration of the region for early Christian remains. Among the researchers to visit these sites were J. G. C. Anderson, William Mitchell Ramsay, and Ramsay's students (among them W. H. Buckler and W. M. Calder). The latter took advantage of the construction of the Berlin-to-Baghdad railway to inspect parts of western and central Asia Minor that western scholars had seldom before seen.[2] Some of this research was embodied in Ramsay's monumental *The Cities and Bishoprics of Phrygia*. Their work, and that of teams of German scholars, resulted in the publication of the ten-volume *Monumenta Asiae Minoris Antiqua*, which contains editions of inscriptions and discussion of literary conventions. A comprehensive edition of the early Christian inscriptions of Asia Minor remains, however, a desideratum; many important editions and commentaries still lie buried in volumes of collected articles and back issues of journals. Synthetic treatments of the subject have often been disappointing in their results and at times controversial. An example of this can be seen in unsuccessful

---

[1] It has proved impossible to offer more than a selection of key texts in this chapter.
[2] Frend, *Archaeology of Early Christianity*, 93–104, 130–4, 193–5, etc.

attempts to find Montanist nuances in the "Christians for Christians" inscriptions and other texts.[3]

The discussion that follows provides a commentary on inscriptions that illuminate key features of Christian self-identification in Asia Minor, as well as the language of monotheism with its related eschatological concerns. It also explores the participation of Christians in the main lines of Anatolian social and economic life, which was inseparable from that of their fellow monotheists, the Jews, and the adherents of traditional Greek religion. A broad consistency of thought, yet at the same time flux of religious ideas, can be traced through surviving vernacular and public documents – the canons of provincial councils, inscriptions, and hagiographic texts – all of which make use of a cognate theological terminology. The flux was partly a consequence of the need for Christian families and church communities to communicate their identities in disguised language. This may have enabled them to evade persecution and defacement of their funerary monuments, but generated an idiosyncratic and sometimes even a heretical tone in their statements about personal and family concerns. With the consolidation of the dynasty of Constantine and his sons after 324, the Christian communities achieved greater consistency in the modes of self-identification; this came with an increasingly coercive response to theological difference, whether it was a matter of pre-Christian attitudes toward the interaction of the divine and material worlds, or conceptions of Christ and the ideal Christian community. The final working of the Anatolian synthesis can be seen in the attempts of the "catholic" and "orthodox" church to regulate the use of the sacred space vis-à-vis pre-Christian cult and to transfer it to the liturgies of Christ, the martyrs, and recognized archangels. It involved the prohibition of sacrifice and reduction of traditional gods to the status of daemons, but also an acceptance of the traditional etiologies and liturgies through Christianization of rite. The final synthesis is at the same time visible in systematic attempts to isolate and repress the public voice of Christians who through cultural habit failed to assimilate the theological consensus expressed in the *horos* of the First Ecumenical Council at Nicaea in their teaching, as with the Montanists, Novatianists, and other sects seen as having a defective concept of the Trinity. Culturally and demographically significant dissenting groups still existed at the beginning of the sixth century, but the repressive policies of Justinian the Great were a critical and final factor in reducing these communities to tiny remnants and driving them underground.

---

[3] Tabbernee, *Montanist Inscriptions, passim.*

ORIGINS

The earliest Christian communities took root in the metropolitan towns of the Aegean coastlands such as Ephesus before the Pauline mission of the 50s CE. The new monotheism grew up in the cultural life of the synagogues of some Hellenized Jews who accepted the messianic status of Jesus and were among the so-called God-fearers (*theoseboumenoi*).[4] The latter were gentiles forming a quasi-catechumenate on the periphery of the synagogue, sharing its monotheism and ethical norms, but abstaining from circumcision and the Mosaic dietary laws. Like Hellenistic Jews, Christians utilized the Septuagint as their scripture until the books of the New Testament canon and other early works came into circulation. The Christians soon became alienated from the synagogues, as documented in Acts of the Apostles and the epistles of Paul, and there began a period of uneasy relations between the two communities that worsened with the coming of the Christian empire under Constantine and his sons.[5]

Apart from the fragments of earlier writers excerpted in Eusebius's *Ecclesiastical History*, the earliest document giving an idea of the social composition and behavioral features of the primitive Christian communities is the account of the martyrdom of Polycarp of Smyrna.[6] Much of the reportage in this work is consistent with the data found in the earliest surviving Christian inscriptions, which begin to appear not later than the end of the second century.[7] Among the phenomena mentioned in the Acta of Polycarp are the presence of Christians on farms and estates in the rural territories of Smyrna, their ownership of multistory residential buildings, and Christian agricultural workers of servile status.[8] The early third-century Christian inscriptions of Phrygia often lay on imperial estates and should be read against the rural background of the church of Smyrna.[9]

The practice of Judaism enjoyed long continuity in Asia Minor, and in many respects it developed in parallel with the local Christianities.[10] The most expressive architectural example of this was the synagogue of Sardis. This pattern is also apparent in the way Hellenized Jews codified

---

[4] On "God-fearers," see van der Horst, Chapter 12 of this volume.
[5] Simon, *Verus Israel*; Neusner, *Age of Constantine*.
[6] Musurillo, *Acts of the Christian Martyrs*, 2–21.
[7] Ramsay, *Cities and Bishoprics*, 388, 390, 500, 534, 545f., 549, 553; Tabbernee, *Montanist Inscriptions*, nos. 1–4.
[8] *Mart. Pol.* 5–7.
[9] Anderson, "Paganism and Christianity," 188–93, 200f.
[10] See van der Horst, Chapter 12 of this volume; also Chaniotis, "Jews of Aphrodisias"; idem, "Zwischen Konfrontation und Interaktion."

and expressed their theological views in places like Acmonia.[11] There is a remarkable verse inscription in a funerary altar (*bōmos*) at Eumeneia (ca.211–34 CE) that reflects a synthesis of philosophical ideas with those of a monotheistic religion. Ramsay was inclined to suggest a Jewish authorship for the inscription. One possible translation is as follows:[12]

> Gaius, a tradesman (*pragmatikos*), who was practiced in (the arts of) the Muses, made this tomb for himself and his dear wife and beloved children while still living. May they have an everlasting home (*aiōnios domos*) with Roubēs, who is a servant of a great god (*megaloio th[eou] therapōn*) and with [---], and as an equal of these two men. I Gaius say openly that I am a holy (*hagios*) (and) good (*agathos*) man. I did not have much wealth in my livelihood or much money, but I was practiced in writing and worked at composing verses (*ta metria*). I imparted these to my friends as much as I was able. I pleased everyone with the talent I possessed. It was a pleasurable art for me to practice if anyone desired it, since the happiness of others brought joy to my heart. So let no one who is blinded by wealth be complacent, for Hades is one (and the same) for all and their end is the same. Is anyone great in consequence of his landholdings? This man exists no more and received this measure of ground for his tomb. You mortals should take care to enjoy life at all times, as life is sweet and (this) is the measure of life. This (comes) after that, my friends, for what more is there? (Then) this (exists) no longer. Stele and stone speak these words, for I am no longer. The gates and roads to Hades are here, and its footpaths have no exit to daylight (*anexodeutoi d' esti es phaos triboi*). All the wretched people [– –] for rising again (*es anastasin*) [– –].

Gaius's statement is at first sight full of paradoxes. One might associate his implied association with the great god, his self-characterization as "holy," and the closing reference to "rising again" with a monotheistic religion. But "great god" was a theologically neutral expression, as was "eternal home," and both turn up at times in clearly non-Christian inscriptions.[13] Ramsay saw Epicurean and Stoic elements in Gaius's characterization of the joys of living, but being a "good" man is if anything a Platonic concept. The observations about the fate of the soul after death were easy to come by for anyone knowledgeable in Greek literature, which Gaius clearly was. It is easier to take Gaius's statement as a contextually mixed synthesis of all the different systems of thought commonly available in early third-century Eumeneia, but with a particular predilection for monotheistic ideas. While one might have anticipated a statement of this type from a member of the Christian catechumenate or "God-fearers" leaning to Judaism, there is strictly speaking no simple way to make an exact identification of Gaius's

---

[11] Ramsay, *Cities and Bishoprics*, nos. 562–4.
[12] Ibid., 386–8, no. 232.
[13] *MAMA* 4, no. 228.

adherence. Eumeneia is one of the few towns to have large concentrations of Christian clergy and lay persons attested in its third-century epigraphy,[14] and the famous Eumeneian formula "he shall be accountable to God" or "the god" is itself of pre-Christian origin and therefore theologically ambiguous,[15] sometimes appearing in contexts where the cult of the persons named is in doubt.[16] The Gaius inscription may be an early indication of the theological flux from which the Christian consensus finally arose in Eumeneia. There is also the possibility that Gaius intended to disguise his adherence to Christian monotheism by using ambiguous or polyvalent theological language, a process William Calder characterized as "crypto-Christian" evasion.

THE DISCOURSE OF CHRISTIAN MONOTHEISM

There was thus a "special relationship" between the primitive Christian local churches of Asia Minor and the non-Christian populations from whom the catechumenate was drawn. In various ways the older etiologies and rituals would become part of a new Christian synthesis that drew on the language of the older ethos, but was ruthlessly monotheistic in its final formulation. While the main period of transition was the third and fourth centuries, experimentation in the new language extended until the time of George the Monk, author of the life of Theodore of Sykeon (d.613). The Christian God was usually conceived in exclusively monotheistic terms. Although the common phrase "one God" seldom appears in the epigraphy of Asia Minor, it has a degree of currency in the letters of Ignatius to the Christian communities of Ephesus and Magnesia.[17] A pre-Christian form of this idea occurs in an inscription of Settae or Saettae in Lydia, and reveals the pre-Christian currency of any number of designations: "(There is) one god in the heavens, (the) great celestial Men (*megas Mēn ouranios*). Great is the power of the immortal god (*athanatos theos*)."[18] There is an important counterfoil to this in a Christian "one God" funerary inscription originally copied by Ramsay: "No one is immortal except only (the) one God himself, the begetter of all things who apportions all things to all."[19] While earlier divinities continued to enjoy their spheres of activity, they fell to the

---

[14] Drew-Bear, *Inscriptions de Phrygie*, nos. 48–9.
[15] Ibid., nos. 44–9.
[16] *MAMA* 4, no. 91.
[17] Ignatius, *Eph.* 7.2 (*heis iatros … theos*); *Mag.* 8.2 (*heis theos estin*). See E. Peterson, *ΕΙΣ ΘΕΟΣ*, 77f.
[18] Cited in Peterson, *ΕΙΣ ΘΕΟΣ*, 268.
[19] Petrie, "Epitaphs," no. 11.

degraded status of daemons (*daimones*), persisting in folklore and ritual of Greece and Asia Minor until the twentieth century.[20]

The religious affiliation of the authorship of a significant number of late second- and third-century inscriptions is ambiguous. Arguments for or against Christian authorship are indecisive. A good example of this is seen in a funerary inscription at Brouzos in the Phrygian Pentapolis (late second century?). After naming the deceased, it adds a curse: "We adjure the greatness of God (or "the god," *to megethos tou theou*) and the subterranean daemons (*katachthonioi daimones*) that no one injure this tomb and no one else be placed in it."[21] This phrasing is based on earlier, pre-Christian formulations, as for example, "If anyone harms the tomb (*to mnēmeion*), he shall be accountable to the celestial gods and to the subterranean <gods> who have been provoked."[22] References to "the god" can also be Christian, as in the case of the Eumenian formula, but not in every instance. The activity of subterranean daemons as the guardian spirits of tombs and buried wealth remained a feature of Christian Anatolian belief for many centuries after this, until the time of Theodore of Sykeon (seventh century).

It should be recognized that pagan and Christian shared an increasingly conventionalized language of discourse in the literature, both epigraphic and literary, about the divine milieu.[23] This was a consequence of the increasingly shared high culture of the Greek *paideia*, which had already made its influence felt in the catechetical school of Alexandria and which Gregory Thaumaturgus promoted in the borderlands of northeastern Anatolia.[24] Clear traces of the *paideia* exist in the Christian funerary inscriptions of Asia Minor from the middle of the third century. An inscription mentions a Christian teacher of grammar (*grammatikos*) in the borderlands of Lycaonia.[25] There is a notable example of this at Aslanapa in the territory of Cotyaeum (ca.250–325), in an inscription that mixes epic meter and morphology with somewhat clumsy late Greek grammar and spelling. A fairly literal translation might run like this:[26]

Suddenly you lie, O young woman, last of all (of our children), after receiving the sting of a terrible Mistress. You were given in marriage to death (*moros*) and your father did not betroth you to a marriage bed, but the deadly Furies in Acheron doubly bewail your name Kyrilla to your parents, Katylla (and) Menandros,

[20] Lawson, *Modern Greek Folklore*, 66–70, 89–91, 120, 146f., etc.
[21] Ramsay, *Cities and Bishoprics*, no. 635.
[22] Ibid., no. 592; see above, note 15.
[23] Jaeger, *Paideia, passim;* Dodds, *Pagan and Christian.*
[24] Altaner, *Patrologie*, 187f.; Young, "Towards a Christian *paideia*," 485.
[25] Callander, "Explorations," no. 73.
[26] *MAMA* 10, no. 275.

and (brother) Onesimos and sister-in-law Alexandria. All of them together were servants of merciless Plouton, for he has laid garlands for this (young woman) over whom it was more proper for revellers to rave. Christians for Christians.

Praise of this sort could please a family whose members enjoyed an education in Greek grammar. The mythological references can only have been understood as an extended metaphor for the grief these people suffered, and perhaps a desire to impress their social and cultural peers in local society. There would have been little question about the monotheistic views of the family in light of the militant closing formula "Christians for Christians."[27]

THE CHRISTIANIZATION OF SPACE

A central feature of Christian institutions in Asia Minor was the construction and use of buildings for liturgical activity. There is little evidence about the use of buildings for primitive Christian liturgical activity. While it is usually supposed that "house churches" were the norm, there is no archaeological evidence to bolster this hypothesis for Asia Minor. The absence of any references to buildings in correspondence between Trajan and Pliny the Younger tends to corroborate the idea that Christians relied on the houses of their community. This is borne out by the epigraphy; not one of the pre-Constantinian inscriptions of Asia Minor mentions the construction of a church. The earliest of these is the funerary altar of Abercius of Hieropolis, a small town in the Upper Tembris valley in Phrygia; it gives the impression of an ecclesiastical organization in the countryside, but no indications of church buildings. Its ostensible author could even observe, "My name is Abercius, disciple of the holy shepherd who feeds his flocks on mountains and plains."[28] It is a clearly literary simile, but may also be a reflection of local practice involving open-air liturgies organized in the countryside to avoid the scrutiny of civil officials. In other inscriptions such as the "Christians to Christians" documents, the community is emphasized rather than the local church or a particular locality. Such buildings as turn up are the "eternal house" (*aiōnios oikos*) of the Christian afterlife, as in the funerary inscription of Aurelios Satorneinos (242/43 CE).[29] The choice of the word *oikos* may be as much an indication of the buildings where Christians assembled

[27] Gibson, *"Christians for Christians,"* 4–98.
[28] Snyder, *Ante Pacem*, 139f.
[29] Gibson, *"Christians for Christians,"* 116–19, no. 42.

as an expression of eschatological hope. The open-air character of the
pre-Christian cults of Asia Minor – which were often associated with
numinous places such as mountain peaks, rivers, sacred springs, trees, and
subterranean rock formations – may have assured a degree of continuity
in this.[30] The later life of Abercius mentions the existence of Christian
buildings in the countryside around Hieropolis. A probably apocryphal
fifth-century tradition has it that Abercius supervised the construction of
these places using funds donated by Plotina, the wife of Marcus Aurelius.
The endowments – which appear to be historical – may well have come
from the wife of Constantius II (337–61). Whatever the case, the historical Abercius may well have used his personal wealth to establish open-air
shrines in the town's territory that later became sites of liturgical focus
and later acquired buildings in the time of Constantine or Constantius.
There is the example of Gonyklisia:[31]

> It happened that [Abercius] was one day on a high mountain that is opposite the
> city of Lysia. When he and the people with him became thirsty, he knelt down
> and prayed. A spring of pure water bubbled up and everyone who was thirsty drew
> satisfaction from it. The place was called Gonyklisia ("spot of kneeling") from that
> time on.

The place may well have been a limestone peak – places where geological forces drove groundwater upward and caused it to exit as a spring.
Detecting potential springs was a well-known practice and is mentioned
as late as the mid-sixth century, when Nicholas of Hagia Sion discovered hidden water on a mountain in the territory of Myra in Lycia. In
pre-Christian lore, the breaking forth of a spring in a "high place" was
considered a numinous event controlled by subterranean divinities, particularly Attis-Men and certain non-Christian "angels." Christian leaders
who discovered or exploited springs attributed these natural phenomena
to the mastery of the Christian God over the forces of nature. Church
leaders sometimes built hydraulic installations in these places, like the
bathhouse at Agros on the River, another place where Abercius had knelt
and prayed, and where "springs of hot water had then bubbled up," as
the fifth-century tradition about him reports.[32] These institutions must
be seen partly in terms of competition with the gods and their priesthoods who dispensed the ground waters at sacred springs. Archaeological
finds could change this view of pre-Constantinian Christianity in Asia
Minor, but until then one must put the construction of the monumental

---

[30] Trombley, *Hellenic Religion and Christianization* 1, 151f., 153f.
[31] *V. Abercii*, §75 (Nissen 52, lines 9–15).
[32] *V. Abercii* §65 (Nissen 46, lines 14–19).

early Christian basilicas in places like Nicomedia not earlier than the late third century.[33]

CHRISTIAN PARTICIPATION IN PUBLIC LIFE

Christians participated fully in the social, political, and economic life of their communities in the century before Constantine. This is borne out by the professions they practiced and the social conventions they observed. Among the status positions mentioned in the Christian inscriptions of Eumeneia in Phrygia are a number of city councillors (*bouleutai*), men who because of wealth in landed property sat in city council and at times served as the local executives, involving themselves in the maintenance of public works and sometimes even funding public spectacles.[34] A number of the Christians of Eumeneia in Phrygia enjoyed formal membership in the traditional tribes of the *polis* and displayed pride in this, like a certain Aurelius Phrontōn, "citizen of Eumeneia of the tribe (*phylē*) of Argias."[35] Aurelius Messalas, a Christian city councillor of Sebaste in Phrygia, was also a physician.[36] Another Christian named Demetrianus from Claudiopolis was city councillor, first archon of the town's executive and agonothete, that is, organizer of the games. In this instance, he may have succeeded in avoiding the public liturgies such as gladiatorial combats and stage productions. For while Christian sponsors of these spectacles were condemned for "murder" and "adultery" at the Council of Elvira in Spain, a family funerary inscription praises Demetrianus and his kin as "faithful to God and most pure."[37]

Many army veterans, who enjoyed higher social status as *honestiores*, settled in Eumeneia.[38] The first Christian soldiers do not appear until perhaps circa 290–300. There were two of them, one of whom allowed his friend to be buried in a tomb he had made for himself and his wife. The inscription gives a good idea of the upward mobility of Christians into the middle ranks as officers in the military and civil hierarchy under the Tetrarchy and thereafter, particularly after Constantine became sole Augustus:[39]

Aurelius Neikerōs prepared the tomb for himself, his wife and children, but I set a friend (in it instead). In this place is buried Aurelius Mannos, soldier, cavalry

---

[33] Gibson, *"Christians for Christians."*
[34] Ramsay, *Cities and Bishoprics*, nos. 359, 361, 368; Johnson, *Early-Christian Epitaphs*, no. 3.3.
[35] Ramsay, *Cities and Bishoprics*, no. 378. Cf. no. 364 = Johnson, *Christian Epitaphs*, no. 3.4.
[36] Ramsay, *Cities and Bishoprics*, no. 451.
[37] Cited by Johnson, *Early Christian Epitaphs*, no. 3.1.
[38] Ramsay, *Cities and Bishoprics*, no. 209 and commentary.
[39] Ramsay, *Cities and Bishoprics*, 372; cf. Johnson, *Christian Epitaphs*, no. 3.9.

archer (and) bearer of the dragon standard (*drakōnaris*) from the headquarters (*ex ophikiou*) of the most brilliant governor (*hēgemōn*) Castrius Constans. If anyone else does this, he will be accountable to God.

Christians were thus found in the *officium* of a civil governor, perhaps of Phrygia. Another example of this was the well-known Marcus Iulius Eugenius, who was a soldier in the *officium* of the governor of Pisidia at the time of Maximinus Daia's decree for Christians to sacrifice and later became a possibly Montanist bishop of Laodicea Combusta.[40] A Christian *protector*, or staff officer attached to a senior military commander or logistic services as the occasion required, is mentioned at Nicaea, probably at the time of the Tetrarchy.[41] A certain Aurelius Mannos was still on active service in Eumeneia, as he does not receive the epithet of "veteran," which commonly appears in other inscriptions there.[42] Among other professions and trades attested in the third and early fourth centuries is an armorer (*hoplopoios*). All this provides additional corroboration for the participation of Christians in the equipping and supplying of armies.[43]

Some Christians practiced lower-status trades, like a certain Antonius Polliōn, who was a dealer in miscellaneous wares (*pantopōlēs*) (256 CE).[44] The butcher's trade (*makellos*) is recognizable because his funerary marker bears the relief sculpture of a meat cleaver.[45] Many of the social values expressed in funerary inscriptions are predictable in families that owned a bit of property and stiffly maintained their property rights, even vis-à-vis their own children. An inscription containing a variation of the Eumeneian formula illustrates this "bourgeoisie" *mentalité* (third century?):[46]

I Phougillianos Auxanōn made the tomb for myself, for my wife Metrodora, and for the children of my blood as long as they are not fully of legal age, but after they become of legal age neither they nor anyone else shall do anything to the bones of their parents. If anyone contravenes this, he shall be accountable to God the judge.

THE LANGUAGE OF CHRISTIAN FUNERARY INSCRIPTIONS

The interpretation of funerary inscriptions is the usual vehicle for identifying Christians, but it is recognized that these documents are frequently

---

[40] Wischmeyer, "M. Iulius Eugenius," 226. Tabbernee, *Montanist Inscriptions*, no. 69.
[41] Johnson, *Christian Epitaphs*, no. 3.10.
[42] Ramsay, *Cities and Bishoprics*, nos. 210, 212, 213, 218.
[43] Johnson, *Christian Epitaphs*, no. 3.11.
[44] Ramsay, *Cities and Bishoprics*, no. 449.
[45] Ibid., no. 388.
[46] Ibid., no. 394.

coded. Because their cult was legally a *religio prava* until the edicts of Galerius (311 CE) and Constantine and Licinius (313 CE) made it a *religio licita,* Christians relied on cryptic language and symbols to avert deface-ment. Recognizable Christian communities emerge in the third-century funerary epigraphy of Apamea and Eumeneia in Phrygia; some Christians partially disguised their identities through the use of coded symbols and terminology.

There are two extraordinary examples at Apamea. The first of them is likely to be contemporaneous with Abercius's funerary altar (late second century CE), and one of the very earliest Christian inscriptions known.[47] After the usual commemorations, it concludes, "Farewell, and may those who pass by offer prayers also for [Artemidorus our son]."[48] The offering of prayers (*euchai*) for the living is also requested in the Abercius inscription and seems normally to have been a particularly Christian practice.[49] Most Christian funerary inscriptions of the third century observe the conven-tions of pagan funerary epigraphy in terms of formulaic language, using terms like *hērōion* (lit. "a hero's temple") for tomb. They also made use of a conventional curse formula against tomb breaking (*tymbōrychia*), requiring the payment of fines to the pagan temple treasury or sometimes invoking the retribution of the gods, as for example, "If anyone harms the tomb, he shall be accountable to the celestial and subterranean divinities who have become enraged,"[50] whether for reasons of burying another corpse or grave robbery.[51] The formula was clothed in monotheistic guise and has become known as the Eumeneian formula because of the large concentration of funerary inscriptions there using the formula "If anyone does this, he shall be accountable to God."[52] The divinity is sometimes characterized in more elaborate terms such as "the living God," "the eternal flail of the immortal God," "the great name of God," "Jesus Christ," "the hand of God," "the justice of God," and "God the judge."[53] Curses were sometimes appended such as "may neither earth nor heaven receive his soul."[54] Others examples

[47] For the date and identity of the persons named, see Ramsay, *Cities and Bishoprics,* 534, no. 387.
[48] Ramsay, *Cities and Bishoprics,* 534, no. 387.
[49] Cf. Buckler, "Asia Minor, 1924 I," no. 24 (fourth to fifth century).
[50] Ramsay, *Cities and Bishoprics,* no. 592.
[51] Ibid., no. 592.
[52] *MAMA* 4, nos. 91, 264, 354–60; Ramsay, *Cities and Bishoprics,* 497–9, nos. 353–62, 364–71, 373–9, 385–6, 388–92, 394–6, 399, 401, 435, 445–6, 448–51, 455–7, 465–6, 651–2, 660, 684; Anderson, "Summer in Phrygia: II," no. 53 *bis*; Drew-Bear, *Nouvelles inscriptions,* nos. 44–8; Tabbernee, *Montanist Inscriptions,* 144–6, nos. 20, 33. On Jewish use of this formula, see van der Horst, Chapter 12 of this volume.
[53] Ramsay, *Cities and Bishoprics,* nos. 353–5, 361, 362, 364, 369, 371, 374, 378, 392, 394, 455–7.
[54] Ibid., no. 435.

include "[The tomb-breaker] shall be accursed before God for eternity,"[55] and "We adjure God that no one should plunder the tomb of our body."[56] The Christian formula first appears in the third century and was still in use as late as 349.[57] A good example of Christian cryptopoiesis combining these features is seen in another inscription of Apamea (259 CE):[58]

In the year 343 (of the Sullan era). I Aurelius Artemas made the tomb for myself and for my wife Tatia and for my children. No one else shall be buried in it. If someone does this, he shall be accountable to the immortal [god].

The authorship makes use of an expanded Eumeneian formula; "immortal" god (*athanatos theos*) is not necessarily a Christian formulation.[59] But in the Anatolian context it probably is, there being few pagan Greek examples of it to hand.[60] Moreover, the stone has a relief sculpture showing a meat cleaver, indicating that the deceased was a butcher, and a vase, a common Christian but perhaps also Stoic symbol.[61] A Christian butcher circa 259 CE would have been less likely to handle sacrificial meats. There is another possible example of Christian encryption at Apamea (third century):[62]

I Aurelius Auxanon twice made the tomb as a gift for myself and for my brother Dosityches with his wife. No one else shall be buried in it. If anyone does this, he shall be accountable to God. Farewell by me, you lovers of the divine and good men newly caught.

The use of the Eumeneian formula lends a specifically Christian identity to the "lovers of the divine" and "good men newly caught" (*philotheoi kai kaloi neothēroi*), the latter a reference to the newly baptized and catechumens.

Inscriptions confessing the *nomen Christianum* and avoiding the types of *cryptopoiesis* just described were a parallel development. Among these were the "Christians" and "Christians for Christians" inscriptions and other simpler examples. There is no particular reason to assign these open and vivid expressions of belief to Montanist Christians, who for the most part shared the views of their catholic-orthodox neighbors.[63] By the second half of the fourth century, Christian funerary conventions would change in a self-conscious way; the use of the Greek cross and Chi-Rho became

[55] Ibid., no. 445.
[56] Ibid., no. 661.
[57] Ibid., 538, no. 399.
[58] Ibid., 534, no. 388; Buckler, "Asia Minor, 1924 I," no. 2.
[59] Peterson, *ΕΙΣ ΘΕΟΣ*, 268–70; see previous note.
[60] The word normally appears in the plural.
[61] Snyder, *Ante Pacem*, 16. M. Ant. 3.3 (*angeion*, "clay vessel" or "pitcher").
[62] Ramsay, *Cities and Bishoprics*, 535, no. 389.
[63] Tabbernee, *Montanist Inscriptions*.

general, and a theologically neutral language was devised to express the concept of the tomb. These words reflected local attitudes; in addition to the very common *mnēmeion* ("memorial"), one finds *thēkē* ("cist tomb") and *sōmatothēkē* ("body box") in the Christian necropolis at Corycus in Cilicia Tracheia,[64] and *soros* ("cinerary urn") in parts of the Lycus valley.[65] The term *hērōon* ("hero's tomb"), and in some instances *mnēmeion* and *hērōon* in combination,[66] were gradually displaced by *koimētērion* ("place of sleep").[67]

CHRISTIAN COMMUNITIES IN LATE ANTIQUITY

The Christian communities of Asia Minor become eclipsed in fourth-century sources. This is partly a consequence of the importance that Eusebius's continuators, Socrates, Sozomen, and Theodoret, give to the Arian controversy. The datable Christian inscriptions decrease in number in Phrygia, but become more widespread in other parts of Asia Minor. Ancyra in Galatia is a good example of an urban site. It possessed a school of rhetoric where Themistius taught, and its Christian inscriptions show a similar preoccupation with the *paideia*. A fourth-century Christian city councillor (*bouleutēs*) seems to have built or repaired bridges and roads in the second half of the fourth century. An inscription celebrating his achievement makes use of flowery language borrowed from the Homeric poems and attests the existence of a Christian sophistic in the provincial capital of Galatia:[68]

+ For a blessing. The divine John, a subject of song among the citizens (and) a bold-hearted man, built a road in front of the city amidst its suburban inhabitants as a man who excelled at wisdom and thought in his decrees. Ancyra found glory (*kleos*) with the help of its godlike citizens, and made things easier for all travellers. + May John, the bridegroom (?) (*euparochos*) of the fatherland, increase in power.

Christians belonging to the churches who signed the decrees of the ecumenical Councils of Nicaea in 325 and Constantinople in 381 acquired a sense of independent identity vis-à-vis the dissenting churches of Asia Minor – among them the Montanists.[69] These "catholic" or "orthodox"

---

[64] *MAMA* 3, nos. 203, 204, etc.
[65] Ramsay, *Cities and Bishoprics*, 416.
[66] Ibid., no. 652.
[67] Ibid., nos. 375, 376, 379, 400, 445, 447, 654, 659, etc.; Ramsay, "Tekmorian guest-friends," no. 28; Johnson, *Christian Epitaphs*, no. 3.10.
[68] *SEG* 27, no. 874.
[69] Cf. Calder, "Julia-Ipsus and Augustopolis," no. 21.

Christians became known not only for public works as city councillors, but for the construction of installations needed by the churches, of which there is a striking fourth-century example in the western province of Lydia:[70]

Gennadius son of Helios built this cemetery (*koimētērion*) of the Christians of the universal church (*katholikē eklēsia* (*sic*)) out of the funds that God gave him. May peace be with him at the hands of the Lord through all the ages.

The so-called sects and heretical churches were also beginning to assert distinctive identities by this time: one sees this in another inscription of perhaps fourth-century date at Nicaea. It is theologically expressive, rather illiterate in spelling, and peculiar in detail:[71]

Gerontiōn of godly mind built this tomb for himself out of his own labors, being of the same name as his father, marking out the foundations and busily completing the entire building (and) being a father (*patēr*) of the church of the Pious (*hē tōn Eusebōn ekklēsia*), hospitably receiving a shelter (and) resurrection (*anastasis*) for his mortal body, and for his most faithful Christ-bearing wife Kyradiē who lived for 28 years, and for his beloved (and) dearest sons Gerontios and also Leonidas who have Christ in their hearts.

It has been suggested that Gerontiōn was perhaps a member of the clergy of the Novatian church, but his clerical rank as "father" is unusual. Funerary inscriptions of presbyters of the churches of Novatian and the Apotactics are reported at Laodicea Combusta in Phrygia, and the detailed funerary narrative of a young woman who adhered to Novatian asceticism is known from the upper Tembris valley in Phrygia.[72] It would be valuable to know the size of the community and whether it possessed ecclesiastical buildings. One last theologically inspired funerary inscription belongs to the second half of the fourth century and reflects the final synthesis of the Anatolian and Judaic ideas of angels with orthodox Christianity in the cult of the angel Michael, supreme commander or *archistratēgos* of the heavenly army. It comes from Yüreme, a place some kilometers from the great church at Germia in Galatia, where the cult was centered:[73]

Here lies Sōtērichos, a man worthy of long memory, who considered that God can raise from the dead and entrusted himself to the *archistratēgos* (and) who (long ago) in this place received the ordinance for the beginning of his life.

---

[70] *SEG* 19, no. 719.
[71] Ibid., no. 1323.
[72] Buckler, "Asia Minor, 1924. IV," 51–7.
[73] *SEG* 6, no. 73.

The last clause might provide a reference to Christian baptism. The inscriptions provide a fragmentary, if revealing, picture of the modes of theological speculation and ritual of later fourth-century Asia Minor. The regionally focused biographies of the founders of monastic communities thereafter become our principal sources of information. These texts have documentary value, and are quite consistent with the epigraphy in their use of vernacular Greek, in the behavioral situations they describe, and in social and institutional structures they depict.

MONTANISM IN ASIA MINOR

The problem of Montanism in Asia Minor has occupied scholars since the beginning of the twentieth century. There are detailed references to the founders of the "sect," its beliefs and practices in Eusebius of Caesarea's *Ecclesiastical History* and in the *Panarion* of Epiphanius of Salamis (d.403). Its agenda is sometimes referred to as the "New Prophecy" because it claimed revealed status for the pronouncements of its prophets and prophetesses. Liturgical innovations developed around the ritual of delivering prophecies. Montanist clerical structure differed from that of the apostolic sees and their suffragans, to the extent that women enjoyed the same status as men in liturgical matters ("gender neutrality").[74] It is true that there was an early tradition in the apostolic churches of a women's diaconate, but the extent to which this entailed ordination to ecclesiastical orders is problematic.[75] There were also the traditions about the prophetic expertise of daughters of the apostle Philip at Laodicea. Female deacons are in any case rare in the Christian epigraphy of Asia Minor, and none have been noted in connection with this study.

The prevailing view is that the existence of "Montanist" inscriptions has been much exaggerated.[76] The indisputably Montanist inscriptions of Asia Minor are few and of relatively late date, circa fifth to sixth century.[77] The superior of many of these communities was known as the *koinōnos*, a term that seems to have the literal sense of "partner" or "participant," and whose functions seem to have been similar to those of a bishop, in the sense that their powers extended over geographically defined districts. Titles like "patriarch," "bishop," and "presbyter" appear also to have been used.[78]

---

[74] Tabbernee, *Montanist Inscriptions*, 70–2.
[75] *PGL, s.v. diakonos.*
[76] Tabbernee, *Montanist Inscriptions*, 553–69.
[77] Ibid., nos. 84–5, 87.
[78] Ibid., nos. 3–8.

Three *koinōnoi* are named in the inscriptions of Asia Minor, all of them from later centuries: "holy Paulinus the 'initiate' (*mystēs*) and *koinōnos*" (Sebaste, fifth century), "holy Praylios the regional *koinōnos* (*kata topon*)" (Philadephia, 8 March 515), and another with the same title (Bagis, fifth to sixth century).[79] It is of some interest that these clearly Montanist prelates made use of conventional catholic-orthodox symbols, including divergent forms of the Chi-Rho and the Latin cross (with serifs). Apart from the prelates' titulature, there is nothing to distinguish these stones from "non-sectarian" Anatolian Christianity. Montanist holy men sometimes bore the epithet *pneumatikos*, or "inspired by the Spirit." It has been proposed that epigraphic expressions like "holy *pneumatikos*" and "Christian *pneu-matikos* " may well refer to Montanists,[80] but the designation could be a product of other motives. Elsewhere, onomastics may provide evidence where the name "Montanus," a common Anatolian name in earlier centuries, was used. Personal names associated with sectarian leaders may well have been avoided in the catholic-orthodox consensus. In consequence, a *prōtodiakonos* Montanus on a marble slab (fifth century), perhaps of Pepuza or Tymion, may well have been an adherent of the group.[81] We are probably also on ground with a funerary inscription mentioning the death of a Stephania who was the leader (*hēgoumenē*) of five lamp-bearing virgins (*lampadiphoroi* (*sic*) *parthenoi*) at Ankara. Following Epiphanius of Salamis, one may well deduce that they were female presbyters who prophesied at liturgical events. Apart from this, however, the titulature and epigraphic symbols are identical with those found on catholic-orthodox inscriptions: *hēgoumenē* was in use for prioresses of Christian female ascetics and *theophilestatos* ("most divinely beloved of Christ") was a normal feature of ecclesiastical titulature. The symbols are conventional Greek crosses typical of the later fifth and sixth centuries.[82] Assuming that the inscription reflects a Montanist community in Ankara at this time, one can see that it used conventional cultural language and symbols to communicate its theological ideas, and was practically indistinguishable from catholic-orthodox Christians except for certain differences in hierarchy and liturgy.

There remains the question of whether the Montanists had church buildings. Before Constantine, their situation was identical with that of catholic-orthodox Christians. The tomb of Montanus and the prophetesses Maximilla and Priscilla lay at Pepuza, where healings were said to

[79] Ibid., nos. 80, 84, 85.
[80] Ibid., nos. 86, 95; cf. ibid., no. 55.
[81] Ibid., no. 77.
[82] Ibid., no. 87.

take place. Successive imperial laws imposed disabilities on their freedom of practice. John of Ephesus definitively looted and destroyed the shrine at Pepuza in 550.[83] The twin sites of Pepuza and Tymion now appear to have been located. The proposed site of Pepuza is a deep and elongated ravine called Ulubey canyon. It has been the object of an intensive architectural and surface survey.[84] Pepuza seems to have been part of a large Roman estate. In its present condition, the site consists of a series of rock-hewn dwellings for solitary monks in the canyon wall and evidence of a "Byzantine" Christian basilica.[85] These installations are likely to have been fitted out after the eradication of the shrine in 550.[86] No decisive epigraphic or material evidence of the proposed Montanist phase of the site (pre-550) has come to light. A recently discovered inscription of Septimius Severus (ca.April 200–209/10) has now given the approximate location of Tymion.[87] Among other things, the stone indicates that this place, probably an imperial estate, had a population of tenant farmers (*coloni*), a characteristic feature of other regions where Christianity arose in second century Asia Minor. The Montanists supposed that New Jerusalem was to come into existence in the intervening area between Pepuza and Tymion, which lie some 10km apart.[88]

CHRISTIANITY AS AN EXPRESSION OF ANATOLIAN CULTURE: CONTINUITY AND INNOVATION

Callinicus of Rufinianae's life of St. Hypatius contains detailed reports about Anatolian Christianity in the province of Bithynia located across the straits opposite Constantinople. The well-constructed internal chronology of the texts allows us to put many of the reported events in the last few years of his life (ca.443–46). There is epigraphic evidence as to the location of the monastery in the rural territory of Chalcedon, a limestone column naming the place (+ *monēs*(*terion*) (*sic*) *Rhouphinianōn*) found between the villages of Kartal and Samandira in the rural territory of Chalcedon not far from the sea of Marmara near the harbor of Chalka (present-day Kartal) and a village or estate apparently named Pion.[89] The place name

[83] Ibid., nos. 1–2.
[84] Tabbernee and Lampe, *Pepouza and Tymion*, 133–265.
[85] Ibid., 97–100, 103f.
[86] Ibid., 93–100.
[87] Ibid., 56–72.
[88] Ibid., 102.
[89] Cf. *SEG* 36, no. 1145, 1146.

Rufinianae derives from the name of a landed magnate named Rufinus who was Praetorian Prefect of Oriens (392–95). The lands were thereafter neglected, and had reverted to the *res privata* of the emperor after Rufinus's dismissal and execution on 27 November 395.[90] Hypatius and a small group of ascetics occupied the site of an abandoned *apostoleion* or shrine of Sts. Peter and Paul, probably as squatters, on 3 April 400, for no landed properties were attached to it. It lay within the same territorial circumscription as another institution, a martyr chapel at Bostancı Köprü, located some 12km southeast of Chalcedon, whose inscription names two of the principal personages who figure in the life of Hypatius:[91]

The foundations of the *martyrion* of St. Christopher were laid in the third indiction, in the month of May, after the consulship of the most splendid Protogenes and Asturius, in the time of Emperor Theodosius and Eulalius, bishop of Chalcedon. It was built by the most suitably pious Euphenia, wife of the *cubicularius*. The act of deposition (*katathesis*) was completed in the fifth indiction, on the twenty-second day of the month of September in the consulship of the most splendid Sphorakios.

The inscription is of considerable interest, because its gives the date of the laying of the foundations and the deposition of relics and other accoutrements of the shrine (May 450–22 September 452). It took some two and a half years to complete the construction work and purchase silver vessels, marble altar screens, and other accoutrements for the shrine.[92] At Rufinianae, an unnamed Christian matron made financial contributions to the monastery there, turning it into a going concern after initially difficult beginnings: the monks earned their money by basket weaving, sack making, and gardening, then selling their products in Chalcedon some 4–5km distant. Among its later patrons was a certain Aetius, who was a relative of the *cubicularius* Urbicius, a man who enjoyed direct access to the emperor and later rose to the office of *praepositus sacri cubiculi*.[93] The careful attention to the consular dating formula of the *martyrion* of St. Christopher and offices of the donors indicates that the families of senior public officials in the capital took a serious interest in subsidizing monastic foundations. The coastlands and mountains of Bithynia were also a refuge for the wealthier element in Constantinopolitan society. Some owned estates and gardens, but others invested their wealth in asceticism, from

---

[90] Bury, *Later Roman Empire* I, 87.
[91] *SEG* 34, no. 1262.
[92] Grumel, *Chronologie*, 243.
[93] *V. Hypatii* §12.8–13.

time to time taking refuge from the burdens of political life by spending time with the monks.

The life of Hypatius provides important information about the cultural links between fifth-century Anatolian Christianity and earlier cultural formations such as the worship of Great Mother divinities like Artemis and Cybele. A festival called the Basket of Artemis was still celebrated in the hilly hinterlands of the Marmara coast of Bithynia. Hypatius saw it as his task to visit the solitary monks who for reasons of enhancing their asceticism had split off from his group and migrated to "inner" Bithynia along the Rebas river.[94] He also came into contact with the local folk, who warned him about the visitations of Artemis, a deity thought to manifest herself in groves around the hour of noon and destroy passersby. The great temple of Artemis at Ephesus had already been transformed into a church, probably at the beginning of the fifth century. A public official there had erected an inscription proclaiming this act, which was nearly contemporaneous with the foundation of the monastery at Rufinianae:[95]

After tearing down the beguiling image of the daemon Artemis, Demeas set up this marker of the truth in honor of God, the expeller of idols, and the cross, the deathless victory-bearing symbol of Christ.

Hypatius's encounter with Artemis Bendis ought to be seen in light of this and other events, like the closure of the Serapeum in Alexandria and Marneion in Gaza. He was susceptible to religious experiences, interpreting natural phenomena sometimes with theistic, at other times with daemonic, criteria. He may also have been inclined to embellish them, as a unique narrative of one of his journeys indicates:[96]

[Hypatius] went to inner Bithynia where the Rebas river is. There was at that time ... the Basket of the defiled Artemis, [a festival] which the countryside keeps every year, and people do not go out onto the main road for fifty days. When he wanted to travel, the locals said to him: "Where are you going, man? The daemon will meet you on the road. Do not travel, for many are caught." When he heard this, he smiled and said: "You fear these things, but I have Christ as my travelling companion." ... [He] met a very aged woman with the height of ten men. She went around spinning and grazed pigs. When he saw [the apparition], he sealed himself [with the sign of the cross] and stood there praying to God. At once she became invisible, and the pigs fled with a great rush and Hypatius came through unharmed.

---

[94] Ibid., §45.1; *SEG* 36 (1984), no. 1147.
[95] Grégoire, *IGC-As. Min.*, no. 104; Guarducci, *Epigrafia Greca*, 400f.
[96] *V. Hypatii* § 45.

There are no signs of cult in this episode, and the "locals" he consulted were in all probability Christians. This connects the religious culture of the mid-fifth century with that of the sixth, when John of Ephesus claimed to have baptized some 80,000 pagans, and the authors of the lives of St. Nicholas of Hagia Sion and St. Theodore of Sykeon knew of sacred groves, springs and trees that still have retained their associations with the pre-Christian belief and ritual. Yet Book 16 of the Theodosian Code, published in 438, repeated a good many of the laws against sacrifice, notwithstanding the boast of an earlier law 9 April 423 mentioning "pagans who have survived, although we believe there are none left."[97] The pre-Christian theistic beliefs and rituals of Asia Minor are mentioned in later centuries.

The continuity of pagan sacrifice in fifth-century Asia Minor is known mainly from the life of Hypatius. The author discreetly observes:[98]

[Hypatius] had zeal for God and converted many places in Bithynia from the error of idol worship. If he heard that there was a tree or some other such object that some people worshiped, he went there at once, taking along his disciples the monks, cut it down and burned it. Thus the rustics became Christian in part (*kata meros*).

It is difficult to say whether "in part" is intended as a demographic term indicating that a portion of the population became Christian, or whether they accepted baptism but retained the etiologies and rituals of the old faith. In some environments, these cultural variants remained in play for a long time. As Callinicus puts it, "Christianity is not a chance thing" (*ouk esti to tychon Christianismos*).[99] Elsewhere, the author paints a more optimistic picture from the standpoint of incipient monotheism:[100]

At that time [ca.April 403] in Phrygia there was not a [monk], apart from one or two here or there. If a church could be found somewhere, the clergy were lazy because of being too close to the land. In consequence the people are catachumens even until today. When they heard about [Hypatius] and becoming amazed that such a man came from their land, they all became Christians in as short a time as necessity required.

If this proposition is taken at face value, it yields the impression that the movement toward the new monotheism penetrated some parts of the countryside only gradually, even if it was overwhelmingly successful elsewhere. It is otherwise difficult to reconcile the author's seemingly vague

97 *CTh* 16.10.22.
98 *V. Hypatii* §30.1.
99 Ibid., §48.1.
100 Ibid., §1.4–5.

estimates for upper or "inner" Bithynia on the one hand, and Phrygia on the other. It may well be that upper Bithynia, including Mount Olympus, proved attractive to ascetics because of its backwardness. The latter will then have been eager to test their regimen against the gods of the old religion whom the new dispensation had reclassified as daemons. There are few firm answers to these questions for the present.

The continuity of sacrifice can be explained for reasons other than adherence to bygone etiologies. It was associated, for example, with divination (*manteia*) and what has been broadly called Greco-Roman magic, but more properly the curse, most commonly the summoning of a daemon or familiar spirit to assist in carrying out acts of erotic intrigue. It was known as the *maleficium* or *pharmakeia*. There is an archetypal example of *manteia* in the life of Hypatius, an alleged transcription of a conversation he had with an old man who was reputed to be a diviner:[101]

Hypatius: "I have heard about you that you can predict the future, and if someone loses something you tell them who took them (*sic*). Tell me, please, how you do it, so that upon learning how, I might worthily honour you."

The man replied with alacrity: "If someone speaks to me about some [such] matter, it is revealed to me at once during the night, and I tell them each to go out and sacrifice a cow, sheep or bird at the idol temple (*eidōleion*), and furthermore, if an angel (*angelos*) tells me something, I tell."

Hypatius is said to have repaid the compliment by arresting the man and confining him to a cell in the monastery, to avoid "Satan teaching men through you to worship idols." It is striking that some presbyters came to Hypatius not long after and asked him to release the old man. This and another incident provide a useful example of the conflicts that frequently arose between ascetics and regular clergy over the most appropriate response to sacrifice and other questionable ritual. It is said that Hypatius agreed to release the man only after the latter had sworn a written oath to eschew all further practice of divination.

The main lines of the development of Christianity in fourth- to fifth-century Asia Minor are expressed in the epigraphy of the local churches and their ecclesiastical officials. It follows particular conventions, but is at the same time varied in the ways it expresses official purpose. Conversely, many inscriptions have no official purpose at all, but are vernacular documents expressing the aspirations of ordinary people, including the monks. The largest number of these texts were cut in the later

---

[101] Ibid., §43.9–15.

fifth or sixth century, but a great many have provisional dates based on stylistic features.

CHRISTIAN SELF-EXPRESSION AFTER CONSTANTINE

A common theme in the epigraphy is the foundation and furnishing of churches. A small number of churches were donated by emperors, archbishops of wealthy sees, senior military commanders, and landed aristocrats. The *martyrion* of St. Christopher mentioned above is a good example of this.[102] Another is found in a monastery at Daskalion on the island of Nesos among the Hekatonesoi, an archipelago in the gulf of Hadramyttion on the west coast of Asia. Although somewhat later than the other texts here under discussion, it provides a good example of the patronage of monastic institutions. Inscription A. appears on lintels, B. on the lower faces of the architraves:[103]

A. The consecration of the church of the Anargyroi (took place) through the zeal and provision of the patrician Solomon and (his wife) Epiphanis and all the holy fathers in the place. Christ was born of Mary. (cross) God.
B. In the time of Epiphanius the lay estate manager and [–] the humble monk, protopresbyter and *syncellus* [–]. Athletes of Christ, physicians of ailments, pray on their behalf!

The holy Anargyroi, "physicians without fees," were Sts. Cosmas and Damian, whose intercessory powers were considered safe insurance against all forms of illness. Solomon combined the offices of Master of Soldiers and Praetorian Prefect in the recently reconquered provinces of Africa until he died in battle in 544, evidently a protective service not covered by the holy Anargyroi. The poor could hardly afford the types of protection sought by Solomon. More often than not they resorted to the prophylaxis of amulets (*phylaktēria*), which were not always sanctioned by the ecclesiastical authorities. The fourth-century synod of Laodicea had forbidden clergy to manufacture amulets – metal apotropaic objects on which syncretistic formulas and the names of unknown angels were sometimes inscribed.[104] Their manufacture and distribution seem to have been allowed only at ecclesiastically sanctioned Christian pilgrimage centers. Bronze amulets contain predictable formulas and plausibly

---

[102] *SEG* 34, no. 1262.
[103] Grégoire, *IGC-As. Min.*, no 47.
[104] C. Laodicea, *Can.* 36.

reflect the concerns of ordinary Christian folk, like two undated objects acquired in late nineteenth th-century Smyrna. The obverse reads, "+ Seal of Solomon. Expel every evil from the bearer!" The reverse has the word "envy" (*phthonos*) inscribed in the center and written round it is "+ Depart, hated thing! Solomon expels you! Sisinnios Sisinnarios."[105] Another amulet of similar type and the same provenance contains the name of an apparently Jewish angel: "+ Depart, hated thing, (for) Araaph expels you! Seal of Solomon. Protect the bearer!"[106] Invocations against the "evil eye" of envy sometimes appear even on churches.[107]

The less wealthy frequently contributed particular elements to the interior of church buildings, such as marble fittings, mosaics, and even sections of the building. A typical donation and its formula come from a church no longer extant in Smyrna, and the inscription is broken at the end: "+ In fulfilment of a vow, Glaukos made the door-posts and lintel (*perithyron*) of the holy church of God. Lord, remember your servant [– –]."[108] Such donors' motives were similar to those expressed by Solomon in the monastic church at Daskalion.

It can be seen from this analysis that Christianity in Asia Minor reached a turning point in the decades after Constantine's unification of the empire. Vernacular documents in the form of funerary inscriptions suggest that adherence to the new monotheism was often expressed in muted terms from earliest times down to the later third century. Expressions like "great God" and "immortal God" were polyvalent and susceptible to the henotheistic and syncretistic constructions common in late Greek Anatolian religion. The open expression of Christianity embodied in the "Christians for Christians" inscriptions was an ephemeral phenomenon characteristic of the new order devised by Diocletian and his colleagues, the Tetrarchy, which lent freedom of expression to most religious systems except Manichaeism. With the establishment of Constantine's rule in Asia Minor after the demise of Licinius, the vernacular expression of Christian ideas took many different routes, sometimes influenced by the Greek *paideia* (which was a continuous strand running from the late second century onward), at other times influenced by the legal reality that Christians now participated openly in civic life with the approval of the emperors. This can be seen in pious contributions to the local churches, in the establishment of privately funded monasteries, and in the increasing use of Christian symbols on public buildings

---

[105] Grégoire, *IGC-As. Min.*, no. 90 *bis*.
[106] Ibid., no. 90 *ter*.
[107] Ramsay, *Cities and Bishoprics*, no. 689.
[108] Grégoire, *IGC-As. Min.* no. 73.

and Christian funerary inscriptions. These tendencies were in full swing by the second half of the fourth century. They arose on a parallel trajectory with the expansion of the local churches and growth of theological literature. The latter was embodied not only in the writings of the Cappadocian fathers, but also in the decrees of the provincial synods and ecumenical councils and in the hagiographic literature, which gave a vernacular interpretation to all this in the languages of the inscriptions.

BIBLIOGRAPHY

Texts

Callinicus of Rufinianae. *De Vita S. Hypatii Liber. BHG* 760, Seminarii Philogorum (Teubner, 1895).
Bonnensis Sodales. *Vie d'Hypatios* (Leipzig, 1895). Ed. and trans. J. M. Bartelink (Paris, 1971).
George the Monk. *Vie de Théodore de Sykéôn*, ed. A.-J. Festugière. *BHG* 1748, 1–2 (Brussels, 1970).
Subsidia Hagiographica. *Hagios Nikolaos. Der heilige Nikolaos in der griechischen Kirche*, ed. Gustav Anrich. *BHG* 1347, 48, 1–2. (Leipzig, 1913–17; Brussels, 1970).
Joannou, Periklès-Pierre, ed. and trans. *Discipline générale antique (IIe-IXe s.)* (Rome, 1962–64).
Pontificia commisione per la redazione del codice di diritto canonico orientale. *Vita S. Abercii*, ed. Theodor Nissen, Fonti 9 (Leipzig, 1912; Rome, 1962).

Epigraphic and Papyrological Collections

Buckler, William H., and David M. Robinson. *Sardis VII. Greek and Latin Inscriptions. Part I* (Leiden, 1932).
Calder, W. M., et al., eds. *Monumenta Asiae Minoris Antiqua* 1–7 (Manchester, 1928–56).
Drew-Bear, Thomas, ed. *Nouvelles inscriptions de Phrygie* (Zutphen, 1978).
Grégoire, Henri, ed. *Recueil des inscriptions grecques-chrétiennes d'Asie Mineure* (Paris, 1922; repr. Chicago, 1980).
Guarducci, Margherita. *Epigrafia Greca IV. Epigrafi sacre pagane e cristiane* (Rome, 1978).
Johnson, Gary J. *Early-Christian Epitaphs from Anatolia.* SBLTT 35. Early Christian Literature 8 (Atlanta, 1995).
Levick, Barbara, and Stephen Mitchell, eds. *Monumenta Asiae Minoris Antiqua X. Monuments from Appia and the Upper Tembris Valley, Cotiaeum, Cadi, Synaus, Ancyra Siera and Tiberiopolis* (London, 1993).
Roueché, Charlotte. *Aphrodisias in Late Antiquity* (London, 1989). Online edition: http://insaph.kcl.ac.uk/ala2004/refer/concord.html.

Secondary sources

Altaner, Berthold. *Patrologie. Leben, Schriften und Lehre der Kirchenvater* (Freiburg, 1960).
Anderson, John G. C. "A Summer in Phrygia: II." *JHS* 18 (1898): 81–128.

"Exploration in Galatia cis Halym." *JHS* 19 (1899): 52–134, 280–318.

"Paganism and Christianity in the Upper Tembris Valley." In *Studies in the Art and Archaeology of the Eastern Roman Provinces*, ed. William M. Ramsay (Aberdeen, 1906): 183–227.

Barnes, Timothy D. *Constantine and Eusebius.* (Cambridge, Mass., 1981).

Bayliss, Richard. *Provincial Cilicia and the Archaeology of Temple Conversion.* BAR Int. Ser. 1281 (Oxford, 2004).

Brixhe, Claude. "Interactions between Greek and Phrygian under the Roman Empire." In *Bilingualism in Ancient Society: Language Contact and Written Text*, eds. James N. Adams, Mark Janse, and Simon Swain (Oxford, 2002): 246–66.

Buckler, W. H., W. M. Calder, and C. W. M. Cox. "Asia Minor, 1924. I.—Monuments from Iconium, Lycaonia and Isauria." *JRS* 14 (1924): 24–84.

"Asia Minor, 1924. V.—Monuments from the Upper Tembris Valley." *JRS* 18 (1928): 21–40.

Bury, John B. *A History of the Later Roman Empire from the Death of Theodosius I to the Death of Justinian* 1–2 (New York, 1958).

Cabrol, Fernand, and Henri Leclercq, eds. *Dictionnaire d'archéologie chrétienne et de liturgie* 1– (Paris, 1903–50).

Calder, William M. "A journey through the Proseilemmene." *Klio* 10 (1901): 323–42.

"Corpus inscriptionum neo-Phrygianum." *JHS* 31 (1911): 161–215.

"Colonia Caesareia Antiocheia." *JRS* 2 (1912): 78–109.

"Julia-Ipsus and Augustopolis." *JRS* 2 (1912): 233–66.

"Corpus inscriptionum neo-Phrygianum. II." *JHS* 33 (1913): 97–104.

"Studies in Early Christian Epigraphy." *JRS* 10 (1920): 42–59.

"Philadelphia and Montanism." *BJRL* 7 (1922–23): 336–54.

"Studies in Early Christian Epigraphy: II." *JRS* 14 (1924): 85–92.

"The Eumenian Formula." In *Anatolian Studies Presented to William Hepburn Buckler*, eds. William M. Calder and Josef Keil (Manchester, 1939): 15–26.

"Early Christian Epitaphs from Phrygia." *AnSt* 5 (1955): 25–38.

Callander, T. "Explorations in Lycaonia and Isauria, 1904." In *Studies in the History and Art of the Eastern Roman Provinces*, ed. William M. Ramsay (Aberdeen, 1906): 155–80.

Chaniotis, Angelos. "The Jews of Aphrodisias: New Evidence and Old Problems." *SCI* 21 (2002): 209–42.

"Zwischen Konfrontation und Interaktion: Christen, Juden und Heiden im spätantiken Aphrodisias." In *Patchwork: Dimensionen multikultureller Gesellschaften*, eds. Andreas Ackermann and Klaus E. Müller (Bielefeld, 2002): 83–127.

"The Conversion of the Temple of Aphrodite at Aphrodisias in Context." In *From Temple to Church: Destruction and Renewal of Local Cultic Topography in Late Antiquity*, eds. Johannes Hahn, Stephen Emmel, and Ulrich Gotter (Leiden, 2008): 243–73.

Coleman-Norton, Paul R. *Roman State and Christian Church: A Collection of Legal Documents to A.D. 535.* 3 vols. (London, 1966).

Cormack, Robin. "The Temple as Cathedral." In *Aphrodisias Papers: Recent Work on Architecture and Sculpture*, eds. Charlotte Roueché, and Kenan T. Erim, eds. *JRA*Sup 1 (Ann Arbor, Mich., 1990): 75–88.

Cox, C. W. M. "Bishop Heortasius of Appia." In *Anatolian Studies Presented to William Hepburn Buckler*, eds. W. M. Calder and J. Keil (Manchester, 1939): 63–6.

Cumont, Franz. "Les anges du paganisme." *RHR* 72 (1915): 159–82.

D'Andria, Francesco. *Hierapolis of Phrygia (Pamukkale): An Archaeological Guide.* Trans. Paul Arthur (Istanbul, 2003).

Deichmann, F. W. "Frühchristliche Kirchen in antiken Heiligtümern." *JDAI* 54 (1939): 105–36.

Dodds, E. R. *Pagan and Christian in an Age of Anxiety* (Cambridge, 1965).

Drew-Bear, Thomas, and Christian Naour. "Divinités de Phrygie." In *ANRW* II.18.3, 1907–2044 (Berlin, 1990).

Feld, Otto, and Hans Weber. "Tempel und Kirche über der korykischen Grotte (Cennet Cehennem) in Kilikien." *IstMitt* 17 (1967): 254–78.

Ferrero, Daria, ed. *Hierapolis Scavi e Ricerche IV. Saggi in onore di Paolo Verzone* (Rome, 2002).

Fleischer, Robert. "Der Fries des Hadrianstempels in Ephesos." In *Festschrift für Fritz Eichler zum achtzigsten Geburtstag,* ed. Egon Braun (Vienna, 1967): 23–71.

Frend, William H. C. *The Archaeology of Early Christianity: A History* (London, 1996).

Geffcken, Johannes. *The Last Days of Greco-Roman Paganism.* Trans. S. MacCormack (Amsterdam, 1978).

Hahn, Johannes. *Gewalt und religiöser Konflikt* (Berlin, 2004).

Halkin, François. *Bibliotheca Hagiographica Graeca* 1–2. Subsidia Hagiographica 8a (Brussels, 1957) (= *BHG*).

Auctuarium Bibliothecae Hagiographicae Graecae. Subsidia Hagiographica 47 (Brussels, 1969).

Hanson, R. P. C. "The Transformation of Pagan Temples into Churches in the Early Christian Centuries." *JSS* 23 (1978): 257–67.

Harl, Kenneth W. "From Pagan to Christian in Cities of Roman Anatolia during the Fourth and Fifth Centuries." In *Urban Centers and Rural Contexts in Late Antiquity,* eds. Thomas S. Burns and John W. Eadie (East Lansing, Mich., 2001): 301–22.

Harnack, Adolf von. *Die Mission und Ausbreitung des Christentums in den ersten drei Jahrhunderten* (Leipzig, 1924).

Hefèle, Charles J., *Histoire des conciles d'après les documents originaux,* 1–3. Ed. and trans. H. Leclercq (Paris, 1907–9).

Hellenkemper, Hansgerd. "Die Kirche im Tempel: Zeustempel und Paulusbasilika am Kalykadnos." In *Orbis Romanus Christianusque ab Diocletiani aetate usque ad Heraclium: travaux sur l'Antiquité tardive rassemblés autour des recherches de Noël Duval,* ed. N. Duval (Paris, 1995): 191–203.

Jaeger, Werner. *Early Christianity and Greek Paideia* (Cambridge, Mass., 1961).

Joannou, Periklès-Pierre. *La legislation imperial et la christianisation de l'empire romain (311–476).* OCA 192 (Rome, 1972).

Jones, A. H. M. *The Later Roman Empire 284–602: A Social, Economic and Administrative Survey* (Oxford, 1964).

Jones, C. P. "A Family of Pisidian Antioch." *Phoenix* 36 (1982): 264–71.

Kirsten, Ernst. "Artemis von Ephesus und Eleuthera von Myra mit Seitblick auf St. Nicolaus und auf Commagene." In *Studien zur Religion und Kultur Kleinasiens: Festschrift für Karl Dörner,* 2, eds. S. Şahin, et al. (Leiden, 1978): 457–88.

Lampe, Peter, and William Tabbernee. *The Discovery and Archaeological Exploration of a Lost Ancient City and an Imperial Estate* (Berlin, 2008).

Lawson, John C. *Modern Greek Folklore and Ancient Greek Religion* (Cambridge, 1910).

Lee, A. D. *Pagans and Christians in Late Antiquity: A Sourcebook* (London, 2000).

Mango, Cyril. "St. Michael and Attis." *Deltion tēs Christianikēs Archaiologikēs Etaireias* 12 (1984): 39–62.

"Germia: a Postscript." *JÖB* 41 (1991): 297–300.

Merkelbach, Reinhold, and Josef Stauber. "'Unsterbliche' Kaiserpriester. Drei Dokumente der heidnischen Reaktion." *EA* 31 (1999): 157–65.

Mitchell, Stephen. "The life of Saint Theodotus of Ancyra." *AnSt* 32 (1982): 93–113.

"Maximinus and the Christians in A.D. 312: A New Latin Inscription." *JRS* 78 (1988): 105–24.

Momigliano, Arnaldo, ed. *The Conflict between Paganism and Christianity in the Fourth Century* (Oxford, 1963).

Mullen, Roderic L. *The Expansion of Christianity: A Gazetteer of Its First Three Centuries* (Leiden, 2004).

Musurillo, Herbert, ed. *Acts of the Christian Martyrs* (Oxford, 1972).

Neusner, Jacob. *Judaism and Christianity in the Age of Constantine: History, Messiah, Israel, and the Initial Confrontation* (Chicago, 1987).

Petrie, A. "Epitaphs in Phrygian Greek." In *Studies in the History and Art of the Eastern Roman Provinces*, ed. W. M. Ramsay (Aberdeen, 1906).

Ramsay, William M., *Cities and Bishoprics of Phrygia* 1–2 (Oxford, 1895).

"The Tekmorian Guest-friends: An Anti-Christian Society on the Imperial Estates at Pisidian Antioch." In *Studies in the History and Art of the Eastern Roman Provinces*, ed. W. M. Ramsay (Aberdeen, 1906): 305–77.

Schneider, C. M. "Leibestätigkeit als Strafe: Bemerkungen zu einer Inschrift an Sardis." In *Polychordia: Festschrift Franz Dölger zum 75. Geburtstag* 1, ed. P. Werth (Amsterdam, 1966): 284–9.

Sheppard, A. R. R. "Pagan Cults of Angels in Roman Asia Minor." *Talanta* 12–13 (1980–81): 77–101.

Simon, Marcel. *Verus Israel. Étude sur les relations entre Chrétiens et Juifs dans l'empire romaine (135–425)* (Paris, 1964). Trans. H. McKeating as *Verus Israel: A Study of the Relations between Christians and Jews in the Roman Empire, 135–425* (Oxford, 1986).

Snyder, Graydon F. *Ante Pacem: Archaeological Evidence of Church Life before Constantine.* Rev. ed. (Macon, 2003).

Tabbernee, William. *Montanist Inscriptions and Testimonia: Epigraphic Sources Illustrating the History of Montanism* (Macon, 1997).

Trombley, Frank R. "Monastic Foundations in Sixth-century Anatolia and their Role in the Social and Economic Life of the Countryside." *GOTR* 30 (1985) 45–59. Reprinted with corrections in *Byzantine Saints and Monasteries*, ed. N. M. Vaporis (Brookline, Mass., 1985): 45–59.

"Paganism in the Greek World at the End of Antiquity: The Case of Rural Anatolia and Greece." *HTR* 78 (1985): 327–52.

Hellenic Religion and Christianization c. 370–529, 1–2 (Leiden, 1993–94; repr. 1995, 2001).

"Religious Experience in Late Antiquity: Theological Ambivalence and Christianization." *BMGS* 24 (2000): 2–60.

"Town and *territorium* in Late Roman Anatolia (late 5th to early 7th c.)." In Luke Lavan, ed. *Recent Research in Late Antique Urbanism.* JRAsup 42 (2001): 217–32.

"Christianisation of Rite in Byzantine Anatolia: F. W. Hasluck and Continuity." In *Anthropology, Archaeology and Heritage in the Balkans and Anatolia: The Life and Times of F. W. Hasluck 1878–1920*, 2, ed. David Shankland (Istanbul, 2004): 55–75.

"The Destruction of Pagan Statuary and Christianization (4th-6th c. C.E.)." In *The Sculptural Environment of the Roman Near East: Reflections on Culture, Ideology, and Power*, eds. Yaron Eliav, Elise Friedland, and Sharon Herbert (Louvain, 2008): 143–64.

Waelkens, Marc. *Die kleinasiatische Türsteine: typologische und epigraphische Untersuchungen der kleinasiatiaschen Grabreliefs mit Scheintür* (Mainz, 1986).

Whitby, Michael. "John of Ephesus and the Pagans: Pagan Survivals in the Sixth Century." In *Paganism in the Later Roman Empire and in Byzantium*, ed. Maciej Salomon. Byzantina et Slavica Cracoviensia (Cracow, 1991).

Wischmeyer, W. "M. Iulius Eugenius. Eine Fallstudie zum Thema 'Christen und Gesellschaft im 3. und 4. Jahrhunderte.'" *ZNW* 81 (1990): 225–46.

Young, Frances M. "Towards a Christian *paideia*.'" In *The Cambridge History of Christianity I. Origins to Constantine*, eds. Margaret M. Mitchell and Francis M. Young (Cambridge, 2006): 485–500.

PART IV

ITALY, ROMAN GAUL, AND SPAIN

14

RELIGION IN ROME AND ITALY FROM THE LATE REPUBLIC THROUGH LATE ANTIQUITY

MICHELE RENEE SALZMAN

In the year 384 CE, the Roman senator Quintus Aurelius Symmachus sent this letter to a colleague:

I am intensely distressed, because, despite numerous sacrifices, and these often repeated by each of the authorities, the prodigy of Spoletum has not yet been expiated in the public name. For the eighth sacrificial victim scarcely appeased Jove, and for the eleventh time honor was paid to Public Fortune with multiple sacrificial victims in vain.[1] You know now where we are. The decision now is to call the colleagues to a meeting. I will make sure you know if the divine remedies make any progress. Farewell.[2]

We do not know the nature of the Spoletum prodigy, but communal fears aroused by natural or manmade disasters, such as earthquakes, drought, and military defeats, were the most frequent reasons for the kind of ritual response mentioned by Symmachus. Following traditional practice, Symmachus refers the matter to the colleagues in the senate who, if they deemed it significant, would then consult with the priestly *augures* or the *quindecimviri sacris faciundis* to determine the appropriate actions to be undertaken by the priests, magistrates, or people as a whole. It is striking that Symmachus's concern as well as the mechanisms to address prodigies had remained in place in Rome at least into the late fourth century, some seventy years after the first Christian emperor, Constantine, claimed the city as his own.[3]

In light of Symmachus's letter, it is hard to defend the notion, which persists in numerous studies on the ancient world, that the Romans lacked

---

[1] Symmachus's reference to Public Fortune suggests this deity had its own cult at Spoletum.

[2] Symmachus, *Ep.* 1.49, can be dated after 360/365 but before Praetextatus's death in December 384 CE. For edition, translation, and commentary in English, see now Salzman and Roberts, *The Letters of Symmachus. Book 1*, 106–7. On the date of this epistle, see ibid., 1.106–7.

[3] Beard, North, and Price, *Religions of Rome*, Vol. 1, 37–8; North, *Roman Religion*, 27–8.

any "real" emotional attachment to their religion, or that their religion consisted of orthopraxy devoid of content. Part of the reason for this view is the nature of the sources, discussed in the following section, and part has to do with the ways in which the historiography on Roman religion developed, which will be discussed at the end of this chapter. My aim here is to challenge these views by considering the key issues raised by Symmachus's letter: how and why the cults, rituals, and beliefs of the peoples living in Rome and Italy thrived, changed, and yet persisted from the late republic circa second century BCE to the Roman empire of the fifth century CE. This is a long time period, and I can consider it only selectively. I will focus on the religious experiences of the people who lived in the city of Rome and whose religious traditions spread throughout Italy and Sicily. This focus on the religion of Rome is justifiable because by the late first century BCE, Roman political hegemony over the peninsula and Sicily was secure. Although the Romans did not stipulate strict conformity to their religious traditions, over the centuries, the cults, practices, and structures of the religious life of the city of Rome came to dominate Italy.

As the Italians incorporated and transformed certain Roman religious traditions, the Romans, for their part, simultaneously incorporated and transformed certain Italic and non-Roman cults and practices (primarily Greek, Egyptian, and Etruscan). This dynamic interchange helps to explain how and why Roman religion flourished for centuries. Although this process of transformation is comparable to the interchange between Romans and foreigners in other regions of the empire, it took a particular turn in Rome and Italy, resulting in a distinctively "Roman" Italic religion.

THE SOURCES

We do not have a set body of shared texts or dogma that can elucidate the religious traditions of Rome and Italy. Instead, we possess a rich array of texts – hymns, poems, prose, philosophical works, magical papyri, oracular statements, histories, and antiquarian texts – that complement the material evidence – coins, tombs, houses, calendars, inscriptions, and temple excavations.[4] For the period before the first century BCE, we depend greatly on two histories dating from the first century BCE to the first century

---

[4] For the most useful sourcebook of Roman religion, see the second volume of Beard, North, and Price, *Religions of Rome*. The first volume provides a chronological analysis of Roman religion, focusing on the city of Rome but also including Italy and its provinces, from its archaic origins down to the Christian empire. This author owes much to this first volume, but does not agree in all respects on particulars or on the processes of religious change and interaction with local cultures.

Map 8. Italy

CE – namely, those of Livy and of Dionysius of Halicarnassus; although based on limited knowledge of the age about which they write, they both reflect the tendency of their contemporaries to idealize the early Roman period as an age filled with piety. In his Greek *Histories,* Polybius (second century BCE) provides only scant information about Roman religion, even while acknowledging the central role that it played in Roman society.

Given the limitations of the textual sources, the archaeological evidence
for the pre-first century BCE is of special import in showing the growth
of early Rome. From this, scholars have come to believe that as early as
the sixth century BCE, Rome was a sophisticated, mainstream city in close
contact with Greeks, Etruscans, and Carthaginians (see Rüpke, Chapter 13
of Volume I).

The last century of the republic is the first period for which we have
enough textual evidence to ground our understanding of the structure
and practices of Roman religion. Yet even the histories of the first century BCE present challenges for understanding Rome's religious traditions.
The aforementioned tendency of Livy and Dionysius of Halicarnassus
to idealize early Rome reflects the perspective of their contemporaries
and inspired some Romans of the first century BCE to gather information on the customs and traditions of their ancestors. Of special note are
the works on Roman religion by M. Terentius Varro (first century BCE),
a scholar whose information has been largely preserved but reshaped by
Augustine in his *City of God*. For instance, Augustine mocks the func-
tionalist principle of Roman religion by citing a lengthy list of minor
deities, many of whom were recovered by Varro. But the aims of the two
writers are worlds apart. When Varro described the three gods necessary
to guard a house – including *Forculus* (the door), *Cardea* (the hinge), and
Limentinus (the threshold) (Augustine, *Civ.* 4.8) – he did so in a display
of antiquarian erudition. Augustine, on the other hand, described them
as if to mock a contemporary practice. Even so, Augustine's misrepresen-
tation of Varro's intent has colored modern accounts of Roman religion,
leading to the tendency, noted earlier, to dismiss Roman religion as concerned solely with orthopraxy and functionalism, empty of deep emotion
or metaphysical meaning.

As John North has observed, Varro's antiquarianism is emblematic of a
more widespread Roman unwillingness to discuss the nature and meaning of contemporary rituals and the character of the priesthood.[5] Roman
writers tend instead to describe the workings of the divine in human matters only obliquely, via, for example, etymologies or, as in the case of the
historian Livy, by listing prodigies and the state's response to them, but
without discussing the religious meaning of these prodigies or miraculous
events. The presence of such lists is worth noting; Livy, like the later historian Tacitus, shared the view that the gods favor those leaders who observe

---

[5] North, *Religions in the Roman Empire*, 330.

proper religious rituals.[6] While Livy is willing to describe the gods or the ways in which the gods communicate to men, both he and ancient philosophers in general are not interested in "internal exegeses of the character of pagan religion."[7] It seems likely that this silence is intentional, representing a more widespread Roman perspective on what is or is not appropriate for discourse. This tendency has certainly also contributed to the misguided modern notion that Roman religion was only about orthopraxy.

Some scholars have contended that Roman religionists became willing to engage in discourse on traditional religion only when they faced challenges from Christian detractors.[8] If this is true, then the problem for historians of traditional Roman religion is even greater, since Christian sources have to be treated as "hostile witnesses." The *Octavius,* for example, a dialogue between a defender of Roman religious traditions and a Christian recounted by the Christian apologist Minucius Felix (130–250 CE?), provides a direct but dismissive discussion of the religious experience of the non-Christian. Yet even such texts cannot be trusted entirely; the Christian poet Prudentius (late fourth to early fifth century) misleads with his exaggerated description of bloody rites of initiation in the cult of Attis and Cybele.[9] Even so, his account has been read by scholars for centuries as a straightforward narrative of the sacrifice and slaughter of a bull. The continued production of texts filled with mockery and attacks against past or imaginary rites rather than contemporary Roman cult practice is in itself an indicator of the vitality of Roman religious traditions in the Christian empire. What did these traditions offer?

CONCEPTUALIZING THE DIVINE: ROMAN AND ITALIC CULTS OF THE REPUBLIC AND EMPIRE

The city of Rome and its public cults

One way to approach Roman religious tradition is to consider the principal cult sites and deities of the city of Rome in the late republic that survived into the late empire. Jupiter/Zeus, the principal god of Rome, was worshipped in the largest temple in the city, placed on the highest hill, the Capitolium, and flanked by his wife, Juno/Hera, along with the goddess Minerva/Athena. Lesser deities had smaller cult sites, but each had a role

---

[6] Liebeschuetz, *Continuity and Change,* 1967; Scott, *Religion and Philosophy,* 1ff.
[7] North, *Religions in the Roman Empire,* 330.
[8] Ibid., 330.
[9] McLynn, "The Fourth-Century Taurobolium," 312–30.

to play in the life of the city. Traditionally, Jupiter/Zeus, as the first god of the state, was in charge of warfare and the sky, the source of nourishing rain or damaging lightning, the latter his attribute. His wife, Juno/Hera, venerated as the protector of childbirth, along with Minerva, goddess of skilled crafts, assisted him on the domestic front. This Capitoline Triad – the collective name of the three dominant deities of the city – represents a central principal of Roman republican religion as well as its politics, namely the sharing of powers in order to ensure the success of Rome.

Because early Rome was dependent on its abilities to fight and farm, Mars, protector of the army and a god originally linked with agriculture, was also a key deity in Rome, especially in the age of Augustus and continuing into the empire. A distinctive female deity was Vesta, the goddess of the communal hearth. Her flame was tended by a group of seven virgins, who were connected from earliest times with the survival of the city-state.

This brief discussion serves to introduce the array of cults and deities that grew to meet contemporary Roman needs (see Table 1). Indeed, Roman writers noted with pride their ability to absorb new cults and divinities into their city. Aesculapius, the god of healing, was brought to Rome from Greece. The historian Livy and the poet Ovid describe how, at the end of the Second Punic War, the Romans transferred the Great Mother, an Anatolian goddess whom the Greeks called Cybele, to the city in the shape of a black stone. Venerated and installed in a temple on the Palatine Hill in Rome, her cult was adapted to Roman religious expectations. Because castration was deemed unmanly and hence not fitting for a Roman, the eunuchs who served her cult were required to be non-Romans (Livy 29.11.7, 14.10–14; Ovid, *Fast.* 4.317). Perhaps the best-known instance of Roman adaptation of a foreign cult was occasioned by the worship of Bacchus in the early second century BCE. The arrival of the cult in Rome and Italy created concern because the rites involved citizens in private meetings with wine present. As in the late fourth-century prodigy at Spoletum noted by Symmachus, the senate, after consultation with priests, decided how best to deal with the new cult and also maintain the *pax deorum*, the good will of the gods. The senatorial decree survives; while imposing restrictions on cultic practice and participation by Romans and non-Romans alike, it did not prevent worship of Bacchus from continuing in Italy or Rome.[10]

---

[10] Livy 39; *ILS* 18 for the senatorial decree; and for further discussion of the event, see North, "Religious Toleration," 1979; de Cazanove, "Some Thoughts," 71–6; Ando, "Exporting Roman Religion," 437. For the convincing argument that the presence of women was not the key issue, see Schultz, *Women's Religious Activity*, 82–93.

Table 1. *Some of the Gods of Rome and Their Greek Equivalents*

Latin Name	Greek Name	Area of Major Activity
Aesculapius	Asclepius	Curing of illness
Apollo	Apollo	Reason; prophecy; health
Liber Pater	Dionysus	Wine and the grape harvest; ecstatic possession
Ceres	Demeter	Corn and agriculture; mother goddess and protector of young girls
Dea Dia		Obscure
Diana	Artemis	The hunt; animals; boundaries
Dis Pater	Hades	The underworld; death
Fortuna	Tyche	Fortune; luck
Isis	Isis	In the Roman period, protector of women and marriage; goddess of maternity and the newborn; guarantor of the fertility of the fields
Juno	Hera	Major goddess of the state; protector of childbirth, marriage
Jupiter	Zeus	Chief god of the state; lightning/weather; warfare
Magna Mater	Cybele	Fertility; ecstatic dancing
Mars	Ares	Agriculture; military matters
Mercury	Hermes	Business; commerce; communications
Minerva	Athena	Major goddess of the state; skilled crafts
Neptune	Poseidon	Water; transport by sea
Quirinus		Identified with Romulus
Saturn	Cronus	Sowing and seed corn; liberation
Sol/Mithras	Helios	Sun
Venus	Aphrodite	Physical love; seduction; conduit between humans and deities
Vesta	Hestia	The hearth
Vulcan	Hephaestus	Metalworking; fire

The second-century-BCE Bacchanalia decree also highlights the personnel in Rome typically responsible for public cult practices. As in this case, the responsibility for maintaining good relations as well as communications between the city-state and its gods fell to the magistrates/ senators, who, in consultation with the colleges of Roman priesthoods, orchestrated the proper rituals for the gods. The magistrates, and later the emperors, relied on the priests for the performance of correct rituals. The high state priesthoods were generally held by the leading senators and magistrates in the city of Rome. Unlike the Christian office of bishop or monk, there never developed at Rome a distinctly separate class of priests who held these offices as a full-time job, as it were. Rather, the same civic elite held the magistracies and the priesthoods; Caesar,

for one, was head priest (*pontifex maximus*) of the priestly colleges at
Rome, a position that members of the top families of the ruling elite
of the republic often held as a starting point in their political careers.
It is a sign of its continuing prestige that from the reign of Augustus
on, emperors held the office of high priest.[11] Nonetheless, Augustus and
subsequent emperors, like the Roman magistrates before them, relied
on the priests of the state's cult for the organization and performance of
public cult ritual.

The priests of Rome's state cults, like the deities they served, were given
specialized functions. They were organized into priestly colleges, the most
important of which were as follows: the *pontifices* or pontiffs (sixteen under
Julius Caesar), who advised the senate and citizens about religious law
and who were responsible for rituals like animal slaughter; the *augures* or
augurs, who sought divine approval by divination through birds; the seven
Vestal Virgins, who served the cult of Vesta; the *quindecimviri sacris faciundis*, fifteen priests who were in charge of and consulted the Sibylline
books for divine guidance; and the *septemviri epulonum,* originally seven
and, after Caesar, ten priests who organized ritual meals for the gods at the
games in honor of Jupiter or of the Capitoline Triad. There were also three
major and twelve minor *flamines,* priests of specific gods and goddesses, as
well as a college of Arval Brethren, twelve priests who performed rituals for
the Dea Dia goddess in her grove outside Rome.

By the late republic, when we have reliable sources, we know that the
priests presiding over public cult rituals had assistants to perform the more
technical work involved. These included killing an animal or reading the
signs of nature, such as the flights of birds or the internal organs of a
sacrificed animal. Within each priestly college, membership depended
on cooptation; emperors could intervene, from Augustus on, but they
tended to do so in less public ways. Each college kept records on membership, responsibilities, and finances; some of them, like those of the Arval
Brethren from the imperial period, have survived, providing a rich source
of information for modern scholars.[12] However, the priests were not independent of state control; the size of the college and changes in their organization were controlled by senatorial legislation and, in the empire, by
imperial influence. The four major priestly colleges – *pontifices, augures,
quindecimviri, septemviri* – fell directly under the control of the senate
in the republic and under the eye of the emperor as *pontifex maximus* in

---

[11] Gordon, "The Veil of Power," 201–31.
[12] For the records of the Arval Brethren, see Scheid, *Romulus et ses frères,* 1ff.

the empire. This same principle of control elucidates why the four major colleges oversaw the lesser priestly colleges.

A mere outline of the cults and priesthoods cannot convey the vitality of religion in Rome, even if it indicates quite clearly how religion was embedded in the political and social institutions of the city. Moreover, scholars have tended to underestimate the appeal of Roman religious traditions because of the structuring of Roman ritual; as long as magistrates and priests performed the rites correctly, the average Roman, citizen or not, was not required to participate in them. Only recently have scholars come to appreciate that the rituals, sacrifices, and holidays associated with the public cults were major civic moments in which the identity of the city and its inhabitants was performed and reinforced.[13] Religious ceremonies and games held for the gods (noted below) were engaging communal moments and religiously meaningful events, bringing with them material as well as spiritual and social benefits for the inhabitants of Rome. The animals sacrificed were then cooked and distributed to participants, one of the few times that most people ate meat in Antiquity.

To get a better sense of the attraction of the traditional cults of Rome, we can turn, briefly, to the information provided by the public calendars of the city. We are extraordinarily fortunate to have a range of calendars from Rome and Italy, beginning with the pre-Caesarean calendar of Antium (84/55 BCE), including multiple first-century calendars from the Julio-Claudian period, along with the remains of an early third-century calendar from S. Maria Maggiore, Rome, and a full calendar from the mid-fourth century CE, the Codex-Calendar of 354; these attest to the rhythms of public cult life in the city and Italy over a five-century period.[14]

In the late republican calendar from Antium, the major holidays were named, along with the days on which the popular assemblies and the senate could meet, or the courts sit. This calendar itself reveals changes over time in Roman religious traditions. The oldest holidays, many of which were to honor deities obscure in the first century, are noted in capital letters. In this way, they are distinguished from holidays added later in the republican period, which are noted in smaller letters in the calendars and which often included sets of games (*ludi*). The games took various forms, including theatrical performances, circus races, physical contests, or, in

---

[13] Gordon, "The Veil of Power," 201–31.
[14] Augustus's (29 BCE–14 CE) reformulation of the city's religious life and his intentional commemorations of the achievements of his family in the annual calendars of the city spurred the Roman penchant for public displays of the Roman calendar that partially explains the great number of extant first-century-CE calendars; see Salzman, *On Roman Time*, 5–8.

some instances, gladiatorial combat. Games were held in conjunction with the holidays along with sacrifices and/or banquets performed by priests and magistrates to honor the deities.

By the first century CE, the games and number of days devoted to their cult rites enable us to determine the major deities of the city. Held in honor of Jupiter and the Capitoline Triad, the *Ludi Romani,* for example, extended from 5–19 September, and the *Ludi Plebeii* from 4–17 November. The symbolic role of Vesta, the goddess of the public hearth, was noted too on calendars with rites on 9 June (the *Vestalia*) and 15 June (*Q.St.D.F.,* literally *Quando stercus delatum fas,* or when it was permitted to carry away the "dung," interpreted as a ritualized cleansing ceremony of the temple precinct). Similarly, Augustus's attention to Mars, especially as Mars the Avenger, led to days and rites for his celebration in the calendars of first-century Rome, including the Birthday of Mars on the first day of March.[15]

Modern interpretations of Roman religious festivals have depended, to a large degree, on the testimonies of ancient sources. Of particular value is the long poem by the Augustan poet Ovid (43 BCE–17 CE), describing Roman holidays for the first six months of the year. Yet his oblique testimony presents problems of interpretation. So, for example, in describing the rites to Vesta on June 9, he writes:

… there is no effigy of Vesta or of the fire [in her temple in the Roman Forum]. The earth stands by its own power; Vesta is so called from standing by power (*vi stando*); and the reason for her Greek name may be similar. But the hearth (*focus*) is so named from the flames, and because it fosters (*fovet*) all things …
in praying we begin by addressing Vesta, who occupies the first place.
It used to be the custom of old to sit on long benches in front of the hearth
and to suppose that the gods were present at table.
Even now when sacrifices are made to ancient Vacuna,
they stand and sit in front of her hearths.
Something of olden custom has come down to our time:
A clean platter contains the food offered to Vesta.
See, loaves are hung from garlanded mules,
And flowery garlands veil the rough millstones.
Husbandmen used formerly to toast only spelt in the ovens,
and the goddess of ovens has her sacred rites:
The hearth of itself baked the bread that was put under the ashes,

[15] See especially Feeney, *Caesar's Calendar,* 176–7 on Augustus's emphasis on Mars Ultor.

And a broken tile was laid on the warm floor.

So the baker honours the hearth, and the mistress of hearths,

And the she-ass that turns the millstones of pumice.[16]

The narrative of this festival is emblematic of Ovid's approach to religion. There is an antiquarian emphasis on etymologies, the significance of which for understanding the contemporary meaning of the rites is not always clear. Ovid proudly recites differing views of the rites. While all of them are valid, some he calls ancient, belonging to Rome or to Italy, as, for example, the way of sacrificing to the obscure deity Vacuna. Others, like Vesta's name, he ascribes to Greek interpretation. Some of the rites seem to have a rationale. We can easily see, for example, why loaves baked on the hearth would honor Vesta, the goddess of the hearth. But there is no particular reason why it is only bread that is the object of ritual attention.

As M. Beard has well argued, the multiplicity of explanations for the rites of Vesta that Ovid and other Roman authors recount is in itself significant. Evidently, the Romans did not expect their festivals to have a fixed canonical meaning. Numerous interpretations survived, and all were valid.[17] Although Roman authors, like Ovid, give the somewhat misleading impression that the rituals themselves were never changing, we can sometimes see changes over time, not just in ritual, but in the meaning for those experiencing such ceremonies. By way of example, M. Beard traced how the festival of the *Parilia,* an early Roman agricultural festival connected with the shepherds who grazed their flocks on the Palatine Hill, came to be interpreted as the date of the foundation of the city of Rome and so celebrated in new ways in connection with building of the temple of Venus Felix and Roma Aeterna by the emperor Hadrian in the early second century CE.[18] Both interpretations survived, and both were relevant to Rome's citizens.[19]

Within such a creative system, the local, topographical context of a cult encouraged multiple interpretations. Introducing a cult to a new site or city could bring different but equally valid meanings to the same rites or could facilitate the addition of novel rituals or places of veneration. At one of Venus's temples on the slope of the Aventine behind the Circus Maximus (Serv. *Ad Aen.* 8.636), this goddess was worshipped as Venus Verticordia (Venus as the "changer of hearts") on 1 April; this temple was dedicated on

---

[16] *Fasti* 6.249–318, trans. J. G. Frazer (LCL; Cambridge, 1956).
[17] Beard, "A Complex of Times," 1–15.
[18] Ibid., 1–15.
[19] Ibid., 1–15.

that day in 114 BCE at the command of the Sibylline books in atonement
for the lack of chastity of three Vestal Virgins. The date, location, and rites
were clearly different from those to celebrate Venus Felix ("Lucky Venus").
In this aspect, this same goddess was venerated at a likely small temple in
the city, this one on the Esquiline Hill, but also at the large, splendid temple constructed by Hadrian dedicated to "Venus Felix et Roma Aeterna,"
("Lucky Venus and Eternal Rome") whose commemoration on 21 April
was associated with the birthday of Rome.[20]

The openness of the Romans to new cults and rites helps to explain the
growing number of days set aside for games as recorded by the calendars
of Rome that exist from the first through the fourth centuries CE. The
undeniable appeal of the games has, however, also contributed to the modern notion that Roman religion had by the mid-fourth century become
nothing more than entertainment; by that time, the calendar recorded
some 177 days devoted to *ludi* and *circenses*, including ten days for gladiatorial contests.[21] That, however, would be a serious misreading of these
commemorations. Admittedly, ambitious politicians made these games as
novel as possible in order to excite and win favor with the populace, but
the intent of the games was to honor the gods. Their religious meaning,
manifested also by the reenacting of the myths of the gods on stage or
in the amphitheaters, explains why Christian bishops preached so loudly
against them, and continued to do so for centuries. In his sermons on the
days devoted to the Collects, annual collections of alms in Rome, Leo I
(440–61 CE), the fifth-century bishop of Rome, stated that he established
this Christian rite on the same days as the *Ludi,* likely the *Ludi Plebeii* to
Jupiter in November, in order to change the behavior of the inhabitants of
Rome who were attending games instead of services in Church.[22]

Italic cults and Roman religion

As the Romans came into contact with Italic and other new peoples and
religions, they tended to "identify gods very closely with specific locales
and to give them distinguishing epithets that linked them to particular
temples, cities, tribes, or topographical features."[23] Upon encountering
Venus Erycina, whose cult originated on Mount Eryx in western Sicily, the
Romans associated the deity with this place even as they erected temples

[20] For more on these temples, see Richardson, *A New Topographical Dictionary,* 408–10.
[21] Salzman, *On Roman Time,* 120–1.
[22] Leo, *Sermones 6–11, Concerning the Collections,* with specific reference to games in *Sermo* 8.
[23] Rives, *Religion,* 281.

to her on the Capitoline Hill and outside the Porta Collina at Rome; this Venus, the embodiment of "impure" love, was the patron goddess of prostitutes.[24] The Roman willingness to integrate local Italic versions of deities and venerate them in Rome typifies the absorptive and creative capacities of traditional Roman religion.

Conversely, the inhabitants of Italy and Sicily assimilated certain aspects of Rome's religions. Indeed, the religion of Rome spread in part because of the establishment of colonies of Roman citizens established in strategic areas in Italy. In the second century CE, Aulus Gellius called colonies "little images, as it were, a sort of representation [of Rome]" (*Noct. att.* 16.13.8–9). We can see this physically insofar as each colony duplicated the positioning of temples and cults to imitate that in Rome. Vitruvius even stipulated this in his instructions for how to lay out a colony: "For the sacred buildings of those gods who seem especially to exercise guardianship over the city – to Jupiter, Juno, and Minerva – plots should be assigned in the loftiest location, from which the greatest part of the walls might be seen" (Vitruvius, *De arch.* 1.7.1). In Roman colonies we find the remains of Capitolia – triple temples to Jupiter, Juno, and Minerva. Even if this way of laying out colonies is largely an early imperial formulation, it shows quite concretely the importation of Roman notions of religion into colonies in Italy and abroad.[25] However, and this should be stressed, even Roman colonies exercised a great deal of local autonomy in religious matters. So, for example, in the charter of the colony of Urso, near Osuna in Spain (*ILS* 6087), founded in 44 BCE, we find the institutionalization of two priesthoods known at Rome, the *pontifices* and *augures*, but no stipulations about their duties. Hence, the local elected officials clearly decided such matters and what their local calendar would look like.[26]

The same combination of assimilation and autonomy in religious practice is apparent too in the cities or municipalities (technically, communities made up of those with partial or so-called Latin citizenship rites, including foreigners) in Italy and Sicily. After the Social War of the late first century BCE, all communities in Italy that were not colonies received this status. These municipalities received charters, one of which, Flavian in date and from Spain, survives. According to this charter, which likely applied across the western empire, the worship of certain gods and the performance of certain religious actions were stipulated by Rome. For example, the oaths

---

[24] For more on her temple, see Richardson, *A New Topographical Dictionary*, 409–10.
[25] Ando, "Exporting Roman Religion," 435.
[26] Ibid., 435.

of magistrates were to be sworn "openly in assembly, by Jupiter, the divine Augustus, the divine Claudius, the divine Vespasian Augustus, the divine Titus Augustus, the Genius of Imperator Caesar Domitian Augustus, and the dei Penates."[27] These deities and their cults were thus present in the community, as per the decree of Rome. Nonetheless, as this Flavian charter indicates, the municipal councils controlled their own calendar and their own pantheon.[28] They could augment their civic rites and add regional deities as desired. Over time, those Roman cults and rituals that made most sense to the inhabitants of the *municipia* and colonies in Italy were maintained, even if the rites and meanings differed from those practiced and understood at Rome. As Roman religion spread through Italy, it changed in a process of what Rives has aptly termed particularization and generalization; this made the religion of Rome look different in different cities in Italy, as in other provinces.[29]

JULIUS CAESAR AND AUGUSTUS: RESTORATION AND REFORMULATION OF PUBLIC CULT IN ROME AND ITALY

Because the public cults were embedded in the state, the demise of the republic in the late first century BCE that resulted in a government by one-man rule – either the perpetual dictatorship of Julius Caesar (45–44 BCE) or the principate (essentially a monarchy) of Caesar's adopted son, Octavian, renamed Augustus (27 BCE–14 CE) – had profound implications for the religious traditions of Rome and Italy. Augustus himself explained these changes when, in his remarkable statement at the end of his life, the *Res Gestae*, he claimed to have restored some eighty-two temples in the city of Rome in 28 BCE (*Res Gestae* 20.4). It was to his advantage to claim such acts of piety, even if these restorations involved little more than a new coat of paint or involved "bogus archaisms."[30] Still, no one man could claim so much *pietas*, devotion toward the gods of the city.

Again, the calendars from Rome and Italy attest to these changes. Under the pressures of the political upheavals of the first century, the Colleges of Priests had allowed the calendar to fall out of sequence with the natural cycle; in 44 BCE, the New Year (1 January) would have fallen on what was actually 14 October 45 BCE according to the sun. To correct this, Caesar, once dictator, called in Egyptian astrologers, and in 46 BCE, "he [Caesar]

[27] Ibid., 440.
[28] Ibid., 439.
[29] Rives, "Graeco-Roman Religion," 240–99.
[30] Cooley, *Res Gestae*, ed. 195.

linked the year to the course of the sun by lengthening it to 365 days, abolishing the short extra month and adding an entire day every fourth year" (Suetonius, *Jul.* 40.1). Following one last correction in 8 BCE, the Caesarean calendar thus functioned like a modern calendar, except that an intercalated day was added every fourth year after 24 February, not after 28 February. This act virtually revolutionized the Roman calendar; "for the first time [it was] feasible in the Mediterranean world to have the civil and natural years in harmony under the same standard of representation."[31] His reform also brought Caesar great glory. As the one who, through his regularization of the times, controlled the cosmos, he was honored by having his name, Iulius, replace the "fifth month" of the old calendar year (that is, beginning in March). Every user of the calendar of Rome – which spread to Italy and the western empire – would be familiar with his name, along with the commemorations and games in his honor.

Expanding on the revolutionary revision of the calendar's chronological system undertaken by Julius Caesar, Augustus (his adopted son) was able to complete a reconfiguration of the Roman calendar year. Indeed, as the republican political institutions, notably the assemblies, continued to decline in significance, Augustus and subsequent emperors, together with their families, took up more time in the civic and religious year. In addition to the annual commemorations of Caesar's victories, Augustus added the commemoration of Caesar's birthday on 12 July.[32] This was the first time that a festival for a human being was incorporated into the public calendar of Rome, an extraordinary accomplishment by the man who completed Caesar's reordering of the Roman calendar. As *pontifex maximus,* the emperor also decided which cults to support and which to downplay, directly influencing public religion.[33] Augustus appreciated the political implications of time. In 8 BCE, after correcting and celebrating Caesar's reformation of the calendar, Augustus accepted the renaming of the month of August in his honor.[34] In 19 BCE, the *Augustalia* of 12 October, the first Roman festival named after a living human being, and the first new festival incorporated in the calendar as a named holiday, was made an annual

[31] Feeney, *Caesar's Calendar,* 196.
[32] The calendars record the addition of public holidays on the anniversaries of Caesar's victories at Munda (17 March), Alexandria (27 March), Thapsus (6 April), Ilerda and Zela (2 August), and Pharsalus (9 August), as well as the birthday of Caesar; see Fraschetti, *Roma,* 15–16.
[33] Salzman, *On Roman Time,* 179–89.
[34] Bennett, "The Early Augustan Calendars," 221–40. This reformation was timed to coincide closely with the dedication of a monumental sundial, the *Horologium,* in the Campus Martius in Rome a year earlier. The gnomon of this massive sundial was an Egyptian obelisk that Augustus, as *Pontifex Maximus,* had brought to Rome and dedicated to the sun; see Buchner, *Die Sonnenuhr,* 10.

event.[35] This commemoration remained in the calendar down through the fourth century.[36]

Honors conferred on the living emperor and the members of the imperial family – the birthdays, death days, accessions to priesthoods, comings of age, dedications of temples, and victories in battle of the *princeps* or the *princeps'* family – contributed to the development in first-century-CE Rome of an elaborate ceremonial in honor of the deceased emperor. Orations in praise of the dead emperor and a parade including members of the elite of Rome accompanied the procession of his body to a funeral pyre. There, as his body was cremated, an eagle was released, symbolizing the ascent of his soul to the heavens. This ceremony only occurred after the senate had recognized that the deceased emperor had become a god; hence, only those emperors whom the senate approved of received this honor. Yet, as Gradel has argued, much of this ceremony was in accord with traditional Roman religion and honors to the civic elite.[37]

The city of Rome maintained the distinction between the deified emperors (*divi*) to whom one offered sacrifice, and the living emperor, whose genius (guardian spirit) was the object of veneration. The deified emperors (*divi*) received the ornate, costly temples and cult honors, whereas worship of the genius of the emperor was less elaborate. The distinction between the living emperor's genius and the deified emperors was not as carefully maintained outside Rome. Inscriptions that indicate sacrifice *for* (that is, on behalf of) rather than *to* the emperor, once thought to be an important indicator of the separation of honors to a divine emperor versus honors on behalf of a mortal ruler, were not consistently employed across the empire, nor was there the traditional Roman hesitation to grant universal honors to the deified emperors and to their living descendants.[38] Over time, even in Rome, the line between veneration of the genius of the emperor versus that of the living emperor blurred.

The cult of the emperor, often in conjunction with the goddess Roma, became firmly fixed in the city and in Italy, as in the empire as a whole. Games, priests, sacrifices, banquets, and processions made real the benefits and powers of the good deified emperors. A clause in a decree from Pisa (*CIL* 11. 1420 = *ILS* 139: ll. 31–33) shows that the religious practices of the imperial cult followed in Rome provided a model for municipalities

---

[35] Michels, *The Calendar*, 1967: 141; Taylor and Holland, *Janus*, 140.
[36] This focus on the *princeps* and his family also explains why no triumphs other than those of Augustus and his family were celebrated in Rome after that of Cornelius Balbus in 19 BCE.
[37] Gradel, *Emperor Worship*.
[38] Rives, "Graeco-Roman Religion," 240–99.

elsewhere in Italy. This did not mean, however, that Rome directly controlled all aspects of Italian or provincial imperial cult. As the *lex coloniae
Genetivae* indicates, municipalities were able to determine which festivals
and accompanying rites they chose to follow in terms of the imperial cult,
as they did for the state cults as well.[39] Diverging localized interpretations
sharpened variations in imperial cult worship.

THE INDIVIDUAL IN ROMAN RELIGION

Public cults, priesthoods, ceremonies, and new cults, as that of the
emperor and his family, did not deprive the individual of the opportunity
and inclination to practice traditional Roman religion in more personal
ways, through private ceremonies and rituals. In early Rome, the family
worshipped the genius (guardian spirit) of the *pater familias*, just as in the
empire, citizens worshipped the genius of the living emperor. In Roman
houses, we find small shrines for offerings of fruit or incense to the spirits
of the family dead, the *lares*, whose images adorned these shrines. Rituals
for the *lares* indicate that the Romans felt the dead needed to be appeased.
Families – at least elite families – also kept alive the memory of dead
ancestors in the form of statues or masks that were kept in full view in
the atria of their family home; at the funerals of nobles, these masks were
worn by actors or family members who, dressed in the appropriate attire
of their dead ancestor, then walked in a procession accompanying the
corpse.[40]

Even the civic calendar of Rome acknowledged the important role that
individual and family religiosity had in the state. Nine days in February
were set aside for the festival of the *Parentalia*, when offerings were made
by families at the tombs or gravesides of their ancestors outside the walls
of the city. After this period, a day was devoted to the reunion and reconciliation of the living members of the family. This peaceful ritual to
honor the ancestors was quite the opposite of the *Lemuria*, the annual festivals on 9, 11, and 13 May; these rituals aimed to placate the hostile spirits
(*Lemures*) of the dead, hearkening back (according to Ovid, *Fast.* 5.419–93)
to Romulus's expiation of his brother's murder. On this day, the father
of every family rose at midnight, purified his hands, tossed black beans

---

[39] Fishwick, *The Imperial Cult in the Latin West*, II.1, 490–1, has argued in favor of direct control of
imperial cult from Rome; but his evidence for Italy suggests that while Rome modeled religious
rituals, municipalities had some degree of independence insofar as they could set their own festivals
and accompanying rites; see the *Lex coloniae Genetivae*: LXIII (*CIL* II.5439 = *ILS* 6087).

[40] Polybius 6.53–4.

for the spirits to gather, and recited entreaties for their departure without harming the living.

Individual religious rituals for the spirits of the deceased suggest that there was, at least on the part of many Romans, a concern with survival after death, as does the formulaic tombstone inscription *dis manibus,* "to the gods of the underworld." Yet such rituals seem at odds with tombstones that proclaim that after death, there is nothing to survive or to be concerned about; the formulaic "I was not; I am; I was; I am no more" ("non fui; sum; fui; non sum") summarizes this attitude. As was the case for Ovid's multiple explanations of holidays, Roman opinions about death and the religious practices associated with it incorporated a range of beliefs. The so-called mystery cults and religions like Christianity and Manichaeism further contributed to the development of a multiplicity of Roman views on the afterlife and on the role of religion in the face of death. Greek philosophers also helped to raise these issues in popular consciousness.

In considering the religious choices of individuals, special attention should be paid to the rise of the mystery cults that came to Rome and Italy and existed in the empire as a whole. These cults offered secret rites of initiation and the promise of their deities' power to help the participant overcome Fate and/or succeed in life, powers that some scholars liken to the offer of personal salvation; hence modern scholars have grouped these cults together and called them "mystery cults," after the Greek word *mystēs* ("initiate").[41] Such cults had been in existence in some form in early Greek society from the sixth century BCE on.[42] But the spread of these rites in conjunction with what were perceived as "foreign" cults is attested as early as the second century BCE in Rome and Italy, as the Bacchic decree noted earlier indicates. These cults differed among themselves; the centrality of initiation rites, for instance, varied by cult, as did the meaning and the message for the worshipper. W. Burkert argued that only in the cults of Bacchus and Demeter do we have evidence for the promise of personal salvation and the power to "overcome Fate."[43] But not all scholars have agreed, arguing that other mystery cults, notably those of Mithras, Cybele, and Isis, offered "the promise of salvation, or more precisely, their deities' power to control fate."[44]

Given these differences, it is worth looking in brief at the mystery cults that appealed most in Rome and Italy. Perhaps most distinctive is the cult

---

[41] Alvar, *Romanizing Oriental Gods*, 26.
[42] On the Greek mysteries, see Roller, Chapter 11 of this volume.
[43] Burkert, *Ancient Mystery Cults*, 1ff.
[44] See, for example, Alvar, *Romanizing Oriental Gods*, who argues against Burkert's view.

of Mithras. Although we have no ancient text that conveys the precise meaning of the initiation to the participant, we do know much about this cult and its organization from archaeological evidence. This cult likely excluded women, and appealed mostly to soldiers in the frontier zones as well as to bureaucrats and freedmen in Rome and Ostia. Based on the floor decorations in underground rooms or caves where initiates most frequently met, scholars have discerned a series of initiations, all associated with astrological signs and with the central iconic scene of Mithras's slaying of the bull. There were seven stages, beginning with the "raven" and then moving up through the male bride, soldier, lion, Persian, sun runner, and finally father; these stages were linked with the planets, starting from Mercury and finishing with Saturn, including as well the sun and the moon. The individual ascent through the seven grades may have reflected the soul's progress through the stars. The deity who controls this progress, Mithras, has a Persian name, but the cult, as it developed in various parts of the empire, assumed a peculiarly Roman form.[45]

Among the mystery cults that appears most vibrant in late fourth-century Rome is that of Attis, the boy-shepherd and consort of the goddess Cybele, whom the Romans brought to the city in the Second Punic War (218–01 BCE) and worshipped as the Magna Mater. The worship of Attis grew with the approval of Roman authorities. In one Latin version of the myth conveyed by the poet Ovid (*Fast.* 4.221–44), Attis was the lover of the goddess who, out of jealousy, drove him mad; in his frenzy, he castrated himself. Variants of this myth appear in Roman sources, but Attis's self-castration, death, and rebirth, often through the intervention of Cybele, are consistent elements (see Arnobius, *Adv. nat.* 5.5–7). Many scholars interpret the evergreen tree that is carried in processions as part of his public rites as a symbol of Attis's rebirth.[46] Other scholars have argued that, rather than a promise of salvation or immortality, the rites and cult myth of Attis, which in some variants were the result of Cybele's pleading with Jupiter, demonstrate the limitations of even the gods over fate.[47] How the myth and the public rites of this cult were linked with private rites of initiation is not certain, but by the late fourth century, a special bull sacrifice (*taurobolium*) was included as part of the individual initiation into this mystery cult. Interestingly, a bull sacrifice was originally performed on behalf of the emperor, and some of that public element may well have remained

[45] Beck, *The Religion of the Mithras Cult.*
[46] Vermaseren, *Cybele and Attis.*
[47] Sfameni Gasparro, *Soteriology and Mystic Aspects.*

in the elaborate private rites attested in fourth-century Rome.[48] Similarly, the mystery cult of the Egyptian goddess Isis, also popular in Rome and Italy, included both public rites and private rites of initiation in a cult that promised its initiates a kind of rebirth in the sacred waters of the Nile.[49]

These and other mystery cults took root in Rome and Italy in ways that reflected their local contexts. Worship of Attis and the Great Mother in fourth-century Rome was linked to late Roman senatorial aristocrats, a local situation that was not duplicated in other cities in Italy. Mystery cults thrived because they met "new spiritual needs that they themselves encouraged and fostered, by which they were sustained in return."[50] But an individual's experiences in mystery cults complemented his/her religious interactions; mystery cults did not replace the state cults, nor were they at odds with the civic religious structures. However, the increasing number of religious options in the Roman empire suggests that the sacred landscape of Rome and Italy, as elsewhere, was changing. As more and different religions became available, some cults expanded and at times, as in the case of Bacchus, they came into conflict with Roman authorities intent on maintaining civic order.

THE END OF TRADITIONAL ROMAN RELIGION?

Given this array of religious options and influences, it would be strange indeed if traditional Roman public cults and priesthoods did not respond. One issue that arose was the question of one god or many – monotheism/henotheism versus polytheism. Traditionalists were generally polytheists, although certain of them, as well as philosophers, came to see the gods as aspects of a single divine principle, whether it be the Logos of the Stoics or the *Theos Hypsistos* (highest god) attested in inscriptions in the East.[51] The neo-Platonists of the second to fourth centuries, who advanced their own notions of a central Logos, did much to articulate and advance monotheistic tendencies among the educated elites, as Augustine's *Confessions*, Book 7, makes clear. Of course, Christians, like Jews, rejected the notion of many gods in favor of one deity. Yet these different religions coexisted in Rome and Italy, generally without incident except for outbursts on

[48] See McLynn, "The Fourth-Century Taurobolium," 312–30.
[49] For the Isis cult, see Takács, *Isis and Sarapis*.
[50] Alvar, *Romanizing Oriental Gods*, 12.
[51] Mitchell, "The Cult of Theos Hypsistos," 81–148. On the veneration of *Theos Hypsistos* in Asia Minor and his assimilation with the god of the Jews and Christians, see Roller in Chapter 11 and van der Horst in Chapter 12 of this volume.

a local level. The most famous expression of the official Roman policy toward monotheistic cults is the letter of the emperor Trajan to the senator Pliny, then acting as a special administrator in Bithynia. In response to Pliny's query about this group, Trajan stated that the Christians not be hunted down and killed; only if denounced and only if they "obstinately" refused to sacrifice to the gods of the state should Christians be punished (Pliny the Younger, *Ep.* 10.97). Neither Pliny nor Trajan were bothered by Christian monotheism; what was at issue was the disruption of traditional religious practices that also affected the local economy and potentially disturbed civic order.

In the third century, however, concern about the gods in relation to the Roman state led to a break with these traditional patterns of religious laissez-faire. The emperor Decius (249–51 CE) attempted to reinforce his position by renewing traditional Roman religion and thereby guarantee the well-being of the state. The edict that he published unfortunately does not survive; but according to Christian sources (see Eusebius, *Hist. eccl.* 6.41.9–13), it ordered every inhabitant in the Roman empire to sacrifice, to taste the sacrificial meal, and to swear that they had always sacrificed. A special commission of local magistrates supervised the sacrifices and wrote a *libellus*, or certificate, as confirmation of the deed. Refusal to sacrifice entailed a steep fine. Such mandatory sacrifice broke with Roman tradition on numerous grounds; most ominously, perhaps, it tried to set a universal policy about individual actions instead of allowing for local and collective action.[52]

As far as we know, Decius's action was not aimed at any one group in the empire, although later Christian writers interpreted it as an attack on them in particular. A number of Christians did reject sacrifice and suffered for their choice. Some died as martyrs, in painful circumstances. The death of Decius in a war against the Goths in 251 brought a reprieve from this policy. But six years later, in 257, the then emperor Valerian (253–61) renewed the idea, now targeting Christians.[53] Those who refused to sacrifice would lose their property and their positions, as well as their lives; imperial officials and freedmen were to be sent to the mines. The aim of the state was to reinvigorate traditional religion among the civic elites. In Rome, the then bishop, Sixtus II, chose martyrdom over sacrifice. Only Valerian's defeat put an end to this policy, and his son Gallienus revoked

---

[52] *Libelli* have been found on Egyptian papyri; see Rives, "The Decree," 135–54.
[53] Valerian's first edict was aimed at Christian clerics (Eusebius, *Hist. eccl.* 7.11; *Acta Proconsularia Cypriani* 1, 4). His second edict was aimed at all Christians.

the edicts in 260/261 (Eusebius, *Hist. eccl.* 7.13). This allowed a return to the *status quo ante*.

Although subsequent third-century emperors were eager to support Roman religion, they did so in more traditional ways. The emperor Aurelian (270–75 CE), for one, focused attention on the cult of the Invincible Sun, Sol Invictus, whose aid he believed had helped him to defeat the queen of Palmyra in 273. In Rome, a magnificent temple and priestly college drawn from the senatorial elite were established to this deity; and a special set of games, the *agon Solis*, held every fourth year, was now made part of the civic calendar. If Aurelian was concerned about Christians, as was alleged by the fourth-century Christian bishop Eusebius (*Hist. eccl.* 7.30.20–1), he did not implement any persecution against them.

It was not until the later years of the reign of the emperor Diocletian (284–303) that the idea of an empire-wide persecution of non-traditionalists reemerged as part of imperial policy. In 297 CE, in response to a request by a proconsul, Diocletian took aim at the Manichaeans, whose leaders were to be burned alive, along with their scriptures. As his edict makes clear, Diocletian associated this group with the enemy, Persia, and considered them a threat to Roman security.[54] After a traditional sacrifice failed, probably around the year 300, Diocletian came to believe that the presence of Christians had incited divine anger and so ordered first the members of the palace and soon all the soldiers and officials to make sacrifices (Lactantius, *Mort.* 10; *Inst.* 4.27.5; Eusebius, *Vit. Const.* 2.50–1). A series of increasingly harsh edicts aimed at Christians who did not sacrifice followed, and many died rather than submit. But Diocletian's attempt to enforce sacrifice failed due to a combination of political, military, and religious reasons, not the least of which was resistance to enforcement on the part of Roman administrators.

In 311, a general edict of toleration was issued by a new emperor, Galerius. After the defeat of Maxentius at the Milvian bridge near Rome, Constantine and Licinius promulgated a policy of toleration, the so-called Edict of Milan; now the victorious emperor Constantine openly embraced the very religion that had only recently been the object of persecution and ushered in a century of religious transformation.[55] Traditional religions were allowed to continue, although they came increasingly under attack as subsequent Christian emperors saw it as their duty to maintain

---

[54] *FIRA* II, 544–89. On Manichaeism in Sasanian Persia, see De Jong in Chapter 1 of this volume.
[55] Drake, *Constantine*, 35–71, for full discussion, bibliography, and documentation of these events discussed most fully by Eusebius, *Vit. Const.* 1.25–41.2.

divine favor by undermining them. Rituals deemed inappropriate for Christians – notably, animal sacrifice – were the first target of imperial legislation. Yet as Symmachus's aforementioned letter, dated before 384, makes clear, enforcement was not uniform in Italy or Rome. Traditional religionists persisted in their practices.

The coercive arm of the state, supported by bishops and monks, over an extended period of time contributed to the demise of the traditional Roman religions. The state met with some resistance. Some traditional religionists argued against imperial efforts at cutting state monies for the public cults and their rituals (with or without animal sacrifice), as Symmachus's famous *Third State Paper* in defense of the maintenance of the Altar of Victory in the Roman senate in 384 makes clear.[56] Only rarely did such resistance erupt into violence in Rome or Italy, as it did in 397 in northern Italy.[57] In Rome, where the ties between the state institutions and the civic elites had been cemented over centuries, the task of disengaging traditional religion from the state extended over the course of the fourth and early fifth centuries. As in the spread of Roman religions throughout Italy, so too the disappearance of traditional Roman religions occurred in different localities at different times, depending on the needs, values, and views of the local communities.[58]

CONCLUSION: WHY DID SCHOLARS BELIEVE THAT THE ROMANS HAD NO RELIGION?

The nineteenth- and twentieth-century scholars who argued that the religions of Rome and Italy were either moribund or merely concerned with orthopraxy were blinded by Judeo-Christian preconceptions that sought genuine "emotion" or systematic doctrine that fit their modern notion of religion.[59] Many historians were greatly influenced by the works of the prestigious scholar Theodor Mommsen, who dismissed the textual descriptions of Roman rites as mere literary artifice.[60]

---

[56] For a recent discussion of Symmachus's *Third State Paper* and the Altar of Victory controversy, see Cameron, *The Last Pagans*, 33–51.

[57] For the incident in the Val di Non, an area just north of ancient Tridentum, modern Trento, see Salzman, "Rethinking Pagan-Christian Religious Violence," 267–73.

[58] Goddard, "The Evolution," 281–308.

[59] Price, *Rituals and Power*, 7–22, is a brilliant exposition and critique of these historiographical perspectives.

[60] For an excellent discussion of the influence of Mommsen's *History of Rome, 3 Volumes* (1854–56) as the source for this view still, see Scheid, "Polytheism Impossible," 303–26.

There was, and still remains even in relatively recent scholarship, the view that Roman religion is synonymous with its political structures, a perspective termed the *polis*-religion model.[61] Hence, the centralization of power by the emperor Augustus made traditional Roman religion no more than an extension of his authority; this emperor's religious reforms were viewed as cynical, politically motivated machinations that led to the establishment of the imperial cult at the expense of traditional religions.[62] Consequently, when the political and military troubles of the third century had undermined the state and changed religious patronage patterns of the civic elites, the resulting structural changes in the administration of cities and the weakening of the government brought with it the demise of traditional Roman religions.[63] The only "real" religious experience presenting individual satisfaction was offered by the mystery cults.[64]

Such views cannot be sustained. A wide range of evidence provided by texts and material culture reveal the vitality of traditional religions in the daily lives of the inhabitants of Rome and Italy into the fourth and early fifth centuries, some of which I have discussed in this chapter. Moreover, interpretation of Roman ritual has advanced beyond the perspective of the individual emotion to require an appreciation of how such rites were important within a system of constructed meanings.[65]

The view that traditional Roman religions were already dead before Constantine's adoption of Christianity in the fourth century is no longer viable. As the civic elites reemerged in Rome in this century in the absence of a resident emperor, they came to play an even greater role in the traditional public cults.[66] Artifacts like the *Codex-Calendar of 354* that depict traditional religious rites do not preserve anachronistic rituals, as was once believed, but lived realities.[67] Despite real changes in the patterns of religious patronage in Rome and Italy, the public cults remained in place. In some places, as in Spoletum, civic patronage persisted even as local leaders turned to wealthy Roman aristocrats like the senator Symmachus to support it.[68] Only because scholars into the latter part of the twentieth

[61] See Introduction to Volume I.
[62] See, for example, Tripolitis, *Religions of the Hellenistic-Roman Age*, 2; and the insightful discussion by Rives, "Graeco-Roman Religion," 231–43.
[63] Rives, *Religion and Authority*, 250–311.
[64] See especially Cumont, *Oriental Religions*, 31–8, whose 1911 edition was republished in 2006, one sign of its lasting influence.
[65] See especially Price, *Rituals and Power*, 7–22; Rives, "Greco-Roman Religion," 240–99.
[66] See, for instance, Chenault, *Rome without Emperors*.
[67] Salzman, *On Roman Time*, 16–19.
[68] Goddard, "The Evolution," 281–308.

century continued to resist attributing meaning to Roman religion were they unwilling to see in this artifact, as in other evidence, proof of the vitality of traditional Roman religion in Late Antiquity.

BIBLIOGRAPHY

Alvar, Jaime. *Romanising Oriental Gods: Myth, Salvation and Ethics in the Cults of Cybele, Isis, and Mithras.* Trans. and ed. R. Gordon. RGRW 165 (Leiden, 2008). Originally published as *Los misterios: Religiones "Orientales" en el Imperio Romano* (Barcelona, 2001).

Ando, Clifford. "Exporting Roman Religion." In *A Companion to Roman Religion,* ed. Jörg Rüpke (Malden, Mass., 2007): 429–45.

Athanassiadi, Polymnia, and Michael Frede, eds. *Pagan Monotheism in Late Antiquity* (Oxford, 1999).

Beard, Mary. "A Complex of Times: No More Sheep on Romulus' Birthday." *PCPhS* n.s 33 (1987): 1–15.

Beard, Mary, John North, and Simon Price. *Religions of Rome.* 2 vols. (Cambridge, 1998).

Beck, Roger. *The Religion of the Mithras Cult in the Roman Empire: Mysteries of the Unconquered Sun* (Oxford, 2006).

Bennett, Chris. "The Early Augustan Calendars in Rome and Egypt." *ZPE* 142 (2003): 221–40.

Buchner, Edmund. *Die Sonnenuhr des Augustus* (Mainz, 1982).

Burkert, Walter. *Ancient Mystery Cults* (Cambridge, Mass., 1987).

Cameron, Alan. *The Last Pagans of Rome* (Oxford, 2011).

Chenault, Robert R. *Rome without Emperors: The Revival of a Senatorial City in the Fourth Century C.E.* diss. Univ. of Michigan, 2008.

Cooley, Alison. *Res Gestae Divi Augusti. Text, Translation, and Commentary* (Cambridge, 2009).

Cumont, Franz. *Oriental Religions in Roman Paganism.* Trans. G. Showerman (Chicago, 1911). Originally published as *Les Religions orientales dans le paganisme romain,* 2nd ed. (Paris, 1909; 5th ed., with an introduction by C. Bonnet and F. van Haeperin. Turin, 2006).

De Cazanove, Olivier. "Some thoughts on the 'religious Romanization' of Italy before the Social War." In *Religion in Archaic and Republican Rome and Italy,* eds. Edward Bispham and Christopher J. Smith (Edinburgh, 2000): 71–6.

Derks, Ton. *Gods, Temples and Ritual Practices: The Transformation of Religious Ideas and Values in Roman Gaul* (Amsterdam, 1999).

Drake, Hal A. *Constantine and the Bishops: The Politics of Intolerance* (Baltimore, 2000).

Feeney, Denis. *Caesar's Calendar: Ancient Time and the Beginnings of History* (Berkeley, 2007).

Fishwick, Duncan. *The Imperial Cult in the Latin West: Studies in the Ruler Cult of the Western Provinces of the Roman Empire.* Vol. II.1 (Leiden, 1991).

Fraschetti, Augusto. *Roma e il principe* (Rome, 1990).

Goddard, Christophe J. "The Evolution of Pagan Sanctuaries in Late Antique Italy (4th-6th centuries A.D): A New Administrative and Legal Framework. A Paradox." In *Les cités de l'Italie tardo-antique, IVe-VIe siècle,* eds. Massimiliano Ghilandi, Christophe J. Goddard, and Pierfrancesco Porena, CEFR 369 (Rome, 2006): 281–308.

Gordon, Richard L. "The Veil of Power: Emperors, Sacrificers, and Benefactors." In *Pagan Priests: Religion and Power in the Ancient World*, eds. Mary Beard and John North (Ithaca, 1990): 201–31.

Gradel, Ittai. *Emperor Worship and Roman Religion* (Oxford, 2002).

Liebeschuetz, J. H. W. G. *Continuity and Change in Roman Religion* (Oxford, 1967).

McLynn, Neil. "The Fourth-Century Taurobolium." *Phoenix* 50 (1996): 312–30.

Michels, Agnes K. *The Calendar of the Roman Republic* (Princeton, 1967).

Mitchell, Stephen. "The Cult of Theos Hypsistos between Pagans, Christians and Jews." In *Pagan Monotheism in Late Antiquity*, eds. P. Athanassiadi and M. Frede (Oxford, 1999): 81–148.

North, John A. "Religious Toleration in Republican Rome." *PCPhS* n.s. 25 (1979): 85–103.

Roman Religion (Greece and Rome: New Surveys in the Classics 30) (Oxford, 2000).

"Religions in the Roman Empire." In *A Handbook of Ancient Religion*, ed. John R. Hinnels (Cambridge, 2007): 318–63.

Noy, David. *Foreigners at Rome: Citizens and Strangers* (London, 2000).

Price, Simon R. F. *Rituals and Power: The Roman Imperial Cult in Asia Minor* (Cambridge, 1984).

Richardson, Lawrence, Jr. *A New Topographical Dictionary of Ancient Rome* (Baltimore, 1992).

Rives, James B. *Religion and Authority in Roman Carthage from Augustus to Constantine* (Oxford, 1995).

"The Decree of Decius and the Religion of the Empire." *JRS* 89 (1999): 135–54.

Religion in the Roman Empire (Malden, Mass., 2007).

"Graeco-Roman Religion in the Roman Empire: Old Assumptions and New Approaches." *CBR* 8.2 (2010): 240–99.

Salzman, Michele Renee. *The Codex-Calendar of 354 and the Rhythms of Urban Life in Late Antiquity* (Berkeley, 1980).

"Rethinking Pagan-Christian Religious Violence." In *Violence in Late Antiquity: Perceptions and Practices*, ed. H. A. Drake (Ashgate, Hampshire, 2006).

Salzman, Michele Renee, and Michael Roberts. *The Letters of Symmachus: Book 1. Translation by Michele Renee Salzman and Michael Roberts. General Introduction and Commentary by Michele Renee Salzman* (Atlanta, 2011).

Scott, Russell T. *Religion and Philosophy in the Histories of Tacitus* (Rome, 1968).

Scheid, John. "Polytheism impossible; or, the empty gods: reasons behind a void in the history of Roman religion." In *The Inconceivable Polytheism: Studies in Religious Historiography, History and Anthropology*. Vol. 3, ed. Francis Schmidt (London, 1987): 303–26.

Romulus et ses frères: le collège des Frères Arvales, modèle du culte public dans la Rome des empereurs. Bibliothèque des écoles françaises d'Athènes et de Rome, fasc. 275 (Rome, 1990).

Schultz, Celia E. *Women's Religious Activity in the Roman Republic* (Chapel Hill, N.C., 2006).

Sfameni Gasparro, G. *Soteriology and Mystic Aspects in the Cult of Cybele and Attis*. EPRO 91 (Leiden, 1985).

Takács, Sarolta. *Isis and Sarapis in the Roman World* (Leiden, 1995).

Taylor, Lily Ross, and Louise Adams Holland. "Janus and the Fasti." *CP* 47 (1952): 137–42.

Tripolitis, Antonia. *Religions of the Hellenistic-Roman Age* (Grand Rapids, Mich., 2002).

Vermaseren, Maarten J. *Cybele and Attis: The Myth and the Cult*. Trans. A. M. H. Lemmers (London, 1977).

15

JUDAISM IN ITALY AND THE WEST

GIANCARLO LACERENZA

In the absence of substantial historical and literary records, an overview of Judaism in the western territories of the Roman empire from the first to the fifth century necessarily relies on epigraphic and archaeological documentation. The limits imposed by the fragmentary state of the material evidence, however, and the random circumstances of its preservation, frustrate any attempt – or temptation – to paint a detailed picture of a reality that must have been internally varied and not always in step with the evolution of rabbinic Judaism in Palestine and Mesopotamia.

From the formative period of the Jewish communities in the West down to the third and fourth centuries, when the Jewish population of Italy and the Iberian Peninsula became a significant component of local society, the western branch of ancient Judaism developed far away from its homeland. Furthermore, Jewish communities in the West were under continuous pressure from a politically and culturally hegemonic environment that rejected, at least in principle, any innovation regarded as barbaric or, in any case, alien. Not surprisingly, Judaism in the West maintained a degree of independence from Palestinian Judaism, with which it began to conform – although the trend was not uniform – only from the fifth century onward and mainly in reaction to the growing success of Christianity.

ROME

The date and circumstances of the appearance of the first Jewish communities in Italy – presumably around the middle of the second century BCE – are still shrouded in uncertainty. 2 Macc 4:1 seems to suggest that the first official contacts between Judea and Rome dated as far back as 174 BCE. However, the earliest securely dated contacts occurred in 161 BCE, the year of the treaties ratified between Rome and the Hasmonean princes and later renewed in 142 (1 Macc 8:17–30; 15:15–17). Although no sources mention a Jewish community in the capital or anywhere else in Italy at this time, by then groups of Jews must have already settled in Rome. In 139 BCE, the *praetor peregrinus* Cn. Cornelius Hispalus repatriated them – together with some astrologers, probably Babylonian – under the accusation of having attempted to spread their religious practices. His act suggests that the local Jewish community was mercantile rather than residential in character. Because the episode, related by Valerius Maximus, survives only in two slightly different epitomes, neither the context nor any other details are known. But the subsequent sending of delegations to Rome under John Hyrcanus between 134 and 112 BCE may be an indication that by that time the crisis had abated (Josephus, *Ant.* 13.260, 266; 14.145–8, 247–55).

The number of Jews in Italy rose suddenly in 63–61 BCE, when Pompey brought back many slaves following his conquest of Judea, including the former pretender to the throne Aristobulus II and his supporters. After the Roman conquest, many more Jews were reduced to slavery under several governors, including Cassius Longinus in 53 (Josephus, *J. W.* 1.8.9). Once Judea fell under direct Roman control, deteriorating relations between the two nations affected even the religious domain. Pompey's sacrilegious entry into the Jerusalem temple was long remembered as one of Rome's most serious affronts to the Jewish cult. Conversely, the Jews' attachment to their traditions and exclusive ritual practices often earned them the accusation of *misanthropia* among the Romans.[1] Given this climate of mutual hostility, one is hardly surprised by Cicero's contemptuous description of a multitude of unruly Roman Jews – apparently an influential lobby – attending the trial of the governor of Asia, L. Valerius Flaccus, in 59 BCE. Among other things, Flaccus was accused of having prevented the sending of funds to the temple of Jerusalem. While heaping scorn on the Jews' *barbara superstitio*, Cicero also informs us that it was a well-established custom at the time to send money to the Temple from Italy. Significantly, in the same period, Varro (quoted in Augustine, *Civ.* 4.31) bears witness to a degree of benevolence toward Judaism. In Varro's case, it was inspired by the "purity" of the Jews' aniconic cult, which for Varro represented *religio* in all respects.

Having sided with the *populares*, the Jews were unaffected by Julius Caesar's decree banning religious *collegia* from Rome (except for the ones established earlier, which were granted the right to assemble, send money

[1] Schäfer, *Judaeophobia*; for deteriorating Jewish perception of Rome, see Hadas-Lebel, *Jérusalem contre Rome*.

to their homelands, and take their meals in common). Many Jews visited the dictator's funeral pyre in gratitude. Octavian later confirmed their religious privileges (Suetonius, *Jul.* 42; 84.5; *Aug.* 32). Judging from the surviving names, there were at least three synagogues in Rome in Julio-Claudian times. They belonged, respectively, to the *Herodiani*, the *Agrippenses*, and the *Augustenses*. To these we must add the synagogue in Ostia, the only one that was certainly active in that period.

It is commonly believed that during the early empire, there were only a few thousand Jews in Rome, out of an estimated population of about one million inhabitants. The evidence, however, is rather scarce. Flavius Josephus, for example, mentions 8,000 Roman Jews who mobilized against Archelaus, heir to Herod the Great (*Ant.* 17.300). First described by Tacitus, Tiberius's expulsion from the city of 4,000 descendants of freedmen, whom he sent away to Sardinia to fight bandits, probably included converts, and members of the Egyptian cults, as well as Jews (Tac. *Ann.* 2.85; Suet. *Tib.* 36). First-century sources report that the Jews of Rome were numerous, but of destitute condition and mostly belonging to the servile class. The Alexandrian philosopher Philo observes that Rome's many Jews, most of whom resided in Trastevere, were former war captives (*Legat.* 155 [23]). The arrival of captives from the war of 68–71 CE must have increased their numbers. According to Josephus, 97,000 people were captured during that campaign. Of these, those under the age of seventeen were reduced to slavery, and at least 700 were selected and sent to Rome for Titus's triumph (Josephus, *J.W.* 6.417–20). Scholars have proposed widely diverging approximations of the size of Rome's Jewish community. For the first century, the estimates were once rather high, between 10,000 and 60,000 individuals. More recent studies based on reexaminations of the archaeological record, however, hypothesize an average of only 500 individuals from the first to the fourth century.[2] This estimate is based on quantitative data deduced from some of the five or six surviving Jewish catacombs. Because it is likely that several more Jewish cemeteries existed, the accuracy of this figure is subject to question.

The first witness to the presence of Palestinian emissaries in Italy dates back to 94/95 CE. In that year, according to written sources, a delegation of four, headed by Gamaliel II, came to Rome, paid a visit to Theudas (or Todos), the capital's main religious leader, and reproached him for not scrupulously following the current precepts of Judea (*y. Mo'ed Qat.* 3.1,

---

[2] Solin, "Juden und Syrer," 698–9, n. 240; McGing, "Population and Proselytism"; Rutgers, "Nuovi dati."

etc.). The principate of Domitian (81–96 CE) was marked by special hostility against the Jews. The aversion to Judaism already visible in the writings of Latin authors such as Quintilian and Martial was in the second century at least partly a reaction to the rebellions that had spread in North Africa and the East ever since 116, and especially the increasing attraction exerted by Judaism on large sectors of Roman society, including the ruling classes. This attraction apparently went hand in hand with active proselytism; because Judaism could not be readily integrated into the Roman tradition, proselytism made the Jewish cult – and Christianity along with it – especially odious in the eyes of those who defended traditional customs against all *externae superstitiones*. The poet Juvenal adopted this attitude, as did the historian Tacitus, who has left us a very negative portrait of Jewish religious *instituta* (*Hist.* 5.5). Tensions created by the steady growth of the Jewish population in the capital were aggravated by a concomitant increase in the number of sympathizers adopting typically Jewish customs – for example, the Sabbath and dietary restrictions. There must have been even less tolerance for the growing number of converts. The latter differed from mere sympathizers in not shrinking from circumcision, a practice abhorrent to Roman traditionalists.

The end of the revolt of 132–35 CE probably brought to Italy many other captives and, according to rabbinic sources, voluntary exiles and scholars as well. On that occasion, a Mattiah ben Heresh reportedly settled in Rome, founding there an academy of Jewish studies (*b. Sanh.* 32b, etc.).[3] Modern scholars have cast doubt on literary traditions about Palestinian sages moving to and remaining in Rome in the first and second centuries. Although these doubts may sometimes be excessive, it is undeniable that the rabbinic account of Roman Judaism in that period is an a posteriori construction. Nor should it distort our understanding of Judaism in Rome. Although literary evidence temporarily wanes at the end of the second century, we begin to see evidence at this time from the Jewish catacombs in Rome.[4] Their variety bears witness to the highly heterogeneous character of local Jewish society. While the complexity of this society's cultural and spiritual orientations still largely eludes us, it can neither be denied nor constrained into halakhic categories unsuitable both to the context and to the period.

Considering the scarcity and ambiguity of written sources, epigraphs are of primary importance for our knowledge of Judaism in the western diaspora in the first few centuries of the common era. Fortunately, Italy

[3] Bokser, "Todos and Rabbinic Authority"; Segal, "R. Matiah ben Heresh of Rome."
[4] Rutgers et al., "Sul problema."

has yielded an abundant epigraphic record comprising, outside Rome, about two hundred inscriptions scattered over the entire national territory. Within current borders, they are mostly concentrated in southern Italy. The catacombs of Rome alone (Monteverde, Villa Torlonia, Vigna Randanini, Conte Cimarra, Via Casilina, and possibly that of Via Appia Pignatelli) have yielded about six hundred epigraphs – about 30 percent of all Jewish inscriptions in the entire Mediterranean area.[5] Any attempt, however provisional, to define the history and character of Judaism in ancient and late antique Italy must, therefore, take account of the abundant and still sometimes overlooked evidence of epigraphic sources. Regrettably, Rome has thus far yielded almost exclusively funerary inscriptions, which can rarely be securely dated. And unlike nearby Ostia, there are no epigraphic or archaeological testimonies about Jewish public life.

The eleven different synagogue communities attested in the city, probably all active at the same time, reflect the diversity of Roman Judaism. Each had its own specific designation, the meaning of which in some cases is uncertain. Several, as we have seen above, were named after illustrious patrons (as in the case of the synagogues of the *Herodiani*, the *Augustenses*, the *Agrippenses*, and the *Volumnenses*); others took their name from their location in the city (*Calcarenses*, *Campenses*, *Sekènoi*, *Suburenses*); and others still were named after the community's place of origin (*Elaei*, *Tripolitani*, and possibly *Vernaculi*). The debated meaning of the expression "synagogue of the Hebrews" (*tōn hebreōn*) may refer to immigrants from Palestine, or members who either used Hebrew as their liturgical language or whose identity was defined by their use of Aramaic. Some funerary inscriptions, not all of them from Rome, contain the epithet *ebreus*, which is, however, even rarer than *iudaeus*.[6]

Epigraphs mentioning community offices, whether real or merely honorific, shed light on the social organization of Italian Jews. Some inscriptions preserve a detailed titulary, in Greek, of synagogue offices. Although the titles are sometimes similar to those found in traditional *collegia*, the actual functions of their bearers remain uncertain. They include *gerusiarchēs* and *archigerusiarchēs*, *archisynagōgos*, *archōn*, *grammateus*, *mellogrammateus*, *psalmōdos*, *patēr sunagōges*, *presbyteros*, *prostatēs*, *frontistēs*, *hypēretes*, and others. It is still debated whether the feminine form of some of these titles – *archēgissa*, *archisynagōgissa*, *mētēr synagōgēs*, *presbytera*, and

---

[5] Lacerenza, "Le iscrizioni giudaiche."
[6] Van der Horst, *Ancient Jewish Epitaphs*, 68–71; *JIWE* II.44; Williams, "The Meaning and Function of *Ioudaios*."

others – represents evidence of the participation of women in communal life, merely honorific designations expressing status, or hereditary titles (for example, in the case of the priestly titles *hiereia* and *hierissa*). All three possible meanings may have variously applied to Jewish women in Rome. While some epigraphs apply such titles even to children and youths, it would be imprudent to assume that the titles borne by women or children were merely honorific.[7]

No epigraphic attestation of the term "rabbi" for a Jewish leader in Rome has yet been discovered. Several inscriptions, however, do mention scholars who apparently exercised the typical functions of the spiritual leader of a community. *JIWE* II 68, an inscription dating from the third or fourth century, is the epitaph of a Eusebius *didaskalos*, "teacher," and *nomomathēs*, "student of the Law," a title also appearing in other texts (*JIWE* II 270, 374, and possibly 390). Another epigraph mentions a *nomodidaskalos*, "teacher of the Law" (*JIWE* II 307), while the designation *mathētēs sofōn*, "disciple of the wise men" (*JIWE* II 544), is probably a calque of the Hebrew *talmid hakhamim*. This evidence, along with other indications we can glean from the rabbinic tradition, sheds light on a statement by Jerome in 384; he reports that Roman Jews were wont to spend time studying, and recalls borrowing scrolls (*volumina*) of the Hebrew Bible from a *hebreus* who in his turn had borrowed them from a synagogue (Jerome, *Ep.* 32.1; 36.1). It is not unlikely, as some scholars have suggested, that this was the milieu in which the *Collatio Legum Mosaicarum et Romanarum* (*Comparison of Mosaic and Roman Laws*) was composed. Indeed, the *Collatio* is the only text of this period that has been ascribed to Roman Judaism.[8]

The extent of conversion to Judaism is still debated. While some scholars have represented it as a mass phenomenon, others have argued against this on various grounds, mostly owing to the lack of evidence.[9] Proselytes (*theosebeis* and *metuentes*) are indeed attested in several inscriptions, but they are usually women. This is possibly due to Hadrian's ban on circumcision, which made female conversion de facto more tolerable, although in 202 a decree of Septimius Severus, reiterated by Constantine in 329, universally prohibited conversion. A third- or fourth-century Latin epitaph to a Veturia Paulla, who had assumed the Jewish name of Sarah, is a remarkable example both of female proselytism and of a woman office-holder: "Veturia Paulla, placed in (her) eternal home, who lived 86 years, six

[7] Brooten, *Women Leaders*; Kraemer, "A New Inscription from Malta"; Zabin, "*Iudeae benemerenti.*"
[8] Cracco Ruggini, "Tolleranza e intolleranza"; Rabello, "La datazione della Collatio."
[9] Feldman, *Jew and Gentile*; Rutgers, "Attitudes to Judaism"; Paget, "Jewish Proselytism"; Rokeah, "Ancient Jewish Proselytism"; Feldman, "Conversion to Judaism."

months, (and) 16 years as a proselyte under the name of Sarah, 'mother of the synagogues' of Campus and Volumnius. May she sleep peacefully" (*JIWE* II 577). This case, however, does not reflect the usual trend of the time. At least as early as the third century, people recorded in inscriptions of the Italian diaspora show a tendency to adopt non-Jewish names, which in Late Antiquity eventually became more common than Jewish names. The preference was for local – that is, Latin – names. This trend has been interpreted as one of the many signs of interaction between Jewish and non-Jewish milieus in late antique Italy.[10]

In the epigraphic and archaeological documentation of the western diaspora, Jewish religious ideology expressed itself predominantly in a visual form – that is, in the iconographic repertory used especially in epitaphs and the decoration of hypogea and catacombs, as well as on a variety of everyday-use objects such as seals, lamps, and the Jewish gilt glass. The subjects do not seem to differ from those found in other places of the diaspora and in Palestine itself: the Temple/synagogue, the menorah, cases for sacred scrolls, and ritual objects for the festival of Succoth (*ethrog, lulav,* and *shofar*). Like the formulas of eulogy and hope in future life that appear in the inscriptions, these signs expressed here an eschatological and soteriological meaning.[11]

The infrequent use of the biblical text in Roman Jewish epitaphs is striking. Only three direct quotations are known. Drawing on the Greek versions of both Aquila and the Septuagint, all three are from Proverbs 10:7: "the memory of the just shall be for a blessing." The formula concluding many epigraphs, "may he/she sleep peacefully," was possibly inspired by the Septuagint version of Psalms 4:9. Such citations cast little light on the liturgical practices of Roman Jews. Originally a bilingual population speaking Aramaic and Greek, Jews settling in Rome had to learn Latin as well, which must have gradually become the primary instrument of everyday conversation. Nonetheless, up until the eve of Late Antiquity, catacomb inscriptions were mainly in Greek, which according to some scholars was, like Latin, regarded as a sacred script. Out of the whole corpus of known Roman Jewish inscriptions, 78 percent are in (usually unpolished) Greek, 21 percent in Latin, and only 1 percent in Hebrew or Aramaic.[12] Although several are bilingual, scholars regard the use of Hebrew, attested

---

[10] Rutgers, *Jews in Late Ancient Rome,* 170–5; idem, "Interactions and its Limits."

[11] Goodenough, *Jewish Symbols,* II, 3–69; Kraemer, "Jewish Tuna and Christian Fish"; Rutgers, "Death and Afterlife."

[12] Leon, "The Language of the Greek Inscriptions"; Solin, "Juden und Syrer," 701–11; van der Horst, *Ancient Jewish Epitaphs,* 25–34; Rutgers, *The Jews,* 176–91; Rosén, "The Language of the Jewish Diaspora of Rome."

in only thirteen cases and limited to stereotyped formulas such as *šalom*, *Yiśraʾel*, or *šalom 'al Yiśraʾel*, as having had a visual rather than a textual significance, reflecting the magical and sacred character traditionally attributed to Hebrew writing.[13]

Ostia

Besides the catacombs – which shed light only on a relatively late period – the most conspicuous archaeological witness to Judaism in Rome and its surroundings is the synagogue of Ostia. This monumental building, discovered in 1961 outside the town walls, was probably founded around the middle of the first century and is hence the oldest synagogue of the western Mediterranean. It remained in use at least until the late fourth century, when it was still being renovated and expanded. The main room of the complex originally had three benches along three walls. The ark containing the Torah stood on a podium leaning against the back wall, which was half-curved and faced southeast. The most striking feature of the synagogue is an apsed and raised aedicule with two seven-armed candelabra gracing the corbels of its architraves. The aedicule, oriented in the opposite direction to the ancient *bimah* in the main hall, was only added in the fourth or possibly the fifth century, after the benches along the wall had been removed. The gradual evolution of religious ritual and ideology reflected in this reorientation of the room has only recently begun to draw the attention it deserves.[14] The synagogue contained various structures with social, religious, and ritual functions built at different times, including rooms for ablutions, a kitchen, and at least one meeting or study room.

The inscriptions found at Ostia and Porto (*JIWE* I 113–18), and the later building phases of the Ostia synagogue, both bear witness to a high degree of Romanization of the local Jewish community, which may have been divided into several distinct groups. The individuals mentioned in the surviving inscriptions (dating from the second and third centuries) include donors and community leaders and bear impressive-sounding names: Plotius Fortunatus (with his sons Ampliatus and Secundinus, and his wife Secunda), Ofilia Basilia, Caius Iulius Iustus, Livius Dionysius, Mindius Faustus, Marcus Aurelius Pylades (whose father, however, was called Iudas). A fourth-century inscription from Porto mentions a ʿEllēl

---

[13] Noy, "'Peace upon Israel'"; Rutgers, "Death and Afterlife," 302–5; Bengtsson, "Semitic Inscriptions in Rome."
[14] Görtz-Wrisberg, "A Sabbath Service in Ostia."

(Hillel; *JIWE* I 17). The synagogue was abandoned and the community gradually dwindled away in the fifth century, when Ostia declined.

The inflow of Jewish slaves into Roman Italy, especially after the campaigns of Pompey, Vespasian, and Titus, boosted the Jewish population both of Rome and of the vast southern Italian region, for a long time the center of important, mainly agricultural, production. Ancient literary sources provide only generic information about this demographic increase, which is described more precisely in late antique and early medieval sources, such as the *Sefer Yosippon*. Various archaeological and especially epigraphic finds, however, mostly from Campania, Puglia, and Sicily, point to a sizeable Jewish presence in southern Italy in Roman times.

Campania

Campania has yielded the earliest evidence of a Jewish presence in Italy. This includes some dubious or fragmentary iconographic and epigraphic materials from Pompeii that have long been either misinterpreted or decidedly overrated. It is beyond doubt, and hardly surprising, that some Jews inhabited this mercantile town of the Campanian coast, which had an active river port and housed several foreign cults. In recent years, however, scholars have cast serious doubts on the reliability, or Jewishness, of these Pompeian testimonies (mostly graffiti with personal names). Thus, although there are clues pointing incontrovertibly to the presence of Jews in Pompeii, and more in the Vesuvian area generally, the actual evidence for this is neither as reliable nor as abundant as once believed.[15]

There is, on the other hand, unequivocal literary and epigraphic testimony establishing the area of Puteoli (present day Pozzuoli), the large Roman port northwest of Naples, as the residence of the most important Jewish community of ancient Campania. Long before Ostia came to the fore, Puteoli, a major grain port and the principal destination of men and merchandise from all over the Mediterranean basin, housed eastern cults and communities even as early as the republican age. Like its counterpart in Rome, the Jewish community of Puteoli may have initially been organized as mercantile unions or *collegia*, as in the case of the Tyrians, whose

---

[15] Lacerenza, "Graffiti aramaici"; idem, "Per un riesame della presenza giudaica a Pompei"; idem, "La realtà documentaria."

community in Puteoli even predates the one in the capital. References in Philo and Josephus confirm the existence of a flourishing Jewish community in Puteoli by the first half of the first century CE. Philo mentions visiting Puteoli with other members of the Jewish *gerousia* of Alexandria, whence he had set sail in the winter of 38/39 or 39/40, possibly landing at the Campanian port, where he stayed for some time to meet Caligula (*Legat.* 185–6). While he does not provide specific information about the local Jewish community, Philo does mention the discussion that followed the report about Gaius's attempt to desecrate the temple of Jerusalem by introducing his statue into it. The Jews of Puteoli informed their Alexandrian guests of this event, about which Philo unfortunately provides no further information. In his autobiography, Josephus mentions journeying to Puteoli around the year 64 to ask Nero to free some priests imprisoned by procurator M. Antonius Felix. During his stay there, he recalls meeting the Jewish actor Aliturus, who introduced him to Poppaea Sabina. Josephus alludes here to her *theosebeia*, which several scholars interpret as sympathy for Judaism (*Life* 16).

Other information about the Jews of Puteoli dates from the late Herodian period, notably from years 4 and 35/36. The episode of the pseudo-Alexander is especially interesting. After succeeding in fooling the Jewish communities of Crete and Melos, this imitator of the homonymous son of Herod the Great did the same thing in Puteoli. He then moved to Rome where Augustus unmasked his imposture (*J. W.* 2.103–4; *Ant.* 17.328–9). Josephus's story provides several bits of information about the Puteolan Jewish elite, which evidently included high-ranking figures who entertained relations with Herod the Great, his sons, and the court. In another passage (*Ant.* 18.159–61) referring to the year 36 CE, Josephus mentions a loan granted to the future king Agrippa I by Alexander, the wealthy alabarch of Alexandria and brother of the philosopher Philo, enabling Agrippa to continue his journey to Campania and meet Tiberius on Capri. Both Philo and Josephus mention locations in the Phlegraean Fields in connection with other historical circumstances, but neither provides any further information about the local Jewish community. The *adelphoi* whom the apostle Paul stayed with in Puteoli sometime between 59 and 61 were presumably Jews (*Acts* 28:13–14).

Epigraphic evidence about Puteolan Jews, while surprisingly meager, is notable for its antiquity. Apart from a brief inscription in which the gerusiarch Ti. Claudius Philippus remembers the erection of a wall (*JIWE* I 23), the most significant record is the epitaph of a young woman called Claudia Aster, *Hierosolymitana*, who arrived from Judea as a slave in the

last quarter of the first century. The inscription (*JIWE* I 26), found in
what was at the time a suburb of Puteoli bordering on the territory of
Neapolis, is of exceptional importance; it shows that at least a portion of
the slaves captured after the conquest of Jerusalem in 70 CE were brought
to Campania (see Fig. 14).[16]

The city of Puteoli is also mentioned in some rabbinic sources referring to the age of Domitian. In the second century CE, the above-cited R.
Mattiah ben Heresh is said to have spent time in Puteoli with some other
scholars before establishing himself in Rome (*Sifra Deut.* 80). Information
about the subsequent centuries is scarce. It is likely that at the time of the
Vandal incursions, most of the Jewish population of Puteoli left the city to
seek refuge in the nearby, better fortified city of Neapolis. The sinking of
Puteoli under the geological effect known as bradyseism may have been an
additional motivation.

In Neapolis, the origin of the local Jewish community was probably
connected to the flourishing local colony of Alexandrians, whose presence
in the city dates at least as far back as the early empire. The Alexandrians
resided in the *Vicus Alexandrinorum* along the lower *decumanus*, in a
neighborhood accordingly called *Regio Nilensis*. The Jews must also have
lived in this area, more specifically near the stretch of the town walls looking out toward the sea, as indicated by several clues: notably, a passage in
Procopius (*Bell. Goth.* 1.8.41, 10.24–6), and medieval sources mentioning a
synagogue that seems to have been active for several centuries.

Sporadic finds within the ancient urban perimeter confirm the presence
of Jews in Naples, but the most important evidence for this comes from
inscriptions from an above-ground cemetery found in an area that was
suburban at the time. Although the graves cannot be dated precisely, they
belong to the period from the fourth to the sixth century (*JIWE* I 27–35).
While the inscriptions – which are all in Latin, except for one in Greek –
draw on a formulaic repertory similar to that of coeval Christian epitaphs,
they also include typical Hebrew expressions such as *shalom, shalom 'al
mᵉnuḥatekha, amen, sela*. In one case, the name of the deceased, Numerius,
is transcribed in Jewish characters. Interestingly, three out of ten of the
individuals mentioned in the epitaphs are qualified as "Jews," including
the above-mentioned Numerius, *ebreus*; a Criscentia, *ebrea*, daughter of
Pascasus; a Flaes, *ebreus*.

It is also significant that all the deceased have Latin names, except for
the *prostatēs* Benjamin "of Caesarea," to whom the only Greek inscription

[16] Lacerenza, "L'iscrizione di *Claudia Aster Hierosolymitana*."

Fig. 14. Epitaph of Claudia Aster from Jerusalem. Puteoli, first century CE. Naples, Museo Archeologico Nazionale. Photograph courtesy of G. Lacerenza.

in the group belongs. The use of this language probably means that "Caesarea" refers here to the Palestinian city of the same name, where, according to some Talmudic sources (such as *y. Ber.* 3:1, 6a), the synagogal liturgy was celebrated in Greek. Still, Caesarea in Mauritania cannot be totally ruled out, considering that the inscriptions indicate, more or less explicitly, a North African origin for several of the deceased, notably [Gau?]diosus, *civis Mauritaniae*, and possibly Erena, a common name at Cyrene. Others were Italian, but not Neapolitan – namely, Barbarus from Venafrum, and Hereni and his father Thelesinus, from Rome. Thus, in spite of its paucity, this late documentation clearly points to a composite character of the Jewish community of Naples. A few epigraphs from other archaeological contexts in Naples probably belong to Neapolitan Jews. One mentions the title "rabbi" (*rebbi*, in the genitive *rebbitis*); because of the contexts in which they appear, some scholars regard this as an honorific title or a sign of social distinction rather than an indication of actual religious leadership.

The introduction of the laws of the Theodosian Code in 438, which drastically curtailed the Jews' social status, had various effects on conversion in the western Mediterranean. The presbyter Uranius's mention, around the mid-fifth century, of the presence of a great number of *neophyti* at the funerary cortege of the bishop of Naples, John I, is plausible in this new juridical and social climate. However, the Ostrogoth Theodoric's later take-over of Campania (494–526) marked a reversal of this anti-Jewish trend. Procopius of Caesarea describes the Neapolitan Jewish community on the eve of Byzantine conquest (536) as flourishing, influential, and economically important. Several fourth- and fifth-century documents bear witness to the presence of Jews in various areas of Campania, such as Capua and Abellinum, and especially in the Nocera-Sarno plain, which has yielded several marble epitaphs, all in Greek. One (*JIWE* I 22, from Brusciano) mentions a *rebbi* Abba Mari, probably of Palestinian origin. Two others found near the ancient town of Nuceria Alfaterna commemorate, respectively, the scribe (*grammateus*) Pedonius and his wife Myrina, *presbytera*.

Venosa

Of all the southern Italian sites that hosted Jewish communities, Venosa (ancient Venusia, in Basilicata) is especially remarkable for its celebrated Jewish catacombs. Discovered in 1853, they yielded an extraordinary epigraphic documentation (*JIWE* I 42–112). The main cemetery stood next to the Christian catacombs in an area outside the town. It consisted of several superimposed tunnels, only a small part of which has been actually explored. More than seventy epigraphs were found here, mostly painted on the plaster used to seal the tombs. The only one bearing a date is from the year 521. The others seem to date from the third or fourth century onward.

Apparently, Venosa was one of the towns in southern Italy with a high concentration of Jewish inhabitants. The inscriptions from the catacomb indicate that Jews were well integrated into local society. Many of them even enjoyed high status, as various references to public offices demonstrate. The influence of Judaism on local society is confirmed by the presence of several proselytes – or at least "God-fearers" – in another cemetery, the so-called Lauridia hypogeum (*JIWE* I 113–16). The titulary attested at Venosa is the same as in Rome. The community included presbyters, gerusiarchs, archisynagogoi, and *patres synagogae*. A bilingual Greek-Hebrew epitaph (*JIWE* I 48) mentions a teacher called Jacob (*Iakōb didaskalos*). Several scholars have identified the *duo apostuli et duo rebbites* ("two apostles and two rabbis") mentioned in the famous epitaph of Faustina (*JIWE* I 86) as envoys of the Jewish Patriarchate to Gothic-Byzantine Italy. The text, probably dating from the mid-sixth century, is clearly later than the suppression of the Patriarchate in 425. It thus probably refers to religious representatives of the local community, whose titulary indeed resembled those used in Jewish communities in Palestine.[17]

The Venosa inscriptions bear witness to strong ties with other Jewish communities, both in southern Italy and throughout the Mediterranean. They also provide clear evidence of a gradual rediscovery of Hebrew in religious contexts and in the liturgical practices of the western diaspora. The earlier inscriptions are all in Greek, after which there is a gradual shift to Latin. Hebrew, which initially makes its appearance in the usual stereotypical formulas, later becomes increasingly common, as the epigraph of the old presbyter Secundinus, written in Hebrew and Greek in Hebrew characters, demonstrates (*JIWE* I 75) (Fig. 15). Indeed, Hebrew is, in percentage, more frequent at Venosa than in Rome: out of seventy-one epigraphs, twenty-nine (or 41 percent) contain Hebrew expressions supplementing the Greek or Latin text, and nine (or 13 percent) are entirely in Hebrew.

Puglia and Calabria

According to an opinion commonly held among medieval Jewish scholars of southern Italy, the Jewish communities of Puglia were the first to establish themselves on Italian soil; they consisted mainly of captives whom Titus brought to Italy after destroying Jerusalem, five thousand of whom were settled in the Salento peninsula, between Taranto and Otranto. It is indeed very likely that a Jewish community existed at Brundisium

---

[17] Lacerenza, "Ebraiche liturgie e peregrini *apostuli*."

Fig. 15. Venosa, Jewish catacombs. Epitaph of the presbyter Secundinus, Greek in Hebrew letters, fifth/sixth century CE. Photograph courtesy of G. Lacerenza.

(present-day Brindisi), an important port of trade with the East and reportedly a destination for ships from Judea. There is no certainly dated evidence, however, of the presence of Jews in Puglia before 398, when the emperor Honorius issued a decree requiring the Jews of many towns of *Apulia Calabriamque* (at the time, the toponym *Calabria* designated the Salento peninsula) to fill the office of decurion. This obligation had been abolished by Constantine but reintroduced by Valentinian II in 383 (*CTh* 12.1.158). Thus, as had already been the case long before under Septimius Severus, the Jews were now required to participate in town *curiae* and assume all the associated duties, both religious and economic.

Honorius's decree indicates that in Puglia there must have been towns where the majority, if not the entirety, of the population was Jewish. It also attests the presence of Jews among the *maiores* of several towns of late antique southern Italy; epigraphic evidence, especially from Venosa, establishes the same point. However, archaeological and epigraphic sources from present-day Puglia and Calabria do not reflect the importance of the Jewish population. Otranto (ancient Hydruntum), at the tip of Salento, has yielded a single epitaph, dated to the third century and containing the Hebrew expression *mishkavam 'im tzaddiqim*, "may they rest with the just"

(*JIWE* I 134). At Lupiae (present-day Lecce), the presence of Jews is indirectly attested by the above-mentioned epitaph from Venosa dated to 521; it remembers the deceased Augusta's father and her grandfather Simon, who was from Lecce: *nepus Symonatis p(atris) Lypiensium* (*JIWE* I 107). At Taranto, the necropolis of Montedoro apparently housed both Christian and Jewish graveyards. Two inscriptions found here, datable between the fifth and sixth centuries, include typically Jewish names: 'Azariah, Daudatos (Natan'el), Elias, Iaakov, and Susannah. The Hebrew text on the verso of the epitaph of Daudatos son of 'Azariah (*JIWE* I 118) is one of the earliest and longest-known epigraphs of this kind, containing several eulogies, including the characteristic "may his soul be bound up in the bundle of life" (from 1 Samuel 25:29).

The most significant evidence of a Jewish presence in Calabria (ancient *Bruttium*), the remains of a synagogue erected around the middle of the fourth century, was discovered at Bova Marina, near *Skyle* on the Peutinger Table. Nothing but the foundations, and fragments of the mosaic decoration of some of the rooms, survive. The symbol of the menorah, oriented southeast toward Jerusalem, is still visible in the prayer hall. Although the local Jewish community probably used an adjacent funerary area where several different forms of inhumation are attested, it has yielded no grave goods and shows no distinctively Jewish features. The remains of several glass lamps, however, have been found in the synagogue, which remained in use until the seventh century. Also discovered were sherds of locally produced amphorae bearing stamped images of the menorah on the handles, probably to certify the *kashruth* of the contents. The discovery of these amphorae in Rome is evidence of the exportation of local products to other Jewish communities in the Italian peninsula.[18]

Sicily and Malta

Although the settlement of Jews in Sicily probably began at an early date, no documents earlier than the imperial period have thus far come down to us. As with almost everywhere else in Italy, the most abundant materials date from late antique times. The earliest testimony, dating from the third or fourth century, actually originates in the catacombs of Villa Torlonia in Rome. This is the epitaph of a Justus, also mentioning his father Amachius from Catania (*JIWE* II 515). Most of the evidence has been found in eastern Sicily, and the island's most important Jewish communities were

---

[18] Arthur, "Some Observations"; Zevi, "Recenti studi e scoperte di archeologia ebraica."

apparently those of Syracuse and Catania. The earliest attestation of a
Jewish presence in that area is a reference to Catanian *iudaei* in the *Passio
Sanctae Agathae*. Referring to the third century, but actually written at a
much later date, it is an unreliable witness. The only surviving epigraphic
sources are a few inscriptions no earlier than the fourth or fifth century. An
especially interesting epitaph of a certain Aurelius Samohil, precisely dated
to 383, reveals Christian influences and possibly a nonconventional use of
the calendar (*JIWE* I 145).[19] The Jews who settled in that area made ample
use of catacombs and rock cemeteries. Many traces of this custom remain,
especially at Syracuse and Noto, but all are badly preserved. In the interior,
in the south-central part of the island, two epigraphs found at Filosofiana,
on the ancient road from Catania to Agrigento, document the presence of
a small Jewish settlement. There may be a connection between this settlement and evidence of a local glass-manufacturing industry.

　　Witnesses to Judaism found in Sicily (not just epigraphs, but also seals,
rings, and lamps) include a number of sources that are magical in character, such as inscriptions and amulets. Some are actually Jewish, while others are Greco-Roman or Christian, with Jewish influence. These finds are
far more numerous in Sicily than in the rest of Italy, where they only occur
sporadically. More abundant parallels from the eastern Mediterranean suggest that they spread from there to Sicily. The dissemination of these artifacts goes hand in hand with the spread and distinctive characteristics of
Jewish communities on the island. The most common amulets, laminas
or small metal plates, are of mixed provenance, form, material, content,
and function. Some are inscribed in Hebrew and/or Aramaic, others –
the most numerous – in Greek; still others bear pseudo-Hebrew inscriptions or magical *charaktēres* or symbols. The Comiso area has yielded some
rock-carved Greek inscriptions, generally datable between the fourth and
sixth centuries. Here Christian formulas and Jewish names are combined
with a wealth of symbols and pseudo-characters to ensure magical protection of agricultural land and assets. Such inscriptions are not isolated
occurrences in late antique Sicily; other examples are attested at Akrai
(Palazzolo Acreide), Noto, and Modica, all featuring, more or less prominently, elements of Jewish-influenced magic and angelology.

　　In the fourth and fifth centuries, on the island of Malta, which in
Roman times was administratively connected to Sicily, a number of Jews

---

[19] Wasserstein, "Calendaric Implications"; Millar, "The Jews of the Graeco-Roman Diaspora"; Stern,
Calendar and Community, 132–6.

were buried inside a Christian cemetery, the so-called catacombs of St. Paul and St. Agatha. The inscriptions scratched in the stucco that sealed the loculi, all in Greek and accompanied by the menorah, confirm the existence of an organized community on the island (*JIWE* I 163–8).

SARDINIA AND NORTHERN ITALY

Sardinia

Other than Josephus's unreliable report about the expulsion of the descendants of freedman devotees of foreign cults from Rome to Sardinia in 19 CE, there are no historical or literary sources about a Jewish presence on the island before the testimony of Gregorius Magnus (540–604). So far, the meager archaeological evidence sheds light, although a dim one, only on a rather late period.

Two Jewish hypogeal cemeteries – which, as in Venosa, adjoined Christian cemeteries – have been identified on the island of Sant'Antioco, at the southeast extremity of Sardinia. One, called "of Beronice," is very small, consisting of a single sepulchral chamber with graves cut into the walls and floor, possibly used by a single family group in the fourth or fifth century. The most significant inscription (*JIWE* I 170), concerning a young woman called Beronice, is painted in red at the back of one of the main arcosolia. It is composed in Latin with some Hebrew formulas also found on the adjacent, unfortunately poorly preserved arcosolium. Nearby is the second hypogeum, which is also not very large. At the time of its discovery in 1920, it still contained an intact burial. The inscription painted on the plaster was difficult to read and was soon lost. It was composed in Latin with some conventional Hebrew expressions, uncharacteristically written from left to right, with some letters reversed or miswritten. The writer was obviously mechanically reproducing a script with which he or she was barely acquainted (*JIWE* I 173). Porto Torres (ancient Turris Libisonis), on the north versant of the island, has yielded several Jewish lamps datable to the fifth century, as well as the Latin epitaphs of two children, Gaudiosa and Anianus, probably from the same period (*JIWE* I 175–6). Of the few other Jewish artifacts found on the island, which include some rings and seals, several appear to be even later.

As is also the case in other areas, the Sardinian evidence parallels coeval Christian materials. The Jewish character of the epigraphs is more often indicated by the addition of figurative elements or eulogies in the

Hebrew script rather than by distinctive features of the text itself or of the name of the deceased.

Northern Italy

To date, there are no traces of the penetration of Judaism into northern Italy earlier than the fourth century, when evidence of Jewish presence first appears in some of the most advanced urban centers, such as Mediolanum (Milan), Brixia (Brescia), Bononia (Bologna), Ravenna, and Aquileia. There is also some evidence from rural areas, but these – unlike the southern Italian countryside – have mostly yielded scarce archaeological and epigraphic materials. In northern Italy, relations between Jews and Christians were apparently unstable and insecure, not favorable to the flourishing of local Jewish culture. The few inscriptions from Mediolanum (*JIWE* I 1–3) do not contain significant information. The famous bishop of Milan, Ambrose, staunchly anti-Jewish, attended the unearthing of the remains of the Christian martyrs Vitalis and Agricola in the Jewish cemetery of Bologna, where they had allegedly been buried around 304 (Ambrose, *Exhort.* 8).

Byzantine Ravenna has yielded more abundant evidence, including a fifth- or sixth-century amphora sherd bearing the inscription *shalom* in Jewish characters (*JIWE* I 10). In this city there were Jewish bureaucrats, slave traders, craftsmen, *milites classiarii* (marines), and shipowners supplying the imperial fleet. As elsewhere in Italy, in late antique times increasing limitations were imposed on Jews, and episodes of intolerance are recorded. A local law issued in 415 addressed the issue of Jewish owners of Christian slaves. It explicitly mentioned the *didascalus* Annas, evidently the religious leader of the community, and the *maiores iudaeorum*. A decree of the following year dealt with the case of Jews who had converted to Christianity in order to benefit, for example, from asylum rights on church grounds. The Ostrogoth Theodoric allegedly buried Odoacer, the first barbarian king of Italy, near a synagogue of Ravenna in 493 (Ioh. Ant. frag. 214a [*FHG* IV.621]). Aquileia, at the northeastern extremity of the Italian coast, yielded a late Republican inscription (*JIWE* I 7) of a L. Aiacius Dama, *iudaeus portor*. The term *portor* has been interpreted as meaning "boatman," or else as an abbreviation of *portitor*, "customs officer." This inscription is the only testimony so far from this early period, although various later sources mention the presence of a rather important Jewish community at Aquileia. While this tradition once led scholars to identify various archaeological finds and epigraphs from Aquileia as Jewish, the Jewishness of almost all this material is now rejected.

Until the fifth century, the literary, archaeological, and epigraphic sources attesting a Jewish presence in Gaul are too sporadic to provide even a sketchy picture. The earliest evidence comes from Avignon, and includes some lamps graced with the menorah and a fourth-century seal bearing the name Ianu(arius). Another seal with the name Aster, from Bordeaux, is only slightly later. This area, too, has yielded lamps with Jewish symbols (*JIWE* I 190–2).

The Spanish evidence is more abundant and earlier, although the precise chronology of the finds is often debated. A first-century amphora from Ibiza bearing a Jewish stamp attests to early relations between the *emporia* of the Balearic Islands and Judea (*JIWE* I 178). The epitaph of the freedman A. Lucius (?) Roscius *iudeus*, from Villamesías (*JIWE* I 188), may date from the first century, but its reading is uncertain. Other epigraphic materials dated by some scholars to the Roman imperial period are in all likelihood medieval instead. The most western evidence is a quartz intaglio with menorah and other symbols found in Ammaia (Lusitania, presently in Portugal; third century).

Thanks to the discovery of funerary inscriptions in various coastal towns, the evidence from the Iberian Peninsula becomes more substantial from the third or fourth century onward. Notably, an organized Jewish community is attested at Ilici (Elche), in southeast Spain, where the remains of a synagogue were found. Its mosaic floor still carried partially preserved Greek dedications referring to the synagogue as "prayer house," and mentioning archons and presbyters. Mention of a merchant or traveler in one text is evidence that local Jews were involved in trading activities (*JIWE* I 182). The participation of Jews in the social life of late imperial Spain is documented by resolutions of the Elvira Council (305/306) seeking a rigid separation between the Jewish and Christian communities, and notably strictly forbidding mixed marriages. The forced conversion of about 540 Jews of the town of Mago (Mahón) on the island of Minorca, recounted in a celebrated epistle by the bishop Severus, is a clear indication of a decline in the living conditions of the Jews.[20] The same source provides valuable insight into the organization of the local Jewish community, which had a

---

[20] Severus Minoricensis, *Epistola ad omnem Ecclesiam de virtutibus ad Iudaeorum conversionem.*

synagogue (later transformed into a church) with rich furnishings and *libri sancti*. Its most eminent member, named Theodorus, held the office of *doctor legis*, an indubitably "rabbinic" role which the Jews, Severus tells us, called *pater patrum*, a title also attested in several southern Italian inscriptions (notably *JIWE* I 68, 85, 90, 114, all from Venosa).

The most original epigraphic testimonies, however, are all rather late. Dating from the Visigoth period, they come from the northeast coast of the Iberian Peninsula. Several sites have yielded bilingual or trilingual epitaphs of the fifth or sixth century featuring Latin side by side not only with Greek – as in various Christian epitaphs from the same area – but also with Hebrew: an eloquent witness to the eastern origins of at least part of the local population. The best known of these epigraphs is the so-called Tortosa trilingual inscription from southern Cataluna. This epitaph of a girl, Meliosa, daughter of Rabbi Yehudah and *domina* (*kúra*) Maria, is notable for its nonbanal use of Hebrew (*JIWE* I 183). An echo of synagogal liturgy appears in a bilingual Latin-Hebrew inscription, apparently not funerary, from Tarragona (*JIWE* I 185). Its Hebrew text contains the expression *shalom 'al Yiśra'el we-'alenu we-'al b^enenu, amen* ("peace on Israel, and on ourselves and our children. Amen"). The mention of scholars (*didascali*) in another epitaph from the same town (*JIWE* I 186) indicates that at least some of the members of this community enjoyed a high social status and cultural standard, and maintained active religious contacts with Palestine.

BIBLIOGRAPHY

Primary

Severus Minoricensis. *Epistola ad omnem Ecclesiam de virtutibus ad Iudaeorum conversionem in Minorcensi insula factis in praesentia reliquarum Sancti Stephani* (*PL* XX.731–46). Trans. Scott Bradbury. *Letter on the Conversion of the Jews* (Oxford, 1996).

Secondary

Arthur, Paul. "Some Observations on the Economy of Bruttium under the later Roman Empire." *JRS* (1989): 133–42.
Bengtsson, Per Å. "Semitic Inscriptions in Rome." In *The Synagogue of Ancient Ostia and the Jews of Rome: Interdisciplinary Studies*, eds. B. Olsson, D. Mitternacht, and O. Brandt (Stockholm, 2001): 151–65.
Bokser, Baruch M. "Todos and Rabbinic Authority in Rome." In *New Perspectives on Ancient Judaism*. Vol. 1: *Religion, Literature, and Society in Ancient Israel, Formative Christianity and Judaism*, eds. Jacob Neusner et al. (Lanham, Md., 1987): 117–30.
Brooten, Bernadette J. *Women Leaders in the Ancient Synagogues* (Atlanta, 1982).

Cracco Ruggini, L. "Tolleranza e intolleranza nella società tardoantica: il caso degli ebrei." *RSSR* 23 (1983): 27–44.

Feldman, Louis H. *Jew and Gentile in the Ancient World: Attitudes and Interactions from Alexander to Justinian* (Princeton, 1993).

"Conversion to Judaism in Classical Antiquity." *HUCA* 74 (2003): 115–56.

Goodenough, Erwin R. *Jewish Symbols in the Greco-Roman Period. Vol. 2: The Archaeological Evidence from the Diaspora* (New York, 1953).

Görtz-Wrisberg, Irene von. "A Sabbath Service in Ostia: What Do We Know about the Ancient Synagogal Service?" In *The Synagogue of Ancient Ostia*, eds. B. Olsson, D. Mitternacht, and O. Brandt (Stockholm, 2001): 168–202.

Hadas-Lebel, Mireille. *Jérusalem contre Rome* (Paris, 1990). Trans. R. Fréchet. *Jerusalem against Rome* (Leuven, 2006).

Kraemer, Ross S. "A New Inscription from Malta and the Question of Women Elders in the Diaspora Jewish Communities." *HTR* 78 (1985): 431–8.

"Jewish Tuna and Christian Fish: Identifying Religious Affiliation in Epigraphic Sources." *HTR* 84 (1991): 141–62.

Lacerenza, Giancarlo. "Graffiti aramaici nella casa del Criptoportico a Pompei (*Regio* I, *insula* VI, 2)." *AION* 56 (1996): 166–88.

"L'iscrizione di *Claudia Aster Hierosolymitana*." In Luigi Cagni, ed. *Biblica et semitica: studi in memoria di Francesco Vattioni* (Naples, 1999): 303–13.

"Per un riesame della presenza ebraica a Pompei." *Materia giudaica* 7 (2001): 99–103.

"Le iscrizioni giudaiche in Italia dal I al VI secolo: tipologie, origine, distribuzione." In *I beni culturali ebraici in Italia*, ed. Mauro Perani (Ravenna, 2003): 71–92.

"Ebraiche liturgie e peregrini *apostuli* nell'Italia bizantina." In *Una manna buona per Mantova. Studi in onore di V. Colorni*, ed. Mauro Perani (Firenze, 2004): 61–72.

"La realtà documentaria e il mito romantico della presenza giudaica a Pompei." In *Pompei, Capri e la Penisola Sorrentina: atti del quinto Ciclo di conferenze di geologia, storia, e archeologia: Pompei, Anacapri, Scafati, Castellammare di Stabia, ottobre 2002-aprile 2003*, ed. Felice Senatore (Capri, 2004): 245–71.

ed. *Hebraica hereditas: Studi in onore di Cesare Colafemmina* (Naples, 2005).

Leon, Harry J. "The Language of the Greek Inscriptions from the Jewish Catacombs of Rome." *TAPA* 58 (1927): 210–33.

McGing, Brian. "Population and Proselytism: How Many Jews were there in the Ancient World?" In *Jews in the Hellenistic and Roman Cities*, ed. John R. Bartlett (London, 2002): 88–106.

Millar, Fergus. "The Jews of the Graeco-Roman Diaspora between Paganism and Christianity, AD 312–438." In *The Jews among Pagans and Christians in the Roman Empire*, eds. Judith Lieu, John A. North, and Tessa Rajak (London, 1992): 97–132.

Noy, David. "'Peace upon Israel': Hebrew Formulae and Names in Jewish Inscriptions from the West Roman Empire." In *Hebrew Study from Ezra to Ben-Yehuda*, ed. William Horbury (Edinburgh, 1999): 135–46.

Olsson, Birger, Dieter Mitternacht, and Olof Brandt, eds. *The Synagogue of Ancient Ostia and the Jews of Rome: Interdisciplinary Studies* (Stockholm, 2001).

Paget, James C. "Jewish Proselytism at the Time of Christian Origins: Chimera or Reality?" *JSNT* 18 (1996): 65–103.

Rabello, Alfredo M. "La datazione della Collatio Legum Mosaicarum et Romanarum e il problema di una sua seconda redazione o del suo uso nel corso del quarto secolo." In *Humana sapit: études d'antiquité tardive offertes à L. Cracco Ruggini*, eds. Jean-Michel Carrié, Rita Lizzi Testa, and Lellia Cracco Ruggini (Turnhout, 2002): 411–22.

Rokeah, David. "Ancient Jewish Proselytism in Theory and in Practice." *TZ* 52 (1996): 206–24.

Rosén, Haim B. "The Language of the Jewish Diaspora of Rome." In *Hebrew at the Crossroads of Cultures: From Outgoing Antiquity to the Middle Ages* (Leuven, 1995): 23–39.

Rutgers, Leonard V. "Attitudes to Judaism in the Greco-Roman Period: Reflections on Feldman's 'Jew and Gentile in the Ancient World.'" *JQR* 85 (1995): 361–95.

——— *The Jews in Late Ancient Rome: Evidence of Cultural Interaction in the Roman Diaspora* (Leiden, 1995).

——— "Interactions and its Limits: Some Notes on the Jews of Sicily in Late Antiquity." *ZPE* 115 (1997): 245–56.

——— "Death and Afterlife: The Inscriptional Evidence." In *Judaism in Late Antiquity* 4, eds. Alan J. Avery-Peck and Jacob Neusner (Leiden, 2000): 293–310.

——— "Nuovi dati sulla demografia della comunità giudaica di Roma." In *Hebraica hereditas*, ed. G. Lacerenza (Naples, 2005): 237–54.

Rutgers, Leonard V., et al. "Sul problema di come datare le catacombe ebraiche di Roma." *BABesch* 81 (2006): 169–84.

Schäfer, Peter. *Judaeophobia: Attitudes Toward the Jews in the Ancient World* (Cambridge, Mass., 1997).

Segal, Lester A. "R. Matiah ben Heresh of Rome on Religious Duties and Redemption." *PAAJR* 58 (1992): 221–41.

Solin, Heikki. "Juden und Syrer im westlichen Teil der römischen Welt." *ANRW* II.29.2. (1983): 587–789, 1222–49.

Stern, Sacha. *Calendar and Community: A History of the Jewish Calendar, 2nd Century BCE – 10th Century CE* (Oxford, 2001).

Van der Horst, Pieter Willem. *Ancient Jewish Epitaphs: An Introductory Survey of a Millennium of Jewish Funerary Epigraphy (300 BCE – 700 CE)* (Kampen, 1991).

Wasserstein, Abraham. "Calendaric Implications of a Fourth-Century Jewish Inscription from Sicily." *SCI* 11 (1991–92): 162–5.

Williams, Margaret H. "The Meaning and Function of *Ioudaios* in Graeco-Roman Inscriptions." *ZPE* 116 (1997): 249–62.

Zabin, Serena. "*Iudeae benemerenti*: Towards a Study of Jewish Women in the Western Roman Empire." *Phoenix* 50 (1996): 262–82.

Zevi, Fausto. "Recenti studi e scoperte di archeologia ebraica." In *La cultura ebraica nell'editoria italiana (1955–1990)* (Rome, 1992): 167–84.

16

CHRISTIANITY IN ITALY

DENNIS TROUT

There were, of course, no Christians in Italy during the principate of Augustus (27 BCE to CE 14), when the public religion of the Romans was being recast and revitalized in tandem with the political and social institutions of the emerging imperial system. Some four and a half centuries later, however, when a bishop of Rome was said to have turned back an invading Hunnic warlord and successfully negotiated with a Vandal king before the gates of his defenseless city,[1] Christianity was the officially sanctioned religion of Rome and Italy. Between these two poles lies, it would seem, a remarkable success story. But the rise of Christianity is a tale marked by deep continuities as well as spectacular contrasts. Pope Leo I's (440–61) alleged victory over Attila and mollification of Gaiseric share certain fundamental assumptions with Augustus's enlistment of the traditional Roman gods in the project of the reconstituted empire. Like many early imperial Romans, many late ancient Romans, too, viewed proper cultivation of the divine as prerequisite to public, as well as personal, welfare. To be sure, by the mid-fifth century the divine power in question was significantly different: Augustus's Rome of Jupiter and Mars and Apollo had become the Rome of Christ, the apostles, and the martyrs, while churches and the memorials of saints now defined a cityscape once commanded by temples and imperial fora. Yet, as Augustus had displayed statues of the heroes of the legendary and recent past in his new Forum, Leo ordered that Rome's churches be decorated with biblical cycles and declared that Peter and Paul had ousted Romulus and Remus as the city's guardians.[2] And although by Leo's day the populace of Rome, like that of most Italian cities, largely

---

[1] Attila: Prosper of Aquitaine, *Epitoma Chronicon, a. 452 (MGH AA* 9 [1892], 482); Stein, *Histoire du Bas-Empire*, 335–6; doubts at Heather, "The Western Empire," 17. Gaiseric: Prosper, *Epitoma Chronicon, a.* 455, 484; Stein, *Histoire du Bas-Empire*, 365–7; Neil, *Leo*, 10–11.
[2] Krautheimer, *Rome*, 52; Leo, *Sermo* 82.1; Neil, *Leo*, 113–18.

421

regulated its ceremonial life by an annual cycle of festivals keyed to the life of Christ and the deaths of the saints, not by holidays linked to the history and legends of a fading age, those same Christian feast days frequently coincided with or overwrote earlier celebrations.[3]

One challenge this chapter faces is to do justice to this deep-seated tension between continuity and change in *Roman* religion in Italy during the first five centuries of the common era. Undoubtedly the success of Christianity in this period significantly altered the cultural landscape. Just as surely, Christianity itself, an imported religion that initially took hold among Greek-speaking inhabitants of the peninsula, was continually naturalized and domesticated across the centuries of this chapter. Moreover, just as the term "Roman religion" gives a false sense of unity and order to a set of much less tidy ideals and practices,[4] so the term Christianity may also mislead. From outset to end, even if a kind of orthodoxy eventually prevailed, Christians debated among themselves the tenets of belief and the guidelines of practice that might define them as Christian. Finally, if it is hard for various reasons to write a "history" of pre-Christian imperial Roman religion, Christianity in Italy lends itself too easily to narratives that privilege triumph and victory. Because imperial Christianity was an exclusive and eventually coercive, if not intolerant, religion that moved from the margins to the center of power,[5] its history would be construed even by contemporaries as the victory of true piety over false. The retreat of paganism in town and countryside was at once both the means and the proof of Christianity's truth and success. Even now such triumphal narratives are seductive, for by the later fourth century not only much political and social leadership but also literary and artistic initiative had come to reside in Christian hands. Indeed, by Leo's day bishops were often the most influential civic authorities in Italy, and Latin literature was largely a Christian enterprise, even if it rested on an educational system and literary culture common to elite pagans and Christians alike.[6]

EARLY IMPERIAL ITALY

Is it possible to write a history of Christianity in Italy during the early imperial age? The difficulties are many. Outside Rome there is very little reliable

[3] Markus, *The End of Ancient Christianity*, 97–135.
[4] Rives, *Religion in the Roman Empire*, 4–7.
[5] Kahlos, *Forebearance and Compulsion*.
[6] Neil, *Leo*, 4–8; Young, Ayres, and Louth, *Early Christian Literature*; Cameron, "Poetry and Literary Culture"; Cameron, *Last Pagans of Rome*.

evidence before the early fourth century. Thus the study of Christianity in early imperial Italy cannot be pursued without recourse to comparative material drawn from other parts of the empire. Furthermore, the very notion of "Italy" masks physical, historical, and cultural boundaries that militate against any attempt to produce a general narrative of the history of pre-Constantinian Christianity on the Italian peninsula. Northern Italy (*Gallia Cisalpina*), for example, was not fully enfranchised until Caesar granted the Transpadani Roman citizenship in 49 BCE. Even in the early imperial period many peoples of this area maintained closer links with areas north of the Alps than with those south of the Apennines.[7] Likewise, although Augustus may have regularized the administration of the peninsula by dividing *Italia* into eleven regions, non-Latin Italic dialects, Greek, and pre-Roman traditions long remained vital to civic identity. Indeed, despite the impulse toward homogeneity of language and civic life that came with Romanization, early imperial Italy was still characterized by influential regional (and intraregional) differences. If Christianity, for example, arrived and spread early in Latium and Campania, it apparently made little headway in the north before the mid-third century, while diffusion in the south appears to have been equally slow and uneven.[8] Moreover, though Rome, home to an ethnically diverse population of several hundred thousand people that included many Greeks, Jews, and other eastern Mediterranean peoples, supplies the bulk of our evidence for Christianity in the nearly three centuries between Paul's letters and Constantine's conversion, few scholars would deem developments at Rome typical of other parts of Italy.

Still, it is possible to discern developments that parallel wider trends and suggest the outlines of a history that might span the regions of Italy. Missionary origins, intracongregational wrangling, doctrinal debate, and institutional definition may characterize the expansion of Christianity here as in other parts of the empire. Likewise, of course, suspicion, animosity, and sometimes violence are among the more evident responses to Christianity (or alleged Christians) by non-Christians. In Italy, as elsewhere, Christians were quickly potential targets of scapegoating and persecution often locally inspired but eventually imperially sanctioned. Nevertheless, documented moments of persecution are relatively rare and Christian congregations grew and expanded despite this environment (though in

[7] Humphries, *Communities of the Blessed*, 22–44.
[8] Otranto, *Italia meridionale e Puglia paleocristiane*, 21–42; Humphries, *Communities of the Blessed*, 101–4.

numbers and proportions impossible to determine), suggesting that the celebrated outbursts of anti-Christian violence were offset by acceptance if not sympathy for men and women who were also neighbors and friends. Finally, in this period in Italy, Christianity began to produce a literature in Latin as well as Greek and to create a visual vocabulary now best preserved in the older sections of the Roman catacombs.[9] In every way, it is clear that practitioners of Christianity moved within the wider cultural horizons of the cities that were the most fertile ground for development and that the religion evolved in dialogue not only with its Jewish background but increasingly with its polyglot Italian milieu. It is thus to be expected that Christianity long drew its adherents from the same social strata and neighborhoods that provided worshipers of Isis, Serapis, Cybele, and similar nonexclusive cults.

Apostolic origins and persecution shaped Christian self-understanding at Rome nearly from the outset and would continue throughout antiquity to be among the most powerful components of Christian communal identity and self-legitimization in Italy at large. The validity of this view is variously vouched for even if still imprecisely understood. Missionary work by both Peter and Paul at Rome is attested, more securely perhaps for the latter but with no condemning doubt for the former.[10] Even before Paul's arrival in Italy about 61 or 62, a Christian community already existed at Rome (as one apparently also did at Puteoli on the Bay of Naples, where Paul disembarked [Acts 28:13–14]). Paul's letter to the Roman community, written from Corinth in 56/57, makes that much clear as it also, especially in the list of greetings with which it ends (chapter 16), attests to the Greek roots and eastern connections of many members of the apostolic Roman church. The Neronian persecution, however, following upon the great fire of July 64, soon weighed heavily on this community. In this context apparently falls the martyrdom of Peter, while Paul's execution may have occurred then or a few years later.[11] More than a half century on both Tacitus (*Ann.* 15.44) and Suetonius (*Nero* 16) document the ferocity of Nero's pogrom, while the slightly earlier (ca.95–100) so-called First Letter of Clement alludes to the deaths of the two apostles in Rome in "our own times" (5–6). The reasons are surely no less complex than obscure: Tacitus credits Neronian scapegoating facilitated by widespread distrust of people known for their "hatred of the human race"; Clement's references

[9] Heine, "Beginnings." Novatian's mid-third-century *De Trinitate* is the earliest theological treatise written in Latin at Rome (Heine, "Cyprian and Novatian," 158).
[10] Bowersock, "Peter and Constantine," 210–12; for doubts see Zwierlin, *Petrus in Rom.*
[11] Légasse, "Paul et l'universalisme chrétien," 144–6; idem, "Les autres voies de la mission," 176–8.

to "rivalry and envy" may hint at friction with Rome's Jews as well as intragroup squabbling. Whether these events in Rome had corollaries in other Italian towns in the later first century is impossible to determine, but in later centuries, as we will see, mission and martyrdom would be dominant themes in the historical memory of many communities throughout the peninsula.

As elsewhere, the language of Rome's Christians remained predominantly Greek well into the third century and outsiders often associated Christians with Jews. Suetonius records that the emperor Claudius (41–54) expelled the Jews from Rome because of disturbances instigated by "Chrestus" (*Claud.* 25.4), a remark that despite its lateness may preserve a memory of Jewish debate at Rome over Christ.[12] Paul's letter to the Roman community, of course, assumes a mixed church of gentiles and Jews; for many decades to come the Roman Christian community apparently drew its membership as well as its inspiration from the Jewish as well as Greek enclaves of the city. Most Roman Christians probably belonged to the ranks of artisans and small traders, though congregations may also have included the destitute.[13] Most, as well, may have been concentrated in the crowded suburban quarters of Trastevere, along the Via Appia beyond the Porta Capena, and near the Via Lata in the Campus Martius.[14] It is reasonable to assume that by the late first century some Christian groups included people of at least moderate means, but evidence of elite membership is elusive. The often-cited case of the former consul Flavius Clemens and his wife Domitilla, who were according to a third-century source executed and exiled respectively by the emperor Domitian (81–96) on charges of "atheism and Jewish sympathies" (Cass. Dio 67.14), is simply too fragile to support claims of Christian allegiance.[15] During the second century, however, the number of "socially elevated" Christians surely increased, though in part this change may reflect broader demographic currents in prosperous Italy.[16] All in all, Christian social life in this period runs largely below our radar.

If details of persecution after Nero are hard to find, animosity is not. Tacitus (*Ann.* 15.44), writing in the early second century about Nero's actions, charged Christians with misanthropy and saw their religion as

---

[12] Légasse, "Les autres voies de la mission," 174–5.
[13] Meeks, *The First Urban Christians*, 51–73; with Green, *Christianity in Ancient Rome*, 23–59, for a relatively early separation of Christianity and Judaism at Rome.
[14] Lampe, *From Paul to Valentinus*, 19–66.
[15] Légasse, "Les autres voies de la mission," 179–80.
[16] Lampe, *From Paul to Valentinus*, 139.

a "deadly superstition (*exitiabilis superstitio*)." Similar sentiments were expressed by two of Tacitus's contemporaries: for Suetonius Christianity was a "new and wicked *superstitio*" (*Nero* 16) while Pliny's famous interrogation of Christians in Bithynia revealed to him nothing but "a depraved and excessive *superstitio*" (*Ep.* 96.8). This may stand as evidence that, nearly a century after the execution of Jesus, the Roman aristocracy still saw Christianity not only as impious and ill-conceived but also as a threat to the social order. This distaste as well as popular prejudice must underlie the vague assertions of pressure and danger that filter through the extant literature, though the persistence of such (mis)judgments may rest to some degree on the reluctance or inability of Christians to make their ideas clear to outsiders in these years.[17]

The simplicity of this external point of view, of course, belies the complexity of Christianity in Italy in this period. Rome was a city of immigrants, travelers, and sojourners. New ideas arrived continually. Institutional unity was slow to emerge. At least through the later second century, the city's house-church communities were still administered by collegial presbyters and not a monarchic bishop, a condition recently dubbed "fractionation."[18] The prestige of the visionary *Shepherd* of Hermas, composed at Rome during this period (dating varies between ca.90 and 150) attests to the continuing viability of charismatic or prophetic voices. The *Shepherd* also makes clear the competition between docetic or gnostic Christianities and other forms of practice and belief. Indeed, the *First Apology* of Justin Martyr, written (in Greek) at Rome and addressed to Antoninus Pius (138–61), acknowledges the confusion that then surrounded the identity of Christians, crediting in particular the disruptive presence and teaching of the "heretic" Marcion (26). Consequently, in his *Against Heresies* (3.4), Irenaeus of Lyon, who spent time in Rome, sought to expose the false teaching of such "apostates" as Valentinus and Cerdo as well as Marcion. Some recent scholars, therefore, prefer to speak of Rome as a city of Christian "cells" or house-churches and deem it misguided to envision Rome's Christians forming a unitary community. Although the proto-orthodoxy of Justin and Irenaeus ultimately obscured and silenced other points of view, including tolerance, their works still reveal the ferment of ideas that blurred the boundaries of loosely affiliated Christian identities in second-century Rome.[19]

---

[17] Lampe, *From Paul to Valentinus*, 379–80.
[18] Lampe, *From Paul to Valentinus*, 397–408; Légasse, "Les autres voies de la mission," 182–3.
[19] Lampe, *From Paul to Valentinus*; Vinzent, "Rome," 410–11; Bowes, *Private Worship, Public Values*, 63–5; Green, *Christianity in Ancient Rome*, 60–119.

The material evidence for early Christianity in Italy is welcome but limited. It is axiomatic that early Christians are archaeologically unidentifiable before the end of the second century. Even long thereafter it is primarily outside the city proper that Christianity becomes visible, in burial contexts associated with cemeteries and venerated tombs. Many of Rome's major fourth-century catacomb complexes, for example, emerge from late second- or early third-century nuclei. This is notably the case at the *memoria apostolorum* on the Via Appia (over which the Basilica Apostolorum would arise in the early fourth century), where third-century graffiti signal both the celebration of funerary banquets (*refrigeria*) and the veneration of Peter and Paul.[20] At the Catacomb of Priscilla on the Via Saleria, the oldest sections preserve important third-century frescoes whose subjects include a Good Shepherd, Old Testament scenes, and a veiled orant figure. Across the city, the first sure stages of the monumental development of the Vatican cult of St. Peter, associated with the apostle's *memoria*, date between the mid-second and mid-third centuries.[21] Such evidence documents the definition of burial areas and cult sites by Christians, with corresponding implications for the construction of a distinct social identity. Yet Christians also still employed traditional motifs – the shepherd, the orant, and the grape vine – whose universality made them suitable vehicles for bearing new Christian meaning while also obscuring difference.[22]

Intramural assembly places are difficult to identify. It can be assumed that Christian cells would initially have gathered for the Eucharist, prayer, study, and singing (Justin, *1 Apol.* 66–7) in private "house churches" fashioned out of unmodified (and thus archaeologically silent) domestic space: in the account of his martyrdom, Justin Martyr claims to have lived and worshipped with his fellow Christians above a bath (*Martyrdom* 3 [Musurillo]).[23] Gradually domestic space, as at Dura-Europos, should have been altered to accommodate larger numbers and liturgical needs, but no undisputed evidence for a pre-Constantinian *domus ecclesiae* (house of the church) remains at Rome.[24] Already in the later third century, some of these assembly places may have been corporately owned. But apart from the post-Constantinian, fourth-century *confessio* complex underlying the early fifth-century *titulus Pammachi* on the Caelian (SS. Giovanni e Paolo), no

[20] Bisconti, "La *Memoria Apostolorum*," 63–8; Mazzoleni, "Pietro e Paolo nell'epigrafia cristiana," 67; Spera, "The Christianization of Space"; Holloway, *Constantine and Rome*, 146–54.
[21] Bowersock, "Peter and Constantine," 211–12; Holloway, *Constantine and Rome*, 154–5.
[22] Snyder, *Ante Pacem*, 19–20; Jensen, "Towards a Christian Material Culture," 572–3.
[23] White, *Building God's House*, 103–10.
[24] Brandenburg, *Ancient Churches of Rome*, 12; Sessa, "*Domus Ecclesiae*," 106–8.

known later *titulus* (community or parish church) in Rome can be shown to have arisen over a previous place of Christian worship. Indeed, the concept of the titular foundation itself appears to be a post-Constantinian phenomenon.[25]

The Christian archaeological record for pre-Constantinian Rome, like the city's literary residue, is remarkably rich in comparison to the rest of Italy. Nevertheless, it is impossible to match the pluralistic Christian presence revealed by the literary sources with the evidence of archaeology. To be sure, even as the Christian population increased over time, congregational unity remained elusive. It is doubtful, for example, that (despite later traditions) a "monarchical bishop" emerged as a recognized leader at Rome much before the mid-third century; it has been suggested that the earliest evidence for this office may only appear in the context of the schism between Cornelius and the rigorist Novatian that followed the martyrdom of Fabian under Decius (250).[26] At the same time, this schism, driven by the problem of reintegrating the lapsed in the wake of persecution, illustrates how the pressure of persecution often forced further definition of the boundaries of identity as well as doctrine.[27]

In sum, though so much of early Roman Christianity remains beyond our reach, internal diversity, tolerance and rivalry, undercurrents of distrust, and evolution toward institutional unity are primary themes of its social history. But however much Rome's early Christians differed in practice and belief among themselves and with their non-Christian neighbors, their apparent tendency for local affiliation and action may have closely conformed to patterns discernible in the loose associations of other socio-religious and study groups in metropolitan Rome. Christian house-church communities, Lampe has suggested, would have looked familiar to others as "schools," mystery cults, or domestic cultic groups, while Humphries has noted parallels between the distribution patterns of cults of Isis and the dissemination of Christianity in northern Italy.[28]

But outside Rome our view is dim. In the south, pre-Constantinian Christian burial areas are manifest at Naples (the catacomb of S. Gennaro), at Nola (Cimitile), and in Sicily (especially at Syracuse), for example, while inscriptions, such as a third-century text from Cluviae in the Abruzzo (*ICI* 3.1) and an assembly of texts from the catacombs of Syracuse, attest to

---

[25] Brandenburg, *Ancient Churches of Rome*, 156; Bowes, *Private Worship, Public Values*, 65–71; MacMullen, *Second Church*, 87.

[26] Vincentz, "Rome," 411.

[27] Heine, "Articulating Identity," 214–18; see also Jensen in Chapter 10 of this volume.

[28] Lampe, *From Paul to Valentinus*, 373–80; Humphries, *Communities of the Blessed*, 99–101.

Christianity's clear presence at these places by the early fourth century.[29] Nevertheless, neither this scattered material nor a luxuriant but untrustworthy late antique hagiographic dossier can underwrite narrative reconstruction. In the north, it is primarily the evidence of early and mid-fourth-century church building, such as the sumptuous Constantinian-age basilica of Bishop Theodore at Aquileia, that suggests the existence of *pre-Constantinian* Christian communities in some of that region's more important economic and administrative centers. The paucity of earlier evidence, however, makes it impossible to access the lives of those communities – although, as in the south, later martyrologies, *passiones*, and saints' lives often highlight the themes of apostolic origins, episcopal succession, and martyrdom that are prominent in the Roman material. Outside these northern urban centers, especially in the countryside, Christianity had apparently made little progress, and persecution had little impact prior to the Tetrarchic period.[30] What we have, then, stops short of satisfying the requirements of a history of Christianity in early imperial Italy. Toleration and imperial favoritism, however, alter the situation.

FROM PERSECUTION TO PRIVILEGE

In October of 312, Constantine defeated a rival claimant for power, Maxentius, on the outskirts of Rome at the battle of the Milvian Bridge (or Saxa Rubra), setting in motion a train of events that would bring Christianity from the edges to the center of Roman history. The inscription on the triumphal arch dedicated in 315 by the senate and Roman people to commemorate Constantine's victory was studiously vague if not evocatively pagan, crediting his defeat of the "tyrant" to "the inspiration of divinity and greatness of mind (*instinctu divinitatis mentis magnitudine*)" (*ILS* 694). But Constantine had already begun to give sharper definition to the source of that inspiration.[31] Early in 313, for reasons political and personal, together with his imperial ally Licinius, Constantine had endorsed the so-called Edict of Milan, a proclamation of religious freedom and property restitution for Christians.[32] In the same year, to handle the fallout from the recent persecutions in North Africa, where churches were split

---

[29] Otranto, *Italia meridionale e Puglia paleocristiane*, 21–42; Stevenson, *The Catacombs*, 131–47; Testini, *Archeologia cristiana*, 499–501; Agnello, *Silloge*; Ferrua, *Note e giunte*.

[30] Humphries, *Communities of the Blessed*, 72–105, 227; Sotinel, *Identité civique et christianisme*, 65–89.

[31] Constantine's arch: Lenski, "Evoking the Pagan Past"; Van Dam, *Remembering Constantine*, 124–32; Bardill, *Constantine*, 222–30; Constantine in Rome: Barnes, *Constantine*, 61–89.

[32] Drake, *Constantine and the Bishops*, 193–8.

over the treatment of *traditores* (clergy who had surrendered sacred texts and objects during the recent persecution), he paid the expenses for bishops to meet first in Rome, then in Arles in 314 (Eus. *Hist. eccl.* 10.5.18–24), foreshadowing the great council he would summon to Nicaea in 325 in an attempt to resolve a different, but no less intractable, internal division. Apparently in 313 as well, Constantine granted Christian clerics the immunity from compulsory services legally claimed by the priests of certain other cults (Eus. *Hist. eccl* 10.7.1–2; *CTh* 16.2.1).[33] Finally, if it was indeed in 315 that Lactantius composed his account of the dream in which Constantine, before his battle with Maxentius, was admonished to set the sign of Christ (perhaps a Chi-Rho) upon his soldiers' shields (*Mort.* 44.5), then it can be assumed that Constantine had announced his personal allegiance to the Christian god relatively soon after his seizure of Rome in 312.

While it is true, as some have noted, that Constantine's favoritism continued a third-century trend toward close association of the emperor with a specific divinity and that Maxentius had shown himself tolerant of Rome's Christians after he gained control of the city in 306, Constantine's reversal of Christianity's fortunes will nonetheless have seemed as abrupt to some as its impact would prove long lasting.[34] There are indications that the Christians of Rome had known relative peace and even a measure of prosperity under the Severan emperors and their immediate successors. Eusebius, for example, reports a claim made by Cornelius, bishop from 250 to 253, that the Roman church then numbered forty-six presbyters, seven deacons, seven subdeacons, and a host of minor officials (*Hist. eccl.* 6.43.11). But in the mid-third century a storm of persecution had broken over the city's Christian groups. Cornelius's predecessor, Fabian, as noted above, was one victim. Moreover, the persecutions associated with the names of Decius (249–51) and Valerian (253–60) – and then Diocletian and Galerius (305–11) – were unlike the locally inspired anti-Christian violence of the early empire. In the mid-third century, for reasons bound up with the empire's military and administrative difficulties, Christians and other apparent religious nonconformists were caught up in novel, centrally directed programs meant to ensure general participation in the public and imperial cults but eventually targeting clerics and church property.[35] While enforcement of these programs was uneven, Rome's Christian communities, like others elsewhere, were left disrupted by the harsh actions of

---

[33] Rapp, *Holy Bishops*, 238.
[34] Drake, "The Impact of Constantine on Christianity"; Cameron, "Constantine and the 'Peace of the Church,'" 540–5; Van Dam, *Roman Revolution*, 9–10.
[35] Lane Fox, *Pagans and Christians*, 450–62; Rives, "The Decree of Decius."

Decius and Valerian, which led some to witness and others to lapse, as well as unbalanced by the competing claims for leadership that followed in their immediate wake.[36] Although the impact of the "Great Persecution" of Diocletian, which flared up in 303, fell most heavily upon the eastern provinces and Rome and Italy apparently escaped relatively unscathed, later sources often portray the effects as severe. Any anguish, however, was soon relieved, in Rome at least, by the usurpation of Maxentius in 306, who (though he would be subsequently demonized) suppressed the persecution and overturned the enabling legislation.[37] Even so, his unpopular fiscal and social policies left Maxentius vulnerable to Constantine's propaganda as well as his arms – and further facilitated the subsequent perception of Constantine as Christianity's champion.

Although Constantine quickly positioned himself as the liberator of the city, the full story of his Christian allegiances emerges slowly. Because he was the emperor of all Romans, the vast majority of whom (perhaps ninety percent) were still non-Christian in 312, it will always seem somewhat ambiguous.[38] Nevertheless, the impact of his decisions is nearly inestimable. By the time of his death in 337, Roman society as well as the church and the imperial office had begun to be reconfigured. Christianity's new-found respectability encouraged conversion, and with the impetus provided by Constantine's legislation bishops embarked on the journey that would eventually transform them into the later empire's leading civic officials.[39] The emperor himself, summoning and addressing the Council of Nicaea (325), assumed a prominent role in the regulation of doctrine and church order.[40] As *pontifex maximus,* he was responsible for ensuring proper worship of those divinities who secured the empire's defense and prosperity. If Christian pluralism might be acceptable, discord and schism were not.

But perhaps the most immediately visible sign of the changing tide in Italy was Constantine's engagement with the Roman cityscape. To be sure, within the city Constantine presented himself as had numerous emperors before him, erecting statues, accepting a triumphal arch, claiming and modifying the great basilica of Maxentius near the *Via Sacra,* building baths on the Quirinal, celebrating his *decennalia,* and triumphing in 315

---

[36] Frend, *Martyrdom and Persecution,* 304–23; Curran, *Pagan City and Christian Capital,* 35–41; Green, *Christianity in Ancient Rome,* 120–69.

[37] Curran, *Pagan City and Christian Capital,* 63–5.

[38] Van Dam, *Roman Revolution.*

[39] Rapp, *Holy Bishops,* 235–60.

[40] Barnes, *Eusebius and Constantine,* 212–19.

(though perhaps forgoing the traditional sacrifice on the Capitoline). It was on the edges of the city, however, that the future was being sketched. Here Constantine and members of his family sponsored building projects whose gravitational pull would slowly reshape the image of the classical city. On the Caelian atop the *castra* of the *equites singulares*, Maxentius's now-disbanded elite horse guard, Constantine erected the Lateran basilica; over the Vatican necropolis where St. Peter was venerated soon appeared a vast basilica with central nave, side aisles, atrium forecourt, and apse; outside the Aurelian walls on the Via Labicana at a spot known as *ad duas lauros,* Constantine sponsored a large U-shaped or ambulatory funerary basilica and built the grand, circular mausoleum that would eventually receive the remains of his mother Helena; on the Via Appia, at the *memoria* of Peter and Paul appeared the similarly designed Basilica Apostolorum (S. Sebastiano); similar but perhaps somewhat later churches were erected on the Via Tiburtina at the tomb of Lawrence and on the Via Nomentana, where another imperial mausoleum arose (Sta. Costanza) adjacent to the ambulatory basilica of the martyr Agnes.[41] Here, in the city's mural zone, Constantine and his kin redirected imperial patronage from temples to churches and from the historic city center to an area then largely given over to cemeteries and suburban estates. Meanwhile, in unison with these changes, other less dramatic ones were underway as the Roman bishops of the Constantinian age, most notably Julius (337–52), joined by lay elites now built more modest basilicas or titular churches on the Esquiline, near the imperial *fora*, and in Trastevere.[42] In the process, Christianity acquired a monumental presence it had never known, and the cityscape was reshaped in ways that would only become more pronounced in time, providing a new index for charting the "growth" of the religion. Surely then Rome's Christians were prominent among those who so grievously lamented the news of Constantine's death and, echoing if not restaging the traditional *consecratio* ceremony that marked the divinization of earlier emperors, honored him with paintings depicting him at home "in an aetherial resort above the vaults of heaven" (Eus. *Vit. Const.* 4.69).[43] It is an image whose appeal should not be underestimated.

[41] Pietri, *Roma Christiana*, 3–69; Curran, *Pagan City and Christian Capital*, 70–115; Bowersock, "Peter and Constantine"; Brandenburg, *Ancient Churches of Rome*, 16–108; MacMullen, *Second Church*, 80–4; Bardill, *Constantine*, 237–51.

[42] Pietri, *Roma Christiana*, 21–5; Curran, *Pagan City and Christian Capital*, 117–27; Brandenburg, *Ancient Churches of Rome*, 110–13; Bowes, *Private Worship, Public Values*, 72.

[43] Translation and commentary at Cameron and Stuart, *Life of Constantine*, 345–6; MacCormack, *Art and Ceremony*, 93–121.

ITALIA CHRISTIANA

About the year 390, the Roman senator and Christian grandee Sextus Petronius Probus was laid to rest in a magnificent mausoleum attached to the apse of the Vatican basilica of St. Peter. Probus's body, clothed in gold-spun fabric, was placed in a marble sarcophagus sculpted with an image of Christ's missionary dispatch of the apostles. His verse epitaph, apparently set out on an interior peristyle, proclaimed Probus's new life among the stars as well as the maturation of aristocratic Christian culture in Italy.[44] In these same years, other nobles appear no less confident about the rewards of baptism into the Christian faith. At Milan, the sepulcher of Manlia Daedalia, probably wife or daughter of the Christian intellectual and consul of 399 Mallius Theodorus, announced her return to Christ "through the lofty stars."[45] During Daedalia's lifetime, Milan, home to other Christians who shared her presumed Neoplatonic sympathies, had risen to prominence not only as an imperial capital but also as the see of the ambitious bishop Ambrose, whose writings and sermons elevated considerably the stock of Christian exegesis and preaching in the West.[46] To the south of Rome, Christianity had made similar headway across the social spectrum. In the mid-390s, the former Roman senator from Bordeaux, Meropius Pontius Paulinus, relocated his household from Spain to Campania, where he had once served as governor, in order to settle at the tomb of the confessor Felix, already the focus of local veneration and papal patronage.[47] By the opening years of the fifth century, widespread changes that go far to explaining the public authority wielded by Leo I at Rome some two generations later were well underway throughout Italy.

The challenge in making sense of Christianity in Italy after Constantine is no longer that presented by the paucity of source material for earlier periods. Literary, documentary, and archaeological evidence now abounds and illuminates regions of Italy and areas of Christian life and practice previously inaccessible. Conversion to Christianity accelerated across the fourth and into the fifth centuries, particularly within the cities and towns, while private wealth and public resources were devoted in increasing measure to devotional and ecclesiastical ends. Although doctrinal and ecclesiological controversies long continued to undermine the unity of Christians in Italy, nevertheless imperial and episcopal leadership began to forge a more

[44] *CIL* 6.1 (1876) ad nos. 1751–56 (= *CIL* 6.8.3 [2000] 4752–53). Trout, "Verse Epitaph(s)."
[45] *CIL* 5.6240 = *ILCV* 1700; *PCBE* 2.1 (Italia), 528.
[46] McLynn, *Ambrose of Milan.*
[47] Trout, *Paulinus of Nola*, 161–3.

monolithic Christian church in these same years. The ideals of Christian
asceticism found an ever-wider audience; the cult of the martyrs claimed
an almost unassailable position in the articulation of piety; and Christian
literary, artistic, and building activity began to transform elite culture as
well as public memory and the cityscape. The Christianization of Roman
society and the Romanization of Christianity are the dominant leitmotivs
of the age.

It is agreed that across the social spectrum, the percentage of Christians
rose significantly in the fourth and fifth centuries. Nevertheless, the rate of
change varied with place and social circumstances, and there were always
some whose religious allegiances were partially if not fully directed elsewhere. Tracking these phenomena is complicated both by the continuing
absence of fully reliable quantitative data and by problems of definition. To
ask who qualifies as Christian raises questions not only about the lines that
might seem to separate orthodox and heterodox Christianities (including
Manichaeism), but also the messy realities of conversion experiences. But
even scholars who prefer an earlier dating overall for the conversion of the
imperial aristocracy typically concede that the senatorial elite of Rome was
relatively slow to adopt Christianity.[48] One recent study concludes that
the aristocracy of Rome and Italy was "predominantly pagan well into
the last decades of the fourth century," while a new study of Aquileia supports the impression given by evidence from other north Italian towns
that elite conversion there, despite the precocious achievements of the
early fourth century, was also a protracted process.[49] Determining the
rate of nonelite conversion is even more difficult, but the epigraphic record offers a rough guide: the number of dated Christian epitaphs from
Rome increases sharply across the fourth century, from forty-one in the
first quarter of the century to 550 in the last with a significant spike in the
third quarter.[50] This boom in epigraphic funerary commemoration buttresses the impression of the Roman church's rapid expansion given as well
by the spate of catacomb construction and church building in the second
half of the fourth century. Other parts of Italy – mountainous zones, the
promontory of Gargano, the Adriatic coast of the Abruzzo and Molise, for
examples – surely lagged behind Rome, as apparently did other regions
of the West whose epigraphic curves rise somewhat later.[51] Yet, although
absolute numbers remain impossible to determine, it seems safe to say that

[48] Barnes, "Statistics and the Conversion of the Roman Aristocracy," 144.
[49] Salzman, *Making of a Christian Aristocracy*, 77–80; Sotinel, *Identité civique et christianisme*, 99–104.
[50] Galvao-Sobrinho, "Funerary Epigraphy."
[51] Otranto, *Italia meridionale e Puglia paleocristiane*, 85–6; Galvao-Sobrinho, "Funerary Epigraphy."

by 400 – subsequent to the strident imperial legislation of the 380s and 390s that again criminalized non-Nicene Christianities as well as many traditional cult practices (for example, *CTh* 16.5.6; 16.10.10)[52] – some form of Christianity was the religion of the majority of the inhabitants of Italy's towns and cities.

The most celebrated examples of the tardy acceptance of Christianity may be found among such conservative Roman families as the Symmachi and Nicomachi or in the grandiose epitaph of the learned Vettius Agorius Praetextatus, who died in late 384 while Praetorian Prefect and consul designate (*CIL* 6.1779).[53] Other evidence, however, reveals the complex interplay of resistance to and assimilation of Christianity in the country-side in this period. In 397, for example, Vigilius of Trent attempted to abolish lustral sacrifices in the partially Christianized Alpine Val di Non north of his city. His efforts provoked the murder of his three clerical agents and the immolation of their bodies before an idol of Saturn on a pyre made from the debris of their missionary church.[54] In contemporary Nola, on the other hand, Paulinus encouraged farmers and husbandmen from the surrounding region to bring to the tomb of St. Felix the vows, prayers, and (sacrificial) offerings for the health and fertility of their herds and fields that they had so long made to the gods and spirits of the pre-Christian countryside.[55] This particular cultural logic is equally evident at Marcellianum in south Italian Lucania. Here, by the sixth century, an ancient festival honoring the sea goddess Leucothea had become a fair of St. Cyprian, the goddess's sacred spring had been turned into a miraculous baptismal pool, and the hand-fed fish once sacred to the goddess were now, Cassiodorus observed, the wards of the Christian God.[56] Though perhaps less spectacular than the plea for the restoration of the Altar of Victory to the Roman Senate House forwarded in 384 to the emperor at Milan by the Urban Prefect Q. Aurelius Symmachus's petition (*Rel.* 3)[57] or the lists of pagan priesthoods and cult initiations of Praetextatus and his wife Fabia Anconia Paulina (*CIL* 6.1778, 6.1780),[58] the events that unfolded in a secluded Alpine valley, at a cemetery outside Nola, and around a fishpond

---

[52] Joannou, *La legislation imperiale*, 43–8.

[53] Matthews, *Western Aristocracies*, 203–11, 238–46; Salzman, *Making of a Christian Aristocracy*, 74–7; Cameron, *Last Pagans of Rome*.

[54] Lizzi, *Vescovi e strutture ecclesiastiche*, 59–70; Lizzi, "Ambrose's Contemporaries," 169–72; Humphries, *Communities of the Blessed*, 181–4.

[55] Paulinus, *Carm.* 20; Trout, "Christianizing the Nolan Countryside."

[56] Cassiodorus, *Variae* 8.33; Barnish, "*Religio in stagno.*"

[57] Matthews, *Western Aristocracies*, 205–11; Sogno, *Symmachus*, 45–57.

[58] *PLRE* 1.772–24 (Praetextatus); 1.675 (Paulina).

in Lucania are reminders that Christianity's triumph in late ancient Italy was neither simple nor complete.

No wonder then that the changes that Christianization did entail defy easy categorization. With Christianity's permeation of society came new expectations for the conduct of public and private life, new modalities of civic leadership and civic identity, altered cityscapes, and the revision of historical memory. Moreover, by the later fourth century, the preeminence of the bishops of Rome ensured that most of the doctrinal and ecclesiastical controversies of this formative but contentious age sooner or later resonated in Rome – as well as in the imperial capitals of Milan and Ravenna. Indeed, the story of the gestation of the papacy merits more consideration than can be given here. By the end of the fourth century, both an imperial law of 380 and the third canon of the general council held at Constantinople in 381[59] had added legal support to the authority Rome's bishops had long been accorded as the successors of Peter residing in the ancient capital of the empire. Across the fourth century, Rome's bishops reinforced to their own advantage their connections to the cult and legacy of Peter and Paul.[60] And when Rome's position was threatened both by imperial claims to ecclesiastical leadership and the rise of Constantinople as the "new Rome," Damasus (366–84) and his successors Siricius (384–99) and Innocent I (401–17) elaborated the latent Petrine doctrine. Christ's words to Peter at Matthew 16:18–19, now supplemented by Rufinus of Aquileia's translation of a pseudonymous letter of Clement I, would provide the crucial juristic, but extra-imperial, basis for Roman primacy. The decretals issued by Roman bishops would crystallize their claim to a divinely sanctioned constitutional authority over other churches.[61] This "primatial monarchic theme," variously accepted and contested even in the West (though carrying relatively little weight in the East), would receive its "final theoretical stamp" during the pontificate of Leo (440–61). No less skilled in ecclesiastical politics than barbarian diplomacy, Leo deftly employed the resources of Roman law to distinguish further the office (rather than the person) of the bishop of Rome as the heir of the legal status and powers of St. Peter.[62]

Commensurate with these ambitions, Rome's bishops were seldom aloof from the challenges that came with the Christianization of Roman society. Indeed, what may be the earliest surviving papal decretal reveals

---

[59] *CTh* 16.1.2; Hefele, *Histoire des conciles*, 2.1, 24–7.
[60] Pietri, "*Concordia Apostolorum*"; Donati, *Pietro e Paolo*.
[61] Ullmann, *A Short History*, 9–18; Schimmelpfennig, *The Papacy*, 24–8.
[62] Ullmann, *A Short History*, 19–21; Neil, *Leo*, 39–44.

Siricius offering Himerius, bishop of Spanish Tarragona, counsel on a wide range of issues, including regulation of the lives of male and female ascetics (*monachi* and *monachae*).[63] The decriminalization of Christianity in the early fourth century had fundamentally changed the relationship between most Christians in Italy and the imperial government. As the age of persecution faded into an age of heroes, with implications to be considered below, asceticism offered Christians a striking means for asserting the depth of their commitment and delineating their religious and social identity in an age of Christian expansion. Rooted in eastern practices, monastic ideals were disseminated in fourth-century Italy by eastern visitors such as Athanasius and Peter of Alexandria, both resident for a time in Rome; by texts, especially the *Life of Anthony*, available in Latin as well as Greek by the 370s; and eventually by returning westerners like Jerome and later Rufinus and Melania the Elder.[64] As the ideals of celibacy, dietary restriction, and the renunciation of wealth and office found an audience among some of Italy's elite families, asceticism emerged as one of the leading forces "shaping the contours of church and society in the late ancient world."[65] The writings of Jerome, who during his sojourn in Rome from 382 to 385 promoted himself along with his vision of ascetic piety and scriptural study, reveal most of what we know of the household asceticism of such notable aristocratic women as Marcella, Paula, and Eustochium.[66] In roughly these same years, in Milan, Augustine was led, in part by the example of Ambrose, to abandon his high-profile teaching post and aspirations for marriage and a political career in favor of ascetic *otium*, sexual continence, and baptism.[67] Soon enough some Roman senators were prepared to adopt ascetic ways as a mark of their determination to win the kingdom of God. Before he declared his secular renunciation and retired with his wife, Therasia, to a necropolis on the outskirts of Nola in the mid-390s, Paulinus of Bordeaux had served as suffect consul at Rome and then governor of Campania in the 380s.[68] He knew other aristocrats, like Turcius Apronianus and Valerius Pinianus, the husband of Melania the Younger, who also preferred to be senators and consuls for Christ.[69] When the senator Pammachius's wife Paulina

[63] Siricius, *Ep.* 1.7 (*PL* 13.1137); Shotwell, Loomis, *The See of Peter*, 697–708. Earlier may be *ad Gallos* (Damasus): see Pietri, *Roma Christiana*, 764–72; Reutter, *Damasus*, 192–247.

[64] Rousseau, *Ascetics, Authority and the Church*, 79–95. On Christian monasticism in Egypt and Syria, see Griffith, Chapter 5 and van der Vliet, Chapter 8 of this volume.

[65] Hunter, *Marriage, Celibacy, and Heresy*, 1–2.

[66] Kelly, *Jerome*, 91–103; Williams, *The Monk and the Book*, 52–62; Cain, *Letters of Jerome*, 68–98.

[67] Brown, *Augustine*, 108–20; O'Donnell, *Augustine*, 59–61.

[68] Trout, *Paulinus of Nola*, 78–103.

[69] Trout, *Paulinus of Nola*, 208–9. PCBE 2.1: 171–3 (Apronianus); 2.2: 1798–1802 (Pinianus).

died in 396, he staged a massive meal for the poor and a distribution of alms at St. Peter's basilica.[70] Thereafter, Pammachius adopted an ascetic lifestyle and further diverted his vast treasure to heaven with the construction of a hostel (*xenodochium*) at Portus, a narthex at St. Peter's, and a titular church on the Caelian (subsequently SS. Giovanni e Paolo).[71] While these cases bear some resemblance to former examples of philosophical retreat from public life and municipal philanthropy, they are also marked by unusual physical rigors and informed by such scriptural admonitions as Christ's call to perfection at Matthew 19:21 and Luke's tale of Lazarus and the rich man (Luke 16:19–31).

Yet these individuals represent exceptional responses to scriptural precepts. Most Christians lived far more conventional lives, and opposition to asceticism was, it seems, widespread.[72] Ambrose, who preached the new asceticism in Milan,[73] predicted a rough welcome in Rome for the news that Paulinus had, it was said, abandoned the senate and his patrimony.[74] The *Life of Melania the Younger* recounts the staunch resistance that met her abnegation of an aristocratic Roman woman's traditional roles and her rejection of a family's vast wealth.[75] Meanwhile, the same epitaph that proclaimed Petronius Probus's privileged afterlife in the heavenly court of Christ boasted of his many secular offices and vast wealth. Probus's seamless transition from terrestrial to heavenly potentate was an implicit rejection of ascetic claims that might seem to undermine the traditional social and family values of the Roman elite. Other critics were more direct. The Roman monk Jovinian, though celibate himself, refused to admit any biblical foundation for basing distinctions of merit solely on degrees of sexual renunciation. His teaching unleashed a firestorm of rebuttals in the mid-390s. Although he was condemned by a Roman synod and savaged by Jerome, he attracted considerable support among the Roman aristocracy. In the aftermath, the ideals of ascetic renunciation were assimilated into elite Christian culture and provided a new idiom for the expression of aristocratic competition and civic munificence. Even so, anxieties about wealth and sexuality informed debates about Christian identity throughout Late Antiquity.[76]

---

[70] Paulinus of Nola, *Ep.* 13.

[71] *PLRE* 1:663; *PCBE* 2.2: 1576–81.

[72] MacMullen, "What Difference Did Christianity Make?"; Hunter, *Marriage, Celibacy, and Heresy*, 51–74.

[73] Brown, *Body and Society*, 341–65.

[74] *Ep.* 6.27.3 (CSEL 82).

[75] Yarbrough, "Christianization," 155–6; Salzman, *Making of a Christian Aristocracy*, 166–77.

[76] Hunter, *Marriage, Celibacy, and Heresy*, 15–50, 74–83.

It is unlikely that asceticism's strictures resonated very far along the socio-economic scale, but other changes were public to a degree that affected the lives and routines of almost all Christians. In fact, funerary banquets and annual commemorations of the dead, now staged in monumentalized suburban cemeteries and often replicating pre-Christian practices with little clerical oversight, may have served many "ordinary" Christians as the primary enactment and expression of their Christianity in this age.[77] Closely linked both to such funerary rituals and to contemporary reconfigurations of urban life and public memory are the burgeoning cult of the saints and the restructuring of civic time and space that had begun to take shape in the Constantinian age. With persecution's recession into the past and new sources of wealth and patronage available, the monumentalized tombs of the martyrs attracted veneration and prayer while the anniversaries of the martyrs' deaths provided a list of feast days to fill out the calendar of Christian holidays. As the tombs of the martyrs were isolated in *martyria* and churches and as, in the course of the later fourth and fifth centuries, the pre-Christian festivals of the towns and cities of Italy were either forgotten or transformed, the image of the late Roman city was remade.[78] Along with these changes came a revised sense of civic identity rooted in new myths of origin.

This phenomenon is evident throughout Italy as bishops joined emperors and aristocrats as builders and donors.[79] At Rome, although the homes of the aristocracy may have continued to serve as centers for worship well into the fourth century,[80] by the fifth century's end there were within the Aurelian walls twenty-five or twenty-six parish churches (*tituli*), Constantine's two foundations at the Lateran and the Sessorian palace (S. Croce), and at least nine other basilicas (including S. Maria Maggiore and S. Stefano Rotondo).[81] Outside the walls, the catacombs rapidly expanded in the later fourth century while the suburbs blossomed with *martyria* and cemetery churches, as many as sixteen of the latter by the end of the fourth century alone.[82] A similar pattern of intra- and extramural church construction unfolded at contemporary Milan and Aquileia and remapped Ravenna in the first half of the fifth century.[83] Though not all north Italian

[77] Rebillard, "The Church, the Living, and the Dead"; MacMullen, *The Second Church*.
[78] Salzman, "Christianization of Time and Space"; Yasin, *Saints and Church Spaces*.
[79] Ward-Perkins, *From Classical Antiquity to the Middle Ages*, 51–84; Bowes, *Private Worship, Public Values*, 65–71.
[80] Bowes, *Private Worship, Public Values*, 73–103.
[81] Reekmans, "L'implantation," 866–8; Guidobaldi, "L'organizzazione dei *tituli*."
[82] Reekmans, "L'implantation," 902–7; Pergola, "Dai cimiteri ai santuari martiriali."
[83] Humphries, *Communities of the Blessed*, 187–202; Sotinel, *Identité civique et christianisme*, 262–70; Deliyannis, *Ravenna in Late Antiquity*, 41–105.

cities kept pace in this environment where paganism and Judaism long retained their vitality, by the mid-fifth century church building had substantially reformed the Italian cityscape.[84]

Moreover, these topographical changes were linked with forms of veneration of the martyrs that distinctly characterize late ancient Christianity.[85] When Ambrose dedicated a new church just outside Milan's walls, he readily complied with his congregation's demand that the basilica be fortified with the earthly remains of thaumaturgic martyr-heroes (who in the event would be the Milanese Gervasius and Protasius).[86] In the course of the next decade, Paulinus transformed the site of Felix's tomb into a complex of ornate basilicas and other structures that impressed visitors from around the empire.[87] No city, however, could rival Rome in the number of its saints and martyrs: by one count the number of feast days for Rome's martyrs and bishops rose from forty-three in the mid-fourth century to 111 by the seventh, paralleling the urbanization of the Roman suburbs in these years.[88] Throughout Italy, rich and poor brought their prayers and gifts to the martyrs' tombs, carried away contact relics, and sought out burial *ad sanctos*. And as episcopal ceremonial incorporated the topography of the saints, these heroes of the age of persecution gradually absorbed or effaced pre-Christian divine and legendary city founders. The narratives of their *passiones* and *acta* filled the reservoir of public memory, displacing older and now irrelevant versions of civic history. Like the rancorous Jovinianist controversy, the honorific *elogia* installed by Damasus in the Roman *martyria* and Ambrose's relic acquisitions are vivid indices of Christianity's centrality in late ancient Italy.[89]

By the time, then, of Leo's negotiations with Gaiseric before the walls of Rome, the Christianization of society had indeed brought considerable change to Italy. As churches came to define the cityscape and the cult of the martyrs to establish the rhythms of civic time, Christian themes dominated the literary and the visual arts.[90] Christianity had now been the religion of Rome's emperors for more than a century. The church had acquired vast wealth from imperial favor and private benefaction and wielded significant public authority. In the days of Damasus, Praetextatus was said to have quipped, "Make me bishop of Rome and I will be a Christian

[84] Humphries, *Communities of the Blessed*, 202–15.
[85] Brown, *Cult of the Saints*; Markus, *The End of Ancient Christianity*, 139–55.
[86] McLynn, *Ambrose*, 209–15.
[87] Trout, *Paulinus of Nola*, 160–97; Lehmann, *Paulinus Nolanus*.
[88] Saxer, "La liturgie," 922–3; Pergola, Valenzani, Volpe, *Suburbium*.
[89] Trout, "Damasus and the Invention of Early Christian Rome"; Brenk, "Il culto delle reliquie."
[90] Elsner, *Imperial Rome and Christian Triumph*, 138–43.

at once,"[91] while shortly thereafter the historian Ammianus Marcellinus caustically condemned the ostentation of those same bishops (27.3.14). In consequence, possession of the episcopal cathedra of Rome was several times contested by violent schisms while at Milan Ambrose faced down the imperial authorities on more than one occasion.[92] Throughout late Roman Italy, bishops were power brokers as well as de facto municipal magistrates, a development that prepared them to assume much of the administration of Italy when in the later sixth century the peninsula reverted to a patchwork of separate regions.[93] By then, however, a common religion, transplanted to Italian soil more than five hundred years before, bridged the political boundaries separating Lombards, Romans, and Byzantines.

BIBLIOGRAPHY

Agnello, Santi Luigi. *Silloge di iscrizioni paleocristiane della Sicilia* (Rome, 1953).
Bardill, Jonathan. *Constantine, Divine Emperor of the Christian Golden Age* (Cambridge, 2012).
Barnes, Timothy. *Eusebius and Constantine* (Cambridge, Mass., 1981).
  "Statistics and the Conversion of the Roman Aristocracy." *JRS* 85 (1995): 135–47.
  Constantine: Dynasty, Religion and Power in the Later Roman Empire (Malden, Mass. and Oxford, 2011).
Barnish, S. J. B. "*Religio in stagno*: Nature, Divinity, and the Christianization of the Countryside in Late Antique Italy." *JECS* 9 (2001): 387–402.
Bisconti, Fabrizio. "La *Memoria Apostolorum*." In *Pietro e Paolo*, ed. Donati (Milan, 2000): 63–6.
Bowersock, Glen. "Peter and Constantine." In *"Humana Sapit,"* eds. J.-M. Carrié and R. L. Testa (Turnhout, 2002): 209–17.
Bowes, Kim. *Private Worship, Public Values, and Religious Change in Late Antiquity* (Cambridge, 2008).
Brandenburg, Hugo. *Ancient Churches of Rome from the Fourth to the Seventh Century* (Turnhout, 2005).
Brenk, Beat. "Il culto delle reliquie e la politica urbanistico-architettonica di Milano ai tempi del vescovo Ambrogio." In *387 d.C.: Ambrogio e Agostino: le sorgenti dell'europa* (Milan, 2003): 56–60.
Brown, Peter. *The Cult of the Saints: Its Rise and Function in Latin Christianity* (Chicago, 1981).
  The Body and Society: Men, Women, and Sexual Renunciation in Early Christianity (New York, 1988).
  Augustine of Hippo: A Biography. New Edition with an Epilogue (Berkeley, 2000).
Cain, Andrew. *The Letters of Jerome: Asceticism, Biblical Exegesis, and the Construction of Christian Authority in Late Antiquity* (Oxford, 2009).

[91] Jerome, *Jo. Hier.* 8.
[92] Pietri, *Roma christiana*, 407–18, 452–60; McLynn, *Ambrose*, 170–219, 291–360.
[93] Humphries, "Italy," 540–4, 550–1.

Cameron, Alan. "Poetry and Literary Culture in Late Antiquity." In *Approaching Late Antiquity: The Transformation from Early to Late Empire*, eds. Simon Swain and Mark Edwards (Oxford, 2004): 325–54.

The Last Pagans of Rome (Oxford, 2011).

Cameron, Averil. "Constantine and the 'Peace of the Church.'" In *Cambridge History of Christianity*. Vol. 1, eds. M. Mitchell and F. Young (Cambridge, 2006): 538–51.

Cameron, Averil, and Stuart G. Hall. *Eusebius: Life of Constantine. Introduction, Translation, and Commentary* (Oxford, 1999).

Cameron, Averil, Bryan Ward-Perkins, and Michael Whitby, eds. *The Cambridge Ancient History.* Vol. 14: *Late Antiquity: Empire and Successors, A.D. 425–600* (Cambridge, 2000).

Carrié, Jean-Michel, and Rita Lizza Testa, eds. *"Humana sapit:" études d'antiquité tardive offertes à Lellia Cracco Ruggini* (Turnhout, 2002).

Curran, John. *Pagan City and Christian Capital: Rome in the Fourth Century* (Oxford, 2000).

Deliyannis, Deborah Mauskopf. *Ravenna in Late Antiquity* (Cambridge, 2010).

Donati, Angela, ed. *Pietro e Paolo: la storia, il culto, la memoria nei primi secoli* (Milan, 2000).

Drake, H. A. *Constantine and the Bishops: The Politics of Intolerance* (Baltimore, 2000).

"The Impact of Constantine on Christianity." In *Cambridge Companion to the Age of Constantine*, ed. N. Lenski (New York, 2006): 111–36.

Elsner, Jaś. *Imperial Rome and Christian Triumph: The Art of the Roman Empire, AD 100–450* (Oxford, 1998).

Ferrua, Antonio. *Note e giunte alle iscrizioni cristiane antiche della Sicilia* (Rome, 1989).

Frend, W. H. C. *Martyrdom and Persecution in the Early Church* (Oxford, 1965).

Galvao-Sobrinho, Carlos. "Funerary Epigraphy and the Spread of Christianity in the West." *Athenaeum* 83 (1995): 431–62.

Green, Bernard. *Christianity in Ancient Rome: The First Three Centuries* (London, 2010).

Guidobaldi, Federico. "L'organizzazione dei *tituli* nello spazio urbano." In *Christiana loca*, ed. L. Pani Ermini (Rome, 2000): 123–9.

Heather, Peter. "The Western Empire, 425–76." In *Cambridge Ancient History*. Vol. 14, eds. A. Cameron, B. Ward-Perkins, and M. Whitby (Cambridge, 2000): 1–32.

Hefele, Karl Joseph von. *Histoire des Conciles d'après les documents originaux.* Vols. 1–2. Trans. H. Leclercq (Paris, 1907–1952).

Heine, Ronald. "The Beginnings of Latin Christian Literature." In *Cambridge History of Early Christian Literature*, eds. F. Young, L. Ayers, and A. Louth (Cambridge, 2004): 131–41.

"Cyprian and Novatian." In *Cambridge History of Early Christian Literature*, eds. F. Young, L. Ayers, and A. Louth (Cambridge, 2004): 152–60.

"Articulating Identity." In *Cambridge History of Early Christian Literature*, eds. F. Young, L. Ayers, and A. Louth (Cambridge, 2004): 200–21.

Holloway, R. Ross. *Constantine and Rome* (New Haven, 2004).

Humphries, Mark. *Communities of the Blessed: Social Environment and Religious Change in Northern Italy, AD 200–400* (Oxford, 1999).

"Italy, A.D. 425–605." In *Cambridge Ancient History*. Vol. 14, eds. A. Cameron, B. Ward-Perkins, and M. Whitby (Cambridge, 2000): 525–51.

Hunter, David. *Marriage, Celibacy, and Heresy in Ancient Christianity: The Jovinianist Controversy* (Oxford, 2007).

Jensen, Robin. "Towards a Christian Material Culture." In *Cambridge History of Christianity*. Vol. 1, eds. M. Mitchell and F. Young (Cambridge, 2006): 568–85.

Joannou, Périclès-Pierre. *La legislation imperiale et la christianisation de l'empire romain (311–476)* (Rome, 1972).

Kahlos, Maijastina. *Forbearance and Compulsion: The Rhetoric of Religious Tolerance and Intolerance in Late Antiquity* (London, 2009).

Kelly, J. N. D. *Jerome: His Life, Writings, and Controversies* (London, 1975).

Krautheimer, Richard. *Rome: Profile of a City, 312–1308* (Berkeley, 1980).

Lampe, Peter. *From Paul to Valentinus: Christians at Rome in the First Two Centuries*. Trans. M. Steinhauser (Minneapolis, 2003).

Lane Fox, Robin. *Pagans and Christians* (San Francisco, 1986).

Légasse, Simon. "Paul et l'universalisme chrétien." In *Histoire du christianisme*, ed. L. Pietri (Paris, 2000): 97–154.

———. "Les autres voies de la mission (de l'Orient jusqu'à Rome)." In *Histoire du christianisme*, ed. L. Pietri (Paris, 2000): 155–87.

Lehmann, Tomas. *Paulinus Nolanus und die Basilica Nova in Cimitile/Nola* (Wiesbaden, 2004).

Lenski, Noel, ed. *The Cambridge Companion to the Age of Constantine* (New York, 2006).

———. "Evoking the Pagan Past: *Instinctu divinitatis* and Constantine's Capture of Rome." *Journal of Late Antiquity* 1 (2008): 204–57.

Lizzi, Rita. *Vescovi e strutture ecclesiastiche nella città tardoantica: l'Italia Annonaria nel IV-V secolo d.C.* (Como, 1989).

———. "Ambrose's Contemporaries and the Christianization of Northern Italy." *JRS* 80 (1990): 156–73.

MacCormack, Sabine. *Art and Ceremony in Late Antiquity* (Berkeley, 1981).

MacMullen, Ramsey. "What Difference Did Christianity Make?" In *Changes in the Roman Empire: Essays in the Ordinary* (New Haven, 1990): 142–55.

———. *The Second Church: Popular Christianity A.D. 200–400* (Atlanta, 2009).

Markus, Robert. *The End of Ancient Christianity* (Cambridge, 1990).

Martin, Dale, and Patricia Cox Miller, eds. *The Cultural Turn in Late Ancient Studies: Gender, Asceticism, and Historiography* (Durham, N.C., 2005).

Matthews, John. *Western Aristocracies and Imperial Court, AD 364–425* (Oxford, 1975).

Mazzoleni, Danilo. "Pietro e Paolo nell'epigrafia cristiana." In *Pietro e Paolo*, ed. A. Donati (Milan, 2000): 67–72.

Meeks, Wayne. *The First Urban Christians: The Social World of the Apostle Paul* (New Haven, 1983).

McLynn, Neil. *Ambrose of Milan: Church and Court in a Christian Capital* (Berkeley, 1994).

Mitchell, Margaret, and Frances Young, eds. *The Cambridge History of Christianity*. Vol. 1: *Origins to Constantine* (Cambridge, 2006).

Musurillo, Herbert. *Acts of the Christian Martyrs*. Vol. 2 (Oxford, 1972).

Neil, Bronwen. *Leo the Great* (New York, 2009).

O'Donnell, James. *Augustine: A New Biography* (New York, 2005).

Otranto, Giorgio. *Italia meridionale e Puglia paleocristiane: saggi storici* (Bari, 1991).

Pani Ermini, Letizia, ed. *Christiana loca: lo spazio cristiano nella Roma del primo millennio*. 2 vols. (Rome, 2000).

Penco, Gregorio. *Storia della chiesa in Italia, Vol. 1. Dalle origini al Concilio di Trento* (Milan, 1977).

Pergola, Philippe. "Dai cimiteri ai santuari martiriali (IV-VIII secolo)." In *Christiana Loca*, ed. L. Pani Ermini (Rome, 2000): 99–105.

Pergola, Philippe, Riccardo Santangeli Valenzani, and Rita Volpe, eds. *Suburbium: il suburbio di Roma dalla crisi del sistema delle ville a Gregorio Magno* (Rome, 2003).

Pietri, Charles. *Roma Christiana: recherches sur l'Eglise de Rome, son organisation, sa politique, son idéologie de Miltiade à Sixte III (311–440)*. 2 vols. (Rome, 1976).

"Concordia apostolorum et renovatio Urbis (Culte des martyrs et propagande pontificale)." Reprinted in *Christiana Republica: éléments d'une enquête sur le christianisme antique*, (Rome, 1997): 1085–1133.

Pietri, Luce, ed. *Histoire du christianisme. Tome I: le nouveau people (des origins à 250)* (Paris, 2000).

Rebillard, Éric. "The Church, the Living, and the Dead." In *A Companion to Late Antiquity*, ed. Philip Rousseau (Malden, 2009).

Reekmans, Louis. "L'implantation monumentale chrétienne dans le paysage urbain de Rome de 300 à 850." In *Actes du XIe congrès international d'archéologie chrétienne* (Rome, 1989): 861–915.

Reutter, Ursula. *Damasus, Bischof von Rom (366–384)* (Tübingen, 2009).

Rives, James B. "The Decree of Decius and the Religion of Empire." *JRS* 89 (1999): 135–154.

Religion in the Roman Empire (Malden, 2007).

Rousseau, Philip. *Ascetics, Authority, and the Church in the Age of Jerome and Cassian* (Oxford, 1978).

Salzman, Michele. "The Christianization of Sacred Time and Sacred Space." In *The Transformations of Urbs Roma in Late Antiquity*, ed. William V. Harris (Portsmouth, R.I., 1999): 123–34.

The Making of a Christian Aristocracy: Social and Religious Change in the Western Roman Empire (Cambridge, 2002).

Saxer, Victor. "L'utilisation par la liturgie de l'espace urbain et suburbain: l'exemple de Rome dans l'antiquité et le haut moyen âge." In *Actes du XIe congrès international d'archéologie chrétienne* (Rome, 1989): 917–1032.

Schimmelpfennig, Bernard. *The Papacy*. Trans. J. Sievert (New York, 1992).

Sessa, Kristina. "*Domus Ecclesiae*: Rethinking a Category of *Ante-Pacem* Christian Space." *JTS* 60 (2009): 90–108.

Shotwell, James, and Louise Ropes Loomis. *The See of Peter* (New York, 1927).

Snyder, Graydon. *Ante Pacem: Archaeological Evidence of Church Life before Constantine* (Macon, Ga., 1985).

Sogno, Cristiana. *Q. Aurelius Symmachus: A Political Biography* (Ann Arbor, Mich., 2006).

Sotinel, Claire. *Identité civique et christianisme: Aquilée du IIIe au VIe siècle* (Rome, 2005).

Spera, Lucrezia. "The Christianization of Space along the Via Appia: Changing Landscape in the Suburbs of Rome." *AJA* 107 (2003): 23–43.

Stein, Ernst. *Histoire du Bas-Empire, Vol. 1. De l'État Romain á l'État Byzantin (284–476)*, ed. Jean-Remy Palanque (Paris, 1959).

Stevenson, James. *The Catacombs: Rediscovered Monuments of Early Christianity* (London, 1978).

Testini, Pasquale. *Archeologia cristiana: nozioni generali dalle origini alla fine del sec. VI* (Rome, 1958).

Trout, Dennis. "Christianizing the Nolan Countryside: Animal Sacrifice at the Tomb of Felix." *JECS* 3 (1995): 281–98.

Paulinus of Nola: Life, Letters, and Poems (Berkeley, 1999).

"The Verse Epitaph(s) of Petronius Probus: Competitive Commemoration in Late-Fourth-Century Rome." *New England Classical Journal* 28 (2001): 157–76.

"Damasus and the Invention of Early Christian Rome." In *The Cultural Turn in Late Ancient Studies*, eds. D. Martin and P. Cox Miller (Durham, N.C., 2005): 298–315.

Ullmann, Walter. *A Short History of the Papacy in the Middle Ages* (London, 1972).

Van Dam, Raymond. *The Roman Revolution of Constantine* (Cambridge, 2007).

Remembering Constantine at the Milvian Bridge (Cambridge, 2011).

Vinzent, Markus. "Rome." In *Cambridge History of Christianity*. Vol. 1, eds. M. Mitchell and F. Young (Cambridge, 2006): 397–412.

Ward-Perkins, Bryan. *From Classical Antiquity to the Middle Ages: Urban Public Building in Northern and Central Italy, AD 300–850* (Oxford, 1984).

White, L. Michael. *Building God's House in the Roman World: Architectural Adaptation among Pagans, Jews, and Christians* (Baltimore, 1990).

Williams, Megan Hale. *The Monk and the Book: Jerome and the Making of Christian Scholarship* (Chicago, 2006).

Yarbrough, Anne. "Christianization in the Fourth Century: The Example of Roman Women." *CH* 45 (1976): 149–65.

Yasin, Ann Marie. *Saints and Church Spaces in the Late Antique Mediterranean: Architecture, Cult, and Community* (Cambridge, 2009).

Young, Frances, Lewis Ayres, and Andrew Louth, eds. *The Cambridge History of Early Christian Literature* (Cambridge, 2004).

Zwierlein, Otto. *Petrus in Rom: Die literarischen Zeugnisse* (Berlin, 2009).

17

RELIGIONS AND CITIES IN ROMAN GAUL
(FIRST TO FOURTH CENTURIES CE)

WILLIAM VAN ANDRINGA

(TRANSLATED BY WILLIAM ADLER)

"Roman domination imposed on Gaul both foreign masters and new styles of governance. Among its habitants, it brought about changes in their way of life, of work, and of material advancement; with the appearance of towns, roads, and monuments, it reshaped the land. But it did even more than that: it altered the beliefs of the people, their language, ways of thinking, and customs. In addition to material transformations of the country, it brought about a revolution in morals." (Jullian, *Histoire de la Gaule*, vol. 2, 133)

INTRODUCTION: TERRITORIAL AND RELIGIOUS DIVERSITY

At the outset, we must clarify our terminology and the geographic area under consideration. Even if the Romans speak readily of "Gaul" and the "Gauls" to describe the territories extending from the Pyrenees to the Rhine, this generic terminology, as recent studies of the Iron Age have demonstrated, masks great local and regional diversity, the evolution of which was shaped in various ways by the Celtic migrations. In effect, the "Gauls" did not exist apart from the reductionist mentality of the conquering Romans. The Romans could not entirely overlook the diversity, however. In the interior of "long-haired Gaul" (*Gallia Comata*), Caesar clearly differentiates the Belgae from the Celts and the Aquitani: "All these people," he states, "differ from one another in speech, customs, and laws."

Beginning with the reign of Augustus Caesar, the *Tres Provinciae Galliae* (as the delegates of the cities assembled at the altar of the Lyon Confluence signed their decree) ultimately became the official designation of the three new provinces of Aquitania, Lugdunensis (Lyonnaise), and Belgica. *Gallia Transalpina*, which was conquered in the second century BCE and which merged the regions of the Midi, received the name *Gallia Narbonensis* (Narbonnaise). A land of colonies and Latin *civitates*,

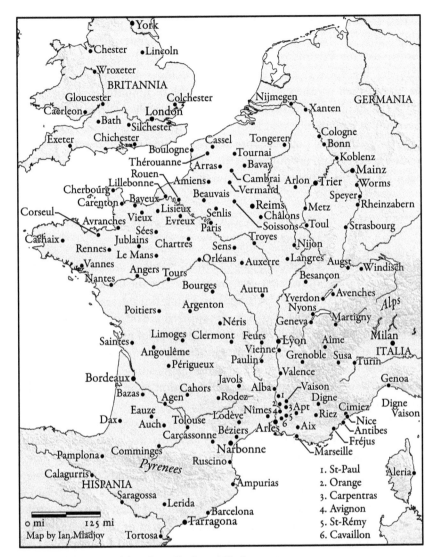

Map 9. The Cities of the Three Gauls and Narbonensis

the Midi, stretching from Narbonne to the Alps, was integrated into the empire at an earlier date. Geographically close to Italy, the Midi did not share the same history as the interior of Gaul conquered by Caesar between 58 and 51 BCE. (See Map 9.)

In the Roman period, Narbonensis and Galliae were divided up into provinces and organized into cities composing a mosaic of autonomous states, each engaged in its own distinctive religious practices. It is thus impossible to study this region as a religious unity. The Bituriges of Bordeaux, the Pictons of Poitiers, the Parisii of Paris, the Ambiani of Amiens, the Vocontii of Vaison, and the Volques Arecomiques of Nîmes fashioned their pantheons in accordance with community needs and their own special history, the result of which is invariably reflected in the preservation of certain ancestral gods. Within the context of this network of city-states, the local populace forged relationships with Rome. Indeed, the gods were indispensable for protecting the community, just as they were in securing the ties between the autonomous city, Rome, and the emperor.

CULTS IN THEIR HISTORICAL CONTEXT: PROVINCIALIZATION AND RAPPROCHEMENT WITH ROME

In the majority of studies of "Gallo-Roman" religion – a term that presupposes a "national" dimension that never existed – the cults are rarely conceived in their community setting. For a long time, research focused on the permanence of Gallic deities in the imperial period, on the *interpretatio Romana,* or on the overall religiosity of the peoples of Gaul. Other longstanding topics concerned the distinctive architectural and monumental features of Gallo-Roman sanctuaries and the meaning of votive offerings, which were understood as the central expression of an essentially popular and local religion.

When we examine these studies, commonly conceived strictly from the "Gallo-Roman perspective," it becomes clear that in many cases hypotheses are generated by culturally determined and modernizing interpretations, which generally fail to recognize the profound uniqueness of ancient religions. Beginning with Camille Jullian, the prevailing image of Gaul is that of harmony between the native and Roman deities, a product of the religious tolerance of the conquerors. Thus, in his study of the "pagan cults in the Roman Empire," Jules Toutain claimed that this Roman tolerance went hand in hand with the favorable reception extended to the Roman gods by the local peoples.[1] In short, the local populations were allowed to "believe and practice as they liked, apart from the State, which built for itself the patchwork character of Gallo-Roman religion."

This representation, which has shaped the studies of the religion of the provinces of Gaul, poses two kinds of problems, both related to the understanding of ancient religious practices. The first of them has to do with

---

[1] Jullian, *Histoire de la Gaule*; Toutain, *Cultes païens*, i, 134.

terminology. The concept of "tolerance," which originated with the history of modern states, is ill-suited to defining religious phenomena associated with the ancient city. The cities of the Roman period were by definition autonomous; this is what makes it possible to refer to the "freedom" of the cults. But the autonomy of communities was defined and circumscribed by Rome. It naturally follows from this that religious change, promoted by the cities themselves, occurred within the framework of the religious ideology of Rome. Integration was inseparable from Roman control over the provinces.[2]

Another problem has to do with the place traditionally assigned to religion in the history of Gaul. Because the study of religious behavior is commonly linked to the spiritual realm, detached from any political context, it becomes a subject of study in isolation, decontextualized, and suspended in a void. As a result, the cults of Roman Gaul have almost always been studied in terms of a personal belief system, detached from their community and institutional setting. Recent analysis of the function of Greco-Roman religions has shown, however, that in Antiquity religious practices cannot be divorced from the political and social context in which they developed, and from which they derived their meaning.

In the provinces of Gaul, as in the empire as a whole, religion was principally community centered. While participation in religious cults was of course contingent upon one's membership in the city, it was also a function of one's membership in a subdivision of the city (the *vicus* or the *pagus*), as well as one's connection to a *collegium* or a family grouping. In other words, if piety played an essential role in maintaining the daily well-being of every individual – witness the thousands of votive offerings of every stripe deposited in the sanctuaries – it played an equally fundamental role in defining societies as a system of communities. Harmony between individuals, as well as the existence of individuals in their communities, was at stake. Among the many examples of this are the public tauroboliums of Lectoure (*CIL* XIII, 520, city of the *Lactorates*) instituted for the preservation of the city, an altar dedicated by the butchers of Périgueux (*CIL* XIII, 941, city of the *Petrocores*) to religious representations of the Roman regime in the form of Jupiter and the *genius* of the emperor Tiberius, and the altar of a house in Autun (*CIL* XIII, 11227, city of the *Aedui*) erected for the guardian (*Tutela*) of the *domus*. Indeed, repeated vows to familiar deities were as crucial to community and individual preservation as was participation in ceremonies or

---

[2] Cf. Beard, North, and Price, *Religions*, 313f.

Fig. 16. Altar of the butchers of Périgueux. The butchers of the urban area gathered together in veneration of Jupiter in the company of the genius of Tiberius.

sacrifices, which were believed to guarantee civic harmony or the social stability of the group to which one belonged (Fig. 16).

These principles are as applicable to the civic religions of Greece and Rome as they are to the Gauls after the Roman conquest, when the Gallic peoples were organized into cities. Aside from the unique case of the Greek settlements of the Midi, which had been established for a long time on the Mediterranean coast, the indigenous peoples were increasingly settled in cities. Notable examples of this policy, which essentially began at the time of Caesar, include the colonies established in *Gallia Transalpina* (Arles and Béziers, for example), and in *Gallia Comata* (Lyon, Nyon, and Augst). During the Augustan era, the system was extended from the Pyrenees to the Rhine. From the beginning of the imperial period, political and religious life was everywhere regulated within the civilized framework of the city-state and the social organization that defined it. The available sources from this period, notably the epigraphic material, require us to pay close attention to the urban context and the evolution of the city from the first to the third centuries CE. Nor should we neglect the connection of the great sanctuaries to a *polis*-based organization of the territories based on new realities such as the *vici* or small towns in general. The result of these fundamental community-based realignments was the creation of new religious systems. Obviously, they did not completely efface the past – the retention of some local deities under the empire demonstrates this.[3] They were, however, adapted to the new times, namely that of autonomous cities incorporated into an empire under the leadership of one ruler.

RELIGION AND INTEGRATION INTO THE EMPIRE: THE TRANSFORMATION OF THE GODS AND THE RECOMPOSITION OF SACRED SPACES

Because the gods of the Greek provinces, clad for a long time in togas, were already integrated into civil life, they could remain essentially unchanged in the imperial period. The situation was different in the West, however. Archaeological and epigraphic records demonstrate that in Gaul the gods evolved and adapted in response to changes brought about by the new organization of the Gauls, beginning already with Augustus. There were of course exceptions. In regions that had been conquered at a much earlier time or in Roman colonies, places where the populace had been Roman for a long time, the cults were for the most part Roman, notwithstanding local variation tied to the history of each community. This is clearly the case with the pantheon of the colony of Narbonne: in the imperial period, the gods venerated were Hercules, the Augustan Lares, Magna Mater, the *numen Augusti, Pax Augusta,* and Vulcan.

The situation was much the same in the private domain. The cults attested in the same town are the *genii* of patrons, fathers and mothers of the family (those last under the form of *Iunones*); as at Rome, the deceased were represented by the *divi manes*. Similarly, in the colony of Vienne, also in Narbonensis, the Roman gods won the day, without having to share power with native deities. Side by side in the capital city are Apollo, Castor and Pollux, Diana, Fortuna, Hercules, Juno, Jupiter, Mars, Mercury,

---

[3] See Van Andringa, *Les dieux indigènes*.

Pluto, Proserpina, Silvanus, Sucellus, Tutela, Venus, and Victoria. With
the exception of the presence of some local deities such as the goddess
Coriotana or the god Limetus, the gods of the outlying territory belong
to the Roman pantheon: Aesculapius, Apollo, Ceres, Diana, Fortuna,
Isis, Juno, Jupiter, Mars, Mercury, Maia, Minerva, Saturn, and Silvanus.
At Saint-Laurent-du-Pont, there is even a temple dedicated to Quirinus
Augustus, the archaic god of Rome.

As demonstrated in recent studies, these practices are in sharp contrast
with the majority of the cities of Gaul.[4] For the most part, the pantheons,
organized during the reign of Augustus, are an amalgamation of indigenous and Roman deities. In addition to Mercury and Minerva, inscriptions from Bourges-Avaricum, the capital of Bituriges Cubes, mention
Mars Mogetius, Mars Rigisamus, Mavida, and Solimara. In the outlying
territory, the register of deities is no different. We encounter Jupiter in
Saint-Ambroix and Magna Mater, Mercury, and Minerva in Argenton;
but Ibosus, Nerius, Magna Mater, and the *Iunones* appear in Neris, Apollo
Bassoledulitanus in Allichamps, Elvontios in Genouilly, Naga in Gièvres,
Apollo Atepomarus in Mauvières, Souconna in Sagonnes and Adacrius at
Vernais. These motley pantheons, the product of community reorganization within the *civitates* and the inevitable rapprochement with Roman
power, attest to a progressive and ongoing reconstitution of local religious
systems.

It is in this context that we can explain the transformation of local deities by means of the *interpretatio romana*. The naturalization of indigenous
deities who had assumed a Roman name ultimately depended on finding a
common link based on perceived similarities in physical appearance or in
the realm in which they operated. Caesar and Tacitus's translation of the
names of certain Gallic and Germanic deities shows that the identification
with Roman gods could be a strictly personal choice (Julius Caesar, *Bell.
gall.* VI, 17; Tacitus, *Germ.* 43). From epigraphic evidence from the *Treveri*
and the *Redones* (*Gallia Belgica* and *Lugdunensis*), however, we can see that
the process became official once the name was used in a city's public cults.
The ancient tribal deity of the *Treveri* thus became Lenus Mars and his
cult was registered in the city's calendar. The organization of a flaminate
and the construction of a great temple some 500m from the city during
the first century CE completed the transformation of the cult.[5] At Rennes,

[4] For example, Häussler, *Pouvoir et religion*; Lavagne, *Les dieux de la Gaule Narbonnaise*; Van Andringa,
La religion en Gaule romaine.
[5] On this material, see Scheid, *Sanctuaires et territoire.*

Fig. 17. Base of a statue discovered at Rennes-*Condate*, mentioning the god Mars Mullo *CIL* XIII, 3149. Source: Museum of Bretagne, Alain Amet, in *À la rencontre des dieux gaulois*, 44.

inscriptions from the reign of Hadrian show that there existed in this city or on its outskirts a temple dedicated to Mars Mullo (*AE* 1969/70 a). It is likely that the naturalization of this local deity, whose name appears in the patronage of three of the four *pagi*, occurred over the course of the first century, perhaps in connection with the acquisition of Latin legal standing (*ius Latinum*) (Fig. 17).

Composing a name by combining the indigenous epithet Mullo with a Roman divine name should not mislead us. It does not indicate that the deity was hybrid, part Roman and part Gallic – to the contrary, the religious language is marked by its exactitude. It means rather that Lenus Mars and Mars Mullo were municipal deities and that their authority was specific to the regions with which they were connected. Indeed, this is implicit in the Gallic names Lenus or Mullo (whatever the exact meaning of those terms – an ancient god's name or a Gaulish attribute). The process

Fig. 18. Stele from Reims showing the Gallic god with stag's horns accompanied by two Roman or Romanized gods, Mercury and Apollo. Source: Museum of Saint-Rémi de Reims, R. Meulle in *À la rencontre des dieux gaulois*, 120.

was decisive once an indigenous deity had adopted a Roman name. This was more than a matter of fusion, syncretism, or simple attire; these gods had changed their name and identity.

Several deities did, to be sure, maintain their local name. This could have been because an equivalent Roman name did not exist. A notable example of this is a god with the horns of a stag, named Cernunnos, on a bas-relief from Paris, whose image is well attested in the Celtic provinces (Fig. 18). The other possible reason is that the deity in question had a native local dimension. In the city of the *Convenae*, the variety of deities with local names that have been counted – a good sixty in all – is very well suited to the division of the lands and communities distinctive of the mountainous regions of the Pyrenees Piedmont.

Another point worth stressing concerns the place of these deities in the city pantheons. At Nuits-Saint-Georges, a *vicus* of the city of the *Aedui*

Fig. 19. Stele of Nuits-Saint-Georges. Source: Museum of Nuits-Saint-Georges, Fasquel, in E. Planson, C. Pommeret, *Les Bolards,* 1 (cover page).

(Eduens), a stele representing three deities has been discovered in the precinct of a great sanctuary of the urban area (Fig. 19).[6] This monument and the gods represented on it have been immediately recognized as "a perfect example of syncretism in Gaul." From left to right, the gods are typically Gallic: a mother goddess, a continuation of a very ancient cult of the mother goddess, source of fertility; a bisexual Cybele (or a *genius*); and above all the three-headed horned god, purveyor of wealth.

---

[6] Planson and Pommeret, *Les Bolards,* 52f.

Informing this reading of the bas-relief is a deep conviction about the permanence of an ancient and native religious substratum, a sentiment supported in this case by the presence of the horned god. However, if we take into account the historical and religious context of this stele, we arrive at another reading. The composition is centered on a god wearing the cornucopia. In our judgment, this can only be a representation of the *genius* of the urban area or its inhabitants, the *vicani*.[7] The *genius* is not here an indigenous deity, but rather the religious expression of an urban area, the *vicus*, which is legally defined as an urban quarter detached from a capital city.[8] The deity represented to the right of the *genius* would appear to be the goddess Fortuna holding the cornucopia and the *patera* in her right hand.[9] The only deity of indigenous appearance is finally the three-headed god with the stag-horns. While he does live on, we now find him in the company of gods who express new civic realities.

The grouping of these gods conveys this religious meaning: while accommodating an ancient ancestral god, the combination points to new realities and new divine relationships. We should also recognize that the stele is not a cult statue; rather, this modestly sized monument doubtlessly commemorated a ceremony celebrated in the great temple of the *vicus*. Beginning in the middle of the first century CE, the sanctuary acquired a monumental appearance, adhering at that time to a classical design. As the epigraphic evidence attests, the god to whom the sanctuary was dedicated was either Apollo or Mars Segomo, namely the major deities of the city of the *Aedui*.[10] The stele and the triad of gods therefore sit enthroned in a secondary position in the sanctuary (Fig. 20).

The notion of a harmonious coexistence between the ancient Gallic gods and the newcomers should be abandoned, because it masks the essential reality: rather than coexistence, we should speak of new religious combinations. These do include some of the ancient ancestral gods and mythological figures; in polytheism in Antiquity it could not be otherwise. But the "Pillar of the *Nautae*" of Paris and the stele of Nuits-Saint-Georges would seem to indicate that in the new combinations created in the imperial period, these gods have either changed their appearance or assumed a secondary position. To decide on the permanence of the gods or the cults is only to return to a practice perfectly consonant with *pietas*, to something

[7] Cf. *LIMC*, VIII, 1997, *s.v.* genius [I. Romeo], 599–607.
[8] Cf. *CIL*, XIII, 1375; 5967; 6433; 7655; 8838. On the meaning of *vicus*, see further in this chapter.
[9] Cf. *LIMC*, VIII, 1997, *s.v. Tychē* [L. Villard], 115–25 ; ibid., *s.v. Tychē/Fortuna* [F. Rausa], 125–41.
[10] Pommeret, *Le sanctuaire des Bolards*.

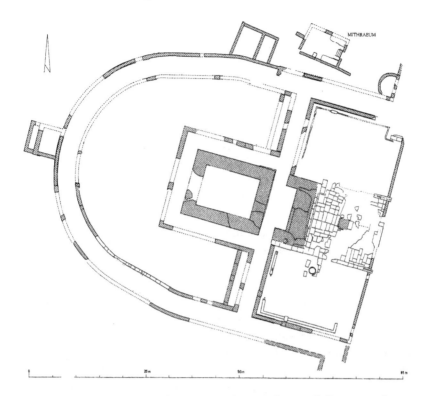

Fig. 20. Plan of the sanctuary of Nuits-Saint-Georges. Source: C. Pommeret, *Le sanctuaire antique des Bolards à Nuits-Saint-Georges*, fig. 7 (24).

obvious. On the other hand, it is fundamental to elucidate the historical context in which these cults had been redefined: Has there been a reformulation of rites? Was a new altar installed? Is there evidence of the construction of a new sanctuary? Of a change in the god's name and standing? Can we observe an association of an ancestral or local cult with new cults? And finally, was there a formation of new pantheons?

The possibilities are numerous, and the witnesses to this development are in most cases meager. One example concerns the sacrifices of horses and dogs in Vertault brought to light by P. Meniel.[11] Although they were local practices, it is noteworthy that such rituals seemed to disappear by the middle of the first century CE, the date of the construction of a temple. Quite obviously, the cult had undergone a change in both form and significance, presumably in connection with the evolution of Vertault, which

[11] Jouin and Méniel, *Le fanum de Vertault*.

had become a *vicus* under the empire. This is not to say that the god or the site of the cult had vanished. Although sacrifice of horses and dogs ceased after 50 CE, the site remained a sanctuary, and the name of the god was able to continue unchanged – this is hardly surprising. In the final analysis, the problem has more to do with the form of the sacrifice than with the continuing sacredness of the site.

Of course, the ancestral gods did not uniformly assume a subordinate place in the pantheon. This is shown by the various forms of Mars in the cities of Gaul.[12] Lenus Mars among the *Treviri*, Mars Mullo among the *Aulerci Cenomani* and the *Redones*, and Mars Caturix among the *Helvetii* are some examples of great local deities established as municipal gods. But in the period to which they belong, these gods are no longer Gallic; they have been officially interpreted and organized in the Roman way. Attesting to this are the flaminates created at Trier and Rennes as well as the construction of new sanctuaries.

In this context – namely, pantheons distinctive of the imperial period and adapted to the history of individual cities of the provinces of the three Gauls and *Narbonensis* – the categories once proposed by Jules Toutain lose their explanatory value.[13] In distinguishing the indigenous gods from the gods of Rome and the so-called Oriental gods, rigid categorization like this fails to take account of the evolution both of the cities and the peoples, ultimately masking the harmony that these gods collectively were thought to represent for each community at a given moment in its existence. Rather than "indigenous" or "Roman" gods, it was a matter of worshipping gods closely linked to the people, whose power was guaranteed by a municipal investiture. These were gods who had forged a link with Rome, adapted to their time, to the situation of the people, and to their place in society. In this way, we can explain how naturalization of deities and their integration into the Roman empire took place in many cities. It also explains the wealth of combinations that helped to keep the gods in touch with their time.

Reconstitution of religious systems in communities of Roman Gaul went hand in hand with the recasting of sacred spaces, which was inevitable, despite the presence of temples architecturally both unique and particular to these regions. Numerous archaeological specimens (more than six hundred have been located or excavated) reveal in fact a main room enclosed by a surrounding gallery. The design on a vase discovered in

---

[12] Cf. Brouquier-Reddé, et al., *Mars en Occident.*
[13] Toutain, *Les cultes païens.*

Fig. 21. Vase from Sains-du-Nord (city of the *Nervii*) representing a Gallo-Roman sanctuary. Source: Cliché de A. Broëz/from Van Andringa, *Archeologie des Sanctuaires*, 2000, p.28.

Sains-du-Nord (city of the *Nervii*), representing a sectional Gallo-Roman temple, confirms that the main room of the temple, elevated in relation to the gallery, was the *cella* containing the cult statue (Fig. 21). This unique layout, once construed as a vestige of an older Celtic design, has long supported the notion of the steadfast perseverance of the religious traditions of the Gallic period. However, excavations of Gallic sanctuaries, which are now numerous, have thus far failed to reveal the expected Celtic model.[14] It is therefore possible that the so-called Gallo-Roman temple is a creation of the Roman period, perhaps adapted to a distinctive liturgy.[15]

[14] For an assessment, Arcelin and Brunaux, *Cultes et sanctuaires*.
[15] See Van Andringa, *Archéologie des sanctuaires*, 14.

Conceivably more important than the architecture of the "Gallo-Roman" temple are the transformations to be observed in the rituals that were performed from the first century CE. Archaeological work shows that, in a general way, and despite occasional local variations, Roman forms of sacrifice gradually began to dominate. In an evocative passage, M. Henig has reconstructed the ceremony of a temple in the province of Roman Britain, which could rightly be adapted to the provinces of Gaul:[16] a procession commences in the sanctuary, leading animals, invariably the three major domestic species (oxen, goats, and pigs), to the sacrificial altar. The gates of the temple are thrown open, making it possible to make out the silhouette of the cult statue in local limestone. The Latin of the prayer is a bit peculiar, and the god has a local epithet. But for the *praefatio,* the *patera* and *oenochoe* are used, filled with a local wine (Gaul had already become a great producer of wine!). Within the temple precinct, formulaic vows are recited; others are paid by sacrifices and offerings. Undoubtedly, this scene is pure fiction; no account of a ceremony has come down to us. Even so, archaeological and epigraphic evidence confirms the architectural framework and the account of the activities that took place in and around the temple. We should also note that in the same forms of the cult, the tableau is not much different from the one that Pliny the Younger draws in connection with the sanctuary of Ceres erected on his domain (*Ep.* 9.39).

The discussion that follows will explain the historical context of the religious transformations we have already described. We shall then return to the conceptual language of the city, which will allow us to situate religious change within the framework of institutional and political transformations.

URBANIZATION AND RELIGIOUS LIFE

The organization of Gallic peoples into cities began with the birth of new towns, designed according to the Roman model of town planning and satisfying the criteria of *urbanitas.*[17] When we speak of Roman town planning, we are reminded, first, that organization into cities arose out of Roman involvement, and, second, that municipal autonomy was defined

---

[16] Henig, *Religion in Roman Britain,* 39–41.
[17] The existence of a "town" in the Gallic period is not at issue here; underlying the Greek or Roman city is a specific cultural context and a different set of standards. When Caesar refers to a town (*urbs* or *oppidum*) in the Gallic states, he has of course adapted his translation to the usage of his readers. On the Roman city in Gaul, see Goudineau, *Histoire de la France urbaine,* vol. 1; Woolf, *Becoming Roman,* 106f.

from the outset in relationship to the imperial regime. Tacitus confirms these principles in his description of the conduct of Agricola, governor of the province of Britain. Agricola extended his program of pacification in the winter of 78–79 by supporting the establishment of capital cities defined by features borrowed from Roman town planning – temples, a forum and domus: "In order, through the charms of luxury, to accustom to peace and tranquility a population scattered and barbarous and therefore inclined to war, Agricola gave private encouragement and public aid to the building of temples, forums, and homes, praising the energetic, and reproving the indolent" (*Agr.* 21). These new towns were meant to promote a civilized and peaceful style of life. What cults were then woven into the fabric of these fully developed urban centers? What deities were invited into the new capital cities and ultimately connected with this new collective enterprise? What role did they play in the design of a network of orthogonal roads, in development of a site set aside for "temples, a forum, and domus," to use Tacitus's terminology?

For the Roman government, a city came into existence only when a sufficient number of decurions could guarantee municipal autonomy (in other words, fund the public coffers). The formation of a local senate required, therefore, the concentration of the elites in an urban center and, from the outset, the establishment of a place for them to gather and administer the government under the guardianship of deities adapted to a new context and capable of forging a connection with Rome. The forum was created for assembly and the administration of the government (Fig. 22).[18] It was only fitting, then, that the public space of towns should accommodate deities embodying the political reality of the new *civitas*: an altar dedicated to the *genius civitatis* as in Bordeaux (*CIL* XIII, 566) or in Bavay (*AE* 1969/70, 410), and an altar to Jupiter, as, for example, in Jublains (*CIL* XIII, 3184). Nor should we overlook the vital role played by the cults dedicated to the imperial regime in shaping the space of the forum. Especially illuminating here are the altars of the *Caesares* discovered in Reims (*CIL* XIII, 3254 and *AE* 1982, 715), in Sens (*CIL* XIII, 2942) and Trier (*CIL* XIII, 3671). Moreover, at Nîmes, a temple dedicated to the two grandsons of Augustus was erected in the public space.

We have, of course, to acknowledge that the paucity of the archaeological evidence at our disposal impedes the identification of sanctuaries dedicated to the emperor in the *fora* of Roman towns of Gaul. While there

---

[18] On the meanings of the forum in the Roman provinces, see above all Gros, *L'architecture romaine*, 207f.

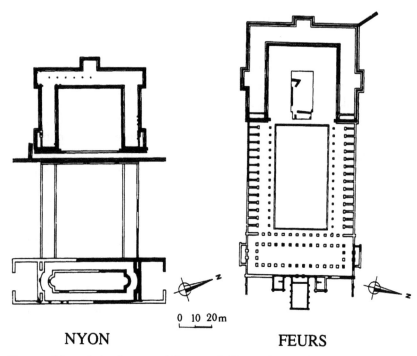

NYON   FEURS

Fig. 22. Plan of the forums of Feurs and Nyon. Source: F. Rossi, in E. Gros, *L'architecture romaine*, 223.

are remains of the podium of temples that dominate the esplanade, con-clusive epigraphic evidence identifying the occupants of the sanctuaries is invariably lacking. Despite this, certain epigraphic and iconographic clues, highlighted by P. Gros in *Narbonensis*, suggest the existence of an altar or a temple erected to Roma and Augustus in the space allotted to the forum of many of the new towns. Elsewhere, the diffusion of the public priesthood of Roma and Augustus, documented from the Augustan era, as, for exam-ple, at Rodez-*Segodunum* (*Ruteni*), allows us to connect it to the temple of the forum (*AE* 1994, 1215 a-b). We might even view the dedication of such a monument as the birth certificate of the town in Gaul, marked by the recognition of Roman authority and thus of the community's integration into the empire.

In the forum, the various cults dedicated to the imperial regime (Roma and Augustus, *numen Augusti, genius Augusti*) could be connected both with the *genius* of the municipality (as for example in Bordeaux), but especially with Jupiter "best and the greatest," the Roman political god *par excellence.* Jupiter is also ubiquitous in the public space of *Lugdunum Convenarum* (Saint-Bertrand-de-Comminges, *AE* 1941, 155; *AE* 1997, 1110–12). An altar discovered in what is presumably the forum of Jublains (*Noviodunum*) pairs Jupiter, the highest-ranking god, with Augustus, the highest-ranking man. Equally suggestive is the discovery of an altar before the main entrance of the forum of Bavay (*Bagacum*); dedicated to Jupiter, it shows him in company with the *genius* of Augustus.[19] Here the two representatives of the official religion who constitute it are joined together: *Jupiter Optimus Maximus*, the supreme god of the Roman state, and the ruling establishment, divinized in the form of the *genius* of Augustus. In city fora and sanctuaries, they embody, as indissolubly linked partners, the Roman civic ideal. They ratify the institution of an established order: the Roman government, an authority that every community integrated into the empire – a city, *vicus,* or *collegium* – was obliged to recognize.

The future of provincial communities was henceforth anchored to that of the Roman state, symbolized by the association between the emperor and the father of the gods. While the cults established in the city center did take account of the selection by local authorities, the evidence compels us to conclude that indigenous or Gallic deities were barred from the civic space. Indeed, the location for deities particular to the urban community was from the very outset situated on the outskirts of the city – hence the creation of suburban sanctuaries attested in most of the towns, for example at Augst (*Augusta Rauricorum*), Jublains (*Neodunum*), Poitiers (*Limonum*), Meaux (*Iatinum*), Beauvais (*Caesaromagnus*), Sens (*Agedincum*), and Chartres (*Autricum*). Sometimes there are veritable religious districts, important remains of which survive at Avenches (*Aventicum*) and Trier (*Augusta Treverorum*) (Figs. 23 and 24). At Limoges (*Augustoritum*), there is in fact an example of a sanctuary of an indigenous tradition set up in the very heart of the town during its construction, but its swift lapse into disuse would seem to confirm that a specific location, at the margins of the urban area, was accorded to community deities in the course of its formation (Fig. 25).[20]

In Roman towns of Gaul, we can therefore speak of coexistence and complementarity between two types of sacred space, each adapted to community ceremonies and each with a distinctive meaning. The first, located in the forum, was intended for cults embodying the new municipal organization, for example, Roma and Augustus, the *genius* of the

[19] Thollard, et al., *Bavay antique,* 57f.
[20] Loustaud, *Limoges antique,* 311f.

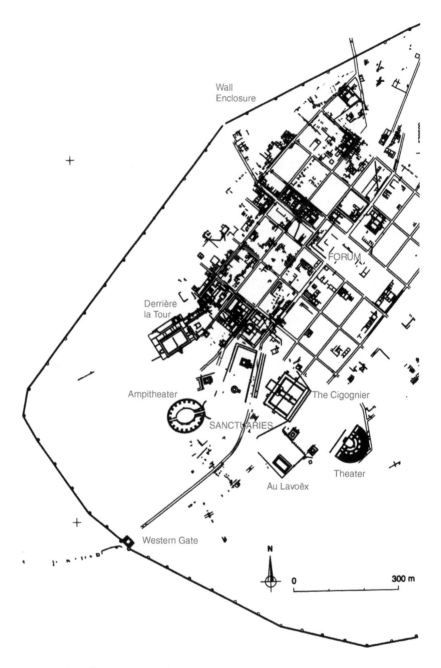

Wall
Enclosure

Derrière
la Tour

FORUM

Ampitheater

The Cigognier

SANCTUARIES

Theater

Au Lavoëx

Western Gate

N

0   300 m

Fig. 23. Plan of *Aventicum* with the site of the religious quarter of the Grange-des-Dîmes. Source: Musée Romain d'Avenches.

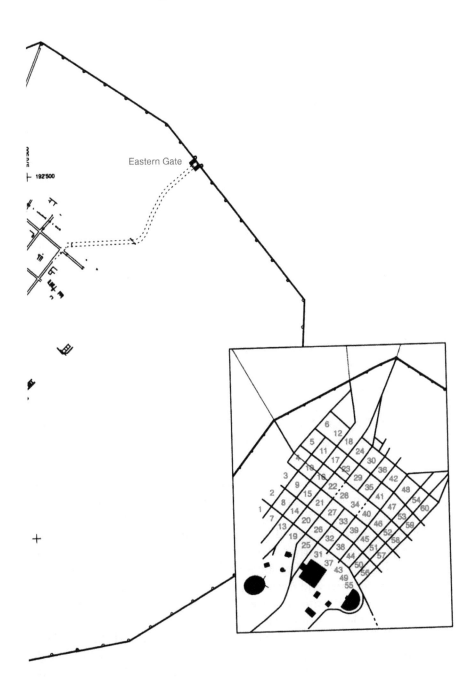

Eastern Gate

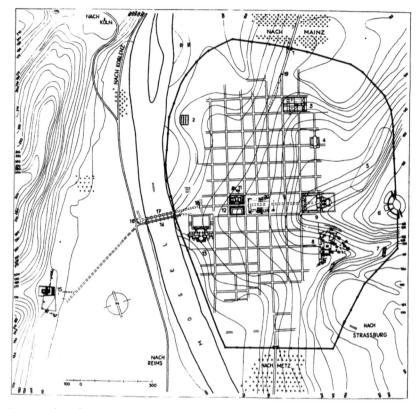

Fig. 24. Plan of *Augusta Treverorum* with the site of the sanctuaries from the urban area. Source: E. Gose, *Der gallo-römische Tempelbezirk im Albachtal zu Trier*, 1972.

civitas, and Jupiter. The second, located at a distance from the city center or in the outskirts, was dedicated to deities intended for the recently settled urban population. The majority of these latter gods, at least at the beginning of the period, were indigenous and unassimilated deities, some of whom had arrived with the groups of people relocated at the site of the new town. The names of the deities attested in the suburban sanctuaries of Trier and Avenches, two towns founded at the same time, appear to indicate this practice. The gods bearing a local name there are in fact at least as numerous as the gods with a Roman name. At the Altbachtal at Trier, Aveta, Intarabus, Ritona, Vorio, and the Dii Casses counter-balance Jupiter, Mercury, and Minerva.[21] At Avenches, in the district of Cigognier, Anextlomara, and Aventia offset Romanized deities

[21] Gose, *Altbachtal.*

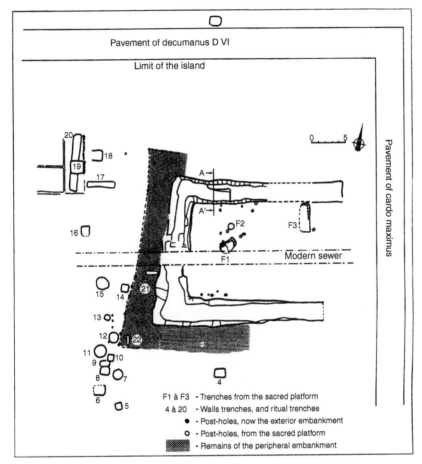

Fig. 25. Indigenous sanctuary of Limoges. Source: J.-P. Loustaud, *Limoges antique*, fig. 1 (312).

such as Mars Caisivus, Mars Caturix, Mercury Cissonius, and deities with a Roman name, such as Apollo, Jupiter, Mercury, Neptune, and Silvanus.[22] Arrangements like this also appear in *Narbonensis*. The suburban sanctuary of the Fountain at Nîmes, dedicated to Nemausus, the god of the spring, is a well-known example. But one could also cite the illustrative case of the Plateau of Poets at Béziers.[23] At this location, situated on the outskirts of the colony, a series of inscriptions mentioning the god Mars along with local deities such as the *Digenes, Menmandutes,*

[22] Bögli, *Aventicum*; Castella and Meylan Krause, *Topographie sacrée*.
[23] Christol, *Les dieux du Plateau des Poètes*.

and *Ricoria* suggest the existence of a suburban sanctuary presided over by Mars and frequented by the inhabitants of the urban area.

TERRITORY AND CIVIC LIFE: THE ORGANIZATION
OF CULTS IN THE CITY

The religious organization of a city closely parallels the complex relations existing between the capital city and its territory.[24] What records are more suggestive of this than the inscriptions of the temple of Mars Mullo at Rennes? During the reign of Hadrian, the *ordo* ratified the installation of statues of patron deities of the various territorial zones of the city (the *pagi*) in a temple of the capital city, namely the temple of Mars Mullo, chief deity of the *Redones* (*AE* 1969/70, 405 a, b, c). The event is of consequence because it signifies that the *pagi* of the city, through the intermediary of tutelary deities, were from that time represented in a public sanctuary belonging to an urban center. The same organization is documented in the colony of the *Treviri*. What this suggests is that the traditional view proposed some time ago by Camille Jullian – namely, that antagonism between the Gallic *civitas* and its *pagi* continued under the empire – needs to be reevaluated. By relocating the population of Gaul in cities, Rome implemented a carefully crafted model of spatial organization in which the town (in the Roman sense of the word) controlled a territory.

When cities had very large territories, or when a capital city did not develop, the countryside did retain some sway. But the available evidence seems to demonstrate that as a rule the different communities constitutive of the cities were little by little organized around common cults represented in the new capital city or in its outskirts; that is to say, the bond between them was very close. This would explain why, among the *Treviri*, for example, the great gods of the territory were also the great urban gods, with Mars, Mercury, and Jupiter continuing to be most popular both in the town and the countryside. Again, this reciprocity reflects the organization of a city. Indeed, the majority of the indigenous gods of Treviran origin are to be found in *Augusta Treverorum*, as we have seen, in the great suburban sanctuaries of the Altbachtal and Irminenwingert.[25] They had, as it were, followed the inhabitants who were increasingly taking up residence in this town, founded in the Augustan era. Included among these gods was Lenus Mars, who was promoted as patron deity of the colony. He then

[24] Cf. Scheid, *Sanctuaires et territoire* and the observations in Woolf, *Polis-Religion*.
[25] Scheid, *Sanctuaires et territoire*; idem, *Les temples de l'Altbachtal*.

received a sanctuary in a suburban location as well as a cult organized and practiced on behalf of the city as a whole.

Conversely, when the authorities of the colony decided to introduce a new god, it appears that the territorial communities, notably the *vici,* similarly recorded the establishment of the new divinity when they erected an altar or a chapel in their own sanctuary. This is clearly the case for Jupiter, a deity widely attested in Trier and patron of numerous urban areas in the surrounding territory, notably, Idenheim, Oberzerf, St-Wendel, Altrier, Bitburg, Dalheim, and Wederath (the last four of which had the standing of *vicus*). In the city of the *Helvetii,* Jupiter, Mercury, and Apollo are the preeminent deities in the chief city, Avenches (*Aventicum*), and in the different *vici* of the city. In Vienne in Narbonensis, Mercury emerges as the best-documented deity, both in the town and in the territory. In this city, Mars, who had a public sanctuary in the capital city – we know of a *flamen* of Mars – was worshipped both at Grenoble and in an important territorial sanctuary, at Passy (Les Outards). An analogous diffusion of the Mars cult is found among the *Sequani.*[26]

A comparison between the cults found in the capital city and in its territory underscores the importance of suburban sanctuaries. Some of them have left impressive remains, for example at Autun-*Augustodunum* (sanctuary of La Genetoye), at Jublains-*Noviodunum*, at Meaux-*Iatinum* (sanctuary of Bauve), at Sens (sanctuary of La Motte du Ciar), at Nîmes (sanctuary of Jardin de la Fontaine), and of course at Trier-*Augusta Treverorum* (Altbachtal and Irminenwingert), and Avenches-*Aventicum* (district of the Cigognier).[27] The position of these last ones, in the *loca suburbana,* made them public places closely dependent on the town. Sometimes, as at Jublains, the new town was deliberately founded in close proximity to a sanctuary presumably of pre-Roman origin. Although the patron deity is not known, the centrality of the sanctuary and its location certainly suggest a public deity of the *Aulerci Diablintes.*[28] As an ancient tribal god or guardian of a Celtic *pagus,* he henceforth presided over the newly interdependent urban center and the *territorium civitatis.* The alignment of the temple with the different public monuments of the new urban area demonstrates that this interdependence was also liturgical. The main road in fact united the sanctuary and the forum, where an altar dedicated to Jupiter and Augustus was erected, along with the theater (Fig. 26).

---

[26] Van Andringa, *Villards d'Héria.*
[27] These various sanctuaries are discussed in Van Andringa, *La religion en Gaule romaine,* 64f.
[28] Naveau, *Recherches sur Jublains.*

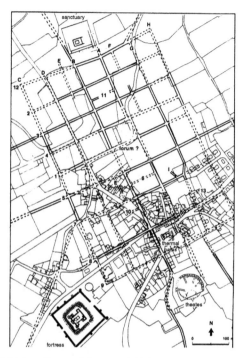

Fig. 26. Plan of Jublains. Source: Naveau, *Jublains.*

At Trier, the status of the sanctuary of the Altbachtal leaves no question about this relationship. Set up at the same time as the town and under public guardianship, it was increasingly populated with gods introduced by the urban community (Fig. 27). Its origin self-evidently accounts for the presence of the principal deities of the *Treviri.* The connection with the territory is even more pronounced in the sanctuary of Lenus Mars, located 500m from the city wall, on the left bank of the Moselle (Fig. 28).[29] Both the inscriptions and the furnishings (*triclinia* and an altar) demonstrate that the various *pagi* of the city were represented in the sanctuary of Lenus Mars and that they had access to a site dedicated to their particular god, situated on the exterior of the enclosure of the sanctuary (Fig. 29). By involving the *pagani* in the public religion of the colony, this arrangement expressed in religious terms the integration of the territorial districts into the municipal system.

[29] Gose, *Lenus Mars.*

Fig. 27. Sanctuary of the Altbachtal at Trier. Source: E. Gose, *Der gallo-römische Tempelbezirk im Altbachtal zu Trier,* 1972.

At specific times, the tutelary deities of different *pagi* (Intarabus and the Mars-Ancamna pair) were part of community ceremonies arranged for Lenus-Mars, the chief god of the city. The sacrifices suggest that the prayers were made on behalf of the imperial house, the guarantor of the municipal building, during ceremonies in which the authorities of the colony and the representatives of the *pagus* jointly participated. This collective celebration took place at the time of the staging of *ludi* in the theater, when the delegates of the *pagi* occupied seats reserved next to the city magistrate and the *flamen* of Lenus Mars. The integration of the *pagi* into the municipal structure was not the only act of the city settling the standing of a colony. The aforementioned epigraphic record of Rennes-*Condate* describes an organization of the cults of the *pagi* that corresponds exactly to the latter. Indeed, the decree of 135 CE already cited makes it possible to locate precisely the installation of bases dedicated to different *numina pagorum.* The statues of the deities were arranged in the *basilica* of the temple of Mars Mullo – that is, in an annex to the sanctuary. Just as at Trier, the *pagi* were thus represented, by means of their guardian deities, in a sanctuary of the main city that was both public and dedicated to the chief deity of the *Redones.*

The appearance of gods of the *pagus* in some of the great sanctuaries of the *civitas* capital raises the question of the religious practices of the *pagi* in the territory of cities. As we have seen, *pagus* is a Roman concept,

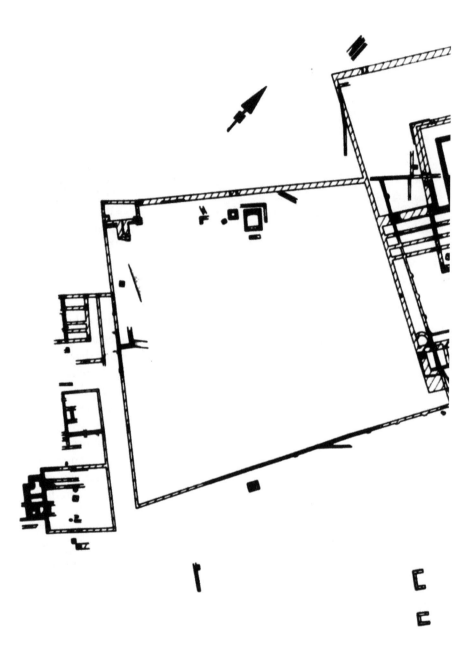

Fig. 28. Sanctuary of Lenus Mars at Trier. Source: E. Gose, *Der Tempelbezirk des Lenus Mars in Trier* (Taf. 37; Abb. 71).

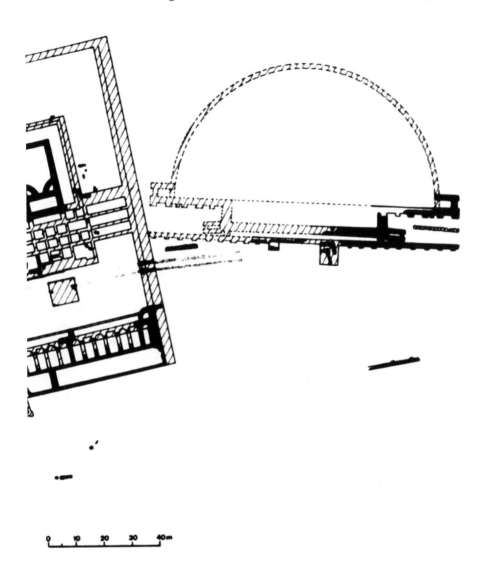

Fig. 29. Cult places of the *pagi* located on the exterior of the sanctuary of Lenus Mars at Trier. Source: E. Gose, *Der Tempelbezirk des Lenus Mars in Trier* (Abb. VII, p. 98).

denoting a territorial subdivision of the city. The meaning is thus the same in Gaul as it is in Capua or in the plain of the Po river. What Caesar calls a *pagus* in independent Gaul denotes autonomous districts, the framework of the Gallic population's social, military, and religious existence. The concentrated minting of coins that took place at the end of the Gallic epoch extended also into these sanctuaries of the *pagi,* and not only in the *oppida* of the main cities. Because these outlying districts were integrated into the construction of cities, they underwent a change both in standing and character as a result. This is why in most cases the invocation was not to an ancestral god, but rather to the *genius pagi.* The *genius pagi* is nothing other than a Roman religious idea, a way to designate the guardian deity of a territorial division of the city.

The placement of the gods of the *pagus* is another indication of change. In the *vicus* of Wederath-*Belginum* among the Treviri, the dedication of the *scaenae frons* of the theater includes the divine house in company with the god Cretus and the *genius* of the *pagus* (Fig. 30). The same scenario is found in the *vicus* of Arlon, among the Treviri, as well as in other cities: for example, Soulosse, the *vicus* of the *Mediomatrici,* and at Eu-Bois l'Abbé (possibly attached to the *Ambiani*). In each case, the dedications belong to a theater that was assuredly a site adapted for an assembly of *pagani.* And the theater was established in the *vicus,* precisely the site for a natural expression of *urbanitas.* This does not imply, however, that we should speak of sanctuaries of the *pagus* erected in the *vici* and thus characterize the *vicus* as the capital of the *pagus.* The two terms denote distinct parts of the city. The *pagus* is in fact a territory, the *vicus* an urban neighborhood association that was integrated into the territory as a community of the

Fig. 30. Inscription from Wederath mentioning the *genius pagi*. Source: H. Cüppers, *La Civilisation romaine de la Moselle à la Sarre* (Mainz, 1983), 241.

district. As a result, each community had access to its own cult places. For example, in the colony of Narbonne in Moux, overseers of a *pagus* (*magistri pagi*) authorized the construction of a temple to the local god Larraso, presumably one of the official gods of the outlying areas (*CIL* XII, 5370), outside the reach of any known vicinal structure.

The *vicani* constitute an urban community that for this reason sheltered many types of cults. The inhabitants of the *vicus* would first provide for the needs that devolve on every collective authority – namely, to celebrate a cult for the appropriate deities, those that were either part of the framework of the capital city (the *vicus* is then a district of the town) or as an urban area within the territory of the city. In Metz-*Divodurum*, capital

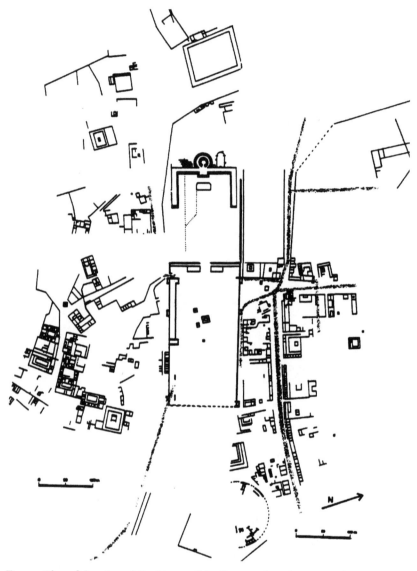

Fig. 31. Plan of the *vicus* of Vendeuvre of the Pictons: the urban area is built around a great sanctuary. Source: *Bulletin de la Société des Antiquaires de l'Ouest*, 19, 1986.

of the *Mediomatrici*, the urban districts bearing the names of districts of Rome erected monuments to Mercury, Maia, and Jupiter. In the sanctuary of the *vicani*, there was also an altar to Jupiter as well as one on the forum. Also among the *Mediomatrici*, but in this case in the territory, at Marsal, the *vicani* erected a statue of Claudius on the occasion of the *dies natalis* of Augustus, quite obviously reflecting a religious festival that had taken place at the capital, in the forum. To be sure, the pantheons of *vici* were varied, a medley of local deities and deities introduced for community needs. But certain cults, which for the most part involved Jupiter or the honors accorded the imperial house, recur in one small town to the next. In a sense, the *vicus* organized its cults as the city did, because it was a subdivision of it and because it made up one part of the *populus*. Its members were thus full-fledged citizens and the notables played roles as benefactors there, just as they did in the capital city: hence the monumental character of these urban clusters. Membership in a *vicus* was also membership in a city, as an article of the Digest also suggests (50,1,30).

One further observation pertains to the archaeological remains. The *vici* have their own individual pantheon, as did any community. In the important urban areas, these gods could be quite numerous, which accounts for the great number of so-called Gallo-Roman temples sometimes observed in the planning of these towns, as, for example, at Gué-de-Sciaux or Vendeuvre-en-Poitou among the Pictons (Fig. 31). Properly speaking, therefore, these were not, as is sometimes imagined, "urban areas intended for a religious function" in the cities of Roman Gaul, but simply areas in which the temples of patron gods of the community were established.

A *vicus* could also accommodate a city's great public sanctuary. One noteworthy example of this is the urban area of Vendeuvre-en-Poitou, situated a score of kilometers to the north of Poitiers-*Limonum*. The urban area was in fact centered on an enormous sanctuary (120m in front), extended by a wide esplanade leading to a theater. Fragments from a monumental inscription discovered in the temple inform us about the standing of this urban area; it is actually a *vicus* of the city of Pictons. The dedication of the theater, which is also partially preserved, suggests that the building had been consecrated *[usibus re]i publicae P[ictonum et vicanorum]* and financed by the city's public priest. This inscription demonstrates that the public monuments of a *vicus* – the temple, basilica, and theater – were also those of the *res publica,* the city. What we further learn from this record is that a great temple of the *civitas*, with a public cult, was erected in the *vicus,* at the time of the founding of this small town. The same scenario is attested at Ribemont-sur-Ancre, among the *Ambiani*. There appears here a great sanctuary that served as the focus of the urban complex. In Villards d'Heria, in the Jura mountains, a great sanctuary to Mars, located 80km to the south of the capital city of Besançon, served as the basis for the development of an urban area, if one can believe an inscription possibly mentioning a *vicus*.[30]

We can infer from these various examples how the ancient sanctuaries of Gallic *pagi* had been assimilated by this means into the religious domain of cities. That is to say, these Gallic sanctuaries became cult centers managed by the city or the *vicus* and its notables. This was a momentous development. It meant that starting in the middle of the first century, in many cities of Gaul, the *pagus* was no longer considered, as it once had been, a political entity in possession of a degree of autonomy. Rather, it constituted a territorial subdivision of the city. In religious terms, the cult of the tutelary god of a *pagus* henceforth figured among the principal cults of the *civitas*: the obvious examples are Mars Mullo among the *Redones*, a deity of the polis and member of the *numina pagorum*, as well as Lenus Mars among the *Treviri*. In the urban territory, the *vici*, integral parts of the *res urbana* of cities, undeniably played the leading role in the organization of cults.

As always, there were exceptions or, rather, special cases that need to be explained. Some native communal structures were in fact able to fashion different organizational schemes, as, for example, in the territory of *Carnutes*, where the only attested subdivision is the *curia*. Although a Roman word, the *curia* in this city is only a veneer covering forms of suprafamilial association of local origin (*CAG* 45, 35, and 38). The cults attested in these groupings show nevertheless that, following the lead of *vici*, the *curiae* integrated the Jupiter cult or cults associated with the imperial house. Occasionally, a few inscriptions, originating from the cities of *Convenae* (*Gomferani* of Saint-Béat), *Lemovici* (*Andecamulenses* of Rancon), and *Carnutes* (*Mocetes* of Orléans) do attest the existence of native communities practicing a cult apart from any reference to a Roman structure, a *pagus*, *vicus*, or *curia*. We can thus suppose that at the time of the composition of these texts (which as far as we can tell belong to the first century CE), some communities in the countryside had not yet satisfied the conditions necessary for assimilation into a subdivision of the city. Even so, the evolution was well underway, as is suggested by the case of the *Andecamulenses* and the *Mocetes* (*CIL* XIII, 1449 and 11280); a reference here to a public and official cult of the imperial god confirms their integration and identity within the city and the empire. The formulation of the religious language according to various subdivisions leads us into familiar territory, that of the ancient city. The evolution that we have delineated shows that the cities of Roman Gaul were gradually

---

[30] Cf. Van Andringa, *Villards d'Héria*.

organized in accordance with classical relationships, distinctive of the system of a city, and joining the town to the countryside.

CONCLUSION

This evolution underscores the advent of the "individual as citizen" in Gaul, acquired by virtue of *urbanitas* and the *Pax Romana*. It is indeed the fundamental change. In the daily life of the Gallic state, warfare was both unceasing and imminent and the bond of political behavior. It explains why so many of the great community gods of the Gallic state had been gods of war, assimilated from the very beginnings of the city to Hercules in the provinces of lower Germania, and to Mars in the provinces of Gaul.[31] If the ancient god of Gaul had lived on after a fashion, it is because he had become a peaceful god, acclimated to civic existence. In the imperial period, Lenus Mars, Mars Mullo, and Mars Cicolluis essentially proclaimed the peaceful existence of people within the framework of the city.

Civic existence was thus increasingly based on the indissoluble partnership between Augustus and the gods of the city, a connection that sanctified the foundations of municipal autonomy. For example, in the second and third centuries CE, the proliferation of religious inscriptions linking a form of the imperial cult to the cult of the gods suggests that adherence to the imperial system was unanimous. Does this then attest to a "false exuberance," a sign of a decline of paganism?[32] Assuredly, the exuberance was here a manifestation of political maturity. On 8 December 241 CE, the city of Lectoure held a celebration with a Magna Mater procession (*CIL* XIII, 511–19). It was the occasion for the *Lactorates* of Aquitania to issue a corporate restatement of their approval of the established order closely linking the fate of the *civitas* to the welfare of the emperor and the imperial household. Between 15 May and 13 June of 253, in an urban area of Trier, a benefactor marked the inauguration of a public monument with a sacrifice to the *genius* of the *vicus* and to the *numen* of Augustus, thereby reaffirming its participation in a system linking the city to the emperor and the gods. Again, in 263, the festival of Magna Mater is observed in the colony of Narbonne (*Narbo Martius*).

While these last epigraphic witnesses are from the imperial religion in Gaul, the official entrance (*adventus*) of Constantine into Autun at the very beginning of the fourth century shows that the religious landscape of cities

---

[31] Derks, *Gods, Temples.*
[32] In the words of Peter Brown, *The Making of Late Antiquity*, 76.

was again in place after the political troubles of the second half of the third century (*Pan. Lat.* VIII, 5). To be sure, the archaeological evidence from the fourth century reveals some signs of the neglect of the sanctuaries here and there. But the late witnesses from Ausone would appear to confirm observations well documented for the African provinces. In spite of the closing of temples and the gradual suppression of sacrifices, the conduct of the city, even in this period, points to the survival of religious language that was formulated in the Augustan period, four centuries before.

BIBLIOGRAPHY

Arcelin, Patrice, and Jean Louis Brunaux (dir.). "Cultes et sanctuaires en France à l'Âge du Fer." *Gallia* 60 (2003): 1–269.

Beard, Mary, John North, and Simon Price. *Religions of Rome, I. A History; II. A Sourcebook* (Cambridge, 1998).

Bögli, Hans. *Aventicum: la ville romaine et le musée.* Guides archéologiques de la Suisse 19 (Avenches, 1989).

Brouquier-Reddé, Veronique, et al., eds. *Mars en Occident: actes du colloque international "Autour d'Allonnes, les sanctuaires de Mars en Occident," Le Mans, 2003* (Rennes, 2006).

Brown, Peter. *The Making of Late Antiquity* (Cambridge, Mass., 1978).

Brunaux, Jean Louis, ed. *Les sanctuaires celtiques et leur rapport avec le monde méditerranean: actes du colloque de Saint-Riquier, 1990* (Paris, 1991).

Les religions gauloises: nouvelles approches sur les rituels celtiques de la Gaule indépendant (Paris, 2000).

Cancik, Hubert, and Jörg Rüpke, eds. *Römische Reichsreligion und Provinzialreligion* (Tübingen, 1997).

Castella, Daniel, and Marie-France Meylan Krause (dir.). *Topographie sacrée et rituels. Le cas d'Aventicum, capitale des Helvètes: actes du colloque international d'Avenches, 2–4 novembre 2006* (Bâle, 2008).

Cattelain, Pierre, and Nicolas Paridaens (dir.). *Le sanctuaire tardo-romain du "Bois des Noël" à Matagne-la-Grande* (Brussels-Treignes, 2009).

Christol, Michel. "La municipalisation de la Gaule Narbonnaise." In *Cités, Municipes, Colonies,* eds. M. Dondin-Payre and M.-Th. Raepsaet-Charlier (Paris, 1999): 1–28.

"L'épigraphie et les dieux du Plateau des Poètes à Béziers." *RANarb* 36 (2003): 411–23.

Christol, Michel, and Dominique Darde (dir.). *L'expression du pouvoir au début de l'Empire. Autour de la Maison Carrée à Nîmes* (Paris, 2009).

Cüppers, Heinz. *Die Römer in Rheinland-Pfalz* (Stuttgart, 1990).

Derks, Ton. *Gods, Temples and Ritual Practices: The Transformation of Religious Ideas and Values in Roman Gaul* (Amsterdam, 1998).

"Le grand sanctuaire de Lenus Mars à Trèves et ses dédicaces privées: une reinterpretation." In *Sanctuaires, pratiques cultuelles et territoires civiques dans l'Occident romain,* eds. M. Dondin-Payre and M.-Th. Raepsaet-Charlier (Brussels, 2006): 239–70.

Dondin-Payre, Monique, and Marie-Thérèse Raepsaet-Charlier, eds. *Cités, Municipes, Colonies: les processus de municipalisation en Gaule et en Germanie sous le Haut Empire romain* (Paris, 1999).

Dondin-Payre, Monique, and Marie-Thérèse Raepsaet-Charlier, eds. *Sanctuaires, pratiques cultuelles et territoires civiques dans l'Occident romain* (Brussels, 2006).

Drack, Walter, and Rudolf Fellmann. *Die Römer in der Schweiz* (Stuttgart, 1988).

Duval, Paul-Marie. *Les dieux de la Gaule*, 4th ed. (Paris, 1993; 1st ed. 1957).

Fauduet, Isabelle. *Les temples de tradition celtique en Gaule romaine* (Paris, 1993).

Ferdière, Alain. *Les Gaules, IIe s. av. J.-C.-Ve s. ap. J.-C.* (Paris, 2005).

Fishwick, Duncan. *The Imperial Cult in the Latin West: Studies in the Ruler Cult of the Western Provinces of the Roman Empire*. 6 vols. (Leiden, 1987–2004).

Gillet, Evelyne, Léonce Demarez, and Alain Henton. *Le sanctuaire de Blicquy "Ville d'Anderlecht"* (Namur, 2009).

Gose, Erich. *Der Tempelbezirk des Lenus Mars in Trier* (Berlin, 1955). *Der gallo-römische Tempelbezirk im Altbachtal zu Trier* (Mainz, 1972).

Goudineau, Christian. "Les villes de la paix romaine. La ville antique." In *Histoire de la France urbaine: la ville antique*. Vol. 1, dir. Georges Duby (Paris, 1980): 233–391.

Goudineau, Christian (dir.). *Religion et société en Gaule* (Paris, 2006).

Gros, Pierre. "Les étapes de l'aménagement monumental du forum, observations comparatives (Italie, Gaule Narbonnaise, Tarraconnaise)." In *La città nell'Italia settentrionale in Età romana*. Collection de l'E.F.R, 130 (Rome, 1990): 29–68.

"Les autels des *Caesares* et leur signification dans l'espace urbain des villes julioclaudiennes." In *L'espace sacrificiel dans les civilisations méditerranéennes de l'Antiquité*, eds. Roland Etienne and Marie-Thérèse Le Dinahet (Paris, 1991): 176–96.

L'architecture romaine du début du IIIe siècle av. J.-C. à la fin du Haut-Empire. 1: les monuments publics (Paris, 1996).

La Gaule Narbonaise de la conquête romaine au IIIe siècle ap. J.-C. (Paris, 2008).

Haffner, Alfred, and Siegmar von Schnurbein, eds. *Kelten, Germanen, Römer im Mittelgebirgsraum zwischen Luxemburg und Thüringen: Akten des Internationalen Kolloquiums zum DFG-Schwerpunktprogramm "Romanisierung" in Trier vom 28. bis 30. September 1998* (Bonn, 2000).

Hatt, Jean-Jacques. *Mythes et dieux de la Gaule, I: les grandes divinités masculines* (Paris, 1989).

Häussler, Ralph. "Pouvoir et religion dans un paysage 'gallo-romain.' Les cités d'Apta Iulia et Aquae Sextiae." In *Romanisation et épigraphie: études interdisciplinaires sur l'acculturation et l'identité dans l'Empire romain*, ed. Ralph Häussler (Montagnac, 2008): 155–248.

Häussler, Ralph, and Anthony C. King, eds. *Continuity and Innovation in Religion in the Roman West*. 2 vols. JRASup 67.1/67 (Portsmouth, R.I., 2007–8).

Henig, Martin. *Religion in Roman Britain* (London, 1984).

Jouin, M., and P. Méniel. "Les dépôts animaux et le fanum gallo-romains de Vertault (Côte-d'Or)." *RAE* 50 (2001): 119–216.

Jullian, Camille. *Histoire de la Gaule*. 2 vols. (Paris, 1993; 1st ed. 1920–26).

Lavagne, Henri. "Les dieux de la Gaule Narbonaise: 'romanité' et 'romanisation.'" *JSav* (1979): 160–75.

Lepetz, Sébastien, and William Van Andringa (dir.). *Archéologie du sacrifice animal en Gaule romaine. Rituels et pratiques alimentaires* (Montagnac, 2008).

Loustaud, Jean-Pierre. *Limoges antique*. TALSup 5 (Limoges, 1999).

Martin-Kilcher, Stefanie, and Regula Schatzmann, eds. *Das römische Heiligtum von Thun-Allmendingen, die Regio Lindensis und die Alpen* (Bern, 2009).

Naveau, Jacques (dir.). *Recherches sur Jublains (Mayenne) et sur la cité des Diablintes*. Documents archéologiques de l'Ouest (Rennes, 1997).

Planson, Ernest, and Colette Pommeret. *Les Bolards: le site gallo-romain et le musée de Nuits-Saint-Georges* (Paris, 1986).

Pommeret, Colette, ed. *Le sanctuaire antique des Bolards à Nuits-Saint-Georges*. RAESup 16 (Dijon, 2001).

Rives, James B. *Religion in the Roman Empire* (Malden, Mass., 2007).

Rodriguez, Laëtitia, and Robert Sablayrolles. *Les autels votifs du musée Saint-Raymond, musée des Antiques de Toulouse. Catalogue raisonné* (Toulouse, 2008).

Rosso, Emmanuelle. *L'image de l'empereur en Gaule romaine: portraits et inscriptions*. CTHS, Archéologie et Histoire de l'Art, 20 (Paris, 2006).

Scheid, John. "Sanctuaires et territoire dans la colonia Augusta Treverorum." In *Les sanctuaires celtiques*, ed. Jean-Louis Brunaux (Paris, 1991): 42–57.

"Epigraphie et sanctuaries guérisseurs en Gaule." *MEFRA* 104.1 (1992): 25–40.

"Les temples de l'Altbachtal à Trèves: un 'sanctuaire national'?" *Cahiers du Centre Glotz* 6 (1995): 227–43.

Spickermann, Wolfgang, ed. *Religion in den germanischen Provinzen Roms* (Tübingen, 2001).

Germania Superior: Religionsgeschichte des römischen Germaniens I (Tübingen, 2003).

Germania Inferior: Religionsgeschichte des römischen Germaniens II (Tübingen, 2008).

Thollard, Patrick, et al. *Bavay antique* (Paris, 1996).

Toutain, Jules. *Les cultes païens dans l'Empire romain. Première partie: les provinces latines*. 3 vols. (Paris, 1907–20).

Van Andringa, William (dir.). *Archéologie des Sanctuaires en Gaule romaine* (Saint-Etienne, 2000).

"Le vase de Sains-du-Nord et le culte de l'*imago* dans les sanctuaires gallo-romains." In *Archéologie des Sanctuaires en Gaule romaine* (Saint-Etienne, 2000): 27–44.

La religion en Gaule romaine: piété et politique (Ier-IIIe siècle ap. J.-C.) (Paris, 2002).

"L'empereur, la cité et les dieux: religion et intégration des *civitates* d'Aquitaine à l'Empire." In *L'Aquitaine et l'Hispanie septentrionale à l'époque julio-claudienne: organisation et exploitation des espaces provinciaux, Colloque Aquitania, Saintes, 2003*, Aquitania, suppl. 13 (Bordeaux, 2005): 113–18.

"Nouvelles combinaisons, nouveaux statuts: les dieux indigènes dans les panthéons des cités de Gaule romaine." In *La romanisation et la question de l'héritage celtique: actes de la table ronde de Lausanne, 17–18 juin 2005*, ed. Daniel Paunier (Glux-en-Glenne, 2006): 219–32. Translated as "New Combinations and New Statuses: The Indigenous Gods in the Pantheons of the Cities of Roman Gaul." In *Oxford Readings in Classical Studies. The Religious History of the Roman Empire*, eds. J. North and S. Price (Oxford, 2011): 109–38.

"Un grand sanctuaire de la cité des Séquanes: Villards d'Héria." In *Sanctuaires, pratiques cultuelles et territoires civiques dans l'Occident romain*, eds. M. Dondin-Payre and M.-Th. Raepsaet-Charlier (Brussels, 2006): 121–34.

"Religion and the Integration of Cities in the Empire in the Second Century AD: The Creation of a Common Religious Language." In *A Companion to Roman Religion*, ed. Jörg Rüpke (Oxford, 2007): 83–95.

ed. *Sacrifices, marché de la viande et pratiques alimentaires dans les cités du monde romain*, Food & History 5.1 (Turnhout, 2008).

Veyne, Paul. *L'Empire gréco-romain* (Paris, 2005).

Woolf, Greg. "Polis-Religion and its alternatives in the Roman provinces." In *Römische Reichsreligion und Provinzialreligion*, eds. H. Cancik and J. Rüpke (Tübingen, 1997): 72–84.

Becoming Roman: The Origin of Provincial Civilization in Gaul (Cambridge, 1998).

18

CHRISTIANITY IN GAUL

WILLIAM KLINGSHIRN

Christianity, as Sulpicius Severus observed circa 400, "was taken up rather late across the Alps" (*Chron.* 2.32.1). Indeed, it was not until the reign of Marcus Aurelius that Gallic Christians entered the literary record. Their first appearance, however, was spectacular, both literally and figuratively, for it occurred in the vivid narrative of persecution that opened book five of Eusebius's *Church History* and both followed and illustrated a prominent statement of historiographical intent. Eusebius based his account on a letter written in Greek by "the servants of Christ sojourning in Vienne and Lyon" to "the churches in Asia and Phrygia" whose purpose was to supply a biblical and theological frame for events that had occurred at Lyon circa 177.[1] Excerpted for the purpose of the narrative and significantly redacted,[2] the letter must be read with caution, but even so, like other documents used by Eusebius, it supplies credible details not available elsewhere.[3]

Despite the arrest of some Christians from Vienne (*Hist. eccl.* 5.1.13), notably "Sanctus, the deacon" (5.1.17) – probably because they were in Lyon at the time[4] – the persecution appears to have arisen from local conditions. As metropolitan capital of Gallia Lugdunensis, site of the altar of Rome and Augustus, and federal capital of the Three Gauls, Lyon was not only an obvious venue for early Christian missionary activity,[5] but also a likely place for confrontation over the state religion. Suspected of atheism and impiety (5.1.9), perhaps in connection with their refusal to participate in celebrations of imperial victory,[6]

---

[1] For doubts about the traditional date, see Barnes, "Eusebius and the Date."
[2] Löhr, "Der Brief der Gemeinden," 135–6.
[3] Barnes, *Constantine and Eusebius*, 140.
[4] Jullian, *Histoire de la Gaule*, 4:494, n. 3.
[5] Humphries, "Trading Gods," 221.
[6] Le Glay, "Le culte impérial," 20.

Christians were barred from public places (5.1.5), denounced to the local authorities (5.1.8), and brought before the governor.[7] He condemned to death those who admitted to being Christians and released those who denied it. Having so far followed the precedent set by Trajan (Pliny the Younger, *Ep.* 10.97), he then went beyond it by affirmatively searching for Christians (*Hist. eccl.* 5.1.14).[8]

In the investigation that followed, some slaves were arrested who charged that their Christian masters practiced what the letter calls "Thyestean feasts and Oedipean intercourse" (5.1.14), a learned insult that may have come from a recent speech by M. Cornelius Fronto.[9] This accusation prompted the governor to detain even those who denied being Christians and to write to the emperor for advice (5.1.44). The emperor's rescript directed the governor to put professed Christians to death, but to release those who recanted (5.1.47), thus dismissing the charges of cannibalism and incest. Some Christians had already died in prison (5.1.27), most prominently the aged Pothinus of Lyon, the first bishop known in Gaul (5.1.29–31). Of those who remained, after one last chance to recant (5.1.47), the governor ordered Roman citizens to be beheaded and noncitizens to be tortured to death at a public festival in the amphitheater. The only exception was Attalus, who despite his citizenship was sent to the amphitheater with the others (5.1.52). The bodies of the martyrs were then put on display for a period of days (5.1.59), burned, and left unburied, their ashes swept into the Rhône (5.1.62). By these acts of public humiliation, the authorities sought to refute claims of a resurrection from the dead and to demonstrate that the god and "strange new cult" for which the Christians had died were powerless to save them from death (5.1.63).

It has often been supposed, from the names of the martyrs in Eusebius's account, that the churches of Lyon and Vienne were composed largely of Greek-speaking immigrants from the East, and that they maintained close ties to their home churches, for instance in Asia and Phrygia. But this view does not seem justified by the evidence.[10] Although the presbyter Irenaeus of Lyon was probably a native of Smyrna, it is difficult to identify the birthplaces of most of the other members of the community. The only two martyrs whose origin is explicitly indicated are Attalus, from Pergamum in the province of Asia, and Alexander, a physician from Phrygia, and this

---

[7] Löhr, "Der Brief der Gemeinden," 143–4.
[8] Sordi, "La ricerca d'ufficio."
[9] Champlin, *Fronto*, 64–6.
[10] Bowersock, "Les églises de Lyon et de Vienne."

information may have been supplied only because it was unusual.[11] The rest of the martyrs, whether their names were Greek (Alcibiades), Latin (Sanctus, Maturus), or both (Vettius Epagathus), were likely natives of Gaul. Their status varied. Some were free; others, like Vettius Epagathus, were probably freed;[12] and still others, such as Biblis, Ponticus, and Blandina, were slaves. This is a striking feature of the letter, at least part of whose appeal for Eusebius was precisely its demonstration that earthly identity did not matter to the power of Christ, who suffered equally in the male body of the deacon Sanctus (5.1.20–4, 37–9) and in the female body of the slave Blandina (5.1.17–19, 40–2, 53–6). Indeed, her torture in the shape of a cross made identification with Christ absolutely explicit, "in order to persuade believers in him that everyone who suffers for the glory of Christ has eternal fellowship with the living God" (5.1.41).[13] All Christians must have sought such fellowship, but to judge from the letter's concern with the lapsed (5.1.11–12, 25–6, 32–5, 45–6, 48) and especially how to treat them afterward (5.2.6–8), many found vicarious suffering through the martyrs preferable to their own.

With the death of Pothinus and the succession of Irenaeus as bishop of Lyon, the history of Christianity in Gaul enters a much more poorly documented phase. Between the end of Marcus Aurelius's reign in 180 and the beginning of Constantine's in 306, the Christians of Gaul are nearly invisible. Irenaeus's writings, although illuminating on a wide range of subjects, contain virtually no information about the city and region over which he presided, described by Eusebius as "the dioceses of Gaul" (5.23.4). Instead, what intermittently surfaces during this period are links between the bishops of Lyon and their colleagues abroad. Irenaeus, for instance, had been absent from Lyon during the persecution because he was visiting Bishop Eleutherus of Rome (5.4.1–2). Later he corresponded with Eleutherus's successor Victor and other bishops over the proper date of Easter (5.24.11–18). In the middle of the next century, Bishop Faustinus of Lyon complained to Cyprian of Carthage that Bishop Marcianus of Arles had associated himself with the rigorist theologian Novatian (Cyprian, *Ep.* 68). Cyprian's assertion that this association was opposed by other bishops in Gaul makes it clear that there were other bishops by this point, and that it was thought important that they share the same beliefs about church order, but the location of their sees is unknown.

---

[11] Wierschowski, "Der Lyoner Märtyrer Vettius Epagathus," 442.

[12] Ibid., 448–51.

[13] The translation and interpretation are based on Goodine and Mitchell, "The Persuasiveness of a Woman."

In the dispute over Easter, Irenaeus had argued that the bishop of Rome should tolerate and not excommunicate the bishops of Asia for celebrating Easter on a different day from that in other regions (Eusebius, *Hist. eccl.* 5.24.13). There is perhaps no better index of how much had changed by the reign of Constantine than the first canon of the first council held in Gaul, which ruled that Easter should be celebrated "by us on one day and at one time throughout the whole world" (CCL 148:9). Constantine had convened this council at Arles in August 314, not even two years after his victory over Maxentius, to resolve the Donatist controversy (Eusebius, *Hist. eccl.* 10.5.21–4). Although its efforts in that regard were unsuccessful, the council did pass several measures of immediate interest to the emperor. Its decision on Easter advanced his Christian, ecumenical, and anti-Jewish priorities,[14] and its third canon, by excommunicating "those who laid down their weapons in peace" (probably deserters[15]), brought church teaching in line with military realities or, from a civilian perspective, security needs.[16] Canons 7 and 8 likewise reflected the new political situation. They permitted Christian governors and other office-holders to remain in the church under the supervision of the local bishop, instead of recusing themselves from church membership during their term in office, as canon 56 of the Spanish Council of Elvira (ca.300) required.[17] The remaining canons, in addition to regulating the movements, ambitions, and activities of deacons, priests, and bishops, treated numerous lay matters. Unseemly employment – chariot racing and acting – was banned for Christians (can. 4, 5), and Christian girls (*puellae fideles*) who married pagans (*gentiles*) were temporarily excommunicated (can. 12). Christian men were told that they could not remarry if they discovered their wives to be adulterers (can. 11). Nonbelievers who were ill were permitted to be admitted to the church by a laying on of hands rather than a more formal entry into the catechumenate (can. 6), and apostate Christians who became ill were required to perform penance before being readmitted (can. 22).

Though in no way comprehensive or definitive, this assortment of regulations does suggest what kinds of membership problems and moral challenges the church in Gaul faced in the early fourth century, not only in the mind of the emperor, but also for the thirty-three bishops and fifty other clerics who attended the council and subscribed to its resolutions.

---

[14] Eusebius, *Vit. Const.* 3.17–20, with the commentary in Cameron and Hall, eds., Eusebius, *Life of Constantine*, 268–72.
[15] Gaudemet, *Conciles gaulois du IVe siècle*, 48, n. 1.
[16] Mehat, "Le concile d'Arles (314)."
[17] *Concilios visigóticos*, ed. Vives, 11.

With twelve bishops, four priests, twelve deacons, six exorcists, and one lector representing sixteen dioceses, Gaul supplied over a third of the delegates, and we can see in their record of attendance an emerging pattern of Christian geography. The oldest centers of Christianity were represented (Lyon, Vienne, Arles), as was Autun, where there may also have been a substantial Christian community in the third century.[18] Also attending were bishops and clergy from smaller dioceses close to Arles (Marseille, Vaison, Orange, Nice, Apt, Javols), as well as from provincial capitals located at some distance: Eauze and Bordeaux in the southwest, and Cologne, Trier, Reims, and Rouen in the north. Where Christianity was not yet much in evidence, at least to judge by the cities represented at the council, was along the upper Rhine, in the Alpine regions, and especially in central Gaul, west of the Rhône and south of the Seine. This pattern changed over time as congregations became large enough to require and recruit a bishop. By the late fourth century, when imperial officials drew up the detailed list of provinces and city-districts known as the *Notitia Galliarum*,[19] it has been estimated that between 70 and 80 of the 113 cities on the list probably had bishops.[20]

It was also at the same time and in part for the same reasons that Christianity in Gaul began to be monumentalized by an imperial architecture suitable to its new public status.[21] This can first be seen in the imperial capital of Trier, where excavations conducted in the present church of St. Mary, adjoining the cathedral, have revealed a three-aisled basilica (I) dated by coin finds to the 320s.[22] Measuring 24.6 by 27.5m and capable of accommodating hundreds of worshippers, it was almost certainly the original cathedral church of Trier. The date indicates that it was built under Bishop Agritius, who had represented Trier at the council of Arles. In the 330s and 340s, three additional basilicas (II, III, and IV) were joined to this structure, probably by Bishop Maximinus, Agritius's successor. At the center of the enormous H-shaped complex stood a baptistery. It would have been this (unfinished) construction project that Bishop Athanasius of Alexandria saw in Trier, probably during his exile there from 335 to 337 (*Apol. Const.* 15).

But churches in the fourth century were more than a practical necessity for Christian communities growing in size and an imperial government

[18] Young, "Sacred Topography," 169–72.
[19] Harries, "Church and State."
[20] Pietri, "Les grandes églises missionnaires," 834, which counts 114 cities. Ammianus Marcellinus surveys the geography of Gaul at this period (*Res gestae* 15.10–11).
[21] Krautheimer, *Early Christian and Byzantine Architecture*, 39–41.
[22] Weber, "Neue Forschungen," 227–8.

determined to express its new religious identity through architecture. They were also perceived as places of holiness and power. This can be illustrated, for Trier, by a collection of 136 graffiti written at two different periods in the fourth century. Located in basilica II, east of basilica I, these inscriptions were scratched into two walls near the altar.[23] Many are too fragmentary to read, but some are relatively complete, such as, from the second quarter of the fourth century, "Verna, may you live in Christ" (*RICG* I.235e), and from the third quarter of the fourth century, "Martius, may you live in God, Christ, always" (*RICG* I.236f).

On one level, such inscriptions serve as a tangible expression of basic Christian beliefs: the divinity of Christ, the efficacy of prayer, and the promise of eternal life.[24] But in their number, location, and variety they also testify to the holiness of the site itself. By placing the believer in proximity to this holiness, the personal names they contain raise expectations of special access to divine power. Parallels to similar graffiti at St. Peter's in Rome have raised the suggestion that this spot in Trier was made holy by relics – of a martyr perhaps or even the Cross.[25] But it is also possible – indeed more likely – that the altar itself was the locus of the holy, the place where Christ's sacrifice was performed over and over again for the faithful. That we cannot answer this question satisfactorily is in part due to a lack of evidence, but more importantly to a debate in the fourth century itself about where holiness was located and how the individual Christian could and should partake in its power. Thoroughly bound up in this question was the continuity of the church with its pre-Constantinian past, especially its martyrs,[26] as well as the continuity of pre-Christian ideas about the holiness of place.[27]

Before the end of the fourth century, Christian pilgrimage in Gaul meant pilgrimage somewhere else, since there were no Christian pilgrimage sites in Gaul. Late in the reign of Constantine an anonymous author from Bordeaux traveled through southern Gaul to Constantinople by way of Milan, and then spent the second half of the year 333 on a pilgrimage to the Holy Land before returning to Milan by way of Rome. The pilgrim's account of the journey is fascinating from many points of view, especially in its Constantinian context,[28] but what is noteworthy from

---

[23] Binsfeld, "Graffiti der frühchristlichen Kirchenanlage," 241.
[24] Ibid., 244.
[25] Ibid., 247–52.
[26] Markus, "How on Earth."
[27] MacCormack, "*Loca Sancta.*"
[28] Elsner, "*Itinerarium Burdigalense.*"

a Gallic perspective is its keen interest in the pools, baths, and rivers of Palestine where healing, miracles, and baptism took place. Gaul too had its sacred waters, where healing cults had long flourished,[29] and the Bordeaux pilgrim's observations seem to hint at a new Christian logic for that ancient practice.

But at the same time theological controversy and the cessation of martyrdom under Constantine were helping to shape and support a Christian logic for two new avenues of holiness that would eventually lead to pilgrimage in Gaul itself. With the rise of monasticism and the cult of the saints, Christians could draw close to the holiness of an ascetic way of life and to the power contained in relics of "the very special dead."[30]

We can see hints of both movements in Gaul as early as the career of Hilary, a well-educated local aristocrat and the first known bishop of Poitiers (ca.350–67). Best known for his theological and exegetical writings, his opposition to Arianism, and his exile to Phrygia by Constantius II, Hilary was the first Latin author in Gaul to make use of the example of the martyrs for theological and polemical ends, especially against opponents who did not share his new-found support for the Council of Nicaea.[31] Hilary was also invoked by Sulpicius Severus as an important mentor for Martin, a discharged Roman soldier from Pannonia with awesome healing powers and a yearning for the monastic life. Ordained an exorcist by Hilary, Martin lived as a monk for several years on the outskirts of Poitiers before being elected bishop of nearby Tours in circa 371 against significant episcopal opposition.[32] There, he established himself as an advocate both of monasticism and of veneration for saints' relics.[33] While at Tours, Martin maintained his reputation as a holy man, performing so many miracles that when he died, according to Gregory of Tours, his body was claimed by the Christians of Poitiers and Tours alike (*Hist.* 1.48). The latter won, and his burial place west of the city walls reportedly became the focal point for further miracles (*Hist.* 2.14).

There were not many men in Gaul like Martin, however, and the future of the cult of the saints in the region lay not in the actual tombs of healing saints, confessors, or martyrs, but in small pieces of their bodies or clothing transmitted by reputable authorities with appropriate ceremonies and narratives of power. In 386, when Bishop Ambrose of Milan discovered

[29] See Rousselle, *Croire et guérir*, esp. 31–6, 65–73.
[30] Brown, *Cult of the Saints*, ch. 4.
[31] Ibid., 56–8.
[32] Sulpicius Severus, *VMartini*; Fontaine, "Hilaire et Martin."
[33] Rousselle, *Croire et guérir*, 172–4.

the bodies of the martyrs Gervasius and Protasius, he sent fragments to a number of prominent Gallic Christians, including Martin of Tours, Victricius, bishop of Rouen, and Paulinus of Bordeaux, the future bishop of Nola. With the right kind of promotion, such relics, like the buried bodies of martyrs or holy men, could transform any place into a venue for miracles. In the earliest sermon known in Gaul, delivered circa 396,[34] Victricius explains how. "If the hem of the Savior's garment cured when lightly touched (Luke 8:42–48), it is beyond doubt that the dwelling places of martyrdom (*domicilia passionum*) will cure when we take them in our arms."[35] Yet it was not just anywhere that Christians could encounter these holy objects. In a sign of what was to come, Victricius built a church for his relics: "Rightly, dearest brothers, did I, a zealous builder, seize a place for the basilica. The arrival of the saints excuses my eagerness. They themselves ... ordered a court to be prepared for them."[36]

The very existence of this sermon alerts us to the controversy raised by Victricius's actions. At issue was not only the illegal disinterment and dismemberment of corpses,[37] but also the profound theological problem of endowing bodies other than Christ's with divine power. In this debate, as David Hunter has argued, the majority of Gallic clergy may have agreed with the criticisms of the priest Vigilantius of Calagurris. Once a close associate of Paulinus of Nola and Sulpicius Severus, this cleric from a small Gallic town near the Spanish border held that the veneration of relics was "almost a ritual of pagans" (*prope ritum gentilium*, Jerome, *Vigil.* 4) and that instead of being scattered everywhere "the souls of the apostles and martyrs" were with God and unable to leave their tombs and be present where they wished (*Vigil.* 6). Easter, he argued, should be the only time when vigils and the Alleluia were permitted, not feasts of the saints (*Vigil.* 1, 9). For what power could the light of candles have in comparison with the splendid majesty of the Lamb of God? (*Vigil.* 4).

Closely related to Vigilantius's opposition to the cult of relics was his criticism of a special holiness for asceticism and monasticism. According to Jerome, Vigilantius argued that it was wrong for monks to withdraw into solitude, for women to shun marriage and children, and for clergy to be celibate, or if married to be required to live apart from their wives after ordination (*Vigil.* 2, 15). What was at issue in these interlocking protests was above all the means of access to divine power. Did it emanate

---

[34] Hunter, "Vigilantius of Calagurris," 422.
[35] *De laude sanctorum* 2, trans. Clark, 378.
[36] *De laude sanctorum* 12, trans. Clark, 399.
[37] For a survey of the laws, see Rebillard, "Violations de sépulture."

exclusively from Christ – freely available to Christians everywhere and at any time – or was it, like secular power, achieved through a combination of hard work and the cultivation of patrons with special access, "friends" not of the emperor, but of God?

There is, as it happens, a Gallic setting for just this concept of the ascetic life, which is relevant whether fictional or not. In his *Confessions*, Augustine relates a story told to him by a high-ranking government official (*Conf.* 8.6.15, trans. Chadwick). When stationed in Trier, "he and three of his colleagues" were at leisure one day while the emperor attended games in the circus. Two of them wandered "into the gardens adjacent to the city wall," probably on the eastern side of the city near the circus. There they discovered the house, or small estate, (*casa*) of some monks. The location of the house in gardens, its ease of discovery, and the fact that its inhabitants were described not as "poor," but as "poor in spirit," suggest an aristocratic milieu. After discovering and reading Athanasius's *Life of Antony* in the house, one of the men began to question his pursuit of a secular career:

> Can we hope for any higher office in the palace than to be Friends of the Emperor? And in that position what is not fragile and full of dangers? How many hazards must one risk to attain to a position of even greater danger? And when will we arrive there? Whereas, if I wish to become God's friend, in an instant I may become that now.

This story has an important role to play in the plot of the *Confessions*, but it also nicely demonstrates the nexus between patronage and saintliness in the late fourth century. At the same time, the status of the participants shows how asceticism, like the cult of the saints, flourished at the highest levels of the Gallic aristocracy. The most spectacular example remains Meropius Pontius Paulinus. Educated at Bordeaux by the grammarian, rhetor, and poet Ausonius, this Roman senator, suffect consul, and governor of Campania renounced his wealth and career, and in 395 moved to Nola (Campania) with his Spanish wife Therasia, where he devoted the rest of his life to asceticism, the local cult of St. Felix, and service to the church.[38] His friend Sulpicius Severus led a similarly ascetic lifestyle on his estate at Primuliacum in southwestern Gaul, where he made Martin his local saint.[39]

A more dangerous ascetic path was taken by followers of the Spanish holy man Priscillian. His emphasis on "moral regeneration emphasizing

---

[38] Trout, *Paulinus of Nola*, is now the standard study.
[39] Stancliffe, *St. Martin and His Hagiographer*.

homogeneity and equality"[40] and promotion of extensive fasting, praying, and reading attracted significant support from pious clergy and laity, but also fierce opposition from bishops who felt their authority challenged.[41] Attacked by twelve bishops at the council of Saragossa in 380 and subsequently consecrated bishop of Avila by two of his episcopal supporters, Priscillian was banished by the emperor Gratian in 381. Efforts to vindicate his name and teachings culminated in an appeal to Magnus Maximus, who had become western emperor in 383 after overthrowing Gratian. Convicted not of heresy (a church matter) but of magic (an imperial crime), Priscillian was put to death in circa 386 (Sulp. Sev. *Chron.* 2.51.3), along with several clerical and lay supporters, including Euchrotia, the widow of a prominent rhetor of Bordeaux (Ausonius, *Prof. Burd.* 5), and the Spanish poet Latronianus (Jerome, *De vir. ill.* 122).

It was a chilling moment in the history of Gallic Christianity, with long repercussions in ascetic aristocratic circles. But most aristocrats found less demanding ways to take advantage of the power of a holy man. One woman from Vienne, for example, was not only baptized by St. Martin, but received further privileges in death. In an early example of inhumation *ad sanctos* in Gaul, Foedula was buried near the relics of Gervasius and Protasius outside the city walls of the city,[42] as her metrical epitaph records: "But now, the martyrs having granted her a fitting place, she venerates saint Gervasius and Protasius.... She has borne witness, who lies associated with the saints" (*RICG* 15.39).

Long before this kind of "privileged inhumation"[43] caught on more widely, in the later fifth and sixth centuries, the wealthiest aristocrats of southern Gaul could afford another medium of saintly association in death: carved marble sarcophagi, occasionally made locally but more often imported from Rome.[44] Vividly illustrated with scenes from Jewish and Christian history, these "prayers in stone"[45] were meant to introduce the deceased, above all, to God, in the company of those already saved.[46]

On one of three sarcophagi found together in Arles in 1974, Marcia Romania Celsa, wife of Flavius Januarinus, ordinary consul of the year

[40] Van Dam, *Leadership and Community*, 99.
[41] See further Chadwick, *Priscillian of Avila*, and Burrus, *The Making of a Heretic*.
[42] *Topographie chrétienne des cités de la Gaule* 3:27.
[43] Duval and Picard, eds., *L'Inhumation privilégiée*.
[44] Immerzeel and Jongste, "Les ateliers de sarcophages," 234–5.
[45] The phrase was originally used in a funerary context: Jane Taylor, "The Squire's Pew" (1816), line 48, ed. Paula R. Feldman, *British Women Poets of the Romantic Era: An Anthology* (Baltimore/London, 1997), 746.
[46] Caillet, "Le message de la sculpture funéraire."

328, is depicted praying in the center, flanked on her right by scenes from the life of Peter and on her left by three miracles of Christ, including the raising of Lazarus.[47] Two scenes on the cover represent the proper worship of the one God by groups of three: on the left the three men in the fiery furnace, together with the angel who rescued them (Dan. 3:25), and on the right the three wise men bearing gifts (Matt. 2:11). Inside the sarcophagus was found the skeleton of a woman aged about forty years – the epitaph lists her age as thirty-eight – whose wrists and hands had been surgically removed, perhaps to be placed in a cenotaph.[48] The excavation report mentions no grave goods, but does note a rectangular opening in the undecorated side of the sarcophagus.[49] The same feature appears on a second sarcophagus from the site; it held the body of a woman about twenty-five years old and a newborn child. The openings may have been used to introduce substances into the tomb, such as perfume[50] or libations,[51] as in traditional burial practice, but their exact function remains unknown.[52] The most elaborately decorated sarcophagus found on the site, dated circa 330/40, depicts an aristocratic couple in the center surrounded by biblical scenes of, among other themes, marriage and children (Fig. 32). Inside were found the remains of a man fifty to sixty years old and of a woman about fifty.[53] Their burial together and the iconography by which they chose to be remembered recalls a similar celebration of conjugality in the *Laudes Domini*, the earliest Christian Latin poem from Gaul.[54] Dating between 317 and 326, this anonymous work commemorates a miracle that took place at Autun when a pious Christian couple was reunited at death. The wife, who had died first, was buried in their common tomb, and when it was reopened at her husband's death she was found to have extended her left hand to welcome him "in a gesture of living love" (line 31). The poem then goes on to celebrate Christ's power and good gifts to humans and ends with a prayer for Constantine and his dynasty.

During the fourth century, at the same time as aristocrats in Trier, Arles, and other Gallic cities were publicly converting to Constantine's religion, in higher proportions than in Italy,[55] Christianity was still far

---

[47] Rouqette, "Trois nouveaux sarcophages," 257–63.
[48] Griesheimer, "Le sarcophage de Marcia Romania Celsa," 170.
[49] Rouqette, "Trois nouveaux sarcophages," 261.
[50] Ibid., 261.
[51] Griesheimer, "Le sarcophage de Marcia Romania Celsa," 170.
[52] Rouquette, "Sarcophage de Marcia Romania Celsa."
[53] Rouqette, "Trois nouveaux sarcophages," 265–73.
[54] Opelt, "Das Carmen *De Laudibus Domini*," 159.
[55] Salzman, *The Making of a Christian Aristocracy*, 86–90.

Fig. 32. Sarcophagus of the Spouses (Sarcophagus of the Trinity). Second quarter of the fourth century CE. Marble. Arles, Musée de l'Arles antique. Photo: Musée départemental Arles antique. Cl. M. Lacanaud.

from commanding the allegiance of the majority of the population. Jews certainly lived in Gaul at this time, especially at Narbonne, Arles, and Marseille, but the evidence for other areas is sparse and difficult to evaluate.[56] Worshippers of Mithras can be identified throughout the century by coin deposits at *mithraea* in frontier zones and rural areas.[57] In cities, traditional Gallo-Roman sanctuaries continued to be attended for much of the fourth century, even when it was no longer legal for animal sacrifice to be conducted there. The massive temple complex of the Altbachtal at Trier, for example, remained active until the last quarter of the fourth century when it was "deliberately destroyed," presumably under Gratian (r.375–83).[58] Sacred sites in the countryside received worshippers even longer, as coin evidence demonstrates.[59] This may have been especially true for shrines located at sacred springs, because of their healing functions,[60] but it also applied to other cult places as well, and not only in central and northern Gaul, but in southern Gaul as well. The sanctuary of Chastelard de Lardiers, excavated between 1961 and 1967, was built in the middle of

[56] Toch, "Jews in Europe," 552–3; Blumenkranz, "Premières implantations de Juifs."
[57] Sauer, *The End of Paganism*, with Gordon, "The End of Mithraism."
[58] Wightman, *Roman Trier*, 229.
[59] Rousselle, *Croire et guérir*, esp. 31–75.
[60] Ibid., 72–3.

the first century CE on the foundations of an abandoned oppidum in the foothills of Mt. Lure (Alpes-de-Haute-Provence), and received ex-votos and coins until the end of the fourth century.[61] About 35km to the southwest, at Lioux on the southern slope of the Vaucluse mountains, a sanctuary of Mars was excavated between 1983 and 1985. It consisted of four small buildings dating to the first century CE and surrounded by a wall, and an additional building outside the wall that was constructed at the beginning of the fourth century. The 317 coins found inside date mainly from the fourth century and suggest that the sanctuary was used until the early fifth century.[62]

The persistence of traditional practices is also suggested by literary evidence. Martin of Tours was famously depicted by his hagiographer in confrontations with local priests, engaged in the violent destruction of temples, idols, and even a tree – most sacred of all – not only in the vicinity of Tours but at Autun as well (Sulpicius Severus, *VMartini* 12–15). That these militant tactics, backed up by the power of Christ, were not matched by other Gallic bishops is due not only to the unusual character of Martin's authority,[63] but also to the low level of active interest in conversion on the part of the clergy. Indeed, Martin's fellow bishops appear to have had their hands full eliminating the last traces of "paganism" from their own congregations. In an early example of what would prove to be a very long series of such pronouncements, the twenty-one bishops who attended the council of Valence in 374 (not including Martin) ordered a lifetime of penance for "people who after the one holy bath [of baptism] were stained either with the profane sacrifices of demons or sinful washing" (can. 3). The *incesta lavatio* of which the bishops spoke could have meant the use of water at Gallic sanctuaries for purification or for healing; the two uses were quite distinct.[64] Aline Rousselle has cited this canon as evidence of the continuing popularity of healing waters among Christians,[65] for which we may also attest the observations of the Bordeaux pilgrim, but the pointed reference to the purification of baptism (also noted by Rousselle) suggests that the bishops clearly had in mind this (far more common[66]) function as well.

---

[61] Barruol, "Lardiers."
[62] Bellet and Borgard, "Plan: Le sanctuaire gallo-romain de Verjusclas," 120–1.
[63] Van Dam, *Leadership and Community*, 132.
[64] Van Andringa, *La religion en Gaule*, 112–14.
[65] Rousselle, *Croire et guérir*, 185.
[66] Derks, *Gods, Temples, and Ritual Practices*, 196–8.

In fact, the lines of division between what was "pagan" and what was "Christian" were very hard to draw, in Gaul or anywhere else, and most Christians, it seems, had no interest in rejecting the large body of customary practices and beliefs that assisted and guided their everyday lives. This is well illustrated by the treatise *De medicamentis* ("Prescriptions") written by the Christian aristocrat Marcellus, one of Theodosius's Gallic supporters and his master of offices in 394/5.[67] Drawing upon earlier medical writers and physicians (including the father of Ausonius) and upon information gathered, apparently firsthand, "from peasants and common people" (pref. 2), Marcellus's book offers remedies for a wide variety of ailments, from headaches (chapter 1) to the gout (chapter 36). Prescriptions generally consist of a list of ingredients, instructions for their preparation, and, in many cases, Greek, Latin, or Gaulish incantations to be recited when ingredients were collected or used, or written on amulets to be worn by the patient. Only one of his prescriptions invokes the name of Christ – an interpolation, to judge by its interruption of the meter[68] – but the remedy is in other respects typical:

Remedy for sciatica. Gather the herb called "British" [probably a variety of sorrel[69]] on the day of Jupiter when the moon is waning and the tide is receding. Dry it and put it away because it does not appear in winter, though it also works when green. Grind it with three grains of salt and five or seven grains of pepper, and add both a large full spoon of honey and a good draft of wine, and if you want you can pour in a little warm water, and in this way administer it as a drink. But while you are holding it, before you gather this herb, you should chant three times as follows:

I hold the earth, I collect the herb, in the name of Christ.

May it benefit [the ailment] for which I gather you.

With your thumb and ring finger (*medicinalibus digitis*) you should cut it without iron or pull it out (Marcellus, *De medicamentis* 25.13, following the German translation of Kollesch and Nickel).

Just as traditional medications, traditionally collected and used, remained important to Gallic Christians like Marcellus, so did other means of controlling for life's uncertainties. It was probably in the fourth century that a Latin divinatory text entitled *The Lots of Saint Gall* (named after the monastery where the manuscript now resides) began to circulate in Gaul with

[67] For his career, see Matthews, "Gallic Supporters of Theodosius," 1083–7.
[68] Zander, *Versus italici antiqui*, 47.
[69] For its name and identity, see Fitzpatrick, "*Ex Radice Britanica*."

definite Christian elements. Loosely adapted from a Greek text of the first or second century CE, this manual provided users with answers to questions such as whether to take on a business partner or whether a fugitive slave would be discovered.[70] Another Latin divinatory text available in the late fourth or early fifth century, and also based on an earlier Greek version, was *The Lots of the Saints*, condemned circa 465 at the Council of Vannes (CCL 148:156).[71] It provided reassuring but generally vague answers, such as "God will help you in what you desire; ask God, and you will quickly arrive at what you desire."[72] For these to work effectively, a diviner was probably required.

Christians who wanted to supplement a knowledge of unseen things with concrete protection against danger could wear or carry a variety of objects. Fourth-century examples from Trier include rings, brooches, fibulae, lamps, and gaming pieces (or counters) decorated with crosses or Christograms.[73] On one small bronze sculpture in Trier, a boy wears a Chi-Rho as his *bulla* (Fig. 33).[74] For those who wanted to take more aggressive measures, magical texts were an option, such as the lead *defixio* written against thieves in the fourth or fifth century and found at Dax in 1976,[75] or the spells found in excavations of the amphitheater in Trier in 1908.[76] Although these magical objects give no indication of religious identity, it would be surprising if none of them was used by a Christian.

During the fourth century, Gaul enjoyed a relatively high degree of imperial attention. Constantius I, Constantine, Constantine II, Constans, Julian, Valentinian I, and Gratian all spent time in the region, as did Magnus Maximus before his defeat by Theodosius at Aquileia in 388, and Valentinian II before his death at Vienne in 392. Trier remained both an imperial capital and the headquarters of the praetorian prefecture, and by its proximity to the Rhine frontier ensured Roman military control of the northern provinces.[77] All that changed with the death of Theodosius in 395. The offices of the praetorian prefect were moved to Arles in 395 or a few years later (the exact date is unknown), and western emperors ruled from Milan, and later Ravenna. Without a significant imperial presence, Gaul was subject to usurpation and invasion, and both occurred in the first

---

[70] Klingshirn, "Christian Divination in Late Roman Gaul."
[71] Klingshirn, "Defining the *Sortes Sanctorum*."
[72] *Sortes Sanctorum* 6.6.4, eds. Montero Cartelle and Alonso Guardo, 70.
[73] Förster, "Katalog der frühchristlichen Abteilung," 77–83 (cat. nos. 59–64).
[74] Ibid., 76 (cat. no. 58).
[75] Marco Simón, Velázquez, "Una nueva defixio."
[76] Schwinden, "Verfluchungstäfelchen aus dem Amphitheater."
[77] Wightman, *Gallia Belgica*, 211–17.

┣━━━┿━━━┿━━━┿━━━┫ cm

Fig. 33. Boy wearing a Christian *bulla*. Fourth century CE. Bronze. Trier, Rheinisches Landesmuseum. C. 4685. Photo: Rheinisches Landesmuseum Trier.

decade of the fifth century.[78] Although the situation was stabilized by 418, with arrangements that included the permanent settlement of the Goths in Aquitaine, it was only southern and southeastern Gaul that remained firmly under imperial control. Territories north of the Loire, although

[78] Drinkwater, "The Usurpers."

notionally part of the empire and still subject to Roman military initiatives, for the most part reverted to control by local aristocrats and barbarian warlords.[79]

In this increasingly decentralized environment, even in areas still under
imperial control, it was most often bishops who were in the best position
to speak and act for their cities. Predominantly drawn from aristocratic
families, they acted as local patrons for their communities, much as their
ancestors had done. They put their wealth to civic use, intervened with
imperial officials, and mobilized help in times of crisis. At the same time,
as religious officials, bishops also offered access to divine power and a theological reinforcement of the moral and social order. Their claims to authority – subject to challenge at any time – were strengthened by alliances
with fellow bishops and clergy; networks of aristocratic support; displays
of literary and rhetorical prowess; and, in Gaul particularly, the acquisition
of ascetic credentials at illustrious monasteries, for instance Martin's foundation at Tours, Honoratus's at Lérins, or Cassian's at Marseille.[80]

An illuminating example is Rusticus, bishop of Narbonne from 427 to
circa 460, who celebrated his career and accomplishments on an inscription for the cathedral he rebuilt in the city.[81] The son of one bishop and
nephew of another (a not uncommon episcopal genealogy in Gaul),
Rusticus had spent time in an unnamed monastery in Marseille (perhaps
Cassian's) before becoming a bishop himself. There he was in good company: his fellow priest and friend in the monastery was Venerius, who later
became bishop of Marseille. Dated 29 November 445, Rusticus's inscription records the stages of reconstruction and the names of the priest, deacon, and subdeacon who managed the work. It also specifies the generous
donors who made the work possible, including Venerius of Marseille, who
contributed one hundred *solidi* (or more – the exact number is uncertain),
and Marcellus, praetorian prefect of Gaul, who contributed 2,100 *solidi*.

At the same time as it illustrates the possibilities of episcopal
self-promotion, Rusticus's inscription also serves as a reminder that,
despite their prominence in the literary and material record, bishops were
not the only Christians who counted in fifth-century Gaul. The rebuilding
of the church in Narbonne clearly required a joint effort, not unrelated
to the consensus of clergy and laity that (ideally at least) elected a bishop
to his lifetime monarchy in the first place and gave him the continuing

---

[79] Halsall, *Settlement and Social Organization*, 7–8.
[80] Mathisen, *Ecclesiastical Factionalism*, offers an excellent analysis of the political aspects. On the role
that asceticism itself played, Rousseau, *Ascetics, Authority and the Church*, remains fundamental.
[81] Marrou, "Le dossier."

capacity to act in the best interests of his city. It is no accident that the clearest expression of this idea occurs in the reform proposal known as the *Ancient Regulations of the Church.* "When having been examined in these [doctrinal] matters he has been discovered fully prepared, then by the consent of the clergy and laity ... let him be ordained bishop. When he has taken up the episcopacy in the name of Christ, let him attend not to his own pleasure or motives but to these regulations of the Fathers" (*Statuta ecclesiae antiqua*, pref., CCL 148:166). Compiled after 475 by an ascetic priest in southern Gaul, probably Gennadius of Marseille,[82] this collection of 102 canons vigorously argues, as do the writings of numerous other fifth-century Gallic Christians, for the vital role of priests, monks, and learned laymen in the definition of true belief and correct practice.[83]

Indeed, an even wider participation was required in the main enterprise of the Gallic church: the erection of a religious infrastructure of protection against the spiritual (and therefore root) causes of disorder. For it was not secular officials, aristocrats, and local clergy, but rather ordinary men and women who collaborated most fully in the ritual activity that made sacred places sacred, holy people holy, and released the divine blessings that healed and saved. As the dangers were spiritual, so too were the weapons. In the words of an anonymous fifth-century preacher, "This man fights by vows, that one by fasts; this one by prayers and heavenly desires, that one by vigils and labors" (Eusebius Gallicanus, *Hom.* 54.6, CCL 101A:632).[84]

For their part, in harnessing the piety of individual Christians, the bishops of Gaul took three main steps. They built up the religious landscape with saints' shrines,[85] baptisteries,[86] and churches;[87] they created and systematized the rituals held in these places; and they began to assemble a professional clergy to operate them. The initiatives of Perpetuus of Tours (458/9–88/9) can serve as an example. As metropolitan of an ecclesiastical province located in one of the most troubled regions in Gaul, Perpetuus built six parish churches and a new basilica over Martin's tomb. He created a schedule of fasts to be observed by all, and vigils to be celebrated on different feast days at the cathedral, baptistery, and churches of the apostles and

---

[82] Munier, *Les Statuta Ecclesiae Antiqua*, 242.
[83] For the entire context of Christian Latin writing in fifth-century Gaul, see above all Vessey, "Peregrinus Against the Heretics," and idem, "The *Epistula Rustici.*"
[84] On this sermon and the role of communal asceticism in spiritual protection, see Bailey, "Monks and Lay Communities," 325.
[85] Beaujard, *Le culte des saints*, 126–41.
[86] Guyon, *Les premiers baptistères.*
[87] For cathedrals, see Loseby, "Bishops and Cathedrals." For parish churches, see Stancliffe, "From Town to Country."

saints (Gregory of Tours, *Hist.* 10.31.6). He further extended this umbrella of divine protection by convincing his suffragan bishops to observe the same order of service (*sacrorum ordo*) and custom of singing psalms (*psallendi ... consuetudo*) throughout the province, just as they shared the same belief in the Trinity (Council of Vannes, can. 15, CCL 148:155).

Around the same time, the liturgy was also being systematized in southern Gaul. At the request of Venerius of Marseille, the priest Musaeus (d.457/61) created a "selection of readings from the holy scriptures suitable for feast days of the whole year" as well as psalm responses "appropriate to the season and the readings" (Gennadius, *De viris illustribus* 80). Later he produced a sacramentary for Venerius's successor Eustasius. It was divided according to the parts of the Mass and seasons of the year, and "suitable in its entirety for making petitions to God and testifying to his blessings" (Gennadius, *De vir. ill.* 80). Although it is probably not by Musaeus,[88] a surviving lectionary in a late fifth-/early sixth-century palimpsest from Wolfenbüttel gives some hint of what his work may have been like. It contains biblical readings and psalm responses for feasts of the church year and special liturgical events.[89] One of its largest groups of readings is for the Rogations, a three-day series of prayers, fasting, sermons, and processions meant to ward away plague, siege, hail, famine, and other calamities. Established by Bishop Mamertus of Vienne in the third quarter of the fifth century, this ceremony joined the bishop and his community (including slaves, women, and children) in a ritual of purification that translated the communal remission of sin into protection for all.[90]

Activated by the liturgy and tied to the land by buildings and their clergy, protection was organized in a series of rings around episcopal cities. The innermost circle was defended by the cathedral, baptistery, and urban basilicas. Outside the city walls the graves of martyrs and confessors provided "a second spiritual ring of defenses, larger and all-embracing."[91] Beyond that were parish churches and privately built villa churches, which formed not a continuous perimeter, but a series of sanctified outposts at strategic locations in the landscape. Each sector was attended by a different group of clergy: at the center, the bishop and his cathedral clergy; in the suburban basilicas, staffs of clergy headed by high-ranking priests later called "abbots of the basilica" (although they were neither monks

---

[88] Vogel, *Introduction aux sources*, 25, 259–60, 290.
[89] Dold, *Das älteste Liturgiebuch*, xc–civ.
[90] Nathan, "Rogation Ceremonies."
[91] Pearce, "Processes of Conversion," 71.

nor heads of monastic communities); and in the countryside, lower-level priests attached to parishes or villas.[92] Although they were denied official status as clergy (Nimes 394/6, can. 2, CCL 148:50; Orange 441, can. 25, CCL 148:84), the deaconesses (*diaconae*) who assisted in the instruction and baptism of female catechumens and in other forms of ministry to women must also be considered part of this cadre of ministers, along with widows, nuns, and the wives of bishops, priests, and other clergymen.[93]

How this army of clergy should conduct itself was a matter of debate. Many clerics in the fifth century would not have lived or thought that they should live much differently from the laity to whom they ministered. Although some clerics were celibate, a large number were married, had children, and to judge by the number of times this was condemned by church councils, did not think it necessary to abstain from relations with their wives. Notions of clerical purity were still very much under construction. The Council of Vannes, for instance, ordered priests, deacons, and subdeacons – the grades of subepiscopal clergy prohibited from marrying after ordination – to avoid others' weddings as well, so as not to pollute their performance of the sacred mysteries with the contagion of obscene love songs and suggestive dancing (can. 11, CCL 148:154). The council also warned clergy to avoid eating with Jews, because the obvious rigor of Jewish food laws could suggest that Christian purity was inferior (can. 12, CCL 148:154). The *Statuta ecclesiae antiqua* reinforces the impression that clerics often lived like laymen, singing at feasts (can. 75, CCL 148:178), wearing fancy clothes and shoes (can. 26, CCL 148:171), and walking around the market with no intention of buying anything (can. 34, CCL 148:172). Ascetic reformers wanted to change this, but it is difficult to see much of a difference in ideals of clerical behavior or standards of pastoral care – the logical corollary of clerical professionalization – until the sixth century, when the work of Caesarius of Arles made this a pressing issue.[94]

These developments in the church, of course, took place in the context of the complete dissolution of imperial control over Gaul. By 476, when Odoacer deposed the emperor Romulus Augustulus in Ravenna, the Visigothic king Euric (466–84) controlled Aquitaine, the Auvergne, and lower Provence; the sons of the Burgundian king Gundioc (d.ca.474) quarrelled over the middle and upper Rhône, and the Frankish king Childeric (d.481) battled Roman and barbarian warlords in northwest Gaul.

[92] Godding, *Prêtres en Gaule mérovingienne*, 209–60; Griff, *La Gaule chrétienne*, 3:283–98.
[93] Barcellona, "Lo spazio declinato al femminile."
[94] Klingshirn, *Caesarius of Arles*; Leyser, *Authority and Asceticism*, 65–100.

Although there were protests from some aristocrats, such as Sidonius, bishop of Clermont,[95] for the most part the disappearance of imperial control was not the result of warfare, betrayal, or invasion, but rather of a shift in Gallo-Roman loyalties from a distant and largely ineffective imperial army and government to nearby barbarian armies and leaders long used to serving as imperial allies. Not only were the cultural, economic, and social effects of the "fall of the Roman empire in the West" therefore minimized, but the "catholic" identity of the population was potentially strengthened. As references to heretics in the *Statuta ecclesiae antiqua* remind us, Visigoths and Burgundians identified themselves as Arian Christians; most Franks only converted to Christianity after Childeric's son Clovis. Those who wanted to differentiate themselves on a religious basis had the means to do so. But this did not lead to religious persecution, and for their part, like good subjects, the Catholic Christians of Gaul prayed for their kings, as at the council convened by Caesarius in 506. "In the name of the Lord by permission of our master the most glorious, magnificent, and pious king [Alaric II] a holy synod has convened in the city of Agde.... We pray to the Lord on behalf of his kingdom, his long life, and his people that the Lord might extend his kingdom with happiness, govern it with justice, and protect it with virtue" (CCL 148:192). It is with this council in the kingdom of the Visigoths, the Council of Orléans (511) in the kingdom of the Franks, and the Council of Epaone (517) in the kingdom of the Burgundians that we can definitively mark the end of the imperial phase of Christianity in Gaul.

BIBLIOGRAPHY

Primary

Ammianus Marcellinus. *Res gestae*, ed. Wolfgang Seyfarth. 2 vols. (Leipzig, 1978).
Athanasius. *Apologia ad Constantium imperatorem*, ed. Jan-M. Szymusiak. *SC* 56 (Paris, 1958).
Augustine. *Confessiones*, ed. Luc Verheijen. CCL 27 (Turnhout, 1981). Trans. Henry Chadwick (Oxford, 1991).
Ausonius. *The Works of Ausonius*, ed. R. P. H. Green (Oxford, 1991).
Concilia Galliae, a.314–a.506, ed. Charles Munier. CCL 148 (Turnhout, 1963).
Concilios visigóticos e hispano-romanos, ed. José Vives (Barcelona, 1963).
Eusebius Gallicanus. *Collectio homiliarum*, ed. François Glorie. CCL 101, 101A, 101B (Turnhout, 1970–71).

[95] Harries, "Sidonius Apollinaris."

Gennadius. *De viris illustribus*, ed. E. C. Richardson. TUGAL, vol. 14, fasc. 1a (Leipzig, 1896): 57–97.
Gregory of Tours. *Historiae*, eds. Bruno Krusch and Wilhelm Levison. *Monumenta Germaniae historica, Scriptores rerum Merovingicarum* 1.1. 2nd ed. (Hanover, 1951).
Itinerarium Burdigalense, eds. P. Geyer and O. Cuntz, *Itineraria et Alia Geographica* CCL 175 (Turnhout, 1965): 1–26.
Jerome. *Contra Vigilantium. PL* 23 (Paris, 1845): 339–52.
    De viris illustribus, ed. E. C. Richardson. TUGAL, vol. 14, fasc. 1a (Leipzig, 1896): 1–56.
Laudes Domini, ed. Pieter van der Weijden, *Laudes Domini: Tekst, vertaling en commentaar* (Amsterdam, 1967).
Marcellus, *De medicamentis*, eds. Max Niedermann and Eduard Liechtenhan, trans. Jutta Kollesch and Diethard Nickel, *Marcellus: Über Heilmittel*, 2nd ed. 2 vols. (Berlin, 1968).
Recueil des inscriptions chrétiennes de la Gaule antérieures à la Renaissance carolingienne (=RICG). Vol. 1, *Première Belgique*, ed. Nancy Gauthier (Paris, 1975). Vol. 8, *Aquitaine première*, ed. Françoise Prévot (Paris, 1997). Vol. 15, *Viennoise du Nord*, ed. Françoise Descombes (Paris, 1985).
Statuta ecclesiae antiqua, ed. Charles Munier. CCL 148 (Turnhout, 1963): 162–88.
Sulpicius Severus. *Chronica*, ed. C. Halm. CSEL 1 (Vienna, 1866) :1–105.
Sulpicius Severus. *Vita Martini*, ed. Jacques Fontaine. 3 vols. SC (Paris, 1967–69): 133–5.
Victricius of Rouen. *De laude sanctorum*, ed. J. Mulders and R. Demeulenaere. CCL 64 (Turnhout, 1985): 69–93. Trans. Gillian Clark, "Victricius of Rouen: Praising the Saints." *JECS* 7 (1999): 365–99.

Secondary

Bailey, Lisa. "Monks and Lay Communities in Late Antique Gaul: The Evidence of the Eusebius Gallicanus Sermons." *JMedHist* 32 (2006): 315–32.
Barcellona, Rossana. "Lo spazio declinato al femminile nei concili gallici fra IV e VI secolo." In *Munera amicitiae: studi di storia e cultura sulla tarda antichità offerti a Salvatore Pricoco*, eds. Rossana Barcellona and Teresa Sardella (Soveria Mannelli, 2003): 25–49.
Barnes, Timothy D. "Eusebius and the Date of the Martyrdoms." In *Les Martyrs de Lyon (177)*, eds. J. Rougé and H. Turcan (Paris, 1978): 137–43.
    Constantine and Eusebius (Cambridge, Mass., 1981).
Barruol, G. "Lardiers." In *The Princeton Encyclopedia of Classical Sites*, eds. Richard Stillwell, William Lloyd MacDonald, and Marian Holland McAllister (Princeton, 1976): 484.
Beaujard, Brigitte. *Le culte des saints en Gaule* (Paris, 2000).
Bellet, M.-E., and P. Borgard. "Plan: Le sanctuaire gallo-romain de Verjusclas à Lioux (Vaucluse)." In *Premiers temps chrétiens en Gaule méridionale*, eds. Paul-Albert Février and François Leyge (Lyon, 1986): 120–1.
Binsfeld, Andrea. "Die Graffiti der frühchristlichen Kirchenanlage in Trier." In *Neue Forschungen zu den Anfängen des Christentums im Rheinland*, ed. Sebastian Ristow (Münster, 2004): 235–52.
Blumenkranz, Bernhard. "Les premières implantations de Juifs en France: du Ier au début du Ve siècle." *CRAI* (1969): 162–74.

Bowersock, Glen W. "Les églises de Lyon et de Vienne: relations avec l'Asie." In *Les Martyrs de Lyon (177)*, eds. J. Rougé and R. Turcan (Paris, 1978): 249–56.

Brown, Peter. *The Cult of the Saints: Its Rise and Function in Latin Christianity* (Chicago, 1981).

Burrus, Virginia. *The Making of a Heretic: Gender, Authority, and the Priscillianist Controversy* (Berkeley, 1995).

Caillet, Jean-Pierre. "Le message de la sculpture funéraire." In *D'un monde à l'autre: naissance d'une Chrétienté en Provence, IVe-VIe siècle*, eds. Jean Guyon and Marc Heijmans (Arles, 2001): 63–7.

Cameron, Averil, and Stuart G. Hall, eds. *Eusebius: Life of Constantine* (Oxford, 1999).

Chadwick, Henry. *Priscillian of Avila: The Occult and the Charismatic in the Early Church* (Oxford, 1976).

Champlin, Edward. *Fronto and Antonine Rome* (Cambridge, Mass., 1980).

Clark, Gillian. "Victricius of Rouen: Praising the Saints." *JECS* 7 (1999): 365–99.

Derks, Ton. *Gods, Temples, and Ritual Practices: The Transformation of Religious Ideas and Values in Roman Gaul* (Amsterdam, 1998).

Dold, Alban. *Das älteste Liturgiebuch der lateinischen Kirche: ein altgallikanisches Lektionar des 5./6. Jhs. aus dem Wolfenbütteler Palimpsest-Codex Weissenburgensis 76* (Beuron in Hohenzollern, 1935).

Drinkwater, John F. "The usurpers Constantine III (407–411) and Jovinus (411–413)." *Britannia* 29 (1998): 269–98.

Drinkwater, John, and Hugh Elton, eds. *Fifth-Century Gaul: A Crisis of Identity?* (Cambridge, 1992).

Duval, Yvette, and J.-Ch. Picard, eds. *L'inhumation privilégiée du IVe au VIIIe siècle en Occident: actes du colloque tenu à Créteil les 16–18 mars 1984* (Paris, 1986).

Elsner, Jaś. "The *Itinerarium Burdigalense*: politics and salvation in the geography of Constantine's empire." *JRS* 90 (2000): 181–95.

Fitzpatrick, A. P. "*Ex Radice Britanica,*" *Britannia* 22 (1991): 143–6.

Fontaine, Jacques. "Hilaire et Martin." In *Hilaire de Poitiers, évêque et docteur (368–1968)* (Paris, 1968): 59–86.

Förster, Else. "Katalog der frühchristlichen Abteilung des Rheinischen Landesmuseums Trier." In *Frühchristliche Zeugnisse im Einzugsgebiet von Rhein und Mosel*, eds. Theodor Konrad Kempf, Wilhelm Reusch, and Maria R Alföldi (Trier, 1965): 17–54, 71–83, 97–112.

Gaudemet, Jean. *Conciles gaulois du IVe siècle.* SC 241 (Paris, 1977).

Godding, Robert. *Prêtres en Gaule mérovingienne* (Brussels, 2001).

Goodine, Elizabeth A., and Matthew W. Mitchell. "The Persuasiveness of a Woman: The Mistranslation and Misinterpretation of Eusebius' *Historia Ecclesiastica* 5.1.41." *JECS* 13 (2005): 1–19.

Gordon, Richard. "The End of Mithraism in the Northwest Provinces." *JRA* 12 (1999): 682–8.

Griesheimer, Marc. "Le sarcophage de Marcia Romania Celsa." In *Premiers temps chrétiens en Gaule méridionale*, eds. Paul-Albert Février and François Leyge (Lyon, 1986): 170.

Griffe, Élie. *La Gaule chrétienne à l'époque romaine.* 3 vols. (Paris, 1964–66).

Guyon, Jean. *Les premiers baptistères des Gaules: (IVe–VIIIe siècles)* (Rome, 2000).

Halsall, Guy. *Settlement and Social Organization: The Merovingian Region of Metz* (Cambridge, 1995).

Harries, Jill. "Church and State in the *Notitia Galliarum*." *JRS* 68 (1978): 26–43.

"Sidonius Apollinaris, Rome and the Barbarians: A Climate of Treason?" In *Fifth-Century Gaul*, eds. J. Drinkwater and H. Elton (Cambridge, 1992): 298–308.

Humphries, Mark. "Trading Gods in Northern Italy." In *Trade, Traders and the Ancient City*, eds. Helen Parkins and Christopher Smith (London, 1998): 203–24.

Hunter, David G. "Vigilantius of Calagurris and Victricius of Rouen: Ascetics, Relics, and Clerics in Late Roman Gaul." *JECS* 7 (1999): 401–30.

Immerzeel, Mat, and Peter Jongste. "Les ateliers de sarcophages paleochrétiens en Gaule: La Provence et Les Pyrénenées." *AntTard* 2 (1994): 233–49.

Jullian, Camille. *Histoire de la Gaule.* 8 vols. (Paris, 1908–26).

Klingshirn, William E. *Caesarius of Arles: The Making of a Christian Community in Late Antique Gaul* (Cambridge, 1994).

"Defining the *Sortes Sanctorum*: Gibbon, Du Cange, and Early Christian Lot Divination." *JECS* 10 (2002): 77–130.

"Christian Divination in Late Roman Gaul: the *Sortes Sangallenses*." In *Mantikê: Studies in Ancient Divination*, eds. Sarah Iles Johnston and Peter T. Struck (Leiden, 2005): 99–128.

Krautheimer, Richard. *Early Christian and Byzantine Architecture*, rev. 4th ed., with Slobodan Ćurčić (New Haven, 1986).

Le Glay, Marcel. "Le culte impérial à Lyon, au IIe siècle ap. J.-C." In *Les Martyrs de Lyon (177)*, eds. J. Rougé and R. Turcan (Paris, 1978): 19–31.

Leyser, Conrad. *Authority and Asceticism from Augustine to Gregory the Great* (Oxford, 2000).

Löhr, Winrich A. "Der Brief der Gemeinden von Lyon und Vienne (Eusebius, h.e. V, 1–2(4))." In *Oecumenica et Patristica: Festschrift für Wilhelm Schneemelcher zum 75. Geburtstag*, eds. Damaskinos Papandreou, Wolfgang A. Bienert, and Knut Schäferdiek (Stuttgart, 1989): 135–49.

Loseby, Simon. "Bishops and Cathedrals: Order and Diversity in the Fifth-Century Urban Landscape of Southern Gaul." In *Fifth-Century Gaul*, eds. J. Drinkwater and H. Elton (Cambridge, 1992): 144–55.

MacCormack, Sabine. "Loca Sancta: The Organization of Sacred Topography in Late Antiquity." In *The Blessings of Pilgrimage*, ed. Robert Ousterhout (Urbana, Ill., 1990): 7–40.

Marco Simón, Francisco, and Isabel Velázquez. "Una nueva *defixio* aparecida en Dax (Landes)." *Aquitania* 17 (2000): 261–74.

Markus, R. A. "How on Earth Could Places Become Holy? Origins of the Christian Idea of Holy Places." *JECS* 2 (1994): 257–71.

Marrou, Henri-Irénée. "Le dossier épigraphique de l'évêque Rusticus de Narbonne." *RAC* 46 (1970): 331–49.

Mathisen, Ralph. *Ecclesiastical Factionalism and Religious Controversy in Fifth-Century Gaul* (Washington, D.C., 1989).

Matthews, John. "Gallic Supporters of Theodosius." *Latomus* 30 (1971): 1073–99.

Mehat, André. "Le concile d'Arles (314) et les Bagaudes." *RSR* 63 (1989): 47–70.

Montero Cartelle, Enrique, and Alberto Alonso Guardo, eds. *Los "libros de suertes" medievales: las* Sortes Sanctorum *y los* Prenostica Socratis Basilei (Madrid, 2004).

Munier, Charles. *Les Statuta Ecclesiae Antiqua; édition, études critiques* (Paris, 1960).

Nathan, Geoffrey. "The Rogation Ceremonies of Late Antique Gaul: Creation, Transmission, and the Role of the Bishop." *C&M* 49 (1998): 275–303.

Opelt, Ilona. "Das *Carmen De Laudibus Domini* als Zeugnis des Christentums bei den Galliern." *RomBarb* 3 (1978): 159–66.

Pearce, Susan M. "Processes of Conversion in North-west Roman Gaul." In *The Cross Goes North: Processes of Conversion in Northern Europe, AD 300–1300*, ed. Martin Carver (Woodbridge, Suffolk, 2003): 61–78.

Pietri, Luce. "Les grandes églises missionnaires: II. La Gaule et la Bretagne." In *Histoire du Christianisme des origines à nos jours*, 2, eds. Jean-Marie Mayeur, et al. (Paris, 1995): 832–60.

Rebillard, Éric. "Violations de sépulture et impiété dans l'Antiquité tardive." In *Impies et païens entre Antiquité et Moyen Âge*, eds. Lionel Mary and Michel Sot (Paris, 2002): 65–80.

Rougé, Jean, and Robert Turcan, eds. *Les Martyrs de Lyon (177)* (Paris, 1978).

Rouqette, Jean-Maurice. "Trois nouveaux sarcophages chrétiens de Trinquetaille (Arles)." *CRAI* (1974): 254–77.

"Sarcophage de Marcia Romania Celsa." In *Du nouveau sur l'Arles antique*, ed. Claude Sintes. *Revue d'Arles* 1 (Arles, 1987): 126.

Rousseau, Philip. *Ascetics, Authority, and the Church in the Age of Jerome and Cassian*, 2nd ed. (Notre Dame, 2010).

Rousselle, Aline. *Croire et guérir: la foi en Gaule dans l'Antiquité tardive* (Paris, 1990).

Salzman, Michele Renee. *The Making of a Christian Aristocracy: Social and Religious Change in the Western Roman Empire* (Cambridge, Mass., 2002).

Sauer, Eberhard W. *The End of Paganism in the North-Western Provinces of the Roman Empire: The Example of the Mithras Cult* (Oxford, 1996).

Schwinden, Lothar. "Verfluchungstäfelchen aus dem Amphitheater." In *Trier, Kaiserresidenz und Bischofssitz: die Stadt in Spätantiker und frühchristlicher Zeit*, ed. Heinz Cüppers (Mainz am Rhein, 1984): 185–9.

Sordi, Marta. "La ricerca d'ufficio nel processo del 177." In *Les Martyrs de Lyon (177)*, eds. J. Rougé and R. Turcan (Paris, 1978): 179–86.

Stancliffe, Claire E. "From Town to Country: The Christianisation of the Touraine, 370–600." In *The Church in Town and Countryside*, ed. Derek Baker. Studies in Church History 16 (Oxford, 1979): 43–59.

St. Martin and his Hagiographer: History and Miracle in Sulpicius Severus (Oxford, 1983).

Toch, Michael. "The Jews in Europe, 500–1050." In *The New Cambridge Medieval History*, vol. 1, ed. Paul Fouracre (Cambridge, 2005): 547–70.

Trout, Dennis E. *Paulinus of Nola: Life, Letters, and Poems* (Berkeley, 1999).

Van Andringa, William. *La religion en Gaule romaine: piété et politique, Ier-IIIe siècle apr. J.-C.* (Paris, 2002).

Van Dam, Raymond. *Leadership and Community in Late Antique Gaul* (Berkeley, 1985).

Vessey, Mark. "The *Epistula Rustici ad Eucherium*: From the Library of Imperial Classics to the Library of the Fathers." In *Society and Culture in Late Antique Gaul: Revisiting the Sources*, eds. Ralph W. Mathisen and Danuta Shanzer (Aldershot, Hampshire, 2001): 278–97.

"Peregrinus Against the Heretics: Classicism, Provinciality, and the Place of the Alien Writer in Late Roman Gaul." Chapter 9 in *Latin Writers in Late Antiquity and their Texts* (Aldershot, Hampshire, 2005).

Vogel, Cyrille. *Introduction aux sources de l'histoire du culte chrétien au Moyen Âge*, 2nd ed. (Spoleto, 1981).

Weber, Winfried. "Neue Forschungen zur Trierer Domgrabung: die archäologischen Ausgrabungen im Garten der Kurie von der Leyen." In *Neue Forschungen zu den Anfängen des Christentums im Rheinland*, ed. Sebastian Ristow (Münster, Westfalen, 2004): 225–34.

Wierschowski, Lothar. "Der Lyoner Märtyrer Vettius Epagathus: Zum Status und zur Herkunft der ersten gallischen Christen." *Historia* 47 (1998): 426–53.

Wightman, Edith Mary. *Roman Trier and the Treveri* (London, 1970).

Gallia Belgica (Berkeley, 1985).

Young, Bailey. "Sacred Topography: The Impact of the Funerary Basilica in Late Antique Gaul." In *Society and Culture in Late Antique Gaul: Revisiting the Sources*, eds. Ralph W. Mathisen and Danuta Shanzer (Aldershot, Hampshire, 2001): 169–86.

Zander, Carl Magnus. *Versus italici antiqui* (Lund, 1890).

19

RELIGIONS OF ROMAN SPAIN

MICHAEL KULIKOWSKI

Dramatic regional differences within the Iberian Peninsula were always characteristic of the religious history of ancient Spain. Although long pre-dating the Roman conquest, these differences are accessible to the modern scholar only as a result of the Roman conquest.[1] Roman conquest brought with it religious practices, chief among them the habit of inscription, which have left traces in the material record. The religious diversity of Iberia followed directly from the enormous cultural differences between the coasts and the interior, the river valleys, the mountain chains, and the vast plateaus of the central peninsula. This cultural diversity was never wholly erased, not even with the spread of Christianity in the fourth and later centuries.

Nonetheless, the arrival of Roman armies in the peninsula, and there-after the slow and bloody process by which Spain was made part of the empire, caused very significant changes to the peninsula's religious life. For many years, these changes were intermittent and highly regional, but three periods of accelerated change affected the whole peninsula. The first of these took place during and immediately after the long reign of Augustus (r.27 BCE–14 CE), who had taken a personal interest in the final conquest of the peninsula and its incorporation into the empire. The Augustan reorga-nization of Spain placed every corner of the peninsula within a framework of Roman government in which Roman religious practices could spread rapidly. The second period of intense religious change began under the Flavian emperors, when Vespasian (r.69–79) extended the Latin right, a subordinate form of Roman citizenship, to every municipality in Spain

---

[1] Richardson, *Romans in Spain*, is the best general account of Spanish history through the early third century CE. Here and throughout, I cite useable English references where they exist, even where less accessible Spanish publications might be more up to date.

that had previously lacked status under Roman law. This had the effect of giving every city in Spain a stake in the Roman system; as a result, both the cult of the Roman emperors and other Roman modes of public religious practice became universalized. The final period of accelerated change came with the imperial conversion to Christianity, as the new religion of the Roman state transformed the religious life of the Spanish provinces just as it did elsewhere. A diachronic perspective on the religious diversity of ancient Spain will perhaps be more useful than a synchronic catalogue of the religions, cults, and divinities of the peninsula, particularly given the necessary superficiality of such surveys. In the first instance, however, it will be worth sketching the broad differences among the various regions of the peninsula.

Despite its long, if not always hospitable, coastlines and its several large river systems, which create swathes of fertile agricultural land, much of the Iberian Peninsula is mountainous and indifferently fertile (see Map 10). Mountain chains, which for the most part run along an east-west axis, have the effect of compartmentalizing the cultural zones of the peninsula both from one another and from ready access to the outer world. What is more, four of the peninsula's five main river systems – the Guadalquivir, Guadiana, Tajo, and Duero – flow from east to west into the Atlantic, away from the heartland of the ancient world. Only the Guadalquivir, which debouches just beyond the Straits of Gibraltar, and the Ebro, which flows from west to east into the Mediterranean itself, were really connected to the archaic Mediterranean. Indeed, long after the first Romans had appeared in Spain, the interior was inaccessible wherever the river valleys did not penetrate, and particularly as one moved further north and west. By the same token, however, the eastern and southeastern coasts of the peninsula were very early incorporated into the broader world of archaic Mediterranean trade and colonization, while the northern coast, along the Bay of Biscay, seems always to have had connections with the Celtic world of the North Atlantic. Yet it was not until the Romans impinged upon this world that the interior and the north began to be systematically linked to the more sophisticated civilizations of the coasts and the river valleys.

Broadly speaking, scholars divide pre-Roman Spain into three major cultural zones. A vast arc of culturally Celtic territory ran in a crescent from southern Portugal and Spanish Extremadura, through Galicia and León-Castile, to the Pyrenees and into Gaul. The Celtiberian zone occupied large parts of the central Meseta and the Ebro valley, while along the lower Ebro valley, parts of Castile-La Mancha, Valencia, and Catalonia, and down into Andalucía, one finds the indigenous Iberian culture. In

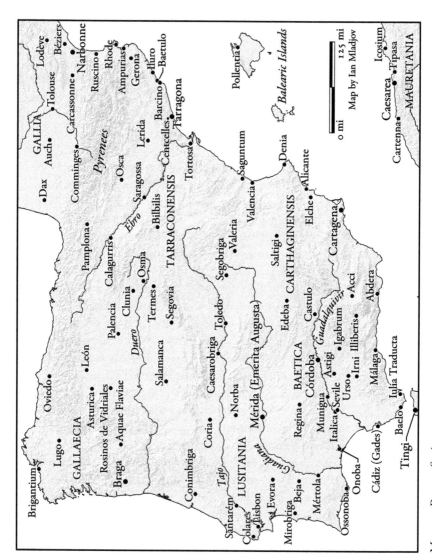

Map 10. Roman Spain

the south, the Iberian civilization, known to the Greeks as the kingdom of Tartessos, ranged alongside, and was heavily influenced by, Phoenician colonies that had been planted around the straits of Gibraltar in the eighth century BCE. Those Phoenician colonies, in turn, were more closely linked to the colonial Phoenician culture of Carthage than to the Levant, and Carthaginian influence on the southern coastal regions of what is now Andalucía was quite heavy.[2] On the northeastern coast of Spain, Greek traders had more influence, both directly and indirectly. Though the only permanent Greek colony on the Iberian Peninsula was Emporion (the Roman Emporiae, modern Ampurias), founded from Massilia in Gaul, the impact of Greek culture on the eastern coast of the peninsula should not be underestimated, because local Iberian sites changed in imitation of Greek models: to take just one example, votive statuettes showing dedicants in Greek poses are known from the third century BCE at indigenous sites like Saguntum.

More than anything else, what separated the Celtic and Iberian interior from the coasts, with their Punic and Hellenic cultural models, was a familiarity with Mediterranean styles of urbanism. The interior of the peninsula had its hilltop sites and refuges, some of them grand enough to be classed as *oppida* by Roman invaders. The closer one came to the coasts, however, the more the indigenous sites looked like archaic settlements or *poleis* anywhere in the Mediterranean. An important feature of all such urban settlements was, naturally enough, sites of public cult. The Greek vision of anthropomorphic deities to whom communities offered public cult in the form of sacrifice was broadly familiar throughout the coastal regions of Spain from an early date, as was the aniconic representation of divinities associated with Syrian cults – like Hercules Gaditanus, the Phoenician Melqaart, whose temple at Gades (Cádiz) was perhaps the most famous cult site in Roman Spain.[3] In the interior, Mediterranean modes of worship, let alone Mediterranean divinities, seem to have made no impact until well into the Roman period. On the other hand, and at first sight paradoxically, it is equally not until well into the Roman period that we begin to have intelligible evidence for the religious life of the interior at all.

<hr />

[2] Harrison, *Spain*, though dated, is the only reliable English introduction to early Spain. Fear, *Rome and Baetica*, is an accessible introduction to the Punic legacy.
[3] García y Bellido, "Hercules Gaditanus." The temple was described by many authors of the imperial period: Philostratus, *Vit. Apoll.* 2.33.2, 5.4–5; Silius Italicus 3.14; Arrian, *Anab.* 2.16.4; Appian, *Bell. civ.* 6.2, 6.65; Arnobius, *Adv. nat.* 1.36; Mela 3.46.

That point is worth stressing, because it underscores how Roman intervention in the peninsula brought its different parts together in ways that had never before been possible. Roman conquest created an overarching framework within which different cultural practices could be exchanged on a constant, rather than sporadic, basis; as a result, cult practices already commonplace on the coasts were exported to and absorbed by the interior. Still more significant was the fact of recording religious activities in a way that makes them accessible to the modern scholar. We know that pre-Roman habits of worship survived in remarkably un-Mediterranean forms well into the Roman period; but the reason we know about them is either because Roman authors tell us or because enough of the Mediterranean religious praxis had been absorbed that the forms of cult become accessible to us – that is to say, coins with images of divinities, votive offerings, or cult sites with forms analogous to those known in the Mediterranean world, and particularly, though at a later date, the habit of inscription. In other words, we gain access to the indigenous religion of the peninsula only as a result of Roman conquest.

That conquest was a very slow process. The first Roman armies appeared in Spain in 218 BCE at the beginning of the Second Punic War (218–02 BCE). The decade of warfare between Romans and Carthaginian forces entangled Roman troops in the peninsula so thoroughly that the Senate could never have countenanced disengagement even had its members wished to do so. They did not, of course, because Spain was an excellent proving ground for generals on the lookout for tribal victims whose chastisement would lend luster to a political career at Rome. What is more, the Punic wars had brought local Spanish obligations with them: not just treaties with a host of local allies, but also the first permanent Roman settlement, Italica; the first Spanish *colonia*, Carteia; and later more permanent establishments for imperial officials, Corduba (modern Córdoba) in the Guadalquivir valley and Tarraco (Tarragona) on the Catalonian coast. In 197 BCE, the peninsula was organized into two provinces, Hispania Citerior and Hispania Ulterior. The next hundred years witnessed more or less continuous campaigning from these bases further into the peninsular interior, with stretches of desultory annual fighting punctuated by more intense violence, as during the Celtiberian wars of the 130s. The process of acculturation, which we may or may not want to describe as Romanization, began in this period, though it was neither as systematic nor as thoroughgoing as it would become in the last century BCE.

What this meant in terms of the history of religion can be seen most clearly in the south and the east, that is to say, the parts of the peninsula in which there was already an urban tradition, one in which Punic and Hellenic models of cult and inscription were familiar to the indigenous population. Capitolium-style temples are known from the republican period at both Roman sites like Italica and native sites like Saguntum. The Greek colony at Emporion remade itself as a Roman city in the first century BCE, not least with a temple long believed, perhaps incorrectly, to have been a Serapeum.[4] Even at an interior site like Azaila, moreover, one can see the free adaptation of Greco-Roman temple forms in the later second and first centuries BCE.[5] Azaila was a wholly indigenous site, lacking in Roman colonists and at a considerable distance from settlements with large Roman populations. It had nevertheless adopted Roman modes of housing native gods, suggesting the kind of influence that the impact of a successful new foreign presence in the peninsula was clearly having. By the Augustan era, when Strabo was writing, he could claim that in the more civilized parts of Spain, by which he meant the Guadalquivir valley, the natives had forgotten their indigenous language and culture, replacing it with Latin and Roman culture.[6]

Strabo's statement gives some idea of what Romanization entailed, but it also introduces us to one of the more difficult evidentiary problems we face in trying to understand ancient religion in Spain. Most of what we know comes from writers of, or who refer to, the last century BCE and the first century CE, and there are a few important obstacles to our applying their evidence. The fact that it imposes an *interpretatio Graeca* or *Romana* on the indigenous religious scene is too obvious to need belaboring, but it is worth stressing that what we learn tends to focus almost exclusively on those peoples or groups who posed the greatest difficulties for Roman authorities.

Even the famous case of the republican rebel Sertorius fits into that category. Sertorius, who opposed the Italian government in the 70s BCE, based himself in Lusitania. We are told that he conspicuously consulted a white deer before acting, and that the deer's oracular abilities helped him retain the trust and support of his native followers.[7] Does this

---

[4] Sanmartí, Castañer, and Tremoleda, "Emporion," for the site; Ruiz de Arbulo, "Santuario," for compelling doubts.
[5] Mierse, *Temples*, 39–44, but in general Ramallo, "Templos," is more reliable on the republican period.
[6] Strabo 3.2.151.
[7] Valerius Maximus 1.2.5; Plutarch, *Sert.* 11; Appian, *Bell. civ.* 1.110; Aulus Gellius, *Noct. Att.* 15.22; Frontinus, *Strat.* 1.11.13.

represent the Roman general's exploitation of local animal worship or an indigenous tradition of divination through the movements of animals? If the Lusitanians saw a native god behind Sertorius deer, what god was it? Plutarch refers to Artemis, Gellius to Diana, but no attempt at identifying the indigenous version thereof has been successful. In a similar vein, Strabo reports that the Lusitanians examined the *viscera* of prisoners as a means of divination, but whether this represents part of the same cult exploited by Sertorius, a different Lusitanian cult, or even mere hostile Roman propaganda, is impossible for us to tell.[8] Other Roman sources are equally opaque. Both Horace and Silius Italicus report equine sacrifice among the mountain peoples of the north, while Juvenal mentions that the Celtiberians worshipped the Celtic horse goddess Epona. But here, too, there is an interpretative problem. Because Epona was widely enough diffused across the Roman empire (the only Celtic divinity of whom this was true), Juvenal's attestation may be describing not an old indigenous cult but rather an import into Spain from neighboring Gaul.[9]

As the foregoing will have suggested, our understanding of the religious life of republican Spain is haphazard and limited, though general regional differences can be discerned without too much difficulty. Even at the very end of the republic, when the end of the civil wars brought really substantial Italian and Roman settlement and the legal status of many urban sites was improved, the peninsula remained very much more a collection of territories than a single place. The reign of Augustus, however, transformed the religious face of the peninsula, as it did so many other things. Augustus, bent on confirming his claim to have brought peace to the whole world, was determined to complete the piecemeal conquest of Spain after two centuries of Roman intervention. What is more, he determined to do so personally, residing in Spain while his generals subjugated the far northwest – the lands of Astures and Cantabri, among other recalcitrant tribes. Resettling those tribes in the lowlands where they could be more readily controlled, he established new administrative centers in the northwest – Asturica Augusta (Astorga), Bracara Augusta (Braga), and Lucus Augusti (Lugo). These foundations illustrate an important point about Augustan policy more generally. Augustus quite deliberately used urbanism as a systematic means of controlling and administering the Iberian Peninsula in a way that was never attempted with the same regularity anywhere else in the Latin West.

---

[8] Strabo 3.3.6.
[9] Horace, *Carm.* 3.4.34; Silius Italicus 3.360; Juv. *Sat.* 8.156.

For Augustus, it was cities and their dependent territories that were to organize peninsular space.[10] Augustus undertook a provincial reorganization that divided the old Hispania Ulterior into a new southern province of Baetica, centered on Corduba and recognizing the difference between the civilized, urban south on the one hand and, on the other, the Guadiana valley and points west, which had not yet been absorbed into Roman provincial culture. This western region was now turned into the province of Lusitania, with a rather grand new city, the veteran colony of Emerita Augusta, as its capital. Citerior, now more generally known as Tarraconensis after its capital, covered much of the peninsula, and encompassed the great cultural divide between the already Romanized coasts, the long-pacified Celtiberian regions, and the distant, just-conquered northwest, where Roman armies would remain stationed for many decades. In all these provinces, and despite the major cultural differences among and within them, it was cities that structured the territory, even if, at the start of the Augustan period at least, they looked nothing like what a Mediterranean person would recognize as a polis.

Yet that fact does nothing to diminish the importance of this Augustan innovation. It meant that, more than any other factor, the setting in which the peninsula would be integrated into the empire was through the city. The privileging of the urban center as the focus of administrative life meant that even in places that had no special status in Roman law, there was a strong impetus to look and behave as Romans. This mimetic impulse struck members of peninsula elites everywhere, and it led to a furious burst of changes to the peninsular landscape. That phenomenon affected religious praxis as it did other spheres of life, beginning in the urban centers themselves – and hence in those regions with the best-established urban traditions – but spreading from there throughout the peninsula. It is thus no surprise that in the Augustan period, many characteristic aspects of pagan religion – from public temples with organized priesthoods, to the universal spread of votive dedications, to the raising of prominent memorials to the dead – either appear in Spain for the first time, or become visible to the modern scholar for the first time.

In part, this is a matter of the spreading of the epigraphic habit, a major part of the phenomenon of Romanization more broadly. The epigraphic corpus of Roman Spain is dramatically larger than that of most other western provinces, and large parts of it are, broadly speaking,

---

[10] Richardson, *Romans in Spain*, 134–78; Kulikowski, *Late Roman Spain*, 5–16, with references to the extensive Spanish literature.

religious – commemoration of religious donations, vows fulfilled, grave-stones, and so on. The distribution of Spanish inscriptions follows a pat-tern similar to that in many of the other Latin regions of the empire: a gradually rising number of inscriptions in the first century, a peak in the second century, and a fairly precipitous decline from the mid-third cen-tury onwards.[11] As always in Spain, however, there are intense regional variations to this overall pattern. Regions with longer experience of Mediterranean traditions saw a much earlier flowering of inscription, but equally witnessed a much earlier dropping off of public commem-oration in stone. Thus, while the epigraphic corpus of an ancient city like Carthago Nova (Cartagena) is concentrated in last century of the republic and the Augustan and Julio-Claudian decades, that of a north-western town like Aquae Flaviae peaks at the turn of the second to the third century.[12] There is, in other words, a close connection between the spread of Roman habits of urban society and the spread of the epigraphic habit.[13] Epigraphy is thus a strong index of the wider adoption of Roman values, and that, in turn, is significant for our understanding of cult in the peninsula. It is, after all, almost entirely through epigraphy that we can establish which gods were worshipped there, and it is possible to compile a list of well over two hundred theonyms from the inscribed evidence.[14]

Some of these theonyms are very common. We possess, for example, nearly a hundred inscriptions to Endovellicus from all over the region that is now central Portugal. Many, however, are *hapaces*, and heated debate among scholars suggests that some cryptic inscriptions that have been read as votive dedications may have nothing to do with cult at all.[15] Still more problematic than the technical difficulties of the epigraphic evidence is the almost total lack of context for understanding the indigenous cults of Spain. Many of the gods whose names survive on inscriptions are charac-terized by scholars on the basis of the location in which their cult objects were found: the divinity named in a votive altar found near a stream must

---

[11] Edmondson, "Epigraphy and History," is an excellent orientation.

[12] Cf. Abascal, Ramallo, *Documentación*; and Rodríguez Colmenero, *Aquae Flaviae*.

[13] See the Spanish essays in Beltrán Lloris, *Roma*.

[14] There is a vast literature on the pre-Roman religions of the peninsula; most multivolume histories of Spain contain useful short chapters on the subject. For Iberian cults, Moneo, *Religio ibérica*, is indispensable. The attempt at a comprehensive catalogue in Crespo and Alonso, *Manifestaciones*, is laudable and could usefully be extended to the whole peninsula. Blázquez, *Diccionario*, remains valuable.

[15] The only way to remain abreast of the changing interpretations of the Spanish epigraphic evidence is via the periodical *Hispania Epigraphica*, now published annually, and currently in its twelfth volume.

be a river god; an altar near a cave belongs to a chthonic deity; the votive statues of bulls and cows that are commonplace in Extremadura and parts of Portugal are fertility offerings for flocks. All of these interpretations are plausible enough, but their tenuousness must be recognized.

The larger point is that the medium through which we learn about these gods is fundamentally Roman. When a second-century dedicant named Veicius dedicated an altar to Deo Bodo at a site near León, he did so with the impeccably Roman formula of *votum solvit libens merito*.[16] Nothing can illustrate the adoption of a Roman technology of worship to a new situation better than that. Even if theonyms of presumably indigenous gods are vastly more numerous in the west, northwest, and north of the peninsula, the technology of worship – ex votos, inscribed dedications, votive altars, and so on – is the same throughout the peninsula, and thus a testament to the normative patterns established by the Roman metropolitan model of cult. One might worship one's own god, but one did so according to Roman models. In that light, it is interesting to find that even a popular indigenous deity like Endovellicus, with a widespread regional cult, seems not to have had an organized cult site until the Roman period.

This key interpretative point is most visible in the north, northwest, and west, where the very phenomenon of inscription was new, arriving with Augustus's legions and cities. Thus, the adoption of inscription was in and of itself symbolic of the new Roman order. The same process is at work in the south and the east, but there, the adoption of explicitly Roman gods, rather than the technology of worship, served to indicate Romanization. For that reason, although indigenous divinities and Punic baals may hide behind some of the Jupiters and Venuses of Baetica, we cannot really find them there: by the late republican period, these regions expressed their integration into the Roman world not by the adoption of Roman technologies of worship, but by assimilation to metropolitan tastes and cults, thoroughly obscuring earlier layers of cultic expression.[17]

In looking at the religions associated with the urbanized regions of the peninsula, it may be helpful to make the distinction, recently stressed by Rives, between emigrant gods, attested because individual immigrant worshippers are present in a region; diaspora cults, imported and supported by large immigrant communities; and assimilated cults, widely adopted by local or indigenous populations even though they may have arrived

---

[16] *CIL* II: 5670 = *IRPL* 53.
[17] It is only on the rarest occasions that we find an indigenous theonym in Baetica, for example, *CIL* II²/5: 309 (near Igabrum).

initially as imports from elsewhere.[18] Apart from the cult of Isis, whose
attestations are concentrated in the second century and in the main cities,
only the chief gods of the Roman pantheon fit into the latter category in
Spain.[19] Which Roman gods predominated in which cities and *territoria*
may have something to do with the earlier history of a particular place. The
Greek Asclepius illustrates such patterns of cultic stratigraphy. Healing deities were perfectly well known in the pre-Roman world of Spain. Indeed,
there is little doubt that the cult of Endovellicus – of whom more than
seventy inscriptions are attested, mainly in the inland parts of Lusitania –
included a strong element of healing ritual and possibly, by the imperial
period, even incubation in temple precincts.[20] But the concentration of
cult to Asclepius in the cities of the Catalonian coast and the Levant, from
Emporiae to Carthago Nova, is striking and undoubtedly reflects the long
Greek influence on these regions.[21] If Pliny the Elder is to be believed, the
Artemis of Ephesus had been worshipped at Saguntum since before the
arrival of the Romans. Like so many of the cults of the classical deities that
were not imperially sponsored, cult to Diana-Artemis, Venus-Aphrodite,
and indeed a lesser god like Cupid-Eros was very much concentrated in
Baetica and the eastern and southeastern parts of Tarraconensis – which
is to say those parts of the peninsula which might plausibly be described
as cosmopolitan.[22] At Saguntum, Diana was Diana Maxima, and there
was a collegium of *cultores Dianae* to look after her worship.[23] Other syncretistic versions of Diana, however, were able to spread much farther;
Diana Venatrix can be found in a wide stretch of the west and northwest,
as can cult of Diana, which has been interpreted as syncretistic with the
old indigenous cult of the moon. A more classical Diana is diffused in the
coastal regions of Catalonia, where it is even found combined with imperial cult.[24] Occasionally, peninsular cult to deities of the Roman pantheon
throws up intriguing oddities, like the cult of Liber Pater. This very Roman
god is largely invisible in the peninsula, but had an old and concentrated
cult at the site of Montaña Frontera, just outside Saguntum. Nearly twenty
votive inscriptions to him have been found there alongside the remains of
a building that is presumed to have been his temple.[25] The inscriptions run

[18] Rives, *Religion*, 132–57.
[19] See Balil, "Culto de Isis"; Alvar, "Culto a Isis," with epigraphic references.
[20] For example, *CIL* II: 129, 138; 5201–2 (Villaviçosa).
[21] For example, *CIL* II: 2407; *CIL* II²/14: 1, 2 (Valentia); 291 (Saguntum).
[22] Pliny the Elder, *Nat.* 16.79.
[23] *CIL* II²/14: 292–4 (Saguntum). Cf. *cultores Iovis* at Segobriga: *HEp.* 9: 315.
[24] *IRC* I: 31 (see also *CIL* II: 4618 = *IRC* I: 30).
[25] See Corell, "Culto a *Liber Pater*."

from the first to the third centuries CE with a heavy concentration in the early part of that period. The interesting point, however, is the preponderance of indigenous names among dedicators of inscriptions, suggesting an intense but localized commitment to the cult of Liber that may dimly reflect pre-Roman, Iberian devotions in the region.

Liber Pater would seem to have had a temple at Montaña Frontera, and hundreds of temples are known either archaeologically or epigraphically from the peninsula. In virtually none of these can the sponsorship of the Roman state be discovered; presumably they sprang up as a result of the euergetism that local elites began to engage in as part of the process of becoming Roman. This underscores how important Augustan urbanism was to the religious transformation of Spain; city elites, following metropolitan models of patronage and largesse, introduced not just new cults, but new settings for old cults in their home towns. In Spain, where the epigraphic record gives us substantial evidence for euergetism of various sorts, temples are the commonest privately constructions on record. In fact, fifty temples built on private initiative are known from Spain, substantial numbers in each province.[26] We would expect such donations in large cities like Emerita, and duly find them, for instance, the Vettilla Paculi who built a temple of Mars.[27] Vettilla and her husband belonged to the senatorial elite, and were not natives of Emerita. In the cases of other major donations – for instance, a temple of Jupiter put up at Malaca (Málaga) by a man with a Greek cognomen – we cannot be sure whether the donor was a local noble or a foreign patron.[28] Nonetheless, we also find this sort of religious euergetism at smaller places like Ulisi, Munigua, or Liria, where the donors are probably locals.[29] Smaller-scale donations, small *aediculae* to the *lares* and *genii* for instance, blur the distinction between private chapel and public temple, and are as characteristic of the big cities as of small sites.[30] That said, the private dedication of temples is overwhelmingly centered on the main privileged cities. What is more, in the northwest, even in the big cities, most private religious patronage seems to have come from members of the imperial administration rather than from locals.[31]

---

[26] Recent survey in Andreu Pintado, "Comportamiento munificente," with references to earlier studies.

[27] *CIL* II: 468.

[28] *CIL* II: 1965.

[29] Ulisi: *CIL* II²/5: 718 (*templum Herculis*); Munigua: *CILA* 2/4: 1058–9 = *HEp.* 7: 916 (Munigua, with very different readings); Liria: *CIL* II: 3786 (*templum Nympharum*), for which cf. *HEp.* 9: 585 (Valentia).

[30] See, for example, *CIL* II: 1980 (Abdera, conv. Malacatensis).

[31] See table at Andreu Pintado, "Comportamiento munificente," 123.

If cult to the gods of the Roman pantheon, and the euergistic construction that supported it, are two important signs of the peninsula's integration into Roman modes of religious behavior, the spread of Roman-style burial in the first century is equally significant. This transformation is most visible among the elite families of urban centers, although there is some reason to believe that it took place at the lower end of the social scale as well. We find Italianate grave monuments at Tarraco from the very end of the second century BCE, and from Corduba a century later, some of them no doubt the work of immigrants. Likewise at Emerita Augusta, and indeed from very shortly after its foundation, the road leading east out of the city was lined with grave markers in exactly the same way as was the Via Appia in Italy. Local variations on the elaborate tomb-markers favored by Roman elites are a marker of regional styles at play: at Baelo, for instance, tall, cubelike monuments capped with pyramids have no parallels in Spain or Italy, but rather in North Africa.[32] Along with the introduction of Roman-style grave monuments came Roman forms of commemorating the dead. The standard vocabulary of death and burial – the inscriptions *dis manibus*, or the exhortations of *sit tibi terra levis* – are omnipresent in peninsula, and in chronological terms follow the general pattern of each local region's epigraphic habit.

The religious trends outlined in the foregoing all have their roots in the Augustan period – they are, indeed, a direct result of his administrative reforms – but they continue under the Julio-Claudians. In many places, in fact, cult sites and urban landscapes that began to be developed under Augustus were completed under his successors. A second period of accelerated change in the religious and cultural life of the peninsula came under the Flavian emperors. Vespasian had to justify his position, and ultimately that of his dynasty, in a way that none of his Julio-Claudian predecessors had found necessary, for the simple reason that he lacked any familial connection to the deified Augustus or even to the nobility of the old Republic.

Just as Vespasian needed to specify his own imperial powers with more precision than had his predecessors, so did the imperial cult receive new impetus under a dynasty that could use emperor worship as a means of emphasizing its legitimacy. The imperial cult did, of course, exist in the peninsula from the time of Augustus onwards, beginning with the obscure and controversial evidence of the three altars, raised in the northwest by

---

[32] Von Hesberg, "Römische Grabbauten" and Beltrán Fortes, "Monumentos," are the basic introductions.

one Sestius and thus called *arae Sestianae*, though our ancient sources disagree about precisely where he put them up.[33] A municipal altar at Tarraco, known from circa 26 BCE, was a local initiative, not the start of the city's public cult to Augustus; however, in 15 CE Tiberius permitted the city to erect a temple to *divus Augustus*, soon commemorated on the local coinage.[34] A decade later, by contrast, the same emperor famously refused the request of an embassy from Baetica to erect a temple to himself and his mother Livia.[35] The provincial cult of the emperors in Spain would thus remain restricted to the *divi*, at least until the major changes of the Flavian period.

In the northwest, Vespasian instituted cult at the level of the *conventus* and either invented, or perhaps merely extended and developed, provincial cult in Baetica. The effects of Flavian efforts in Tarraconensis are equally impressive. For one thing, Vespasian seems to have resolved the problem of worship of a living emperor by allowing for *flamines divorum et Augustorum*, so that both dead and living emperor(s) could be worshipped simultaneously in one place.[36] More dramatically, the Flavian emphasis on imperial cult in the peninsula's great cities could produce massive construction projects and consequent transformation of how religion functioned within the confines of the city.[37] The case of Tarragona is most striking: Roman Tarragona was built at the base of a tall hill several hundred meters from the seashore. The city was walled in the republican period, but under the Flavians, the hill was transformed into the site of an enormous imperial precinct that dominated the old republican *colonia* at its foot.[38] Built on three terraces, this complex included a temple of the imperial cult, a forum in which the council of the *provincia Tarraconensis* met, and a vast circus. This large complex was accessible only through the vaults of the circus, separated from the rest of the city by the passage of the Via Augusta through the town at this point.[39] Within the city but separate from it, Tarragona's imperial complex was undoubtedly the grandest monument of the *pax Romana* in all of Spain, and it was very much a religious monument, centering as it did on the cult of the Roman emperors. Yet in

---

[33] Ptolemy, *Geogr.* 2.6.6; Mela 3.13; Pliny the Elder, *Nat.* 4.20.111. Étienne, *Culte impériale* and Fishwick, *Imperial Cult*, are the main studies, but see Delgado, "Flamines," for Lusitania, and idem, *Elites y organización*.
[34] Tacitus, *Ann.* 1.78; Mierse, *Temples*, 135–41, for the coins.
[35] Tacitus, *Ann.* 4.37.
[36] *CIL* II: 4217 = *RIT* 316. See Alföldy, *Flamines*, 46–9.
[37] Garriguet Mata, "Culto imperial."
[38] There is a good historical sketch in Carreté, Keay, and Millett, *Roman Provincial Capital.*
[39] For the forum, see generally TED'A, "Foro provincial."

providing a central meeting place for the display of imperial cult, it is only a hypertrophied example of a phenomenon that was nearly universal in the cities of Spain.

Imperial cult, more than anything else, functioned to tie the different parts of each province together, and to provide a single focus for communal activity amid the great diversity of Spanish cities. Priesthoods of the imperial cult seem to have attracted those members of the Spanish elite who were most willing to participate in other key aspects of Roman aristocratic behavior, for instance, by way of euergistic display. Priests of the imperial cult, not just those who had reached the apex of their local civic careers, but also freedmen whose access to power was especially mediated via imperial cult, were among the many prominent donors of religious foundations in Spanish cities,[40] both to the imperial cult itself and to other deities whose worship they especially favored.[41] For the freedman population, the sevirate represented the apex of the public career to which they could aspire, and we find quite a lot of inscriptions by sevirs from most of the main cities of the peninsula, though with a noticeable concentration in Baetica.[42] Imperial cult often went along with other forms of religious worship. Cult to Jupiter and the Capitoline triad, or the personified Roma, is to be expected,[43] but there was also cult to a wide variety of other divinities, particularly universalizing ones, whose rites might be performed *pro salute* of the reigning emperor. Thus, a marble altar at Colares (Sintra, Portugal) is dedicated to *Sol Aeternus* and *Luna*, but for the well-being of the emperor Septimius Severus.[44] From Córdoba, half a peninsula away, we find *taurobolia* being conducted for the same purposes.[45] This focus on the emperor is something that affected Spain just as it affected the rest of the Roman world: with the rise and consolidation of imperial government, and particularly after the years of experimentation under the early Julio-Claudians, the centrality of the emperor's person and image was itself a transformative force in religious life. For that reason, the giving of imperial attributes to various intangible and impersonal characteristics spreads across the peninsula in the second and third centuries, for instance, in cult to *Bonus Eventus Augustus*.[46]

---

[40] *CIL* II: 35 = *IRCP* 184 (Salacia Imperatoria); *CIL* II 1934 = *ILMM* 8 (Lacippo); *CIL* II: 3279 (Castulo).

[41] For example, *CIL* II²/7: 240 (Corduba); *CIL* II: 964 (Arucci); *CILA* 2/4: 1056 (Munigua).

[42] See Rodríguez Cortés, *Sociedad y religión*.

[43] For example, *HEp.* 1: 391. Roma: for example, *CIL* II: 3279.

[44] *CIL* II: 259 (Olisipo).

[45] *CIL* II²/7: 233–6 (Corduba).

[46] *CIL* II: 4612 = *IRC* I: 97 (Mataró).

Just as the Flavian period underscored the importance of imperial cult in the peninsula, so too did it emphasize the importance of the cities and their governments to the organization and practice of public cult. Vespasian's tenure of the censorship granted Latin rights (*ius Latii*) to every community in the peninsula that had previously lacked them, effectively transforming *civitates* into *municipia*.[47] This revolution is nowadays known to us in detail thanks to the discovery of multiple fragments of Flavian municipal laws, the actual bronze tablets on which municipal charters were inscribed and posted for the regulation of the new municipalities.[48] While substantial fragments of two such laws were well known already in the nineteenth century,[49] the recovery in the 1980s of the larger part of the constitution of Irni, the so-called *Lex Irnitana*, shows us how a hierarchy of local magistrates presided over the life of local cities and their dependent territories. Chance finds since then have demonstrated that the *Lex Irnitana* is, with its cognates, just one example of a model constitution that was applied with minor modifications to newly constituted *municipia* across the peninsula. These municipal laws give us some insight into the religious role of urban magistrates and the religious life of the cities. We learn, for instance, that the temples and other sacred places were to be maintained by the aediles, who could use public slaves for this purpose.[50] The duumvirs of the municipality were to oversee the religious festivals of the town, with the approval of a majority of the curia, and public funds could be used to support such ceremonies.[51] And festival days, both imperial and local, were similarly under the control of the duumvirs and, through them, the curia.[52] The Flavian municipal laws – which went along with the reinscription and modest revision of older colonial charters like that of the Caesarian colony of Urso (Osuna), with their own religious provisions – show very clearly how urbanism and the transformation of the peninsula's religious life went hand in hand.[53]

Second only to the cities in its effect on peninsula religion was the army; its religious role has been studied far more intensively than has

---

[47] Richardson, *Romans in Spain*, 179–213.
[48] See González Fernández, "*Lex Irnitana*"; idem, *Bronces jurídicos*; idem, "*Lex Villonensis*"; idem, "Nuevos fragmentos."
[49] *ILS* 6088, 6089 and now González Fernández, *Bronces jurídicos*, 101–26.
[50] *Lex Irn.* 19. Edition in either González Fernández, "*Lex Irnitana*" or idem, *Bronces jurídicos*, 51–99.
[51] *Lex Irn.* 77, 79.
[52] *Lex Irn.* 92.
[53] E.g. *Lex Urson.* 66–7, 72, edited at *ILS* 6087 and now González Fernández, *Bronces jurídicos*, 19–49. See Mangas, "Financiación," for religious financing in the *Lex Ursonensis*.

that of urbanism.[54] This is perhaps surprising, given that the military establishment of Spain was considerably smaller than that of other western provinces: the peninsula housed several legions during the Augustan period, no more than three under the Julio-Claudians, until, with the success of the Flavians, only a single legion remained. This *Legio VII Gemina* survived into the fourth or perhaps even the fifth century, giving its name to the medieval and modern city of León, where it was headquartered. A number of auxiliary units were also stationed in the peninsula, many of them recruited locally. In the first and second centuries, quite a lot of Spaniards enlisted in auxiliary units for service elsewhere in the empire as well.[55] It is unsurprising then, that we find a process of synthesis taking place in the vicinity of legionary and auxiliary camps. On the one hand, we find evidence for the full panoply of military gods and cult that were a standard part of army life across the empire – cults of the *signa*, dedications to the *genii* of various bases or units, Mars in any number of forms, and an omnipresent Jupiter.[56] Given the exclusive concentration of the Spanish army in the peninsular north, it seems clear that this military worship of Jupiter formed the basis for his cult's wide diffusion in the three *conventus* of the northwest, whence derive more than half the known peninsular dedications to Jupiter Capitolinus. Alongside such dedications, we find cult to Jupiter Optimus Maximus Anderon, Jupiter Cadamius, and Jupiter Ladicus.[57] These local syncretic Jupiters are probably the result of the army and its favored cults having served as the primary model of Roman behavior and practice in the north. It is a reminder that the role played by cities, with their imperial and provincial cults, in the south and east, was more often played by the army in the north.

In the same way that the soldiers influenced the religious behavior and even the actual gods worshipped in the Spanish north, so too did the local gods of the interior enter the legions and the auxiliaries, unsurprisingly given the number of locals who joined the standards. We have a substantial corpus of indigenous theonyms commemorated in votive inscriptions set up by soldiers, including some to important peninsular divinities like Ataecinae, Cossue, Larocuo, and Naviae, whose cults are

[54] Most recently Andrés Hurtado, *Aproximación* and Moreno Pablos, *Religión*, cover much the same ground, the former rather more thoroughly, both with extensive bibliographies.
[55] Le Roux, *L'armée*; Roldán Hervas, *Hispania y el ejército*.
[56] Domaszewski, "Religion," is still basic; see also Helgeland, "Roman Army Religion," and Andrés Hurtado, *Aproximación*, 426–95, for a corpus of military votive inscriptions.
[57] Respectively *CIL* II: 2598 (prov. unknown); 2695 (Asturia, prov. unknown); 2525 = *HEp.* 2: 578 (civitas Limicorum).

equally well attested in civilian contexts in the interior.[58] This interchange
between army and civilian life in the interior is entirely what one would
expect, and for the same reasons, we find soldiers donating temples to the
civilian settlements that grew up beside the camps.[59] The officers in charge
of these units, and imperial administrators more generally, provide some
of our most significant evidence for the introduction of foreign religions
into Spain. One third-century procurator, Julius Silvanus Melanion, commemorated at Legio his own personal pantheon; consisting of Serapis, Isis,
Kore, Apollo Granius, and Mars Sagatus, they reflect nobody's religious
inclinations but his own.[60] While it has always been presumed that soldiers
were mainly responsible for spreading mystery cults throughout the peninsula, there is evidence for Mithraic cult at Can Modolell in which one
of the dedicatees is an *aliarius*, or garlic merchant.[61] This example is a useful caution against overconfident generalizing. Indeed, it would seem that
the influence of the army on Spain was, in some respects, less significant
than in others of the Latin provinces. It is surely noteworthy that the cult
of Mithras, which spread so widely and so rapidly with the Roman army
from the later first century onward, should be dramatically less common
in Spain than in Britain, Pannonia, or Dacia. Likewise, and even in the
northwest, there are many varieties of syncretism that cannot be traced
directly to the army. Thus we find in the three northwestern *conventus* a
very widespread popular cult to *lares viales (augustales)*. This must have
been a Romanized form of a particularly significant local belief in the protective spirits of roads; as late as the sixth century CE, we find Martin of
Braga specifically condemning the habit of lighting tapers at crossroads in
a region where high imperial dedications to *lares* are most numerous.[62]

By the later second century, we have evidence of more or less every
cult ever attested in Roman Spain, including Christianity. While in the
long term the spread of Christianity constitutes the next major transformation in the religious history of the peninsula, as throughout the empire,
this transformation was slow in coming. Spain did not, during the third
century, witness the sort of crisis evoked in traditional historical accounts
of the period. Although the great building projects of the second century slackened considerably, this was in part because every city of any size
already had a full complement of large, Roman-style public buildings,

---

[58] Andrés Hurtado, *Aproximación*, 217–67, lists all the evidence.
[59] E.g., *CIL* II: 2915 (Segisamo); *CIL* II: 2660 (León).
[60] Alvar, "Cultos mistéricos," 32.
[61] *IRC* I: 85.
[62] *De corr. rust.* 16.4–5. For the cult, Portela Filgueiras, "Dioses Lares," to which add *HEp.* 1: 78; 4: 67, 341, 342; 5: 189; 6: 747.

temples very much among them. It was the fourth century, far more than the third, that really altered the textures of life in Roman Spain. The tetrarchic reorganization of the peninsula into five provinces, and the increased imperial supervision of local government that additional layers of bureaucracy brought with it, created real changes to the urban life of Spain. By the end of the fourth century, cities without imperial patronage had ceased to be maintained, and their infrastructures, temples, and fora included, began to deteriorate in ways that we can still detect in the archaeological record. By the time this happens, Christianity has become much the most visible religion in the literary record of the peninsula.

The earliest genuine evidence for Spanish Christianity is a letter of Cyprian of Carthage adjudicating a dispute brought on by the Decian persecution, in which two Spanish bishops who had compromised with imperial authorities were deposed by their communities and then objected to this treatment.[63] From the reign of Valerian, we possess the indisputably authentic *acta* of Fructuosus, bishop of Tarragona, but Christianity as a larger social phenomenon is for the most part invisible.[64] By the time of the Diocletianic persecutions, by contrast, faint traces of Christian cult can be discovered archaeologically. While many martyr stories relate to Diocletian's persecution and suggest a substantial Christian community, very few of these can be proved to be authentic: the great Spanish martyr cults – those to Felix of Gerona, Vincentius of Valencia, or Eulalia of Mérida, for instance – are not attested in the literary record until Prudentius's early fifth-century *Peristephanon*. Only the *acta* of Marcellus, a legionary of *Legio VII Gemina* who had thrown away his insignia because a Christian ought not to bear arms, are clearly authentic; the fact that Marcellus was executed in Tingitania, a province that Diocletian had attached to the Spanish diocese, helps corroborate them.[65] The canons of Elvira, which must date to just before the outbreak of Diocletian's persecution, are a rich source of evidence for the difficulties faced by observant Christians living in a still-vibrant urban culture suffused with non-Christian gods and their rites.[66] By the middle of the fourth century, by contrast, our literary sources imply that non-Christian cult was nothing but a marginal aberration to be stamped out by devoted bishops like Pacianus of Barcino.[67]

---

[63] Cyprian, *Ep.* 67.

[64] See Musurillo, *Acts*, 176–85.

[65] See Musurillo, *Acts*, 250–9.

[66] Best edition of the canons in Martínez Díez, *Colección*, 235–68. Despite continued assertions of a Constantinian date for Elvira, Duchesne, "Concile," long ago proved that the absence of any reference to persecution must place the council before 303.

[67] See in particular Pacianus, *De paenitentia*.

But the physical landscape of the cities shows this literary evidence to be misleading. Most datable evidence for church building in Spain comes from the second half of the fourth century at the earliest. The great Christian cemetery at Tarragona was excavated too early in the twentieth century to provide any reliable evidence about its origin, let alone the date of its basilica. By contrast, the exemplary excavations at the church of Santa Eulalia at Mérida show that several early fourth-century mausolea became the core of a pilgrimage and burial site around which a sixth-century basilica was later constructed.[68] More significant, however, is the date at which church buildings began to penetrate the core of the old Roman cities – the fora, the cult sites, and the public spaces more generally. Intramural Christian cult sites in general are rarely visible before the later fourth century, as at Barcino, and then they are on the peripheries of the walled zone. By contrast, churches begin to appear in the fora and around the old temple precincts only when those areas have ceased to possess any social meaning for local communities. At Tarragona, for instance, while the old imperial precinct of the upper town began to deteriorate from the 440s, it was not until the turn of the fifth to the sixth century that a Christian church and probable *episcopium* were put up where the temple of the imperial cult had once stood.[69] What is more, we can see the same regional differences in the spread of Christianity that had always existed within the peninsula: the north and west are much slower to develop a visibly Christian culture, despite the fact that Gallaecia provides – in the shape of Orosius and Hydatius – two of the earliest Christian writers from Spain. In other words, the physical Christianization of Spain is the last stage in the Roman phase of the peninsula's religious life. The process of becoming Christian was long and slow, set in motion by the Roman government, but lasting well into the medieval period – as long and slow, in fact, as the original acculturation of Spain to the Roman conquest itself.

BIBLIOGRAPHY

Alföldy, Géza. *Flamines provinciae Hispaniae Citerioris* (Madrid, 1973).
Alvar, J. "El culto a Isis en Hispania." In *Religión romana*, ed. CSIC (Madrid, 1981): 311–19.
"Los cultos mistéricos en la Tarraconense." In *Religio Deorum*, ed. M. Mayer (Sabadell, 1993): 27–46.
Andrés Hurtado, Gloria. *Una aproximación a la religión del ejército romano imperial: Hispania* (Logroño, 2005).

---

[68] Mateos Cruz, *Basílica*.
[69] Extensive exposition with references in Kulikowski, *Late Roman Spain*, 220–55.

Andreu Pintado, J. "El comportamiento munificente de las élites hispano-romanas en materia religiosa: la construcción de templos por iniciativa privada en *Hispania*." *Iberia: Revista de la Antigüedad* 3 (2000): 111–28.

Arce, Javier, Serena Ensoli, and Eugenio La Rocca, eds. *Hispania Romana: desde tierra de conquista a provincia del imperio* (Milan, 1997).

Balil, Alberto. "El culto de Isis en España." *Cuadernos de Trabajos de la Escuela Española de Historia y Arqueología en Roma* 7 (1956): 3–13.

Beltrán Fortes, Jose. "Monumentos funerarios." In *Hispania*, eds. J. Arce, S. Ensoli, and E. La Rocca (Milan, 1997): 119–25.

Beltrán Lloris, Francisco, ed. *Roma y el nacimiento de la cultura epigráfica en Occidente* (Zaragoza, 1995).

Blázquez, José María. *Diccionario de las religiones prerromanas de Hispania* (Madrid, 1975).

Carreté, Josep María, Simon J. Keay, and Martin Millett. *A Roman Provincial Capital and Its Hinterland: The Survey of the Territory of Tarragona, Spain, 1985–1990* (Ann Arbor, Mich., 1995).

Corell, J. "El culto a *Liber Pater* en el sur del *conventus Tarraconensis* según la epigrafía." In *Religio Deorum*, ed. M. Mayer (Sabadell, 1993): 125–43.

Crespo Ortiz de Zárate, Santos, and Ángeles Alonso Ávila. *Las manifestaciones religiosas del mundo antiguo en Hispania romana: el territorio de Castilla y León I: fuentes epigráficas* (Valladolid, 1999).

C. S. I.C. *La religión romana en Hispania (Symposio organizado por el Instituto de Arqueología "Rodrigo Caro" del C.S.I.C. del 17 al 19 de diciembre de 1979)* (Madrid, 1981).

Delgado, José A. *Elites y organización de la religión en las provincias romanas de la Bética y las Mauritanias: sacerdotes y sacerdocios*. BAR Int. Ser. 724 (Oxford, 1998).

"Flamines Provinciae Lusitaniae." *Gerión* 17 (1999): 433–61.

Domaszewski, Alfred von. "Die Religion des römischen Heeres." *Westdeutsche Zeitschrift für Geschichte und Kunst* 14 (1895): 1–128.

Duchesne, L. "Le Concile d'Elvire et les flamines chrétiens." *Melanges Renier. Bibliothéque de l'École des Hautes Études* 73 (1887): 159–74.

Edmondson, Jonathan C. "The Epigraphy and History of Roman *Hispania*: The New Edition of *CIL* II." *JRA* 12 (1999): 649–66.

Étienne, Robert. *Le culte impériale dans la péninsule ibérique d'Auguste à Diocletien* (Paris, 1958).

Fear, A. T. *Rome and Baetica* (Oxford, 1996).

Fishwick, Duncan. *The Imperial Cult in the Latin West*. Vol. 2.1 (Leiden, 1991).

García y Bellido, A. "Hercules Gaditanus." *Archivo Español de Arqueología* 36 (1963): 70–153.

Garriguet Mata, J. A. "El culto imperial en las tres capitales provinciales hispanas: fuentes para su estudio y estado actual del conocimiento." *Anales de Arqueología Cordobesa* 8 (1997): 43–68.

González Fernández, Julián. "The Lex Irnitana: a new Flavian municipal law." *JRS* 76 (1986): 147–243.

Bronces jurídicos romanos de Andalucía (Seville, 1990).

"*Lex Villonensis*," *Habis* 23 (1993): 97–119.

"Nuevos fragmentos de la *lex Flavia municipalis* pertenecientes a la *Lex Villonensis* y a otros municipios de nombre desconocido." In *Ciudades privilegiadas en el occidente romano* (Seville, 1999): 239–45.

Harrison, Richard J. *Spain at the Dawn of History: Iberians, Phoenicians and Greeks* (London, 1987).

Helgeland, John. "Roman Army Religion." *ANRW* II 16.2 (1978): 1470–1505.

Hesberg, Henner von. "Römische Grabbauten in den hispanischen Provinzen." In *Hispania Antiqua*, ed. Annette Nünnerich-Asmus (Mainz, 1993): 159–92.

Le Roux, Patrick. *L'armée romaine et l'organisation des provinces ibériques d'Auguste à l'invasion de 409* (Paris, 1982).

Mangas, J. "Financiación y administración de los *sacra publica* en la *Lex Ursonensis.*" *Studia Historica. Historia Antigua* 15 (1997): 181–95.

Martínez Díez, Gonzalo, and Félix Rodríguez. *La Colección Canónica Hispana IV: Concilios Galos, Concilios Hispanos: Primera Parte* (Madrid, 1984).

Mateos Cruz, Pedro. *La basílica de Santa Eulalia de Mérida. Arqueología y urbanismo* (Madrid, 1999).

Mayer, Marc, ed. *Religio Deorum: actas del Coloquio internacional de epigrafía Culto y Sociedad en Occidente* (Sabadell, 1993).

Mierse, William E. *Temples and Towns in Roman Iberia* (Berkeley, 1999).

Moneo, Teresa. *Religio ibérica: santuarios, ritos y divinidades (siglos VII-I a.C.)* (Madrid, 2003).

Moreno Pablos, Ma. José. *La religión del ejército romano: Hispania en los siglos I-III* (Madrid, 2001).

Musurillo, Herbert. *Acts of the Christian Martyrs* (Oxford, 1972).

Portela Filgueiras, M. I. "Los dioses Lares en la Hispania romana." *Lucentum* 3 (1984): 153–80.

Ramallo, S. "Templos y santuarios en la Hispania republicana." In *Hispania*, eds. J. Arce, S. Ensoli, and E. La Rocca (Milan, 1997): 253–66.

Richardson, J. S. *The Romans in Spain* (Oxford, 1996).

Rives, James B. *Religion in the Roman Empire* (Oxford, 2007).

Rodríguez Cortés, Juana. *Sociedad y religión clásica en la Bética romana* (Salamanca, 1991).

Roldán Hervas, José M. *Hispania y el ejército romano: contribución a la historia social de la España Antigua* (Salamanca, 1974).

Ruiz de Arbulo, J. "El santuario de Asklepios y las divinidades alejandrinas en la Neapolis de Ampurias (s. II-I a.C.). Nuevas hipotesis." *Verdolay* 7 (1995): 327–38.

Sanmartí i Grego, E., P. Castañer i Masoliver, and J. Tremoleda i Trilla. "Emporion: Un ejemplo de monumentalización precoz en la Hispania republicana (los santuarios helenísticos de su sector meriodional)." In *Stadtbild und Ideologie: die Monumentalisierung hispanischer Städte zwischen Republik und Kaiserzeit*, eds. Walter Trillmich and Paul Zanker (Munich, 1990): 117–44.

TED'A. "El foro provincial de Tarraco, un ejemplo arquitectónico de época flavia." *Archivo Español de Arqueología* 62 (1989): 141–91.

Epigraphic Corpora

Abascal Palazón, Juan Manuel, and Sebastián F. Ramallo Asensio. *La ciudad de Carthago Nova, 3: la documentación epigráfica* (Murcia, 1997).

Alföldy, Géza, ed. *Die römischen Inschriften von Tarraco*. 2 vols. (Berlin, 1975) (= *RIT*).

Almagro, Martin A. *Las inscripciones ampuritanas* (Barcelona, 1952).

Arias Vilas, Felipe, Patrick Le Roux, and Alain Tranoy. *Inscriptions romaines de la province de Lugo* (Paris, 1979).

Corpus Inscriptionum Latinarum: *Inscriptiones Hispaniae* (Berlin, 1869). *Supplementum* (Berlin, 1892) (= *CIL* II).

Corpus Inscriptionum Latinarum: *Inscriptiones Hispaniae, editio altera, V: conuentus Astigitanus* (Berlin, 1998) (= *CIL* II²/5).

Corpus Inscriptionum Latinarum: *Inscriptiones Hispaniae, editio altera, VII: conuentus Cordubensis* (Berlin, 1995) (= *CIL* II²/7).

Corpus Inscriptionum Latinarum: *Inscriptiones Hispaniae, editio altera, XIV: conuentus Tarraconensis, fasciculus I, pars meridionalis conventus Tarraconensis* (Berlin, 1995) (= *CIL* II²/14,1).

Corpus de inscripciones latinas de Andalucía. 6 vols. (Seville, 1989–1996) (= *CILA*).

Corpus de Inscricións romanas de Galicia. 4 vols. (Santiago de Compostela, 1994-) (= *CIRG*).

Diego Santos, Francisco. *Epigrafía romana de Asturias,* 2nd ed. (León, 1985).

Inscripciones romanas de la provincia de León (León, 1986) (=*IRPL*).

d'Encarnaçao, José. *Inscriçoes romanas do conventus Pacensis* (Coimbra, 1984) (=*IRCP*).

Espinosa Ruiz, Urbano. *Epigrafía romana de La Rioja* (Logroño, 1986). (*HEp. = Hispania Epigraphica.* 12 vols. to date.)

Hübner, Emil, ed. *Inscriptiones Hispaniae christianae* (Berlin, 1871). *Supplementum* (Berlin, 1901) (= *IHC*).

Iglesias Gil, José M., and Alicia Ruiz. *Epigrafía romana de Cantabria* (Bordeaux, 1998).

Inscriptions romaines de Catalogne. 5 vols. (Paris, 1984–2002) (= *IRC*).

Inscripciones romanas de Galicia. 4 vols. (Santiago de Compostela, 1954–1968) (=*IRG*).

Muñoz, Mauricio Pastor, and Angela Mendoza Eguaras, eds. *Inscripciones latinas de la provincia de Granada* (Granada, 1987) (= *ILPG*).

Ramos, Encarnación Serrano, and Rafael Atencia Paez. *Inscripciones latinas del Museo de Málaga* (Madrid, 1981) (= *ILMM*).

Rodríguez Colmenero, Antonio. *Aquae Flaviae I: Fontes epigráficas da Gallaecia meridional interior,* 2nd ed. (Chaves, 1999).

Vilas, Felipe Arias, Patrick Le Roux, and Alain Tranoy. *Inscriptions romaines de la province de Lugo* (Paris, 1979) (= *IRPLugo*).

Vives, José. *Inscripciones latinas de la España romana.* 2 vols. (Barcelona, 1975) (= *ILER*).

SUGGESTIONS FOR FURTHER READING

I. RELIGIONS OF IRAN

Boyce, Mary, and Frantz Grenet. *A History of Zoroastrianism 3: Zoroastrianism under Macedonian and Roman Rule.* HO. Abt. 1: Der Nahe und der Mittlere Osten. Bd. 8 (Leiden, 1991).
Be Duhn, Jason, ed. *New light on Manichaeism: Papers from the Sixth International Congress on Manichaeism* (Leiden, 2009).
Yarshater, Ehshan, ed. *The Cambridge History of Iran.* Vol. 3 (1): *The Seleucid, Parthian and Sasanian Periods* (Cambridge, 1983).

II. RELIGIONS OF THE NEAR EAST

Ball, Warwick. *Rome in the East: The Transformation of an Empire* (London, 2000).
Butcher, Kevin. *Roman Syria and the Near East* (London, 2003).
Eliav, Yaron Z., Elise A. Friedland, and Sharon Herbert, eds. *The Sculptural Environment of the Roman Near East: Reflections on Culture, Ideology, and Power* (Leuven, 2008).
Healey, John F. *The Religion of the Nabataeans: A Conspectus.* RGRW 136 (Leiden, 2001).
Kaizer, Ted, ed. *The Variety of Local Religious Life in the Near East in the Hellenistic and Roman Periods* (Leiden, 2008).
Sartre, Maurice. *The Middle East under Rome* (Cambridge, Mass., 2005).

Judaism in Judea and the Near East

Primary Sources

Frey, Jean-Baptiste. *Corpus Inscriptionum Iudaicarum* (Rome, 1936).
Naveh, Joseph, and Shaul Shaked. *Amulets and Magic Bowls: Aramaic Incantations of Late Antiquity* (Jerusalem, 1985).
Magic Spells and Formulae: Aramaic Incantations of Late Antiquity (Jerusalem, 1993).
Noy, David, and Hanswulf Bloedhorn. *Inscriptiones Judaicae Orientis.* Vol. 3: *Syria and Cyprus.* TSAJ 102 (Tübingen, 2004).
Reinach, Théodore. *Textes d'auteurs grecs et romains relatifs au judaïsme* (Paris, 1895; repr. Hildesheim, 1963).

Stern, Menahem, ed. *Greek and Latin Authors on Jews and Judaism*. 3 vols. (Jerusalem, 1974–84).

Secondary Sources

Cotton, Hannah M., Robert G. Hoyland, Jonathan J. Price, and David J. Wasserstein, eds. *From Hellenism to Islam: Cultural and Linguistic Change in the Roman Near East* (Cambridge, 2009).
Fonrobert, Charlotte Elisheva, and Martin S. Jaffee, eds. *The Cambridge Companion to the Talmud and Rabbinic Literature* (Cambridge, 2007).
Hezser, Catherine. *The Oxford Handbook of Jewish Daily Life in Roman Palestine* (Oxford, 2010).
Kalmin, Richard. *Jewish Babylonia between Persia and Roman Palestine* (Oxford, 2006).
Linder, Amnon. *The Jews in Roman Imperial Legislation* (Detroit, 1987).

Syriac Christianity

Baarda, Tjitze. *The Gospel Quotations of Aphrahat the Persian Sage*. 2 vols. (Meppel, 1975).
Brock, Sebastian. *The Syriac Fathers on Prayer and the Spiritual Life* (Kalamazoo, Mich., 1987).
"Eusebius and Syriac Christianity." In *Eusebius, Christianity and Judaism*, eds. Harold W. Attridge and Gohei Hata (Detroit, 1992): 212–34.
Brock, Sebastian, et al., eds. *Gorgias Encyclopedic Dictionary of the Syriac Heritage* (Piscataway, N.J., 2011).
Garsoïan, Nina G., ed. *East of Byzantium: Syria and Armenia in the Formative Period* (Washington, D.C., 1982).
Mansour, Tanios B. *La pensée symbolique de Saint Ephrem le Syrien* (Kaslik, 1988).
Reinink, G. J. *Syriac Christianity under Late Sasanian and Early Islamic Rule* (Aldershot, Hampshire, 2005).
Richardson, Christine T., *Anti-Judaism and Christian Orthodoxy: Ephrem's Hymns in Fourth-century Syria*. NAPSPMS 20 (Washington, D.C, 2008).
Voobus, Arthur. *History of the School of Nisibis* (Louvain, 1965).
Zetterholm, Magnus. *The Formation of Christianity in Antioch: A Social-Scientific Approach to the Separation between Judaism and Christianity* (London, 2003).

III. RELIGIONS OF EGYPT

Arslan, Ermanno A., ed. *Iside, il mito, il mistero, la magia* (Milan, 1997).
Bagnall, Roger S., and Dominic W. Rathbone. *Egypt from Alexander to the Copts* (London, 2004).
Bakhoum, Soheir. *Dieux égyptiens à Alexandrie sous les Antonins: recherches numismatiques et historiques* (Paris, 1999).
Ballet, Pascale. *La vie quotidienne à Alexandrie, 331–30 av. J.C.* (Paris, 1999).
Bataille, André. *Les inscriptions grecques et latines du temple d'Hatshepsout à Deir el-Bahari* (Cairo, 1951).
Bergman, Jan. *Ich bin Isis: Studien zum memphitischen Hintergrund der griechischen Isisaretalogien* (Uppsala, 1968).

Bierbrier, Morris L., ed. *Portraits and Masks: Burial Customs in Roman Egypt* (London, 1997).

Bowman, Alan K. *Egypt after the Pharaohs, 332 BC – AD 642* (London, 1986).

Cauville, Sylvie. *Essai sur la théologie du temple d'Horus à Edfou* (Cairo, 1987).

Clarysse, Willy, Antoon Schoors, and Harco Willems, eds. *Egyptian Religion: The Last Thousand Years: Studies dedicated to the memory of Jan Quaegebeur* (Leuven, 1998).

Dunand, Françoise. *Religion populaire en Égypte romaine: les terres cuites isiaques du Musée du Caire* (Leiden, 1979).

Durand, A. *Égypte romaine, l'autre Égypte* (Marseille, 1997).

Fowden, Garth. *The Egyptian Hermes: A Historical Approach to the Late Pagan Mind* (Cambridge, 1986).

Gutbub, Adolphe. *Textes fondamentaux de la théologie de Kom Ombo* (Cairo, 1973).

Hölbl, Günther. *A History of the Ptolemaic Empire*. Translated by Tina Saavedra (London, 2001).

Hornbostel, Wilhelm. *Sarapis: Studien zur Überlieferungsgeschichte, den Erscheinungsformen und Wandlungen der Gestalt eines Gottes* (Leiden, 1973).

Ikram, Salima, and Aidan Dodson. *The Mummy in Ancient Egypt: Equipping the Dead for Eternity* (New York, 1998).

Kákosy, László. "Probleme der Religion im römerzeitlichen Ägypten." *ANRW* II.18.5 (1995): 2894–3049.

Lewis, Naphtali. *Life in Egypt under Roman Rule* (Oxford, 1983).

Lippert, Sandra L., and Maren Schentulheit, eds. *Tebtynis und Soknopaiu Nesos: Leben im römerzeitlichen Fajum: Akten des Internationalen Symposions vom 11. bis 13. Dezember 2003 in Sommerhausen bei Würzburg* (Wiesbaden, 2005).

Otto, Walter G. A. *Priester und Tempel im hellenistischen Ägypten* (Rome, 1971).

Perdrizet, Paul, and Gustave Lefebvre. *Les Graffites grecs du Memnonion d'Abydos* (Nancy, 1919).

Perpillou-Thomas, Françoise. *Fêtes d'Égypte ptolémaïque et romaine d'après la documentation papyrologique grecque* (Leuven, 1993).

Pinch, Geraldine. *Magic in Ancient Egypt* (London, 1994).

Ray, John D. *The Archive of Hor* (London, 1976).

Riggs, Christina. *The Beautiful Burial in Roman Egypt: Art, Identity and Funerary Religion* (Oxford, 2005).

Whitehorne, J. W. "The Pagan Cults of Roman Oxyrhynchus." *ANRW* II.18.5 (1995): 3050–91.

Judaism in Egypt

Primary Sources (papyri and inscriptions)

Boffo, Laura. *Iscrizioni Iscrizioni greche e latine per lo studio della Bibbia* (Brescia, 1994).

Cowey, James M. S., and Klaus Maresch. *Urkunden des Politeuma der Juden von Herakleopolis (144/3 – 133/2 v. Chr.) (P.Polit.Iud.). Papyri aus den Sammlungen von Heidelberg, Köln, München und Wien* (Wiesbaden, 2001).

Horbury, William, and David Noy, eds. *Jewish Inscriptions from Graeco-Roman Egypt* (Cambridge, 1992).

Tcherikover, Victor, Alexander Fuks, and Menahem Stern, eds. *Corpus Papyrorum Judaicarum*. 3 vols. (Jerusalem, 1957–64).

Secondary Sources

Barclay, John M. G. *Jews in the Mediterranean Diaspora: From Alexander to Trajan (323 BCE – 117 CE).* HCS 33 (Berkeley, 1991). (For Egypt, see Part One.)

Gambetti, Sandra. *The Alexandrian Riots of 38 C.E. and the Persecution of the Jews: A Historical Reconstruction.* JSJSup 135 (Leiden, 2009).

Kasher Aryeh. *The Jews in Hellenistic and Roman Egypt: The Struggle for Equal Rights* (Tübingen, 1985).

Niehoff, Maren. *Philo on Jewish Identity and Culture* (Tübingen, 2001).

Pearce, Sarah J. K. *The Land of the Body: Studies in Philo's Representation of Egypt* (Tübingen, 2007).

Smallwood, E. Mary. *The Jews under Roman rule: from Pompey to Diocletian.* SLJA 20 (Leiden, 1981). (For Egypt, see chapter 10.)

Christianity in Egypt

Bagnall, Roger S. *Early Christian Books in Egypt* (Princeton, 2009).

Bowman, Alan K. *Egypt after the Pharaohs, 332 BC–AD 642: From Alexander to the Arab Conquest* (Berkeley, 1989).

Davis, Stephen J. *Coptic Christology in Practice: Incarnation and Divine Participation in Late Antique and Medieval Egypt.* OECS (Oxford, 2008).

Goehring, James E., and Janet Timbie, eds. *The World of Early Egyptian Christianity: Language, Literature, and Social Context: Essays in Honor of David W. Johnson* (Washington, D.C., 2007).

Pearson, Birger A. *Gnosticism, Judaism, and Egyptian Christianity* (Minneapolis, 1990).

Török, Laszlo. *Transfigurations of Hellenism: Aspects of Late Antique Art in Egypt AD 250–700.* Probleme der Ägyptologie 23 (Leiden, 2005).

IV. RELIGIONS OF NORTH AFRICA

Dubabin, Katherine. *The Mosaics of Roman North Africa: Studies in Iconography and Patronage* (Oxford, 1979).

Lipínski, Edward. *Dieux et déesses de l'univers phénicien et punique* (Leuven, 1995).

Shaw, Brent. *Rulers, Nomads, and Christians in Roman North Africa* (Aldershot, Hampshire, 1995).

Judaism in North Africa

Applebaum, Shimon. *Jews and Greeks in Ancient Cyrene.* SJLA 28 (Leiden, 1979).

Chouraqui, Andre. *Between East and West: A History of the Jews of North Africa* (Philadelphia, 1981).

Hirschberg, H. Z. *A History of the Jews in North Africa.* Vol. 1 (Leiden, 1974).

Iancu, Carol, and Jean Marie Lassère. *Juifs et judaisme en Afrique du Nord dans l'antiqueé et le haut Moyen-Age* (Montpelier, 1985).

Le Bohec, Yves. "Inscriptions juives et judaïsantes de l'Afrique romaine." *AntAfr* 17 (1981): 165–207.

Lüderitz, Gert, and Joyce Maire Reynolds. *Corpus jüdischer Zeugnisse aus der Cyrenaika* (Wiesbaden, 1983).

Setzer, Claudia. "The Jews in Carthage and Western North Africa, 66–235." In *CHJ*. Vol. 4: *The Late Roman-Rabbinic Period*, ed. Steven T. Katz (Cambridge, 2006): 68–75.

Stern, Karen B. *Inscribing Devotion and Death: Archaeological Evidence for Jewish Populations of North Africa* (Leiden, 2008).

Christianity in North Africa

Barnes, Timothy D. *Tertullian: A Historical and Literary Study* (Oxford, 1971).

Brown, Peter. *Religion and Society in the Age of Saint Augustine* (London, 1972).

Augustine of Hippo. Revised edition. (Berkeley, 2000).

Burns, J. Patout. *Cyprian the Bishop* (London, 2002).

Conant, Jonathan. *Staying Roman: Conquest and Identity in the Mediterranean, 439–700* (Cambridge, 2012).

Kaegi, Walter. *Muslim Expansion and Byzantine Collapse in North Africa* (Cambridge, 2010).

Lancel, Serge. *St. Augustine*. Translated by Antonia Nevill (London, 2002).

V. RELIGIONS OF GREECE AND ASIA MINOR

Athanassiadi, Polymnia, and Michael Frede, eds. *Pagan Monotheism in Late Antiquity* (Oxford, 1999).

Cosmopoulos, Michael, ed. *Greek Mysteries: The Archaeology and Ritual of Ancient Greek Secret Cults* (London, 2003).

Hoff, Michael C., and Susan I. Rotroff, eds. *The Romanization of Athens: Proceedings of an International Conference held at Lincoln, Nebraska (April 1996)* (Exeter, 1997).

Koester, Helmut, ed. *Pergamon, Citadel of the Gods: Archaeological Record, Literary Description, and Religious Development* (Harrisburg, Pa., 1998).

Schowalter, Daniel N., and Steven J. Friesen, eds. *Urban Religion in Roman Corinth* (Cambridge, Mass., 2005).

Small, Alistair, ed. *Subject and Ruler: the Cult of the Ruling Power in Classical Antiquity* (Ann Arbor, Mich., 1996).

Judaism in Asia Minor

Fine, Steven, and Leonard Rutgers. "New Light on Judaism in Asia Minor during Late Antiquity: Two Recently Identified Inscribed Menorahs." *JSR* 3 (1996): 1–23.

Kraabel, A. Thomas. *Judaism in Western Asia Minor under the Roman Empire*. Th.D. diss. Harvard University, 1968.

"The Diaspora Synagogue: Archaeological and Epigraphic Evidence since Sukenik." *ANRW* II.19.1 (1979): 477–510.

Trebilco, Paul. "The Jews in Asia Minor: 66-c. 235 CE." In *CHJ*. Vol. 4: *The Late Roman-Rabbinic Period*, ed. Steven T. Katz (Cambridge, 2006): 75–82.

Christianity in Greece and Asia Minor

Belayche, Nicole. "La politique religieuse 'païenne' de Maximin Daia, de l'historiographie a l'histoire." In *Politiche religiose nel mondo antico e tardoantico. Poteri e indirizzi, forme del controlle, idee e prassi di tolleranza. Atti del Convegno internazionale di studi*

(Firenze, 24–26 settembre 2009), eds. Giovanni A. Cecconi and Chantal Gabrielli (Bari, 2011): 235–59.

Frend, W. H. C. *Martyrdom and Persecution in the Early Church* (Oxford, 1965).

Johnson, Sherman E. "Asia Minor and Early Christianity." In *Christianity, Judaism and Other Greco-Roman Cults*, Vol. 1, ed. Jacob Neusner. (Leiden, 1975): 77–145.

MacMullen, Ramsay. *Christianizing the Roman Empire* (New Haven, 1981).

Tellbe, Mikael. *Christ-Believers in Ephesus: A Textual Analysis of Early Christian Identity Formation in a Local Perspective*. WUNT 242 (Tübingen, 2009).

Trebilco, Paul. *The Early Christians in Ephesus from Paul to Ignatius* (Grand Rapids, Mich., 2007).

Trevett, Christine. *Montanism: Gender, Authority, and the New Prophecy* (Cambridge, 2002).

——— "Asia Minor and Achaea." In *The Cambridge History of Christianity I: Origins to Constantine*, eds. Margaret M. Mitchell and Francis M. Young (Cambridge, 2006): 314–29.

VI. RELIGIONS OF ITALY, GAUL, AND SPAIN

Roman Spain

Cardim Ribeiro, J. *Religiões da Lusitania: loquuntur saxa* (Lisbon, 2002).

Diez de Velasco, Francisco. *Termalismo y Religión: la sacralización del agua termal en la Península Ibérica y el norte de África en el mundo antiguo* (Madrid, 1998).

García y Bellido, Antonio. *Les religions orientales dans l'Espagne romaine* (Leiden, 1967).

Rodríguez Colmenero, Antonio, and L. Gasperini, eds. *Saxa Scripta (Inscripciones en Roca): actas del Simposio Internacional Ibero-Itálico sobre epigrafía rupestre* (La Coruña, 1999).

Rodríguez Neila, Juan Francisco, and F. Javier Navarro, eds. *Élites y promoción social en la Hispania Romana* (Pamplona, 1999).

Judaism in Italy, Southern Gaul, and Spain

Primary Sources

Feldman, Louis H., and Meyer Reinhold, eds. *Jewish Life and Thought among Greeks and Romans: Primary Readings* (Minneapolis, 1996).

Frey, Jean-Baptiste, ed. *Corpus Inscriptionum Judaicarum, I: Europe* (Vatican City, 1936). Reprinted as *Corpus of Jewish Inscriptions*, with a prolegomenon by B. Lifshitz (New York, 1975).

Noy, David. *Jewish Inscriptions of Western Europe:* Vol. I. *Italy (excluding the City of Rome), Spain and Gaul* (Cambridge, 1993).

Jewish Inscriptions of Western Europe: Vol. II. *The City of Rome* (Cambridge, 1995).

Williams, Margaret H. *The Jews among the Greek and Romans: A Diasporan Sourcebook* (London, 1998).

Secondary Sources

Applebaum, Shimon. "The Organization of the Jewish Communities in the Diaspora." In *The Jewish People in the First Century: Historical Geography, Political History, Social,*

Cultural and Religious Life and Institutions, eds. S. Safrai and M. Stern. CRINT 1 (Assen, 1974): 464–503.

Barclay, John M. G. *Jews in the Mediterranean Diaspora: From Alexander to Trajan (323 B.C.E. – 117 C.E.)* (Berkeley, 1999). (For Rome, see chapter 10.)

Bartlett, John R., ed. *Jews in the Hellenistic and Roman Cities* (London, 2002).

Beinart, Haim. "The Jews in Spain." In *The Jewish World: Revelation, Prophecy and History*, ed. Elie Kedourie (London, 1979): 161–7.

Benbassa, Esther. *Histoire des Juifs de France*. 3rd ed. (Paris, 2004). Translated by M. B. DeBevoise as *The Jews of France: A History from Antiquity to the Present* (Princeton, 1999).

Blázquez Martínez, José M. "Relations between Hispania and Palestine in the Late Roman Empire." *Assaph* (1998): 163–78.

Blumenkranz, Bernhard. "Les premières implantations de juifs en France: du Ier au début du Ve siècle." *CRAIBL* (1969): 162–74.

"Premiers témoignages épigraphiques sur les juifs en France." In *S. Wittmayer Baron Jubilee*, Vol. 1, ed. Saul Lieberman (Jerusalem, 1974): 229–35.

Bowers, W. Paul. "Jewish Communities in Spain in the Time of Paul the Apostle." *JTS* 26 (1975): 395–402.

Bradbury, Scott. "The Jews of Spain, c. 235–638." In *CHJ*. Vol. 4: *The Late Roman Rabbinic Period*, ed. Steven T. Katz (Cambridge, 2006): 508–18.

Buhagiar, Mario. *Late Roman and Byzantine Catacombs and Related Burial Places in the Maltese Islands* (Oxford, 1986).

Donfried, Karl P., and Peter Richardson, eds. *Judaism and Christianity in First-Century Rome* (Grand Rapids, Mich., 1998).

Goodman, Martin. "Jews and Judaism in the Mediterranean Diaspora in the Late-Roman Period: The Limitations of Evidence." *JMS* 4 (1994): 208–24.

Goodnick Westenholz, Joan, ed. *The Jewish Presence in Ancient Rome* (Jerusalem, 1994).

Hunt, E. D. "St. Stephen in Minorca: An Episode in Jewish-Christian Relations in the Early Fifth Century AD." *JTS* 3 (1982): 106–23.

Leon, Harry J. *The Jews of Ancient Rome* (Philadelphia, 1960).

Niquet, Heike. "Jews in the Iberian Peninsula in Roman Times." *SCI* 23 (2004): 159–82.

Noy, David. "The Jewish Communities of Leontopolis and Venosa." In *Studies in Early Jewish Epigraphy*, eds. J. W. van Henten and Pieter W. van der Horst (Leiden, 1994): 162–82.

"Writing in Tongues: The Use of Greek, Latin and Hebrew in Jewish Inscriptions from Roman Italy." *JJS* 48 (1997): 300–11.

"'Letters out of Judaea': Echoes of Israel in Jewish Inscriptions from Europe." In *Jewish Local Patriotism and Self-Identification in the Graeco-Roman Period*, eds. Siân Jones and Sarah Pearce (Sheffield, 1998): 106–17.

"Where Were the Jews of the Diaspora Buried?" In *Jews in a Graeco-Roman World*, ed. Martin Goodman (Oxford, 1998): 75–89.

"Jewish Inscriptions of Western Europe: Language and Community." In *XI Congresso Internazionale di Epigrafia Greca e Latina. Roma 1997. Atti.* Vol. 2 (Rome, 1999): 603–12.

"Jews in Italy in the 1st-6th Centuries C.E." In *The Jews of Italy: Memory and Identity*, eds. Bernard Dov Cooperman and Barbara Garvin (Bethesda, Md., 2000): 47–64.

Foreigners at Rome: Citizens and Strangers (Duckworth, 2000).

Rabello, Alfredo M. *The Jews in Visigothic Spain in the Light of the Legislation* (Jerusalem, 1983) (Heb.).

Rocca, Samuel. "A Jewish Gladiator in Pompeii." *Materia Giudaica* 11/1–2 (2006): 287–301.

Rutgers, Leonard V. "The Legal Position of Jews in Ancient Rome, with Special Emphasis on the First Century." *CA* 13 (1994): 56–74. Repr. in *Judaism and Christianity in First-Century Rome*, eds. K. P. Donfried and P. Richardson (Grand Rapids, Mich., 1998): 93–116.

The Hidden Heritage of Diaspora Judaism: Essays on Jewish Cultural Identity in the Roman World (Leuven, 1998).

Subterranean Rome: Searching for the Roots of Christianity in the Catacombs of the Eternal City (Leuven, 2000).

"The Jews of Italy, c. 235–638." In *CHJ*. Vol. 4: *The Late Roman-Rabbinic Period*, ed. Steven T. Katz (Cambridge, 2006): 492–508.

Slingerland, Dixon. "Modern Historiography on the Early Imperial Mistreatment of Roman Jews." In *The Most Ancient of Minorities: The Jews of Italy*, ed. Stanislao G. Pugliese (Westport, Conn., 2002): 35–50.

"The Shaping of the Identity of the Jewish Community in Rome in Antiquity." In *Christians as a Religious Minority in a Multicultural City: Modes of Interaction and Identity Formation in Early Imperial Rome*, eds. Jürgen Zangenberg and Michael Labahn (London, 2004): 33–46.

Williams, Margaret H. "The Contribution of Jewish Inscriptions to the Study of Judaism." In *CHJ*. Vol. 3: *The Early Roman Period*, eds. W. Horbury, John Sturdy, and W. D. Davies (Cambridge, 1999): 75–93

"The Structure of the Jewish Community in Rome." In *Jews in a Graeco-Roman World*, ed. Martin Goodman (Oxford, 1998): 215–28.

"The Jews of Early Byzantine Venusia: The Family of Faustinus I, the Father." *JJS* 50 (1999): 38–52.

Christianity in Gaul

Primary Sources (material and textual)

Constantius, *Vita Germani*, ed. René Borius. *SC* 112 (Paris, 1965). Trans. F. R. Hoare, *The Western Fathers* (New York, 1954): 283–320.

Cüppers, Heinz, ed. *Trier, Kaiserresidenz und Bischofssitz: die Stadt in Spätantiker und früh-christlicher Zeit* (Mainz am Rhein, 1984).

Duval, Noël, ed. *Les premiers monuments chretiens de la France.* 3 vols. (Paris, 1995–98).

Duval, Noël, et al., eds. *Naissance des arts chrétiens: Atlas des monuments paléochrétiens de la France* (Paris, 1991).

Février, Paul-Albert, and François Leyge, eds. *Premiers temps chrétiens en Gaule méridionale: antiquité tardive et Haut Moyen Age, IIIème-VIIIème siècles* (Lyon, 1986).

Gauthier, Nancy, J-Ch Picard, and Noël Duval, eds. *Topographie chrétienne des cités de la Gaule, des origines au milieu du VIIIe siècle.* 13 vols. to date. (Paris, 1986–).

Guyon, Jean, and Marc Heijmans, eds. *D'un monde à l'autre: naissance d'une Chrétienté en Provence, IVe-VIe siècle* (Arles, 2001).

Hilary of Arles, *Sermo de vita Sancti Honorati*, ed. Marie-Denise Valentin. *SC* 235 (Paris, 1977). Trans. F. R. Hoare. *The Western Fathers* (New York, 1954): 247–80.

Kempf, Theodor Konrad, Wilhelm Reusch, and Maria R Alföldi, eds. *Frühchristliche Zeugnisse im Einzugsgebiet von Rhein und Mosel* (Trier, 1965).
Provost, Michel, ed. *Carte archéologique de la Gaule* (Paris, 1988–).
Sidonius Apollinaris, ed. André Loyen. 3 vols. (Paris, 1960). Trans. W. B. Anderson. LCL (Cambridge, Mass., 1936–65).

Guides to Written Sources

Hamman, Adalbert. "Writers of Gaul." In *Patrology*, Vol. 4, ed. Angelo Di Berardino. Trans. Placid Solari (Westminster, Md., 1988): 505–63
Handley, Mark A. *Death, Society, and Culture: Inscriptions and Epitaphs in Gaul and Spain, AD 300–750* (Oxford, 2003).
Murray, Alexander Callander, ed. and trans. *From Roman to Merovingian Gaul: A Reader* (Peterborough, Ont., 2000).

GENERAL INDEX

Gildo, Mauretanian prince (fourth cent.), 274
Gnomon of the Idios Logos, 168
Gnosticism,
  in Egypt, 213–17, 220, 224
  in North Africa, 269
  self-legitimating strategies, 13, 220.
    See also Sethianism
"God-fearers," non-Jewish sympathizers with
  Judaism,
  in Asia Minor, 9, 328–31, 343–4
  connections with cult of Theos Hypsistos,
    333–4
  religious practices, 329–31
  in Rome, 403
Goeleon, village of Asia Minor, Jews of, 335
Gog and Magog, war of, 103
Gonyklisia, bubbling spring of, 348–9
  Christian shrine, 348–9
Gordian III, Roman emperor (r. 225–244),
  39, 77
gosans, professional ministrels of Iran, 24
Gospel of Judas, 214, 220
Gospel of Philip, 214
Gospel of Thomas, 141, 214, 220
Gradel, I., 386
Gratian, Roman emperor (r. 375–383), 15, 493,
  495, 498
Great Mother. *See* Magna Mater
"Great Sabbath," 336
Greek, language,
  Christian use, 139, 212
  in Hellenistic and Roman Egypt, 5, 173,
    175–6
  Jewish use, 92, 105, 192–5, 197, 207, 404
  as *lingua franca*, 64
Gregory, exarch of Africa (seventh cent.),
  287–8
Gregory I, bishop of Rome (590–604),
  suppression of Donatism by, 286–7
Gregory of Nazianzus, Christian theologian and
  bishop of Constantinople (329–ca. 390),
  description of Hypsistarians by, 333
Gregory Thaumaturgus, Christian bishop of
  Neocaesarea (ca. 213–ca. 270), 346
Gregory of Tours, Christian historian and
  bishop (ca. 538–594), 490
Gulia Runa, *presbyterissa* of North Africa, 281
Gunderic, Vandal king (379–428), 277
Gundioc, Burgundian king (d. ca. 474), 503
Gunthamund, Vandal king (r. 484–496), 280
Gurzil, Berber deity, 285

Hadad, Semitic deity, 56, 61
Hadaran, Syrian deity, 62
Hadrian, Roman emperor (r. 117–138), 3–4,
  76–7, 207, 305, 312, 381
  dealings with Judaism, 205–6, 403
  dedication of temples, 381
  divine cult, 312
  participation in Greek religions, 304–5, 308,
    316
  urban re-organization in Roman Gaul, 468
Hadrumetum, Phoenician colony of North
  Africa, 244, 256
Hagne. *See* Kore
Hapy, Egyptian demigod of the Nile, 181
Harnack, A. von, 119
Haroeris, Egyptian deity, 172
Harpocrates, son of Isis, 174, 181
Harran, Mesopotamian city, 62
Hasideans, Jewish religious party (second cent.
  BCE), 94
Hasmoneans, Jewish high priestly dynasty, 94
  decline, 104
  political policies, 94, 118
  treaties with Rome, 398–9
Hathor, Egyptian goddess, 179
  temple at Dendara, 173
Hatra, ancient city of Mesopotamia, 34, 47,
  79–80
  gods, 65–6, 80
  temple complex, 79–80
Hatrean, Aramaic dialect, 64
Hatshepsut, mortuary temple of, 211
  conversion to a monastery, 211
Hauran, region of Syria,
  judgment of Paris relief, 72
  statue of military deity, 54–6 and Fig. 1
Hebrew, language, 10, 106, 207, 404, 411, 418
Hekhalot literature, esoteric/mystical Jewish
  texts, 124
Helen, wife of Menelaus, 4, 182
Heliopolis, city of ancient Egypt, 174, 203
Helios, 314
  depicted in synagogues, 123
Hellenistic culture
  and Christianity, 16, 17, 214–17
  and Egyptian religion, 4–5, 175–81
  and Judaism, 91–2, 94
  and the Near East, 4, 65, 91
Helvetii, gods of, 458, 469
Henig, M., 460
Hephaestus, 300

Marcellianum, city in southern Italy, religious
  festival in honor of Leucothea at, 435–6
Marcellus, Christian aristocrat of Gaul (late
  fourth cent. CE) and author of *De
  medicamentis*, 497
Marcellus, Christian Roman legionary, *acta* of,
  528
Marcia Romania, fourth century Christian
  noblewoman of Gaul, sarcophagus of,
  493–4
Marcian, 148
Marcianus, bishop of Arles (mid-third cent.),
  486
Marcion of Sinope (ca. 86–160), 14, 140, 146,
  426
Marcionites, followers of Marcion, 13, 140, 146,
  269
Marcus Aurelius, Roman emperor (r. 161–180),
  169, 304, 484
Marcus Iulius Eugenius, Christian soldier of
  Pisidia, 350
Marcus Turbo, Roman general (second cent.
  CE), 206
Marduk-Bel, Babylonian high god, battle with
  Tiamat, 74. *See also* Bel
Maren, deity of Hatra, cult of, 80.
  See also Marten, Bar-Maren
Mari, Syriac bishop, 149
Mark, St., 227
  Acts of, 227
  and Egyptian Christianity, 13, 213, 221
Mark Antony (83–30 BCE), divine cult of, 312
Marneion, temple to Zeus Marnas in Gaza,
  closure of, 359
Mars, 247, 380, 451–2, 468
  cult, 299
  rites, 380
  in Roman Africa, 257
  in Roman Gaul, 451–2, 458, 467–8, 479, 496
  in Roman Pantheon, 376
  in Roman Spain, 521, 527. *See also* Ares,
  Lenus-Mars
Mars, epithets of
  Caisivus, 467
  Caturix, 458, 467
  Cicollius, 479
  Mogetius, 452
  Mullo, 453, 458, 468, 471, 478–9
  Rigasimus, 452
  Sagatus, 527
  Ultor, 380
Marseille, Jewish community at, 495

Marten, deity of Hatra, cult of, 80.
  See also Maren and Bar-Maren
Martial, 401
Martin, Christian holy man of Gaul, 490–1
Martin I, bishop of Rome (640–655), 288
Martin of Tours, bishop of Tours (fourth cent.),
  490–3, 496
  acts against traditional religion, 496
  monastic foundations, 500
martyrs, Christian, 12, 226–9, 243, 265, 269–71,
  439–40
  authority, 221, 269–71
  cult, 12, 18, 212, 221, 227–9, 270, 439–40
  Donatist, 274–5
  glorification, 14, 269–71
  intercessory role, 270–1
  martyria, 226–7, 439–40
  martyrologies, 227
  relics, 18, 221, 227–9, 439–40, 490–1
Maruta of Tagrit (d. 649), 151
Masada, 104–5, 108
Masiden, African deity, 239
Massidicca, African deity, 239
Matar. *See* Meter
Mater Matuta, Latin goddess, identified as
  Leucothea, 71
Matilam, African deity, 238
Matthew, gospel according to, 200, 438
Matthias, apostle, 13, 220
Mattiah ben Heresh, 401, 408
Mauretania, 247
Mauretania Tingitana, 248
Mauri, uprisings in North Africa by, 285
Mauricius, Byzantine emperor (582–602), 286
Mauvières, inscriptions from, 452
Maxentius, Roman emperor (r. 306–312), 392,
  429–2, 487
Maximilla, Montanist prophetess, 356–7
Maximinus, Arian bishop (fifth cent.), 278
Maximinus, bishop of Trier, 488
Maximus the Confessor, Byzantine theologian
  (580–662), 287–8
Maximinus Daia, Roman emperor (r. 270–313),
  decrees against Christians, 221, 350
Mazdak, movement of, 45–6
Meaux (*Iatinum*), suburban sanctuary at, 463, 469
Medea, children of, shrines to, 299
Mediomatrici, gods of, 474
Megaloi Theoi, at Samothrace, 304–6
  diffusion of cult, 305
Melania the Elder, Christian ascetic (fourth
  cent.), 437

INDEX OF CITATIONS

Section I ("Literary Sources"), which includes legal texts, is subdivided into the following categories: Greek and Roman, Biblical, Jewish, Christian, Manichaean, and Arabic. Section II ("Non-literary Sources") encompasses, among other things, coins, epitaphs, inscriptions, monuments, and amulets. Citations of works in individual chapters may occasionally depart from the conventions used in the index. Abbreviations are enclosed in parentheses.

I. LITERARY SOURCES

Greek and Roman

Ammianus Marcellinus, *Res Gestae*
    (Amm. Marc.)
      22.11.3–10   185
      27.3.14   441
Apollodorus, *Bibliotheca* (*Bibl.*)
      2.4.3   72, n. 40
Appian
    Bella civilia (*Bell. civ.*)
      1.110   515, n. 7
      2.90   206
      6.2   513, n. 3
      6.65   513, n. 3
    Hannibalica (*Hann.*)
      5.27   308, n. 46
Arrian, *Anabasis* (*Anab.*)
      2.16.4   513, n. 3
Athenaeus, *Deipnosophistae* (*Deipn.*)
      6.253   310, n. 60
Augustus, *Res Gestae*
      20.4   384
Aulus Gellius, *Attic Nights*
    (*Noct. att.*)
      15.22   515, n. 7
      16.13.8–9   383

Cassius Dio, *Historia Romana* (Cass. Dio)
      57.10   165
      67.14   425
Cicero
    De legibus (*Leg.*)
      2.14.26   307
    Pro Balbo (*Pro Balb.*)
      43   241, n. 22
    Pro Flacco (*Flac.*)
      28.68   325
Clearchus
    ap. Jos. *Ag. Ap.* 1.179–82   323, n. 8
Cornelius Labeo, *De oraculo Apollinis*
    Clarii, ed. Mastandrea
      fr. 18   334, n. 60

Damascius, *Life of Isidore*
    ap. Photius, *Bibliotheca,* cod. 242
      (348a–b)   69, n. 30
Dio Chrysostom
    Or. 12.25   301
    Or. 12.33   306
Diodorus Siculus, *Bibliotheca*
      1.21.7   167

Biblical

Josephus *(cont.)*

19.278–312	324, n. 11
20.34	121
20.38	121
20.41	121, 122

Jewish War (J.W.)

1.8.9	399
1.33	93, n. 28
1.190	203
2.103–4	407
2.117–119	104, n. 75
2.119	97
2.285–92	127, n. 48
2.433	104, n. 75
2.433–6	124, n. 25
2.461–80	119, n. 16
2.487	192
2.490–97	205
2.560	329
3.490–97	205
6.417–20	400
7.41–2	119, n. 16
7.43–5	329
7.44	127, n. 48
7.54–62	119, n. 16
7.110–15	119, n. 16
7.323–88	105, n. 81
7.420–36	204
7.426–30	204

Life

16	407
277	127, n. 48
280	127, n. 48
293	127, n. 48

Megillat Ta'anit

12 (scholion to)	120, n. 18

Philo

De providentia (Prov.)

2.64	95

De specialibus legibus (Spec).

3.72	200

De vita contemplative (Contempl.)

1–90	98

Hypothetica

11.1–18	97

In Flaccum (Flacc.)

46	118

Legatio ad Gaium (Legat.)

134	201
155	400
185–6	407
245	325
281	325

Quod omnis probus liber sit (Every good man is free)

75–91	97

Psalms of Solomon

17:23–51	102

Qumran and related texts

CD I:18	100, n. 56
1QHa X:15.32	100, n. 56
1QpHab II:1–10	100
1QpHab VII:3–5	100
1QpNah, frgs. 3–4 I:2	100, n. 56
1QS 3:13–4:26	98
4ApNah, frgs. 3–4 Col. 1:2	98
4Q255–264	96, n. 41
4Q266–273	97, n. 47
4QpNahum	100
5Q12	97, n. 47
6Q15	97, n. 47
11QMelchizedek	102

Rabbinic (m. = Mishnah; t. = tosepta; b. = Babylonian Talmud; y = Jerusalem Talmud)

m. Abot

1.3	92, n. 21
1.10–11	92, n. 21

b. 'Abodah Zarah (b. 'Abod. Zar.)

43b	123
52b	204

b. Baba Qamma (b. B. Qam)

59b	125, n. 37

b. Berakot (b. Ber.)

33b	98, n. 50
57b	125

m. Berakot (m. Ber)

1:3	92, n. 21

t. Berakot (t. Ber.)

3:25	125, n. 27

y. Berakot (y. Ber.)

3:1,6a	409
9:1,12d	125

t. Beṣah

2:15	124, n. 25

y. Demai (y. Dem.).

2:1, 22d	118, n. 7

y. Ḥagigah (y. Ḥag.)

1:8, 76c	126, n. 44

t. Ḥullin (t. Ḥul.)

2:13	124, n. 25

t. Ketubbot (t. Ketub.)

4,9	200

Massekhet Soferim, 7–10 — 195

b. Menaḥot (Menaḥ.)

109b	204

Christian

Arabic sources

Ibn Hishaq, tr. Guillaume		3:79	131, n. 64
Sīra I, 12–24	122, n. 25	5:44	131, n. 64
Sīra I, 287	124, n. 36	5:63	131, n. 64
Sīra I, 352	124, n. 36	9:30–1	131, n. 64
Sīra I, 383	124, n. 36	al-Tabari, *History*, tr. Bosworth	
Sīra I, 387	124, n. 36	I, 901–6	122, n. 25
Sīra I, 659	124, n. 36	I, 919–20	122, n. 25
Qu'ran		I, 924–6	122, n. 25

Zoroastrian

Gathas	
Y. 30.3	44

II. NON-LITERARY (COINS, EPITAPHS, INSCRIPTIONS, MONUMENTS, AMULETS, ETC.)

Aegyptische Urkunden aus den königlichen (staatlichen) Museen zu Berlin, Griechische Urkunden, I-IV (BGU)		1917: 227–38 nos. 227–38	238, n. 8
V, 1210	168, n. 3	*Carte archéologique de la Gaule (CAG)*	
Amulets and Magic Bowls: Aramaic Incantations of Late Antiquity, ed. Naveh and Shaked		35	478
		38	478
Amulet 13	126, n. 42	45	478
Amulet 15	126, n. 42	*Catalogue of Greek coins in the British Museum, Phoenicia (BMC Phoenicia)*, ed. Hill	
Bowl 5.5, 6	126, n. 42	No. 11	71, n. 34
Anatolia. Land, Men, and Gods in Asia Minor, ed. Mitchell		*A Catalogue of the Greek and Roman Sculptures*, ed. Budde and Nicholls	
No. 233 (= *SEG* 27 no. 933)	334	No. 126	56, n. 2
L'Année epigraphique (AE)		*Le Chettaba et les grottes à inscriptions latines de Chettaba et du Taya*, ed. J. and P. Alquier	
1901: 54	238, n. 8		
1941: 155	463	Nos. 1–70	238, n. 8
1969: 70 a	453	*The "Christians for Christians" Inscriptions of Phrygia*, ed. Gibson	
1969/70: 405 a,b,c	468		
1969/70: 410	461	No. 42 (116–19)	347, n. 29
1982: 715	461	*The Cities and Bishoprics of Phrygia*, ed. Ramsay	
1984: 933	256, n. 76	No. 209	349, n. 38
1994: 1215 a, b	462	No. 210	350, n. 42
1997: 1110–12	463	No. 212	350, n. 42
"Asia Minor, 1924 I," Buckler		No. 213	350, n. 42
No. 2	352, n. 58	No. 218	350, n. 42
Augustus, *Res Gestae*		No. 232	344, n. 11
20.4	384	No. 353–5	351, n. 53
		No. 353–62	351, n. 52
Bulletin archéologique du Comité des travaux historiques et scientifiques (BCTH)		No. 359	349, n. 34

For EU product safety concerns, contact us at Calle de José Abascal, 56–1°,
28003 Madrid, Spain or eugpsr@cambridge.org.

www.ingramcontent.com/pod-product-compliance
Ingram Content Group UK Ltd.
Pitfield, Milton Keynes, MK11 3LW, UK
UKHW020346140625
459647UK00019B/2325